Lecture Notes in Computer Science 14398

Founding Editors

Gerhard Goos
Juris Hartmanis

The series Lecture Notes in Computer Science (LNCS), including its subseries Lecture Notes in Artificial Intelligence (LNAI) and Lecture Notes in Bioinformatics (LNBI), has established itself as a medium for the publication of new developments in computer science and information technology research, teaching, and education.

LNCS enjoys close cooperation with the computer science R & D community, the series counts many renowned academics among its volume editors and paper authors, and collaborates with prestigious societies. Its mission is to serve this international community by providing an invaluable service, mainly focused on the publication of conference and workshop proceedings and postproceedings. LNCS commenced publication in 1973.

Sokratis Katsikas · Frédéric Cuppens ·
Nora Cuppens-Boulahia ·
Costas Lambrinoudakis · Joaquin Garcia-Alfaro ·
Guillermo Navarro-Arribas · Pantaleone Nespoli ·
Christos Kalloniatis · John Mylopoulos ·
Annie Antón · Stefanos Gritzalis
Editors

Computer Security

ESORICS 2023 International Workshops

CyberICS, DPM, CBT, and SECPRE
The Hague, The Netherlands, September 25–29, 2023
Revised Selected Papers, Part I

 Springer

Editors
Sokratis Katsikas (iD)
Norwegian University of Science
and Technology
Gjøvik, Norway

Nora Cuppens-Boulahia (iD)
Polytechnique Montréal
Montreal, QC, Canada

Joaquin Garcia-Alfaro (iD)
Télécom SudParis
Palaiseau, France

Pantaleone Nespoli (iD)
University of Murcia
Murcia, Spain

John Mylopoulos
University of Toronto
Toronto, ON, Canada

Stefanos Gritzalis
University of Piraeus
Piraeus, Greece

Frédéric Cuppens
Polytechnique Montréal
Montreal, QC, Canada

Costas Lambrinoudakis
University of Piraeus
Piraeus, Greece

Guillermo Navarro-Arribas (iD)
Universitat Autonoma de Barcelona
Bellaterra, Spain

Christos Kalloniatis (iD)
University of the Aegean
Mytilene, Greece

Annie Antón
Georgia Institute of Technology
Atlanta, GA, USA

ISSN 0302-9743   ISSN 1611-3349 (electronic)
Lecture Notes in Computer Science
ISBN 978-3-031-54203-9   ISBN 978-3-031-54204-6 (eBook)
https://doi.org/10.1007/978-3-031-54204-6

Preface

The 28th edition of the European Symposium on Research in Computer Security (ESORICS) was held in The Hague, The Netherlands, September 25-29, 2023. In addition to the main conference, 12 workshops were organized and held in the same time period.

This volume includes the accepted contributions to 4 of these workshops, as follows:

- the 9th Workshop on the Security of Industrial Control Systems and of Cyber-Physical Systems (CyberICPS 2023);
- the 18th International Workshop on Data Privacy Management (DPM 2023);
- the 7th International Workshop on Cryptocurrencies and Blockchain Technology (CBT 2023); and
- the 7th International Workshop on SECurity and Privacy Requirements Engineering (SECPRE 2023).

While each of the workshops had a high-quality program of its own, the organizers opted to publish the proceedings jointly; these are included in this volume, which contains 29 full papers. The authors improved and extended these papers based on the reviewers' feedback as well as the discussions at the workshops.

We would like to thank each and every one who was involved in the organization of the ESORICS 2023 workshops. Special thanks go to the ESORICS 2023 Workshop Chairs and to all the workshop organizers and their respective Program Committees who contributed to making the ESORICS 2023 workshops a real success. We would also like to thank the ESORICS 2023 Organizing Committee for supporting the day-to-day operation and execution of the workshops.

December 2023

Sokratis Katsikas
Frédéric Cuppens
Nora Cuppens-Boulahia
Costas Lambrinoudakis
Joaquin Garcia-Alfaro
Guillermo Navarro-Arribas
Pantaleone Nespoli
John Mylopoulos
Christos Kalloniatis
Annie Antón
Stefanos Gritzalis

Contents – Part I

SECPRE 2023

Contents – Part II

CyberICPS 2023

CyberICPS 2023 Preface

This book contains revised versions of the papers presented at the 9th Workshop on Security of Industrial Control Systems and Cyber-Physical Systems (CyberICPS 2023). The workshop was co-located with the 28th European Symposium on Research in Computer Security (ESORICS 2023) and was held in The Hague, The Netherlands, on September 28th, 2023.

Cyber-physical systems (CPS) are physical and engineered systems that interact with the physical environment, whose operations are monitored, coordinated, controlled, and integrated by information and communication technologies. These systems exist everywhere around us, and range in size, complexity, and criticality from embedded systems used in smart vehicles, to SCADA systems in smart grids, to control systems in water distribution systems, to smart transportation systems, to plant control systems, engineering workstations, substation equipment, programmable logic controllers (PLCs), and other Industrial Control Systems (ICS). These systems also include the emerging trend of Industrial Internet of Things (IIoT) that will be the central part of the fourth industrial revolution. As ICS and CPS proliferate, and increasingly interact with us and affect our lives, their security becomes of paramount importance.

CyberICPS 2023 brought together researchers, engineers, and governmental actors with an interest in the security of ICS and CPS in the context of their increasing exposure to cyberspace, by offering a forum for discussion on all issues related to their cyber security. CyberICPS 2023 attracted 18 high-quality submissions, each of which was assigned to 3 referees for Single-blind review; the review process resulted in 8 papers being accepted to be presented and included in the proceedings i.e., the acceptance rate was 44%. The chairs and members of the Program Committee had no involvement with or visibility of the reviewing process of submissions authored or co-authored by them. The accepted papers cover topics related to many aspects of cyber security in cyber-physical and industrial control systems, ranging from threats, to risks that such systems face, to cyber-attacks that may be launched against such systems, to ways of detecting and responding to such attacks.

We would like to express our thanks to all those who assisted us in organizing the event and putting together the program. We are very grateful to the members of the Program Committee for their timely and rigorous reviews. Thanks are also due to the ESORICS Workshop Chairs and to the ESORICS Organizers. Last, but by no means least, we would like to thank all the authors who submitted their work to the workshop and contributed to an interesting set of proceedings.

October 2023

Sokratis Katsikas
Frédéric Cuppens
Nora Cuppens-Boulahia
Costas Lambrinoudakis

CyberICPS 2023 Organization

General Chairs

Sokratis Katsikas   Norwegian University of Science and Technology, Norway

Frédéric Cuppens   Polytechnique Montréal, Canada

Program Chairs

Costas Lambrinoudakis   University of Piraeus, Greece

Nora Cuppens-Boulahia   Polytechnique Montréal, Canada

Publicity Chair

Nikolaos Pitropakis   Edinburgh Napier University, UK

Program Committee

Habtamu Abie	Norsk Regnesentral, Norway
Cristina Alcaraz	University of Malaga, Spain
Marios Anagnostopoulos	Aalborg University, Denmark
Samiha Ayed	University of Technology of Troyes, France
Mauro Conti	University of Padua, Italy
David Espes	University of Brest, France
Khan Ferdous Wahid	Airbus Group, France
Joaquin Garcia-Alfaro	Institut Polytechnique de Paris, France
Vasileios Gkioulos	Norwegian University of Science and Technology, Norway
Dieter Gollmann	Hamburg University of Technology, Germany
Georgios Kavallieratos	Norwegian University of Science and Technology, Norway
Youssef Laarouchi	EDF R&D, France
Stefano Longari	Politecnico di Milano, Italy
Michail Maniatakos	NYU-Abu Dhabi, UAE
Sjouke Mauw	University of Luxembourg, Luxembourg
Weizhi Meng	Technical University of Denmark, Denmark
Pankaj Pandey	Norwegian University of Science and Technology, Norway

Nikolaos Pitropakis	Edinburgh Napier University, UK
Indrakshi Ray	Colorado State University, USA
Rodrigo Roman	University of Malaga, Spain
Andrea Saracino	Consiglio Nazionale delle Ricerche, Italy
Georgios Spathoulas	University of Thessaly, Greece
Nils Ole Tippenhauer	CISPA, Germany
Stefano Zanero	Politecnico di Milano, Italy
Jianying Zhou	Singapore University of Technology and Design, Singapore

External Reviewers

Denis Donadel	University of Padua, Italy
Ankit Gangwal	University of Padua, Italy
Pavlos Papadopoulos	Edinburgh Napier University, UK
Federico Turrin	University of Padua, Italy

Effects of Organizational Cyber Security Culture Across the Energy Sector Supply Chain

Susanne Barkhald Sandberg(✉) 📵, Aida Akbarzadeh📵,
and Vasileios Gkioulos📵

Norwegian University of Science and Technology, Gjøvik, Norway
`susanne.bs@outlook.com`, {`aida.akbarzadeh,vasileios.gkioulos`}`@ntnu.no`

Abstract. In critical infrastructure, cyber incidents can have significant impact not only on an organization itself but also on the security of society and safety of the public. In recent years, there has been an increasing number of supply chain cyber attacks, with weak links in the chain commonly exploited as points of penetration. For this reason, it is crucial for organizations to start managing cyber security not only within their own organization, but also across the entire supply chain. To shed light on this challenge and bridge existing gaps, this study investigated the effects of cyber security culture within and among organizations across the energy sector supply chain. Our findings indicate that cultivating a robust security culture can significantly enhance supply chain security practices. Therefore, it is of paramount importance to prioritize efforts towards aligning organizations through the promotion of common understanding and shared values. These concerted efforts are not only advantageous but also indispensable as we strive toward a more secure future for the supply chain.

Keywords: Cyber security · Cyber security culture · Organizational culture · Supply chain security · Supply chain cyber security · Human factors · Critical infrastructure · Supply chain risk management

1 Introduction

In the energy sector, many organizations have a technical environment that consists of both administrative systems and operational systems. With increasing digitization, the dependencies on these systems, as well as their supply chains, are becoming increasingly crucial. In these environments, there is often a combination of new and old technology, including industrial control systems and legacy systems. Traditionally, many of these systems were physically separated from other systems through *airgapping* [1]. However, with the increasing interconnection between them today, the distinction is becoming less prominent [2,3]. This results in increased risk for the organizations, especially considering that many legacy systems were not designed with security in mind. Also the increased use of Industrial Internet of Things (IIoT) has raised concerns about vulnerabilities in operational technology (OT) environments [4].

© The Author(s), under exclusive license to Springer Nature Switzerland AG 2024
S. Katsikas et al. (Eds.): ESORICS 2023 Workshops, LNCS 14398, pp. 5–24, 2024.
https://doi.org/10.1007/978-3-031-54204-6_1

Additionally, the vulnerabilities in the supply chain are increasing with its complexity. In a complex supply chain, organizations lack visibility and control, which in turn exposes them to a wide range of threats [5]. According to ENISA [6], the number of supply chain attacks has increased rapidly in the last years, and this number is expected to continue to increase further in the years to come. This is challenging as it becomes necessary not only to consider cybersecurity within the borders of an organization, but also to take into account the relations and dependencies with other organizations in the chain. Meanwhile, the mentioned complexity and lack of visibility and transparency in the chain can make it difficult to discover and identify such relations and dependencies. In addition, the consequences of a security incident or an attack may extend beyond the affected organization. As a part of critical infrastructures, the energy sector is of significant importance for modern society. Many of the organizations within the sector rely on the same large vendors, creating interdependencies among them [7]. Hence, the ripple effect of large-scale targeted attacks could have serious impact on society. The relation and dependencies between the different sectors and critical infrastructures further makes it possible for incidents to propagate and have detrimental effects even across different industries. Consequently, supply chain cyber security risk is something to consider not only for the individual organizations or the energy sector, but also for national security [5]. The question is then, how can organizations in the energy sector mitigate these risks? Previous research has mainly been focused on the technical aspects of cyber security, while human aspects have been more neglected [8]. Human and organizational aspects of cyber security does however play an important role.'

Therefore, to fill this gap, this study aims to investigate the effects of cyber security culture on supply chain security practices and the relation between entities in the chain. In more detail, this work attempts to provide insights into:

- How organizational cyber security culture affects the overview and control of dependencies to other organizations in the supply chain from a preparedness perspective (RQ1).
- How organizational cyber security culture affects the level of trust in other organizations in the supply chain (RQ2).

In addressing RQ1, the study explores security practices related to dependencies to other organizations in the chain, such as the procurement process and security revision. It aims to examine how organizational cyber security culture influences the extent to which organizations have a clear understanding of dependencies and maintain control over them. Regarding RQ2, the research delves into the relationship between organizations in the supply chain and the role of organizational cyber security culture in shaping the level of trust. It seeks to uncover the explicit and implicit mechanisms that contribute to trust-building, including policies, agreements, contracts, and revisions. By examining these research questions, the study aims to shed light on the various dimensions of cyber security culture and how they intersect with supply chain relations and practices. The findings will provide valuable insights for organizations in the energy sector to mitigate cyber security risks and strengthen their supply chain security by emphasizing the significance of organizational cyber security culture. In summary, the main contribution of this paper is as follows:

- Bridges the gap between technical aspects of cyber security and human/organizational aspects in the supply chain;
- Investigates the significance of cyber security culture on supply chain security;
- Enhances supply chain security practices;
- Studies trusted relationships among entities in the supply chain and their impact on supply chain security.

The rest of the paper is organized as follows: In Sect. 2, we review the related work conducted on supply chain cyber security and cyber security culture. Section 3 describes the methodology used in this study. In Sect. 4, we present and provide a detailed explanation of the findings. We discuss the implications of our findings and their significance in Sect. 5. Finally, Sect. 6 summarizes our conclusions and indicates possible directions for future research.

2   Related Work

2.1   Supply Chain Cyber Security

A literature review conducted by Safa et al. [9] investigates the different aspects of cyber security in the supply chain. The findings highlight the multi-dimensional and complex nature of supply chain cyber security. The authors also notably emphasize the significance of organizational and human aspects of security, in particular the importance of risk awareness, risk identification and security policies. Employee compliance with existing policies is also identified as a crucial factor in this work. In more recent reviews of literature, it has been observed that there has been relatively less research conducted on human factors in supply chain cyber security compared to technical factors [8].

Furthermore, Ghadge et al. [8] conducted a systematic literature review in 2019 to explore cyber risk management in the supply chain. The review encompassed 41 articles published between 2000 and 2017. The study emphasizes that the links within a supply chain can serve as vulnerable points of penetration if they are not sufficiently secured, underscoring the importance of identifying these weak links within the organization. Additionally, the findings also highlight the significant role of employees as a major cyber security risk in the supply chain. As stated in the review, "In both the negligent and premeditated mode, the human factor can pose the biggest and most unpredictable threat to a company's cybersecurity" [8]. Moreover, it has been found that the risk increases when employees from different organizations interact [8]. In the year 2022, Melnyk et al. [12] identified small-to-medium sized enterprises (SMEs) as weak links within the scope of their investigation. They conducted an exploratory research study with the aim of developing a research framework for cyber security across the supply chain.

In addition to cyber security risks and challenges within the supply chain, potential mitigations have also been proposed in research. Ghadge et al. [8] classified such mitigations into three distinct categories, based on the phases of an attack: Pre-attack, trans-attack and post-attack. The mitigations related to the pre-attack phase are further divided into those addressing technical factors and those addressing human factors, where the latter being particularly relevant for this study. Among the mitigations mentioned in the study [8], the following examples are noteworthy:

- Awareness training for employees
- Accreditation against standards
- Information sharing
- Standard guidelines for collaboration
- Formalised agreements between organizations
- Supplier audit
- Risk classification and identification
- Zero-trust policy

Roman et al. [10] additionally proposed international cooperation and coordinated actions by government institutions, as well as establishing guidelines to ensure transparency within and between organizations in the supply chain. They point out that this might also include awareness and security training. More specifically, for preparedness, they suggested approaches using cyberrange and digital twins (DTs).

ENISA also provided recommendations in their 2021 report [6]. They presented good practices for both customers and suppliers in the supply chain to manage supply chain cybersecurity risk, as well as the customer-supplier relationships. However, regarding certain threats, they also highlighted that there might be a need for actions to be taken at a higher level than the organizational one, such as at the national or European level.

2.2   Cyber Security Culture

In a recent structured literature review, Uchendu et al. [11] presented the current work and future needs for developing a cyber security culture. Following the PRISMA protocol [12], the study examined 58 papers from the last ten years, focusing on four specific areas: Definitions, Factors, Frameworks, and Metrics. The findings reveal that a significant part of previous research on security culture primarily focuses on information security culture, with only 10 of the 58 articles specifically examining cyber security culture. Figure 1 demonstrates the distinction between cyber security and information security [13].

Uchendu et al. [11] also show that questionnaires and surveys are the most common research instruments along with theoretical research. The study indicates that a significant portion of the research encompasses a diverse range of participants, while a smaller number of studies focus solely on top management. An interesting finding is that, similar to research on supply chain cyber

Fig. 1. Difference between Information Security, ICT Security and Cyber Security [13]

security, there has been relatively limited investigation into SME's compared to larger organizations. Besides, there is a lack of research examining the long-term effects of cultural frameworks and approaches in practice.

This literature review also revealed that top management support is the most frequently mentioned factor associated with the development of a cyber security culture, appearing in 34 out of the 58 papers [11]. Other factors are depicted in Fig. 2, scaled based on the frequency of their mention in research. It is worth mentioning that while top management support is crucial, it alone is insufficient to build a culture. Other factors, such as trust, awareness, training, and policies, are also vital components in establishing a comprehensive cyber security culture. Notably, regulations are mentioned in only four papers, which is of particular interest in the context of this study.

Fig. 2. Factors of security culture [11]

Understanding the underlying factors that contribute to the development of a cyber security culture is of paramount importance for this study as it facilitates the examination of potential associations with supply chain security practices. The review of related work revealed a significant overlap between the key factors of security culture and the mitigations of supply chain cyber risk. Notably, there are areas of convergence that encompass elements such as awareness, training, and risk management. This overlap is illustrated in Fig. 3. This finding highlights the interconnectedness and shared importance of these factors in addressing challenges within the supply chain context. We will elaborate more on that in the subsequent sections.

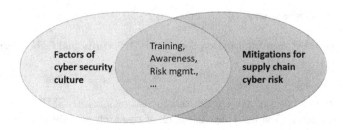

Fig. 3. Overlapping factors

3   Method

In this section, we describe the methodology used in the study. The process is divided into three phases including *Problem Identification and Literature Review*, *Data Collection and Analysis*, and *Data Interpretation and Reporting*. Figure 4 provides a visual summary of this section.

3.1   Problem Identification and Literature Review

In the first phase of the study, empirical data from the Norwegian energy sector was used as starting point for the research. The objective was to identify challenges, risks and areas in need of improvement in relation to supply chain security. This was studied through publicly available reports from different actors, among others The Norwegian Water Resources and Energy Directorate (NVE), The Office of the Auditor General of Norway (OAG) and The Norwegian National Security Authority (NSM) [5,7,14,15]. Subsequenly, a literature study of related academic research was performed to place the empirical information into a broader context and to shape the theoretical concepts. ENISA's definition of cyber security culture was used as the basis for the theoretical model. In their report, cyber security culture "...refers to the knowledge, beliefs, perceptions, attitudes, assumptions, norms and values of people regarding cybersecurity and how they manifest in people's behavior with information technologies" [16]. SME's were also added as a variable to the study at this point, as both reports from the sector and the review of academic research had pointed out challenges around these and their role in the supply chain. In this study we define the term small-to-medium sized as an organization having 500 employees or less.

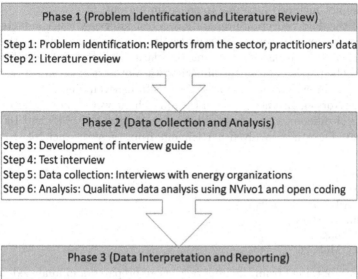

Fig. 4. Process

3.2 Data Collection and Analysis

Related work has shown that surveys and questionnaires are the most commonly used tools for assessing cyber security culture. Furthermore, reviewing recent studies also revealed several tools for assessing security culture that had already been developed and validated. However, due to the limited research on the combination of cyber security culture and supply chain cyber security in the past, and the need to thoroughly explore the relationship between these concepts, a qualitative approach in the form of interviews was chosen for our study. A selection of the mentioned assessment tools were used as a foundation in the development of an interview guide. In particular, questions and statements from the following references were used to create a database of a total of 245 sample statements: the adjusted Information Security Culture Assessment (ISCA) [17], the Norwegian Digitalisation Agency's method for assessing security culture [18], CheckIT [19], the "Workforce", "Response", and "Third-Parties" dimensions of the Cybersecurity Capability Maturity Model (C2M2) [20]. As a first iteration, all questions that could be relevant to the research questions were identified, categorized and put into a first draft. The number of questions were then reduced in an iterative process. The final interview guide contained a total of 54 questions in four different categories including *Background* (5 questions), *Perceptions of Management and Control* (14 questions), *Incidents and Incident Response* (10 questions), and *Supply Chain Management* (25 questions). Interested readers can refer to [21] for more details on the collected data and questionnaire items, as they are not included here due to space limitations.

As part of the data collection preparation, a test interview was conducted. This was done for several reasons, with a particular emphasis on verifying the anticipated interview duration and ensuring the clarity and comprehensibility of the questions. The participant in this interview was not part of the study sample. In the next step, interviews with representatives from seven different organizations within the Norwegian energy sectors supply chain were made. The organizations were of different sizes, divided into the categories of SME and LE (Large Enterprise). The study involved participants from these distinct roles:

- CEO
- IT Manager
- Security Architect
- Senior Advisor (Security)
- IT Administrator
- Sales Manager
- Security Manager

The data obtained from the interviews were prepared and analyzed in accordance with Creswell's data analysis spiral [22], a well-referenced approach for analyzing qualitative data (see Fig. 5).

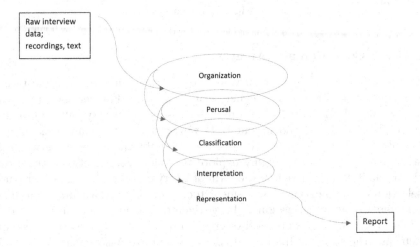

Fig. 5. Creswell's Data Analysis Spiral [22]

During the initial review process, in line with Creswell's data analysis spiral, initial thoughts and interpretations were documented in separate comments, distinct from the interview data. In order to further classify the data, the software tool NVivo[1] was used to perform open coding in an iterative process. As a starting point, cases were created for each of the organizations. Responses from each

---

[1] More information about NVivo can be found at https://www.alfasoft.com/en/products/statistics-and-analysis/nvivo.html.

organization was then coded to the respective case. Subsequently, the classifications "SME" and "LE" were created and assigned to cases from small-to-medium sized organizations and large organizations, respectively. Due to their relevance to the RQ's, the codes "Cyber security culture", "Supply chain cyber security practices", "Preparedness", "Trust". "Organization size" were also created. Data relevant to these elements were assigned to the respective codes. Continuing the iterative process, new codes and sub-codes were generated based on the collected data. The goal of this step was to identify any other relevant subjects and potentially uncover any unknown underlying patterns. Figure 6 presents the resulting codes compared by number of references they received.

3.3   Data Interpretation and Reporting

In the final step of the classification, identified codes were grouped into themes, marking the readiness of the data for interpretation and reporting. In Sect. 4 we will delve into a comprehensive exploration of the outcomes derived from these interpretive processes, offering a detailed analysis and insights into the patterns, trends, and key findings encapsulated within the gathered data.

4   Results

In this section, we provide a detailed explanation of the outcomes, which will be presented in eight distinct subsections. Each subsection will focus on a specific aspect of the findings, providing a comprehensive analysis of the interview data and their implications.

4.1   Governance

The results indicate that cyber security policies and procedures are well established in the energy organizations. With one exception, the results also show that the responsibility for cyber security is perceived to be placed at the top management. Top management support, however, differs much more among the organizations. While most of the larger organizations explain that their top management clearly communicates that cyber security is important for the organization, several from the SME-category express ambiguity regarding their expectations towards employees in terms of cyber security. One explain that top management never challenges them if they are secure enough, but that they rather question if they are spending too much money on security.

Fig. 7 illustrates the participants' perception of the most significant motivation for engaging in cyber security work within their respective organizations. The most frequently mentioned aspect was the possible consequences for society in case of a large breach. Legal and regulatory requirements are also important factors, as well as audits, privacy and the EU General Data Protection Regulation (GDPR).

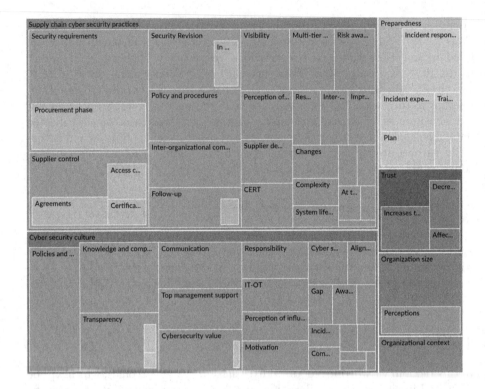

Fig. 6. Comparison of Codes by Number of References.

4.2 Preparedness and Incident Response

The results indicate that all participants are familiar with cyber security incidents in the sector, and that these incidents affect their respective organizations to a variating degree. In case of an incident in the sector, at the least, the organizations need to take measures in the form of checking or verifying possible consequences for their own organization. Information sharing among the organizations in the sector is therefore important. A common CERT for the sector stands out as a central point of information sharing, which is highly valued by the organizations. Vendors, however, are not necessarily under the same restrictions and requirements as the energy organizations, and information sharing from vendor to customer organizations might be less structured unless agreed upon.

From a preparedness perspective, vendor control and follow-ups are directly related to the regulatory requirements. The regulatory framework makes strict requirements to power organizations regarding the protection of sensitive power information, and the organizations need to make sure that their vendors fulfill the information security and confidentiality requirements, as well as ensuring the right to control and revise. The results suggest that all organizations have embedded this aspect in their contracts and agreements. They also have

Fig. 7. Key motivations for cyber security efforts in organizations

important dependencies included in their preparedness plans. In general, policies and procedures that relates to cyber security requirements seem to be well established in the organizations. However, some participants express uncertainty about the extent to which these plans are actually implemented in practice.

4.3 Supply Chain Challenges

Most of the participants state that they only have visibility of the supply chain up to one tier down, two tiers down at the maximum. The depth and complexity of the supply chain, as well as the traceability of components, presents a great challenge for the organizations. More specifically, the following points are mentioned:

- **To know what you are buying.** There are many tiers in the chain and many components in each product. One participant explained this was more challenging in OT than in IT. Another expressed a feeling that vendors barely know what they are selling.
- **Complexity and number of suppliers.** It is challenging and resource-intensive to maintain an overview over time, particularly when dealing with a large number of suppliers, especially those that are primarily focused on delivery.
- **Lack of standardization.** Lack of standardization makes it challenging to know where to make effort.
- **Lack of common understanding.** This was pointed out as a current challenge, particularly when it comes to vendors understanding what it means to deliver to critical infrastructure. A common understanding could push suppliers in the right direction and benefit in the implementation of frameworks.
- **Lifecycle of systems and components.** Keeping all components up-to-date can be a challenge, as some reach end-of-life and are no longer patchable.
- **Gap in competency.** Buyer competency is important in a supply chain. The organization is always responsible for their own data. Misunderstandings

of where the responsibility lies is a common challenge from a vendor's point of view.

Further, our results indicate that the organizations have well established policies and procedures to verify that vendors fulfill security requirements when entering agreements, although the specific practices vary from organization to organization. Active follow-ups within the period of contract is however less common, and change management is connected with the following challenges:

– **Updates:** Software/firmware updates from the vendor might be installed without question, vulnerability patches in particular. If these updates are somehow compromised or faulty, it is rarely possible to discover before damage is done.
– **Resources:** Keeping track of the supply chain(s) over time is perceived extremely challenging and resource demanding from the organizations' perspective. It needs to be decided how far down in the chain one should go. Tools and methods for keeping an overview should be considered/developed.
– **Communication:** Communication regarding updates and changes from vendor to customer organizations is challenging and sometimes lacking. Internal communication within organizations is also mentioned as an important point, as the information needs to get to the right people.

4.4   Trust

The term *Trust* was frequently mentioned during interviews when speaking of the supply chain. There were also a collection of factors that the participants believed influenced the trust between organizations in the supply chain. The factors are shown in Fig. 8.

Transparency and openness, along with dialogue, communication, and relationship, were the most frequently mentioned aspects. These are closely related with honesty. These factors refer not only to the vertical communication of vulnerabilities and incidents within the chain, but also to the exchange of information between the different organizations in the sector. A culture of sharing and openness is necessary across the sector, and the majority of participants feel that this culture is already present today. Some, however, also highlighted that there is room for improvement. The following points were mentioned:

– There is less sharing in OT than IT.
– There have been improvements, but there are still glossy pictures out there when incidents occur.
– Information sharing relies on individuals - Information needs to be lifted to the right people to a larger degree.

A common CERT-function is also highlighted as an important aspect of the information flow. Direct contact between suppliers and their customers appears to be less structured and may benefit from improvement.

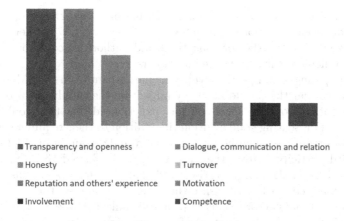

Fig. 8. Factors that affect Trust

4.5 Looking Towards Others and Propagation of Trust

Our results show that especially SME's have a tendency to look to other organizations to a large degree when choosing vendors or making security-related decisions. Vendors with many larger size customers seem to be perceived as more trustworthy. This is built on an assumption that larger organizations have a higher level of security. In organizations where cyber security value was perceived to be at a medium or lower level, the external focus was perceived as a security challenge. This could be due to the fact that decision makers may (1) look to organizations with lower security requirements without fully understanding the difference it makes and (2) look to others to find justification for choosing less expensive systems.

4.6 The Impact of Organization Size

SME's were intentially included in the study both because they have been considered weak links in the chain in previous works and that less studies have focused on smaller organizations compared to larger ones [8,23]. For this reason, the answers were categorized into two groups: SME's and LE's when presenting the results. At first glance, the results seem to support the findings of related work, as they suggest that cyber security is valued higher in larger organizations, and that top management in these organizations have communicated their expectations regarding cyber security to a larger degree compared to SME's. However, there are nuances to consider. Based on the results, participants from both smaller organizations and larger organizations see both benefits and drawbacks of having the organizational size that they have. As already mentioned there are also some assumptions among the organizations that relates to other organizations' size. While the results show that the larger organizations in this study generally take cyber security very seriously, with some of them making efforts to influence their vendors, the findings also reveal that supply chain cyber security poses challenge for them as well. One participant emphasized that they might be large on a national scale, but not on an international scale. They further suggested standing together with other organizations and authorities could be a possible approach to increase their influence on vendors.

Another interesting finding is that while one participant from the SME-category did not believe that they could have any impact on the supply chain because of their size, another from the same category experienced that they could, but by suggesting and presenting good solutions in addition to their requirements. This, however, does require some in-house competency and certain priorities from their side. A third participant from the same category explained that requirements could be stricter in their organization, and that security evaluations were not necessarily followed up by the risk owner even if it showed that the vendor's security was not satisfactory. This is primarily linked to the focus and priorities of decision makers. The diversity of answers suggests that an organization's influence on the chain is determined by a complex combination of factors, rather than solely relying on size and resources.

5   Discussion

In this section, we will first discuss the results in relation to the main research questions mentioned in the Introduction. Then, we will also explore additional findings that, although not initially part of the research questions, are still relevant to the topic of cyber security culture across the energy sector supply chain.

5.1   Discussion of Main Research Questions

Here, we focus on the discussion of the research questions:

RQ1: Our results show that the awareness around the risk of third-party collaboration is high, however many of the organizations are strongly depending on their vendors. The need for what the vendor can offer to the organization outlines the risk or leads to an acceptance of the excess risk. Moreover, organizations in the energy sector find keeping control of their dependencies in the supply chain challenging, both within IT and OT. The visibility is low below the first tier of the chain.

According to the results, organizations have well established policies and procedures for the procurement process. However, the results also indicate that change management and regular follow-ups within contract lifetime is less structured. This is also very resource-demanding for the organizations, considering the number of vendors. Still, it is difficult to discover breaches to the security requirements if they are not actively followed up on. If not, one has to make the assumption that the conditions that are present at the point of entering contract will stay constant throughout the contract lifetime. It needs to be decided how far down in the chain one should go to keep control and how this should be carried out over time. This depends on knowledge, competency, resources and willingness of both organizations and vendors, and also the perceived cyber security value and priorities within the organization.

From the preparedness perspective, vendor control is directly related to the regulatory requirements that organizations in the energy sector need to comply with. Organizations need to ensure that vendors fulfill the security and confidentiality requirements and they also need to ensure the right to revise. Our results generally indicate that organizations have well established policies and procedures for cyber security and supply chain management, and that they keep control of their vendors through contracts and agreements. However, for some, it is more unsure how well this is followed up in practice. This is a crucial point, as a policy will not be of any value to an organization unless it has an actual effect on practices, especially in a preparedness situation. This suggests that there is still room for improvement, and that building a good cyber security culture could be a way for organizations to cover this gap between policy and practice. However, it would be important for organizations to investigate further the underlying reasons for lack of compliance with policies. There might be several causes, for example risk perception or lack of knowledge, resources or competency. Research has also shown that policy compliance increases when employees are not only aware of the content of the policy, but also why the policies are important [24]. Efforts to identify these factors would ease the improvement process.

RQ2: In our study, we have found several factors that are of importance for the trust between different organizations in the supply chain. With the exception of turnover, all the factors are all closely related to the different dimensions of cyber security culture reviewed in related work. As trust itself can be seen as a cultural factor, this is not surprising [25]. Not much related work has looked at cyber security culture beyond the borders of an organization, thus there is a need to separate between the internal trust within the organization and external trust towards other organizations. Transparency, openness and communication stands out among the most frequently mentioned factors that affect the trust between oranizations. It is also found that organizations in many cases could benefit from increased awareness regarding *where* shared information ends up within their own organization. Depending on the nature of the information, it may need to be raised and distributed beyond IT or security personnel. Thus, based on the factors found and their relation to cyber security culture, results suggest that the trust in a third-party would be affected by the third-party's security culture. Nevertheless, the results do not give any clear suggestions to how an organization's own cyber security culture affect the trust in third-parties. The importance of trust in supply chain relations and management is nonetheless remarkable, based on the collected data.

Several participants tended to use phrasings like *"We have to trust our vendors"* or *"We are at the mercy of our vendors"*. The choice of words could indicate that this is more "forced" trust than "earned" trust, in the way that the only alternative is to trust the vendor. For instance, some pointed to the fact that they have little to no possibility to do security revisions in practice. However, the same participants do feel that they might influence the supply chain through making requirements or in other ways. A possible explanation to this could be that there are alternatives in theory, but not in practice. Many vendors have large, international organizations. It is also worth noting that all participants described to have the regulatory requirements fulfilled through contracts, but that the challenges are more related to how compliance can be verified and followed up in practice.

Our findings also show that trust can propagate within the supply chain. As an example, a participant from the SME-category described that it was common to look to larger organizations in the sector when choosing vendors. Vendors with many large customers are perceived more trustworthy based on an assumption that larger organizations have stricter requirements and a higher level of security. Thus, this assumption leads to implicit trust in vendors. However, the collected data also revealed that the larger organizations find supply chain cyber security challenging. One of the participants from the LE-category also pointed out that simply being large does not necessarily mean that you are great, even if you have some good prerequisites. This is an important point. Every organization is different, and there will be a complexity of factors that have an impact on the general lever of cyber security. Two organizations of the exact same size might have very different values, structure and distribution of resources. It is risky to make assumptions solely based on size, in particular when trust propagates within the chain. Also internally, the focus should be shifted towards other factors. By breaking it down, it is possible to both assess and improve. An assumption that an organization cannot influence their supply chain simply because they are small might lead to less focus on requirements and accepting lower levels of security at the vendor. However the challenge of standing independently should not be underestimated, and it is crucial for all organizations within the sector to be aligned. Efforts to build a strong security culture throughout the sector would in this case be beneficial and would also have vertical effects in the supply chain by a larger influence on the vendors. One of the participants summarized it effectively:

> " It has to do with raising up those with very low maturity with the help of those with high maturity and make sure it is aligned"

Finally, a supply chain attack is an attack that takes advantage of the trust between parties. For this reason, organizations need be aware of how, when and why they put their trust in a third-party. Considering the results of our study, it could also be considered to which degree a Zero Trust Architecture (ZTA) approach could be beneficial for supply chain security. The ZTA was developed by National Institute of Standards and Technology (NIST) as a technical approach to cyber security in which there is no implicit trust between parties [26]. However, as stated in an security blog post by Edward Kost, "for the ZTA to have maximum potential, this framework should be implemented both within an organization and throughout its vendor network" [27]. This implies a significant demand and necessitates a cultural shift towards a zero-trust philosophy throughout the supply chain.

5.2 Exploration of Additional Findings

Comparisons to HSE: During the interview, several of the participants compared their cyber security practices with those related to health, safety and the environment (HSE). The first comparison was related to the value of cyber security, where one participant expressed that they wished that cyber security efforts would be reinforced and supported in the organization in the same way as for HSE. In their organization, HSE was the first point on the agenda at all board meetings. In recent years, the industry organization Energy Norway[2] has focused on HSE, with the aim of making the Norwegian renewable energy industry the best in HSE. In particular, they presented "HMS-Løftet", which is a pledge to lift[3] the level of HSE [28]. The CEOs of the participating organizations must sign and accept five points related to the responsibilities and attitudes they have towards HSE. Energy Norway also made board presentations and guidelines available to the organizations to ease implementation. It is clear that this approach focuses on several of the same factors that are important when developing a cyber security culture, in example top management support, accountability and responsibility[11, 28]. Responsibility is a key word here, as our results have shown that vendors experience confusion from the organizations as to where the responsibility for cyber security lies. Regardless of third-parties, organizations should be aware that they are responsible for the security of their own assets, also those reachable through cyber space. Furthermore, there should be no doubt that top management has the responsibility within each organization. It could be interesting to study the effects of a similar approach as "HMS-Løftet" for improving the cyber security culture across the sector. Of course, this would require efforts from a higher level than the individual or organizational level.

Alignment: Alignment is another key word related to the supply chain. Internal alignment is an important factor for internal culture, in terms of the perceptions, assumptions, values and behaviours that exist within the organization. As some of the participants mentioned during interviews, organizations might have different maturity in the different parts of their organization. Some also pointed out that the alignment between IT or cyber security personnel and other employees can be a challenge, which might be caused by a lack of common understanding and a different view on the value of cyber security efforts. Misalignment in organizations can possibly also be caused by conflicting goals, as explained by Parsons et al. [29] in a study of information security decision making. In their study, top management scored less on knowledge, awareness and self-reported behaviour. In our case, some of the participants pointed out the two axes of usability and security.

---

[2] Energy Norway merged with Norwea in January 2023, creating the new organization Renewables Norway (www.fornybarnorge.no/om-oss/in-english/).
[3] Both "Pledge" and "Lift" can be translated to "Løfte" in Norwegian.

In addition to the importance of internal alignment, our results also clearly show that the alignment between the different organizations in the sector is of great value for the security of the supply chain. A common understanding and shared values should be a goal for the future. This includes not only a vertical alignment (supplier-to-vendor, vendor-to-vendor, and vendor-to-customer), but also a horizontal alignment between peer organizations. Continued development of a culture of openness and transparency should facilitate this process.

6   Conclusion and Future Work

Organizations in the energy sector hold significant importance as part of critical infrastructure in the modern society. With digitization and increased interconnection, these organizations are experiencing increased risk of cyber incidents. Due to the dependencies between organizations and also between different industries, large scale incidents might have wide-reaching consequences. These consequences extend beyond the individual organizations and can impact society as a whole, as well as pose risks to national security. Therefore, it is crucial to gain more knowledge on how supply chain cyber risks may be managed and mitigated.

In this study, we have investigated the relation between organizational cyber security culture and supply chain cyber security through a qualitative empirical approach. Interviews were performed with representatives from different organizations within the Norwegian energy sector and its supply chain. Our findings indicate cultivating a robust security culture can significantly enhance supply chain security practices. Furthermore, it is of great importance to make efforts towards alignment within the sector though common understanding and shared values.

The study has also revealed several possible areas in need of more research. As participants have pointed out, some organizations experience gaps in maturity and security subcultures within their own organization. It would be interesting for future research to investigate the impact of subcultures on supply chain security to gain a deeper understanding of their effects. Another area of future work would be to identify and investigate a specific cyber supply chain vertically starting from a focal organiziation. Expanding the research to include other EU and non-EU countries and conducting a comparative analysis of the results would provide valuable insights for future research in this field.

References

1. Krutz, K.R.L.: Securing SCADA systems. Wiley-Blackwell (2015)
2. Colbert, E.J.M., Kott, A. (eds.): Cyber-security of SCADA and Other Industrial Control Systems. AIS, vol. 66. Springer, Cham (2016). https://doi.org/10.1007/978-3-319-32125-7
3. Akbarzadeh, A.: Dependency based risk analysis in Cyber-Physical Systems. PhD thesis, NTNU (2023)

4. Topping, C., Dwyer, A., Michalec, O., Craggs, B., Rashid, A.: Beware suppliers bearing gifts!: analysing coverage of supply chain cyber security in critical national infrastructure sectorial and cross-sectorial frameworks. Comput. Secur. **108**, 9 (2021)
5. Nasjonal Sikkerhetsmyndighet (NSM). Risiko 2021 - helhetlig sikring mot sammensatte trusler (2021)
6. European Union Agency for Cybersecurity (ENISA). Enisa threat landscape for supply chain attacks. Technical report (July 2021)
7. Riksrevisjonen. Riksrevisjonens undersøkelse av nves arbeid med ikt-sikkerhet i kraftforsyningen, dokument 3:7 (2020–2021). Technical Report Dokument 3:7 (2020–2021), Riksrevisjonen (2021)
8. Ghadge, A., Weiß, M., Caldwell, N.D., Wilding, R.: Managing cyber risk in supply chains: a review and research agenda. Supply Chain Manag. Inter. J. **25**(2), 223–240 (2019)
9. Safa, N.S., Maple, C., Watson, T.: The information security landscape in the supply chain. Comput. Fraud Sec. **16–20**, 2017 (2017)
10. Roman, R., Alcaraz, C., Lopez, J., Sakurai, K.: Current perspectives on securing critical infrastructures' supply chains. IEEE Sec. Priv. **21**(4), 29–38 (2023)
11. Uchendu, B., Nurse, J.R.C., Bada, M., Furnell, S.: Developing a cyber security culture: current practices and future needs. Comput. Sec. **109**, 102387 (2021)
12. PRISMA. Prisma transparent reporting of systematic reviews and meta-analyses
13. Malmedal, B., Røislien, H.E.: The norwegian cyber security culture (2016)
14. Kirkebø, E., Ljøsne, M.: Ikt-sikkerhet ved anskaffelser og tjenesteutsetting i energibransjen. Report 90/2018, NVE (2018)
15. Nasjonal Sikkerhetsmyndighet (NSM). Risiko 2022 - Økt risiko krever økt årvåkenhet (2022)
16. The European Union Agency for Cybersecurity (ENISA). Cyber security culture in organisations. ENISA, Heraklion (2017)
17. Da Veiga, A.: An approach to information security culture change combining ADKAR and the ISCA questionnaire to aid transition to the desired culture. Inform. Comput. Sec. **26**(5), 584–612 (2018)
18. Digitaliseringsdirektoratet. Veileder for kartlegging av sikkerhetskultur
19. Johnsen, S.O., Hansen, C.W., Nordby, Y., Dahl, M.B.: Measurement and improvement of information security culture. Measurem. Control **39**(2), 52–56 (2006)
20. Office of Cybersecurity, Energy Security, and Emergency Response. Cybersecurity Capability Maturity Model (C2M2)
21. Sandberg, S.B.: Effects of organizational cyber security culture across the energy sector supply chain [unpublished manuscript]. Master's thesis, Norwegian University of Science and Technology, Gjøvik, Norway (December 2022)
22. Creswell, J.W., Poth, C.N.: Qualitative inquiry & research design : choosing among five approaches (2018)
23. Melnyk, S.A., Schoenherr, T., Speier-Pero, C., Peters, C., Chang, J.F., Friday, D.: New challenges in supply chain management: cybersecurity across the supply chain. Int. J. Prod. Res. **60**(1), 162–183 (2022)
24. Parsons, K., McCormac, A., Pattinson, M., Butavicius, M., Jerram, C.: A study of information security awareness in Australian government organisations. Inform. Manag. Comput. Sec. **22**, 334–345 (2014)
25. Georgiadou, A., Mouzakitis, S., Bounas, K., Askounis, D.: A cyber-security culture framework for assessing organization readiness. J. Comput. Syst. 1–11 (2020)
26. Rose, S., Borchert, O., Mitchell, S., Connelly, S.: Zero trust architecture (2020)

27. Kost, E.: Zero trust as a defence against supply chain attacks
28. Norge, E.: Kom i gang med hms-løftet. https://www.energinorge.no/publikasjoner/veileder/kom-i-gang-med-hms-loftet/
29. Parsons, K.M., Young, E., Butavicius, M.A., McCormac, A., Pattinson, M.R., Jerram, C.: The influence of organizational information security culture on information security decision making. J. Cognitive Eng. Decision Making 9, 117–129 (2015)

METRICS: A Methodology for Evaluating and Testing the Resilience of Industrial Control Systems to Cyberattacks

Lennart Bader[1,2], Eric Wagner[1,2], Martin Henze[1,3], and Martin Serror[1(✉)]

[1] Cyber Analysis and Defense, Fraunhofer FKIE, Wachtberg, Germany
{lennart.bader,eric.wagner,martin.henze,
martin.serror}@fkie.fraunhofer.de
[2] Communication and Distributed Systems, RWTH Aachen University,
Aachen, Germany
{bader,wagner}@comsys.rwth-aachen.de
[3] Security and Privacy in Industrial Cooperation, RWTH Aachen University,
Aachen, Germany
henze@cs.rwth-aachen.de

Abstract. The increasing digitalization and interconnectivity of industrial control systems (ICSs) create enormous benefits, such as enhanced productivity and flexibility, but also amplify the impact of cyberattacks. Cybersecurity research thus continuously needs to adapt to new threats while proposing comprehensive security mechanisms for the ICS domain. As a prerequisite, researchers need to understand the resilience of ICSs against cyberattacks by systematically testing new security approaches without interfering with productive systems. Therefore, one possibility for such evaluations is using already available ICS testbeds and datasets. However, the heterogeneity of the industrial landscape poses great challenges to obtaining comparable and transferable results. In this paper, we propose to bridge this gap with METRICS, a methodology for systematic resilience evaluation of ICSs. METRICS complements existing ICS testbeds by enabling the configuration of measurement campaigns for comprehensive resilience evaluations. Therefore, the user specifies individual evaluation scenarios consisting of cyberattacks and countermeasures while facilitating manual and automatic interventions. Moreover, METRICS provides domain-agnostic evaluation capabilities to achieve comparable results, which user-defined domain-specific metrics can complement. We apply the methodology in a use case study with the power grid simulator WATTSON, demonstrating its effectiveness in providing valuable insights for security practitioners and researchers.

Keywords: Industrial control systems · Security evaluations · Testbeds · Datasets · Resilience

1 Introduction

The ongoing shift from local, isolated ICSs toward highly interconnected networks currently affects all areas of industrial automation, such as manufacturing

S. Katsikas et al. (Eds.): ESORICS 2023 Workshops, LNCS 14398, pp. 25–45, 2024.
https://doi.org/10.1007/978-3-031-54204-6_2

systems, process control, and power grids [39]. This trend fosters enhanced productivity, higher flexibility, and potentially better safety while reducing installation and maintenance costs [9]. On the downside, however, it increases the dependence between individual components and amplifies the harmful impact of cyberattacks. Even worse, it is largely known that ICSs exhibit significant cybersecurity deficits, mainly due to the challenges of retrofitting modern security mechanisms to long-lived legacy hardware with stringent latency and availability requirements [29]. Furthermore, ICSs are an attractive target for financially or politically motivated criminals who make use of constantly evolving attack vectors [24]. Cybersecurity research for ICSs must hence continuously adapt countermeasures and responses to keep pace with this development and even anticipate new threats when proposing preventive measures.

As a first step toward this ambitious goal, researchers and security practitioners need a profound understanding of current cyberattacks and countermeasures in ICSs and how these affect the underlying physical processes. Based on such resilience evaluations, they can identify and address existing weaknesses and, in the event of a cyberattack, select the best available response, i.e., repelling the attack while maintaining the operation of the ongoing industrial process as best as possible. Nevertheless, conducting cybersecurity research in productive ICSs is, in most cases, not a viable option due to safety concerns and the high availability requirements of the involved systems [10]. Consequently, cybersecurity researchers increasingly rely on ICSs testbeds and datasets for performing resilience evaluations, e.g., the Secure Water Treatment (SWaT) testbed [23] or the HIL-based augmented ICS security (HAI) dataset [30]. However, using these tools to conduct comparable cybersecurity research remains challenging due to their heterogeneous landscape manifesting in substantial discrepancies regarding accuracy, scalability, and flexibility [12]. Moreover, the gained insights depend on made assumptions, the necessary abstractions, and the considered use cases, emphasizing the need for comparative evaluations. Hence, a general evaluation methodology for (available) ICS testbeds is missing, facilitating comprehensive and comparable resilience evaluations of such systems.

Therefore, in this paper, we propose METRICS, a combined Methodology for Evaluating and Testing the Resilience of ICSs to cyberattacks. Our proposed methodology facilitates automated resilience evaluations for given ICS testbed environments with defined attacker's capabilities and response mechanisms by systematically testing different options and configurations. A given ICS testbed may range from a physical setup to an entirely virtual environment (e.g., a simulator) where the respective testbed exposes its capabilities and configuration possibilities to METRICS in a cross-domain environment description format. For the evaluation, we distinguish between domain-agnostic metrics, such as the reachability of system and network components, which independently apply to every testbed, and domain-specific metrics, which individually apply to the given testbed and thus must be provided along with the testbed description. The *evaluation control* then enables users to configure distinct scenarios and facilitates manual and automated interventions in running evaluations.

The evaluation results eventually converge into a *presentation layer*, providing insights and visualizations of ongoing evaluations. Moreover, METRICS retrieves datasets of each evaluation run, enabling subsequent analyses. This methodology thus helps to systematically identify weaknesses in current ICS deployments, assess the potential impact of cyberattacks, and improve the respective countermeasures.

In particular, this paper covers the following *contributions*:

- We analyze the requirements for an evaluation methodology concerning cybersecurity research for ICSs (Sect. 2);
- We propose METRICS, a comprehensive methodology to facilitate the resilience evaluation of ICSs to cyberattacks by providing comparable evaluation metrics (Sect. 3); and
- We present and discuss initial evaluation results by extensively studying a use case within the power grid simulator WATTSON [1] consisting of distinct attack vectors and countermeasures (Sect. 4).

Our use case evaluation demonstrates that METRICS offers valuable insights for security practitioners and researchers by facilitating a systematic iteration through possible configuration options while allowing manual and automatic interventions. Moreover, we identify the remaining challenges toward achieving universal resilience evaluation of ICSs in Sect. 5. In the following, we take a closer look at the fundamentals of cybersecurity research for ICSs before deriving the requirements and challenges for a comprehensive evaluation methodology.

Availability Statement. For better transparency of our conducted evaluation and enabling further research, our evaluation artifacts are publicly available: https://wattson.it/METRICS.

2 Cybersecurity Research for ICSs

Productive ICSs are typically unavailable for cybersecurity research due to the high availability requirements and safety concerns [10,12]. Security researchers and engineers thus rely on testbeds and datasets to model ICSs and conduct the evaluations in a safe environment. Figure 1 depicts the interplay between security research, testbeds, and datasets for ICSs [6]. Testbeds model real ICS in prototypical deployments using hardware, virtual components, or a combination. Furthermore, they can provide relevant recordings of network traffic and process states in the form of datasets, which, in turn, represent specific evaluation scenarios. Both concepts are thus valuable means for security research, facilitating testing and evaluation, depending on the respective level of abstraction and the considered research questions. Several literature surveys confirm the increasing availability of ICS testbeds and datasets and, moreover, summarize the complementary benefits of the distinct concepts [6,16]. In the following, we briefly present the methodological features of each concept in the ICS domain while putting a special focus on evaluating the resilience to cyberattacks.

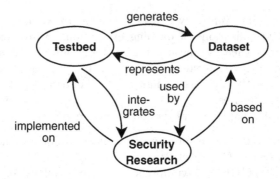

Fig. 1. Interplay of security research, testbeds, and datasets for ICSs showing that they mutually depend and benefit from each other. (Figure adapted from [6].)

2.1 Testbeds

ICS testbeds offer a protected research environment for cybersecurity research by replicating (parts of) productive ICS. They typically consist of physical or virtual components where any combination and level of abstraction are possible [6, 16]. Thus, their concrete design depends on their individual purpose and the requirements for the considered research questions.

While testbeds relying on physical components are generally close to reality and provide high accuracy, they are typically limited in flexibility and scalability. Moreover, their deployment is costly and sometimes requires extensive maintenance. In turn, testbeds relying on virtual components, which can be realized by simulation or emulation approaches, are significantly cheaper and more flexible but sometimes do not provide real-time capabilities. Moreover, scalability must often be traded against achieved accuracy when designing a virtual testbed. Examples of the broad range of possible ICS testbeds include the Secure Water Treatment (SWaT) testbed [23], the security-focused yet universal EPS-ICS testbed [10], and the power grid co-simulator WATTSON [1].

When striving to evaluate the resilience to cyberattacks, the respective ICS testbed needs to fulfill specific requirements to assess the impact of cyberattacks and the effectiveness of possible countermeasures. These mainly refer to achieving high accuracy of the modeled ICS, i.e., a comprehensive representation of the physical processes and the underlying information and communication technologies, to also capture unanticipated side effects. Moreover, extensive traceability of the conducted experiments facilitates complex resilience analyses, where recording datasets plays a decisive role, as further explained in the following.

2.2 Datasets

ICS datasets represent specific scenarios of the considered systems, resulting from a particular configuration and a predefined measurement time. They typically include recordings of network traffic, process states, and possibly meta-information about the scenario [6]. Such recordings facilitate, on the one hand, systematically analyzing the impact of cyberattacks and countermeasures post hoc. On the other hand, recorded datasets may help to improve the prevention and detection of cyberattacks, most prominently for training and testing of intrusion detection systems (IDSs) [35]. Although desirable, ICS datasets are rarely available from productive ICSs, mainly for protecting the confidentiality of industrial processes. Therefore, their generation and provision are typically closely related to the availability of ICS testbeds.

Generally, two possibilities exist to generate ICS datasets with cyberattacks [5]. One is to perform the cyberattacks directly in an ICS testbed and record the respective data. The other is to record a scenario without cyberattacks and inject (synthetic) attack data into the recordings afterward. While the latter is also possible for datasets from productive ICSs during normal operation, there is a risk of obtaining inaccurate or inconsistent data [6]. Regardless of how the dataset was obtained, labeling normal and abnormal data within the dataset is extremely helpful, e.g., when using the data for IDSs. Examples of such ICS datasets are the HIL-based augmented ICS security (HAI) dataset [30] or the PowerDuck dataset focusing on GOOSE traffic in an electrical substation [38].

Concerning resilience evaluations, ICS datasets thus provide evidence for a detailed assessment of the countermeasures' effectiveness. Nevertheless, their full potential can only be exploited in combination with their ICS testbed, facilitating flexible adaptions of the measurement scenarios and, therefore, systematic resilience evaluations. In the following, we review related work and derive the requirements for such a comprehensive evaluation methodology.

2.3 Related Work

Evaluating and assessing system resilience, and especially the resilience of ICSs, has been identified as an important topic by both past and ongoing research [3]. Related work can be divided into research that *conducts* resilience evaluations of respective systems [1] and research proposing *evaluation methodologies* [27], where both aspects are also *combined* for certain research areas [37]. As the resilience of physical systems, e.g., buildings, railway networks, or power grids, has been an active research area for multiple decades [4], ICS-related research can seize the gained insights and transfer them into the ICS domain. For instance, Haque et al. [13,14] adapt the well-known framework for seismic resilience by Bruneau et al. [4], defining *sub-metrics* ("the four *Rs*") for ICS resilience in three dimensions (physical, organizational, technical) [13]. While their approach targets the whole ICS domain, it does not provide a concrete definition of sub-metrics, e.g., *redundancy*, as such a metric heavily depends on the concrete ICS. On the other hand, related work focusing on the resilience of a specific ICS [1] provides concrete metrics for the respective ICS without considering the transferability of results to other domains. Thus, a cross-domain methodology for comparably evaluating the resilience of ICSs is still missing.

2.4   Toward a Cross-Domain ICS Evaluation

We recognize the need for a methodology allowing systematic analyses of ICSs with comparable and reproducible results, especially concerning resilience evaluations. Such a methodology combines testbeds and datasets to facilitate the creation of accurate and safe research environments, an invaluable feature for the ICS domain. While testbeds enable modeling of ICS and realistic impact evaluations, datasets are especially useful for post hoc analyses. Moreover, we identify the following desirable design requirements for such a methodology:

Universality. It applies to diverse testbeds facilitating resilience evaluations for the entire ICS domain.
Accuracy. It supports precise representations of specific ICSs, enabling meaningful modeling of cyberattacks and countermeasures.
Assessability. It allows the integration of domain-agnostic and domain-specific metrics to promote the comparability between distinct testbeds.
Traceability. It has the ability to export datasets for retracing the evaluation results, conducting post hoc analyses, and verification by others.

Hence, the evaluation methodology must cater to the wide range of ICSs, all exhibiting distinct susceptibilities and resiliencies to various cyberattacks. Further, different countermeasures and responses might be of varying success for such systems. Thus, universally evaluating their resilience to cyberthreats remains an open challenge. Despite their differences, potential cyberattacks and countermeasures are applicable and relevant across multiple ICSs, but their actual implementations might vary. Similarly, an evaluation metric must always be defined based on domain-specific knowledge to account for the actual *impact* of attacks and countermeasures. In the next section, we propose such a comprehensive evaluation methodology while also providing details on the distinct design components and the challenges when implementing them.

3   METRICS: A Cybersecurity Evaluation Methodology for ICSs

In this section, we present METRICS, a two-layered approach for achieving an ICS domain-spanning evaluation methodology. METRICS leverages the commonalities of attack and countermeasure strategies while respecting the differences and specifics of each ICS domain to allow directly evaluating cyberattacks and responses as well as generating datasets for subsequent analyses.

Figure 2 depicts the design overview of METRICS, where we distinguish between a domain-specific *evaluation environment* and a (mostly) domain-agnostic *evaluation control*. When considering a specific ICS, a corresponding evaluation environment is required, which may range from a physical testbed over a hybrid setup to a simulation. This environment allows evaluating the desired system under test (SUT) by representing the ICS, implementing adversaries and responses, and providing insights into the system's state. In turn,

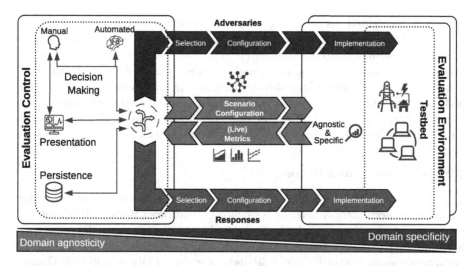

Fig. 2. METRICS' design leverages a *domain-agnostic* evaluation control which interacts with a *domain-specific* evaluation environment. This environment wraps a testbed for representing the desired ICS, implements adversaries and responses, and provides insights into their effects in the form of metrics. In evaluation control, decisions for adjustments of adversaries and responses are made based on these metrics which are further presented to the user, and persisted for later analyses.

the evaluation control manages the evaluation environment by configuring the desired scenario, including adversaries and responses, and receiving reported (live) metrics. Configuration options and received metrics are visualized for user interaction. Based on metrics reported to the evaluation control, manual and automated decisions may adjust the current evaluation or schedule new ones. We now detail METRICS' components and their interactions.

3.1 Exchangeable Evaluation Environment

To fulfill the design requirements of Sect. 2.4, METRICS supports exchangeable, domain-specific evaluation environments in the form of physical or virtual testbeds (cf. Sect. 2.1). Consequently, a supported testbed must be (i) *accurate* w.r.t. its real-world equivalent, (ii) *observable* w.r.t. both the network traffic and the physical processes, and (iii) *cybersecurity-focused* to allow conducting cyberattacks and integrating individual responses. Moreover, depending on the considered use cases, there might be some additional desirable properties: (iv) *flexibility* w.r.t. the domain-specific scenarios that can be reproduced, and (v) *scalability* w.r.t. the supported network size and number of components.

The evaluation environment must expose its capabilities and configuration options for METRICS in a universally applicable *environment description file (EDF)*. This file defines available topologies, metrics, assets and their roles, as well as adversary and response actions and their configurations. Appendix A provides an example illustrating the structure of such an EDF.

When configured for a specific scenario with potential *adversaries* and *responses*, the evaluation environment then implements the behavior of the SUT and provides insights into the state and effects of all components and their interactions. The adversaries, responses, and metrics all have domain-specific and domain-agnostic aspects. While abstract metrics, e.g., the availability of network nodes, can be applied to several domains, their concrete definition depends on the domain-specific context. Thus, we now specifically focus on the implications for adversaries and responses as well as cross-domain metrics.

3.2   Adversaries and Responses

The evaluation environment needs to represent cyberattacks *and* potential responses to *accurately* enable the resilience evaluation of ICSs. In this context, cyberattacks range from simple physical attacks, e.g., destroying or disconnecting hardware [17], over to network attacks, e.g., denial-of-service (DoS) attacks [31], up to process-aware attacks, e.g., false data injection (FDI) attacks [18]. Consequently, potential responses may include, e.g., external perimeter security systems [28], IDSs [33], or lightweight authentication schemes [22]. While most concepts of attacks and responses apply to various ICSs, their technical details, implementations, and effects differ between scenarios. Thus, we explicitly consider the resulting implications within METRICS to combine both, domain-specific implementations with domain-agnostic and generalizable concepts to comparably evaluate different ICSs. Hence, the evaluation environment provides concrete implementations for adversaries and responses, defines valid configuration options, and maps them to common concepts. To exemplify these design aspects, we now discuss them for both adversaries and responses in more detail.

Adversaries. A critical attack on ICSs is an FDI attack [26]. Here, attackers interfere with the ongoing communication to manipulate exchanged (application-layer) information, e.g., sent measurements or control commands as a machinein-the-middle (MitM). For METRICS, this inline network payload manipulation concept is quite domain-agnostic, as such attacks apply to various ICSs. Their implementation, however, is very specific and depends on the actual ICS and its individual properties. First, establishing the technical requirements for conducting an FDI attack differ. While an ARP-spoofing attack might be appropriate for Ethernet-based networks [25], bus-based networks might require dedicated timing techniques [36], whereas base station spoofing might be applicable for wireless networks [20]. Second, the manipulation of process information depends on the used application-layer protocol as well as the use of encryption and message authentication mechanisms. Thus, successfully implementing an FDI attack depends on the domain and might differ within a given heterogeneous domain.

Responses. Like the adversary design, preventive and reactive responses follow domain-agnostic concepts but require domain- and scenario-specific realizations: Integrity protection, encryption, or intrusion detection apply to various ICSs,

while their implementation and configuration require domain-specific information. A process-aware IDS is specific to its target domain, i.e., IDSs related
to manufacturing follow different approaches than, e.g., an IDS for power grid
networks. Consequently, we divide adversaries and responses into a domain-
agnostic (concept) selection, a concept-specific configuration, and a domain-
specific implementation (cf. Fig. 2). Similarly, we propose a cross-domain approach for metrics for comparative evaluations of different ICSs, as detailed in the
following.

3.3   Cross-Domain Metrics

Comparably assessing the impact of cyberattacks and the effectiveness of countermeasures requires appropriate metrics as desired by the *assessability* design
requirement. For ICSs, defining such metrics is particularly challenging since
effects can cover both the networking and the physical part of the system. The
differences and specifics of each ICS further exacerbate the comparability of
results across different ICSs. Thus, we propose differentiating between domain-
specific and domain-agnostic metrics, similar to the adversary and response definitions.

Metric Requirements. For each ICS, the evaluation environment should provide domain- or even instance-specific metrics. Such metrics provide valuable and
detailed insights into the system, allowing in-depth evaluations of system-specific
characteristics and effects. However, they complicate automated decision-making
when selecting (iterative and reactive) adversaries and responses, further hin-
dering comparing certain results from different domains or instances. In MET-
RICS, we flexibly address these challenges in three ways: (i) each evaluation
environment may provide automated decision-making algorithms that enhance
its domain awareness, (ii) implementations and configurations of adversaries and
responses may include domain-specific metrics to adjust their behavior automatically, and (iii) each evaluation environment should provide abstract concepts
for its domain-specific metrics. While the two former aspects primarily require
implementation effort, the latter focuses on conceptual aspects.

The domain-specific metrics provide detailed insights into the specific system.
However, their interpretation often requires specific knowledge of the SUT, which
hinders comparability across domain boundaries. Therefore, we encourage the
domain experts to provide domain-agnostic abstractions from these detailed metrics that follow a *normalized cross-domain specification* and allow non-domain
experts to understand and interpret them.

Exemplary Cross-Domain Metric. We use a metric for *network operability*
as an example. Such a metric applies to various ICSs and provides insights
into potential impairments of the network's desired operation. While, for some
domains, the number or fraction of operational network nodes might be well-
suited to represent the network's operability, other ICSs might define this metric

based on available network paths between application layer nodes or even the number of reachable nodes from a single source.

While their abstract design enables such metrics to apply to multiple independent ICSs and allows researchers to compare them across different domains, they cannot provide the in-depth details that domain-specific metrics can. Thus, we explicitly include both domain-agnostic and domain-specific metrics in METRICS to enable cross-domain comparisons as well as in-depth evaluations.

3.4 Evaluation Control

METRICS includes an evaluation control to provide a cross-domain interface for researchers to evaluate different ICSs under different adversary and response concepts. Designed as a primarily domain-agnostic component, it allows researchers to define their desired ICS scenario, choose from adversaries, responses, or abstracted concepts of those, and control the evaluation environment. It fulfills three primary tasks, as detailed in the following.

Scenario Configuration. Before starting the evaluation, researchers must select and configure the desired ICS scenario. By selecting the targeted domain (e.g., power grids) and the domain-specific scenario (e.g., the grid's actual topology), the adversary concepts and implementations as well as responses, researchers can precisely define their evaluation parameters. For generic yet comparable cross-domain evaluations and detailed domain-specific insights, this configuration process allows both the selection of domain-agnostic adversary and response concepts and the choice of domain-specific variants based on the *environment description*. Besides this *static* (e.g., playbook-based) configuration of adversaries and responses, METRICS also considers on-demand decision-making for live interactions and adjustments. METRICS defines the *scenario description file (SDF)* analogously to the EDF to allow the configuration of distinct evaluation scenarios. In Appendix B, we provide an example of an SDF.

Decision-Making. For in-depth research, *dynamically* influencing the running evaluation represents a valuable feature. On-demand decision-making, e.g., based on live metrics, can influence the running evaluation and instantiate new adversaries and responses or re-configure existing ones. Researchers can make these decisions directly or automate them with domain-agnostic and domain-specific implementations. Examples of such automated decision-making include rule-based approaches [7] or machine learning [2]. Further, the human-in-the-loop could also re-configure the automated decision-making to follow different strategies.

The metrics provided by the evaluation environment are of particular importance for the decision-making process. While domain-specific metrics allow respective experts to choose corresponding adversaries and responses carefully, more generic and domain-agnostic metrics allow for cross-domain automation implementations, easing large-scale evaluations of multiple ICS domains. Since these insights into the ongoing evaluation are the primary input for all decisions, METRICS has to also present these insights to the human-in-the-loop.

Scenario and Result Presentation. We include a dedicated *presentation layer* within the evaluation control providing (live) insights and visualizations into the ongoing evaluation. Comparing metrics and observing their variation during the evaluation eases the human-based decision-making processes, providing a desirable feature for the evaluations. Besides the presentation and visualization of (live) metrics, the presentation layer also covers the scenario configuration, i.e., it provides insights into the domain-specific scenario, offers viable configuration options, and presents applicable adversary and response concepts to the researchers. Moreover, it allows researchers to extract datasets from completed simulation runs, thus covering the *traceability* design requirement.

Overall, all metrics of the evaluation environment are (i) used as input for decision-making, (ii) presented to and visualized for researchers, and (iii) persisted for later in-depth analyses. Thus, METRICS enables researchers to conduct individualized, in-depth evaluations of specific ICS domains and scenarios, to implement flexible yet automated evaluations of different scenarios and multiple domains, and to compare their results with analyses from other researchers with potentially different focuses. We now present a concrete use case example to emphasize the concept of METRICS and evaluate its value.

4   Use Case: **METRICS** for Power Grids

We apply the concepts and methodologies of METRICS to evaluate the effects of cyberattacks and respective countermeasures in a power grid network. To represent the SUT, we use WATTSON [1], a co-simulator focusing on cybersecurity for power grids. We use a small medium-voltage reference grid (Cigre MV [32]) along with the corresponding information and communication technologies (ICT) network as the base scenario. Figure 3 visualizes the power grid with the corresponding ICT network. Moreover, we provide the EDF for WATTSON and the SDF of the considered use case in the evaluation artifacts[1].

Our evaluation consists of multiple phases, where adversaries and responses are iteratively established or adjusted, following METRICS' basic idea of dynamic adjustments based on (live) insights into the SUT's behavior. In particular, the evaluation phases alternate between adversary and response actions.

4.1   Evaluation Phases

We now emphasize the details of each phase in our exemplary use case, the effects on both the network and the physical process, and how the phases interconnect. In Fig. 4, we visualize domain-specific and domain-agnostic metrics for both the ICT network and the power grid during the evaluation.

---

[1] https://wattson.it/METRICS.

Phase 1: Reference. The first phase is the reference phase, where the power grid operates normally without adversaries. We program the control center to issue control commands to keep the grid connected, i.e., closing or opening circuit breakers as needed. In this phase, all RTUs are connected to the control center, and all buses in the power grid operate normally, resulting in grid availability and network operability metrics of 100%.

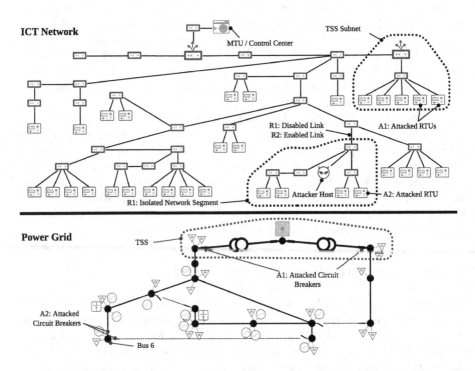

Fig. 3. The ICT network follows a tree-like topology consisting of three different subnets. The attacker host is attached to a switch within a DSS, a common attack vector for power girds [19]. In the first phase (**A1**), it connects to RTUs in the TSS and disconnects the majority of the grid. After its connection to these RTUs is blocked (**R1**) by isolating the network segment of the attacker host, the attack targets a still-reachable RTU to disconnect Bus 6 (**A2**). Finally, the operator configures all RTUs to block unauthorized connections (**R2a**) before reenabling the previously disabled link (**R2b**).

Phase 2: Industroyer (A1). The first attack is conducted at 20 s into the evaluation. A new host is connected to a switch at a (remote) DSS. On this host, a variant of the infamous *Industroyer* [8] malware is executed. This malware targets power grid networks by connecting to RTUs and issuing malicious control commands. In past attacks [15], these control commands were crafted to disconnect circuit breakers at TSSs, essentially disconnecting entire parts of the power grid. During our evaluation, we follow its real-world behavior, such

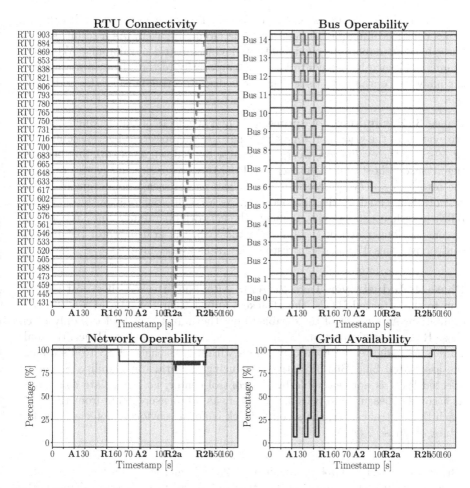

Fig. 4. The initial Industroyer attack (**A1**) repeatedly opens the circuit breakers at the transformers in the TSS. Although the control center issues respective counter commands, the grid's availability repeatedly drops significantly as most of the grid is disconnected. In contrast, the ICT network is not negatively affected during this phase. After the operator disables a link in response to the ongoing attack (**R1**), four RTUs lose their *connectivity* (domain-specific), resulting in reduced *network operability* (domain-agnostic). Since the grid operator gains back control over the previously attacked RTUs, the grid availability returns to 100%. The second Industroyer attack (**A2**) only targets a single DSS RTU as the first response (**R1**) blocks the attacker from connecting to the TSS RTUs. As a result, Bus 6 becomes inoperable, and the grid's availability drops slightly. During the reconfiguration of all RTUs to enable client authentication (**R2a**), all previously connected RTUs shortly lose their connection to the control center. After the link is re-enabled (**R2b**), the grid is fully available again and all RTUs re-establish their connections to the control center, resulting in a network operability of 100%. While the domain-specific *RTU connectivity* and *bus operability* metrics provides more detailed insights, the domain-agnostic *network operability* and *grid availability* metrics allow insights into the attack effects for non-experts.

that the malware connects to two RTUs at the power grid's central TSS and issues control commands to open multiple circuit breakers. As a result, several buses become inoperable, significantly reducing the grid's availability. While the commands issued by the control center temporarily restore the grid availability, the malware continues to issue commands disconnecting most of the grid.

Phase 3: Preliminary Response (R1). The effects of the conducted attack are evident to the grid operator as large parts of the power grid get disconnected. At 50 s into the evaluation, the grid operator takes down a network link between the attackers' host and the attacked RTUs. However, since the precise origin of the attack is not (yet) determinable by the operator, a whole segment of the network is affected by the disabled link. As a result, four previously unaffected RTUs lose their connectivity, reducing the network operability. Since the attackers can no longer attack the RTUs in the TSS, the grid operator regains sole control over this TSS and can restore the grid's availability.

Phase 4: Industroyer Take 2 (A2). After the attackers' host lost connection to the attacked RTUs, the attackers adjust their behavior at 80 s into the evaluation. As a result of the disabled link, the Industroyer host can only reach those RTUs that are part of the disconnected network segment. Hence, the malware is reconfigured to attack an RTUs within a reachable DSS to disconnect the associated bus (Bus 6), actively reducing the grid's availability. Since the affected RTU is not reachable by the control center, no immediate commands as a countermeasure are possible. Further, as no measurements from the RTU reach the control center, the second attack is not as obviously detectable as the attack of Phase 2 (A1).

Phase 5a: Client Authentication (R2a). While the preliminary response (Phase 3) reduced the impact of the attack on the grid's availability significantly, it is not sufficient to recover the reference state (Phase 1) as several RTUs are unavailable and one DSS is inoperable. Since the Industroyer malware connects as a secondary IEC 60870-5-104 client to the RTUs, this revised response enables (simple) client authentication within the network. To this end, the operator reconfigures all (reachable) RTU to only accept connections from the IP address of the master terminal unit (MTU) in the control center. Starting at ≈111 s, each RTU is reconfigured individually, which resets all active connections. This process is visible in Fig. 4, where these short connection losses are observable.

Phase 5b: Link Reactivation (R2b). As soon as all RTUs are reconfigured, the operator reactivates the previously disabled link at ≈140 s. Connections to the previously unreachable RTUs can be reestablished and the client authentication can be enabled. Therefore, the Industroyer malware, which is still active, is disconnected from the targeted RTU and can no longer establish a new connection. Consequently, the grid operator regains full control over all RTUs and can restore the grid's availability. After all network and power grid effects are averted, the malicious host can be permanently physically removed based on its position in the network.

4.2 Discussion

The evaluation of the presented use case provides valuable insights concerning the specific SUT, i.e., the cybersecurity of power grids, and the methodological approach and application of METRICS. In the following, we equally discuss these different aspects.

Cybersecurity in Power Grids. Past cyberattacks against power grid networks highlight the potentially drastic effects of such attacks and common vulnerabilities within such networks [19,34]. Our use case evaluation highlights multiple aspects relevant to cybersecurity in power grids. First, the geographical size of such networks represents a unique challenge for securing such networks. Numerous potentially unmanned remote locations increase the risk of physical access to network assets [19]. Physical protection and the appropriate configuration of such assets are required to minimize this risk. Second, remote visibility and controllability are of paramount importance [40]. While fine-granular visibility allows identifying attacks early, controllability of network assets provides the possibility to remotely implement appropriate countermeasures to ongoing attacks. Third, the protection of process information is essential but challenging [1]. The lack of encryption and command authentication enables attackers to conduct attacks such as the presented Industroyer attack or more advanced false data injection attacks [21]. Cryptographic authentication of control commands can prevent semantic attacks that aim to manipulate the physical process over the communication network [1]. However, since power grids have stringent real-time requirements and must always ensure process safety and availability, adapted security solutions are necessary, fully adhering to these requirements.

Specific and Agnostic Metrics. In METRICS' design, we introduced both *domain-specific* and *domain-agnostic* metrics to provide insights into the SUT. For the exemplary evaluation, we follow this concept and provide a domain-specific and domain-agnostic metric for the communication network and the power grid states. The domain-specific metrics, i.e., the *Bus Operability* and the *RTU Connectivity*, provide detailed insights into the SUT. They show the number of covered assets and individually state their respective states. These insights are especially valuable for domain experts and when comparing several variants of the same scenario during an evaluation series. However, their interpretation for researchers from different domains is challenging. Consequently, we include domain-agnostic metrics for the network and the physical process: With a normalized value range (0%–100%) and abstraction from the actual number of assets, these metrics offer comparability and eased interpretation for non-experts at the cost of reduced specificity. Since both variants of metrics offer valuable insights into the SUT, we assess their combined usage as favorable: While domain-agnostic metrics offer comprehensibility and comparability, detailed evaluations always require using domain-specific metrics.

METRICS' Iterative Methodology. The phase-based use case evaluation highlights the potential for METRICS' iterative evaluation methodology. While distinct phases allow us to observe the effects of each attack and response, their iterative structure enables flexible evaluation of different adversary and response behaviors. As visualized in Fig. 4, we can observe the delay of certain effects (e.g., as for phase **A2**) as well as effects that span across multiple phases (e.g., multiple disconnected nodes after **R1**). Thus, METRICS provides a flexible yet structured approach for conducting cybersecurity evaluations for complex ICSs. In particular, they support grid operators in understanding the varying impact of cyberattacks on their configurations and consequently reacting more effectively in case of actual attacks.

5   Toward Cross-Domain Resilience

With METRICS, we address the demand for a cross-domain evaluation methodology regarding the resilience of ICSs against cyberattacks. Acknowledging the need for domain-specific metrics and insights as well as domain-agnostic (i.e., comparable and transferable) insights, METRICS considers individual requirements for adversary, response, and metric designs. However, deriving a comprehensive *resilience score* from metrics and evaluation results remains an open challenge. As identified by related work from the ICS domain and different research areas [4,13], *resilience* depends on and consists of multiple aspects. While these aspects, such as robustness or redundancy, have been identified to influence the resulting system resilience, their respective definitions and weights still depend on the concrete ICS domain or even the specific instance of an ICS. Thus, we assess the derivation of concrete yet universal resilience definitions as an essential research area, which can be divided into several aspects.

First, for a concrete instance of a specific ICS, a comprehensive measure or metric for resilience has to be derived by identifying and assessing factors that influence the system's resilience. Here, *resilience* depends on the specific scenario, e.g., the tasks and features of the ICS and the presence of specific adversaries and response mechanisms. Further, multiple definitions of a system's *resilience* might be appropriate or even necessary.

Second, combining these ICS- and scenario-specific insights into an overall resilience score, i.e., a resilience measure for a specific ICS, is necessary. Since different adversaries and responses might affect various aspects of a complex ICS, weighting individual resilience measures is particularly challenging.

Third, abstracting the definitions for a specific ICS or ICS domain to enable cross-domain comparisons promises valuable and comparable insights into the strengths and weaknesses of different ICS domains. Identifying different resiliencies of distinct domains paves the way for applying successful concepts from different ICSs to strengthen the overall security and resilience of ICSs. In this context, we plan to apply METRICS to further industrial domains, starting with aquaponics [11], to identify universally applicable concepts as well as incompatibilities between acquaponics and power grid ICSs.

With METRICS, we thus foster the proposed research areas by providing a comprehensive evaluation methodology, enabling researchers to gather comparable insights into various ICSs under flexible scenarios. Based on these results, assessing the *resilience* of a specific instance, a single ICS domain, and ICSs as a whole are the next steps toward enhanced resilience of ICSs.

6   Conclusion

Spurred by the current need to improve cybersecurity in complex, interconnected ICSs, we propose METRICS, a methodology for evaluating and testing the resilience of ICSs to cyberattacks. Our approach provides a framework to integrate existing ICS testbeds while obtaining comparable evaluation results. We introduce domain-specific and domain-agnostic metrics considering the specific properties of an ICS, as well as a normalized cross-domain assessment. Security researchers and practitioners can perform systematic resilience evaluations by specifying distinct scenarios consisting of adversaries and responses and including manual and automatic interventions to influence the running evaluations.

In a preliminary case study, we demonstrate the feasibility and potential of METRICS using the power grid simulator WATTSON. The results are twofold: On the one hand, they reveal the benefits of an iterative approach to understanding the impact of a cyberattack and figuring out the best possible responses. On the other hand, they help identify (recurring) weaknesses in current ICS deployments, which can be subsequently addressed to prevent actual attacks. However, leveraging METRICS' full potential requires further advances in the specification of applicable resilience metrics and, as a next step, we intend to use METRICS for performing comparative evaluations using different ICS testbeds. With this in mind, we are convinced that METRICS represents a valuable contribution toward addressing the long-neglected security deficiencies in ICSs.

Acknowledgements. This paper was supported by the EDA Cyber R&T project "CYBER ELECTROMAGNETIC RESILIENCE EVALUATION ON REPLICATED ENVIRONMENT (CERERE)", funded by Italy and Germany.

Appendix A   Environment Description File Example

```
 {"name": "power grid",
1 "host": "https://example.org",
2 "port": 443,
3 "topologies": ["cigre_mv"],
4 "devices": {
```

```
 5   "cigre_mv": [
 6      {"device-id": "1016",
 7      "type": "switch",
 8      "info": {}},
     . . .
787  "links": {
788    "cigre_mv": [
789      {"link-id": "1003",
790      "type": "digital",
791      "connection": ["994","614"],
792      "info": {}},
     . . .
1623 "adversaries": {
1624   "kill device": {
1625     "parameters": {
1626       "device-id":
1627         {"type": "string",
1628         "description": "The ID of the device to kill"},
         . . .
```

Appendix B   Scenario Description File Example

```
 {   "environment": "power grid",
 1   "topology": "cigre_mv",
 2   "duration": 200,
 3   "adversaries": [
 4       {"type": "add_host",
 5   "start-time": 15,
 6   "parameters": {"name": "industroyer",
    . . .
81   "responses": [
    . . .
91       {"type": "link_action",
92       "start-time": 60,
93       "parameters": {
94       "action": "down",
    . . .
```

References

1. Bader, L., et al.: Comprehensively analyzing the impact of cyberattacks on power grids. In: European Symposium on Security and Privacy. IEEE (2023)

2. Bhattacharya, A., Ramachandran, T., Banik, S., Dowling, C.P., Bopardikar, S.D.: Automated adversary emulation for cyber-physical systems via reinforcement learning. In: IEEE International Conference on Intelligence and Security Informatics (ISI) (2020)
3. Bodeau, D.J., Graubart, R.D., McQuaid, R.M., Woodill, J.: Cyber resiliency metrics, measures of effectiveness, and scoring: enabling systems engineers and program managers to select the most useful assessment methods. Technical report, Mitre Corp Bedford Ma Bedford United States (2018)
4. Bruneau, M., et al.: A framework to quantitatively assess and enhance the seismic resilience of communities. Earthq. Spectra **19**(4), 733–752 (2003)
5. Choi, S., Yun, J.H., Min, B.G.: Probabilistic attack sequence generation and execution based on MITRE ATT&CK for ICS datasets. In: Cyber Security Experimentation and Test Workshop, CSET 2021. ACM (2021)
6. Conti, M., Donadel, D., Turrin, F.: A survey on industrial control system testbeds and datasets for security research. IEEE Comm. Surv. Tutorials **23**(4), 2248–2294 (2021)
7. Deloglos, C., Elks, C., Tantawy, A.: An attacker modeling framework for the assessment of cyber-physical systems security. In: Casimiro, A., Ortmeier, F., Bitsch, F., Ferreira, P. (eds.) SAFECOMP 2020. LNCS, vol. 12234, pp. 150–163. Springer, Cham (2020). https://doi.org/10.1007/978-3-030-54549-9_10
8. ESET Research: Industroyer 2: Industroyer reloaded. We Live Security (2022). https://www.welivesecurity.com/2022/04/12/industroyer2-industroyer-reloaded/
9. Galloway, B., Hancke, G.P.: Introduction to industrial control networks. IEEE Commun. Surv. Tutorials **15**(2), 860–880 (2013)
10. Gao, H., Peng, Y., Jia, K., Dai, Z., Wang, T.: The design of ICS testbed based on emulation, physical, and simulation (EPS-ICS Testbed). In: International Conference on Intelligent Information Hiding and Multimedia Signal Processing. IEEE (2013)
11. Goddek, S., Körner, O.: A fully integrated simulation model of multi-loop aquaponics: a case study for system sizing in different environments. Agric. Syst. **171**, 143–154 (2019)
12. Green, B., Lee, A., Antrobus, R., et al.: Pains, gains and PLCs: ten lessons from building an industrial control systems testbed for security research. In: USENIX Workshop on Cyber Security Experimentation and Test, CSET 2017 (2017)
13. Haque, M.A., De Teyou, G.K., Shetty, S., Krishnappa, B.: Cyber resilience framework for industrial control systems: concepts, metrics, and insights. In: International Conference on Intelligence and Security Informatics (ISI). IEEE (2018)
14. Haque, M.A., Shetty, S., Krishnappa, B.: ICS-CRAT: a cyber resilience assessment tool for industrial control systems. In: International Conference on Big Data Security on Cloud (BigDataSecurity), International Conference on High Performance and Smart Computing (HPSC), and International Conference on Intelligent Data and Security (IDS). IEEE (2019)
15. Hjelmvik, E.: Industroyer2 IEC-104 Analysis. NETRESEC AB (2022). https://www.netresec.com/?page=Blog&month=2022-04&post=Industroyer2-IEC-104-Analysis
16. Holm, H., Karresand, M., Vidström, A., Westring, E.: A survey of industrial control system testbeds. In: Buchegger, S., Dam, M. (eds.) Secure IT Systems. NordSec 2015. Springer, Cham (2015). https://doi.org/10.1007/978-3-319-26502-5_2
17. Hossain, M.J., Rahnamy-Naeini, M.: Line failure detection from PMU data after a joint cyber-physical attack. In: IEEE Power & Energy Society General Meeting. PESGM (2019)

18. Kosut, O., Jia, L., Thomas, R.J., Tong, L.: Malicious data attacks on the smart grid. IEEE Trans. Smart Grid **2**(4), 645–658 (2011)
19. Krause, T., Ernst, R., Klaer, B., Hacker, I., Henze, M.: Cybersecurity in power grids: challenges and opportunities. Sensors **21**(18), 6225 (2021)
20. Lichtman, M., Rao, R., Marojevic, V., Reed, J., Jover, R.P.: 5G NR jamming, spoofing, and sniffing: threat assessment and mitigation. In: International Conference on Communications Workshops (ICC Workshops). IEEE (2018)
21. Liu, Y., Ning, P., Reiter, M.K.: False data injection attacks against state estimation in electric power grids. ACM Trans. Inf. Syst. Secur. **14**(1), 1–33 (2011)
22. Mahmood, K., Chaudhry, S.A., Naqvi, H., Kumari, S., Li, X., Sangaiah, A.K.: An elliptic curve cryptography based lightweight authentication scheme for smart grid communication. Futur. Gener. Comput. Syst. **81**, 557–565 (2018)
23. Mathur, A.P., Tippenhauer, N.O.: SWaT: a water treatment testbed for research and training on ICS security. In: International Workshop on Cyber-Physical Systems for Smart Water Networks. CySWater (2016)
24. Miller, T., Staves, A., Maesschalck, S., Sturdee, M., Green, B.: Looking back to look forward: lessons learnt from cyber-attacks on industrial control systems. Int. J. Crit. Infrastruct. Prot. **35**, 100464 (2021)
25. Ramachandran, V., Nandi, S.: Detecting ARP spoofing: an active technique. In: Jajodia, S., Mazumdar, C. (eds.) ICISS 2005. LNCS, vol. 3803, pp. 239–250. Springer, Heidelberg (2005). https://doi.org/10.1007/11593980_18
26. Reda, H.T., Anwar, A., Mahmood, A.: Comprehensive survey and taxonomies of false data injection attacks in smart grids: attack models, targets, and impacts. Renew. Sustain. Energy Rev. **163**, 112423 (2022)
27. Reed, D.A., Kapur, K.C., Christie, R.D.: Methodology for assessing the resilience of networked infrastructure. IEEE Syst. J. **3**(2), 174–180 (2009)
28. Serror, M., Bader, L., Henze, M., Schwarze, A., Nürnberger, K.: Poster: INSIDE - enhancing network intrusion detection in power grids with automated facility monitoring. In: ACM SIGSAC Conference on Computer and Communications Security, CCS 2022 (2022)
29. Serror, M., Hack, S., Henze, M., Schuba, M., Wehrle, K.: Challenges and opportunities in securing the industrial Internet of Things. IEEE Trans. Ind. Inform. **17**(5), 2985–2996 (2021)
30. Shin, H.K., Lee, W., et al.: HAI 1.0: HIL-based augmented ICS security dataset. In: USENIX Conference on Cyber Security Experimentation and Test, CSET 2020 (2020)
31. Srikantha, P., Kundur, D.: Denial of service attacks and mitigation for stability in cyber-enabled power grid. In: IEEE Power Energy Society Innovative Smart Grid Technologies Conference (ISGT) (2015)
32. Strunz, K., Abbasi, E., Fletcher, R., Hatziargyriou, N.D., Iravani, R., Joos, G.: Benchmark systems for network integration of renewable and distributed energy resources. Cigre Task Force C **6**(04–02), 119 (2014)
33. Upadhyay, D., Manero, J., Zaman, M., Sampalli, S.: Intrusion detection in SCADA based power grids: recursive feature elimination model with majority vote ensemble algorithm. IEEE Trans. Network Sci. Eng. **8**(3), 2559–2574 (2021)
34. Whitehead, D.E., Owens, K., Gammel, D., Smith, J.: Ukraine cyber-induced power outage: analysis and practical mitigation strategies. In: Conference for Protective Relay Engineers (CPRE) (2017)

35. Wolsing, K., Wagner, E., Saillard, A., Henze, M.: IPAL: breaking up Silos of protocol-dependent and domain-specific industrial intrusion detection systems. In: International Symposium on Research in Attacks, Intrusions and Defenses. ACM (2022)
36. Young, C., Zambreno, J., et al.: Survey of automotive controller area network intrusion detection systems. IEEE Des. Test **36**(6), 48–55 (2019)
37. Yuan, X., Wang, L., Liu, T., Zhang, Y.: A methodology for continuous evaluation of cloud resiliency. Am. J. Eng. Appl. Sci. **9**(2), 264–273 (2016)
38. Zemanek, S., Hacker, I., Wolsing, K., Wagner, E., Henze, M., Serror, M.: PowerDuck: a GOOSE data set of cyberattacks in substations. In: Cyber Security Experimentation and Test Workshop, CSET 2022. ACM (2022)
39. Zhang, X.M., Han, Q.L., Ge, X., et al.: Networked control systems: a survey of trends and techniques. IEEE/CAA J. Automatica Sinica **7**(1), 1–17 (2020)
40. Zhao, J., Netto, M., Huang, Z., et al.: Roles of dynamic state estimation in power system modeling, monitoring and operation. IEEE Trans. Power Syst. **36**(3), 2462–2472 (2020)

Threat Analysis in Dairy Farming 4.0

Karl Jonatan Due Vatn⬤, Georgios Kavallieratos⬤,
and Sokratis Katsikas$^{(\boxtimes)}$⬤

Department of Information Security and Communications Technology,
Norwegian University of Science and Technology, Gjøvik, Norway
Jonatan.Vatn@protonmail.com,
{georgios.kavallieratos,sokratis.katsikas}@ntnu.no

Abstract. In the era of digital transformation and automation, cyber-security has become a critical concern in various sectors, including dairy farming. As dairy farms increasingly adopt cyber-physical systems, understanding and mitigating relevant cyber threats is paramount. This work identifies typical cyber-physical systems in a dairy farm and their interconnections to analyze potential cyber threats and risks. Regarding cyber risk, the farm management system is the most critical system of the dairy farm IT-OT infrastructure. This study provides insights into the relatively underexplored cybersecurity domain in dairy farming, establishing a foundation for future research and evidence-based policy development in this vital food production sector.

Keywords: Threat analysis · Cyber physical-systems · Dairy farms · Cyber risk

1 Introduction

"Industry 4.0" was initially coined to describe manufacturing technologies, process automation, and data exchange trends. Nowadays, it encompasses several industry sectors beyond manufacturing, including agriculture. It describes the trend towards increasing automation and connectivity by leveraging technologies such as the Internet of Things (IoT), Artificial Intelligence (AI), and Big Data Analytics, regardless of the application domain. Accordingly, the term "Dairy Farming 4.0" describes the adoption of emerging technologies in dairy farms to facilitate functions and operations such as real-time health monitoring, real-time tracking, real-time disease detection, real-time nutrition monitoring, real-time animal welfare, real-time monitoring of milk hygiene, and vision node-based furious animal attack detection [12].

The agriculture industry is witnessing significant changes with the advent of modern technology. This transformation integrates advanced technologies such as the IoT, robotics, cyber-physical systems (CPS), and AI into farming practices. This digital transformation influences dairy farming processes and procedures. Today's dairy farms are characterized by sophisticated operations to

S. Katsikas et al. (Eds.): ESORICS 2023 Workshops, LNCS 14398, pp. 46–63, 2024.
https://doi.org/10.1007/978-3-031-54204-6_3

manage and monitor livestock, optimize feeding, and automate milking processes. These operations are performed by CPSs that increase milk yield and improve livestock health, leading to higher productivity and profitability. The employed CPSs can seamlessly share data with partners, suppliers, and governmental entities.

The integration of the CPSs constitutes a central element of the digital transformation process in any application domain. The integration is unavoidably accompanied by the enlargement and diversification of the domain's cyber risks, with existing risks being increased and new risks being introduced. The reason for this is that whereas traditional operations were designed with no need for cyber security in mind, modern IT-enabled operations are allowed to be accessed and controlled by information systems connected to the internet through interfaces that are only partially secured [9]. The vulnerabilities inherent in CPSs make dairy farms potential targets for cyber attacks. This situation poses a novel threat to the agriculture industry, which historically is accustomed to dealing with environmental threats, but not with cyber attacks.

As agriculture transitions into a more technologically advanced era, it becomes increasingly important to recognize the vulnerabilities of the infrastructure. Identifying and analyzing cyber threats becomes a crucial step to ensure the security and integrity of the CPSs that make up the infrastructure. Several attacks have already targeted the agricultural industry. One of the largest tractor companies in the world, John Deere, was shown to be vulnerable. As a result, the console of the tractors was jailbroken [16]. Researchers tested off-the-shelf dairy farm equipment, and it was found to have inadequate security, or in some cases, no security at all [2]. The FBI warned against timed attacks against the food and agricultural sector after several ransomware attacks against the sector [9,10] that, in some cases, resulted in considerable production downtime [10]. Additionally, some parts of the dairy industry, such as retailers and suppliers, have been attacked [1] without affecting the dairy farms themselves to a great extent.

Given the significant economic role of the dairy farming industry, the number of people it employs, and its critical role in society, any disruption could have far-reaching consequences for the industry and the broader society and economy. Therefore, it is vital to consider potential cyber threats against dairy farms, towards enhancing the cybersecurity of the sector at large.

This research has been motivated by the need to improve the understanding of the cybersecurity landscape in the dairy farming industry. By first identifying the CPSs used in dairy farms and then analyzing their potential threats through a threat analysis, this study seeks to provide an overview of the system-level threats. This knowledge will help stakeholders, including farmers, equipment manufacturers, and policymakers, to take informed actions toward safeguarding the operations and the overall resilience of the dairy farming industry.

The study first identifies the CPSs deployed on a typical dairy farm to provide an understanding of the technological landscape and the attack surface. Then the research systematically explores the potential threats associated with these systems using the STRIDE threat modeling method. Finally, these threats' potential impact and likelihood are assessed to estimate the accordant cyber risks. The contributions of the paper are as follows:

- A system-level model of CPSs deployed in dairy farms. The model is built based on information from high-level technical documents from the dairy farming industry.
- Based on this model, a STRIDE-based threat analysis for each CPS included in the model. This approach systematically evaluates potential cyber threats that may compromise the security attributes of the CPSs in the dairy farm.
- An assessment of the risk of CPSs in a dairy farm, based on the identified threats.

The remainder of this article is structured as follows: Sect. 2 reviews related work. Section 3 presents the proposed CPSs model for a dairy farm. Section 4 briefly discusses STRIDE, the reasons that led us to use it, and the results of its application to the case at hand. Finally, Sect. 5 summarizes our conclusions and proposes directions for future work.

2 Related Work

The applications and architectures of the CPSs in agriculture have been explored in the literature. The potential of CPSs in a dairy farm is analyzed in [14], focusing on the new possibilities of product and process quality. Further, a framework for cyber-physical agricultural systems (CPASs) is proposed in [5] to analyze the integration of contemporary technology in the infrastructure. However, the literature only partially discusses the CPSs in dairy farms. I. A. Katsko et al. [18] discussed monitoring CPSs in milk production. The CPSs, sensors, and data exchanged in a milking production process are described in [8]. The application of CPSs in smart farming is also discussed in [13]. The technological developments and the parts of the advanced systems of dairy farms are discussed in [12]. Although the above works provide information regarding the CPSs used, a model of CPSs that describes the main functions, data flows, interconnections, and dependencies is yet to be developed.

Agarwal et al. designed a testbed to test the security of components in a dairy farm [2]. By leveraging the testbed, several vulnerabilities and open cybersecurity issues were discussed and the lack of reference architecture models in the literature was highlighted. Nikander et al. in [24] described the network of six dairy farms in Finland, emphasizing the farms' local area networks and connected devices. The analysis focused on general security threats and recommendations such as lack of awareness and implementation of firewalls. An analysis of networks in dairy farms is provided in [23,24].

Several threats against technology in the agriculture industry were identified in [4], and several threats against confidentiality, integrity, and availability in the agriculture industry were presented in [3]. The FBI warned that farm-level data was at risk in the US and that farmers should take action to secure their data

[9]. Nikander et al. argue that most threats to dairy farms materialize through internal rather than external attacks [24].

A systematic literature review [26] identified 28 threat analysis methods or approaches. The commonly used techniques were STRIDE, attack trees, graphs and paths, MUCs (misuse cases), problem frames, and threat patterns. Another review of threat modeling techniques [27] showed that the identified techniques had widely different characteristics. The STRIDE method is selected as the most appropriate for this study, as it is widely used within the domain because of its relevance and applicability [27] and its ability to be used in combination with other methods, due to its flexibility [17, 19].

Although several works have analyzed cybersecurity in agriculture infrastructures, the security threats in dairy farming are under-researched. The research described above is primarily on general farming, not dairy farming. The systems used on a dairy farm are highly specialized and are different from other use cases. Additionally, the risks that potential threats may pose to the dairy farm infrastructure have only partially been discussed.

3   CPSs of a Dairy Farm 4.0

A graphical depiction of a dairy farm's IT-OT infrastructure model is shown in Fig. 1. The graph nodes represent CPSs, and the solid line edges represent *main* information flows. The dotted line edge from the node labeled "SS" to the node labeled "FMS" indicates *possible* information flows. The following model description includes the CPSs, their functionality, data flows, and dependencies. The CPSs have been analyzed based on information in existing system descriptions in academic literature and technical reports from the dairy farm industry, as discussed in the related work section. For each CPS, the following elements are provided: its functionality and a brief description of the system, its purpose, and its primary function within the farm. Data flows, i.e., an outline of the flow of data, including inputs and outputs to other CPSs, are also included in the model. Finally, dependencies on other *internal* systems are also included in the model. *External* systems or entities are excluded.

Farm Management System (FMS): The FMS in a dairy farm is a software solution designed to optimize and streamline the operations of a dairy farm. Its primary function is to manage and monitor various aspects of dairy farming, including herd management, milk production, animal health, nutrition, and financial and staff management. In addition, the system helps dairy farmers improve their overall efficiency, productivity, and profitability, by providing a centralized data analysis and decision-making platform. The farmer and the workers on the farm operate the system [2, 6, 21]. *Functionality:* The FMS plays a critical role in four areas of the farms' operation, namely (1) Animal health management: The system helps monitor the health of each animal by tracking vaccinations, medical treatments, and regular check-ups. (2) Milk production tracking: The FMS records each cow's daily milk production data. (3) Breeding and reproduction management: The system keeps track of breeding cycles,

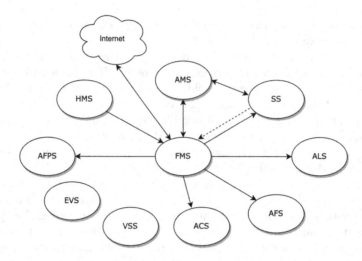

Fig. 1. Overview of systems on a dairy farm, with information flows. Legend: FMS - Farm management system, AMS - Automatic milking system, SS - Segregation system, ALS - Automatic lighting system, ALS - Automatic feeding system, ACS - Automatic cleaning system, VSS - Video surveillance system, EVS - Environment ventilation system, AFPS - Automatic feed pushing system, HMS - Herd management system.

insemination dates, and calving history. (4) Food and nutrition management: The system calculates the nutritional requirements of the herd and of each individual cow, helping farmers create balanced diets and monitor food consumption. *Data flow:* The FMS receives information from all systems on the dairy farm except the Environmental Ventilation System (EVS) [2]. The FMS is the single point in the model where all data are stored, processed, and visualized. The system is connected to the internet and receives data from cloud storage. It sends quality control data of the milk to the buyer. *Dependencies:* The FMS is connected to all CPSs in the farm except the EVS.

Automatic Milking System (AMS): The AMS is an advanced robot system that milks the cow. The AMS is preferred over other methods because it can optimize the milking process, reduce labor requirements, and improve overall productivity and animal welfare [15]. The system typically offers various functionalities and connects with others, relying on them for seamless and efficient operation. *Functionality:* The cow must go through the Segregation System (SS0 before the AMS. The system's primary purpose is to milk the cow. The AMS uses advanced sensors and technologies to perform its functions [7,11,22]. *Data flow:* The AMS sends data about milk production, quality analysis, health monitoring, feeding data, and alerts and notifications to the FMS. Health monitoring data is typically the cow's weight and body temperature. Feeding data contain the amount of concentrate the cow is fed during the visit to the AMS. *Dependencies:* The AMS depends on the FMS to send and receive data and perform its functions.

Herd Management System (HMS): The primary function is to collect data from sensors attached to the cow [2]. *Functionality:* According to [2], the HMS gathers information such as "eating habits, lying time, stand-up counts, step counts, and temperature." The system consists of sensors placed around the neck or leg of the cow and processes and stores data about the cows' health. These sensors also function as electronic identification tags, helping identify individual cows for interactions with other systems like segregation gates or the AMS. Such data facilitate the monitoring of health aspects such as detecting abnormal walking patterns, frequency of laying down, or changes in rumination activity. *Data flow:* The data is transmitted from the sensor to the reader via RFID and then to the controller on the Controller Area Network (CAN) bus. The controller sends the data to the FMS through Ethernet [2]. The sensors send the data to receivers in the barn at regular intervals. *Dependencies:* The HMS does not rely on other systems.

Automatic Cleaning System (ACS): A self-driving robot is responsible for cleaning the space where the animals live by removing the manure from the cows [20]. *Functionality:* The robot must go between the cows to perform the necessary functions. To this end, it is equipped with advanced sensors. *Data flow:* The ACS communicates with the FMS about the planned cleaning. To enhance its operation, it can use information on the whereabouts of the cows from the HMS received through the FMS. *Dependencies:* The ACS relies on information from the FMS to identify the target area for cleaning.

Automatic Feed-Pushing System (AFPS): The AFPS is a robot that moves around the feed alley and pushes the food toward the cows so that they can get easier access to it. *Functionality:* The routes for the robot can be programmed manually, or the robot can autonomously navigate its path. It then uses sensory technology to identify the location of the food [20]. *Data flow:* The AFPS is connected to the FMS and gets its routes from there. *Dependencies* The AFPS relies on the FMS to get its routes from and when it should and should not operate.

Automatic Feeding System (AFS): The AFS provides an efficient and precise means of delivering feed to the cows, improving productivity, and optimizing resources on the farm [20]. *Functionality:* Robots mix different feeds that suit the herd on the farm. The mixed feed is then transported to the cows via conveyor belts or by a robot. The robot distributes the feed along a path from which only the cows can eat. The cows are fed at regular intervals. When the cows eat, some of the feed gets pushed out and the cows cannot access it. *Data flow:* The AFS communicates to the FMS about the type of food and the amount needed for cows. As a result, the FMS has detailed information about how many cows will be fed and if a particular group needs more. *Dependencies:* The AFS relies on precise data from the FMS concerning the animals' dietary requirements.

Automatic Lighting System (ALS): The ALS automatically adjusts the light inside the barn according to a predefined schedule or input from light sensors [20]. *Functionality:* The ALS uses sensors and control algorithms to adjust the lighting intensity and duration based on various factors, such as the time of day, cow activity, and environmental conditions. The ALS detects the light level inside and outside the barn to adjust for the proper light setting inside the barn. *Data flow:* The system sends data to the FMS about the current state of operation, including information about the lighting condition inside the barn. It receives data on when the light should be on or off. *Dependencies:* The system depends on the light setting information from the FMS to set the correct light level.

Environmental Ventilation System (EVS): The EVS adjusts the temperature inside the barn via ventilation [2]. *Functionality:* The EVS is disconnected from the rest of the network and the FMS and can be accessed and adjusted via Bluetooth to a mobile phone app. *Data flow:* The EVS receives weather data such as temperature, precipitation, wind direction, and speed from sensors on the farm. Based on information from those, it adjusts the ventilation to set the right conditions inside the barn. The system is adjusted by phone and returns data about the conditions inside and the weather conditions. *Dependencies:* The system is not dependent on other systems as it is not connected to any.

Segregation System (SS): The segregation system allows the cows to pass through the farm's gates. *Functionality:* The gates are in place to ensure that only the right cows can pass through. They can move to the grazing and feeding areas, the milking robot (AMS), and the resting areas [2]. The SS ensures that the cows are only allowed to be milked a certain number of times daily [2]. *Data flow:* The system receives the cow's identity through the RFID chip on the cow. The RFID reader picks up the information at the gate [7]. Next, the system communicates with the FMS and asks if the cow is allowed through the gate or where it is supposed to go (in case of multiple gates). Finally, the FMS tells the gates to open or not [2]. *Dependencies:* When a cow enters the gate, the SS depends on the FMS to give it the correct information about whether to allow the cow through or not.

Video Surveillance System (VSS): The VSS is responsible for monitoring dairy farms. *Functionality:* Video surveillance is a common feature on dairy farms [23]. The VSS is an analog or digital (IP) camera connected to a dedicated surveillance PC or IP recorder. The VSS allows the farmer to monitor the farm from one place and ensure that it operates as it should. *Data flow:* The cameras are sometimes connected to the rest of the network. Live video is transmitted from the cameras to the recorder or personal computer to facilitate the monitoring. The VSS does not need to communicate with the FMS or any other system on the farm. *Dependencies:* The VSS is not dependent on other systems in the farm.

4   Threat Modeling and Risk Assessment

This section presents the methodology used to identify security threats and the accordant risks. The results of the analysis and of the risk assessment are discussed.

4.1   Methodology

STRIDE describes six threats: Spoofing, Tampering, Repudiation, Information Disclosure, Denial of Service, and Elevation of Privilege [25]. *Spoofing* is the capability of the adversary to pretend to be someone or something else. *Tampering* is the alteration or disruption of a disk, network, or memory of the system. *Repudiation* is a threat that refers to someone's allegation that did not do something which influenced the system's operation or was not responsible for the results derived from their actions. *Information disclosure* refers to the revelation of confidential information to unauthorized entities. *Denial of Service* refers to a violation of the availability of the system. *Elevation of Privilege* is the threat of an adversary executing unauthorized actions by abusing existing privileges. STRIDE attempts to discover potential threats and vulnerabilities as early as the design phase and analyzes each threat by answering questions corresponding to specific security properties. STRIDE facilitates the analysis of both active and passive threats. Threats that manipulate the physical environment of a sensor have not been considered in this paper.

The STRIDE threats and the CPS risk assessment are performed by using a revised form of the impact and likelihood criteria of [17,19], as depicted in Tables 1 and 2. The risk is calculated using the risk matrix depicted in Table 3.

Table 1. Impact criteria.

Level of impact	Impact description
High (H)	Threats that could result in the loss of human life. Threats that could result in the loss of animal life. Threats that could result in large energy loss. Threats that may cause damage to the infrastructure. Threats that will result in economic damage and client loss. Threats that will result in system malfunction.
Medium (M)	Threats that could cause process disruption in real-time. Threats that could result in miscalculations in the systems. Threats that could result in a bad reputation for the company. Threats that could result in serious harm to animals. Threats that could influence the system's integrity. Threats that could influence the system's availability. Threats that could result in legal sanctions.
Low (L)	Threats that could result in operation delay or disruption in noncritical processes. Threats that could result in leakage of non-sensitive data.

Table 2. Likelihood criteria.

Likelihood level	Likelihood description
Very likely (V)	The adversary is highly motivated and capable, with no deployed countermeasures. Existing popular exploits which can be executed at any time. High system exposure to the internet.
Moderate (M)	The adversary is highly motivated and capable, while the system's attack prevention countermeasures are insufficient. The system's vulnerability is widely known, but the attacker has to gain physical access. Systems are not directly exposed to the internet.
Rare (R)	The attacker is not highly motivated or does not have the necessary knowledge to perform an attack, or the deployed countermeasures are sufficient. An attacker must have administrative rights to perform the attack. The system is not connected to external networks or systems.

Table 3. Risk matrix

	Impact		
	High	Medium	Low
Very likely	High	High	Medium
Moderate	High	Medium	Low
Rare	Medium	Low	Low

Likelihood

4.2 Threats and Risks in the Dairy Farm 4.0

The threat analysis of the CPSs of the dairy farm is presented in the following tables. The threats shown in the tables are indicative. In these tables, "T" stands for "Threat", "I" stands for "Impact," "L" stands for "Likelihood," and "R" stands for "Risk" (Tables 4, 5, 6, 7, 8, 9, 10, 11, 12 and 13).

Table 4. Threats to the farm management system (FMS)

T	Description of threat	I	L	R
S	Since the system is exposed to the internet, an attacker could spoof the identity of a legitimate user, such as a farm employee or the farmer, to remotely gain unauthorized access to the FMS. This could lead to unauthorized modifications or theft of valuable data.	M	V	H
T	An attacker could tamper with the data stored in the FMS, such as changing milk production numbers, breeding cycles, or nutritional requirements, leading to inefficiencies in the farm operation or even financial losses and affecting the cows' health.	H	V	H
R	Without a strong system of logging and verification, an attacker could manipulate data in the FMS, such as milk production statistics or animal health records, and deny the action. This lack of accountability may raise legal issues for the company.	M	V	H
I	Information about the cows' health could be leaked, possibly leading to a disadvantage for the farmer against competitors.	M	V	H
D	An attacker could launch an attack against the system, overwhelming the FMS with traffic and causing the farm's operations to cease.	H	V	H
E	An attacker could, either on-premise or remotely, exploit vulnerabilities to elevate their privileges within the FMS, allowing them to perform actions typically reserved for privileged users. This could result in significant operational disruptions or damage to the farm's infrastructure.	H	V	H

Table 5. Threats to the automatic milking system (AMS)

T	Description of threat	I	L	R
S	An attacker could spoof ID tags so that the system thinks another cow is in the AMS. This could result in improper feeding, incorrect medication dosing, or inappropriate milking schedules.	M	M	M
T	Tampering with the milk quality control systems could result in the delivery of poor-quality milk, posing significant damage to the farmer's reputation. Tampering with the quality control data could lead the system to allow infected or bad milk into the milk tanks, potentially destroying all the milk in the tank.	H	M	H
R	In the absence of robust logging and audit trails, harmful changes made in the AMS, such as adjusting milk schedules or medicine doses, could be denied by the attacker. This could lead to issues in tracing accountability and in resolving adverse effects on cows' health and milk production.	M	M	M
I	Attackers could leak data related to milk production, quality analysis, or health monitoring. Since the milking process is a crucial part of the dairy farms' operation, this could impact the farm's competitiveness if competitors received the data.	H	M	H
D	An adversary may disrupt the communication between the AMS and the FMS. This may cause damage to productivity, animal welfare issues, and potential revenue loss.	H	M	H
E	An attacker may exploit vulnerabilities within the AMS to gain unauthorized access and control over system functionalities. This could lead to the manipulation of medicine dosages or interference with milking processes, ultimately affecting productivity and animal welfare.	M	M	M

Table 6. Threats to the herd management system (HMS)

T	Description of threat	I	L	R
S	An attacker could spoof the system by changing the cow's identity when communicating with other systems, leading to a false identification of the cow in various contexts. This can lead to incorrect health monitoring and possibly incorrect treatment decisions.	M	M	M
T	An attacker could manipulate data such as eating habits, temperature readings, and rumination activity, leading to incorrect assessments of cow health.	M	M	M
R	A threat actor denying their unauthorized alterations to sensor data, such as feeding or rumination patterns, could adversely affect the well-being of the cows and disrupt farm operations.	M	M	M
I	Data from the sensors to the receivers and from receivers to the FMS could be intercepted if improperly encrypted. This could lead to the unauthorized disclosure of sensitive information about the cows and their health.	M	M	M
D	Attackers could jam the wireless signals between the sensors and the receivers, leading to a denial of service. This could prevent the system from receiving any data from the cows, causing a disruption in monitoring and decision-making for the farmer.	L	M	L
E	If an attacker can exploit vulnerabilities in this transmission process, they could escalate their access privileges, enabling them to view and alter the transmitted data. This could lead to incorrect data being sent to the receivers and subsequently to the FMS, affecting the decisions based on this data.	M	M	M

Table 7. Threats to the automatic cleaning system (ACS)

T	Description of threat	I	L	R
S	An attacker could spoof the identity of the ACS and transmit fake location signals to the FMS, causing the FMS to not know where the robot is and consequently giving the robot incorrect cleaning routes in return, leading to incomplete or ineffective cleaning or driving into cows.	M	M	M
T	An attacker could intercept or modify the input between the ACS, FMS, and HMS, leading to erroneous cleaning schedules, wrong path planning, or loss of real-time cow location data.	L	M	L
R	In this system, any unaccounted modifications to the cleaning process of the ACS may compromise the sanitary conditions in the barn, thereby threatening the health of the animals.	L	M	L
I	An attacker could access operational data such as cow locations, cleaning schedules, or facility layout, potentially compromising the barn's operational security.	M	M	M
D	An attacker could stop the robot from working by targeting critical components (e.g., power supply, communication systems) or overloading the system with excessive or incorrect data, rendering it unable to perform its cleaning tasks.	H	M	H
E	An attacker could exploit a vulnerability in the robot's security mechanisms to gain unauthorized access, allowing them to control the robot and alter its settings.	M	M	M

Table 8. Threats to the automatic feed pushing system (AFPS)

T	Description of threat	I	L	R
S	An attacker could spoof a legitimate connection from the FMS and change the settings or routes of the AFPS. This could result in disrupting the feeding process and wasting energy.	L	M	L
T	An attacker could inject malicious data into the sensor network or the location module of the AFPS, altering the robot's sensing capabilities. This could result in incorrect movement and physical damage to the equipment or the animals.	M	M	M
R	An attacker could send unauthorized commands to the AFPS without leaving a trace of their actions. This would make it difficult to identify the cause of any resulting problems, such as incorrect feed-pushing patterns.	L	M	L
I	Sensory data collected by the AFPS could be intercepted by an attacker. This could reveal information about the conditions within the farm, such as the cows' health or the feed's quality.	M	M	M
D	An attacker could shut down the AFPS by overloading it with requests or exploiting a system vulnerability. This could disrupt the feed delivery process, leading to potential health issues for the cows.	M	M	M
E	An attacker could exploit a vulnerability in the AFPS to take control of its operation. This could allow them to modify the robot's behavior, potentially causing harm to the cows and disrupting the feeding process.	M	M	M

Table 9. Threats to the automatic feeding system (AFS)

T	Description of threat	I	L	R
S	An attacker may spoof the identity of FMS and make the robot dispense excessive or inadequate amounts of feed, potentially disrupting the farm's operations and affecting the cows' health.	M	M	M
T	An attacker may tamper with the feeding intervals programmed into the AFS, causing the cows to be overfed or underfed, resulting in poor health or reduced milk production.	L	M	L
R	In the case of alterations in the feed's composition or quantity, every action must be traceable to the person or system who performed it since it could disrupt the nutritional balance of the cows.	M	M	M
I	An attacker may expose data such as feed types and feeding schedules, potentially causing harm to the farm's operations or reputation.	L	M	L
D	A threat actor could cause a denial of service by disrupting the AFS by overloading the system with requests, preventing the cows from receiving adequate feed.	H	M	H
E	An attacker could gain control over the AFS robot, enabling them to manipulate the feeding process, cause damage to the robot or facilities and harm the cows.	H	M	H

Table 10. Threats to the automatic lighting system (ALS)

T	Description of threat	I	L	R
S	An attacker could impersonate an authorized user and manipulate the automatic lighting system. By altering the lighting schedules, they could create undesirable conditions for the cows, leading to stress, reduced milk production, and potential health issues.	L	M	L
T	An attacker could physically or remotely tamper with the input from the light sensors, causing them to provide false readings or alter them. Improper lighting may lead to inadequate lighting conditions, negatively impacting the cows' health and productivity.	L	M	L
R	Untraceability to a specific user of actions in the ALS could lead to undetected malicious activities or repeated system faults, adversely affecting the cows' health.	L	M	L
I	An attacker could gain unauthorized access to the lighting schedules and configurations of the ALS, revealing operating patterns of the farm that could be used for potential malicious activities.	L	M	L
D	An attacker could flood requests to the controllers in the lighting system, possibly causing the lights to be faulty. This attack requires physical access to the infrastructure.	M	M	M
E	If an attacker gains administrative access to the system, they could misuse this to disrupt the lighting schedules. This could cause damage to health and productivity and, in the worst-case scenario, create unsafe working conditions for farm workers.	M	M	M

Table 11. Threats to the environment ventilation system (EVS)

T	Description of threat	I	L	R
S	An attacker could spoof the Bluetooth connection to the system and pretend to be a legitimate user. This would give the attacker access to the actuators or manipulate the EVS settings, potentially leading to harmful conditions for the animal.	M	R	L
T	By manipulating the data sent to the EVS from the app, an attacker could adjust the ventilation adjustments or give wrong temperature information from the temperature sensors.	L	R	L
R	Lack of logging events on the system could lead to the users denying having made specific EVS adjustments through the mobile app.	L	R	L
I	An interception of the communications may lead to information leakage about the farm's operating conditions; this could be used for malicious purposes.	L	R	L
D	An attacker could block the source of the weather data, causing the EVS to operate with outdated or incorrect information. This could lead to unsuitable conditions inside the barn for the animals.	H	R	M
E	An attacker with administrative rights could turn off the ventilation, making the cows overheat in warm weather.	H	R	M

Table 12. Threats to the segregation system (SS)

T	Description of threat	I	L	R
S	An attacker could clone an RFID tag, tricking the system into thinking an unauthorized cow is authorized to enter the AMS or other restricted areas. This can lead to improper segregation, causing disruptions in the milking process and potential conflicts among the cows.	M	M	M
T	An attacker could tamper with the gate's control system to disable or force it to open/close unexpectedly. This could lead to hurting the cows when they are in the segregator, letting them in or out where they do not belong, or disabling them altogether.	H	M	H
R	The repudiation of actions within this system is not permitted, as improper or unauthorized manipulation of the control system or RFID readings could jeopardize the cows' well-being and farm processes' efficiency.	M	M	M
I	An attacker may collect the usage statistics for the gates for malicious purposes. The attacker could maximize the impact of their activities by targeting the farm at the most vulnerable times.	M	M	M
D	An attacker could jam RFID signals near the gates, preventing RFID readers from accurately identifying cows and causing delays to the milking operation.	M	M	M
E	If an attacker has high privilege on the system, they can use it to override the gates and let every cow that wants to pass through to do so. This could lead to cows queuing up and ending up in the wrong place on the farm.	M	M	M

Table 13. Threats to the video surveillance system (VSS)

T	Description of threat	I	L	R
S	An attacker could replace the genuine video feeds with recorded or manipulated footage, misleading the farmer and obscuring any activities happening in the farm.	L	R	L
T	A threat actor could tamper with the video recordings stored on the recorder or PC, altering or deleting critical evidence of incidents on the farm.	M	R	L
R	Any action carried out within the video surveillance system that impacts its function, such as manipulating video feeds or tampering with video recordings, should be attributable. Denial of responsibility for such actions could mislead the farmer and possibly lead to security breaches.	M	R	L
I	An attacker could leak feeds or recordings, potentially disclosing information about the farm's operations or personnel. The footage can be selected only to show negative incidents on the farm, damaging the farm's reputation.	H	R	M
D	An attacker could intentionally overload the system, causing the video feeds to become unavailable. This would hinder the farmer's ability to monitor the farm remotely.	L	R	L
E	An attacker could exploit vulnerabilities in the VSS to gain unauthorized control over the cameras, allowing them to manipulate the camera settings or disable them entirely.	M	R	L

Considering the above threat analysis results, we notice that the FMS gathered six high-risk scores. Further, three high-risk threats are identified for the AMS and two for the AFS. Therefore, these three systems are among the most critical ones. The SS and the AFPS gathered five and four, respectively, medium risk scores. This is due to their high dependence on the critical CPSs. Finally, the ALS, EVS, and VSS are characterized by low-risk levels.

The threat analysis focuses on attacks against each CPS's main properties, as described in the previous section, namely functionality, data flow, and dependencies. An essential aspect of the identified threats is the potential for harming animals; an example is the tampering threat against the segregation system. Similarly, a tampering or spoofing threat to the ACS may inflict physical damage to the infrastructure since the cows' health is highly dependent on the ACS. Furthermore, these threats may hurt the business continuity of the organization. As mentioned earlier, the FMS is crucial in the network model and acts as the central node in the model graph. However, this role makes it potentially vulnerable, as threats against the FMS could compromise the entire system due to the high dependencies on the other CPSs. A consequence is that if the FMS is compromised, wide-reaching effects across the overall system might occur. For instance, numerous spoofing threats have been identified, where an attacker could pretend to be the FMS, issuing false commands or injecting incorrect data into other systems.

Tampering and *Denial of service* threats are among the most critical for the dairy farm as they are rated as critical in four out of the ten CPSs. *Spoofing* and *Elevation of Privileges* are rated as medium lever threats while *Repudiation* and *Information Disclosure* are low level threats.

By leveraging the risk assessment performed per CPSs and per STRIDE threat, the criticality of each CPS is determined. The overall risk analysis results are depicted in Table 14 where twenty low, twenty-seven medium, and thirteen high-risk threats in the dairy farm are shown. The impact and likelihood values are estimated based on the criteria presented in Tables 1 and 2. It can be noticed that the CPSs that are exposed to the internet received the highest risk values. The AFS, ACS, HMS, and ASPS received medium-level risk scores. This is because the functions of and data flows between these CPSs are only partially exposed to the internet, hence less vulnerable to cyber attacks. Finally, the ALS, EVS, and VSS have received low-level risk scores due to limited dependencies.

Table 14. Risk assessments for all systems

System	Low	Medium	High	System risk score
FMS			6	3.0
AMS		3	3	2.5
SS		5	1	2.2
AFS	2	2	2	2.0
ACS	2	3	1	1.8
HMS	1	5		1.8
AFPS	2	4		1.7
ALS	4	2		1.3
EVS	4	2		1.3
VSS	5	1		1.2
Total	20	27	13	

Table 14 illustrates the system's low, medium, and high-risk scores. The risk score itself for each threat is calculated by the matrix shown in Table 3. The risk score per CPS and per threat is calculated by assigning numerical values to the risk scores for each threat. The threat scores were given the following values: Low = 1, Medium = 2, High = 3. By adding these together and dividing them by the number of threats (six for each CPS), the average risk score of the system is shown. For example, the FMS gets the highest possible score of 3 (6 high-risk threats, calculated as $(6*3)/6 = 3$). Table 14 sets the CPSs in a priority list based on their criticality (Fig. 2).

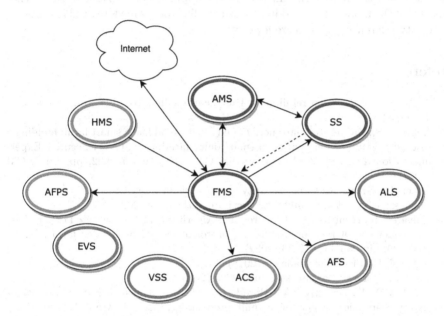

Fig. 2. Overview of systems on a dairy farm, with information flows, high-risk systems marked with red, medium-risk with orange, low-risk with green. Legend: FMS - Farm management system, AMS - Automatic milking system, SS - Segregation system, ALS - Automatic lighting system, ALS - Automatic feeding system, ACS - Automatic cleaning system, VSS - Video surveillance system, EVS - Environment ventilation system, AFPS - Automatic feed pushing system, HMS - Herd management system. (Color figure online)

The FMS is characterized as the most critical CPSs since it is central to the model and directly connected to the internet. The AMS scored high on the risk scale due to its integral role in the farm's operations and its potential to cause significant harm to the cows if compromised. The interdependence between the AMS and the FMS also implies that a compromise in the AMS could spread to other interconnected systems. Four out of ten CPSs have received medium-level risk scores. The likelihood of attacks in such systems is low due to their low interconnectedness. Last, three systems have received low-level risk scores.

5   Conclusions

This paper discussed cybersecurity aspects of contemporary dairy farms employing IT-OT integrated technology. The CPSs of the dairy farm were presented and analyzed, considering functions, data flows, and dependencies. The cyber threats per CPSs were identified by employing the STRIDE method and analyzing attack scenarios per STRIDE threat. Tampering and Denial of service threats are among the most critical, whilst Spoofing and Elevation of Privileges are characterized as medium-level threats. Additionally, the risks per STRIDE threat and per CPSs were assessed to identify the most critical components. In future work, further analysis of the model presented in this work will be performed, towards proposing a security reference architecture for dairy farms 4.0.

References

1. Abrams, L.: Pan-Asian retail giant Dairy Farm suffers REvil ransomware attack, January 2021
2. Agarwal, S., Rashid, A., Gardiner, J.: Old MacDonald had a smart farm: building a testbed to study cybersecurity in smart dairy farming. In: Cyber Security Experimentation and Test Workshop, Virtual CA USA, August 2022, pp. 1–9. ACM (2022)
3. Baker, L., Green, R.: Cyber security in UK agriculture (2019)
4. Boghossian, A., et al.: Threats to precision agriculture (2018)
5. Chivarov, S., Dimitrov, K., Chivarov, N.: Algorithms for cost oriented cyber physical system (COCPS) for intelligent control of animal husbandry farms. IFAC-PapersOnLine **55**(11), 31–36 (2022)
6. DeLaval: DelPro Farm Manager (2018)
7. DeLaval. DeLaval Landbrukskatalog 2023 (2023)
8. Dmytriv, V.T., Dmytriv, I.V., Horodetskyy, I.M., Yatsunskyi, P.P., et al.: Adaptive cyber-physical system of the milk production process. INMATEH Agric. Eng. **61**(2), 199–208 (2020)
9. FBI: Smart farming may increase cyber targeting against US food and agriculture sector (2016)
10. FBI: Ransomware attacks on agricultural cooperatives potentially timed to critical seasons, April 2020
11. GEA: GEA product catalogue (2017)
12. Gehlot, A., Malik, P.K., Singh, R., Akram, S.V., Alsuwian, T.: Dairy 4.0: intelligent communication ecosystem for the cattle animal welfare with blockchain and IoT enabled technologies. Appl. Sci. **12**(14), 7316 (2022)
13. Gkoulis, D., et al.: An event-based microservice platform for autonomous cyber-physical systems: the case of smart farming. In: 2021 16th International Conference of System of Systems Engineering (SoSE), pp. 31–36. IEEE (2021)
14. Höhendinger, M., Schlereth, N., Treiber, M., Höld, M., Stumpenhausen, J., Bernhardt, H.: Potential of cyber-physical systems in German dairy farming. In: 2019 ASABE Annual International Meeting, p. 1. American Society of Agricultural and Biological Engineers (2019)
15. Hårstad, R.M.B.: Bonden, familien og melkeroboten - en ny hverdag. Technical Report 2/2019, RURALIS - Institutt for rural- og regionalforskning (2019)

16. Jarvis, W.: Sick Codes talks tractor hacks, September 2022
17. Jelacic, B., Rosic, D., Lendak, I., Stanojevic, M., Stoja, S.: Stride to a secure smart grid in a hybrid cloud. In: CyberICPS/SECPRE@ESORICS (2017)
18. Katsko, I.A., Kremyanskaya, E.V.: Cognitive monitoring of cyber-physical systems in agriculture. In: Arseniev, D.G., Overmeyer, L., Kälviäinen, H., Katalinić, B. (eds.) CPS&C 2019. LNNS, vol. 95, pp. 422–430. Springer, Cham (2020). https://doi.org/10.1007/978-3-030-34983-7_41
19. Kavallieratos, G., Katsikas, S., Gkioulos, V.: Cyber-attacks against the autonomous ship. In: Katsikas, S.K., et al. (eds.) SECPRE/CyberICPS -2018. LNCS, vol. 11387, pp. 20–36. Springer, Cham (2019). https://doi.org/10.1007/978-3-030-12786-2_2
20. Lely: Lely dairy equipment (2014)
21. Lely: Horizon brochure (2020)
22. Lely: Astronaut A5 operator manual (2022)
23. Manninen, O.: Cybersecurity in agricultural communication networks: case dairy farms. Master's thesis, JAMK University of Applied Sciences (2018)
24. Nikander, J., Manninen, O., Laajalahti, M.: Requirements for cybersecurity in agricultural communication networks. Comput. Electron. Agric. **179**, 105776 (2020)
25. Shostack, A.: Threat Modeling: Designing for Security, 1st edn. Wiley, Hoboken (2014)
26. Tuma, K., Calikli, G., Scandariato, R.: Threat analysis of software systems: a systematic literature review. J. Syst. Softw. **144**, 275–294 (2018)
27. Xiong, W., Lagerström, R.: Threat modeling - a systematic literature review. Comput. Secur. **84**, 53–69 (2019)

Overview of Social Engineering Protection and Prevention Methods

Konstantinos Kontogeorgopoulos$^{(\boxtimes)}$ ⓘ and Kyriakos Kritikos ⓘ

Department of Information and Communication Systems Engineering,
University of Aegean, Mytilene, Greece
{kontogeorgopoulosk,kkritikos}@aegean.gr

Abstract. Recently, with the increasing use of social networks, services, and computers in general plus the enhanced capabilities of remote working, especially during quarantine periods due to Covid-19, social engineering attacks are a growing phenomenon. These attacks are, nowadays, the most common, since no matter how protected an information system is from security attacks, the weakest link is the human factor. As such, it is imperative to address and prevent such attacks. This paper reviews the most common social engineering attack prevention and protection methods and classifies them based on various criteria. Based on the analysis, it identifies the most effective methods in their protection degree, while it supplies some challenges to maximise such degree.

Keywords: Social engineering · attacks · protection methods · review

1 Introduction

Social engineering is the manipulation of individuals to extract information, especially confidential and sensitive data. These attacks are so widespread as no matter how strong the security of an information system and the strength of its protection mechanisms are, the system can be penetrated due to external factors, such as people [1]. The social engineering attack methods used do not require as much time and effort as other types of attacks that exploit system vulnerabilities, since humans are dominated and operate based on emotions. This makes these attacks among the most dangerous [1] since they cannot be yet addressed with a complete and definitive security solution while their confrontation also requires the proper training of the people who access and operate the systems in question.

As such, social engineering protection and prevention methods have witnessed significant advancement. Organizations are increasingly investing in security awareness and training programs, which aim to educate employees about the risks of social engineering attacks and how to identify and respond to them. Further, new technologies, such as machine/deep learning and natural language processing (NLP) are being developed to address social engineering attacks in

Supported by organization x.

real-time. The increasing adoption of these protection methods has significantly reduced the success rate of social engineering attacks and improved the overall security posture of organizations [2].

Systemizing protection methods allows organizations to streamline processes and standardize practices. Categorizing and evaluating different protection methods helps identify effective approaches and prioritize their implementation. This promotes efficiency, reduces effort duplication, and ensures consistent application of social engineering protection measures. By understanding the methods' effectiveness, organizations can allocate resources and prioritize measures based on risk levels, aligning strategies with their objectives. Documenting and categorizing effective protection methods facilitates sharing best practices and lessons learned, fostering collaboration and enhancing defence against social engineering attacks. Having a comprehensive understanding of social engineering protection and prevention methods is crucial so as to achieve this vision.

Our paper introduces significant advancement and value by exploring machine, deep and hybrid learning plus scenario-based attack detection methods. By extending from [3] and [4], our study goes beyond the existing scope to delve into the realm of deep learning algorithms, harnessing their potential to enhance attack detection accuracy and robustness. Moreover, by incorporating hybrid learning techniques the detection system's effectiveness is further strengthened. Our paper also introduces the concept of scenario-based attack detection, which considers real-world scenarios and contextual information to improve the system's ability to identify and mitigate emerging threats.

Our paper adds extra value by introducing original criteria for comparing protection methods. By applying such criteria, our research goes beyond the existing literature and provides a comprehensive and objective framework to assess the protection approaches effectiveness. This novel contribution allows for a more systematic understanding of the strengths and weaknesses of various methods, enabling researchers and practitioners to make informed decisions when selecting and implementing cybersecurity measures. Further, creating such criteria opens up new avenues for future research, as they can serve as a benchmark to evaluate and refine protection techniques in an evolving threat landscape.

The remainder of this paper is structured as follows. Section 2 explains the methodology used to select the defence and prevention methods. Section 3 introduces the evaluation criteria, evaluates the methods based on them and analyzes the evaluation results. Finally, Sect. 4 concludes the paper.

2 Method Selection Methodology

The selection of suitable social engineering protection and prevention methods is critical to ensure the security of an organization's sensitive information and systems. In this paper, a systematic literature review was conducted to evaluate existing measures and methods (policies and tools) to address social engineering attacks. The review's main research questions to answer were the following:

- What are the main categories of methods utilized to protect against social engineering attacks?
- What are the main pros and cons of each protection method in each category?
- Which is the best protection method based on which criteria and aspects?

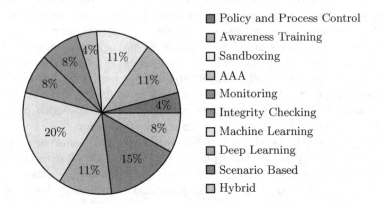

Fig. 1. The distribution of different protection and prevention methods.

The search strategy employed used keyword patterns to search relevant literature on Google Scholar, Science Direct, and Web of Science. The keywords used were "Social Engineering || Phishing || Impersonation" &&·"Attack" && "Detection || Prevention || Protection." || means logical OR, while && logical AND.

Several articles and studies appearing with the above keywords were examined. To separate and filter the studies, eligibility criteria (exclusion, inclusion and quality) were applied to determine whether to include or exclude each identified article from the subsequent analysis.

The inclusion criteria were as follows:

- Literature publications which include research articles from scientific journals, conferences and workshops and doctoral theses.
- Publications proposing techniques, tools, methodologies, strategies and solutions focusing on social engineering attacks prevention and addressing.

The exclusion criteria were as follows:

- Exclusion of publications published before 2008. By focusing on more recent literature, we capture the latest advancements, trends, and insights in the field.
- Exclusion of publications written in a language other than English.
- Exclusion of publication with charged access to their content

The quality criteria were as follows:

- Exclusion of publications supplying an unmeaningful solution.

– Exclusion of publications with no kind of assessment of their contribution.
– Exclusion of publications with unverifiable assessment results.

The articles originally identified were 367 while the ones retained after the application of the eligibility criteria were 66. Of these 66 articles, 50 mapped to Protection and Prevention Methods that we chose to examine while the rest were literature review ones, kept for respective knowledge extraction and utilization by our paper. The 50 methods are approximately distributed based on their protection method category in Fig. 1 while their distribution based on their publication kind is shown in Fig. 2.

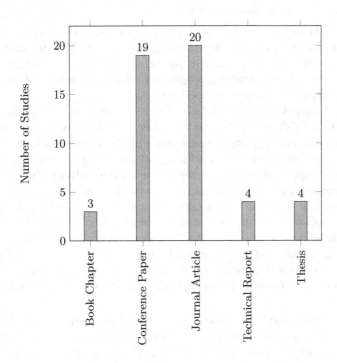

Fig. 2. The publication distribution of the different studies.

3   Analysis

This section overviews the main method categories. Based on this categorization, it then classifies the protection methods selected according to the methodology in Sect. 2. It also evaluates these methods based on some key evaluation criteria.

3.1   Overview of Protection Method Categories

This sub-section analyzes the main categories of social engineering protection methods by extending the method categorisation in [3] with the categories of Deep Learning, Hybrid Learning and Scenario-based Attack Detection.

Policy and Process Control. Policy and process control provide hierarchical control via some management and process frameworks, as opposed to technical systems, such as security software. They are essential in an organisation as they provide a comprehensive protection approach. Most importantly, they are procedures to prevent and detect potential attacks, but also steps and procedures to react to such attacks. They are designed to reduce exposure to social engineering attacks. Well-maintained policy and organizational procedures help mitigate the occurrence of an exploit without relying on the technical capabilities of the system users. Policy and Procedure Control are the backbone of the organizations' security, while the overall security countermeasures and tools to protect against such attacks are decided based on them.

Awareness Training. Since attacks target the system's users, attacks can be greatly reduced by proper user training and awareness. Education is a key defence model element. In particular, in social engineering attacks, it concerns introducing and applying training programs to compensate for and mitigate the technical security mechanisms inadequacy.

Empirical studies and research have shown that awareness training programs can enhance individuals' ability to recognize and identify social engineering attacks. Training participants become more alert to common tactics, such as phishing emails, impersonation attempts, and phone scams. Further, awareness training encourages individuals to report suspicious activities or social engineering attempts. This can lead to quicker incident response and mitigation of potential security breaches. When employees are educated about the risks and consequences of social engineering attacks, they become more proactive to safeguarde information and are more likely to adopt secure behaviors [5].

Social engineering tactics evolve rapidly such that individuals require regular and updated training to stay informed. One-time training sessions may not be sufficient to combat the ever-changing landscape of social engineering attacks.

Technical. "Technical" are those protection and prevention methods in which the human factor is either irrelevant or has little significance in addressing social engineering attacks. These methods create mechanisms that either prevent and protect against social engineering attacks entirely on their own or create an infrastructure helping the user to identify and defend against such attacks.

We categorize Technical Protection and Prevention Methods into:

Sandboxing Mechanisms. In sandboxing, an isolated computer environment is created, usually via virtualization, to test unreliable functions. It has been effectively applied in various IT domains, from specific code platforms to browsers, plus in the field of smartphone security to improve defence against malware. Sandboxing can be used to help in protecting against social engineering attacks by isolating potentially malicious programs or actions from the rest of a system. For example, if a user clicks on a link or opens an email attachment that contains malware, sandboxing can prevent that malware from spreading beyond the sandboxed environment. This can help prevent the attacker from gaining access to sensitive data or causing damage to the system [6].

Authorisation, Authentication, and Accounting (AAA). AAA is a framework for intelligent computer access, enforcing authentication and authorization-related policies, controlling usage, and providing the information needed for service billing. It is typically applied in controlled environments, especially where there is a diverse user landscape that compromises data control and protection. The framework provides controls for accessing resources (Authentication), enforcing organizational policies (Authorization), and controlling resource usage (e.g., devices accessed). Its use is intended to ensure that organisations have a detailed assurance and control level over who has access to a system, based on data about names, roles, skill sets, etc. By using strong authentication methods, such as multi-factor authentication, organizations ensure that only authorized users access sensitive data or systems. Further, by implementing strong accounting policies, logging and monitoring of user activities are enabled, providing an audit trail to be used for post-incident analysis and forensic investigations. This can help detect and mitigate the effects of social engineering attacks, as organizations can identify respective suspicious behaviour.

Monitoring. Monitoring concerns observing a computer system's behaviour, generated by user/programmer actions, programs, services and processes, via collection, aggregation and analysis mechanisms. Monitoring is a key security mechanism for social engineering attacks, as new attacks can be identified by logging and analysis of network traffic and effective security control where they can be detected by juxtaposition to normal/legal user actions in the system.

Effective monitoring enables timely alerts and notifications when potential social engineering attacks are detected. These alerts can trigger incident response procedures, allowing security teams to investigate and mitigate the attacks before causing significant harm [7].

Social engineering attacks evolve over time; thus, monitoring should be an ongoing process. Regularly reviewing and updating monitoring systems, staying informed about new attack vectors, and adapting monitoring strategies are critical to maintaining an effective defence against social engineering attacks.

Integrity Checking. The integrity of applications and data is difficult to ensure without proof or analysis. Integrity checking provides the user with a visual response and technical assurance as to whether the file, site, or data should be trusted through various tools like Intrusion Detection Systems (IDS).

Integrity checking can effectively identify instances where malware has been injected into files or system components. By regularly verifying file integrity and detecting unexpected modifications, organizations can detect and mitigate the impact of social engineering attacks involving malware injection. Further, it can also help ensure the integrity and authenticity of data by using cryptographic hashing or digital signatures such that organizations can verify data integrity at rest or during transmission. This helps protect against social engineering attacks that involve tampering with sensitive information or data manipulation [8].

Machine Learning. Research has demonstrated that malware detection via machine learning (ML) can be dynamic, where appropriate algorithms, such as support vector machines and neural networks can be applied to profile files against known and potential exploits and distinguish between legitimate and illegitimate data. ML algorithms have been successfully applied to detect malicious emails using anomaly classification techniques, thus demonstrating their potential for further application to other areas of social engineering attacks.

The effectiveness of ML algorithms in detecting social engineering attacks relies heavily on the availability of high-quality and diverse training data. Collecting data sets that encompass a wide range of social engineering attack scenarios can be challenging. Further, maintaining up-to-date data sets to keep pace with evolving attack techniques is crucial for ML model accuracy [9].

Deep Learning. Similar to ML, Deep Learning (DL) algorithms can prevent social engineering attacks by analyzing patterns in user and system behaviour and detecting anomalies indicative of an attack. DL algorithms can be used to analyze the language used in emails, social media messages, and other communication channels to detect phishing and other social engineering attacks. Natural language processing (NLP) can identify suspicious language patterns or unusual word usage indicative of an attack. These algorithms can also be used to analyze images and videos for signs of social engineering attacks, such as phishing sites, fake login pages, or malware. Recent developments in approaches have suggested that the classification of phishing websites using neural networks should outperform traditional ML algorithms.

DL techniques, e.g., convolutional neural networks (CNNs), have been used to analyze visual content, such as images or video frames, to detect social engineering-related cues or visual elements. For example, DL models can identify spoofed websites or altered images used in social engineering attacks [10].

Hybrid Learning. Hybrid learning (HL) is a training approach that combines different types of learning algorithms or architectures to improve a DL model's performance. By utilizing the advantages of various learning architectures or algorithms, HL seeks to improve upon each one's shortcomings. An example HL approach is to combine supervised and unsupervised learning methods or different types of deep learning architectures, such as CNNs and recurrent neural networks (RNNs). HL can improve detection model accuracy and reduce false positives, whereas multi-modal data analysis models can combine multiple data types, such as images, and speech, to analyze the different aspects of a social engineering attack. The models can also adapt and learn from new attack types and update their detection algorithms accordingly [11].

Scenario-Based Attack Detection. By simulating various attack scenarios and examining user behaviour for signals of an attack, scenario-based attack detection is a technique used to identify and stop social engineering attacks. It involves creating hypothetical situations and common attack patterns that closely resemble strategies and procedures employed by attackers and then keeping an eye on user behaviour to spot potential risks. Red team assessments, involving simulated attacks performed by specialized teams, are often used to evaluate an organization's resilience against social engineering attacks. Such assessments provide empirical evidence by demonstrating how effective existing security measures are in detecting and mitigating real-world social engineering threats [12].

Scenario-based attack detection should be an ongoing process that evolves alongside emerging social engineering techniques. Regularly updating and refining attack scenarios based on new threats and attack vectors is crucial to maintain the effectiveness of this protection method.

3.2 Criteria for Method Evaluation

This section defines newly devised criteria for evaluating the protection and prevention methods selected. Some of these criteria focus on the applicability of the protection methods to be evaluated.

Method of Protection - MoP. Refers to a specific approach, technique, or countermeasure implemented to safeguard individuals, organizations, or systems against social engineering attacks.

Method of Treatment - MoT. Indicates whether the method of treatment targets *Prevention P, Reaction R, Detection D* or a mix of these.

Degree of Protection - DoP. Evaluates the effectiveness of a protection method in addressing the attacks it specializes in. The evaluation can lead to assessing that the provided degree of protection is either *Small, Medium,* or *Great.* "Small" means that extra measures or improvements are necessary to enhance the protection level and strengthen the security posture, "Medium" indicates that the method offers a satisfactory protection level under typical circumstances while "Great" suggests that the method surpasses the average protection level and is considered highly reliable and secure.

Ease of Implementation - EoI. Assesses how easily the response suggested by a protection method can be implemented in an information system or incorporated into an organization's plan. EoI can be categorised as *Small, Medium,* or *Great,* based on the level of effort, resources, and complexity required to deploy and integrate the suggested response. "Small" indicates that the implementation process is straightforward, requiring minimal changes or adjustments, "Medium" implies a balanced effort level without posing overwhelming obstacles while "Great" suggests that the response can be quickly adopted without causing disruptions or significant changes to existing systems or processes.

Application Part - AppP. Identifies the areas or components to which the proposed method applies. These areas are: *The architecture, Policies and Procedures, Security Mechanisms, People, and Systems.* This categorization clarifies the scope and context in which the method can be effectively implemented.

Implementation Time - ImplT. Refers to the estimated duration, measured in *Hours, Days, Months,* or *Years,* required to fully implement the proposed method. It represents the time investment needed to deploy and integrate the method into an organization's existing infrastructure, processes, and security framework. While time estimation can be quite challenging, several factors can be considered to facilitate it: the method complexity, organization size, resource availability, complexity and integration, plus the training and familiarization. By breaking down the implementation tasks, identifying dependencies, and considering the above factors, a reasonable implementation time estimation can be derived. However, it must be noted that unforeseen challenges or unexpected circumstances may impact the actual implementation time, and regular monitoring and adjustment of the implementation plan may be necessary.

Application Effort - AppE. Evaluates the amount of effort required to fully implement the proposed method. AppE can be assessed as *small, medium,* or *great,* based on the resources, time, and complexity involved in the implementation process. "Small" indicates that the method can be readily implemented efficiently without significant disruptions or resource-intensive activities with the available resources and within a reasonable time frame. "Medium" indicates that it can be accomplished within a manageable time frame and with a reasonable resource allocation. Thus, the method is implementable with the organization's existing capabilities and may require a moderate coordination and planning level. A "Great" value suggests that the implementation may require significant changes to the existing infrastructure, processes, or systems. So, the method is resource-intensive, complex, and may require extra expertise or support for successful implementation. Thus, implementing such a method may involve extensive planning, coordination, and resource allocation.

Implementation Cost - ImplC. Refers to the expenses associated with implementing and maintaining a protection method. It quantifies the financial resources required for the method's setup, deployment, and ongoing management. A method's ImplC can be categorized into three general categories: *Small, Medium,* and *Great,* representing different cost ranges. "Small" indicates that the method can be implemented without significant financial burden or extra investments. Thus, the cost is manageable and aligns with the organization's budgetary constraints. "Medium" indicates that the cost is within a balanced range, considering the value provided by the method and the organization's financial capabilities. Thus, the implementation cost is justifiable and can be accommodated with appropriate budget planning. A "Great" assessment value suggests that the cost may exceed the average budget allocation and might require extra financial resources or long-term commitments. As such, the method may involve expensive infrastructure, specialized tools, or ongoing licensing fees.

3.3   Evaluation Results

The evaluation results are presented via a set of tables. Each table showcases how well each method within a specific category satisfies the above criteria.

3.4   Analysis of Evaluation Results

This section analyses the methods' effectiveness in terms of their performance against the devised criteria. The analysis is performed per method category.

Table 1. Policy and Process Control

MoP	MoT	DoP	EoI	AppP	ImplT	AppE	ImplC
[13]	D, P, R	Great	Medium	Policies and Procedures	Months	Medium	Medium
[14]	P	Medium	Medium	Policies and Procedures	Months	Medium	Medium

Table 2. Awareness Training

MoP	MoT	DoP	EoI	AppP	ImplT	AppE	ImplC
[15,16]	P	Medium	Great	People	Days	Great	Great
[17]	P, R	Small	Great	Systems, People	Hours	Great	Great
[18]	P	Medium	Great	Systems, People	Hours	Great	Great
[19]	P	Medium	Medium	Systems, People	Hours	Medium	Great
[20]	D	Great	Small	Systems, People	Days	Medium	Great

Policy and Process Control deals with all security levels (Technical Attacks - Social Engineering Attacks, etc.) but every category method is quite time-consuming to implement. It is a general method of security that stands out in overall organisational security approaches. It is defined around the business and the user environment. However, the security frameworks introduced to address attacks have been added as extra elements to the broader security architecture, rather than to the strategic policy and process control development (i.e., by-design) [62]. More importantly, policy must be inherently structured with people management and embedded at the core of all information systems.

As can be seen in Table 1, EoI is moderate and implementation time corresponds to months since it takes some time to implement such security approaches as a whole. There is a fairly good protection degree but mainly only general guidelines for security procedures are provided for the whole information system and the people participating in it. The application part is Policies and procedures and the implementation costs are moderate.

More effective policies may be developed identifying gaps in current policies and introducing new policies better tailored to social engineering threats. There is also a need to measure more accurately policies and process control effectiveness in preventing and mitigating social engineering attacks with new metrics and evaluation methods. Such data can also be used to train ML and DL models.

Awareness Training is probably the most basic response to social engineering attacks since the weak system link is the human user. As can be seen in Table 2, this method category is mainly concerned with prevention, while its main application targets are humans and systems. The protection degree, ease of implementation, implementation time and cost can vary depending on the program and training type each organization-organization will follow.

There are various training modes, where beyond a simple presentation or seminar, they can take the form of interactive games or training systems, which make the process more interesting and reward the user in the learning process. Training has shown good results as a way of protection as it reduces social engineering attacks to a fairly satisfactory degree, but it must be done thoroughly

Table 3. Technical - Sandboxing

MoP	MoT	DoP	EoI	AppP	ImplT	AppE	ImplC
[21]	D, P, R	Great	Medium	Systems	Months	Medium	Medium
[6]	D	Medium	Medium	Systems	Days	Medium	Medium
[22, 23]	P	Small	Medium	Systems	Weeks	Medium	Medium
[24]	R	Great	Great	Systems	Weeks	Great	Medium
[25]	R	Great	Great	Systems	Days	Great	Great

Table 4. Technical - AAA

MoP	MoT	DoP	EoI	AppP	ImplT	AppE	ImplC
[26]	D	Medium	Medium	Systems, Policies and Procedures	Days	Medium	Medium
[27]	R	Medium	Medium	Systems, Policies and Procedures	Days	Medium	Great

and properly implemented in an organisation to attain such results. It must be also continuously applied to cover new attacks and exploitation modes [63].

Sandboxing mechanisms represent a good protection way at a low cost compared to what they offer. As can be seen in Table 3 the protection provided is *Medium* to *High*, except for some methods in a more experimental stage. The EoI is *Moderate* to *Great* since the system supports the user in making correct decisions as to how to run applications of dubious origin in such an environment via a UI without being obscure and difficult for the ordinary user. Implementation time ranges from days to months depending on the approach taken and the environment choice (widespread and quickly accessible, or experimental-research in development) while implementation effort ranges from *Medium* to *Great* in the examined methods, as they did not use an already existing infrastructure with some exceptions. The application target is systems while cost again varies depending on the environment choice, but ranges towards *Moderate*.

The attack range addressed is wide as many key attack features are covered [64]. The Sandboxing mechanisms already in use are widespread as a security solution, with a fairly good defence rate against large-scale attacks but there is room for improvement in enhancing their detection capabilities and performance.

AAA: It is a moderate protection mode and specific towards large organisations as it provides a centralized management framework for access control, making it easier to manage a large number of users, resources and permissions, and can easily be scaled depending on the use case. As can be seen in Table 4, the coping mode is mainly in detection and reaction with medium protection and EoI as there are many established infrastructures and implementations that are accessible (FreeRADIUS, Globberry, etc.). EoI is also moderate since once the AAA infrastructure is built, it is very easy to cover many people in the organisation. Implementation time is usually within hours and the implementation effort is moderate. The application targets are systems, policies and procedures while the implementation cost is moderate to low if open-source solutions are used. However, the cost of implementation is Medium to Great in the solutions

Table 5. Technical - Monitoring

MoP	MoT	DoP	EoI	AppP	ImplT	AppE	ImplC
[28]	D	Medium	Medium	Systems	Weeks	Medium	Medium
[29]	D	Great	Great	Systems	Hours	Small	Great
[30]	D	Medium	Great	Systems, Policies and Procedures	Hours	Medium	Great
[31]	D	Great	Great	Systems	Hours	Small	Great

Table 6. Technical - Integrity Checking

MoP	MoT	DoP	EoI	AppP	ImplT	AppE	ImplC
[32]	D	Medium	Medium	Security Mechanisms	Months	Small	Medium
[33]	P	Small	Medium	Security Mechanisms	Months	Medium	Medium
[34]	P	Medium	Great	Security Mechanisms	Weeks	Medium	Medium
[35]	D	Medium	Medium	Security Mechanisms	Weeks	Medium	Small

we examined as they require extra resources, such as storage, bandwidth, and processing power, to collect and analyze data.

The authentication methods can be improved to better protect against social engineering attacks relying on credential theft or account takeover. While AAA solutions typically include some authentication form, they may not be sufficient to protect against the latest social engineering techniques. Research in this area could focus on developing new authentication methods more resistant to social engineering attacks, such as biometric authentication or behavioural analysis. While AAA solutions typically include authorization controls, these controls may not be sufficient to prevent social engineering attacks that exploit weaknesses in the authorization process. Research in this area could focus on developing new authorization methods more resistant to social engineering attacks, such as adaptive authorization that considers user behaviour and context.

Monitoring: As can be seen in Table 5, response mode is *Detection* while EoI is medium to great, as there are many open-source implementations (e.g., Wireshark, OSSEC). It is mainly applied to systems. The implementation time depends on the solution and tool choice (Hours - Days - Months) but the monitoring data, to be meaningful, must be collected over a long time period. The implementation cost is from moderate to none as there are several monitoring programs even for free (e.g., SolarWinds IP Monitor). Monitoring delivers good protection results [29] It is one of the most effective protection ways, if there is a cyber security specialist or a mechanism (Software, Model, etc.) in the organization that manages the network traffic, system logs, user activity, etc.

Monitoring may not be always able to detect the latest social engineering attacks. As such, research in this area could focus on developing new, more effective monitoring techniques, such as user activity monitoring, network monitoring, and endpoint monitoring. Further research is needed to compare the effectiveness of different monitoring approaches and identify best practices.

Integrity Checking. As can be seen in Table 6, response mode is prevention and detection, since users are warned of any malicious actions. The protection degree is moderate since the final decision beyond warning is at the user's discretion. EoI

Table 7. Technical - Machine Learning

MoP	MoT	DoP	EoI	AppP	ImplT	AppE	ImplC
[36]	D	Medium	Great	Security Mechanisms	Months	Great	Medium
[37]	D	Medium	Medium	Systems	Weeks	Medium	Medium
[38]	D	Great	Medium	Security Mechanisms	Months	Medium	Medium
[39]	D	Small	Medium	Security Mechanisms	Months	Medium	Great
[40]	D	Small	Medium	Architecture	Months	Medium	Medium
[41]	D	Medium	Great	Systems	Hours	Medium	Great
[42]	D	Great	Great	Systems	Hours	Medium	Great
[43]	D	Great	Medium	Systems	Months	Medium	Small

Table 8. Technical - Deep Learning

MoP	MoT	DoP	EoI	AppP	ImplT	AppE	ImplC
[44]	P	Small	Small	Architecture	Months	Medium	Small
[45]	D	Small	Medium	Security Mechanisms	Months	Medium	Medium
[46]	D	Great	Small	Systems	Months	Medium	Small
[47]	P	Small	Medium	Security Mechanisms	Weeks	Medium	Medium
[48]	P	Small	Medium	Security Mechanisms	Weeks	Medium	Medium
[49]	D	Great	Medium	Security Mechanisms	Days	Medium	Medium

is medium as there are existing tools (e.g., Tripwire, AIDE); but it may vary in some methods depending on what stage they are and how experimental is their approach. The application target is Security mechanisms. Implementation effort is usually moderate as the existing tools are easily integrated and there is sufficient documentation for such an integration, with some exceptions depending on the research and the algorithms under consideration. Implementation time is moderate - mostly months as there was no existing infrastructure in the examined methods. The cost of implementation is *Medium*.

Integrity checking can be improved by enhancing the methods' scalability to protect against large-scale attacks. The existing methods should be also extended, e.g., by using ML algorithms to identify anomalous behaviour, so as to address attacks that involve manipulation of data or systems.

Machine Learning becomes increasingly common with great research interest since the use and invention of ML algorithms have been quite widespread recently. As shown in Table 7, the coping mode is *Detection*. The protection degree, implementation time and implementation cost vary depending on the approach followed and the volume of data selected each time for learning. The application target varies (Security Mechanisms, Systems, Architecture) in the examined methods. EoI is moderate to high, as once the algorithm has acquired the necessary 'knowledge', it can be included in systems with relative ease.

Using feature variables with behavioural input data sets (usually collected through monitoring), accurate predictions and indicator measurements can be achieved in terms of the significance of a file or user behaviour effect on a system.

Table 9. Technical - Scenario Based

MoP	MoT	DoP	EoI	AppP	ImplT	AppE	ImplC
[50]	D	Small	Medium	Security Mechanisms	Weeks	Medium	Medium
[51,52]	P	Small	Medium	Security Mechanisms	Months	Great	Medium
[53]	R	Medium	Medium	Security Mechanisms	Weeks	Small	Medium
[54]	P	Small	Medium	Security Mechanisms	Weeks	Medium	Medium
[55]	D	Medium	Great	Security Mechanisms	Days	Small	Great
[56]	D	Small	Small	Security Mechanisms	Weeks	Medium	Great
[57]	D	Small	Medium	Security Mechanisms	Weeks	Small	Medium

Table 10. Technical - Hybrid

MoP	MoT	DoP	EoI	AppP	ImplT	AppE	ImplC
[58]	P	Medium	Medium	Security Mechanisms, Policies and Procedures	Weeks	Medium	Great
[59]	R	Great	Medium	Security Mechanisms, Policies and Procedures	Weeks	Medium	Medium
[60]	D	Medium	Medium	Security Mechanisms, Policies and Procedures	Days	Medium	Medium
[61]	D	Great	Medium	Security Mechanisms, Policies and Procedures, People	Days	Medium	Medium

While ML tools have been built, tested and evaluated in research, their application has largely focused on countering phishing attacks [65,66].

There is room to further optimize ML methods. Developing more effective feature engineering methods is a potential research gap so as to more accurately extract relevant features from social engineering attack data. The interpretability of ML models could be also improved by utilising, e.g., explainable artificial intelligence (XAI) methods [67].

Deep Learning. With neural networks being increasingly used and slowly replacing traditional ML algorithms, DL approaches are becoming more and more common. As can be seen in Table 8, DL methods supply detection and prevention abilities since they are similar to ML methods. The protection degree can vary from small to great as it depends on the model created and the data used to create it. EoI is moderate as it depends on the way the problem is approached and the amount of data to be learned. The application target can vary (Architecture, security mechanisms, and systems). Implementation time varies from weeks to months, as it is quite time-consuming to train a neural network with a large data volume. Implementation effort is medium and the cost is small to medium in the studied methods, as suitable, advanced tools to train the models already exist (e.g., Tensorflow, Keras). These values may vary depending on the integration requirements of each implementation effort.

The DL research results are modest at present but may improve further due to the intensity of research being conducted. DL solutions can be improved by more diverse and relevant data collection, incorporating contextual information into DL models and developing DL models that can detect and respond to social engineering attacks in real-time. It is also worth addressing the potential for bias in the DL algorithms so as to increase prediction accuracy.

Scenario-Based. It can be seen from Table 9 that the response mode varies while the application target is security mechanisms. The protection degree, EoI, implementation time and effort can vary as they depend on the kind and complexity of the scenario chosen by the researchers. As such, such methods can be used for more specific situations and organisation needs; however, we can use combinations of scenario-based attack detection methods to get better results and attain a larger coverage.

Research must be conducted for the more accurate measurement of the methods' effectiveness via the use of objective and standardized metrics. Further, there is a need to develop personalized training scenarios that are tailored to the specific needs and vulnerabilities of individual employees or employee groups.

Hybrid. As shown in Table 10, the response mode varies. The implementation effort is medium in the examined methods as hybrid proposals with specific use cases can have great cost-benefit analysis and a well-defined incident-response plan. The application target is Security mechanisms, policy and processes plus people, as hybrid methods use a union of technical and non-technical approaches. The implementation time ranges from days to weeks. The cost can vary from little to great depending on the method complexity and integration. Hybrid protection methods are quite effective but with a slightly higher implementation cost due to the expertise and infrastructure needed.

Hybrid approaches often involve integrating multiple solutions and technologies, which can be challenging. Thus, there is a need to develop standardized frameworks and protocols to enable seamless integration of different protection methods. There is also the need to develop optimization algorithms that can take into account the strengths and weaknesses of the different protection methods to achieve optimal hybrid approach performance.

Overall Analysis: Determining a single method category as universally better than the others based on all criteria is challenging, as the methods' effectiveness against social engineering attacks depends on various factors. Different criteria hold different weights of importance for different organizations or systems, making it difficult to establish a definitive superiority across all categories. However, there are categories that may be deemed better than others based on specific criteria. For instance, ML methods promise to detect and mitigate social engineering attacks by utilizing advanced algorithms and pattern recognition. They can adapt and evolve to new attack vectors, making them highly effective in certain scenarios. Similarly, categories like Policy and Process Control, focusing on establishing robust security procedures and guidelines, can provide comprehensive protection and help organizations maintain a strong defence against attacks. In terms of EoI, some categories may require significant effort and time to fully implement, such as Policy and Process Control. These methods typically involve developing comprehensive security procedures and guidelines for the entire information system, which can be time-consuming and resource-intensive. On the other hand, categories like Monitoring and Integrity Checking may have a relatively easier implementation process, as there are existing tools and open-source solutions available. Similarly, the protection degree can vary across categories. While some methods may offer great protection against social engineering attacks, such as Sandboxing Mechanisms and ML, others may provide only moderate or small protection levels. It depends on the specific features and capabilities of each method in addressing the attacks they specialize in.

It is also challenging to pinpoint a specific category as generally worse than others. Each category has its own strengths and weaknesses, and their effectiveness can vary depending on the context and specific criteria. For example, categories like Awareness Training, aiming to educate and empower users to recognize and resist social engineering attempts, can be highly effective only when implemented correctly. However, if not properly executed or lacking regular updates, their impact may be limited.

In real-world scenarios, the implementation of social engineering prevention methods often requires a hybrid approach that combines multiple strategies to address the multifaceted nature of social engineering attacks. These hybrid solutions leverage a combination of technological, procedural, and educational measures to create a robust defence against ever-evolving threats. For instance, an organization might employ advanced email filtering systems to detect and block phishing attempts, complemented by periodic security awareness training for employees to identify and report suspicious messages. Additionally, access controls and multi-factor authentication mechanisms can be integrated to prevent unauthorized access to critical systems, mitigating the risk of social engineering attacks that exploit human error. The adoption of hybrid solutions allows organizations to create a layered defence, where each protective measure reinforces the effectiveness of others, thereby significantly reducing the likelihood of successful social engineering attacks.

To determine the most suitable category or combination of methods, organizations should carefully evaluate their needs, assess the potential risks they face, and consider those criteria that hold the highest priority for their operation. By conducting thorough assessments and understanding the strengths and limitations of each category and method especially against the devised criteria, organizations can make informed decisions on which methods are most suitable for their needs to establish a multi-layered defence against social engineering attacks.

4 Conclusion

This paper has supplied an analysis of protection and prevention methods against social engineering attacks, facilitating the selection of such methods based on the user/organisation needs as well as the development of countermeasures and conduction of further research in this area. It has classified the methods based on some key dimensions by extending the work in [3] and assessed them based on specific evaluation criteria. The evaluation results obtained were then analysed to infer some interesting conclusions, such as how effective these methods are.

References

1. Klimburg-Witjes, N., Wentland, A.: Hacking humans? Social engineering and the construction of the "deficient user" in cybersecurity discourses. Sci. Technol. Hum. Values **46**, 1316–1339 (2021)
2. Khalid, A., Nazir, M., Hussain, S., Asim, M.: A comprehensive review of social engineering attacks and defense mechanisms. J. Inf. Secur. (2016)
3. Heartfield, R., Loukas, G.: A taxonomy of attacks and a survey of defence mechanisms for semantic social engineering attacks. ACM Comput. Surv. **48**(3), 1–39 (2016). https://doi.org/10.1145/2835375
4. Odeh, A.E.N.A., Eleyan, D.: A survey of social engineering attacks: detection and prevention tools (2021)
5. Aldawood, H., Skinner, G.: Reviewing cyber security social engineering training and awareness programs—pitfalls and ongoing issues. Fut. Internet **11**(3), 73 (2019). https://doi.org/10.3390/fi11030073
6. Greamo, C., Ghosh, A.: Sandboxing and virtualization: modern tools for combating malware. IEEE Secur. Priv. **9**(2), 79–82 (2011)
7. Ghafir, I., Prenosil, V., Svoboda, J., Hammoudeh, M.: A survey on network security monitoring systems, pp. 77–82, August 2016
8. Subha, T., Jayashri, S.: Efficient privacy preserving integrity checking model for cloud data storage security. In: 2016 Eighth International Conference on Advanced Computing (ICoAC), pp. 55–60 (2017)
9. Xue, M., Yuan, C., Wu, H., Zhang, Y., Liu, W.: Machine learning security: threats, countermeasures, and evaluations. IEEE Access **8**, 74720–74742 (2020)
10. Samakovitis, G., Petridis, M., Lansley, M., Polatidis, N., Kapetanakis, S., Amin, K.: Seen the villains: detecting social engineering attacks using case-based reasoning and deep learning, July 2019
11. Sedjelmaci, H., Senouci, S.-M., Ansari, N., Boualouache, A.: A trusted hybrid learning approach to secure edge computing. IEEE Consum. Electron. Mag. **11**(3), 30–37 (2022)
12. Krombholz, K., Hobel, H., Donko-Huber, M., Weippl, E.: Advanced social engineering attacks. J. Inf. Secur. Appl. **22**, 10 (2014)
13. Peltier, T.R.: Information Security Policies, Procedures, and Standards: Guidelines for Effective Information Security Management (2001)
14. Frauenstein, E.D., von Solms, R.: An enterprise anti-phishing framework, March 2011
15. Kumaraguru, P.: PhishGuru: a system for educating users about semantic attacks, p. 199, April 2009
16. Arachchilage, N.A.G., Love, S., Scott, M.: Designing a mobile game to teach conceptual knowledge of avoiding 'phishing attacks'. Int. J. e-Learn. Secur. **2**(1), 127–132 (2012). https://doi.org/10.20533/ijels.2046.4568.2012.0016
17. Lin, E., Greenberg, S., Trotter, E., Ma, D., Aycock, J.: Does domain highlighting help people identify phishing sites?, pp. 2075–2084, May 2011
18. Lee, J., Bauer, L., Mazurek, M.: Studying the effectiveness of security images in internet banking. IEEE Internet Comput. **13** (2015)
19. Kritzinger, E., von Solms, S.H.: Cyber security for home users: a new way of protection through awareness enforcement. Comput. Secur. **29**(8), 840–847 (2010)
20. Anderson, B., Kirwan, B., Jenkins, J., Eargle, D., Howard, S., Vance, A.: How polymorphic warnings reduce habituation in the brain: insights from an fMRI Study, pp. 2883–2892, April 2015

21. Barth, A., Reis, C.: The security architecture of the chromium browser (2009)
22. Mozilla Wiki-Security/Sandbox (2015)
23. The chromium projects-sandbox (2015)
24. Lu, L., Yegneswaran, V., Porras, P., Lee, W.: BLADE: an attack-agnostic approach for preventing drive-by malware infections, pp. 440–450, October 2010
25. Bianchi, A., Corbetta, J., Invernizzi, L., Fratantonio, Y., Kruegel, C., Vigna, G.: What the app is that? Deception and countermeasures in the android user interface, pp. 931–948, July 2015
26. Desmond, R.A.B., Richards, J., Lowe-Norris, A.G.: Active Directory, 5th edn. (2013)
27. Motiee, S., Hawkey, K., Beznosov, K.: Do windows users follow the principle of least privilege? Investigating user account control practices, July 2010
28. Salem, M.B., Stolfo, S.J.: Modeling user search behavior for masquerade detection. In: Sommer, R., Balzarotti, D., Maier, G. (eds.) RAID 2011. LNCS, vol. 6961, pp. 181–200. Springer, Heidelberg (2011). https://doi.org/10.1007/978-3-642-23644-0_10
29. Lu, L., Perdisci, R., Lee, W.: SURF: detecting and measuring search poisoning, pp. 467–476, October 2011
30. Li, Z., Alrwais, S., Xie, Y., Yu, F., Wang, X.: Finding the linchpins of the dark web: a study on topologically dedicated hosts on malicious web infrastructures, pp. 112–126, May 2013
31. Lee, S., Kim, J.: WARNINGBIRD: detecting suspicious URLs in Twitter stream, January 2012
32. Udzir, N., Samsudin, K.: Towards a dynamic file integrity monitor through a security classification. Int. J. New Comput. Archit. Appl. (IJNCAA) 3, 789–802 (2011)
33. Dhanalakshmi, R., Chellappan, C.: Detection and recognition of file masquerading for e-mail and data security. In: Meghanathan, N., Boumerdassi, S., Chaki, N., Nagamalai, D. (eds.) CNSA 2010. CCIS, vol. 89, pp. 253–262. Springer, Heidelberg (2010). https://doi.org/10.1007/978-3-642-14478-3_26
34. Hara, M., Yamada, A., Miyake, Y.: Visual similarity-based phishing detection without victim site information, pp. 30–36, May 2009
35. Bhardwaj, T., Sharma, T.K., Pandit, M.R.: Social engineering prevention by detecting malicious URLs using artificial bee colony algorithm. In: Pant, M., Deep, K., Nagar, A., Bansal, J.C. (eds.) Proceedings of the Third International Conference on Soft Computing for Problem Solving. AISC, vol. 258, pp. 355–363. Springer, New Delhi (2014). https://doi.org/10.1007/978-81-322-1771-8_31
36. Singhal, P., Raul, N.: Malware detection module using machine learning algorithms to assist in centralized security in enterprise networks. Int. J. Netw. Secur. Appl. 4, 61–67 (2012)
37. Sandouka, H., Cullen, A., Mann, I.: Social engineering detection using neural networks, pp. 273–278, January 2009
38. Basnet, R., Mukkamala, S., Sung, A.H.: Detection of phishing attacks: a machine learning approach. In: Prasad, B. (eds.) Soft Computing Applications in Industry. Studies in Fuzziness and Soft Computing, vol. 226, pp. 373–383. Springer, Heidelberg (2008). https://doi.org/10.1007/978-3-540-77465-5_19
39. Raskin, V., Rayz, J., Hempelmann, C.: Ontological semantic technology for detecting insider threat and social engineering. In: Proceedings New Security Paradigms Workshop, September 2010
40. Xiang, G., Hong, J., Rose, C.P., Cranor, L.: CANTINA+: a feature-rich machine learning framework for detecting phishing web sites. ACM Trans. Inf. Syst. Secur. 14(2), 1–28 (2011)

41. Cova, M., Krügel, C., Vigna, G.: Detection and analysis of drive-by-download attacks and malicious JavaScript code, pp. 281–290, April 2010
42. Aggarwal, A., Rajadesingan, A., Kumaraguru, P.: PhishAri: automatic realtime phishing detection on Twitter. In: eCrime Researchers Summit, eCrime, January 2013
43. Stringhini, G., Thonnard, O.: That ain't you: blocking spearphishing through behavioral modelling. In: Almgren, M., Gulisano, V., Maggi, F. (eds.) DIMVA 2015. LNCS, vol. 9148, pp. 78–97. Springer, Cham (2015). https://doi.org/10.1007/978-3-319-20550-2_5
44. Basit, A., Zafar, M., Liu, X., Javed, A.R., Jalil, Z., Kifayat, K.: A comprehensive survey of AI-enabled phishing attacks detection techniques. Telecommun. Syst. 76(1), 139–154 (2020). https://doi.org/10.1007/s11235-020-00733-2
45. Maurya, S., Jain, A.: Deep learning to combat phishing. J. Stat. Manag. Syst. 23, 07 (2020)
46. Subasi, A., Molah, E., Almkallawi, F., Chaudhery, T.J.: Intelligent phishing website detection using random forest classifier, pp. 1–5, November 2017
47. Abdelhamid, N., Thabtah, F., Abdel-jaber, H.: Phishing detection: a recent intelligent machine learning comparison based on models content and features, pp. 72–77, July 2017
48. Mao, J., et al.: Detecting phishing websites via aggregation analysis of page layouts. Procedia Comput. Sci. 129, 224–230 (2018)
49. Lansley, M., Polatidis, N., Kapetanakis, S.: SEADer: a social engineering attack detection method based on natural language processing and artificial neural networks. In: Nguyen, N.T., Chbeir, R., Exposito, E., Aniorté, P., Trawiński, B. (eds.) ICCCI 2019. LNCS (LNAI), vol. 11683, pp. 686–696. Springer, Cham (2019). https://doi.org/10.1007/978-3-030-28377-3_57
50. Begum, A., Badugu, S.: A study of malicious URL detection using machine learning and heuristic approaches. In: Satapathy, S.C., Raju, K.S., Shyamala, K., Krishna, D.R., Favorskaya, M.N. (eds.) Advances in Decision Sciences, Image Processing, Security and Computer Vision. LAIS, vol. 4, pp. 587–597. Springer, Cham (2020). https://doi.org/10.1007/978-3-030-24318-0_68
51. Chouhan, A.Y., Fatima, R., Liu, L., Yasin, A., Wang, J.: Contemplating social engineering studies and attack scenarios: a review study. Secur. Priv. 2, e73 (2019)
52. Al-Hamar, Y., Kolivand, H., Tajdini, M., Saba, T., Ramachandran, V.: Enterprise credential spear-phishing attack detection. Comput. Electr. Eng. 94, 107363 (2021)
53. Fatima, R., Chouhan, A.Y., Liu, L., Wang, J.: How persuasive is a phishing email? A phishing game for phishing awareness. J. Comput. Secur. 27, 1–32 (2019)
54. Chiew, K.L., Yong, K., Tan, C.C.L.: A survey of phishing attacks: their types, vectors and technical approaches. Exp. Syst. Appl. 106, 1–20 (2018)
55. Yao, W., Ding, Y., Li, X.: LogoPhish: a new two-dimensional code phishing attack detection method, pp. 231–236, December 2018
56. Mao, J., et al.: Phishing page detection via learning classifiers from page layout feature. EURASIP J. Wirel. Commun. Netw. 2019, 43 (2019). https://doi.org/10.1186/s13638-019-1361-0
57. Sahingoz, O., Buber, E., Demir, O., Diri, B.: Machine learning based phishing detection from URLs. Exp. Syst. Appl. 117, 345–357 (2019)
58. Adebowale, M., Lwin, K., Sanchez, E., Hossain, A.: Intelligent web-phishing detection and protection scheme using integrated features of images, frames and text. Exp. Syst. Appl. 115, 300–313 (2018)

59. Pandey, A., Gill, N., Sai Prasad Nadendla, K., Thaseen, I.S.: Identification of phishing attack in websites using random forest-SVM hybrid model. In: Abraham, A., Cherukuri, A.K., Melin, P., Gandhi, N. (eds.) ISDA 2018 2018. AISC, vol. 941, pp. 120–128. Springer, Cham (2020). https://doi.org/10.1007/978-3-030-16660-1_12
60. Niranjan, A., Haripriya, D.K., Pooja, R., Sarah, S., Deepa Shenoy, P., Venugopal, K.R.: EKRV: ensemble of kNN and random committee using voting for efficient classification of phishing. In: Pati, B., Panigrahi, C.R., Misra, S., Pujari, A.K., Bakshi, S. (eds.) Progress in Advanced Computing and Intelligent Engineering. AISC, vol. 713, pp. 403–414. Springer, Singapore (2019). https://doi.org/10.1007/978-981-13-1708-8_37
61. Patil, V., Thakkar, P., Shah, C., Bhat, T., Godse, S.P.: Detection and prevention of phishing websites using machine learning approach, pp. 1–5, August 2018
62. Flowerday, S.: Information security policy development and implementation: a content analysis approach, July 2014
63. Lee, J., Bauer, L., Mazurek, M.L.: The effectiveness of security images in internet banking. IEEE Internet Comput. 19(1), 54–62 (2015)
64. Heartfield, R., Loukas, G.: A taxonomy of attacks and a survey of defence mechanisms for semantic social engineering attacks. ACM Comput. Surv. 48, 02 (2016)
65. Rifat, N., Ahsan, M., Chowdhury, M., Gomes, R.: BERT against social engineering attack: phishing text detection, pp. 1–6, May 2022
66. Wang, Z., Ren, Y., Zhu, H., Sun, L.: Threat detection for general social engineering attack using machine learning techniques, March 2022
67. Arrieta, A.B., et al.: Explainable artificial intelligence (XAI): concepts, taxonomies, opportunities and challenges toward responsible AI. Inf. Fusion 58, 82–115 (2019)

Skade – A Challenge Management System for Cyber Threat Hunting

Teodor Sommestad$^{(\boxtimes)}$, Henrik Karlzén, Hanna Kvist, and Hanna Gustafsson

Swedish Defence Research Agency FOI, Stockholm, Sweden
teodor.sommestad@foi.se

Abstract. When cyber security analysts believe their computer network has been compromised, or feel uneasy about potential intrusions, they might initiate a threat hunting process. The success of a threat hunt is largely dependent on the threat hunter's ability to determine what to investigate, sift through logs, and distinguish normal events from threats. However, these abilities are hard to come by, and it is therefore important to find ways to improve peoples' ability to threat hunt. This paper presents the blueprint for Skade, a system to manage threat hunting challenges. Skade is designed to meet a number of established theories in the field of pedagogy: ensuring constructive alignment, motivating trainees by meeting Turner and Paris' six Cs, providing useful feedback, and covering multiple learning dimensions. Mockups of the user interface of Skade and requirements on supporting scenario emulators are presented, e.g. the data they need to provide to enable generation of feedback to trainees. Seven required functions are identified, e.g. the ability to produce assessment questions based on logs from emulators.

Keywords: cyber security · threat hunting · education · cyber range

1 Introduction

Large parts of our society's critical infrastructure depend on the industrial control systems and cyber-physical systems. There are many potential cyber threats to these systems, and governing bodies often have specific policies addressing this aspect of cyber security. For instance, the European Network and Information Security Agency (ENISA) have released specific guidance on how to build computer emergency response capabilities for industrial control systems [16]. In line with this, critical infrastructure and related cyber-physical systems are reoccurring themes in cyber defence exercises. For example, various departments within the US government exercised incident handling in the exercise Cyber Storm 2022 [13], and in Locked Shields the "typical scenario relates to the disruption or destruction of critical infrastructure by an adversarial actor" [43].

One type of incident handling activity becoming increasingly popular is *threat hunting*. In threat hunting, an analyst works in hypothesis-driven fashion and looks for things that are suspicious in relation to normal events (e.g. are of

S. Katsikas et al. (Eds.): ESORICS 2023 Workshops, LNCS 14398, pp. 84–103, 2024.
https://doi.org/10.1007/978-3-031-54204-6_5

unusual frequency), have a connection to some threat intelligence (e.g. a known malware), or otherwise fit the hypothesis about the threat (e.g. some presumed goal of the threat agent). In general, threat hunting is concerned with finding threats that have evaded the detection systems and signatures already in place. Because many industrial control system environments lack standardized security measures threat hunting is especially relevant to those managing such systems. More specifically, a higher portion of the threats against industrial control systems will need to be detected by human analysts. In addition, critical infrastructure's dependency on industrial control systems suggests that advanced persistent threats such as nation states are targeting industrial control systems. These threat actors have resources and patience to wait for the right moment to use or elevate the privileges they have obtained. For example, the 2015 attack on the systems controlling Ukraine's power grid was preceded by months of attacker-activity within the power company's networks [53]. Similarly, threat agents may aim to degrade the industrial process in ways that do not make cyber attacks the obvious explanation for the problems. For instance, Stuxnet is believed to have been active for years before it was detected [38]. Thus, the hypothesis that someone unauthorized has obtained access to the control system network without making this apparent is plausible.

Thus, it can be argued that threat hunting is particularly relevant to those managing systems running critical infrastructure. Unfortunately, threat hunting is inherently dependent on human expertise. Miazi et al. [37] describe threat hunting as a "highly unstructured task that demands deep technical know-how, data analytics savvy, and out of the box thinking". This paper presents the blueprints for Skade, a challenge management system designed to address the need for human competence in threat hunting within the industrial control system community. Skade, which draws its name from the goddess of hunting in Norse mythology, integrates three main components: a user interface for the trainee, an environment emulator, and a threat emulator (cf. Fig. 1). These are used to create synthetic threat hunting scenarios where all details concerning the threat and its traces are known. These scenarios and the ground truth associated with them are used to train people in the process of threat hunting.

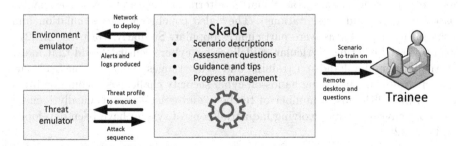

Fig. 1. Illustration of the components of Skade.

Skade's user interface probes trainees for information used to instrument the two emulators, and the user interface is thereafter guided by the user interface to solve the challenge. For example, Skade may probe about the trainee's proficiency level to generate a scenario aimed for this particular proficiency level, probe the trainee with evaluative questions, and assist the trainee with hints in case progress is slow. The contribution of the paper is twofold:

1. Established theories from the field of pedagogy are used to identify how threat hunting training ought to be designed to produce an effective learning experience. This results in a set of hypotheses concerning threat hunting training.
2. The hypotheses are used to identify how the user interface, the environment emulator, and threat emulator should be instrumented to produce training. This results in a blueprint for Skade.

The remainder of this paper is structured as follows. Section 2 provides a brief overview of other initiatives pertaining to threat hunting training, incident scenario generators, and emulators of relevance to threat hunting. Section 3 presents four hypotheses believed to be associated with the learning effect produced in hunting training. Section 4 describes how Skade is designed to address these four hypotheses, and exemplifies how Skade could have been used to realize a recently arranged threat hunting exercise. Section 5 discusses the prospect of Skade as well as future work aimed at developing and evaluating Skade.

2   Related Work

Skade will manage technical challenges designed to train people in the process of threat hunting, specifically people working with computer networks involving industrial control systems. The challenges Skade is designed to manage will be emulated to be technically relevant and realistic. To produce technical challenges or technical environments of this type is by no means a new idea. After reviewing the state-of-the-art in cyber security training for critical infrastructure protection, Chowdhury and Gkioulos [12] "found that delivery methods that offered hands-on experience, in the form of training scenarios and team-based exercises were often preferred over traditional or alternative methods" (such as paper-based teaching and presentations). They also concluded that simulation and virtualization platforms were particularly popular. Similarly, Hajny et al. [21], who reviewed existing curricular guidelines for cyber security, found that many curriculum employ hands-on training and cyber ranges. Thus, to construct virtual environments involving hands-on cyber security challenges is common practice. In line with this, a number of testbeds and emulators specifically focused on cyber environments involving industrial control system have been developed [2,33,36,42].

Skade focuses on building virtual environments containing challenges related to cyber threat hunting. Threat hunting is closely related to incident handling, e.g. the type of processes addressed in exercises such as Cyber Storm [13], Locked Shields [43], SAFE Cyber [34] and Cyber Czech [49]. However, as described above, the process of threat hunting is highly unstructured and requires considerable technical competence. This is somewhat different from the typical incident handling exercise, which tends to focus on following incident handling processes and collaboration between organizations or team members. Threat hunting challenges tend to focus more on technical analyses. For instance, the threat hunting framework presented in [26] uses the techniques described in MITRE ATT&CK for ICS as basis for log analysis.

There are a few simulations focusing explicitly on producing challenges for threat hunting. Miazi et al. [37] describe experiences from a threat hunting competition arranged on a university campus, concluding that the competition can act as a start for academic threat hunting. Wei et al. [51] developed a university course in threat hunting, with six hands-on assignments. In these assignments, attacks were simulated on virtual machines, and students were given written instructions and pre-prepared questions. The aim was to cover the skills needed during threat hunting across multiple difficulty levels. Both the competition described in [37] and the course described in [51], use pre-defined static scenarios.

A number of platforms have been developed to manage such static scenarios and handle their difficulty etc. Beuran et al. [4] developed CyTrONE, a laboratory scenario management system for cyber security scenarios with automated progression management. The competition platform i-tee [18] has automated handling and scoring for a set of incident handling scenarios in a fictitious cyber environment. The cyber range Kypo [48] is also managing capture-the-flag-tasks, with hints, time limits, and scoring. TopoMojo [10] is another example of a scenario management system, were labs can be built and associated with correct answers. Unlike CyTrONE and i-tee, Skade will manage progress and provide hints to trainees and generate scenarios dynamically by interacting with emulators. Unlike the solutions in CyTrONE, the capture the flag challenges in Kypo, and TopoMojo, Skade focuses on the defensive element and produces threat hunting challenges by emulating threats.

A considerable number of tools and platforms have been developed to emulate cyber environments, and a few have been developed to emulate cyber threats. Examples of environment emulators include ICSTASY [32], Crate [20], CRACK [41], and KYPO [48]; while examples of threat emulators include CARTT [39], SVED [25], Lore [24], and CALDERA [3]. Platforms that combine both environment emulation and threat emulation in an integrated framework have also been developed, e.g. TESTREX [15], Kyoushi [30], and LARIAT [40]. Unlike Skade, these integrated frameworks focus on generating datasets and technical test cases. Skade will instead combine environment emulation and threat emulation in an integrated framework to produce learning outcomes. In other words, Skade aim to combine the ambition of challenge management systems (e.g. TopoMojo) with fully automated scenario emulators (e.g. Kyoushi). Section 3 of this paper outlines requirements that arise from this objective.

3 Hypotheses Concerning Threat Hunting Training

We here present hypotheses concerning threat hunting training. The hypotheses are drawn from well-established theories from the field of pedagogy, and concern ensuring constructive alignment, supporting motivating setting, providing feedback and assessment, as well as covering multiple learning dimensions. The underlying theories were chosen to be common in pedagogy, empirically validated, reasonably concretely applicable to threat hunting, and adequately distinct from each other.

3.1 Ensuring Constructive Alignment

Constructive alignment emphasizes both that knowledge is created by the student, rather than merely passed on by the teacher, and that alignment is needed between curriculum objectives, aims, learning activities, and assessments of performance and understanding [6]. Tests also demonstrate that courses designed with constructive alignment in mind foster a deeper understanding in the students [50]. Furthermore, the alignment of learning objectives with learning activity has been found to increase students' motivation to learn, the effort put in, and perceived use of the knowledge [45]. Despite these effects, teachers often forget using constructive alignment, or are not aware of the importance of using it [8]

The usefulness of constructive alignment is widely established in the educational domain, and it has been recommended for security training efforts [11]. Thus, it makes sense to consider constructive alignment when threat hunters are trained. For example, constructive alignment in threat hunting training could start with a clear idea of the purpose of the learning, e.g. training hypothesis-driven threat hunting. From that purpose, a number of learning objectives are defined, e.g. the trainee will be able to 1) understand what hypothesis-driven threat hunting is, 2) use hypothesis-driven threat hunting in Windows environments, and 3) identify known threat actors. From the objectives, a number of learning activities are planned, e.g. 1) watching a recorded lecture on hypothesis-driven threat hunting, 2) practice and perform threat hunting on a small virtual Windows environment and mark machines that are interesting to an attacker, and 3) read about common threat actors in a specific industry. Finally, learning can be assessed in a number of ways, e.g. providing feedback in right/wrong marking of interested machines and grading an essay or quiz relating to threat hunting. Based on constructive alignment theory, it is hypothesized that:

H1 Threat hunting training with constructive alignment will produce larger learning effects than training without constructive alignment.

3.2 Supporting Motivating Setting

Turner and Paris [46] introduced the "six Cs": choice, challenge, control, collaboration, constructing meaning, and consequences. These six features are said to be critical to creating a motivating learning environment. Based on the theory described in [46], the text below summarizes what each C entails and how it can be addressed to motivate threat hunting trainees.

Choice concerns to what extent students get the opportunity to select activities based on their interests, benefitting their commitment and personal responsibility. In threat hunting training, trainees could be provided a choice of what tasks to focus on in the training. *Challenge* emphasizes the importance of an appropriate difficulty level of the tasks, with tasks that are neither too easy and boring nor frustratingly challenging. In threat hunting training, struggling trainees could be provided clues, in terms of additional threat intelligence. *Control* focuses on student involvement and control over their own learning, e.g. by letting students select tasks and objectives. In threat hunting training, trainees could be provided a selection of scenarios and learning objectives to focus on. *Collaboration* underscores motivation by communication and social interaction, e.g. by having students inspire each other. In threat hunting training, trainees could be provided scenarios that promote collaboration and teamwork. *Constructing meaning* ensures that students understand the value of what they are learning and why, increasing their motivation, e.g. by relating course materials and objectives to real life situations or explaining task rationale. In threat hunting training, trainees could be provided an explanation of constructive alignment (cf. Sect. 3.1). *Consequence* underlines the students' sharing of their successes and failures, letting them take responsibility of choices in training. In threat hunting training, trainees could be provided their own scores and other trainees' scores for comparison purposes.

There are other ways to classify and describe variables that determine students' motivations. For instance, Epstein introduces the TARGET-framework [17], consisting of the six dimensions Task, Authority, Recognition, Grouping, Evaluation, and Time. However, there is a considerable overlap between these six dimensions and the six Cs. For instance, Task emphasizes a mixture of difficulty among tasks, similar to Challenge in the six Cs. Based on the theory of the six Cs of motivating setting, it is hypothesized that:

H2 Threat hunting training designs that aim to meet the six Cs will motivate trainees more, and produce larger learning effects, than training that does not consider the six Cs.

3.3 Providing Feedback and Assessment

Feedback and assessments are known to have a positive impact on learning [22,31]. Distinctions are often made between summative and formative assessments, with the former constituting assessment *of* learning, and the latter assessment *for* learning [7]. Summative assessments judge the result after the learning process, and constitute a sort of feedback, while formative assessments give pointers during the training process. Summative assessments indicate when the learning goals are fulfilled, while formative assessments increase motivation and encourage self-assessment [52]. Effective assessment can result in better learning and make the student "take better ownership of its learning, as opposed to coasting as surface learners" [7]. Research suggests that learning outcomes are higher when the feedback (summative assessment) is given as an explanation, rather than as an evaluation of correctness [28,35].

The formative assessment in the threat hunting process should reflect how the trainee is performing in the threat hunt. This can be shown in the learning environment as a progress bar, and points or stars given by sub-tasks, e.g. based on how many parts of the threat hunting challenge that have been completed. For the tasks that the trainee failed, hints or correct solutions can be shown to indicate the change in behavior needed for success. Such hints can be made authentic by framing them as threat intelligence, or as anomaly reports by system administrators. The summative assessment at the end of the learning process can indicate to the trainee if the score or level achieved was enough to pass, how the trainee performed compared to other trainees, how the trainee could have done better, and recap the tasks. Based on the theories on feedback and assessments it is hypothesized that:

H3 Threat hunting training with formative and/or summative assessments is associated with greater learning outcomes than training without assessments.

3.4   Covering Multiple Learning Dimensions

Kolb's experiential learning theory (ELT) [29] states that learning is a continuous process where each person enters the learning process with various skills and life experiences. In ELT, Kolb defines two primary dimensions of the learning process. The first dimension represents information gathering, which could be accomplished by either concrete experience or abstract conceptualization. The second dimension describes how the information is processed, either by active experimentation or by reflective observation. The two dimensions are also described as a cyclic learning process, divided in the four phases of concrete experience, reflective observation, abstract conceptualization, and active experimentation.

Kolb's ELT has stood the test of time and has a positive impact on learning [9], has been deemed relevant in cyber security training [27], and has been used to design games in cyber ranges [21]. Figure 2 illustrates how Kolb's process can be related to the "hunting loop" described in [44].

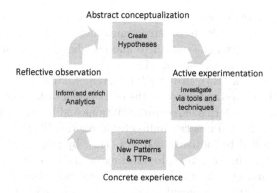

Fig. 2. Kolb's four phases, synthesized with the process of threat hunting from [44]

As Fig. 2 suggests, trainees will be required to do abstract conceptualization by constructing hypotheses concerning benign and malicious processes in the computer network. Further, the whole idea of generating hands-on scenarios with emulators is to support active experimentation and foster concrete experience, e.g. to use analysis tools to uncover patterns generated by threat emulators, thus testing the hypotheses and recording the outcome. Finally, reflective observation can be supported, e.g. by encouraging trainees to automate the process with scripts and presenting the ground truth after the challenge. Based on the theory of Kolb, it is hypothesized that:

H4 Threat hunting training that covers all steps in the learning process will produce larger learning effects than designs focusing on individual steps in the learning process.

4 Realization of the Challenge Manager Skade

This section presents how Skade will implement scenarios that address the hypotheses, using an user interface, as well as employing emulators for the environment and for threats. This section will provide concrete examples of trainee interaction and emulator interaction.

4.1 Features

The four hypotheses (H1–H4) presented in Sect. 3 require a user interface with the ability to present (or not present) information and options. To reflect this, Skade will have a web based user interface where trainees have user accounts and where their progress is recorded. Table 1 summarizes other features of Skade and how they relate to the four hypotheses. To ensure constructive alignment (i.e. H1), threat hunting scenarios in the database will be related to learning objectives, tasks and requirements, e.g. with a data structure such as Blumberg's course alignment table [8].

Backstories and real-world examples related to the scenario, will also be presented to trainees, in order to construct meaning and motivate learning (H2). Trainees will also be given the option to choose what they should train on, in order to promote a feeling of control (H2).

Summative feedback (H3), in terms of current fulfilment of learning objectives, will be displayed to the trainee at the end of each task. Formative feedback (H3) will be displayed in terms of recommendations and hints. By requesting tips and recommendations, trainees can indirectly lower the difficulty of a task. This mechanism is intended to motivate trainees (H2), by adapting the tasks to be the right kind of challenging, while also offering both choice and control. Recommendations, tips, and options will be related to learning objectives and tasks in order to provide constructive meaning (H2), and ensure constructive alignment (H1). For instance, it will be clearly stated what part of the learning the trainee can skip by choosing to ask for a hint.

Kolb's learning cycle suggests that trainees should be encouraged to go through all steps of the learning process (H4). Skade will therefore include follow-up tasks that encourage trainees to reflect on what they have done. For instance, trainees may be given time to write scripts that automate the threat hunting process they have performed, and thereby be encouraged to recap the more successful parts of their hunting.

The user account of the trainee will record trainee progress. Trainees will be able to compare their accomplishments to other trainees and to predefined benchmarks. This summative feedback (H3) is meant to highlight the consequences (H2) of the learning. Trainees will have the option of measuring their progress on an individual level by taking on scenarios alone, or to form a team with other users to work on scenarios. This option of collaboration (H2) will be made available because it triggers motivation, and because many threat hunting efforts in real life consist of teamwork.

Table 1. Features in Skade and their relationships to the four hypotheses.

Feature	H1	H2	H3	H4
Presentation of the alignment table for each challenge	•	•		
Displaying the current fulfilment of learning objectives	•	•	•	
Backstories and real-world examples related to the scenario		•		
Giving trainees the option to choose what they should train on		•		
Enabling optional recommendations and hints at all stages		•	•	
Presenting the ground truth after the challenge				•
Follow-up tasks that encourage trainees to reflect				•

4.2 Functions

All the features described above require the storage of data about scenarios and trainees in a structured manner. The features will also require internal logic that can iterate over scenarios, objectives, and tasks, in order to measure a trainee's progress or a team's progress. More specifically, the internal logic of Skade needs functions capable of providing:

[F1] Textual and visual presentation of scenarios, their objectives, tasks, and requirements.

[F2] Textual and visual descriptions of the emulated networks, e.g. machine names, topology maps, operating systems, users, and settings for log collection.

[F3] Questionnaires for each task, based on the instantiated network, and the threat, e.g. as evidenced by the machines that have been compromised in the network.

[F4] Textual and visual descriptions of the progress of a trainee or team, as provided by querying previously executed scenarios and the objectives the trainees have met.

[F5] Textual tips or recommendations for each task that helps the trainee complete the task, e.g. produce threat intelligence that reveals parts of the attack sequence.

[F6] Textual and visual descriptions of the attack sequence executed by the threat emulator and how this could have been detected, e.g. a bullet point list with time stamps describing the actions taken and artifacts produced.

[F7] Possibility to re-instantiate whole scenarios again, e.g. by instrumenting emulators the same way.

The mapping between the features and the functions can be seen in Table 2.

Table 2. Features in Skade and their relationships to the seven functions.

Feature	F1	F2	F3	F4	F5	F6	F7
Presentation of the alignment table for each challenge	•						
Displaying the current fulfilment of learning objectives			•	•			
Backstories and real-world examples related to the scenario	•	•			•		
Giving trainees the option to choose what they should train on							
Enabling optional recommendations and hints at all stages			•	•			
Presenting the ground truth after the challenge						•	
Follow-up tasks that encourage trainees to reflect							•

Functions [F1] enables the presentation of the scenario to the trainee as in Fig. 3a and function [F2] is needed to provide the type of background information illustrated in Fig. 3b. Functions [F3] and [F4] are needed to provide the functionality related to assessments and feedback as in Fig. 3c. Function [F5] is needed to provide the trainee with hints as illustrated in Fig. 3d and to create a reasonable backstory, e.g. providing information about the network and its assets. Function [F6] is required to provide ground truth to trainees after they have completed their hunt, and thereby support reflection and self-evaluation. Function [F7] will allow the creation of follow-up tasks were trainees try again using different methods or try to automate successful parts of a threat hunt.

(a) Illustrates the panel where challenges are selected

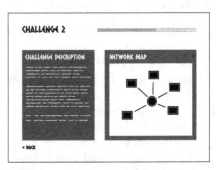

(b) Presents the scenario and its backstory

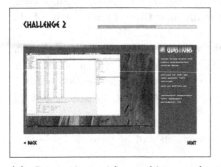

(c) Interaction with machines and challenge questions

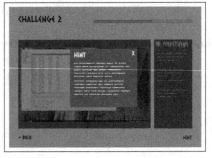

(d) Hint provided to a trainee

Fig. 3. Mockups of the user interface.

4.3   Example Based on the Nordic-US Exercise of 2023

To illustrate the type of challenges Skade will be able to manage, we here present an example drawn from a cyber defence exercise arranged in 2023. The exercise was held in Sweden hosted by The Swedish Civil Contingencies Agency (MSB) [1]. It included participants from government CSIRT (Computer Security Incident Response Team) of the Nordic countries and the USA. The simulated environment was representing a fictive country with vital societal functions and critical infrastructure that were the target of several cyber attacks, were each attack was treated as separate challenge. In one of these challenges, an insider connected a laptop to the company network and obtained credentials from a domain controller by exploiting the vulnerability CVE-2020-1472 (often referred to as ZeroLogon). Participants were tasked to hunt, report and manage this threat. The text below will explain how Skade could have been used to deliver this challenge in an automated manner, and how the seven functions ([F1]–[F7]) could have been implemented if Skade would have been used.

Function [F1] and [F2] involves giving participants the necessary background information in textual and visual forms. It is straightforward to implement these functions based on the information the exercise management used to instruct trainees (e.g. power point presentations). For instance, Skade could have shown the participants a network topology map and a textual description of the task. The difficulty of this challenge could have been varied by deploying computer networks with more or less logging capabilities or by providing trainees with threat intelligence of different detail. In the Nordic-US exercise standard logging was enabled and the training was initiated by giving participants intelligence suggesting that credentials of the organization had leaked on the dark web.

Functions [F3] and [F4] are straightforward to implement if objectives are defined in a way that is measurable using web forms. Skade could have been loaded with objectives such as: 1) identify obtained credentials by entering the machine they were taken from, 2) identify the MITRE ATT&CK techniques involved in the attack, and 3) attribute the attack to a user or IP address. All of these can be known beforehand or extracted from logs. The attacks in the exercise were scripted using the threat emulator SVED [25]. When the attacker's laptop is connected to the network, SVED produces several logs, for instance as follows:

```
{
    "data": "{\"event\": \"VLAN switch completed.\",
\"new_ip\": \"59.21.4.150\"}",
    "id": 43391680,
    "log_source_id": 5358730,
    "log_source_type": "VLANSwitch",
    "status": "EntityState.SUCCESSFUL",
    "time_stamp": "2023-06-27 15:28:30"
}
```

The IP address (i.e. "59.21.4.150") and the time stamp ("2023-06-27 15:28:30") can be extracted from the log using the following regular expressions in python.

```
r'VLAN switch completed\D*(.*?)\\\"}'
r'VLAN switch completed[\D\d]*\"time_stamp\": \"(.*)\"'
```

Function [F5] requires Skade to have information that can be used to help trainees. The logs from SVED can be used to generate clues to a trainee in a predictable way. For example, intelligence concerning the use of CVE-2020-1472 to target other critical infrastructure, could have been presented as a clue; the time of events could have been read from SVED's logs and presented as a clue;

the IP address of the insiders laptop could have been read from SVED's logs and presented as a clue; and the name of the target domain is a parameter of the attack in SVED and could have been given as a clue. Furthermore, the predictability that comes from managing the attack with a threat emulator makes it straightforward to identify logs that are generated by the attack. For instance, in the network of the exercise, the laptop generated logs in the DHCP server when it requested an IP address and the ZeroLogon exploit could be detected through logs of multiple connection requests and Windows event with ID 4742 with certain content. This could have been stored as clues in Skade. Alternatively, the logs collected in the targeted systems could have been queried using information about the attack (e.g. IP address and timestamp) to identify specific log entries to direct the trainee to.

Function [F6] involves presenting the ground truth in a way that the trainee understands. The logs from SVED's execution contain all the information needed, e.g. machines involved, timestamps and the exploits used. However, to implement this function, Skade would need to process SVED's output and simplify it. For instance, when SVED connects a machine to the network, it produces 15 logs like the one above, including printouts on preparation of different actions and their status at different points in time. Only the completed and successful actions need to be summarized to the trainee.

The use of emulators makes [F7] simple to implement. In this particular exercise the network was emulated using the cyber range Crate [20] and the attack was scripted using the tool SVED [25]. It has already been re-instantiated multiple times with different networks etc.

5   Discussion

This paper has presented the overall idea of Skade, the theory related to the training of threat hunters, and outlined how Skade can be realized using emulators and a user interface. The sections below discuss to what extent Skade meets the requirements of design science suggested by Hevner et al. [23], expand on topics relating to the trainees, elaborate on what the emulators need to cover, give more detail on learning objectives, and outlines a plan to test the hypotheses.

5.1   Skade as a Design Science Effort

Hevner et al. [23] proposed seven guidelines for design science, i.e. research that aims to create new and innovative artifacts. The intention of this project is to create the new and innovative artifact Skade, and the project's compliance with these seven guidelines is therefore of relevance.

The *first* guideline states that a viable artifact must be produced in the form of a construct, a model, a method, or an instantiation. This is straightforward for the project to fulfill. The Skade system, illustrated in the mock-ups of Fig. 3, intends to be an artifact in the shape of a concrete instantiation. The *second* guideline concerns problem relevance. In Sect. 1, we argued for the case that threat hunting training is an important and relevant business problem. Section 5.2 further discusses the need for training. *Third*, Hevner et al. stress that the efficacy of a design artifact must be rigorously demonstrated. The evaluation of Skade is far from complete, but plans for validations of utility are outlined in Sect. 5.5. *Fourth*, design-science research shall make contributions in the areas of the design artifact, design foundations, and/or design methodologies. Skade will be an artifact that solves a previously unsolved problem, i.e. scalable automated training in threat hunting. The *fifth* guideline concerns the rigor of the construction and evaluation of the artifact. Skade has not been constructed or evaluated yet, but Sect. 5.5 outlines the plans for validation and Sect. 5.3 outlines the plan for implementation using emulators. The *sixth* guideline stresses that design science is an iterative search process. Accordingly, research on Skade will consider different emulators and solutions within the boundaries given by the theories described in this paper. Further, the boundaries will be set differently if other theories show promise. Finally, the *seventh* guideline concerns communication to both technology-oriented and management-oriented audiences. The overarching project already has a communication plan that covers both of these types of audiences.

5.2 Trainees and Requirements on Challenges

The suitable content for the challenges that Skade provides will depend on the level of expertise of the trainees that use Skade. Our initial analysis is that senior threat hunters will be difficult to please with the type of challenges Skade can provide. This is because experts can be expected to require a high level of realism and fidelity to learning something useful. This would pose extreme requirements on emulated environments, threat emulation, and toolsets provided to trainees. Our initial analysis also suggests that novices, e.g. those unfamiliar with log management, security threats, and basic system administration, will struggle with basic parts of the challenges and gain little from a system such as Skade. Accordingly, Skade will focus on a target audience of intermediate learners.

There is no clear definition of an intermediate learner, but there are several frameworks classifying cyber security practitioners into roles and levels of proficiency. In addition, a survey by Fuchs and Lemon suggests that the most valuable professional background for threat hunting team members, is knowledge in baseline network communications and activity; incident response; threat intelligence and analysis; knowledge in baseline endpoint applications, users and access; and network and endpoint forensics (c.f. Figure 8 in [19]). Based on this, we consider the target audience of Skade to include: senior system administrators from organizations that meet the minimal level of the Threat Hunting Maturity Model (THMM) of organizations [44]; tier 1 and tier 2 of Security Operation Centers [47]; as well as personnel in the roles of Cyber Incident Responder and Cyber Threat Intelligence Specialist in the European Cybersecurity Skills Framework [14].

5.3   Interaction with Emulators

As described in the introduction, there are a large number of emulators available. The functional requirements of Skade appear to be met by many of these. For example, Kyoushi [30] stores data on the network in configuration files and supports [F4]. CALDERA [3] produces operation reports that support [F5] and [F6]. Skade also requires the possibility of representing meaningful challenges for a threat hunter. Using the number of procedure examples for different attack techniques in MITRE ATT&CK as a proxy for relevance, the following techniques could piece together a relevant partial scenario: initial access via spearphishing attachment (T1566.001), execution via Windows command shell (T1059.003), persistence and escalation via registry run keys (T1547.001), evasion using obfuscated files (T1027), and credential access using keylogging (T1056.001). These types of techniques can be employed in many types of networks and are common in threat emulators. Thus, they do not restrict Skade or threat hunting challenges to a particular set of emulators.

The overall idea of Skade is agnostic to the emulators used, and Skade requires little from the emulators. However, Skade will need to interact with emulators, e.g. send instructions to emulators and interpret logs to generate assessment items. The current plan is focused on the environment emulator Crate [20] and the threat emulator Lore [24]. This choice of emulators is primarily due to practical reasons related to development resources, but also because of the high level of automation that these two emulators offer. Crate has an extensive API for configuration and deployment, which makes it possible to deploy new, diverse, and complex networks, adjusted to fit relevant scenarios. For instance, Crate has scripts that configure collection and signatures in the networks that could be used by Skade. Lore automates the construction of attacks in SVED [25] and the logs can be extracted in the same way as in SVED (the tool mentioned in Sect. 4.3). It enables multiple profiles with different pre-existing knowledge, differing targets etc. in order to enable the threat hunting scenarios to be created dynamically in a manner appropriate for Skade.

5.4   Learning Objectives and Learning Activities

Section 3 describes hypotheses regarding threat hunting derived from the field of pedagogy. The objectives could relate to planning and communication, or more concrete hands-on-keyboard actions. We envision that Skade cover all three of these, and offer challenges designed for different levels of expertise. Examples of what the learning objectives may entail are described below, together with a brief note on how to adjust the difficulty level of reaching the objectives.

Planning objectives could be to create and evaluate threat or detection hypotheses, in a cyclic manner as described in Fig. 2. The hypotheses could be formed from different focal points, such as identified vulnerabilities, critical systems, crown jewel assets, binaries, indicators of compromise, attack techniques, or threat intelligence. Planning can also include structuring the thought process using the pyramid of pain [5] in order to strike a balance between the most valuable indicators (e.g. attack techniques and tools) and the easiest identifiable indicators (e.g. IP addresses and hash values). Thus, scenarios with different indicators on different levels in the pyramid of pain will need to be emulated.

Communication objectives could include documenting, reporting incidents or communicating with team members. The communication could also concern requests for further information, such as information about vulnerable systems, threat intelligence, or other tools needed, as well as requests to remediate vulnerabilities or perform endpoint hardening. To enable communication learning, Skade will require some way of checking trainee documentation and communication, e.g. by recommending a practice of structuring reports, and automatically checking if trainee reports align with this structure.

Hand-on-keyboard objectives could include the detection of things such as vulnerabilities, insecure practices, misconfigurations, and attack techniques already used in the network. Some examples of the detection of attack techniques in a few attack phases are given in the following. Persistence might be detected by finding which objects use Run and RunOnce or login scripts, as well as which objects that have historically initialized network connections. Command and control (C2) might be detected by looking for anomalies in HTTP requests (e.g. URLs and User-Agent strings), bytes transferred, and duration of connections. Internal reconnaissance might be detected by looking for certain commands spawned by a script (e.g. automated ipconfig). The Skade platform will need to be aware of how trainees could detect things like this in each scenario. In addition, to ensure that training can be transferred to operational contexts, the attack techniques used and the indicators provided will need to be representative of those in operational networks.

A later step in the threat hunting process, as mentioned previously, is to automate each part of the process once the parts have been performed manually. This might include the improvement of automatic detection mechanisms by reducing their false positives and false negatives, or by placing new sensors. To provide such training opportunities, the scenarios, or variants of them, will need to executed on request to test trainee attempts to automate the threat hunt.

One aim of Skade is to offer training for trainees with different levels of expertise by adjusting the difficulty level of the scenario. The difficulty level can be altered by the allotted time to hunt, the provided threat intelligence and logging mechanisms, the complexity and size of the system, the level of background noise, the hunter's familiarity with system, the need to ask for more permissions etc. in the system, and how much the evidence must stack up in order to count as proof.

5.5   Experiment Plan and Tests of Hypotheses

While the prospect of training individuals and teams in threat hunting in a partially automated fashion is appealing, it is not obvious that it is possible to obtain clear learning effects from the type of training that Skade will support. *First*, the threat hunting process is typically thought of as unstructured, making it difficult to create an automated training software for training. *Second*, threat hunting is sometimes said to require some degree of "thinking outside the box", and this is difficult to learn in training. *Third*, threat hunting requires extensive in-depth technical knowledge in terms of normal system behavior, cyberattacks, logging etc. Skade will focus on the ability to combine different kinds of knowledge relating to threat hunting, but it is unclear if this is worthwhile in case individuals lack the various kinds of knowledge that are to be combined. Thus, the utility of Skade will need to be evaluated properly.

The four high-level hypotheses presented in Sect. 3 can all be tested by comparing Skade to some alternative that is not designed to meet the underlying theory. This alternative could be an instance of Skade purposely modified to be inconsistent with the theory. For instance, H3 states that feedback is important. An experiment can be applied to test the learning outcomes in two conditions: a) training with feedback by Skade and b) training where the feedback is removed. Learning outcomes can be evaluated by simply asking trainees if they learned anything after being exposed to each condition. Previous meta-analyses suggest that feedback improves learning effects with approximately 0.5 standard deviations [28]. Tentative power calculations ($\beta = 0.8, \alpha = 0.05$) suggest that a sample size of 65 trainees will be sufficient in order to detect such effect sizes in a crossover design. The same approach is possible to use for tests of the other hypotheses: the alternative condition for H1 can be scrambled relationships between objectives and tasks; the alternative condition for H2 can be removal of various options for the trainee; and the alternative condition for H4 can be to focus on individual steps.

6 Conclusion

This paper has identified four basic ideas that can be used to guide the design of training in the field of threat hunting: the idea of constructive alignment [6], Turner and Paris' six Cs related to motivation [46], the general idea of providing meaningful feedback, and the four learning dimensions from experiential learning theory [29]. The blueprint of Skade meets these theories, e.g. by presenting challenges in a good way and offering trainees the option to get hints on what to do. A number of publicly available emulators would meet the requirements of Skade. A suitable target audience for a challenge management system is intermediate learners, e.g. senior system administrators. The efficacy of Skade and the design guidelines can be tested in experiments with samples of approximately 65 such trainees.

References

1. MSB hosts international cybersecurity exercise in Sweden (2023). https://www.msb.se/en/news/2023/may/msb-hosts-international-cybersecurity-exercise-in-sweden/
2. Almgren, M., et al.: RICS-el: building a national testbed for research and training on SCADA security (Short Paper). In: Luiijf, E., Žutautaitė, I., Hämmerli, B.M. (eds.) CRITIS 2018. LNCS, vol. 11260, pp. 219–225. Springer, Cham (2019). https://doi.org/10.1007/978-3-030-05849-4_17
3. Applebaum, A., Miller, D., Strom, B., Korban, C., Wolf, R.: Intelligent, automated red team emulation. In: Proceedings of the 32nd Annual Conference on Computer Security Applications, pp. 363–373 (2016)
4. Beuran, R., Inoue, T., Tan, Y., Shinoda, Y.: Realistic cybersecurity training via scenario progression management. In: 2019 IEEE European Symposium on Security and Privacy Workshops (EuroS&PW), pp. 67–76. IEEE (2019)
5. Bianco, D.: The pyramid of pain. Enterprise Detection & Response (2013)
6. Biggs, J.: Enhancing teaching through constructive alignment. High. Educ. **32**(3), 347–364 (1996)
7. Bin Mubayrik, H.F.: New trends in formative-summative evaluations for adult education. Sage Open **10**(3) (2020)
8. Blumberg, P.: Maximizing learning through course alignment and experience with different types of knowledge. Innov. High. Educ. **34**, 93–103 (2009)
9. Burch, G.F., Giambatista, R., Batchelor, J.H., Burch, J.J., Hoover, J.D., Heller, N.A.: A meta-analysis of the relationship between experiential learning and learning outcomes. Decis. Sci. J. Innov. Educ. **17**(3), 239–273 (2019)
10. Carnegie Mellon University: TopoMojo: A VM Topology Manager (2019)
11. Chanussot, T., Schürmann, C.: Cyber awareness training for election staff using constructive alignment. In: Krimmer, R., et al. (eds.) E-Vote-ID 2021. LNCS, vol. 12900, pp. 63–74. Springer, Cham (2021). https://doi.org/10.1007/978-3-030-86942-7_5
12. Chowdhury, N., Gkioulos, V.: Cyber security training for critical infrastructure protection: a literature review. Comput. Sci. Rev. **40**, 100361 (2021)
13. CISA: Cyber storm viii: After-action report, Tech. rep. (2022)
14. For Cybersecurity (ENISA), T.E.U.A.: European cybersecurity skills framework, Tech. rep. (2022)
15. Dashevskyi, S., Dos Santos, D.R., Massacci, F., Sabetta, A.: Testrex: a testbed for repeatable exploits. In: CSET (2014)
16. Dufkova, A., Budd, J., Homola, J., Marden, M.: Good practice guide for certs in the area of industrial control systems. European Network and Information Security Agency (ENISA) (2013)
17. Epstein, J.L., for Research on Elementary, J.H.U.C., Schools, M.: Target, an Examination of Parallel School and Family Structures that Promote Student Motivation and Achievement. Report (Johns Hopkins University. Center for Research on Elementary and Middle Schools), Center for Research on Elementary and Middle Schools, Johns Hopkins University (1987)
18. Ernits, M., Tammekänd, J., Maennel, O.: i-tee: a fully automated cyber defense competition for students. ACM SIGCOMM Comput. Commun. Rev. **45**(4), 113–114 (2015)
19. Fuchs, M., Lemon, J.: Sans 2019 threat hunting survey: The differing needs of new and experienced hunters, Tech. rep. (2019)

20. Gustafsson, T., Almroth, J.: Cyber range automation overview with a case study of CRATE. In: Asplund, M., Nadjm-Tehrani, S. (eds.) NordSec 2020. LNCS, vol. 12556, pp. 192–209. Springer, Cham (2021). https://doi.org/10.1007/978-3-030-70852-8_12

21. Hajny, J., Ricci, S., Piesarskas, E., Levillain, O., Galletta, L., De Nicola, R.: Framework, tools and good practices for cybersecurity curricula. IEEE Access 9, 94723–94747 (2021)

22. Hattie, J.: The applicability of visible learning to higher education. Scholarsh. Teach. Learn. Psychol. 1(1), 79 (2015)

23. Hevner, A.R., March, S.T., Park, J., Ram, S.: Design science in information systems research. Manage. Inform. Syst. Q. 28, 75–106 (2004)

24. Holm, H.: Lore a red team emulation tool. IEEE Trans. Depend. Secure Comput. 20, 1596–1608 (2022)

25. Holm, H., Sommestad, T.: SVED: scanning, vulnerabilities, exploits and detection. In: MILCOM 2016–2016 IEEE Military Communications Conference, pp. 976–981. IEEE (2016)

26. Jadidi, Z., Lu, Y.: A threat hunting framework for industrial control systems. IEEE Access 9, 164118–164130 (2021)

27. Karjalainen, M., Siponen, M.: Toward a new meta-theory for designing information systems (IS) security training approaches. J. Assoc. Inf. Syst. 12(8), 3 (2011)

28. der Kleij, F.M.V., Feskens, R.C.W., Eggen, T.J.H.M.: Effects of feedback in a computer-based learning environment on students' learning outcomes. Rev. Educ. Res. 85(4), 475–511 (2015). https://doi.org/10.3102/0034654314564881

29. Kolb, D.: Experiential Learning: Experience As The Source Of Learning And Development, vol. 1. Prentice Hall (1984)

30. Landauer, M., Frank, M., Skopik, F., Hotwagner, W., Wurzenberger, M., Rauber, A.: A framework for automatic labeling of log datasets from model-driven testbeds for HIDS evaluation. In: Proceedings of the 2022 ACM Workshop on Secure and Trustworthy Cyber-Physical Systems, pp. 77–86 (2022)

31. Lau, A.M.S.: 'Formative good, summative bad?' - a review of the dichotomy in assessment literature. J. Furth. High. Educ. 40(4), 509–525 (2015). https://doi.org/10.1080/0309877x.2014.984600

32. Lee, D., Kim, D., Lee, C., Ahn, M.K., Lee, W.: ICSTASY: an integrated cybersecurity training system for military personnel. IEEE Access 10, 62232–62246 (2022)

33. Lemay, A., Fernandez, J., Knight, S.: An isolated virtual cluster for SCADA network security research. In: 1st International Symposium for ICS & SCADA Cyber Security Research 2013 (ICS-CSR 2013) 1, pp. 88–96 (2013)

34. Lif, P., Varga, S., Wedlin, M., Lindahl, D., Persson, M.: Evaluation of information elements in a cyber incident report. In: 2020 IEEE European Symposium on Security and Privacy Workshops (EuroS&PW), pp. 17–26. IEEE (2020)

35. Mandouit, L., Hattie, J.: Revisiting "the power of feedback" from the perspective of the learner. Learn. Instr. 84, 101718 (2023)

36. Mathur, A.P., Tippenhauer, N.O.: Swat: a water treatment testbed for research and training on ICS security. In: 2016 International Workshop on Cyber-Physical Systems for Smart Water Networks (CySWater), pp. 31–36. IEEE (2016)

37. Miazi, M.N.S., Pritom, M.M.A., Shehab, M., Chu, B., Wei, J.: The design of cyber threat hunting games: a case study. In: 2017 26th International Conference on Computer Communication and Networks (ICCCN), pp. 1–6. IEEE (2017)

38. Nakashima, E., Warrick, J.: Stuxnet was work of US and Israeli experts, officials say. The Washington Post 2 (2012)

39. Plot, J., Shaffer, A., Singh, G.: CARTT: cyber automated red team tool. HICSS (2020)
40. Rossey, L.M., et al.: LARIAT: Lincoln adaptable real-time information assurance testbed. In: Proceedings, IEEE Aerospace Conference, vol. 6, p. 6. IEEE (2002)
41. Russo, E., Costa, G., Armando, A.: Building next generation cyber ranges with crack. Comput. Secur. **95**, 101837 (2020)
42. Sitnikova, E., Foo, E., Vaughn, R.B.: The power of hands-on exercises in SCADA cyber security education. In: Dodge, R.C., Futcher, L. (eds.) WISE 2009/2011/2013. IAICT, vol. 406, pp. 83–94. Springer, Heidelberg (2013). https://doi.org/10.1007/978-3-642-39377-8_9
43. Smeets, M.: The role of military cyber exercises: a case study of locked shields. In: 2022 14th International Conference on Cyber Conflict: Keep Moving! (CyCon), vol. 700, pp. 9–25. IEEE (2022)
44. SQRRL: A framework for cyber threat hunting, Tech. rep. (2018)
45. Stamov Roßnagel, C., Fitzallen, N., Lo Baido, K.: Constructive alignment and the learning experience: relationships with student motivation and perceived learning demands. High. Educ. Res. Develop. **40**(4), 838–851 (2021)
46. Turner, J., Paris, S.G.: How literacy tasks influence children's motivation for literacy. Read. Teach. **48**(8), 662–673 (1995)
47. Vielberth, M., Böhm, F., Fichtinger, I., Pernul, G.: Security operations center: a systematic study and open challenges. IEEE Access **8**, 227756–227779 (2020)
48. Vykopal, J., Ošlejšek, R., Čeleda, P., Vizvary, M., Tovarňák, D.: KYPO cyber range: design and use cases. In: 12th International Conference on Software Technologies. SciTePress (2017)
49. Vykopal, J., Vizvary, M., Oslejsek, R., Celeda, P., Tovarnak, D.: Lessons learned from complex hands-on defence exercises in a cyber range. In: 2017 IEEE Frontiers in education conference (FIE), pp. 1–8. IEEE (2017)
50. Wang, X., Su, Y., Cheung, S., Wong, E., Kwong, T.: An exploration of Biggs' constructive alignment in course design and its impact on students' learning approaches. Assessment Eval. High. Educ. **38**(4), 477–491 (2013)
51. Wei, J., Chu, B.T., Cranford-Wesley, D., Brown, J.: A laboratory for hands-on cyber threat hunting education. J. Colloquium Inform. Syst. Secur. Educ. **7**, 1 (2020)
52. Yüksel, H.S., Gündüz, N.: Formative and summative assessment in higher education: opinions and practices of instructors. Eur. J. Educ. Stud. (2017)
53. Zetter, K., et al.: Inside the cunning, unprecedented hack of Ukraine's power grid. Wired **9**, 1–5 (2016)

On the Usage of NLP on CVE Descriptions for Calculating Risk

Thrasyvoulos Giannakopoulos[1]([✉])[iD] and Konstantinos Maliatsos[2][iD]

[1] Department of Digital Systems, University of Piraeus, Piraeus, Greece
tgian@unipi.gr
[2] Department of Information and Communication Systems Engineering,
University of the Aegean, Mytilene, Greece
kmaliat@aegean.gr

Abstract. In order to conduct a risk analysis on an ecosystem the potential threats to its assets must first be identified. The Risk Modelling Tool (RMT) of the CitySCAPE Project uses CWE - CAPEC - threat relationships that were mapped for identifying the threats that vulnerabilities can pose on specific assets, namely in the context of multimodal transport use cases, based on already existing vulnerabilities. However, nearly one third of all CVEs do not have any CWEs assigned to them or have generic CWEs like "NVD-CWE-Other" that do not offer any information about that vulnerability, to then be linked back to a threat. This paper proposes the use of a Natural Language Processing model and more specifically a text classification model to be trained on CVE descriptions that can be traced back to a threat using the created mapping. The model will therefore be able to extrapolate the threat that a specific vulnerability will expose and be detected earlier, allowing security analysts to be able to deploy countermeasures to combat that risk. The resulting model has an accuracy of over 90% across a ten-fold validation process. As such a more complete and accurate risk analysis can be performed using the larger number of applicable vulnerabilities found using our ML model.

Keywords: Text Classification · Natural Language Processing · Threat Analysis · CVE · CWE · CAPEC · Risk Analysis

1 Introduction

In today's interconnected world, various systems are becoming more reliant on computer services and automation. Such systems include Intelligent Transport Systems (ITSs), Cyber-Physical Power Systems (CPPSs), precision agriculture systems, digital healthcare, etc. They typically have a digitised/computerised aspect and a physical component that are linked to create what are called Cyber-Physical Systems (CPSs). These systems typically use Industrial Control Systems (ICSs). Due to their nature and widespread adoption, CPSs significantly

S. Katsikas et al. (Eds.): ESORICS 2023 Workshops, LNCS 14398, pp. 104–123, 2024.
https://doi.org/10.1007/978-3-031-54204-6_6

impact critical infrastructures, so their protection from potential cyberattack incidents is of the utmost importance.

Cyber-Physical Systems Security is not a new domain, since there have been plenty of incidents and attacks targeting CPSs, with Stuxnet being one of the most famous, where a malware targeted Iran's Natanz nuclear enrichment facility [16], as well as the compromise of the Colonial Pipeline in 2021 that led to a disruption of the US's oil supply [24]. As such, a holistic risk analysis is important, as it can identify such threats.

The City-level Cyber-Secure Multimodal Transport Ecosystem (CitySCAPE)[1] is a research project sponsored by the European Union's Horizon 2020 research & innovation programme. It features two pilot sites, one in Tallinn, Estonia and one Genoa, Italy. Through both of those pilot sites various Cyber-Physical Systems are present, namely among others: connected AV Shuttles and networks, ticketing and passenger information systems, and more. As enhancing the cybersecurity aspect of those CPSs is key, a software toolkit was developed to assist in the areas of financial impact assessment, collaborative threat investigation, incident response and IDS/IPS engines along with SIEMs, all in the context of CPSs and multimodal transport. Another part of the software toolkit is the Risk and Impact Assessment (RITA), with the Risk Modeling Tool (RMT)[2, 3] being a subcomponent. Its objective is to find vulnerabilities in various ecosystems comprised of a multitude of heterogeneous components with various interconnections. Once these vulnerabilities are discovered, it identifies possible threats that can exploit them, posing risks to the various components of the ecosystem, based on relationships among Common Weakness Enumeration(s) (CWEs), Common Attack Pattern Enumeration(s) and Classification(s) (CAPECs) and Threats. It is then able to produce a risk score for that ecosystem. Those threats are derived from various publications and reports affecting ITSs, IoT devices, 5G networks etc. While working on the RMT, both the amount of unlabeled weaknesses (such as "NVD-CWE-noinfo" and "NVD-CWE-Other" as shown in Table 3) and the time it takes to for NIST to publish and analyze new CVEs, as [25] also states, were identified as issues in using and utilizing the National Vulnerability Database (NVD) as a public database for vulnerability identification.

This paper aims to solve both of those problems by identifying the threats that both new and unlabeled CVEs pose, as well as identify the threats of CVEs that cannot be mapped using CWE - CAPEC - threat relationships, as shown in Fig. 3 and explained in detail in [17]. This paper, thus, acts as an extension to the existing risk calculation methodology presented in [17], where a greater percentage of CVEs is included in the risk calculation. This is accomplished

---

[1] https://www.cityscape-project.eu/.

[2] https://www.cityscape-project.eu/wp-content/uploads/2022/07/D2.3-Multimodal-Transport-System_-System-Modelling-Risk-Analysis-and-Management-GDPR-Compliance-1.pdf.

[3] https://www.cityscape-project.eu/wp-content/uploads/2022/07/D2.4-Cascading-risks-in-the-multimodal-transportation-platforms-1.pdf.

by training a Natural Language Processing (NLP) model on CVE descriptions with the threats that were matched using CWE and CAPEC information in the CVE record. This enables a threat identification mechanism for CVEs without CWEs or with non descriptive CWEs such as "NVD-CWE-noinfo". The rest of the paper is structured as follows. Section 2 provides the necessary cybersecurity background; Sect. 3 showcases related works; Sect. 4 presents the relative NLP technical background; Sect. 5 presents the actual implementation; finally, Sect. 6 concludes this paper.

2   Cybersecurity Related Background

2.1   Common Vulnerabilities and Exposures (CVE)

Common Vulnerabilities and Exposures (CVE) is a dataset with the objective of identifying, defining, and cataloguing publicly disclosed cybersecurity vulnerabilities. Several U.S. Government agencies, including the National Institute of Standards and Technology (NIST) in "NIST Special Publication (SP) 800-51, Use of the CVE Vulnerability Naming Scheme" [6] or the Cybersecurity and Infrastructure Security Agency (CISA) of the Department of Homeland Security (DHS) in its Log4j Vulnerability Guidance [4], recommend, use and utilize the CVE catalogue. Currently, CISA also sponsors the program, alongside NIST's National Vulnerability Database (NVD). CVEs are assigned from CVE Numbering Authorities (CNAs). Such authorities are partners to the CVE Program and include software vendors, bug bounty programs and others. As of June 5th, 2023, a total of 203,968 vulnerabilities have been disclosed using the CVE Program.

Each CVE with a tag has it appended in the beginning of the description field. The majority of all CVE entries do not have any tags. The existence of a tag in a CVE description does not affect the calculated risk that RMT produces. Table 1 shows the CVE tags found in CVEs as of writing, with the number of corresponding entries.

Note: Reserved CVEs are not contained in the NVD data feeds that were used to generate Table 1, thus no information is available. Moreover, there is a slight discrepancy between the content of the cve.org website and NISTs data feed, because cve.org is updated in real time, whereas NVD data feeds are updated daily. As we can see from Table 1, the most common CVE tags are "REJECT", "DISPUTED" and "UNSUPPORTED WHEN ASSIGNED". Rejected CVEs are entries where a CVE ID should not have been assigned. Such is the case when, for example, upon further inspection, the reported issue is not a vulnerability, or when the researcher wants to keep the vulnerability private. Disputed entries occur when an authoritative source such as a vendor, coordinator or researcher, disputes the vulnerability [5]. "UNSUPPORTED WHEN ASSIGNED" are entries where the vendor no longer supports the vulnerable product or version. In most cases, the general "UNSUPPORTED WHEN ASSIGNED" tag is used, however, there are handful of examples where more specific tags indicating lack of support for a product or version have been selected (i.e., "PRODUCT NOT SUPPORTED WHEN ASSIGNED", and "VERSION

Table 1. CVE Tags

Tag	Entries
** RESERVED **	N/A
** REJECT **	12,748
** DISPUTED **	1,035
DISPUTED	2
** DISPUTED *	1
** UNVERIFIABLE **	5
** UNVERIFIABLE, PRERELEASE **	2
** UNSUPPORTED WHEN ASSIGNED **	158
** UNSUPPPORTED WHEN ASSIGNED **	31
** Unsupported When Assigned **	1
UNSUPPORTED WHEN ASSIGNED	1
VERSION NOT SUPPORTED WHEN ASSIGNED	5
** PRODUCT NOT SUPPORTED WHEN ASSIGNED **	6
Resolved	2
** SPLIT **	1

NOT SUPPORTED WHEN ASSIGNED" respectively) [7]. Typically, vendors do not issue patches on End-of-Life (EOL) products, however in extreme cases vendors have issued patches to critical vulnerabilities. An example of this is Microsoft with Windows XP, following the WannaCrypt outbreak [19]. As of writing, 202 CVEs with the "UNSUPPORTED WHEN ASSIGNED" tag have been released. The single occurrence of a "SPLIT" tag appears in CVE-2005-2759. The "MERGE" tag indicates that there were multiple CVE IDs issued to the same vulnerability, whereas the "SPLIT" tag indicates that a single CVE ID was issued when multiple CVE IDs should have been issued [5]. In practice, the "MERGE" tag is not used in the beginning of CVE descriptions but rather inside the explanation using a "REJECT" tag.

2.2 Common Platform Enumeration (CPE)

Common Platform Enumeration (CPE) is a standardized record dataset for describing products, applications and hardware from vendors. Initially maintained by "The MITRE Corporation", CPE has been transferred to NIST, that currently maintains it. Labeling it as part of their Security Content Automation Protocol (SCAP), NIST highlights its importance for usage within IT management tools, in order to actively monitor new vulnerabilities for deployed products, applications and hardware [20]. Currently, multiple network and vulnerability scanning utilities report identified products using the CPE format. Such utilities include Nmap, Nessus and OpenVAS. In CitySCAPE's RMT, CPE has been used for identifying which vulnerabilities are related to specific hardware, software or network assets. In August of 2011, NIST released CPE Version 2.3, which is still in use today. There are three naming schemes for CPEs [3]:

1. Well-Formed CPE Name (WFN): It is defined as comma-separated attribute - value pairs as shown below:

$$wfn : [attribute\_1 = ``value\_1", attribute\_2 = ``value\_2"]$$

with the allowed attributes being: part, vendor, product, version, update, edition, language, software edition (sw_edition), target software (target_sw), target hardware (target_hw), other. The allowed values for the part attribute are: "a" for applications, "h" for hardware, and "o" for operating systems. An example representing the 64-bit version of Microsoft Windows 10 is shown below:

$$wfn : [part = ``o", vendor = ``microsoft"product = ``windows\_10", target\_hw = ``x64"]$$

2. Uniform Resource Identifier (URI) binding: Also associated with CPE 2.2, it is a string defined as shown below:

$$cpe:/part:vendor:product:version:update:edition:language$$

The representation in URI binding format of the same product as with WFN yields:

$$cpe:/o:microsoft:windows\_10 :::\sim\sim\sim\sim x64 \sim$$

From the specification [3], and by looking at the above CPE, we can see that for future CPE versions the tilde character ($\sim$) is used to add in the missing fields that CPE 2.3 contains. Specifically it states that the tilde character is used to "pack" multiple attribute values into the edition component.

3. Formatted string binding: It is most commonly used to describe CPE 2.3 entries. It is defined as shown below:

$$cpe : < cpe\_version >:< part >:< vendor >:< product >:< version >:< update >:$$
$$< edition >:< language >:< sw\_edition >:< target\_sw >:< target\_hw >:< other >$$

The same product, the 64-bit version of Windows 10, for any language, version or edition, can be specified in formatted string binding as:

$$cpe:2.3:o:microsoft:windows\_10:*:**:*:*:*:x64:*$$

Asterisks denote wildcards and colons denote the field change. Colons can be delimited using a backslash (\). For example, in CVE-2016-0380[4], the product sterling_connect:direct that contains a colon, is represented as:

$$cpe:2.3:a:ibm:sterling\_connect\backslash : direct:4.1.0.0:*:*:*:*:unix:*:*$$

---

[4] https://nvd.nist.gov/vuln/detail/CVE-2016-0380.

2.3   Common Weakness Enumeration (CWE)

Common Weakness Enumeration (CWE) is a public list of weaknesses. It is managed by the Homeland Security Systems Engineering and Development Institute (HSSEDI), which is operated by "The MITRE Corporation". Launched in 2006, it initially focused on software issues, however following the LoJax rootkit and the Meltdown/Spectre exploits, in 2020 CWE included hardware weaknesses [9]. CWEs are assigned to CVEs from NIST in their NVD database.

It has 6 main lists of weaknesses, namely:

- CWE-1000: Research Concepts (it contains all the weaknesses in the CWE list)
- CWE-1194: Hardware Design
- CWE-699: Software Development
- CWE-1003: Weaknesses for Simplified Mapping of Published Vulnerabilities
- CWE Top 25 Most Dangerous Software Weaknesses
- CWE Most Important Hardware Weaknesses

NVD analysts use CWE-1003 to categorize the weaknesses used in vulnerabilities as of 2016. It is a joint effort of NIST and the CWE Team, in order for analysts to be able to easily categorize the most common and impactful weaknesses into newly discovered vulnerabilities. As such, it is not a comprehensive list, and it contains only 130 weaknesses out of a total of 933, as of writing [10]. Prior to using CWE-1003 as a weakness list for CVEs, NVD used CWE-635, containing only 13 weaknesses, that was used from 2008 until it was replaced [11]. Nevertheless, 384 weaknesses were found to have been in use in CVEs, i.e., more than double the amount that are supposed to be used during categorization. This increases the amount of manual mapping required and is another case where our methodology can assist in the threat categorization.

CWE and the representrative lists and views are constantly updated, in order to be up-to-date with the current state of software and hardware weaknesses. For that reason, it uses a versioning system, with the latest version being version 4.11 as of writing.

The CWE Top 25 Most Dangerous Software Weaknesses is a yearly list that is formulated as a result of the most common and impactful weaknesses. Initially launched in 2009 and updated in 2010 and 2011, it remained the same until 2019, where the list was updated once more, and has been updated yearly ever since. It serves as a reference to report to users the most important weaknesses. In order to generate the list, data from CVE and NVD are used. The two most important metrics for generating the CWE Top 25 are the number of CVE occurrences and their overall severity using Common Vulnerability Scoring System (CVSS) as the vulnerability severity metric [8]. CVE records can contain 0, 1 or more CWE entries, with Table 2 showing the distribution of the number of CWEs found in CVEs. Note that the total number of entries adds up to 216,694, which is the number of CVEs in the NVD JSON feeds as of June 5th, 2023.

Table 2. Number of CWE entries in CVEs

No. of CWE Entries	CVE Count	Percent of Entries
0	13,094	6.04%
1	200,174	92.37%
2	3,194	1.47%
3	219	0.10%
4	9	<0.00%
5	4	<0.00%

The number of CVE entries that have zero CWEs assigned to them fluctuates, depending on the number of CVEs that have yet to be analyzed. There are however, a lot of old CVE entries that may never get assigned a CWE.

Table 3 contains the 15 most used CWE entries in CVEs and the number of occurrences of those weaknesses in the vulnerabilities.

Table 3. 15 most used CWE entries

CWE ID	CWE Name	No. of occurrences
NVD-CWE-Other	Other	28,046
NVD-CWE-noinfo	Insufficient Information	23,577
CWE-79	Improper Neutralization of Input During WebPage Generation ('Cross-site Scripting')	22,836
CWE-119	Improper Restriction of Operations within theBounds of a Memory Buffer	11,453
CWE-89	Improper Neutralization of Special Elementsused in an SQL Command ('SQL Injection')	9,718
CWE-20	Improper Input Validation	9,250
CWE-787	Out-of-bounds Write	8,422
CWE-200	Exposure of Sensitive Information to anUnauthorized Actor	6,837
CWE-264	Permissions, Privileges, and Access Controls	5,279
CWE-22	Improper Limitation of a Pathname to aRestricted Directory ('Path Traversal')	5,168
CWE-125	Out-of-bounds Read	5,087
CWE-352	Cross-Site Request Forgery (CSRF)	4,489
CWE-416	Use After Free	3,579
CWE-287	Improper Authentication	2,982
CWE-94	Improper Control of Generation of Code('Code Injection')	2,954

Note that there are two CWE entries that are not included in CWE Lists. They are "NVD-CWE-Other" and "NVD-CWE-noinfo" that are used by NVD analysts. These two special CWEs make up 23.82% of all CVE entries. Combined with the CVE entries that do not have a CWE assigned to them, they make up nearly a third (29.86%) of all CVEs that are impossible to analyze using CWE data alone. This was a key rationale for this paper.

2.4   Common Attack Pattern Enumeration and Classification (CAPEC)

Common Attack Pattern Enumeration and Classification (CAPEC) is a list of common attack patterns that help users understand how the most common weaknesses are exploited, that in turn create vulnerabilities. Initially released in 2007, it is currently managed by "The MITRE Corporation" [2]. While there is no direct link between CVEs and CAPECs, each attack pattern contains related weaknesses (CWEs) in its information page. There are two CAPEC Views:

- CAPEC-1000: Mechanisms of Attack
- CAPEC-3000: Domains of Attack

Both CAPEC views contain all the current attack patterns, 559 as of writing, with the differences being in how they are categorized. More specifically, CAPEC-1000 categorizes attacks based on how they occur, and CAPEC-3000 based on what they affect. The current version of CAPEC is 3.9.

2.5 National Vulnerability Database (NVD)

NIST's National Vulnerability Database (NVD) is an extension to the CVE Program. Introduced in 1999 as the "Internet Category of Attack Toolkit" (ICAT), it initially hosted attack scripts, before shifting its focus onto vulnerabilities with the first analysts being students of the SANS Institute (SysAdmin, Audit, Network, and Security). In 2004, ICAT received funding from DHS, and in 2005 it was rebranded as NVD [21].

Both CVE and NVD are vulnerability databases that contain the same vulnerabilities. While CVE simply lists the vulnerabilities, with a description, some references and the assigning CNA, NVD performs an analysis of each vulnerability to extract relevant CPE names, CVSS scoring information, as well as CWE mappings. However, all the extra information has to be extracted by NVD analysts, and therefore, there is usually a delay between the initial CVE publication and the NVD entry that includes other information such as CVSS scoring. The delay itself can pose a critical threat for vendors and users that need to be aware of new vulnerabilities and their potential impact, despite the fact that they have not yet been analyzed by the NVD. It is for that reason that companies like Tenable have created solutions in order to get that relevant information from CVE descriptions using natural language processing and machine learning [25].

NVD provides both an API for making relatively fast queries for vulnerabilities related to a specific CPE, as well as JSON feeds that are updated daily. The JSON feeds from NVD were used in order to get all the information necessary to map and consequently train our model with the specific threats.

2.6 Common Vulnerability Scoring System (CVSS)

Common Vulnerability Scoring System (CVSS) is a standardized system for assessing the severity of computer vulnerabilities. Initially created by the National Infrastructure Advisory Council (NIAC), CVSS v1 was released in February 2005, with the Forum of Incident Response and Security Teams (FIRST) chosen to be the custodian of CVSS in April 2005 [12]. In June of 2007, CVSS v2 was launched after feedback received from vendors. It reduced inconsistencies, increased granularity and reflected a wider variety of vulnerabilities [14]. CVSS v3.0 was released in June 2015 and included several changes including:

- In the Base Metric Group Group, confidentiality, integrity and availability metrics were changed from Low (L), Medium (M), High (H) to None (N), Low (L) or High (H).
- The Attack Vector (AV) metric added the Physical (P) metric value, to include vulnerabilities that require physical access, like cold boot attacks.
- The metric User Interaction (UI) was added, with 2 options, None (N) or Required (R). It represents whether the user must interact with a malicious payload in order for it to infect a system or not (e.g. zero-click exploits).
- The Privileges Required (PR) metric was also added with the None (N), Low (L) or High (H) options, to reflect the privilege level the attacker must obtain in order to successfully exploit the vulnerability.

Finally, metric severity ratings depending on the metric score, were changed as presented in Fig. 1.

CVSS v2 Ratings	
Low	0.0 - 3.9
Medium	4.0 - 6.9
High	7.0 - 10.0

CVSS v3.0 Ratings	
None	0.0
Low	0.1 - 3.9
Medium	4.0 - 6.9
High	7.0 - 8.9
Critical	9.0 - 10.0

Fig. 1. CVSS v2 vs CVSS v3.0 Metric Severity Ratings

The current version, CVSS v3.1, was launched in June 17th 2019 and it was adopted by the NVD on September 2019. It focused on making clarifications and improvements to the 3.0 standard without making significant changes to the formulas [13]. The biggest change was the publishing of a clarification in the CVSS specification that specifies that CVSS measures severity and not risk. This was due to the fact that the CVSS Base Score was solely used as a method to measure risk and since the CVSS Base Score only takes into account the constant characteristics of vulnerabilities, the calculated risk would not include the evolution of the vulnerability or potential existing countermeasures. Temporal and Environmental Metrics are recommended for use in risk calculation, that involve, among others, the exploit code maturity and the remediation level that can change across the timeline of a vulnerabilities discovery, as well as, the specific CIA requirements in the case of Environmental Metrics. However many CNAs do not provide Temporal metrics and neither does NIST on its API on the rare occasions that CNAs do provide them, for example in CVE-2019-9516[5] [6].

---

[5] https://nvd.nist.gov/vuln/detail/CVE-2019-9516.
[6] https://kb.cert.org/vuls/id/605641/.

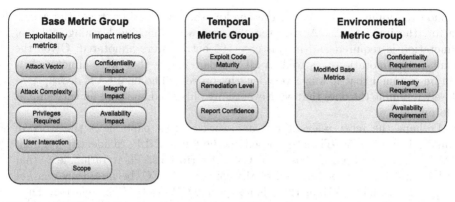

Fig. 2. CVSS v3.1 Metric Groups.   https://www.first.org/cvss/v3.1/specification-document

3   Related Work

This section provides a brief introduction into Natural Language Processing (NLP) and showcases relevant related works. NLP refers to a branch of computer science that aims to make computers understand written and spoken words like a human would. It combines multiple fields of computer science including computational linguistics, machine learning (ML), and deep learning models. There is a plethora of tasks that can be accomplished using NLP, such as named-entity recognition (NER), that identifies entities in sentences; sentiment analysis, that can extract subjective information; speech-to-text; text-to-speech; AI-powered translations; and the task of interest for this paper: text classification.

There have been several cases where NLP and ML techniques have been applied on CVE descriptions to extract information [15,24,25]. However, to best of our knowledge threat extraction as presented in this paper has not been proposed. In this section we will briefly analyze these related works, where NLP was applied on CVE or other vulnerability related descriptions, however no other work has tried to accomplish what is presented in this paper.

Tenable, the company that created Nessus, a popular vulnerability assessment tool, uses NLP on CVE descriptions as part of their vulnerability priority rating (VPR) [25]. VPR is a vulnerability impact tool that aims to accurately analyze the impact of vulnerabilities, since, according to Tenable, CVSS has high proportion of High and Critical vulnerabilities, thus making prioritization difficult [26]. In their VPR tool, they use NLP in order to calculate CVSS impact metrics from CVE descriptions. Another reasoning for their approach is that it takes some time between a CVE disclosure and NVD publication, which can take more than 30 d in some cases.

The work of Sun et al. [24] showcased a methodology for the extraction of information from sometimes lengthy ExploitDB posts, with ExploitDB being a public database of exploits. This includes the title, the description, metadata, etc. Using this information, they are able to generate CVE descriptions that include the vulnerable product, the vendor, the vulnerability type, the attack vector, the impact, etc. As is often the case with machine learning, a lot of annotation is required and in this case 765 entries were annotated. Given the number of annotations, as well as all the parameters that were annotated, it can be assumed that it was a very lengthy process. The final CVE descriptions closely resemble the ones that were eventually published and contain very similar information.

Perhaps the most relevant relevant work to this paper is is the work of Kanakogi et al. [15]. Their proposed method uses NLP to identify relevant CAPEC Attack Patterns, based on CVE descriptions. Their rationale is that CVEs cannot always be mapped to the correct CAPEC, because they can not be traced through CWE, as there is no specific CWE - CAPEC relation. Their methodology compares the similarity of CAPEC descriptions with CVE descriptions and rank them based on it, in order to find the most suitable CAPEC.

In our work, NLP is used to identify relevant threats to CVEs, since nearly one third of the CVEs do not have CWEs assigned to them and, consequently threats. Thus, it provides an enriched and more accurate basis for the performance of risk analysis, since more CVEs are taken into account.

4   Natural Language Processing Background

This section will further elaborate on text classification, and explain some key metrics that are used to measure the effectiveness of our implementation. Finally it will present the library that was used.

4.1   Text Classification

Text classification is the process of categorizing text into certain categories. When a computer model classifies information, the result will fall into four categories of prediction correctness, depending on the predicted label and the actual label. In Table 4 a confusion matrix that shows the different categories is presented.

Table 4. Confusion Matrix of Classification Results

		True Label	
		Positive	Negative
Predicted Label	Positive	True Positive (TP)	False Positive (FP)
	Negative	False Negative (FN)	True Negative (TN)

It can be seen that when the predicted label matches the true label, the result is classified as a true positive or a true negative, when the true label is positive or negative, respectively. Otherwise, it is classified as a false negative when the true label is positive and the predicted is negative, and as a false positive when the true label is negative and the predicted is positive. Using these categories we can evaluate the performance of the model. The most common metric for classification models is accuracy, which is calculated using Formula 1.

$$Accuracy = \frac{Number\ of\ correct\ predictions}{Total\ number\ of\ predictions} \tag{1}$$

Using the categories, that can be generated by the confusion matrix shown in Table 4, accuracy can also be expressed as:

$$Accuracy = \frac{True\ Positives + True\ Negatives}{True\ Positives + True\ Negatives + False\ Positives + False\ Negatives} \tag{2}$$

Another common metric is precision, that measures the ratio of True Positives to the total number of positives (true or false) predicted by a model. It is calculated using Formula 3:

$$Precision = \frac{True\ Positives}{True\ Positives + False\ Positives} \tag{3}$$

Along with precision, another common metric is recall that is the fraction of the True Positives to all actual positives, that include true positives and false negatives. It is calculated using Formula 4:

$$Recall = \frac{True\ Positives}{True\ Positives + False\ Negatives} \tag{4}$$

Finally, another common metric is F1-score, the harmonic mean of precision and recall [23], which is defined as:

$$F1 - score = 2 \times \frac{Precision \times Recall}{Precision + Recall} \tag{5}$$

There are other metrics to measure the effectiveness of classification models, however, for the purposes of this paper, only the ones mentioned above will be used. The classification problem is defined as a binary decision, where the two hypotheses are the existence or not of a certain threat. Since the output of the model is a probabilistic value between 0 and 1, a classification threshold is set to be able to distinguish between the two outcomes of the binary decision.

4.2 spaCy

spaCy[7] is an open-source Python library focused on natural language processing (NLP). It is built and maintained by the company Explosion, and uses transformers for its deep learning models. Among other things, it features:

---

[7] https://spacy.io/.

- Named-entity recognition (NER)
- Text Classification
- Lemmatization

It was selected for its ease of use, since it does not require too much technical knowledge of NLP. During the initial research phases of this paper, NER was considered in order to identify the threats, which required a manual annotation in order to train the ML model to recognize threats. For the purpose of manual annotation of CVE descriptions, the Prodigy[8] program was used which, alongside NLP, features computer vision annotation tools. Prodigy was kindly provided for our research by Explosion, however the effort of finding examples of all the threats in CVEs and annotating a large enough set to use for training and validation, was deemed substantial. Through the CitySCAPE project, a mapping of threats with CWEs and CAPECs was compiled for the RMT subcomponent as shown in Fig. 3 and analyzed in depth in the paper "A Hybrid Dynamic Risk Analysis Methodology for Cyber-Physical Systems" [17]. The creation of such a mapping allowed us to prefer it to manual annotation at this stage due to the substantial amount of work required.

5   Implementation

As mentioned previously and from the data presented in Tables 2 and 3, 64,717 CVEs or nearly one third of all CVE entries do not have a CWE mapped to them. Moreover, the delay between a CVE disclosure and the NVD analysis could be substantial, leaving a potential risk undetected by the RMT or any risk analysis tool utilizing public datasets. As such it is important to be able to get information about new vulnerabilities as soon as possible, since along with the CVE ID, a description is also included on new disclosures.

Our research for identifying threats in CVE descriptions began using NER, with an initial proof of concept being created. For example in CVE-1999-0011[9] that has a description of "Denial of Service vulnerabilities in BIND 4.9 and BIND 8 Releases via CNAME record and zone transfer.", "Denial of Service" would be marked as the impact of the vulnerability and then mapped to the corresponding threat. However, a combination of the substantial annotation effort needed, and the fact that a mapping for threats to CVEs was already under development specifically for the CitySCAPE project (see [17] and Fig. 3), we opted to shift our focus to text classification, in order to identify threats in CVE descriptions.

The mapping used for the training and validation of our text classification model was a snapshot of the mapping used for the RMT, which was embedded on the Risk and Impact Assessment Tool of the CitySCAPE project. As such not all threats of the CitySCAPE taxonomy are present in Table 5. The mapping uses the CWE(s) found in the CVE entry, and the CAPEC(s) that can be mapped to the assigned CWE(s) to then extract the related threat(s) that the vulnerability

---

[8] https://prodi.gy/.
[9] https://nvd.nist.gov/vuln/detail/CVE-1999-0011.

can expose. The reason that the CAPEC(s) are derived from the CWE(s) in the CVE record is that CAPEC(s) are not available in NIST's CVE information feed.

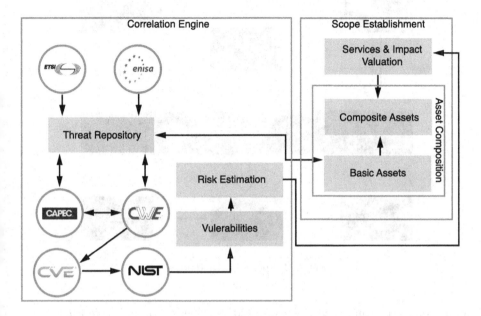

Fig. 3. Risk Managment Tool high-level overview

The objective of our work is to establish an intelligent and automated relationship between CVEs and threats as shown in Fig. 4. Under favourable conditions, mapping between CVEs and threats can be achieved using the mapping in Fig. 3 [17], where the relations of CVEs to CWEs and CWEs to CAPECs, as well as the relations of CWEs and CAPECs to threats can be used. However, in many cases as presented in Tables 2 and 3, this mapping cannot occur for one third of the CVEs, while there is also the risk of the notable delays by the NVD. Therefore, an alternative shall be devised to cover such cases.

Our proposed solution uses text classification to accomplish this, while utilizing the implemented mapping of CVEs to threats through CWEs and CAPECs of Fig. 3 for model training and validation. More specifically, in order to train our text classification model we need an input, the CVE description, and the corresponding labels, in this case the mapped threats. The end result is a list containing all the CVE descriptions of the CVEs that can be mapped, with their respective threats. This is then passed on to the ML model for it to train on as depicted in Fig. 4. More specifically the input for the ML model is a list of CVE descriptions, along with a list of tuples for each description containing all the identified threats in the threats taxonomy and a numerical representation of each threat's applicability to a specific description (0 for not applicable and 1 for

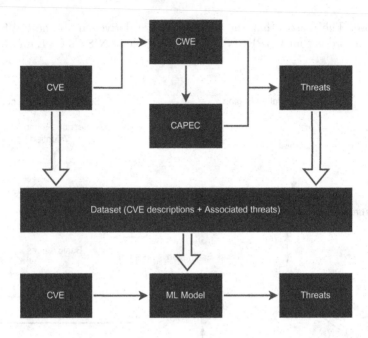

Fig. 4. Proposed methodology

applicable). An example entry for CVE-2023-22809 is: *"In Sudo before 1.9.12p2, the sudoedit (aka -e) feature mishandles extra arguments passed...", ['TH-28': 0, 'TH-24': 0, 'TH-26': 0, 'TH-09': 0, 'TH-11': 0, 'TH-19': 0, 'TH-25': 1, 'TH-27': 0, 'TH-03': 0, 'TH-05': 0, 'TH-23': 0, 'TH-02': 0, 'TH-14': 0, 'TH-08': 0, 'TH-21': 0, 'TH-06': 0].* Similarly the output is the same list of threats with the probability of the threat applicability on the input CVE description.

The reason that CAPECs are not directly mapped to CVEs is due to the fact that CAPECs are not mapped to CVEs, but rather CWEs. In the end, the mapped dataset contains 136,421 CVEs that have one or more threats assigned to them. In order not to confuse the model, only CVEs that have one or more threats are used, because unannotated CVEs would be automatically assigned as not containing any threats and would reduce our model's accuracy. For example, if a denial of service CVE was published but could not be mapped to the denial of service threat using the aforementioned mapping, it would automatically assign that CVE as not posing a denial of service threat, with the model being trained with that incorrect information. As such overall accuracy would be reduced.

With that initial mapping in place, a program was written in python 3 using the spaCy library to train a ML model to extract threats from CVE descriptions, using the mapping stated above. We conducted three experiments:

- Using CVE descriptions, without any modifications.
- Using CVE descriptions that had been stemmed using the Natural Language Toolkit (NLTK) [1].

– Using CVE descriptions that had been lemmatized using spaCy.

Stemming and lemmatization are both word normalization techniques [18] that are capable of reducing the inflectional forms of words. The difference is that stemming is a more unrefined process as it trims words in order to find the root word, while lemmatization takes into account the context the word is used in. For example, as Manning et al. [18] state, "the word *saw* using stemming would become *s*, while lemmatization would return *see* or *saw*, depending on whether the original token was a verb or a noun". Since spaCy does not support stemming, the Natural Language Toolkit (NLTK)[10] was used to create a file containing the stemmed descriptions and the CVE ID. The goal was that using either stemmed or lemmatized descriptions would yield a better accuracy, however that was not the case.

All three experiments were run using k-fold cross-validation. The dataset consisted of 136,421 CVE descriptions along with their corresponding threats, which were generated through the approach shown in Fig. 3. It is also important to note that only CVEs that could be mapped to threats are present in the dataset. The dataset was divided into 10 subsets, and for each fold, one subset was used for validation, while the rest were used for training. Particular attention was given to ensuring that all data points in the initial dataset were used for both training and validation. This means that the process of training and validation was performed ten times as shown in Fig. 5.

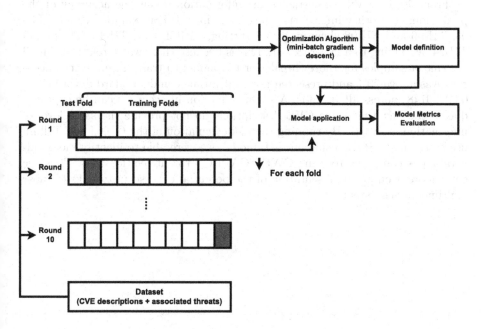

Fig. 5. Used 10-fold cross-validation process

---

[10] https://www.nltk.org/.

There are plenty of optimization algorithms, but the main ones are batch gradient descent, stochastic gradient descent (SGD) and mini-batch gradient descent. Batch gradient descent optimizes on the entire dataset at once requiring a lot of memory to run on large datasets, SGD optimizes for each item, while mini-batch gradient descent uses a batch of data to perform an update on, with the main advantage being a reduction in variance on the updates and faster runtime using matrix optimizations [22]. Optimization algorithms are ways to find the minimum or maximum of a function. In this case, the optimization objective is to minimize loss or the error in the model. In our model, training used compounded mini-batches found in spaCy, with an initial size of 4, a max size of 32 and a compounding rate of 1.001. Finally, mini-batch gradient descent was used as the optimising function with a 0.2 dropout rate.

We noticed that stemming and lemmatization had a minimal effect on our model, with the differences being within margin of error for the different models. As such, only the results of the unaltered CVE descriptions are presented. Note that multiple threats can be identified per CVE.

Table 5, shows the accuracy of the predictions after a 10-fold cross-validation. Accuracy is the average accuracy across the ten folds with its variance and standard deviation. Precision, recall and F1-score are the average values across the ten folds, while TP (True Positives), TN (True Negatives), FP (False Positives) and FN (False Negatives) are the results of the addition of the respectable values for the ten folds. The total number of CVEs used is 136,421.

From Table 5, we can extract some information about the accuracy of the predictions and other information about our model. For example, threats TH-05, TH-06 and TH-08 show major overfitting, with TH-14, TH-19, TH-23 and TH-24 overfitting to a lesser extent. This is because there was a relatively small amount of samples for those threats for the model to train from. Overall accuracy was above 90% and presented minimal variance and standard deviation ($\sim$ 0,00129748) across all 10 folds. A slight reduction in accuracy can be expected due to the fact that some CVE descriptions do not provide the same level of information as others. By running the risk calculation of the Genoa and Tallinn use cases on the RMT using our ML model, we were able to identify more vulnerabilities compared to using CWE - CAPEC - threat relationships. Thus, we get a more accurate representation of the potential cybersecurity risks of those multimodal ecosystems.

Table 5. Results after 10-fold cross validation

Threat ID	Threat Name	Accuracy	Variance	Standard Deviation	Precision	Recall	F1	TP	TN	FP	FN
TH-02	Denial of Service	0.9327	0.00000469	0.00216603	0.9365	0.8657	0.8996	41,162	86,078	2,801	6,380
TH-03	Modification of Information / Data Manipulation	0.9764	0.00000026	0.00051292	0.9275	0.6529	0.7661	5,281	127,920	415	2,805
TH-05	Interception of Information	0.9966	0.00000009	0.00029722	0.7864	0.0521	0.0939	24	135,933	10	454
TH-06	Replay of Messages	0.9992	0.00000004	0.00019792	-	-	-	0	136,312	0	109
TH-08	Failures of Devices	1.0000	0.00000000	0.00003359	-	-	-	0	136,418	0	3
TH-09	Failure of System	0.9672	0.00000364	0.00190915	0.8650	0.7793	0.8189	10,150	121,790	1,598	2,883
TH-11	Software Exploitation / Malicious Code Injection	0.9132	0.00000892	0.00298686	0.9403	0.9283	0.9342	84,110	40,471	5,342	6,498
TH-14	Device Modification	0.9964	0.00000048	0.00069614	0.9568	0.5420	0.6895	546	135,382	25	468
TH-19	Phishing Attacks	0.9966	0.00000028	0.00053364	0.9583	0.4212	0.5643	324	135,627	24	446
TH-21	Resource Exhaustion/Lack of resources	0.9238	0.00000680	0.00260782	0.9286	0.7989	0.8585	31,587	94,435	2,452	7,947
TH-23	Management Interface Compromise	0.9973	0.00000047	0.00068609	0.7831	0.5523	0.6267	328	135,720	102	271
TH-24	Unauthorized Access To Premises	0.9922	0.00000028	0.00052652	0.4401	0.0613	0.1030	65	135,296	60	1
TH-25	Abuse of Authorisation / Privilege Escalation	0.9285	0.00000714	0.00267142	0.7938	0.7313	0.7600	15,461	111,209	4,074	5,677
TH-26	Loss/Leakage of Information	0.9438	0.00000698	0.00264103	0.8825	0.6756	0.7645	12,467	116,293	1,678	5,983
TH-27	Abuse of Authentication	0.9714	0.00000120	0.00109543	0.8965	0.6856	0.7765	6,806	125,708	792	3,115
TH-28	Identity Theft	0.9712	0.00000143	0.00119785	0.8652	0.7377	0.7955	7,652	124,843	1,207	2,719

6 Conclusion

As we have discovered, threat identification based on vulnerabilities is not always possible, since there is not always a link between CVEs to CWEs in order to be able to take advantage of CWE - CAPEC - threat relations. Using the proposed methodology on the Tallinn and Genoa CitySCAPE use cases, the number of identified vulnerabilities assigned to Cyber-Physical and other assets was higher, leading to a more accurate risk score. With NLP, we are able to take into account CVEs that NIST has not been able to assign proper CWEs (such as "NVD-CWE-Other" and "NVD-CWE-noinfo"), and CVEs where no appropriate CWE was selected during analysis. Furthermore, we are able to timely include new CVEs that have not yet been analysed in the risk analysis. Using text classification we were able to identify threats with an accuracy of over 90%. As new vulnerabilities are discovered, and the threat landscape evolves, more effort will be required in order to accurately perform a risk analysis with the proposed methodology in this paper being a possible option, and is in fact implemented into the CitySCAPE project's Risk Modelling Tool. Future work may include manual annotation of threats in vulnerabilities in order to rely fully on text classification and reduce reliance on the predetermined list of weaknesses present in CWE, as well as the integration of ExploitDB entries for early vulnerability discovery as presented by [24], while also taking into account exploit code maturity and remediation level that is absent from most CVSS entries. Finally, with the future addition of automatic asset discovery and asset relation discovery, the work of replicating the entirety of the ecosystem can be automated, thus reducing the time required to perform a risk analysis and increase accuracy due to automation.

Acknowledgment. This work is a part of the CitySCAPE project. CitySCAPE has received funding from the European Union's Horizon 2020 research & innovation programme under grant agreement no 883321. Content reflects only the authors' view and European Commission is not responsible for any use that may be made of the information it contains.

References

1. Bird, S., Klein, E., Loper, E.: Natural language processing with Python: analyzing text with the natural language toolkit. O'Reilly Media, Inc. (2009)
2. CAPEC: About CAPEC. https://capec.mitre.org/about/index.html 04 Apr 2019
3. Cheikes, B., Waltermire, D., Scarfone, K.: Common Platform Enumeration: Naming Specification Version **2**, 3 (2011). https://doi.org/10.6028/NIST.IR.7695, https://tsapps.nist.gov/publication/get_pdf.cfm?pub_id=909010
4. CISA: Apache Log4j Vulnerability Guidance. httpo://www.cisa.gov/uscert/apache-log4j-vulnerability-guidance Accessed 27 Apr 2022
5. CVE: CVE Numbering Authority (CNA) Rules. https://www.cve.org/ResourcesSupport/AllResources/CNARules 05 Mar 2020
6. CVE: History. https://www.cve.org/About/History Accessed 27 Apr 2022
7. CVE: Process for Assigning CVE IDs to End-of-Life (EOL) Products. https://cve.mitre.org/cve/cna/CVE_Program_End_of_Life_EOL_Assignment_Process.html 11 Dec 2020
8. CWE: 2021 CWE Top 25 Most Dangerous Software Weaknesses. https://cwe.mitre.org/top25/archive/2021/2021_cwe_top25.html 13 Oct 2022
9. CWE: About CWE. https://cwe.mitre.org/about/index.html 06 June 2023
10. CWE: CWE VIEW: Weaknesses for Simplified Mapping of Published Vulnerabilities. https://cwe.mitre.org/data/definitions/1003.html 27 Apr 2023
11. CWE: Weaknesses Originally Used by NVD from 2008 to 2016. https://cwe.mitre.org/data/definitions/635.html 27 Apr 2023
12. FIRST: Common Vulnerability Scoring System v1 Archive. https://www.first.org/cvss/v1/ 14 Apr 2005
13. FIRST: Common Vulnerability Scoring System version 3.1: User Guide. https://www.first.org/cvss/user-guide Accessed 5 May 2022
14. FIRST: New version of Common Vulnerability Scoring System released. https://www.first.org/cvss/v2/ 20 June 2007
15. Kanakogi, K., et al.: Tracing CVE Vulnerability Information to CAPEC Attack Patterns Using Natural Language Processing Techniques. Information **12**(8), (2021). https://doi.org/10.3390/info12080298, https://www.mdpi.com/2078-2489/12/8/298
16. Kushner, D.: The real story of stuxnet. IEEE Spectr. **50**(3), 48–53 (2013). https://doi.org/10.1109/MSPEC.2013.6471059

17. Lyvas, C., et al.: A hybrid dynamic risk analysis methodology for cyber-physical systems. In: Kastsikas, S., et al. (eds.) Computer Security. ESORICS 2022 International Workshops: CyberICPS 2022, SECPRE 2022, SPOSE 2022, CPS4CIP 2022, CDT&SECOMANE 2022, EIS 2022, and SecAssure 2022, Copenhagen, Denmark, September 26–30, 2022, Revised Selected Papers, pp. 134–152. Springer International Publishing, Cham (2023). https://doi.org/10.1007/978-3-031-25460-4_8

18. Manning, C.D., Raghavan, P., Schütze, H.: Introduction to Information Retrieval. Cambridge University Press (2008). https://doi.org/10.1017/CBO9780511809071

19. Microsoft Security Response Center: Customer Guidance for WannaCrypt attacks. https://msrc-blog.microsoft.com/2017/05/12/customer-guidance-for-wannacrypt-attacks/ 12 May 2017

20. NIST CSRC: Common Platform Enumeration (CPE). https://csrc.nist.gov/Projects/Security-Content-Automation-Protocol/Specifications/cpe 20 Apr 2023

21. NVD: A Brief History of the NVD. https://nvd.nist.gov/general/brief-history Accessed 27 Apr 2022

22. Ruder, S.: An overview of gradient descent optimization algorithms (2016). https://doi.org/10.48550/ARXIV.1609.04747, https://arxiv.org/abs/1609.04747

23. Sammut, C., Webb, G.I. (eds.): Encyclopedia of Machine Learning and Data Mining. Springer US, Boston, MA (2017). https://doi.org/10.1007/978-1-4899-7687-1

24. Sun, J., et al.: Generating Informative CVE Description From ExploitDB Posts by Extractive Summarization (2021). https://doi.org/10.48550/ARXIV.2101.01431, https://arxiv.org/abs/2101.01431

25. Tai, W.: How to Use VPR to Manage Threats Prior to NVD Publication. https://www.tenable.com/blog/how-to-use-vpr-to-manage-threats-prior-to-nvd-publication 22 May 2020

26. Tai, W.: What Is VPR and How Is It Different from CVSS?. https://www.tenable.com/blog/what-is-vpr-and-how-is-it-different-from-cvss 16 Apr 2020

Evaluation of an OPC UA-Based Access Control Enforcement Architecture

Björn Leander[1,2(✉)] ⓘ, Aida Čaušević[1,3] ⓘ, Hans Hansson[1] ⓘ,
and Tomas Lindström[2]

[1] Mälardalen University, Västerås, Sweden
{bjorn.leander,aida.causevic,hans.hansson}@mdu.se
[2] ABB Industrial Automation, Process Control Platform, Västerås, Sweden
tomas.lindstrom@se.abb.com
[3] Alstom Rail AB, Västerås, Sweden
aida.causevic@alstomgroup.se

Abstract. Dynamic access control in industrial systems is becoming a concern of greater importance as a consequence of the increasingly flexible manufacturing systems developed within the Industry 4.0 paradigm. With the shift from control system security design based on implicit trust toward a zero-trust approach, fine grained access control is a fundamental requirement.

In this article, we look at an access control enforcement architecture and authorization protocol outlined as part of the Open Process Communication Unified Automation (OPC UA) protocol that can allow sufficiently dynamic and fine-grained access control. We present an implementation, and evaluates a set of important quality metrics related to this implementation, as guidelines and considerations for introduction of this protocol in industrial settings. Two approaches for optimization of the authorization protocol are presented and evaluated, which more than halves the average connection establishment time compared to the initial approach.

1 Introduction

Within industrial systems, such as industrial control systems, logistics, manufacturing, etc., cybersecurity is a factor of growing concern. The industrial automation systems of today are growing increasingly complex, heterogeneous, dynamic and interconnected [1–3], which implies that the currently used cybersecurity models based on implicit trust are no longer tenable. Instead using a zero-trust approach to cybersecurity is gaining ground [4,5]. Access Control [6] is one of the major cybersecurity mechanisms in any information system and fine-grained access control is a basic requirement for a zero-trust architecture [7].

When conducting research on access control, it can be useful to structure the research according to Policy-, Enforcement- and Implementation-models (PEI), as suggested by Sandhu *et al.* [8], where the P-models describe how to the rules are formulated, E-models describe the enforcement architecture, and I-models describe the implementation of the components of the enforcement architecture.

S. Katsikas et al. (Eds.): ESORICS 2023 Workshops, LNCS 14398, pp. 124–144, 2024.
https://doi.org/10.1007/978-3-031-54204-6_7

Expressing sufficiently fine-grained access policies for dynamic industrial systems is a challenging task, but in this work we assume that such rules can be expressed, e.g., following the approach described by Leander *et al.* [9] or Knorr [10]. The mechanisms of enforcing access control policies are of great importance, and should ideally exhibit the same level of flexibility as the expressed policies.

In the previous work [11], different policy enforcement models for dynamic manufacturing systems have been introduced and discussed. The goal of this article is to describe and evaluate the implementation models for one of the most promising enforcement models from that article. The enforcement architecture uses a combination of local and centralized policy decision points, where the local decisions are static and the central decisions are dynamic, allowing a flexible and efficient architecture. The implementation uses Open Process Communication Unified Automation (OPC UA) [12] as a communication protocol, since it is the only available industrial protocol supporting policy-delegation mechanisms (to the best of our knowledge).

There are several previous works looking at quality metrics related to the OPC UA protocol, further discussed in Sect. 2. However, none of them look at the impact of the enforcement architecture, which we tackle in this article.

Problem Statement. There is an increasing need for fine-grained and dynamic authorization in industrial manufacturing systems. There are available solution on how to express such policies. However enforcing the policies, and how the enforcement affects different quality metrics of the system is so far not widely explored.

Paper Objectives. This article focuses on describing and evaluating the implementation of a policy enforcement architecture that deals with dynamic access control in industrial systems, using a workflow-based approach for policy decisions, and the widely adopted OPC UA protocol for communication.

Contributions. The following are our main contributions:

- Description and analysis of a tokens-based OPC UA authorization protocol, described in Sect. 3.
- Description of required implementations, described in Sect. 4.
- Experimental evaluation of impact of enforcement: (Sects. 5 and 6)
  - Time to completion for session creation and resource requests.
  - Impact of token expiry time on resource requests.
  - Impact of token size on session creation.
- Two approaches on optimization of the connection establishment protocol, described and evaluated in Sects. 7.
- Recommendations and considerations, discussed in Sect. 8.

Conclusions and ideas for potential future work are presented in Sect. 9.

2   Related Work

The enforcement architecture used in this article is based on suggestions from a previous work [11], there are however other suggestions and approaches of access control enforcement architectures for industrial systems. E.g., Alcaraz et al. [13], discuss a policy enforcement system for the distributed smart grid, using authentication tokens similarly as us. Martinelli et al. [14] describes an alternative enforcement architecture for OPC UA supporting the Usage Control (UCON) policy model [15], adding an extra protocol layer for handling the UCON policy decisions. The focus of these works are on the description and formalization of the enforcement architecture, while we in this paper focus on performance evaluation of an architecture based on the OPC UA standard.

Several previous works look at performance metrics for different aspects of the OPC UA protocol. Cavalieri et al. [16] model a part of the OPC UA stack in a network simulator, evaluating the impact of, e.g., signing and certificate validation on connection establishment and data read, similarly as our work. Kohnhäuser et al. [17] investigate the feasibility and performance of secure OPC UA communication including e.g., connection establishment time for different combinations of security policies.

Rocha et al. [18] compare the performance of the OPC UA publish/subscribe mechanism with the Message Queue Telemetry Transport protocol (MQTT) [19]. Similarly, Burger et al. [20] look the OPC UA publish/subscribe, investigating memory and CPU consumption, reaching the conclusion that memory and network overhead are small, as well as usage of data encryption, while CPU utilization is identified as the bottleneck. The publish/subscribe mechanism is not covered in this article, but the observations on network and memory load v.s. CPU utilization are similar.

Silva et al. [21] evaluate a series of Internet of Things protocols, including MQTT and OPC UA, in an experiment measuring completion times related to data transport, similarly as this done in this article.

Ladegourdie and Kua [22] investigate the performance in terms of CPU and memory consumption on different sets of traffic scenarios, in an experiment also utilizing a RasberryPi as the OPC UA server.

All of these mentioned related articles investigate important aspects of the OPC UA protocol, and several of them evaluate similar performance metrics as done in our article, e.g., time for connection establishment and response time of signal reads. However, none of these previous works include the authorization flow in their measurements, which is the focus of this work.

3   Architecture

In this section the system architecture is briefly described and the authorization protocol analyzed to provide the theoretical foundation for the work to be presented. The goal of this article is to study how these theoretical constructs behave when deployed in practice.

An **Access Control Enforcement Architecture** describes required mechanisms and components related to access control, together with their respective placement in the system architecture. The architecture used in this work is based on the approach suggested in [11], with basic components and placements as depicted in Fig. 1. The architecture is using components from the eXtensible Access Control Markup Language (XACML) reference architecture [23,24], with the main Policy Decision Point (PDP) outsourced to an authorization service. It makes the active policy decisions upon a client request and returns the policy decision in the form of an authorization access token (AuthZ token). The client transfers the policy decision to the resource server that makes a local policy decision, based on the access token content and local policy data. The policy decision is enforced by the resource servers' Policy Enforcement Point (PEP).

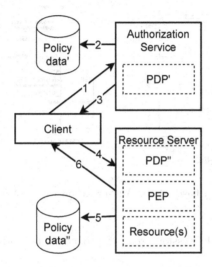

Fig. 1. An access control enforcement architecture, from [11].

The **Authorization Protocol** used in the architecture is based on the implicit authorization flow of OPC UA[1], executed in two different phases. The primary policy decisions are taken during session establishment phase using the protocol described in Fig. 2a in which the authorization server makes the high-level decisions on valid permissions for the duration of the session encoded in an access token. The client acts as a mediator of the policy decisions by sending the access token as a part of the Activate Session call. The resource server validates the access token before the session is activated.

The second phase of the authorization protocol is executed when the client requests a resource from the resource server through the active session, following the protocol shown in Fig. 2b. The resource server validates token expiry and

---

[1] `reference.opcfoundation.org/GDS/v105/docs/9`.

checks whether the requested resource permissions are included in the set of permissions granted by the central policy decision. If the resource is not granted, the client may attempt to fetch a new AuthZ token from the authorization service and refresh the session. If there are changed conditions implying new permissions the resource may be granted. The client must then refresh the session with a new token before token expires to avoid a new round of a session establishment.

The refresh token flow is identical to the session creation flow, except that the Client does not need to Open Session. The Client directly requests a new AuthZ token from the authorization service, and call Refresh Session, instead of Activate session.

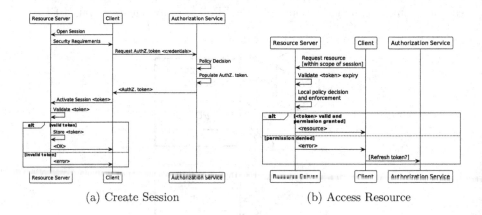

(a) Create Session   (b) Access Resource

Fig. 2. Phases of the Authorization Protocol Flow.

Session Creation. The session creation procedure is conducted in three separate stages:

1. Open session.
2. Request AuthZ token.
3. Activate session.

Opening a session includes the following steps: 1) establishing a channel with the server; 2) sending client instance certificate; 3) receiving service instance certificate along with connection options for the server, including security options for secure communication and user authentication/authorization.

If the options for user authentication/authorization indicate that an AuthZ token is required, the client needs to request a token from the endpoint as designated in the security information received from the the resource server. The token is then used to activate a session with the resource server.

From the resource server perspective, the session establishment is done in two steps: 1) an open session requests arrives and the resource server replies with the list of security configurations it supports, including options for authorization; and 2) upon session activation, the received access token is validated and associated with the active session, if accepted. Several other checks are also done on session establishment, e.g., the client application instance certificate must be directly or indirectly trusted by the server. AuthZ token validation includes: 1) decryption (if encrypted); 2) validation of the token signature and expiry time; and 3) control that the token is issued for the client of the session and for the resource server.

Communication Through Active Session. Once the session is activated, the client may access resources if permitted by the resource server, e.g., browse the name-space, read values, write values and execute methods. In due time before session expiry, the client can request a new access token from the authorization service and refresh the active session. An expired session, regardless of content, cannot be used for resource requests.

3.1 Protocol Modeling

To verify some basic properties of the authorization protocol, a model is created using the UPPAAL [25] tool environment, illustrated in Fig. 3. The model has separate templates for a client, a resource server and an authorization service. This model does not contain any details on access token content, instead we assume that a correctly issued token will contain permissions for the desired resource. The client and resource server models contain all states and transitions related to the authorization protocol outlined above.

Using this model we show that resource requests are not possible unless the model is in an active session. Furthermore we show that outlined protocol must be followed in order for the client to be granted access resources.

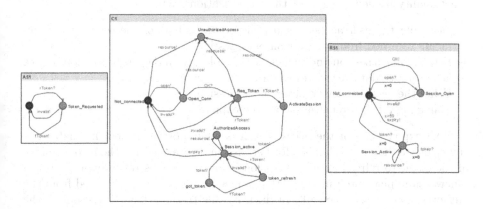

Fig. 3. Resource Server (RS1), Client (C1) and Authorization Service (AS1), modeled in UPPAAL.

Using the temporal logic we can verify that the modeled protocol works as expected, i.e., that the protocol is free from deadlocks (A[] not deadlock)

and that it is possible to activate a session (E<> RS1.SessionActive and
C1.SessionActive). Further, we check that the resource server cannot be in *not
connected* state while the client is in *session active* (A[] RS1.NotConnected imply
not C1.SessionActive). Also, we were interested to see whether it is possible
for the client to access a resource only by the *authorized access* state (E<>
C1.AuthorizedAccess, A[] not C1.UnauthorizedAccess). All the checks have been
successfully performed, showing no deviations.

4 Implementation

This section provides detailed information on the implementation done to support the evaluation work. Even though the authorization flow, as described in
the previous section, is part of the standard, no available software stack fully
supports the flow yet. The required implementation for supporting the authorization flow according to the standard is outlined below. The implementation
uses the .NET stack implementation from the OPC foundation[2], as it currently
has the best support for the outlined authorization flow, and, being open source
it is quite easy to extend.

Resource Server. All the basic logic for transmitting and receiving access
tokens are implemented in the stack. However, token validation and handling
of permissions based on token content has been implemented as part of this
evaluation, as well as the behavior for handling token expiry.

Client. The available base-class for an OPC UA client is extended with the
functionality needed to support the authorization flow:

- Decoding the user access token policy data as part of the security require-
  ments returned from a server on open session.
- Establishing a session and request access token from the Authorization service
  according to data received from a resource server.
- Using the access token to activate the session.
- Managing a token renewal before the expiry.

The expiry time of the access token is an important aspect in enabling a
sufficiently dynamic mechanism for permission delegation. It is the responsibility
of the client to refresh an active session before the access token expires. Token
renewal is implemented in a way that a new access token is requested from the
authorization service when 80% of the token life-time has passed. As soon as the
new access token is received, the session is refreshed.

---

[2] github.com/OPCFoundation/UA-.NETStandard.

Authorization Service. To support the evaluation experiment, a simple authorization service is implemented following the OPC UA standard[3], with the authorization service being accessible through an OPC UA server endpoint. On an AuthZ token request from a client, the implemented authorization service will always return a valid access token, with a configurable expiry time and a configurable size. This means that we have minimized the policy inference time of the authorization service.

JSON Web Tokens (JWT) [26] is used for encoding the policy decision, which is the preferred encoding according to the OPC UA standard.

5 Experiment

In order to evaluate the two phases of the authorization protocol, as outlined in Sect. 3, a set of experiments are constructed and they are executed twice, first in a system configured to use no authorization as a baseline, and second following the authorization protocol. Measuring the time to complete for different parts of the protocol allows a quantitative estimation of the operational properties of the authorization protocol, compared to the baseline.

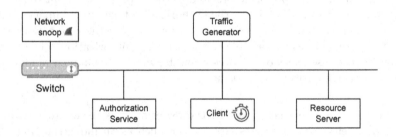

Fig. 4. Experiment setup.

In order to understand the sensitivity of the architecture in relation to traffic load, indicating its scalability, experiments are executed using two traffic load scenarios, *High traffic load* and *Low traffic load*. In the *Low traffic load* scenario, no additional traffic is generated. In the *High traffic load* scenario the client has additional connections to 5 other servers, where each accesses variables on 10 ms intervals, representing approximately 5000 reads/s. Additionally, two clients are connected to the resource server, one making 6 resource requests (2 read, 2 write, 2 execute) on a 15 ms clock, and one making 7 reads on a 10 ms clock, representing approximately 1100 additional resource requests per second towards the resource server. Measuring network load, the high-load scenario generates approximately 1.2 Mbps traffic to the resource server and 2.1 Mbps from the server. The high-load scenario pushes the CPU load of the resource server to about 40% for each of its' four processor cores.

---

[3] reference.opcfoundation.org/GDS/v105/docs/9.6.5.

The *High traffic load* scenario is meant to represent a realistically high load for the resource server and client respectively.

The experiments are executed in a system containing a resource server, a specially developed client which can execute and measure the completion times, an authorization service, and a variable subsystem for generating the traffic load scenario. The system setup for the experiment is illustrated in Fig. 4.

During the experiments related to session establishment, the completion time for the three stages of the session establishment protocol is measured (i.e., open session, handle token, activate session). For the resource access phase of the protocol, experiments are performed for read and write of signals and execution of methods.

In total, this sums up to 16 individual experiments, with results summarized in Sect. 6. Each instance of the experiment is executed a fixed number of times, i.e., 1000 times for the connection experiments and 4000 times for the access resource experiments. The client is designed to perform experiment repetitions on a clock with some randomization. The time interval between each experiment sample is between 10 ms and 2000 ms. This is done so that the samples are not accidentally coinciding with any of the fixed-frequency cycles of the traffic generators.

Experiments are also performed related to the impact of different token sizes and token expiry times. The size of the authorization token may impact connection establishment time, prompting an additional run of the connection establishment experiment, using variable token size. An authorization token refresh may impact response times of resource requests, which is examined in an experiment using variable token expiry time.

Equipment. The equipment used in the experiment is meant to mirror the scenario of a relatively simple resource server, such as an industrial controller, communicating with a Human-Machine Interface (HMI) client running on a standard PC, and the authorization service running on a server machine.

A Raspberry Pi 4 Model B (ARM Cortex-A72) with Ubuntu 22.04 is used for running the resource server. The ARM Cortext-A72 is normally clocked at 1.5 GHz and the majority of the experiments are performed using that configuration. A set of experiments is also performed with the processor down-clocked to 600 MHz, to get performance comparable to that of a CI845[4], which is an industrial hardware platform used for running control and connectivity services.

The client and the authorization service are both running on separate commodity hi-spec PCs (Intel i7-11850H (8 cores), 2.5GHz, 32GB RAM, Windows 10). The Switch is a ZYXEL GS1915-8.

6   Results

In the following sections, the detailed results of the performed experiments are presented.

---

[4] 800xahardwareselector.com/product/ci845.

6.1   Results on Connection Experiments

The connection experiments are executed for low and high load scenarios, with and without token-based authorization, with each test executed 1000 times. In order to perform a more detailed analysis, the total connection time is separated into open session, request token and activate session, following the protocol flow in Fig. 2a. Results for the experiments are presented in Table 1.

Table 1. Results from connection experiments. All results are given in milliseconds where μ is the average value and σ the standard deviation.

Authorization	None		Token	
	μ	σ	μ	σ
Low load				
Open session	15.0	3.3	15.1	3.3
Request Token	0	0	115.2	12.8
Activate session	100.0	12.3	193.9	12.9
Total	115.0	13.2	324.3	19.3
High load				
Open session	17.0	10.5	18.7	14.4
Request Token	0	0	213.8	69.0
Activate session	124.8	23.2	223.1	25.1
Total	141.6	29.0	455.6	88.6

When looking at the connection test results, an obvious additional cost when using access tokens is the time related to requesting the token from the authorization service. In our experiment this adds time representing a whole additional connect cycle, on average 115 ms in the low load scenario and as much as 213 ms in the high load one. For all these experiments, the client is creating a new session for each access token request. This points towards a first idea for optimizing the client implementation of the protocol by keeping the session to the authorization service open in the client.

Connections using access tokens not only increase in cost by the amount related to authorization service interactions of the client, a significant increase in time is needed also for the session activation, almost doubling the average session creation time. The experiment is not constructed to directly measure what in the session activation is most expensive, but a theoretical analysis of the protocol suggests the following possible sources for this extra time:

- Transport of the AuthZ token (which in this example is 1536 bytes after encryption).
- Encryption of the token on the client side.

- Decryption of token data on server side.
- Validation of token on server side.

The access token is already transported over an encrypted channel, so a second potential optimization of the protocol would be to remove the explicit encryption of the access token, which is added by the client.

There is a clear impact of the traffic loads for both authorization scenarios, especially on Activate Session and Request Token. By analyzing different traffic scenarios, we notice that network utilization and memory consumption for both the resource server and client are only marginally affected by the high load. What is hugely affected is the CPU load of the resource server, jumping from an average of 4% CPU utilization on each core in the low traffic scenario to about 40% for high traffic load.

6.2 Results on Access Resource Experiments

To evaluate the impact of the authorization protocol on accessing resources, three separate experiments are performed, for reading, writing and execution of a method, each one being executed 4000 times, for each of the different traffic scenarios. The results are presented in Table 2.

Table 2. Results from the resource access experiments, All results are given in milliseconds, where μ is the average value and σ the standard deviation.

Authorization	None		Token	
	μ	σ	μ	σ
Low load				
Read	3.2	1.5	3.3	1.7
Write	3.2	1.5	3.3	1.5
Execute	12.3	4.0	12.7	3.3
High load				
Read	2.2	1.6	2.2	1.7
Write	2.3	1.6	2.3	1.6
Execute	10.0	4.5	10.3	4.1

From the resource access experiment results, we can see that resource requests have similar completion time regardless of the used authorization protocol. This is expected, since the major overhead of the authorization protocol is related to session creation. In our experiment, a resource request related to read or write will on average take from 2 ms to 3 ms to complete, while the method execution has a completion time between 10 ms and 13 ms. It is worth noting that the method execution call is designed to return directly, i.e., there is a minimal amount of internal processing within the resource server related to executing the method.

The resource request times for the high-load scenario consistently outperform the low load scenario in our experiments. A theoretical analysis shows that the resource server handling of access requests is done by pulling working threads from a thread pool. A hypothesis is that in the low load scenario, the threads will be inactive before the next resource request arrives, while when there is a high load, this will not happen, meaning that the thread creation time is increasing the completion time of the low load resource requests. This is however out of the scope for this article to investigate, and is therefore not further explored.

6.3   Results on Different Token Expiry Times

Before an access token expires, the client of the session has the option to fetch a new AuthZ token from the authorization service, and use that to refresh the session. As demonstrated, session activation is a relatively expensive operation, the impact of token refresh is however not evaluated. By lowering the session expiry time, the amount of session refresh calls are increased. However, measuring the completion time for a session refresh explicitly is not very interesting, as it is executed during the time a session is already open, i.e., it does not directly affect session establishment.

The token expiry time may however impact resource requests. To investigate this, the read-resource experiment is repeated, but this time using sessions with different token expiry times. The client is configured to automatically refresh the tokens. Results from 1000 runs for three different expiry times are summarized in Table 3, for the low-traffic scenario. Additionally, we also report the maximum time to completion.

Table 3. Results for read resource experiment with different token expiry times. μ is the average value and σ is the standard deviation.

Token expiry time	μ	σ	max	min
8 s	4.6 ms	9.7 ms	139 ms	2.0 ms
28 s	3.3 ms	3.1 ms	60 ms	1.9 ms
96 s	3.1 ms	1.8 ms	45 ms	1.5 ms

Based on the gathered results, we can conclude that the expiry time does not affect the average value considerably, but the standard deviation is substantially increased with shorter expiry times. When a resource request coincides with a session refresh call to the resource server, the request may be delayed until the refresh is completed. The likelihood for such a coincidence is to a large extent depending on the expiry time, with a higher risk for a lower expiry time.

6.4   Result on Different Token Sizes

It is most likely the case that the different token sizes have impact on the session activation time, because of the cost for encryption and decryption of the token. To evaluate how the token size affects the connection time, the connection experiments are repeated, but with the issued AuthZ token having different sizes. A claim with configurable size has been added, after which the total token size was calculated (i.e., after encryption). For each token size, the connection experiment has been repeated 100 times. Results for average connection time in relation to size of the token are provided in Fig. 5. Please note that the session activation time remains stable (at around 220 ms) until token size reaches 4000 bytes, after which the time to connect increases proportionally.

6.5   Results on Lowering the CPU Clock Frequency of the Resource Server

CPU utilization of the resource server seems to be a determining factor for the completion time for at least the session establishment part of the protocol. The experiments so far have been done using a 1.5 GHz processor. In the following we repeat some of the experiments, but with the clock frequency of the CPU of the resource server lowered to 600 MHz (the lowest supported frequency of the Cortex A72), i.e., to 40% of the nominal performance. The aim is to get results comparable to the ones of an CI845, an industrial hardware platform developed by ABB used for various control service applications. Connection experiments results are given in Table 4.

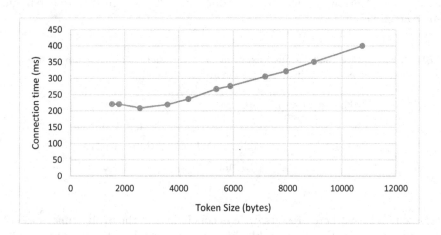

Fig. 5. Session activation time vs. token size

Table 4. Results on connection experiment using downgraded resource server CPU. All numbers are provided in milliseconds, μ is the average value and σ is the standard deviation. Percentages in parenthesis are compared to the original experiment.

Authorization	None		Token	
	μ	σ	μ	σ
Low load				
Open session	18.4 (+23%)	6.1	19.9 (+32%)	10.0
Request Token	0	0	149.8 (+30%)	31.9
Activate session	163.5 (+63%)	31.4	216.7 (+12%)	33.7
Total	182.0 (+58%)	33.7	386.7 (+14%)	51.1
High load				
Open session	21.6 (+27%)	7.2	33.8 (+81%)	85.5
Request Token	0	0	216.1 (+1%)	84.5
Activate session	196.0 (+57%)	22.0	364.7 (+63%)	58.7
Total	217.7 (+54%)	25.2	614.7 (+35%)	211.7

Compared to the previous experiments in Sect. 6.1, the total completion time for connection establishment increases between 14% and 60%.

As the completion time for the different experiments related to accessing resources are very similar, only the read experiment using token authorization has been repeated in this setting, for low and high traffic scenarios. For low traffic, the average time for read was 4.4 ms (+38%), with $\sigma = 3.2$ ms and for high traffic average completion time was 3.8 ms (+72%), with $\sigma = 1.8$ ms. The results follow the patterns of the initial experiments, but with completion times increasing on a similar scale as the connection establishment experiment.

This confirm the assumption that the completion time in our experiment is highly dependent on the CPU power of the resource server. The standard deviation also increases significantly, especially in the high-load scenario. This implies that our selected high-load scenario may be beyond the limit of what this configuration of the resource server can handle while staying within predictable operational boundaries.

7   Suggestions on Optimizations of Session Activation

Based on the analysis of the experiment results, we suggest two potential optimizations for the authorization protocol implementation: 1) In the client to keep the session to authorization service(s) open, and 2) to remove the explicit encryption of the access token if it is already being transported using an encrypted channel.

Both suggested optimizations are implemented and then evaluated using the same experimental setup as the initial experiments related to connection establishment. Results are provided in Table 5. As the optimization only affects the session establishment, the experiments for resource requests are not repeated.

Table 5. Experimental results of optimization of session activation. All numbers are given in milliseconds, μ is the average value and σ is the standard deviation.

Improvement	Keep session		Single encryption		Combined	
	μ	σ	μ	σ	μ	σ
Low load						
Open session	14.1	3.0	13.8	5.5	15.0	6.3
Request Token	7.3	4.4	128.5	32.7	7.1	4.1
Activate session	191.0	10.9	142.6	13.6	143.6	15.8
Total	212.5	13.4	285.0	38.3	165.8	20.8
High load						
Open session	15.4	9.8	16.1	15.0	13.1	3.5
Request Token	10.8	7.5	160.3	50.7	8.2	3.4
Activate session	208.3	25.2	151.8	35.5	148.1	12.5
Total	234.4	32.9	328.2	69.0	169.5	15.5

As can be seen, keeping a session to the authorization service provides a large performance increase on the token request part of the protocol, going from an average of 115 ms (Table 1, low load req. token) down to 7 ms in our experiment. Removing the double encryption enables a significant gain during the session activation phase, down to about 50 ms in our experiment.

The best performance gain is reached by combining these two approaches, both caching the authorization service session and removing the double encryption. Using this combination cuts the connection time to between 50% and 37% of the initial implementation. This results in the total difference between using no authorization and using the authorization protocol with access tokens to be reduced to about 50 ms in our experiment (115.0 ms with no authorization compared to 165.8 ms), and is even lower for the high-traffic scenarios.

Repeating the experiment with different token sizes with the single encryption optimization in place indicates that the size of the token no longer has an impact on the session activation time, i.e., in our experiments all the measurable additional time related to the size of the AuthZ token is related to the explicit token encryption.

8 Discussion

The performed experiments have shown some important and interesting properties of the authorization protocol. Authorization in the way it is implemented in this architecture, will have no measurable impact on individual resource requests, but have significant impact on session establishment. For sporadic resource requests that include establishing a new session to a resource server, a majority of the response time will be related to the session establishment. This is also the case for scenario without using the enforcement architecture.

The session establishment time is increasing when the traffic load towards the resource server is increasing. In particular, the standard deviation for the high-load scenario is increasing for the connection time when the enforcement architecture is used. This due to the authorization protocol containing several additional steps in which uncertainty is introduced. However, for resource requests, the higher traffic load has no adverse effect on completion times in our experiment. The architecture scales well with regards to resource requests, but may have issues for session establishment. This is even more visible for the results with a lower resource server CPU clock frequency. The completion time increases and are on average in the same order as the CPU performance downgrade, but the standard deviation for connection establishment using the enforcement architecture is almost tripled.

When analyzing the impact of using short-lived access tokens, the results point in a similar direction. The average completion time related to resource requests is close to the initial experiments, but the standard deviation increases as the expiry time is decreased. The risk of a resource request coinciding with the session re-activation call increases with a short token expiry time. For minimizing this impact, the client could be implemented to avoid resource requests while a session-reactivation is on-going. With a shorter token expiry time, the flexibility of the access control mechanism increases. Generally, using a short expiry time in a large system will generate a lot of traffic both between clients and authorization services, and clients and resource servers.

For the initial experiments on session establishment, the completion time is on average three times higher when using the described authorization protocol. The majority of additional time is spent during token request and session activation. Combining two simple suggestions of performance optimization, the session establishment phase of the authorization protocol is brought to numbers comparable to the baseline scenario when using no authorization.

The first performance optimization is a pure client implementation, and is using the assumption that many resource servers will outsource their policy decisions to the same authorization service. Therefore it is a good idea to keep a session of an authorization service open to be used for subsequent AuthZ token requests. This will have a slight memory consumption hit for the client and authorization service. The exact impact for the authorization service is not further evaluated in this article. However, for a larger systems with many clients there may be negative scalability effects of that approach for the authorization service, especially on memory consumption. On the other hand, establishing a new session with the authorization service for each resource request and client will have a much higher impact on the authorization service CPU utilization.

The second performance optimization is related to encryption and decryption of the AuthZ token. If the client is communicating with the resource server using an unencrypted session, it is important that the AuthZ token is encrypted. Otherwise this provides an opportunity for token to be stolen and misused by a threat actor. However, if the session is already encrypted, there is no obvious need for the AuthZ token to also be encrypted. The default behavior of the .NET stack is to use asymmetric encryption of the AuthZ token, which leads to a huge additional time needed for the resource server to perform decryption of the token. Removing this "double encryption" is possible within the resource server OPC UA configuration. However, using this option may lead to other unwanted behavior of the server, e.g., the same option is used to remove validation of the client nonce on session establishment. This optimization will therefore need some additional rounds of analysis before being used in a real-world system.

If keeping the encryption of the AuthZ token, the size of the token will have a direct impact on the completion time for session establishment, as shown in Sect. 6.4. Therefore it is desirable to attempt to minimize the size of the token. For dynamic access control this may be a challenging task, as the policy decision from the authorization service will have to be expressed in a very detailed way. Further investigations by continuing the work in [11] are needed to find the right balance between the high granularity and sufficiently compact token encoding. Furthermore, there is a practical size limitation of the AuthZ token in the OPC UA .NET stack is set to 256 kb, which should be sufficient for most needs, but may be an actual limitation in more complex scenarios.

8.1   Recommendations

Based on the experimental results and experiences from implementing the enforcement architecture, a few basic advice and recommendations can be provided.

From the client side one should **keep sessions active**, if several resources requests are likely to be performed towards the same resource server. This recommendation is applicable regardless of the enforcement architecture. It provides extra benefits with regards to authorization service sessions as described above.

Avoid double encryption, especially asymmetric encryption/decryption that is CPU intensive, and can cause a high penalty on a low resource embedded device.

If using token encryption, **keep token size small** as time to perform encryption/decryption increases with token size.

Find the **right balance for token expiry times**. A short expiry time will have an impact on scalability properties of the system, including resource request performance, as session refresh can interfere with ordinary resource requests. The longer the expiry time, the higher the risk of outdated permissions being used in the system. In the performed experiments, an expiry time of a few minutes have a rather low likelihood of negatively impacting performance, but this will depend on the size and complexity of the system.

If using the described enforcement protocol in a control-loop with real-time requirements, the completion time should be carefully measured in the target system, to guarantee that deadlines can be met and that the jitter for resource requests are kept at acceptable levels. In such a scenario it is most likely that there is no need for short token expiry times. Please note that there are other potentially more deterministic methods for real-time control in OPC UA, e.g., using the publish/subscribe pattern, which however cannot provide as flexible access control possibilities.

The typical use-case for this enforcement architecture would be for high level control and supervision, i.e., on the communication between an operator HMI and (several) resource servers, or for the workflow orchestration part of, e.g., modular automation, as described in [9]. In these use-cases the cycle-times are often not that high and may even be event-based, while the access control policies are more dynamic in nature, based on the currently executing workflows in the system.

8.2 Limitations and Impact

The precise results of the described experiments are limited to the materialization and implementation of the hardware and software components used. For different system with other components, the completion times most likely will differ. However, we believe that the results provide good indications of the completion times for the described phases of the authorization protocol, especially the relative performance of the protocol compared to the baseline.

A drawback of using .NET to measure quality metrics is its lack of real-time characteristics, as e.g., memory management is out of control for the programmer. A garbage collection may occur at any time, which can have huge effect on a particular measurement. Furthermore, operating system overhead may be larger and more unpredictable when using Windows (for the client) and Ubuntu for the resource server, as compared to using real-time operating systems. To counter these issues, we have repeated the experiments a large number of times to decrease the impact of sporadic disturbances.

As mentioned, the inference time of the authorization service is set to a minimum in the experimental setup. In reality, this inference time will of course be larger and have an impact on the performance of the session establishment. Measuring this impact is out of scope for this work, but may be interesting to look at as part of a future experiment.

9 Conclusions

Dynamic fine-grained authorization is a requirement for the future industrial automation and control systems, which will be network-centric, dynamic and flexible, using a Zero-trust security model. Very few technologies are available which can provide such characteristics for industrial systems. The OPC UA protocol is currently the best option, if using the authorization flow based on outsourced policy decisions to an authorization service.

In this work, we have analyzed, implemented and evaluated several aspects of this variant of access control enforcement architecture, something that is not previously done.

The experiments show that for resource requests there is no measurable additional cost of the authorization protocol. However for short AuthZ token expiry times, which will result in frequent session refresh calls, the standard deviation of the resource request is increasing. The expiry time is therefore one important design decision which is a trade-off between the level of dynamicity of the architecture and the standard deviation of resource requests.

There is a large difference in the connection establishment times between using fine-grained access control and no authorization, which is further impacted by increasing traffic load. However, two suggestions for optimizations are provided that limit this impact. One is related to the session handling in the client, while the other is related to avoiding double encryption of the AuthZ token. Combining these two optimizations more than halves the average connection establishment time compared to the initial approach.

Limitations. The experimental evaluation required a number of implementations to fully support the described authorization protocol. These implementations clearly have an impact on the results of the evaluations and any misinterpretations of the standard, or bad design decisions can limit the validity of the results.

In this article we aim to have an experimental scenario were the resource server and client are similar to what could be expected in an industrial system. However, the required implementation was not possible to run on an embedded real-time system. To partly counter this, the CPU-, memory- and network-utilization are measured during the experiments, leading to the realization that the CPU-frequency is the deciding factor. This was confirmed by repeating some of the experiments with the CPU of the resource server clocked down to 40%, leading to results with equally longer completion time.

Future Work. The inference time of the Authorization Service is not accounted for in our evaluation, as the authorization service always returns the same claims, encoded in a correct token. Therefore, it is our plan to include the inference time for different variants of policy decision mechanisms in the authorization service in our future work.

Once there exist commercial or open-source implementations of the authorization flow, we would like to repeat the evaluation using a resource server running a real-time operating system on an embedded device.

Detailed threat modeling and analysis is not covered in this work, but is another important future investigation.

Acknowledgements. This work is supported by ABB AB; the industrial postgraduate school Automation Region Research Academy (ARRAY), funded by The Knowledge Foundation; and the Horizon 2020 project InSecTT. InSecTT (www.insectt.eu) has received funding from the ECSEL Joint Undertaking (JU) under grant agreement No 876038. The JU receives support from the European Union's Horizon 2020 research and innovation programme and Austria, Sweden, Spain, Italy, France, Portugal, Ireland, Finland, Slovenia, Poland, Netherlands, Turkey[8] (The document reflects only the author's view and the Commission is not responsible for any use that may be made of the information it contains.)

References

1. Sigov, A., Ratkin, L., Ivanov, L.A., Xu, L.D.: Emerging enabling technologies for industry 4.0 and beyond. Inform. Syst. Front. 1–11 (2022). https://doi.org/10.1007/s10796-021-10213-w
2. Thoben, K.D., Wiesner, S., Wuest, T.: Industrie 4.0 and smart manufacturing - a review of research issues and application examples. Intl. J. Autom. Technol. **11**(1), 4–16 January (2017)
3. Lu, Y.: Industry 4.0: a survey on technologies, applications and open research issues. J. Ind. Inf. Integr. **6**, 1–10 (2017)
4. Zanasi, C., Magnanini, F., Russo, S., Colajanni, M.: A zero trust approach for the cybersecurity of industrial control systems. In: 2022 IEEE 21st International Symposium on Network Computing and Applications (NCA), vol. 21, pp. 1–7, (2022)
5. Leander, B., Johansson, B., Lindström, T., Holmström, O., Nolte, T., Papadopoulos, A.V.: Dependability and Security Aspects of Network-Centric Control. In: 28th IEEE International Conference on Emerging Technologies and Factory Automation (ETFA), IEEE (2023)
6. Saltzer, J.H., Schroeder, M.D.: The Protection of Information in Computer Systems. In: proceedings of the IEEE, vol. 63, pp. 1278–1308, September (1975)
7. Rose, S., Borchert, O., Mitchell, S., Connelly, S.: Zero Trust Architecture tech. rep., National Institute of Standards and Technology, Gaithersburg, MD. Aug (2020)
8. Sandhu, R., Ranganathan, K., Zhang, X.: Secure information sharing enabled by trusted computing and PEI models. In: Proceedings of the 2006 ACM Symposium on Information, Computer and Communications Security, ASIACCS '06, vol. 2006, pp. 2–12 (2006)
9. Leander, B., Čaušević, A., Hansson, H., Lindström, T.: Toward an ideal access control strategy for industry 4.0 manufacturing systems. IEEE Access **9**, 114037–114050 (2021)
10. Knorr, K.: Dynamic access control through Petri net workflows. In: Proceedings - Annual Computer Security Applications Conference, ACSAC, vol. 2000-January, pp. 159–167 (2000)
11. Leander, B., Čaušević, A., Lindström, T., Hansson, H.: Access control enforcement architectures for dynamic manufacturing systems. In: 2023 IEEE 20th International Conference on Software Architecture (ICSA), pp. 82–92 (2023)
12. IEC 62541 OPC unified architecture, standard, International Electrotechnical Commission, Geneva, CH (2016)
13. Alcaraz, C., Lopez, J., Wolthusen, S.: Policy enforcement system for secure interoperable control in distributed smart grid systems. J. Netw. Comput. Appl. **59**, 301–314 (2016)

14. Martinelli, F., Osliak, O., Mori, P., Saracino, A.: Improving security in industry 4.0 by extending OPC-UA with usage control. In: 15th International Conference on Availability, Reliability and Security, ACM, (2020)
15. Park, J., Sandhu, R.: The UCON$_{ABC}$ usage control model. ACM Trans. Inform. Syst. Secur. **7**(1), 128–174 (2004)
16. Cavalieri, S., Chiacchio, F.: Analysis of OPC UA performances. Comput. Stand. Interfaces **36**(1), 165–177 (2013)
17. Kohnhäuser, F., Coppik, N., Mendoza, F., Kumari, A.: On the feasibility and performance of secure OPC UA communication with IIoT Devices. Lecture Notes in Computer Science, vol. 13414 LNCS, pp. 189–203 (2022)
18. Rocha, M.S., Sestito, G.S., Dias, A.L., Turcato, A.C., Brandao, D.: Performance comparison between OPC UA and MQTT for Data Exchange. In: 2018 Workshop on Metrology for Industry 4.0 and IoT, MetroInd 4.0 and IoT 2018 - Proceedings, pp. 175–179 (2018)
19. MQTT Version 5.0, OASIS Standard, March 2019. Edited by Andrew Banks, Ed Briggs, Ken Borgendale, and Rahul Gupta
20. Burger, A., Koziolek, H., Rückert, J., Platenius-Mohr, M., Stomberg, G.: Bottleneck identification and performance modeling of OPC UA communication models. In: ICPE 2019 - Proceedings of the 2019 ACM/SPEC International Conference on Performance Engineering, pp. 231–242 (2019)
21. Silva, D., Carvalho, L.I., Soares, J., Sofia, R.C.: A performance analysis of internet of things networking. Appl. Sci. **11**(4879), 1–30 (2021)
22. Ladegourdie, M., Kua, J.: Performance analysis of OPC UA for industrial interoperability towards industry 4.0. IoT **3**(4), 507–525 (2022)
23. eXtensible Access Control Markup Language (XACML) Version 3. 0 Plus Errata 01, OASIS Standard incorporating Approved Errata., July 2017. Edited by Erik Rissanen
24. Hu, V.C.: Guide to Attribute Based Access Control (ABAC) Definition and Considerations. tech. rep., NIST (2014)
25. Bengtsson, J., Larsson, F., Larsen, K., Pettersson, P., Yi, W.: "UPPAAL - a Tool for Automatic Verifictation of Real-Time Systems," DoCS Technical Report Nr 96/97, Uppsala University, January (2016)
26. Jones, M., Bradley, J., Sakimura, N.: JSON Web Token (JWT). RFC 7519, May (2015)

HoneyEVSE: An Honeypot to Emulate Electric Vehicle Supply Equipments

Massimiliano Baldo$^{(\boxtimes)}$, Tommaso Bianchi⬡, Mauro Conti⬡, Alessio Trevisan, and Federico Turrin⬡

University of Padova, Padua, Italy
{massimiliano.baldo,alessio.trevisan.2}@studenti.unipd.it,
{tommaso.bianchi,federico.turrin}@phd.unipd.it, mauro.conti@unipd.it

Abstract. To fight climate change, new "green" technology are emerging, most of them using electricity as a power source. Among the solutions, Electric Vehicles (EVs) represent a central asset in the future transport system. EVs require a complex infrastructure to enable the so-called Vehicle-to-Grid (V2G) paradigm to manage the charging process between the smart grid and the EV. In this paradigm, the Electric Vehicle Supply Equipment (EVSE), or charging station, is the end device that authenticates the vehicle and delivers the power to charge it. However, since an EVSE is publicly exposed and connected to the Internet, recent works show how an attacker with physical tampering and remote access can target an EVSE, exposing the security of the entire infrastructure and the final user. For this reason, it is important to develop novel strategies to secure such infrastructures.

In this paper we present HoneyEVSE, the first honeypot conceived to simulate an EVSE. HoneyEVSE can simulate with high fidelity the EV charging process and, at the same time, enables a user to interact with it through a dashboard. Furthermore, based on other charging columns exposed on the Internet, we emulate the login and device information pages to increase user engagement. We exposed HoneyEVSE for 30 days to the Internet to assess its capability and measured the interaction received with its Shodan Honeyscore. Results show that HoneyEVSE can successfully evade the Shodan honeyscore metric while attracting a high number of interactions on the exposed services.

Keywords: Honeypot · V2G · EVSE · Measurement · Security

1 Introduction

To fight climate change, novel technologies are emerging to reduce the emission footprint. Among the different promising solutions, Electric Vehicle (EV) aims at substituting traditional fossil-fueled vehicles to achieve better performances and fewer emissions. According to Statista [33], by 2027, the number of EV sold in the market will be around 16.21 m. To manage such a huge amount of vehicles is required an ad-hoc infrastructure. Indeed, to deliver the energy needed to

© The Author(s), under exclusive license to Springer Nature Switzerland AG 2024
S. Katsikas et al. (Eds.): ESORICS 2023 Workshops, LNCS 14398, pp. 145–159, 2024.
https://doi.org/10.1007/978-3-031-54204-6_8

recharge EVs, a connection between the EV and the power grid is required. The paradigm that regulates such a connection is called Vehicle-to-Grid (V2G). V2G paradigm includes three main entities: 1) the smart grid, which generates and distributes electric energy; 2) the EV that represents the end-user asking for a recharge 3) the charging column, or Electric Vehicle Supply Equipment (EVSE), that authenticate the EV and deliver the energy.

Managing a distributed and complex architecture is very challenging, including from the cybersecurity perspective. In fact, recent works showed the feasibility of a wide range of attacks on V2G infrastructure, particularly the EVSE devices. EVSE are publicly exposed and therefore subject to physical manumission by malicious actors. Attacks that have been proven effective in targeting EVSE include relay attack [11], charging traces profiling [8], eavesdropping [6], and denial of service [18]. The threats affecting EVSE are even more emphasized by recent work highlighting the lack of security policies and the exposition to the Internet, opening dangerous vulnerabilities surfaces to the user [27].

Motivation. Being a relatively recent technology, the security of V2G paradigm and, in particular, EVSE devices is still under investigation, several novel attacks have been identified, and therefore research still requires contribution in this direction. To this end, honeypots can support the research of new security mechanisms. The goal of a honeypot is twofold: it can be used to deceive the attackers, making them think they are interacting with a real device and collecting data about the attackers' movements. To develop more robust defense mechanisms, data collected from honeypot can then be analyzed to understand the typical attackers' strategies and scanning campaigns. Honeypots, are widely adopted to emulate Information Technology (IT) devices or services. However, their application in the Cyber-Physical System (CPS) domain is still under development, mainly due to the difficulty in replicating devices and physical processes with high fidelity [12].

Contribution. In this paper, we present HoneyEVSE, the first honeypot conceived to emulate an EVSE. To build an effective honeypot with high fidelity, we based our implementation on the exposed EVSE device we identified and the related work analyzing the exposure of such systems [27]. To mimic a realistic charging process, we leveraged the ACN-sim simulator, while the network personality engine is managed by a customized version of Honeyd that incorporated EVSE functionalities. We exposed HoneyEVSE for 30 days on a local Internet Exchange Point (IXP), and we measured different engagement results, as commands exchanged with the Web app, the time spent on each page by the user, and the origin of the IPs. Results show that HoneyEVSE can successfully evade Shodan's Hoenyscore while receiving a high number of interactions from users. We release the source code of HoneyEVSE on github[1], and we summarize the contribution of the paper in the following:

- We present HoneyEVSE, the first honeypot conceived to emulate an EVSE. In HoneyEVSE, we integrate a high-fidelity physical process and the possibility for an attacker to interact with the dashboard.

---

[1] Repository: https://github.com/spritz-group/HoneyEVSE.

- We exposed HoneyEVSE to the Internet for 30 days, and we report the results of the interactions received. The results highlight the good level of interaction received by HoneyEVSE.

Organization. The paper is organized as follows. Section 2 briefly recalls the concepts useful to understand the remainder of the paper, while Sect. 3 discusses the related work. Section 4 introduces HoneyEVSE honeypot structure and functionalities, then Sect. 5 presents the measurement study we performed by exposing HoneyEVSE to the Internet. Finally, Sect. 6 concludes the paper.

2   Background

In the following, we briefly recall the main concepts useful to understand the remainder of the paper. In particular, Sect. 2.1 recalls the IXP infrastructure, where we based our evaluation phase. Then Sect. 2.2 and Sect. 2.3 briefly recall, respectively, the concept of honeypot and V2G infrastructure.

2.1   Internet Exchange Point

An IXP is a network facility that enables the interconnection and Internet traffic exchange between two or more independent Autonomous Systems (ASs) through specific peering agreements and according to the Border Gateway Protocol (BGP) routing configurations. Its typical architecture consists of single or multiple switches connected to the adherent's border routers of the adherent ASs, ensuring bandwidth, costs, and latency benefits. An AS comprises a group of IP prefixes controlled by a single Internet Service Provider (ISP), which defines the routing policies. The Interior Gateway Protocol (IGP) enables the routing within an AS, while communication with other ASs relies on the BGP. An IXP network facility enables Internet traffic interconnection between more than two independent ASs.

Our analysis relies on *VSIX* [3], an IXP which manages the traffic circulating in the North East of Italy. In this work, we installed a honeypot in VSIX and exposed it to the Internet. The system architecture of the IXP representation, together with the honeypot, is represented in Fig. 1. Thanks to their infrastructure VSIX allows us to integrate many interesting features to the honeypot exposed. In particular, the IP dedicated to the honeypot has been announced worldwide thanks to the transit provider, allowing high visibility worldwide. Furthermore, VSIX offers high resilience thanks to a BGP multihomed system and supports a connection speed of up to 1 Gb/s.

2.2   Honeypot

Honeypots are systems designed to protect systems and, at the same time, collect information related to attacker actions. Once deployed, honeypots are exposed

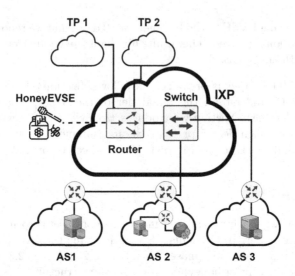

Fig. 1. IXP System representation and corresponding installation point of the honeypot.

over the Internet and may include exploitable vulnerabilities and services. If carefully monitorod, honeypots allow for obtaining a lot of information and insights about the attacks registered.

Honeypots are classified based on the level of interaction they offer to an attacker. *Pure Honeypots* are real machines installed and exposed in the production network (e.g., PLC exposed but not employed in controlling processes). Although this seems to be the best approach to installing a honeypot, it also has disadvantages, most notably its cost. *High-Interaction Honeypots* are generally real computers, or virtual machines, that simulate with high fidelity all the services of the emulated machine. They allow a high level of interaction with the emulated system. *Low-Interaction Honeypots* are software that emulates the operating system and services provided by the simulated device. They are easy to install and maintain but, due to the lower degree of engagement it provides, make it possible to capture less information. Furthermore, honeypots can also be classified based on their scope. *Production Honeypots* are usually low-interaction and simple to install and use. They are located within an enterprise production network along with production servers. Their primary function is not to collect information but to raise the alarm if detecting an attacker's presence. *Research Honeypots*, contrary to the previous typology, aims at collecting as much information as possible about potential attackers. For this reason, they require a higher level of interaction.

In our work, we developed a *High-Interaction Research* honeypot specifically designed to simulate an EVSE.

2.3 Vehicle-to-Grid (V2G)

The V2G paradigm (depicted in Fig. 2) creates a bidirectional communication between an EV and a power grid. Among the different advantages, the bi-directionality of communication allows smart management of the charging process and enables the EV to create a bidirectional power flow with the grid.

The V2G paradigm includes different entities: the power grid, responsible for generating electricity, the distribution network, which involves all the infrastructures to deliver the energy demanded to the final user; the EVSE that authenticates the end user and deliver the energy, and the EV that represents the end user and requires the energy delivery. To authenticate the user, the EVSE is generally connected to an energy provider and accounts for the EV energy demand. EVSEs include different components: charging station, charging cable, and charging connector. The last one is usually attached to the cable [5]. The EVSE performs all the actions required to recharge the EV and interface it with the V2G infrastructure. Moreover, an EVSE usually integrates a graphical interface to allow users to monitor and control the state of the charge of their vehicle. The technology implemented in an EVSE can differ from manufacturers, but it usually relies on an HTTP service for a Web App interface, an SSH connection for remote access by an administrator, and different kinds of connectivity such as WiFi or Bluetooth [2]. Additionally, an EVSE can support MQ Telemetry Transport (MQTT) connection in the case of aggregated EVSE, for example, as a charging station with multiple columns. We can divide the V2G communication into the front-end and back-end. Back-end communication enables the exchanges of data and energy between the EVSE and the distribution network. The most adopted protocol in this type of communication is the Open Charge Point Protocol (OCPP) [14]. Similarly to back-end communication, front-end communication includes both power and data delivery. Different standards have been proposed for front-end communications to regulate the communication between the EV and the EVSE. The most widely adopted protocols for the front-end communication between the vehicle and the EVSE are ISO 15118, SAE J2847, and CHAdeMO. Among them, the most advanced standard is ISO 15118 [15,16] which supports many services, including secure authentication, vehicle firmware update, and plug-and-charge [9].

3 Related Work

To the best of our knowledge, HoneyEVSE is the first honeypot conceived to emulate an EVSE; therefore, there is no other literature to compare with. However, honeypots are a warm topic, and significant efforts have been produced in this research direction [13]. In the IT domain, honeypots have been used to emulate common IT services such as Databases [10], Web Servers [31], or Internet of Things (IoT) devices [22]. This family of honeypots is the most commonly investigated in the literature also due to its simplicity of emulation: they are just required to replicate a service in a protected environment. Other than the IT domain, honeypots are highly studied in the CPS domain [13]. Particular focus

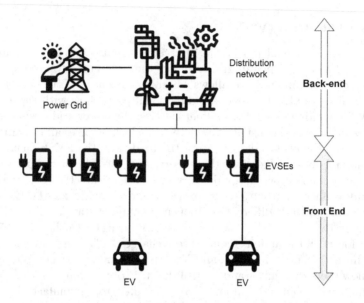

Fig. 2. The basic architecture of a V2G environment.

has been dedicated to the Industrial domain, which has been shown to be dramatically exposed to cyberattacks in recent years [7]. To protect such systems, several honeypots have been proposed [21] ranging from water systems [26, 29] to smart grids [4, 23]. The most difficult part in developing this type of honeypot is emulating a real physical process with the possibility of interacting with it by the attacker. Indeed only a few honeypots aim at addressing this challenge [12]. A few Honeypots have also been proposed to replicate a vehicular domain [28, 32]. However, these honeypots are specifically designed to replicate vehicular ad-hoc networks, but none consider the V2G communication paradigm together with its specific devices.

Among the other numerous CPS domains, the EV field is nowadays under the spotlight. This is mainly due to the pervasive proliferation of this technology in daily life but also due to research highlighting the current security flaws of such a system. Indeed, different researchers have successfully proven attacks on V2G infrastructure, where the entry point is mostly the EVSE. These attacks include relay attack [11], charging traces profiling [8], eavesdropping [6], and denial of service [18]. Furthermore, recent research has shown the problematic exposure of the EVSE to the internet [27]. Driven by this emerging threat, we present HoneyEVSE to support the security community to protect EVSE and, at the same time, collect data about attackers' moves.

4 HoneyEVSE Honeypot

HoneyEVSE, as a honeypot, is designed to deceive attacks targeting real EVSE and retrieve information about the techniques used by attackers. It emulates the charging process of electric vehicles, exposing information through a web application accessible from the Internet. The general functioning and architecture are inspired by two previous projects: HoneyPLC [21] and ICSPot [12].

In this Section, we first introduce HoneyEVSE. In Sect. 4.1, we describe the honeypot architecture and, in Sect. 4.2, Sect. 4.3, and Sect. 4.4, the technical aspects of HoneyEVSE concerning the physical process, the exposed services, and the logs, respectively.

4.1 Architecture

HoneyEVSE integrates different components to generate the physical process, the network exposition, and the interaction logging. In Fig. 3, we show the graphical representation of the honeypot architecture. The core part of HoneyEVSE is Honeyd [30], a tool that emulates the TCP/IP network stack and defines the honeypot network profile. It allows the system to differentiate the IP and MAC addresses from the ones of the hosting computer and trigger the different components of the systems once the interaction is received.

The only necessary step to use Honeyd is to provide, in a configuration file, the parameters for the implemented services, the IP address on which we want to route the honeypot communication, and the physical interface (MAC address) of the IP of the hosting machine. Honeyd module is then linked to the physical process simulating the charging activity and a logging system.

4.2 Physical Process

To make the honeypot as real as possible from an external perspective, we introduce a physical process emulating the vehicle's charging. The physical process leverages ACN Portal [17], a tool suite that allows EV researchers to develop and test practical solutions. ACN Portal, accessible via public API, combines ACN-Data [20] and ACN-Sim [19]. The former is a dataset containing a data collection of charging sessions of real EV, gathered by the authors through EVSE installed at the Caltech Institute of Technology. The latter is a simulation environment for EV charges which enables the study of algorithms for scheduling the power and the time of the charging processes. HoneyEVSE uses ACN Portal to simulate the underlying physical process and create reliable and truthful charging operations to deceive the attacker. In particular, we leveraged these tools to generate real-time EV charging traces and build a GUI with an interactive dashboard to monitor and interact with the charging process, similar to what happens in real life. However, the default charging traces generation of the ACN Portal presents some limitations. The representation of the EV and the EV is limited to a single case: a completely discharged vehicle with a single static template of charging parameters; therefore ACN-Sim does not allow for including

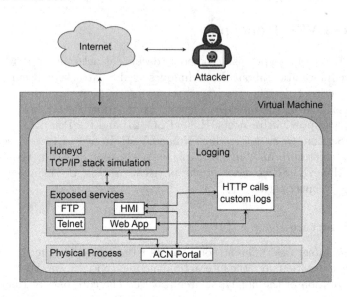

Fig. 3. HoneyEVSE architecture.

variability in the charging process. Furthermore, ACN-Sim charging parameters do not include helpful information to replicate a real-world scenario: energy required to fill the battery, current completion percentage, and the recharge cost. Excluding this information does not allow to achieve a high fidelity level of the physical process. In the HoneyEVSE physical process, we address these limitations by improving the data generation and estimating the parameters from the traces generated. In particular, we associate each charging trace generated by fictional vehicles with random arrival and departure times, energy requests (e.g., the power required by the vehicle), and battery parameters (e.g., capacity). In this way, an external viewer has the feeling to interact with a real environment. As previously said, ACN-Sim does not include the case where the initial charge of the car's battery is greater than zero. This may raise some warning in the attacker that would always see a completely discharged vehicle. We addressed this limitation by developing a heuristic to calculate a random plausible initial status using the default information provided by ACN-Sim and considering the charging demand of the specific vehicle and its overall requested energy.

4.3   Services and Interaction

HoneyEVSE exposed three different services: a web interface to let the attacker interact with and the traditional Telnet and File Transfer Protocol (FTP) services to mimic the possibility of remotely updating or controlling charging columns. The web interface is built by taking as a reference the EVSE we found in the wild using Shodan [25] upon a preliminary analysis.

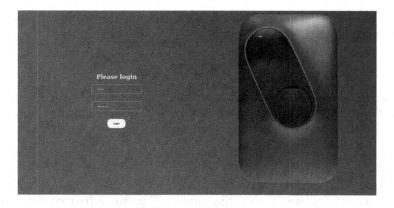

Fig. 4. Login page replicated from Etrel EVSE

HTTP. Inspired by what we and related work found exposed on the Internet, we mock a web application of a charging column. The web interface reports the data generated by the physical process, the EVSE technical details of the charging column, and a login page. On the root page, the interface shows technical information about the EVSE. We copied the layout and template of such information from existing exposed EVSE and modified the existing information. We implemented a dedicated dashboard with a real-time charging process to monitor the physical process from the perspective of the EV owner that is recharging the car. This dashboard includes three buttons: Stop, Pause, and Resume Charge, and they represent the possible interaction of a user with the charging column. Furthermore, we implemented an admin dashboard with information and statistics on the different vehicles attached and the demands from the grid. This page represents the overview of the different processes occurring on the EVSEs that the admin generally monitors. These three pages are hosted on port 5000. On port 80, we also implemented a *login* and *registration* pages to mock login and logon procedures of users and company employees. The actions performed using these forms are logged, and every login attempts returns an error by default. We copied the login page template from Etrel EVSE exposed on the Internet. Indeed, according to our preliminary analysis and related work [27], this type of charging column is widely exposed on the Internet.

FTP. The FTP allows the file transmission over TCP/IP connections. The service is open on port 21, waiting for commands. This behavior emulates an administrator's ability to remotely perform firmware updates or web application changes. The exposed service waits for a user to log in but always retrieves an error during the login phase. Thanks to this service, we can monitor the possible attempts of an attacker to access the EVSE.

Telnet. This protocol allows two-way unencrypted text-based communication between two machines. It provides access to a virtual terminal in the remote system, and it can be used to control the EVSE. This service uses port 23. As for FTP, the system returns an error during the communication to avoid possible exploits. Meanwhile, it collects data about the attacker's attempts to access the EVSE through Telnet.

4.4 Data Logging

HoneyEVSE includes a logging module connected to the Web App interface to record the interaction with the accessible services. The web app logger intercepts different communications and divides the logs into three main categories:

- **Port**. We store in the logging file the number of port with wich the attacker interact;
- **Actions**. The physical process dashboard contains three buttons that enable a user to manipulate the charging process. The three buttons are "Stop," "Pause," and "Resume" and they include a javascript linked to them to log in when a person clicks on them. Furthermore, to simulate a user's interaction with the charging columns, the buttons trigger the corresponding actions in the physical process.
- **HTTP Requests**. We log the HTTP requests directed to the honeypot. The log file includes the specific page requested, the Uniform Resource Locator (URL) that can contain a malicious payload, the request code, and the request result;
- **Timing**. We also report each user's time on a specific page. To do this, we use the TimeMe.js[2] javascript library.

In all of these log types, we store the IP of the remote host generating the action, along with the time and date of the log.

5   Results

We exposed for 30 days an instance of HoneyEVSE through a virtual machine hosted by VSIX IXP. We verified the honeyscore assigned from Shodan to HoneyEVSE as a preliminary analysis. The honeyscore is a score from 0 to 1 that Shodan assigns to an IP address and corresponds to the likelihood that a specific IP is a honeypot. Ideally, the goal is to achieve a lower Honeyscore as possible. In this way, an attacker cannot understand that it is interacting with a honeypot. Unfortunately, Shodan has not released detailed information on the computation of the honeyscore. However, in [24], the author states that the computation is based on a combination of metrics: (1) the number of open ports; (2) matching between services and the environment (3) honeypots default settings; (4) the IP history; (5) a not disclosed Machine Learning algorithm. Shodan could not assign a score to HoneyEVSE, meaning our honeypot can successfully camouflage to Shodan's detection. In the following, we describe the results by means of interaction received on the web application and the IPs originating the scan. We present first in Sect. 5.1 an analysis of the interaction received by HoneyEVSE, then in Sect. 5.2 we present an analysis of the actors we registered.

---

[2] https://github.com/jasonzissman/TimeMe.js.

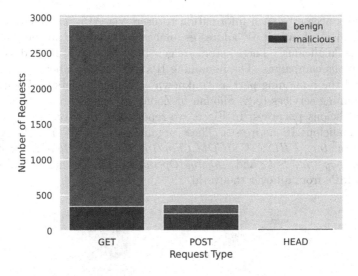

Fig. 5. Type of interactions received.

5.1 Interactions Analysis

After 30 days of data collection, we report a total of 3293 HTTP requests
on the three different pages. Specifically, we found 2899 GET requests, 366
POST requests, and 28 HEAD requests. In the following, we analyze the type of
HTTP requests received. We define a request as malicious if it contains patterns recalling an attack behavior or attempt. For instance, the request for
the URL *"/shell?cd+/tmp;rm+-rf+*;wget+167.71.210.63/jaws;sh+/tmp/jaws"*
seeks a remote code execution followed by a remote file upload attack. Also, different requests try to invoke *cgi-bin* scripts, a common folder with programs aiming to interact with a Web browser. Lastly, many requests target the database,
trying to exploit MySQL or PHP vulnerabilities, in line with the vulnerabilities EVSE vulnerabilities identified in [27]. Among all the requests, we classified
as malicious 340 GET and 236 POST actions. Almost all of them seem to be
directed by automatic tools or bots due to the absence of a specific target. However, we have not identified requests tailored specifically for HoneyEVSE charging process. Instead, all the scans and attacks were directed against the web
interface. We show the results in Fig. 5. We have not found significant activities
regarding the time spent on each page. Indeed, on average, the visitors spent
about 2 s on each page. This may imply that they were visited through automatic navigation tools, not humans. Finally, we have not identified particular
activities on FTP and Telnet ports, and on the login page form.

5.2 Interactions Origin

To analyze the presence of malicious actors among the IP sources, we leveraged
GreyNoise [1]. Greynoise is a company that collects, labels, and diagnoses data

and provides access to such information to users via API. The analysis shows that about 51% of unique IP addresses analyzed are labeled in the GreyNoise database as "malicious". These actors are generally IP sources flagged as attackers in previous campaigns. The remaining IPs were 23.5% labeled as "benign" sources and the remaining part as "unknown". "benign" refers to research centers or scanning services (e.g., Shodan or Zoomeye) that scan the IP addresses without malicious purposes. In Fig. 6, we report the top-5 organizations with the most malicious IP addresses. These organizations are *DigitalOcean, LLC, Amazon.com, Inc., CHINA UNICOM China169 Backbone, Hong Kong Zhengxing Technology Co., Ltd.*, and *Aggros Operations Ltd.*. Other actors include numerous ISPs from all over the world.

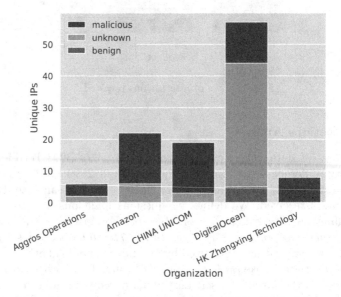

Fig. 6. Most frequent organization together with IPs label of Greynoise.

GreyNoise can also identify the actor related to an IP address, i.e., the entity using the IP address. The actor can differ from the organization to which the address belongs since it commonly happens that ISPs and companies offering cloud computing services or IP addresses block which are used for malicious activities. All the actors analyzed belong to hosts categorized as "benign" and represent legitimate organizations scanning the network to identify exposed and vulnerable services, sometimes also notifying the owners about the dangers they incur. The most frequent benign scanners in both the honeypot include *Stretchoid, Censys, Bitsight, ShadowServer, Cortex Xpanse*, and *Shodan*. All the malicious scanner actors are instead unknown by Greynoise except for some IPs belonging to *Stretchoid, XMCO.fr*, and *LeakIX*.

In Fig. 7, we report the country of origin of the unique IPs labeled as malicious. We can note that most of the malicious IPs belong to China, Russia, and

India. However, we must note that this may not be the original source of the scan but may be the last hop of a VPN.

Fig. 7. Country of origin of malicious IPs.

6   Conclusion

This paper presents HoneyEVSE, the first honeypot conceived to emulate a charging column. HoneyEVSE leverages tools like ACN-Sim to simulate the EV charging process and Honeyd as a network personality engine. We developed HoneyEVSE to mimic existing EVSE that related work found exposed on the internet, and we performed a data collection 30 days after exposing it. Results show that HoneyEVSE obtained a satisfying level of engagement during the data collection, confirming its capability in effectively reproducing a EVSE device. In this direction, future works include the development of more sophisticated EVSE functionalities and services to increase emulation fidelity.

We believe that HoneyEVSE can support the security research on the V2G field by enabling novel applications and analysis on EVSE functioning.

Acknowledgment. We thank *VSIX* [3] for enabling us to install the honeypot and collect data at their IXP.

References

1. GreyNoise Intelligence. https://greynoise.io/
2. Openenergymonitor. https://openenergymonitor.org/. Accessed 05 Aug 2023
3. Vsix Internet Exchange Point. https://www.vsix.it/. Accessed 15 May 2023
4. GridPot Github Project (2015). https://github.com/sk4ld/gridpot. Accessed 02 May 2023

5. What is Evse? (2023). https://ev-lectron.com/blogs/blog/what-is-evse. Accessed 03 Aug 2023
6. Baker, R., Martinovic, I.: Losing the car keys: wireless PHY-layer insecurity in EV charging. In: USENIX (2019)
7. Barbieri, G., Conti, M., Tippenhauer, N.O., Turrin, F.: Assessing the use of insecure ICS protocols via IXP network traffic analysis. In: 2021 International Conference on Computer Communications and Networks (ICCCN), pp. 1–9 (2021). https://doi.org/10.1109/ICCCN52240.2021.9522219
8. Brighente, A., Conti, M., Donadel, D., Turrin, F.: Evscout2. 0: electric vehicle profiling through charging profile. ACM Trans. Cyber Phys. Syst. (2021)
9. Buschlinger, L., Springer, M., Zhdanova, M.: Plug-and-patch: secure value added services for electric vehicle charging. ACM Int. Conf. Proc. Ser. (2019)
10. Cenys, A., Rainys, D., Radvilavicius, L., Bielko, A.: Development of honeypot system emulating functions of database server. Tech. rep, Semiconductor Physics Inst Vilnius (Lithuania) (2004)
11. Conti, M., Donadel, D., Poovendran, R., Turrin, F.: EVExchange: a relay attack on electric vehicle charging system. In: Atluri, V., Di Pietro, R., Jensen, C.D., Meng, W. (eds.) ESORICS 2022, pp. 488–508. Springer, Cham (2022). https://doi.org/10.1007/978-3-031-17140-6_24
12. Conti, M., Trolese, F., Turrin, F.: Icspot: a high-interaction honeypot for industrial control systems. In: 2022 International Symposium on Networks, Computers and Communications (ISNCC), pp. 1–4. IEEE (2022)
13. Franco, J., Aris, A., Canberk, B., Uluagac, A.S.: A survey of honeypots and honeynets for internet of things, industrial internet of things, and cyber-physical systems. IEEE Commun. Surv. Tutor. 23(4), 2351–2383 (2021)
14. Garofalaki, Z., Kosmanos, D., Moschoyiannis, S., Kallergis, D., Douligeris, C.: Electric vehicle charging: a survey on the security issues and challenges of the open charge point protocol (OCPP). IEEE Commun. Surv. Tutor. (2022)
15. Road Vehicles—Vehicle-to-Grid Communication Interface—Part 1: General information and use-case definition. Standard, International Organization for Standardization, Geneva (2019)
16. Road Vehicles—Vehicle-to-Grid Communication Interface—Part 2: Network and application protocol requirements. Standard, International Organization for Standardization, Geneva (2014)
17. Johansson, D., Lee, Z.J., Sharma, S.: ACN Portal (2021). https://github.com/zach401/acnportal
18. Köhler, S., Baker, R., Strohmeier, M., Martinovic, I.: Brokenwire: wireless disruption of ccs electric vehicle charging. arXiv preprint arXiv:2202.02104 (2022)
19. Lee, Z., Sharma, S., Johansson, D., Low, S.: ACN-sim: an open-source simulator for data-driven electric vehicle charging research. IEEE Trans. Smart Grid PP (2020). https://doi.org/10.1109/TSG.2021.3103156
20. Lee, Z.J., Li, T., Low, S.H.: ACN-data: analysis and applications of an open EV charging dataset. In: Proceedings of the Tenth ACM International Conference on Future Energy Systems, pp. 139–149 (2019)
21. López-Morales, E., Rubio, C., Doupé, A., Shoshitaishvili, Y., Bao, T., Ahn, G.J.: Honeyplc: A Next-Generation Honeypot for Industrial Control Systems, pp. 279–291 (2020). https://doi.org/10.1145/3372297.3423356
22. Luo, T., Xu, Z., Jin, X., Jia, Y., Ouyang, X.: Iotcandyjar: towards an intelligent-interaction honeypot for IoT devices. Black Hat 2017, 1–11 (2017)

23. Mashima, D., Li, Y., Chen, B.: Who's scanning our smart grid? empirical study on honeypot data. In: 2019 IEEE Global Communications Conference (GLOBE-COM), pp. 1–6. IEEE (2019)
24. Matherly, J.: Complete Guide to Shodan. https://ia800705.us.archive.org/17/items/shodan-book-extras/shodan/shodan.pdf
25. Matherly, J.: Complete Guide to Shodan (2016). https://ia800705.us.archive.org/17/items/shodan-book-extras/shodan/shodan.pdf
26. Murillo, A.F., Cómbita, L.F., Gonzalez, A.C., Rueda, S., Cardenas, A.A., Quijano, N.: A virtual environment for industrial control systems: a nonlinear use-case in attack detection, identification, and response. In: Proceedings of the 4th Annual Industrial Control System Security Workshop, pp. 25–32 (2018)
27. Nasr, T., Torabi, S., Bou-Harb, E., Fachkha, C., Assi, C.: Chargeprint: a framework for internet-scale discovery and security analysis of EV charging management systems. In: NDSS (2023)
28. Panda, S., Rass, S., Moschoyiannis, S., Liang, K., Loukas, G., Panaousis, E.: Honeycar: a framework to configure honeypot vulnerabilities on the internet of vehicles. IEEE Access 10, 104671–104685 (2022). https://doi.org/10.1109/ACCESS.2022.3210117
29. Petre, C.A., Korodi, A.: Honeypot inside an OPC UA wrapper for water pumping stations. In: 2019 22nd International Conference on Control Systems and Computer Science (CSCS), pp. 72–77. IEEE (2019)
30. Provos, N.: Honeyd: a virtual honeypot daemon (extended abstract) (2003)
31. Rahmatullah, D.K., Nasution, S.M., Azmi, F.: Implementation of low interaction web server honeypot using cubieboard. In: 2016 International Conference on Control, Electronics, Renewable Energy and Communications (ICCEREC), pp. 127–131. IEEE (2016)
32. Sharma, S., Kaul, A.: A survey on intrusion detection systems and honeypot based proactive security mechanisms in vanets and vanet cloud. Vehicul. Commun. 12, 138–164 (2018)
33. Statista. Electric Vehicles - Worldwide (2023). https://www.statista.com/outlook/mmo/electric-vehicles/worldwide. Accessed Apr 2023

DPM 2023

Foreword from the DPM 2023 Program Chairs

This volume contains the post-proceedings of the 18th Data Privacy Management International Workshop (DPM 2023), which was organized within the 28th European Symposium on Research in Computer Security (ESORICS 2023). The DPM series started in 2005 when the first workshop took place in Tokyo (Japan). Since then, the event has been held in different venues: Atlanta, USA (2006); Istanbul, Turkey (2007); Saint Malo, France (2009); Athens, Greece (2010); Leuven, Belgium (2011); Pisa, Italy (2012); Egham, UK (2013); Wroclaw, Poland (2014); Vienna, Austria (2015); Crete, Greece (2016); Oslo, Norway (2017); Barcelona, Spain (2018); Luxembourg (2019); Guildford, UK (2020); Darmstadt, Germany (2021); and Copenhagen, Denmark (2022).

The 2023 edition of DPM was held in The Hague, The Netherlands. The workshop took place on the 28th of September as part of the ESORICS 2023 workshops. All presentations where in person, and the workshop was organized with relatively big time slots to boost discussions and engagement of attendees with each of the presented papers.

We received 18 submissions. All papers were assigned to at least 3 PC members to handle reviews, and all reviews were returned. Each submission was evaluated on the basis of significance, novelty, and technical quality. The program committee performed a thorough review process and selected 4 regular papers, complemented with 6 additional short papers.

The workshop was complemented with an invited keynote by Michal Choras from the Bydgoszcz University of Science and Technology. This was a joint keynote together with the workshops CBT 2023 (7th International Workshop on Cryptocurrencies and Blockchain Technology), CyberICPS 2023 (9th Workshop on the Security of Industrial Control Systems & of Cyber-Physical Systems), and SECPRE 2023 (7th International Workshop on SECurity and Privacy Requirements Engineering). We believe that this joint keynote contributed to establish synergies and a great atmosphere between the workshops attendees. An important novelty with respect to past editions is that the post-proceedings of DPM are now in this volume, which covers most of the ESORICS workshops. We think that having a joint proceedings volume will be beneficial for all authors at ESORICS workshops, helping them to gain more relevance and presence, and will also contribute to more stable and consistent publication of future workshops.

We would like to thank everyone who helped to organize the event, including all the members of the organizing committees of both ESORICS and DPM 2023. Our gratitude goes to Kaitai Liang and Georgios Smaragdakis, General chairs of ESORICS 2023, Jérémie Decouchant and Stjepan Picek, Workshop chairs of ESORICS 2023, and all the people in the ESORICS 2023 organization. We also want to thank Ken Barker for chairing a session and contributing to the smooth running of the workshop. Very special thanks go as well to all the DPM 2023 Program Committee members, additional reviewers, and, most notably, all the authors who submitted papers, and to all the workshop attendees.

Finally, we want to acknowledge the support received from the sponsoring institutions: Institut Mines-Télécom, Institut Polytechnique de Paris (Télécom SudParis and SAMOVAR Confiance Numérique), Universitat Autònoma de Barcelona (UAB), and Cybercat. We acknowledge support as well from the Spanish Government project SECURING/NET PID2021-125962OB-C33, CiberSec+ RED2022-134603-T, and the UNESCO Chair in Data Privacy.

October 2023

Joaquin Garcia-Alfaro
Guillermo Navarro-Arribas

18th International Workshop on Data Privacy Management – DPM 2023

PC Chairs

Joaquin Garcia-Alfaro	Intitut Polytechnique de Paris, France
Guillermo Navarro-Arribas	Universitat Autònoma de Barcelona, Spain

Program Committee

Esma Aïmeur	University of Montreal, Canada
Ken Barker	University of Calgary, Canada
Jordi Casas-Roma	Universitat Oberta de Catalunya, Spain
Jordi Castellà-Roca	Universitat Rovira i Virgili, Spain
Mauro Conti	University of Padua, Italy
Mathieu Cunche	University of Lyon, France
Frédéric Cuppens	Polytechnique Montréal, Canada
Nora Cuppens-Boulahia	Polytechnique Montréal, Canada
Mila Dalla Preda	University of Verona, Italy
Sabrina De Capitani di Vimercati	Università degli Studi di Milano, Italy
Josep Domingo-Ferrer	Universitat Rovira i Virgili, Spain
Nicolás E. Díaz Ferreyra	Hamburg University of Technology, Germany
Jose Maria de Fuentes	Universidad Carlos III de Madrid, Spain
Sebastien Gambs	Université du Québec à Montréal, Canada
Lorena González Manzano	Universidad Carlos III de Madrid, Spain
M. Emre Gursoy	Koç University, Turkey
Guy-Vincent Jourdan	University of Ottawa, Canada
Marc Juarez	University of Edinburgh, UK
Christos Kalloniatis	University of the Aegean, Greece
Bruce Kapron	University of Victoria, Canada
Sokratis Katsikas	Norwegian University of Science and Technology, Norway
Christophe Kiennert	Télécom SudParis, France
Hiroaki Kikuchi	Meiji University, Japan
Evangelos Kranakis	Carleton University, Canada
Romain Laborde	Université Paul Sabatier, France
Patrick Lacharme	EnsiCaen, France
Costas Lambrinoudakis	University of Piraeus, Greece
Giovanni Livraga	University of Milan, Italy

Brad Malin	Vanderbilt University, USA
Lukas Malina	Brno University of Technology, Czech Republic
David Megias	Universitat Oberta de Catalunya, Spain
Chris Mitchell	Royal Holloway, University of London, UK
Benjamin Nguyen	INSA Centre Val de Loire, France
Martín Ochoa	AppGate Inc., USA
Gerardo Pelosi	Politecnico di Milano, Italy
Isabel Praça	GECAD / ISEP, Portugal
Kai Rannenberg	Goethe University Frankfurt, Germany
Ruben Rios	University of Malaga, Spain
Pierangela Samarati	Università degli Studi di Milano, Italy
Nadia Tawbi	Laval University, Canada
Alexandre Viejo	Universitat Rovira i Virgili, Spain
Isabel Wagner	University of Basel, Switzerland
Jens Weber	University of Victoria, Canada
Lena Wiese	Fraunhofer Institute for Toxicology and Experimental Medicine, Germany
Nicola Zannone	Eindhoven University of Technology, The Netherlands
Melek Önen	EURECOM, France

Steering Committee

Joaquin Garcia-Alfaro	Intitut Polytechnique de Paris, France
Guillermo Navarro-Arribas	Universitat Autònoma de Barcelona, Spain
Josep Domingo-Ferrer	Universitat Rovira i Virgili, Spain
Vicenç Torra	Umeå University, Sweden

Additional Reviewers

Federico Turrin	University of Padua, Italy
Morteza Sargolzaei Javan	Goethe University Frankfurt, Germany
Gaetan Pradel	Royal Holloway, University of London, UK

Not Only Security and Privacy: The Evolving Ethical and Legal Challenges of E-Commerce

Michał Choraś[1], Aleksandra Pawlicka[2(✉)], Dagmara Jaroszewska-Choraś[3], and Marek Pawlicki[1]

[1] Bydgoszcz University of Science and Technology, Bydgoszcz, Poland
[2] University of Warsaw, Warsaw, Poland
a.pawlicka5@uw.edu.pl
[3] Kazimierz Wielki University, Bydgoszcz, Poland

Abstract. The coronavirus pandemic has influenced nearly all the aspects of people's lives, including their shift to purchasing online. Along with the changes, the known ethical and legal issues of the e-commerce grew in significance; there also appeared a number of new, unprecedented challenges. This paper presents the results of a novel study aimed at identifying the most significant ethical and legal issues of e-commerce that appeared alongside the COVID-19 pandemic, or grew in significance because of it. The study also sheds light on the evolution of human knowledge and understanding of these challenges, driven by an unprecedented reliance on e-commerce during the pandemic.

Keywords: E-commerce · Ethics · Information Systems · Pandemic · Privacy · Security

1 Introduction

The outbreak of the coronavirus (COVID-19) pandemic in March 2020 [10] has influenced nearly all the aspects of people's lives. One of the most dramatic shifts was caused by strict lockdowns and the necessity to depend on digital services in order to be able to continue working, studying or shopping. Electronic commerce (e-commerce), understood as a business model enabling selling and purchasing goods and services by means of the Internet [13] has been one of the sectors which have witnessed some dramatic, unprecedented transformations.

Ethics is the study of morality, the ultimate goal of which is to objectively determine what is right and what is wrong. It aims at finding such behaviour patterns which would be generally approved by most people. Unlike law, which must be obeyed by everyone even if they disagree with it, ethics principles are personal and defined by each individual. Thus, it can so happen that a person finds their own actions justifiable despite others refusing to condone them [32,34].

In the times of the pandemic, an enormous increase in popularity of the e-commerce services was observed: the e-commerce's global retail share increased from 14% to 17% just within the year of 2020 [45]. Resultantly, it seems natural

S. Katsikas et al. (Eds.): ESORICS 2023 Workshops, LNCS 14398, pp. 167–181, 2024.
https://doi.org/10.1007/978-3-031-54204-6_9

that providing cybersecurity to e-commerce has never been more important
before. Yet, as it turns out, in the light of the ethical dilemmas there arise
in relation to this matter [5,23], so has been adhering to ethics standards. In
fact, the ethical issues have been dubbed one of the most pressing challenges of
e-commerce besides the strictly technical ones [29,35], especially in the light of
some of the recent e-commerce-related scandals [42]. Businesses are starting to
realize that their unethical behaviour not only is a disservice to their clients, but
also to themselves [9,11]. As the ethics of e-commerce has attracted the interest of scientists [12], it has already been confirmed experimentally that the way
ethical guidelines is followed affects customers' trust, satisfaction, loyalty [24],
attitude, positive experience as well as the fact if they will be willing to revisit
and purchase again [27,43,51]; it also influences how healthy the atmosphere
is for the customers [39]. In other words, with the growing maturity of the e-
commerce's users, who are increasingly more mindful of the fact that beside a
product, they buy the company's business practices as well [41], their awareness
of the significance of ethical behaviour has also increased, and many of them
will feel reluctant to engage with the services of a provider who behaves in an
unethical way [37]. Simply put, if the e-commerce companies wish to stay relevant today, they simply cannot afford risking losing their customers' trust [49].
Consequently, in the light of the above, the ethical dilemmas which had been
typically related to the e-commerce services have taken a new significance since
the beginning of the pandemic. Additionally, mainly due to the situation being
unprecedented, there emerged some further, unforeseen e-commerce related ethical dilemmas. This work presents selected ethical challenges that are relevant
to e-commerce in the context of the COVID-19 pandemic.

The main contribution of this paper is that, to the Authors' best knowledge,
to date there has been no scientific paper that would do it. The article is structured as follows: firstly, the background for the paper is presented. Then, the
Methodology of this paper is outlined. The Results' Section first discusses the
identified *classical* ethical issues of e-commerce; the following Section outlines
the newer ethical dilemmas, which may either have been made more significant
by the pandemic, or resulted directly from it. Both sections contain a number
of suggestions and recommendations on how to solve the particular challenges.
Then, the paper closes with a number of final remarks.

2   Background

As Lunka believes, engaging in e-commerce has become *a new norm and must-
have for retail* [26]. Owing to its being so available, for some individuals it has
turned out to be the favoured way of purchasing goods. Moreover, for vendors,
it proves much more affordable to start selling online to customers worldwide
than to open a number of physical shops.

The pandemic triggered the turning point of e-commerce. 2020 will be remem-
bered as the time when everything changed. The digital and e-commerce sectors boomed amid the crisis, and the growth they experienced has been both
unprecedented and unforeseen. Although the economy as a whole slowed down,

e-commerce has been thriving. Lockdowns made businesses turn more digital, as they started offering more goods and services by cyber means. E-commerce has expanded towards new companies, product types (e.g., groceries) and customer segments (e.g., the elderly). In parallel, a partial switch in the e-commerce transactions has been observed, namely from luxury goods and services to more common, everyday necessities [30].

According to the report by UNCTAD, the organizations and individuals who *were able to 'go digital' have helped mitigate the economic downturn caused by the pandemic (. . .) but they have also sped up the digital transition that will have lasting impacts (. . .)—for which not everyone is prepared* [45]. The shift to online shopping was the most profound in emerging economies, where it saw the increase in the number of items sold online even as high as double the amount as compared to the previous year.

The pandemic has shown that e-commerce may play a special role in the times of crisis, by offering an alternative to the brick-and-mortar shops. The crisis has also made e-commerce more dynamic. However, it also exposed some challenges to e-commerce—or rather, exposed the pre-existing challenges and created a number of new challenges. They range from physical ones, such as reliable and stable electricity and internet connections to the things such as visibility in online searches, advertising or access to online payment services [46].

Prior to the pandemic, technophiles used to claim that if people are not satisfied with online services, there is always the possibility to opt out. Even before the coronavirus outbreak, quitting the net was not really a viable option, though. It is so, as some services have become unavoidable, and a person who does not use them may find themselves at a competitive disadvantage, and not taking full part in society. Amid strict lockdowns, the *lingering illusion of voluntariness in the use of technology has disappeared* [48]. Communication apps have become the main or sole means of social interaction, and people started relying on digital tools for work, education, getting medical help, etc. Besides individuals, organizations, universities, hospitals and even governments have needed technology to maintain their functions. Thus, the digital technologies became a substitute channel for maintaining business activities, providing and receiving education, socializing and purchasing necessities amidst strict lockdowns [46].

This unprecedented situation caused a number of new ethical dilemmas to emerge. Additionally, the shifts in the hitherto prevailing order of things made the ethical issues present before becoming more profound, or different. The aim of this paper is to present the results of the study which aimed at identifying the new, unprecedented ethical issues of e-commerce that the COVID-19 pandemic begot.

3   Methodology and Research Strategy

3.1   Research Questions

This study aimed at answering the following research questions:
RQ 1 - What were the major ethical issues of e-commerce before the COVID-19 pandemic?

This work will refer to them as the *old*, or *classical* dilemmas.

RQ 2 - What major ethical issues of e-commerce have been related to or reinforced by the COVID-19 pandemic?

Research Strategy

In order to be able to answer the Research Questions, the ethical dilemmas of e-commerce had first to be identified and collected from the subject literature, in the course of a targeted search. The selected research method was the limited literature review [40].

The strings used in the research was "ethical", "issues/dillemmas" and "e-commerce", and "ethical", "issues/dillemmas" "e-commerce", and "covid", each of them combined using Boolean "AND"; the strings were used for browsing in the titles, keywords, and abstracts.

In this part of the study, the specific inclusion and exclusion criteria were applied to screen through the search results. The inclusion criteria were as follows: peer-reviewed scientific articles or quality and relevant magazine articles and blog posts, not older than 5 years old, in English. In turn, the exclusion criteria were: poor quality, irrelevant contents, older than 5 years old (unless very relevant), in other languages.

After applying these criteria to the search results, 48 sources were identified as potentially relevant. After removing duplicates, there remained 39 papers and articles, which were then examined in-depth. The papers and other sources have been gathered in Table 1. Then, the ethical issues mentioned in the sources have been mapped. If a source concerned the ethical issues of e-commerce but did not name any specific ones, it was put in the *general* category.

The analysis of the sources allowed identifying the ethical issues of e-commerce which were discussed before, or without the context of the pandemic, as well as the ones which were either introduced or made more prominent alongside it. The findings are presented below.

4   Results

4.1   The 'old' Ethical Dilemmas of E-Commerce

Back in 2005, Fontrodona divided the ethical challenges of e-commerce into four broad categories: security, privacy, identity and transaction non-refutability [18]. All of them are still valid and still more than relevant today. In fact, they have risen in importance during the pandemic.

Security. Even before the pandemic, the secure processing of personal information was amongst the most vital concerns [32]. As [25] remarks, what makes the security of e-commerce so troublesome, is the number of various exchanges related to data. And the e-commerce services indeed gather and process plenty of data. Credit card credentials seem to be particularly valuable and sought for by threat actors, as this information allows stealing the money from victims' accounts; nevertheless, all of this data, if breached, can be used by wrongdoers

Table 1. The ethical issues of e-commerce as identified in the subject literature and other relevant sources.

	security	privacy	identity	non-refutability	bad service	counterfeits	compliance	cybersquatting	fake products	greenwashing	inequalities	intellectual property	no accessibility	profiling and tracking	spam	general
Fortcrodeca (2008) [18]	X	X	X	X												
Babu (2011) [4]	X	X						X							X	
AbuRaya (2020) [2]																X
Himani, Shivani (2020) [21]		X						X							X	
Velä (2021) [48]	X	X										X		X		
D'Cruz, Du, Noronha et al. (2022) [12]																X
Kethan, Basha (2022) [24]																X
Kumar (2022) [25]	X															
Nayak, Dev Rroy (2022) [29]	X	X		X		X						X			X	
Yusiart, Arief, Meydia, Yevis (2022) [51]	X	X	X													
Mainarden, Coutinho, Alves (2023) [27]	X	X														
Lunia (2019) [26]	X		X			X	X						X			
Petersen (2019) [36]	X				X	X	X					X				
Garg (2020) [19]									X					X	X	
OECD (2020) [30]										X						
RSI Security (2020) [38]	X	X													X	
UNODC (2020) [47]									X							
de Passerio (2021) [31]																X
Micheal (2021) [28]	X	X										X				
Tareque (2021) [42]			X							X						
UNCTAD (2021) [45]																X
UNECE (2021) [46]				X						X						
Drishti (2022) [13]																
Tako (2022) [5]									X			X			X	
Crudo (2022) [9]		X		X					X	X						
Dave (2022) [11]	X	X		X	X	X			X							
Teolin (2022) [43]													X			
Shantia (2022) [39]																X
Stephenson (2022) [41]										X						
Qureshi (2022) [37]		X							X	X				X		
Wallace (2022) [49]	X															
Azim (2022) [3]	X				X	X		X				X		X	X	
Burks (2022) [7]														X		
Clift (2022) [8]										X						
30Acres (2022) [1]																X
Blackman, Ammanath (2022) [6]												X				
Iyer (2022) [23]											X		X			
Wibken (2022) [50]										X						
Uddin (2022) [44]										X						

for malicious purposes, such as identity fraud [36]. Even one's purchase history could be used in a malicious way, especially if one buys sensitive products [26].

E-commerce sellers need to bear that in mind, that they take full responsibility for protecting the data the customers trusted them with. Some of the actions which could be taken in order to protect the customers' data are using TSL/SSL for the e-commerce websites; particularly important if the pages gather sensitive data, as well as adding further layers of protection (such as a firewall), etc. [26]. One of the ways of making sure the customers' data is as safe as possible is choosing trustworthy and reliable e-commerce platforms, capable of ensuring security. This alone is not enough, as such services need regular patching and updating, as well as staying up to date with firewalls and plug-ins. A security-aware e-commerce vendor also needs to be prepared for the moment when the platforms and the servers they are hosted on may become vulnerable after they have reached their end-of-life and are not updated anymore [38].

The COVID-19 pandemic saw a global increase in cybercrime in fraud. In 2020, the cybercrime reports almost doubled in the US; were more than 30% higher in the UK, whilst in particular places of Latin America there were 60% more cybercrimes than in the relevant period of 2019. All this has been the direct result of malicious actors taking advantage of the unusual circumstances and the fact that millions of individuals have been particularly vulnerable. The wrongdoers did not stop there; conversely, it seems that they have been coming up with new ways of exploiting a broader and deeper range of individuals and organizations. It is highly unlikely that this trend will be halted anytime soon [22].

Privacy. In the recent years, the problem of privacy has become so burning, that it resulted in introducing the General Data Protection Regulation (GDPR), aimed at making the personal data as secure as possible [33]. If a person was still not willing for their data to be gathered or processed, they had some choice not to share the information, for example by frequenting local corner shops and paying by cash, rather than shopping online. However, the introduction of lockdowns, often in a rapid manner, made it impossible for many people not to share their data—they faced the dilemma of either ordering things from online shops and sharing their data, or being locked up at homes, without necessities.

Indeed, a lot of Personally Identifiable Information is gathered in e-commerce. Although using it for profit is not illegal, it raises much discussion when it comes to data ethics [38]. Typically, online shops collect customers' names, addresses and credit card numbers, but also their phone numbers, birthday dates [38] or purchase history [26]. If an e-commerce website allows customers set up an account, they have to come up with a username and a password [36]. In the context of e-commerce, the ethical challenge of privacy mainly relates to the question of processing customers' personal information; it must be processed in a lawful way—but ideally, it should also be done ethically. As RSISecurity puts it, data processing is not only what one does to the data technically; what one does with it, becomes the question of ethics [38].

The issue of processing data in e-commerce relates to a number of aspects. Firstly, the data must be gathered with its purpose in mind. In other words, it is not advisable to gather information *just in case*, forming the so-called *data lakes* [3], which are *the organization's equivalent of a hoarder's closet* [38]. Maintaining such data is not only a nuisance to the organization itself, but it is also deeply unethical and illegal. According to the GDPR, keeping unnecessary data poses a security concern and is lawfully penalized. As RSISecurity notices, despite that, there are large companies which keep storing vast data sets on individuals anyway. They argue that this may be caused by the companies' business models trumping over humanitarian issues, although this too proves to be really unethical owing to the fact that organizations mission is to *help its customers or fix their problems not to create new ones* [38]. The same is true for storing the data—it may be stored securely and legally, yet still in an unethical manner.

A further aspect of e-commerce which raises questions about ethics is web tracking. Companies are able to examine one's web activity by analysing cookies and using tracking software. As this data may also be used unethically, the misuse of cookies raises privacy concerns, too [4].

Identity. According to Fontrodona et al., this challenge is related to the fact that computer systems are only able identify one's *virtual* identity. Due to this fact, it becomes possible to impersonate someone, or to steal the said identity, as when purchasing goods from on-line shops, people are somehow forced to expose themselves [18]. Protecting the customers' identity is as important as making all of their other personal information secure.

Non-refutability. In their work, Fontrodona et al. have described this challenge as verifying the transaction or *what really happened online* [18]. In the contemporary e-commerce, a number of challenges fall under this umbrella, one of the problems being inaccurate product listings.

One of the major differences between traditional and e-commerce is that the customers of the latter do not have the possibility to touch, smell, feel the products before buying. They usually do not see the exact item they are going to receive; especially during lockdowns, the customer has to put full trust in the seller that they will send them products matching the pictures and descriptions on the website [36]. However, the pictures or videos that are presented to them may be heavily edited, or present the product in best possible lighting. The product information may be scarce, or may be meticulously crafted, so that it discusses the positives only and omits the possible flaws. As Lunka warns, ruining the moment of excitement the customer experiences before opening the package, for example by the product's lower quality or attributes different from what the listing promised, leads to disappointment [26]. Taking advantage of the distance between the customer and the product in order to sell inferior items is severely unethical [36]. Supposedly, in most cases the listings are not incorrect on purpose; their being inaccurate results from lack of experience or troubles with data management. Nevertheless, the vendors have to make sure a product is presented in the most accurate, complete and honest way possible. If any errors or inaccuracies in the listings are spotted, they must be corrected in a timely manner [26].

Another point to consider that has been brought by Petersen is the fact that the combination of available technologies and relative anonymity on the internet make it possible for some companies to pretend to be larger and better-experienced than in fact they are. In other words, in the struggle of creating a strong brand, an e-business owner may misrepresent the organization and be dishonest to their customers. For example, putting stock images of large office buildings may contribute to the impression that the company owns the facilities. Similarly, buying social media *likes* or followers is not considered ethical, as it gives the impression of having a greater following and better interaction with the customer base. Finally, lack of transparency regarding the information about company is unethical to its customers, too [36].

4.2   The 'New' Ethical Dilemmas of E-Commerce

This section highlights the newer, more recent ethical dilemmas of e-commerce. The emergence of some of them has been directly caused by the coronavirus pandemic.

Fake COVID-19-Related Products. One of the most obvious ethical problems related to e-commerce is that a number of companies have claimed to sell various products that could allegedly cure or prevent the virus. The *miraculous* remedies have varied, from bogus drugs [47] to vitamin drips, sauna sessions and energy healing, to name just a few [16, 20]. This kind of listings prey on people's vulnerabilities - fears, lack of knowledge, or uncertainty, which is deeply unethical. Indeed, Gerg deemed such practices *social engineering at its worst* [19].

Spam. In the context of e-commerce, e-mail spam means any unnecessary communication with customers. Most online shops collect client e-mails, in order to be able to contact them or track their orders. Plus, organizations often suggest becoming a subscriber; they will be receiving special offers or information concerning the business. As RSISecurity remarks, gathering e-mails is also a form of information processing and as such should be ethical. If the company spams the customer's inbox with communication which is not necessary, the balance between good marketing and unethical behaviour may be disrupted [38]. On top of that, since 2020, there have been companies which resorted to spamming their customers with COVID-19 related e-mails. Even if the e-mails were not malicious lures [32], they usually were just social engineered in hope to make people open them and/or click the links they contained.

The Lack of Web Accessibility. The pandemic forced everyone to stay home—the young and the old, the able and the disabled ones; no matter the gender or ethnicity, no one was safe to leave home. This means that the people who experience some specific problems whilst browsing the traditional web pages were also forced to use them—no matter if the vendor had made the website accessible or not. As Lunka remarks, although web accessibility is a concept which has existed for some time now, it still tends to get neglected. By accessibility one understand the standards which may be applied to websites to ensure people with certain disabilities are able to use them [26]. It is particularly crucial, as equal access and opportunities as far as the web is concerned, to the disabled, contributes to their more active participation in society. Conversely, if e-commerce websites are not accessible enough, they discriminate against the disabled and refuse them equal access to the services. Especially in the times of pandemic, when people were deprived of any alternative means of purchasing goods, this becomes an issue of ethics.

Bad Customer Service. Unlike in traditional retail, in e-commerce there is the barrier which separates customers from vendors. Thus, in case a client requires assistance, claims a refund, or is sent a faulty item, they are not able to simply walk into the shop to seek for help. Rather, they have no other choice but to rely on the contact methods that the e-commerce vendor provides. Quality customer service may encompass phone-based service, online chats, e-mail assistance, etc. However, if a company makes it hard to receive help, for example by ignoring e-mails and other attempts at contacting them, then it is deemed not to be ethical behaviour. Similarly, it is deeply unethical to deliberately delay dealing with the customer's case, so that they either give up, or it gets too late for the customers to be refunded by the credit card operator [36]. Due to social distancing and lockdowns, the customers of unethical businesses were left to their own fate to a greater degree.

Violations of Intellectual Property. Another aspect of e-commerce which may lead to ethical issues, or rather, where some kinds of illegal actions may result in the *ethical fallouts*, are any violations of intellectual property [26,28]. As Babu notices, protecting intellectual property in e-commerce is a daunting task [4].

The vast category of intellectual property violations encompasses such infringements as using stolen images instead of purchasing them or hiring a professional photographer to take them[1] stealing content from blogs or catalogues rather than hiring professional copywriters, adapting unoriginal, copied logos, or using audio and video content without proper permissions or buying the rights to it. No matter if the violations result from ignorance, lack of sensible advice or deliberate actions, they may lead to legal actions, but also to the ethical consequences, such as public shaming, or customers' losing trust or actively trying to "cancel" the vendor[2]

Counterfeit Products. Similarly to other violations of intellectual property, selling unauthentic, counterfeit products, besides being against the law, is also deeply unethical. All the more, if the client has no opportunity to check the product themselves, before making the purchase. Although the fact that products are counterfeit may not be the fault of the vendor, as they might not be aware of the fact themselves, the retailers should make sure that the products they sell are authentic. This can be done by checking the lists of common signs of counterfeit products, verifying the products with the manufacturer, working only with trusted suppliers, whose credibility can be verified, and being especially vigilant when making international deals. Again, if a vendor learns that they sold counterfeit goods, they must handle the situation immediately and definitively [26].

Vendor Compliance. Vendor compliance may also lead to ethical concerns arising. The owner of a brand may establish stipulations for third-party sellers, concerning the ways of selling their products. This means that the retailers need to obtain permission to sell the product in an authorized way, use company-approved content, such as logos or photographs, or respect the prices that the vendor establishes. Not all sellers honour the requirements of this kind. This

---

[1] See: C. Raadio, "'It has been a battle': Montreal artist says her designs were stolen by online companies," CBC Raadio, 2020; Laser Gallery, "Stolen Listing Photos Appear on AliExpress," Etsy, 2017. [Online]. Available: https://community.etsy.com/t5/Photography-Tips/Stolen-Listing-Photos-Appear-on-AliExpress/td-p/14911802.,.

[2] See: LMA, "Zara Accused Of Stealing Designs From Independent Artists, And Here's The Evidence" Boredpanda, 2016. [Online]. Available: https://www.boredpanda.com/zara-stealing-designs-copying-independent-artists-tuesday-bassen/.

challenge may seem to be purely of legal nature when concerning the brand owners and third party vendors. Yet, if it leads to confusion and customers losing trust in the brand, it becomes an ethical problem [36].

Cybersquatting/Domain Squatting. Another situation in e-commerce which may be perceived as unethical has been mentioned by [4,21]. It is the so-called cybersquatting. By this term, one means registering the domain names which belong to someone else or could possibly interest them, and wishing to sell them at substantially higher prices [4]. Although not illegal, it also takes advantage of people's lack of technical knowledge or forgetfulness in a calculated way, so many see believe it to be unethical.

Inequalities. As the International Federation of Accountants points it out, *every entity, sector and jurisdiction* will emerge from this global crisis differently [22]. One of the factors driving this might be the drastically varying levels of vaccination in particular countries, which will in turn result in them being at various stages of recovery. Even after an economy reopens fully, it will take months, or even years, to rebuild and catch up. The pandemic *created myriad opportunities for unethical behaviour*, and the uneven recovery will give birth to even more of them.

As stated in [45]'s report, there were some major obstacles which prevented the world's least developed countries from capitalizing on the e-commerce opportunities that the pandemic induced. These barriers encompassed expensive internet connection services, overreliance on cash, lack of consumer's trust, as well as the governments not being particularly attentive to e-commerce. Another crucial aspect has been poor digital skills of the population. This has led to a situation, where the countries which were able to utilize the benefits that e-commerce brings will be able to gain more from global markets, whilst the ones that were unable to turn more digital have fallen behind even further. Thus, the digital inequalities have become even more profound. In fact, according to the report, many e-commerce solutions are provided by a relatively small number of US- and China-based companies; in other words, the pandemic has mostly benefitted the world's leading platforms, not the small players [45].

As Veliz believes, the changes worsened the vulnerabilities of ordinary citizens, *from the interaction with government to ordering food online, and almost everything in between* [48]. They argue that workers experienced increased surveillance, whilst students are subjected to more scrutiny; *privacy losses disempower citizens and often lead to further abuses of power* [48]. They also claim that the shifts during the coronavirus pandemic have promoted authoritarian tendencies, as it has been observed that in several dozen countries democracy has been in retreat during the pandemic. Recently, OECD have announced a list recommendations addressing these ethical issues. They emphasize the need of closing the digital divides between individuals, by providing affordable and quality internet access to the areas in need, and building trust in e-commerce, as well as

develop the necessary skills. They also recommend fostering e-commerce participation by the most vulnerable population, and protecting them from unethical
or illegal practices and unsafe products [30].

New Technologies for Advanced Profiling. Profiling is one of the typical
aspects of privacy mentioned e.g. in the Articles 21 and 22 of GDPR. Still, in
recent years, new techniques for data discovery, machine learning, correlation
engines etc. are even better equipped to profile citizens, especially customers in
e-commerce; these tools will gradually become even more powerful. The analysed
observable features can be either unchangeable or changeable, and in correlation
can offer better commercials, products and services, even if unwanted by customers. Therefore, both consumers and e-commerce companies should remember
that, as stated in the GDPR, the Subject can at any time object to processing
of personal data for marketing and profiling.

As [7] highlights, there are other ways in which the gathered data on customer
behaviour may be used unethically. Firstly, the data may be manipulated in order
to meet any business goals. Then, it can be mined from varied sources, without
the customers' consent and knowledge, e.g., by tracking users' activity across
different sites using the cookies on their computers. Lastly, they warn that *failed
transparency is (...) worse than no transparency*, i.e., leaving consumers unaware
of how the data is utilized makes them vulnerable to exploitation.

Ethical E-Commerce Means Green and Eco!...But Not Greenwashed.
With the raising challenge of climate change (or crisis), both e-commerce consumers and companies should take into account the need to evolve into ecological and green, which also means ethical. There are several practical aspects that
should be considered, such as: improving packaging (less plastic), consolidating
packaging, improving and optimizing shipping processes to make them greener
and more efficient, introducing carbon efficient processes, working on consumers
awareness (e.g. explaining ecological costs of free returns), etc. [8]

On the other hand, this demand often leads to *greenwashing* - that is, businesses falsely claiming to be ethical or green when in fact they are not. A study
showed that up to 40% of "green businesses" are not as "green" as they claim to
be [50].

5 Conclusions

This paper has identified some of the major ethical challenges of e-commerce that
have been relevant before the pandemic, and the new ones, which had appeared
or become more significant in the context of the COVID-19 pandemic; thus, the
Research Questions 1 and 2 have been answered. The scale of those issues are
often closely related to the fact that millions of people have had no other choice
but to rely on digital services, in order not to lose their jobs, fail classes or starve.
Similarly, for businesses, turning to e-commerce has also ceased to be a choice;
they will simply perish if they do not adopt online strategies [2].

Nonetheless, there are some reasons to stay optimistic, as *we have reached a stage where ethical issues in e-commerce, and the tech industry at large, can no longer be ignored* [38]. All the more, as shifting from the traditional, business-centric view to a user-focused, ethical one, proves to be the best for the business anyway [1]. The society also seems to be more and more aware of the ethical challenges surrounding e-commerce. In one study, 62% of the respondents claimed the pandemic made them value the ethics of retailers to a greater extent [31].

There are many legal regulations which pertain to e-commerce and the related activities. Many of these legislations overlap with ethical issues. In other words, ensuring compliance with most of the regulations, at the same time guarantees that the business operates ethically, too. Some of such regulations are GDPR [15], the e-commerce Directive [14], the CAN-SPAM act [17], as well as data compliance and privacy laws, regulations that are product-specific, and so on [26]. On top of that, in the industry, where profit is directly related to collecting and processing individuals' personal information, any possible solutions to this problem must be sought for in close cooperation of individuals, organisations and governments [38]. As [6] notice, due to the nature of the situation there are no "quick fixes", though.

As it is the misuse of data which may lead to deepening inequalities, creating mistrust, posing risks to national security, to eroding the democracy [48], or spelling *economic disaster* [44], even though it is rather improbable for the e-commerce to entirely outplace the unique experiences and social aspects that traditional, physical shops offer [31], the ethical use of data should become the driving factor of the post-pandemic recovery, not only in e-commerce [38]. The pandemic did increase the risk of unethical behaviour; in the process of recovery, there will be many chances to evolve for the better, though [22].

References

1. 30Acres: Creating Ethical User Experience in E-Commerce. 30Acres (2022). https://www.30acres.com.au/blog/creating-ethical-user-experience-in-e-commerce. Accessed 18 May 2023
2. AbuRaya, R.: Business analytics of e-commerce policy and practice: an ethical perspective. In: 2020 International Conference on Decision Aid Sciences and Application (DASA), pp. 761–767 (2020). https://doi.org/10.1109/DASA51403.2020.9317117
3. Asim, L.: Ethical Issues in eCommerce: 9 Biggest Problems You Need to Know and Avoid. Debutify (2022). https://debutify.com/blog/ethical-issues-in-ecommerce-9-biggest-problems-you-need-/to-know-and-avoid/. Accessed 18 May 2023
4. Babu, R.: E-Commerce Ethical and Legal Issues (2011). http://blog.qburst.com/2011/03/e-commerce-ethical-and-legal-issues/. Accessed 04 Feb 2013
5. Bijelic, Z.: AI Ethics & eCommerce 101. Tako Stand (2022). https://blog.takoagency.com/tako-stand/ai-ethics-ecommerce-101. Accessed 18 May 2023
6. Blackman, R., Ammanath, B.: Ethics and AI: 3 Conversations Companies Need to Have. Harvard Business Review (2022). https://hbr.org/2022/03/ethics-and-ai-3-conversations-companies-need-to-be-having. Accessed 18 May 2023

7. Burke, S.: The ethics of customer behavioral tracking. Lytics (2022). https://www.linkedin.com/pulse/ethics-customer-behavioral-tracking-jascha-kaykas-wolff/. Accessed 18 May 2023
8. Clift, S.: The Ins & Outs of Ethical Ecommerce. Good Carts (2022). https://goodcarts.co/the-ins-and-outs-of-ethical-ecommerce/. Accessed 18 May 2023
9. Crudo, B.: 3 Ways We Can Make Online Shopping More Ethical. LinkedIn (2022). https://www.linkedin.com/pulse/3-ways-we-can-make-online-shopping-more-ethical-benjamin-.crudo/. Accessed 18 May 2023
10. Cucinotta, D.V.M.: WHO declares COVID-19 a pandemic. Acta Biomed. **91**(1), 157–160 (2020). https://doi.org/10.23750/abm.v91i1.9397
11. Dave, T.: Why Acting Ethically Matters in E-Commerce. Forbes (2022). https://www.forbes.com/sites/forbesbusinesscouncil/2022/09/01/why-acting-ethically-matters-in-e-commerce/. Accessed 18 May 2023
12. D'Cruz, P., et al.: Technology, megatrends and work: thoughts on the future of business ethics. J. Bus. Ethics **180**(3), 879–902 (2022). https://doi.org/10.1007/s10551-022-05240-9
13. Drishti Mains Question: Ethical E-Commerce. Drishi IAS (2022). https://www.drishtiias.com/daily-news-editorials/ethical-e-commerce. Accessed 18 May 2023
14. EUR-Lex: Directive 2000/31/EC of the European Parliament and of the Council of 8 June 2000 on Certain Legal Aspects of Information Society Services, in Particular Electronic Commerce, in the Internal Market ('Directive on Electronic Commerce') (2000)
15. EUR-Lex: Regulation (EU) 2016/679 of the European Parliament and of the Council of 27 April 2016 on the Protection of Natural Persons with Regard to the Processing of Personal Data and on the Free Movement of Such Data, and Repealing Directive 95/46/EC (General Data Protection Regulation) (2016)
16. Fair, L.: Advertisers: stop unproven COVID claims or face penalties under new law (2021). https://www.ftc.gov/news-events/blogs/business-blog/2021/04/advertisers-stop-unproven-covid-claims-or-face-penalties. Accessed 18 May 2023
17. Federal Trade Commission: Can-Spam Act: A Compilance Guide for Business (2009). https://www.ftc.gov/tips-advice/business-center/guidance/can-spam-act-compliance-guide-business. Accessed 18 May 2023
18. Fontrodona, J.: Ethical Aspects of e-Commerce: Data Subjects and Content. IESE Business School Working Paper No. 586, SSRN Electronic Journal (2005). https://doi.org/10.2139/ssrn.884377, https://papers.ssrn.com/sol3/papers.cfm?abstract_id=884377. Accessed 18 May 2023
19. Gerg, C.: How Hackers are Exploiting COVID-19. Security Magazine (2020). https://www.securitymagazine.com/articles/92411-how-hackers-are-exploiting-covid-19. Accessed 18 May 2023
20. Gragnani, J.: The Brazilian doctor offering bogus covid remedies for social media likes (2021). https://www.bbc.com/news/blogs-trending-57276286. Accessed 18 May 2023
21. Grewal, H., Shivani: a study on ethical and social issues in E-commerce. Int. J. Adv. Res. Comput. Sci. Softw. Eng. **2**(7) (2020). https://doi.org/10.37896/sr7.10/075
22. International Federation of Accountants: 5 Ethics Challenges that Will Intensify as the Pandemic Wanes (2021). https://www.ifac.org/knowledge-gateway/building-trust-ethics/discussion/5-ethics-challenges-will-intensify-pandemic-wanes. Accessed 04 Feb 2023

23. Iyer, U.: Should E-commerce be renamed as ethical-commerce? In: SiFy (2022). https://www.sify.com/digital-transformation/should-e-commerce-be-renamed-as-ethical-commerce/. Accessed 18 May 2023
24. Kethan, M., S, M.B.: Relationship of ethical sales behaviour with customer loyalty, trust and commitment: a study with special reference to retail store in Mysore City. East Asian J. Multidiscip. Res. 1(7), 1365–1376 (2022)
25. Kumar, A.: Legal and ethical issues in E-commerce. In: E-Commerce And Global Marketing Course (CO2 23) (2022)
26. Lunka, R.: Ethical Issues in eCommerce: Are You Violating Any of Them? (2019). https://www.nchannel.com/blog/ethical-issues-in-ecommerce/. Accessed 18 May 2023
27. Mainardes, E.W., Coutinho, A.R.S., Alves, H.M.B.: The influence of the ethics of E-retailers on online customer experience and customer satisfaction. J. Retail. Consum. Serv. **2023**, 103171 (2023). https://doi.org/10.1016/j.jretconser.2022.103171
28. Micheal, J.: 5 growing ethical issues in online marketing you need to be aware of. Growth Animals (2021). https://growthanimals.com/5-growing-ethical-issues-in-online-marketing-you-need-to.-be-aware-of/. Accessed 18 May 2023
29. Nayak, P., Rroy, A.D.: Perception of customers towards ethical issues in online shopping. Int. Manag. Rev. Supl. Spec. Issu. **18** (2022). http://www.americanscholarspress.us/journals/IMR/pdf/IMR-SP-2022/SpecV18-art6.pdf. Accessed 18 May 2023
30. OECD: E-commerce in the time of COVID-19. Tech. rep., OECD (2020). https://www.oecd.org/coronavirus/policy-responses/e-commerce-in-the-time-of-covid-19-3a2b78e8/. Accessed 18 May 2023
31. de Passorio, P.: Future of payments and e-commerce: lessons from the COVID-19 pandemic. euronews.next (2021). https://www.euronews.com/next/2021/06/16/future-of-/-payments-and-e-commerce-lessons-from-the-covid-19-pandemic. Accessed 18 May 2023
32. Pawlicka, A., Choraś, M., Pawlicki, M., Kozik, R.: A $10 million question and other cybersecurity-related ethical dilemmas amid the COVID-19 pandemic. Business Horizons **64**(6), 729–734 (2021). https://doi.org/10.1016/j.bushor.2021.07.010, https://linkinghub.elsevier.com/retrieve/pii/S0007681321001336
33. Pawlicka, A., Jaroszewska-Choras, D., Choras, M., Pawlicki, M.: Guidelines for Stego/malware detection tools: achieving GDPR compliance. IEEE Technol. Soc. Magaz. **39**(4), 60–70 (2020). https://doi.org/10.1109/MTS.2020.3031848
34. Pawlicka, A., Pawlicki, M., Kozik, R., Choraś, M.: What will the future of cybersecurity bring us, and will it be ethical? The hunt for the black swans of cybersecurity ethics. IEEE Access **11**, 58796–58807 (2023). https://doi.org/10.1109/ACCESS.2023.3283791, https://ieeexplore.ieee.org/document/10145795/. Accessed 18 May 2023
35. Pawlicki, M., Kozik, R., Choraś, M.: A survey on neural networks for (cyber-) security and (cyber-) security of neural networks. Neurocomputing **500**, 1075–1087 (2022). https://doi.org/10.1016/j.neucom.2022.06.002
36. Petersen, L.: The ethical problems in E-business. Chron (2019). https://smallbusiness.chron.com/ethical-problems-ebusiness-62037.html. Accessed 18 May 2023
37. Qureshi, V.: The Importance of Ethics in eCommerce. TechBullion (2022). https://techbullion.com/the-importance-of-ethics-in-ecommerce/. Accessed 18 May 2023
38. RSI Security. Ethical Issues in E-Commerce: Handling Customer Data (2020). https://blog.rsisecurity.com/ethical-issues-in-e-commerce-handling-customer-data/. Accessed 18 May 2023

39. Shanika, S.: The 8 Best Factors Of Online Business Ethics. Smartiac (2022). https://smartiac.org/online-business-ethics/. Accessed 18 May 2023
40. Snyder, H.: Literature review as a research methodology: an overview and guidelines. J. Bus. Res. 333–339 (2019). https://doi.org/10.1016/j.jbusres.2019.07.039
41. Stephanson, A.: Avoid amazon ethics: 5 little-known ways to buy straight from the seller. In: Circuit Blog (2022). https://getcircuit.com/package-tracker/blog/avoid-amazon-ethics. Accessed 18 May 2023
42. Tareque, A.: Ethics in online business: there is no grey area. In: The Business Standard (2021). https://www.tbsnews.net/features/panorama/ethics-online-business-there-no-grey-area-305434. Accessed 18 May 2023
43. Toolin, M.: Privacy, data ethics and the 'seismic shift' in consumer trust. In: eCommerce News (2022). https://ecommercenews.com.au/story/privacy-data-ethics-and-the-seismic-shift-in-consumer-trust. Accessed 18 May 2023
44. Uddin, A.S.M.A.: The Moral Dilemmas Facing Evaly: A Call for Justice in E-Commerce in Bangladesh (2022). https://www.researchgate.net/publication/360773934_The_Moral_Dilemmas_Facing_Evaly_A_Call_for_Justice_in_E-_commerce_in_Bangladesh. Accessed 18 May 2023
45. UNCTAD. How COVID-19 triggered the digital and e-commerce turning point. UNCTAD (2021). https://unctad.org/news/how-covid-19-triggered-digital-and-e-commerce-turning-point. Accessed 18 May 2023
46. UNECE. Harnessing e-commerce post-COVID-19: opportunities and challenges for transition economies (2021). https://unece.org/trade/events/harnessing-e-commerce-post-covid-19-opportunities-and-.challenges-transition-economies. Accessed 18 May 2023
47. UNODC. COVID-19: Cyber Threat Analysis. Tech. rep., UNODC (2020). https://www.unodc.org/documents/middleeastandnorthafrica//2020/COVID19/COVID19_MENA_Cyber_Report_EN.pdf. Accessed 18 May 2023
48. Véliz, C.: Privacy and digital ethics after the pandemic. Nat. Electron. 4(1), 10–11 (2021). https://doi.org/10.1038/s41928-020-00536-y
49. Wallace, F.: Ethical guidelines for the use of E-commerce data. PaymentsJournal (2022). https://www.paymentsjournal.com/ethical-guidelines-for-the-use-of-e-commerce-data/. Accessed 18 May 2023
50. Wilcken, S.: What Exactly Is Ethical eCommerce? Eclipse (2022). https://www.eclipsegroup.co.uk/what-exactly-is-ethical-ecommerce/. Accessed 18 May 2023
51. Yuniarti, F., Arief, R., Meydia, H., Yevis, M.O.: Online retailers' ethics and its effect on repurchase intention: the mediating role of perceived risk. Cogent Bus. Manag. 1 (2022). https://doi.org/10.1080/23311975.2022.2051691

Synthetic Is All You Need: Removing the Auxiliary Data Assumption for Membership Inference Attacks Against Synthetic Data

Florent Guépin⬤, Matthieu Meeus⬤, Ana-Maria Creţu⬤,
and Yves-Alexandre de Montjoye$^{(\boxtimes)}$⬤

Department of Computing and Data Science Institute, Imperial College London,
London, UK
{florent.guepin20,m.meeus22,a.cretu,deMontjoye}@imperial.ac.uk

Abstract. Synthetic data is emerging as one of the most promising solutions to share individual-level data while safeguarding privacy. While membership inference attacks (MIAs), based on shadow modeling, have become the standard to evaluate the privacy of synthetic data, they currently assume the attacker to have access to an auxiliary dataset sampled from a similar distribution as the training dataset. This is often seen as a very strong assumption in practice, especially as the proposed main use cases for synthetic tabular data (e.g. medical data, financial transactions) are very specific and don't have any reference datasets directly available. We here show how this assumption can be removed, allowing for MIAs to be performed using only the synthetic data. Specifically, we developed three different scenarios: (S1) Black-box access to the generator, (S2) only access to the released synthetic dataset and (S3) a theoretical setup as upper bound for the attack performance using only synthetic data. Our results show that MIAs are still successful, across two real-world datasets and two synthetic data generators. These results show how the strong hypothesis made when auditing synthetic data releases – access to an auxiliary dataset – can be relaxed, making the attacks more realistic in practice.

Keywords: Synthetic Data · Privacy · Membership Inference Attacks

1 Introduction

Data is crucial in statistical modeling, machine learning systems, and decision-making processes, driving research and innovation. However, data often pertains directly or indirectly to individuals and may contain sensitive information, such as medical records and financial transactions, raising privacy concerns.

F. Guépin and M. Meeus—These authors contributed equally to this work.

S. Katsikas et al. (Eds.): ESORICS 2023 Workshops, LNCS 14398, pp. 182–198, 2024.
https://doi.org/10.1007/978-3-031-54204-6_10

Synthetic tabular data is a promising solution to share data while limiting the risk of re-identification [4]. A synthetic data generator is a statistical model trained on the original, private dataset and used to generate synthetic records. The generated synthetic records would then not be linkable to any specific individual while retaining most of the statistical utility of the original dataset. Extensive research has been dedicated to exploring a wide range of techniques for generating synthetic data [13,16,17,29,32]. Since, if truly anonymous, synthetic data would fall outside the scope of data protection legislation such as the European Union's General Data Protection Regulation (EU GDPR) [1] or California Consumer Privacy Act [5], various sectors including finance [3], healthcare [28], and research [11] have expressed significant interest in its adoption in practice.

However, synthetic data alone does not necessarily preserve privacy. First, it is long known that aggregation alone does not effectively safeguard privacy [9,22]. Second, achieving formal privacy guarantees for synthetic data generation models poses implementation challenges and currently comes at a cost in utility [2,27].

Membership inference attacks (MIAs) have thus been used to evaluate the privacy preservation capabilities of synthetic data in practice. An MIA aims to infer if a specific target record is part of the generative model's training set. Recent work has shown that synthetic data is vulnerable to MIAs, with state-of-the-art attacks relying on the shadow modeling approach [15,26,27]. This approach involves training a membership classifier to distinguish between synthetic datasets generated from so-called shadow datasets with or without a particular target record. Importantly, these attacks require the attacker to have access to an auxiliary dataset that follows the same distribution as the original, private dataset, from which the attacker will sample their shadow datasets.

We here argue that this is often a strong assumption in practice [24]. While general datasets of images are widely available, medical datasets or datasets of financial transactions – some of the main use cases for synthetic tabular data – are not only not widely available but also very specific e.g. to certain geographies, type of diseases, etc. The practical feasibility of an attack is also an important criterion from a legal perspective when assessing what constitutes anonymous data. Recital 26 of the EU GDPR [1] indeed states that "account should be taken of *all the means reasonably likely to be used*, such as singling out, either by the controller or by another person to identify the natural person directly or indirectly."

Contribution. In this work, we show how synthetic data can effectively replace the auxiliary dataset when running MIAs, removing the strong assumption made by attacks so far and making our attack –in our opinion– more reasonably likely from a legal perspective.

First, we consider an attacker with black-box access to the synthetic data generator, which is used to generate shadow datasets for running the MIA. We evaluate the shadow modeling attacks of Houssiau et al. [15] and Meeus et al. [18] on two real-world datasets, two synthetic data generators and across ten target records identified by the vulnerable record identification method of Meeus et al. [18]. Our results show that MIAs based on synthetic data alone leak the membership of their most vulnerable records 65.5% of the time on average across datasets and generators. This is 15.5 percentage points (p.p.) better than the random guess baseline. We then compare the MIA performance to the traditional setting that assumes access to an auxiliary dataset from the same distribution. We find that our attacker only loses 11.6 p.p. when compared to this much stronger assumption.

Second, we consider an even weaker attacker that exclusively uses the released synthetic data to perform shadow modeling-based MIAs. This attacker obtains an average accuracy of 62.8%. This result is especially meaningful as having access to the released synthetic dataset is an assumption almost always met in practice. Even here, we show the attack to still work 12.8 p.p. better than the random guess baseline.

Third, we identify a potential *double counting* issue which might lower the accuracy of an attack when using synthetic data to replace the auxiliary dataset. We formalize the problem and propose an empirical setup, where we artificially solve the double counting issue, to compute an upper-bound on the accuracy of an attack using only synthetic data. We show the upper-bound to reach 85.8%, 8.7 p.p. higher than the auxiliary data scenario, emphasizing how synthetic only attacks might in the future outperform what is today considered the risk posed by a strong attacker.

MIAs are the main tool to evaluate the privacy-preserving capabilities of synthetic data. However, the strong auxiliary data assumption they currently rely on might lead some to question the practical risk posed by these attacks [8, 24] and whether they are 'reasonably likely'. We here show how this assumption can be relaxed, as attackers having solely access to the synthetic data generator or even released synthetic data are still able to develop meaningful attacks. We finally find that future attacks based on synthetic data might outperform traditional attacks if the double counting issue can be resolved.

2   Background and Related Work

2.1   Synthetic Data Generation

Suppose that an entity (e.g. governmental institution, company) seeks to grant a third party access to a private, tabular dataset D for analysis. This dataset consists of a collection of records, each corresponding to an individual, which we denote by $D = \{x_1, \ldots, x_n\}$. Each record consists of F features, where a feature is the value for a given attribute.

To address privacy risks, realizing that anonymizing record-level data often fails [19], an increasingly popular approach involves training a synthetic data generator and publishing a synthetic dataset [4]. Synthetic data is created by (1) fitting a statistical model to the original data, and (2) using this model to generate artificial ("synthetic") records by sampling new values. Ideally, the synthetic data should preserve key statistical properties of the original dataset D without disclosing private information of the individuals in D.

The statistical model employed for generating synthetic data is referred to as the *synthetic data generator* ϕ, and we write $D^s \sim \Phi, |D^s| = m$ to denote that a synthetic dataset of m records is sampled i.i.d. from the generator Φ, fitted on a dataset D. We write $\Phi = \mathcal{G}(D)$ to say that a certain fitting procedure $\mathcal{G}$ (e.g., parameter fitting of a Bayesian network) was applied to the original dataset D to obtain the generator Φ. The generator can take various forms, such as a probabilistic model like Bayesian networks (BayNet) [32] and Synthpop [20] or a generative adversarial network like CTGAN [29].

2.2   Membership Inference Attacks Against Synthetic Tabular Data

Membership inference attacks (MIAs) have become the standard to evaluate the privacy of synthetic data, machine learning (ML) models, and aggregation mechanisms more broadly. Given the output of an aggregation mechanism, e.g., a synthetic dataset or a set of aggregate statistics computed on a private dataset D, the aim of an MIA is to infer whether a given target record x_T was part of D or not. Successful MIAs have been developed against aggregate statistics of e.g. location data [22], genomic data [14,25], and against ML models [6,24,26].

For MIAs against synthetic tabular data, a first class of methods directly compares the synthetic records to the original records, searching for exact or near-matches [10,12,30,31]. Stadler et al. [27] argue, however, that the studies relying on similarity testing severely underestimate the risk and instead propose an attack using the shadow modeling approach. First introduced to evaluate the privacy of ML models [26], the shadow modeling approach is now the state-of-the-art in evaluating the privacy of synthetic data [15,18,27].

Shadow modeling typically assumes that the attacker has knowledge of the model Φ_T used to generate the synthetic data and has access to an auxiliary dataset D_{aux} that comes from the same distribution as the original dataset $(D_{aux} \sim \mathcal{D})$. The attacker then constructs multiple shadow datasets D_{shadow} utilizing D_{aux}. First, the attacker randomly samples $|D| - 1$ records from D_{aux}, to then add the target record x_T to 50% of the shadow datasets, and a random record x_R to the other 50% instead. Next, by using the knowledge of the model Φ_T, the attacker will train multiple shadow generators Φ_{shadow}, which in turn produce synthetic shadow datasets D^s_{shadow}. The attacker knows which D^s_{shadow} have been derived from a shadow dataset containing the target record x_T and which were not. This enables the attacker to train a binary meta-classifier on features extracted from the synthetic shadow datasets to predict membership. Figure 1 illustrates how the shadow modeling technique is used to train the meta-classifier. Lastly, the meta-classifier is evaluated on synthetic test datasets that are similarly constructed (with 50% having seen the target record during training), but on a disjoint set of records.

Different techniques have been proposed to extract meaningful features from the synthetic shadow datasets to predict membership. Stadler et al. [27] proposed to extract aggregate statistics, specifically the mean and standard deviation of

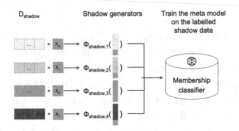

Fig. 1. Illustration of the shadow modeling technique

the attributes, and correlation matrices and histograms. Houssiau et al. [15] extended this work with a *query-based* feature extractor, using k-way marginal statistics computed over the values of the target record for randomly selected subsets of attributes. Lastly, Meeus et al. [18] developed the first trainable feature extractor, which uses the synthetic dataset directly as input to an attention-based classifier. The authors compared the two approaches, showing that the *query-based* method is the state-of-the-art attack on tabular records.

In previous work, attacks against machine learning models using synthetically generated data have been developed [7,26]. In one experiment, Shokri et al. [26] assumed knowledge of the dataset marginals in order to generate synthetic data. In another experiment, the same authors generated this data using local search techniques but the method was shown to only be effective when applied to binary records [24]. Finally, Cretu et al. [7] generated synthetic datasets using the copula generative model that satisfy a subset of the correlations present in the private training dataset D. Differently from these approaches targeting ML models, our work concerns attacks targeting synthetic data and makes no additional assumptions on the attacker's knowledge about the original dataset.

3   Attack Scenarios

We exclusively consider state-of-the-art MIAs, which are based on the shadow modeling technique. We assume that the attacker has access to the synthetic dataset $D^s \sim \phi_T(\mathcal{G}(D))$, where ϕ_T is referred to as the target generator. We will refer to the size of the synthetic dataset as $n_{synthetic}$. The attacker aims to infer whether a particular record, referred to as the target record x_T, was part of the original dataset, i.e., whether $x_T \in D$ or $x_T \notin D$. In line with the literature, we consider the standard setting under which the attacker knows the fitting procedure $\mathcal{G}$ used to train the statistical model on the original data.

To model the uncertainty of the attacker about the dataset, we consider four attack scenarios. First, **(S0) Auxiliary** is the traditional setup where the attacker has access to an auxiliary dataset sampled from the same distribution as the private dataset. We then propose two new scenarios assuming a weaker attacker: **(S1) Black-box**, where the attacker has access to the target generator ϕ_T and can query the generator an arbitrary number of times to sample synthetic records and **(S2) Published**, where the attacker has only access to a released synthetic dataset D^s of the same size as the private dataset. Lastly, as a fourth scenario, we construct an artificial setup **(S3) Upper bound** to evaluate the upper bound of MIAs against synthetic data while only using synthetic records.

3.1   (S0) Auxiliary

As a baseline, we consider the traditional attack scenario [15,27] where the attacker has access to an auxiliary dataset D_{aux} sampled from the same distribution $\mathcal{D}$ as the private dataset D, i.e. $D_{aux} \sim \mathcal{D}$. D_{aux} is then used to construct the n_{shadow} shadow datasets by uniformly sampling records from D_{aux} without replacement. The meta-classifier is then trained to predict membership with as input features extracted from the synthetic shadow datasets.

Next, the meta-classifier is evaluated on n_{test} synthetic datasets, synthesized from test data that is disjoint from the data used for training. The binary membership prediction is then aggregated across all n_{test} synthetic datasets to a final accuracy used as the MIA performance metric.

3.2   (S1) Black Box

Next, we remove the auxiliary dataset assumption. We consider an attacker who is able to query the target generator Φ_T for synthetic records, i.e. has black-box access to the generator. This scenario could, for instance, arise when the end user of the synthetic data would require access to more synthetic records than there were present in the original dataset, e.g. to train ML models. The attacker will here use the black box access to generate m synthetic records to directly construct the shadow datasets.

Note that, unlike the baseline setting (S0) Auxiliary, the shadow datasets and (consequently) the meta-classifier are now specific to the target generator on which it is evaluated. In other words, this setup requires the attacker to train $n_{shadow} \times n_{test}$ generators and n_{test} meta-classifiers while in the standard setting (S0), an attacker needs to train $n_{shadow} + n_{test}$ generators and only one meta-classifier.

Again, an attacker will query the trained meta-classifier for one binary prediction for membership per test dataset, which we aggregate to a final accuracy across all n_{test} generators.

For computational reasons, we sample $m > |D|$ synthetic records for every target generator Φ_T, which we use to sample the shadow datasets in our experiments.

3.3   (S2) Published

In this scenario, we further remove the access to the target generator Φ_T assumption. The only knowledge about the original data available to the attacker is the released synthetic dataset D^s. We here assume that the size of the released synthetic dataset is the same as the original, private set, formally $n_{synthetic} = |D^s| = |D|$.

In this scenario, the attacker trains another generator Φ_S, using the synthetic dataset as training points, i.e., $\Phi_S = \mathcal{G}(D^s)$. With this new generator Φ_S, the attacker generates m new synthetic records to be used to construct the shadow datasets.

We evaluate the MIA performance for this scenario in the same way as in scenario (S1) Black box above.

3.4 (S3) Upper Bound

When an MIA against synthetic data for a particular target record is successful, the meta-classifier is able to distinguish whether the target record was part of the original dataset or not. In other words, the meta-classifier is able to detect the effect of the presence of the target record in the original dataset on the generated synthetic data. As shown by Meeus et al. [18], this effect is more significant for records more distant to their closest neighbours.

In scenarios (S1) and (S2), the attacker uses this synthetic data to construct the shadow datasets. When the target record x_T was part of the target generator's training dataset, we hypothesize that using these synthetic records to construct the shadow datasets could deteriorate the performance of the meta-classifier in two ways. First, as we use synthetic data that is likely impacted by the presence of x_T already to construct the shadow datasets, the two "worlds" (presence or absence of x_T) in the shadow datasets are likely to be less distinguishable overall by the meta-classifier. Second, this could create a discrepancy in the training (on the shadow datasets) and inference task (on the target generator) of the meta-classifier. We call both effects the *double counting issue* and hypothesize that this could impact the attack performance.

We formalize this issue by first defining the concept of adjoining synthetic datasets to then define the *trace* of x_T.

Definition 1. *Let $D = (x_1, \cdots, x_n)$ be a dataset, then an **adjoining dataset** with respect to x_T will be such that $\exists \ k \mid D^T = (x_1, \cdots, x_k, x_T, x_{k+2}, \cdots, x_n)$ and $x_{k+1} \neq x_T$. We call **adjoining synthetic datasets** the resulting synthetic datasets generated by the same generator model $\mathcal{G}$ trained on the respective datasets. Namely, $D^{s,T} \sim \Phi = \mathcal{G}(D^T)$ and $D^s \sim \Phi = \mathcal{G}(D)$ are called two adjoining synthetic datasets.*

Definition 2. *Let $\mathcal{D}^s$ and $\mathcal{D}^{s,T}$ be two adjoining synthetic datasets with respect to x_T. Then, the **trace** of x_T is defined as the impact of excluding (respectively including) the target record in the training dataset D ($D \cup \{x_T\} = D^T$) of a synthetic data generator $\Phi = \mathcal{G}(D)(\Phi = \mathcal{G}(D^T))$ on the generated synthetic data $D^s \sim \Phi$ ($D^{s,T} \sim \Phi$), written $|.|_\Phi$. Formally, $trace(x_T) = |\mathcal{D}^s - \mathcal{D}^{s,T}|_\Phi$.*

At inference time, the meta-classifier is expected to recognize the trace of x_T i.e. $|\mathcal{D}^s - \mathcal{D}^{s,T}|_\Phi$. When synthetic data is used to construct the shadow datasets and the target record has not been part of the training data for the target generator, the meta-classifier has been trained to recognize this same trace and hence, the attacker does not encounter the double counting issue.

However, when the target generator has seen the target record during training, the attacker uses the synthetic dataset $\mathcal{D}^{s,T}$ to construct shadow datasets, each of which will contain x_T with 50% probability as well. In other words, the synthetic shadow datasets will now be either $\mathcal{D}_2^s \sim \Phi = \mathcal{G}(\mathcal{D}^{s,T} \cup \{x_{random}\})$ or $\mathcal{D}_2^{s,T} \sim \Phi = \mathcal{G}(\mathcal{D}^{s,T} \cup \{x_T\})$ with 50% probability. The meta-classifier is hence trained to recognize the trace of trace of x_T i.e. $|\mathcal{D}_2^s - \mathcal{D}_2^{s,T}|_\Phi$, while at inference time it is still expected to recognize the trace of x_T, i.e. $|\mathcal{D}^s - \mathcal{D}^{s,T}|_\Phi$.

To avoid the double counting issue, we here design a hypothetical attack as a slight modification from scenario (S1). We now artificially ensure that the target x_T is never seen during the training of the generator, to then use the same setup as in (S1). Specifically, when the target is not seen during training, nothing changes, and the attacker has black box access to Φ. In contrast, for a target generator that has seen the target record during training (the target generator will generate $\mathcal{D}^{s,T}$ with D^T as training dataset), we ensure the attacker to have access to an adjoining synthetic dataset $\mathcal{D}^s$, by training the same generator Φ on an adjoining dataset D of D^T.

This scenario serves as an **upper bound** for an MIA with access only to synthetic data, since now we artificially avoid the double counting issue. We further evaluate this scenario in the same way as in scenario (S1).

4   Experimental Setup

In this section, we describe the experimental setup for the attacks: the synthetic data generation models, datasets, the meta-classifier methods used and the exact attack parameters.

4.1   Synthetic Data Generators

Synthpop has been introduced by Nowok et al. [20] as an R package for synthetic data generation. It uses classification and regression trees to estimate conditional probabilities from the training dataset, then used to generate synthetic data. In our work, we utilize the Python re-implementation of Synthpop [13] from the reprosyn repository [16].

BayNet uses a Bayesian Network to generate synthetic data. It represents the attributes of the training data as a Directed Acyclic Graph, capturing causal relationships. Each node in the graph has a conditional distribution $\mathbb{P}[X|Parents(X)]$ estimated from the available data. Synthetic data is generated by sampling from the joint distribution obtained by multiplying the computed conditionals. We also use the implementation from the reprosyn repository [16].

4.2   Real World Datasets

UK Census, or the 2011 Census Microdata Teaching File [21], was published by the Office for National Statistics and consists of a random sample representing 1% of the 2011 Census output database for England and Wales. This dataset comprises a total of $n = 569,741$ records and includes $F = 17$ categorical attributes.

Adult [23] is extracted from the 1994 US Census database. The dataset comprises $n = 45,222$ records with $F = 15$ attributes, 9 of which are categorical and 6 continuous.

4.3   Meta-classifier Methods

We consider two previously proposed methods to extract features from the synthetic shadow datasets and to train the meta-classifier.

Query Based. Introduced by Houssiau et al. [15], this state-of-the-art attack uses k-way marginal statistics, or count queries, computed over subsets of the attribute values of the target record from the synthetic dataset. We use 100,000 randomly sampled count queries of the 2^F possibilities and use a random forest classifier with 100 trees and maximum depth of 10 to predict membership.

Target Attention. Introduced by Meeus et al. [18], this method takes as input (part of) the synthetic dataset, and is the first trainable feature extractor for MIAs against synthetic data. The method first computes record-level embeddings. Next, through a custom attention mechanism, these embeddings are aggregated to a dataset-level embedding, which is used to predict binary membership. We use the exact implementation and parameters as laid out in the paper [18].

Table 1. Parameters used throughout experiments.

Dataset	Scenario	$|D_{aux}|$	$|D_{test}|$	m	n_{shadow}	n_{test}
Adult	S0	10000	5000	1000	2000	100
	S1	0	5000	20000		
	S2	0	5000	1000		
	S3	0	5000	20000		
UK Census	S0	50000	25000	1000	2000	100
	S1	0	25000	20000		
	S2	0	25000	1000		
	S3	0	25000	20000		

4.4 Parameters of the Attack

Table 1 shows the parameters used throughout our experiments. Here, D_{aux} represents the auxiliary dataset and D_{test} the dataset that is used to sample the test datasets. Both are random and disjoint subsets of the entire dataset. Further, m represents the number of synthetic records queried from the trained generator, n_{shadow} the number of shadow datasets used for training the meta-classifier, and finally n_{test} the number of datasets used for testing.

Throughout our experiments, the size of the released synthetic dataset is equal to the size of the private dataset D, i.e., $n_{synthetic} = |D| = 1000$, and similarly for the shadow datasets, i.e. $|D_{shadow}| = |D^s_{shadow}| = 1000$. In scenarios (S1) and (S3) where $m > n_{synthetic}$, we train the meta-classifier using shadow datasets randomly sampled from the m synthetic records. At inference time, we use a random subset of $n_{synthetic} = 1000$ synthetic records to query the trained meta-classifier.

When constructing both the n_{shadow} shadow datasets for training and n_{test} datasets for testing, we ensure that the target record x_T is present with 50% probability. This ensures that the evaluation of the attack on the n_{test} datasets is balanced, with a random guess baseline of 50% accuracy for binary prediction of membership.

Lastly, for each dataset, we run the attack on 10 target records selected using the vulnerable record identification method proposed by Meeus et al. [18]. For each record in the original dataset, the method computes its vulnerability score as the mean cosine distance, generalized across attribute types, to its five closest neighbours. The records that are the most distant from their closest neighbours, i.e. have the largest mean distance, are selected as vulnerable records.

5 Results

In this section, we evaluate how the performance of the MIA varies across our attack scenarios over two synthetic data generators and two datasets.

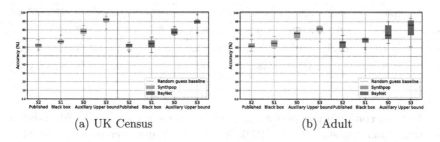

(a) UK Census   (b) Adult

Fig. 2. Comparison of MIA accuracy for the query based attack method across the 4 different scenarios (S0, S1, S2 and S3), for both generators Synthpop and BayNet. Figure (a) shows results for UK Census, while figure (b) displays results for Adult.

5.1 Query Based Attack

We first use the state-of-the-art, query based attack method as introduced by Houssiau et al. [15] to compare the MIA performance across different scenarios.

We start by evaluating our weak attackers (S1) Black box and (S2) Published, where the attacker has only access to the target generator Φ_T or the released synthetic dataset respectively.

Figure 2 and Table 2 show that, across datasets and generators, an attacker in the (S1) Black box scenario achieves an average accuracy of 65.5%. This is 15.5% better than the random guess baseline of 50%. This shows that the traditional, strong assumption of having access to an auxiliary dataset can be removed while still successfully inferring membership.

Next, we aim to make the attack as realistic as possible. To achieve that goal, we weaken the assumptions for the attacker to only have access to the published synthetic dataset ((S2) Published). Remarkably, we find that the MIA performance remains fairly constant when compared to the (S1) Black box scenario. Figure 2 shows that across datasets and generators, we achieve an average accuracy of 62.8%, which is only 2.7 p.p. lower than the (S1) Black box scenario. These results show that MIAs against synthetic data can still be successful, i.e. 12.8 p.p. better than the random baseline, when the released dataset is the only information available to the attacker. Given that releasing synthetic data instead of the original dataset is often the ultimate goal of generating synthetic data, we argue that scenario (S2) Published represents a minimal assumption that is almost always met in practice. Our results show that even in this realistic case, records detected by the vulnerable record identification method of Meeus et al. [18] are at risk.

Table 2. MIA accuracy results (mean and standard deviation for 10 target records) across datasets and generators, for the query based attack.

Scenario	UK census		Adult		Average
	Synthpop	BayNet	Synthpop	BayNet	
S0: Auxiliary	78.6 ± 3.5 %	78.4 ± 3.4 %	74.3 ± 6.2 %	77.0 ± 8.6 %	77.1 ± 5.4 %
S1: Black-Box	66.3 ± 3.0 %	64.6 ± 5.3 %	64.1 ± 6.6 %	67.2 ± 4.4 %	65.6 ± 4.8 %
S2: Published	61.9 ± 3.3 %	61.8 ± 3.3 %	63.1 ± 4.9 %	64.4 ± 5.1 %	62.8 ± 4.2 %
S3: Upper Bound	91.1 ± 4.0 %	89.3 ± 5.0 %	80.3 ± 5.1 %	82.5 ± 1.1 %	85.8 ± 3.8 %

We then compare the performance of our weak attacker (S1) Black-box to the traditional strong attacker (S0), where we assume access to an auxiliary dataset D_{aux} of real records from the same distribution as the target dataset D. Figure 2 shows that our (S1) attacker achieves an accuracy 11.6 p.p. lower compared to the baseline scenario (S0), on average across datasets and generators. This is expected for two possible reasons. First, the synthetic data might not be perfectly representative of the original distribution $\mathcal{D}$. Thus, the training distribution of the meta-classifier from scenario (S1), consisting of features extracted from shadow generators trained on not perfectly representative data, might be quite different from the one on which it is evaluated, leading to worse performance. Scenario (S0) does not suffer from this issue, since the meta-classifier is trained on features extracted from shadow generators trained on subsets of D_{aux}, which was itself sampled from the underlying distribution $\mathcal{D}$. Second, there is the potential double counting issue, which we investigate next.

Figure 2 shows that (S3) Upper Bound achieves an MIA performance of 20.3 p.p. more than (S1) Black Box. These results suggest that the double issue might be significantly affecting the performance of the weaker attackers and that fixing this issue could, in the future, bridge the gap between our weak attackers and the (S3) Upper bound scenario.

Lastly, we find that on average, as reported in Table 2 across datasets and generators, this attacker achieves an accuracy of 85.8%, which is 8.7 p.p. higher than in the (S0) Auxiliary scenario. This suggests that synthetic data is representative enough to construct shadow datasets for a successful MIA, and potentially more representative than an auxiliary dataset allowing to outperform scenario (S0).

5.2 Target Attention Attack

In this section, we evaluate if our results and conclusion are consistent across attack methods. To do this, we run the target attention attack method as proposed by Meeus et al. [18] using the same generator and datasets, with the same attack scenarios (S0-3). Figure 3 and Table 3 summarize the results.

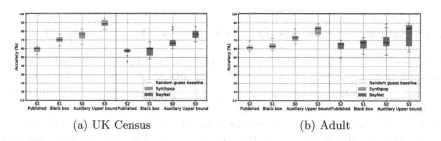

(a) UK Census   (b) Adult

Fig. 3. Comparison of MIA accuracy for the target attention attack method across the 4 different scenarios S0, S1, S2 and S3, for both generators Synthpop and BayNet. Figure (a) shows results for UK Census, while figure (b) displays results for Adult.

First, we find that the attacker from scenario (S1) is still successful using the target attention attack. Across datasets and generators, the average accuracy of the MIA lies at 63.3 %, which is 13.3 p.p. better than the random baseline. This confirms that after removing access to the auxiliary dataset, records remain vulnerable against MIAs, even when using a distinct attack method.

Second, in scenario (S2), the MIA using the target attention method achieves 60.2%, a drop of 3.1 p.p. compared to scenario (S1). These results show that the most realistic scenario, even across attack methods, can be considered as a realistic threat with a performance significantly above the random guess baseline.

Next, we find that the difference between the baseline scenario (S0) Auxiliary and scenario (S1) is on par with the results for the query-based attack. Across datasets and generators, the average accuracy drops by 8.5 p.p. while still achieving an average score of 63.3%.

Finally, in scenario (S3), we confirm our findings that the double counting issue is the main reason affecting the performance of the weaker attackers, also when using the target attention method. The MIAs achieve an average of 81.2% accuracy, which is 9.4 p.p. higher than (S0) and 17.9 p.p. higher than (S1).

The fact that our findings are consistent across two very distinct attack methods suggests that even when new attack methods are developed, MIAs against synthetic data using only synthetic data will be successful.

Table 3. MIA accuracy results (mean and standard deviation for 10 target records) across datasets and generators, for the target attention attack.

Scenario	UK census		Adult		Average
	Synthpop	BayNet	Synthpop	BayNet	
S0: Auxiliary	75.4 ± 5.4 %	68.7 ± 7.9 %	73.2 ± 4.7 %	69.7 ± 10.3 %	71.8 ± 7.1 %
S1: Black-Box	61.5 ± 3.3 %	62.1 ± 6.3 %	64.1 ± 4.3 %	65.5 ± 6.2 %	63.3 ± 5.0 %
S2: Published	58.9 ± 3.0 %	56.4 ± 4.3 %	61.5 ± 3.3 %	63.8 ± 5.6 %	60.2 ± 4.1 %
S3: Upper Bound	88.9 ± 4.4 %	76.8 ± 5.2 %	82.0 ± 4.9 %	77.2 ± 13.0 %	81.2 ± 6.9 %

5.3   Robustness Analysis for Number of Synthetic Records m

In scenario (S1) Black Box, we assume the attacker to have black box access to the target generator, i.e. the attacker can query the generator for synthetic records an arbitrary number of times. In our experiments we set the number of synthetic records m to $20,000$.

We now evaluate the effect of the value of m on the attack performance. Across the two datasets, for the BayNet generator, Fig. 4 shows how the MIA performance for scenario (S1) varies for increasing m.

Across datasets, the MIA accuracy remains fairly robust for varying number of synthetic records made available to the attacker. For m varying from $5,000$ to $100,000$, the mean MIA accuracy does not change significantly. First, this shows that $m = 20,000$, as used in our experimental setup, is a good approximation for black box access to the generator. Further, along with the MIA results for scenario (S2) Published, this confirms that releasing a number of synthetic records m larger or equal to the number of original records, allows the attacker to build meaningful MIAs.

6   Future Work

6.1   Impact of Releasing Less Synthetic Records

Intuitively, for a training dataset of fixed size, the more synthetic records we generate, the more information the synthetic dataset might start leaking.

In scenarios (S0) and (S2), the attacker only has access to a limited number of synthetic records $m = |\mathcal{D}|$. As synthetic data is often used to replace the original dataset, we argue that it is reasonable in practice to generate the same amount of synthetic records as the number of training records.

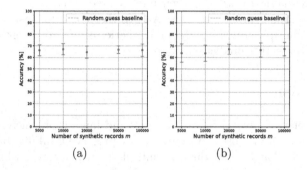

(a)   (b)

Fig. 4. Mean and standard deviation of MIA accuracy for scenario (S1) Black-Box for varying number m synthetic records available to the attacker. Results for BayNet and the query-based attack using (a) UK Census (b) Adult.

However, we hypothesize that releasing fewer synthetic records for a fixed size of the training dataset, namely $m < |\mathcal{D}|$, could reduce the accuracy of our attack. Of course, releasing less synthetic records typically comes at a cost in utility. We leave the evaluation of this potential trade-off between m and the accuracy of our attack on the released synthetic data for future work.

6.2   Differentially Private Synthetic Generation Methods

As main contribution in this work, we show that it is possible to attack a synthetic data generator based only on the generated synthetic data.

We leave for future work to confirm whether these effects translate to synthetic data generators with formal privacy guarantees, such as differentially private generators proposed in the literature [17,32]. Previous work has shown that Differential Privacy (DP) comes at a cost in utility [2,27] and that the MIA accuracy drops for decreasing value of the privacy budget ϵ [18]. We expect that, while exhibiting similar trends, our findings would translate to DP generators.

6.3   Bridging the Gap with the Upper Bound

Our results show that scenario (S3) achieves a significant MIA accuracy, namely higher than scenarios (S1) and (S2), and even higher than scenario (S0). We leave for future work to address the double counting issue we identified in practice, to bridge the gap between scenarios (S1, S2) and the upper bound scenario (S3).

Potentially, an attacker could remove the synthetic records close to the target record, prior to using the synthetic data to construct the shadow models. This could reduce the impact of the double counting issue, but might also introduce bias into the shadow datasets. Additionally, note that in scenario (S1) we currently train the meta classifier using shadow datasets randomly sampled from $m = 20000$ synthetic records, to then infer a prediction on a random subset of $n_{synthetic} = 1000$ synthetic records. An attacker could for instance infer the prediction on multiple subsets of the m synthetic records to potentially make a more optimal, ensemble prediction.

7   Conclusion

Sharing data plays a pivotal role in research and innovation. Increasingly, synthetic data has been proposed to share privacy-preserving tabular data, by synthesizing records that are not directly linkable to real records, while retaining data utility.

Membership Inference Attacks (MIAs) are the standard to audit the privacy preservation of synthetic data, and recent work has shown that these attacks can successfully infer the membership of certain records in the private dataset. State-of-the-art MIAs rely on shadow modeling, which traditionally assumes an attacker to have access to an auxiliary dataset.

First, this auxiliary data assumption is hard to meet in practice. Second, GDPR Recital 26 [1] states that, to legally meet anonymization standards, all means reasonably likely for an attacker to possess should be considered.

We here proposed a more realistic attack by removing the auxiliary data assumption. Across two real world datasets and two synthetic data generators, we find that MIAs are still successful when only using synthetic data.

Specifically, we find that on average, an attacker with black box access to the generator achieves 65.5% accuracy, while an attacker with only access to the released synthetic dataset attains an accuracy of 62.8%. The latter result is particularly significant as it demonstrates that an attacker can extract sensitive information from released synthetic data without any additional information.

Moreover, we identify a double counting issue and establish an upper bound for MIA accuracy against synthetic data when only synthetic data is available. Using current state-of-the-art attacks, this upper bound stands at 85.8%, which is, remarkably, higher than traditional attacks using auxiliary data. This finding highlights the potential for future researchers to bridge the existing gap of MIA performance between realistic scenarios and the upper bound.

Our results provide compelling evidence that MIAs against synthetic data pose a realistic threat in practice. We hope this helps researchers and practitioners to better evaluate risks associated with releasing synthetic data, while encouraging the development of methods to address these concerns.

Acknowledgements. We acknowledge computational resources and support provided by the Imperial College Research Computing Service (http://doi.org/10.14469/hpc/2232.).

References

1. General data protection regulation (2016). https://gdpr-info.eu/
2. Annamalai, M.S.M.S., Gadotti, A., Rocher, L.: A linear reconstruction approach for attribute inference attacks against synthetic data. arXiv preprint arXiv:2301.10053 (2023)
3. Authority, F.C.: Synthetic data to support financial services innovation (2022). https://www.fca.org.uk/publication/call-for-input/synthetic-data-to-support-financial-services-innovation.pdf. Accessed 02 June 2023
4. Bellovin, S.M., Dutta, P.K., Reitinger, N.: Privacy and synthetic datasets. Stan. Tech. L. Rev. **22**, 1 (2019)
5. Bukaty, P.: The California Consumer Privacy Act (CCPA): An Implementation Guide. IT Governance Publishing (2019). http://www.jstor.org/stable/j.ctvjghvnn
6. Carlini, N., Chien, S., Nasr, M., Song, S., Terzis, A., Tramer, F.: Membership inference attacks from first principles. In: 2022 IEEE Symposium on Security and Privacy (SP), pp. 1897–1914. IEEE (2022)
7. Crețu, A.M., Guépin, F., de Montjoye, Y.A.: Correlation inference attacks against machine learning models. arXiv preprint arXiv:2112.08806 (2021)
8. Deng, Z., Chen, K., Meng, G., Zhang, X., Xu, K., Cheng, Y.: Understanding real-world threats to deep learning models in android apps. In: Proceedings of the 2022 ACM SIGSAC Conference on Computer and Communications Security, pp. 785–799 (2022)
9. Dinur, I., Nissim, K.: Revealing information while preserving privacy. In: Proceedings of the Twenty-Second ACM SIGMOD-SIGACT-SIGART Symposium on Principles of Database Systems, pp. 202–210 (2003)
10. Domingo-Ferrer, J., Ricci, S., Soria-Comas, J.: Disclosure risk assessment via record linkage by a maximum-knowledge attacker. In: 2015 13th Annual Conference on Privacy, Security and Trust (PST), pp. 28–35. IEEE (2015)
11. Edge, D., et al.: Design of a privacy-preserving data platform for collaboration against human trafficking. arXiv preprint arXiv:2005.05688 (2020)
12. Giomi, M., Boenisch, F., Wehmeyer, C., Tasnádi, B.: A unified framework for quantifying privacy risk in synthetic data. arXiv preprint arXiv:2211.10459 (2022)
13. Hazy: Synthpop (2019). https://github.com/hazy/synthpop
14. Homer, N., et al.: Resolving individuals contributing trace amounts of DNA to highly complex mixtures using high-density SNP genotyping microarrays. PLoS Genet. **4**(8), e1000167 (2008)
15. Houssiau, F., et al.: TAPAS: a toolbox for adversarial privacy auditing of synthetic data. In: NeurIPS 2022 Workshop on Synthetic Data for Empowering ML Research (2022)

16. Alan Turing Institute: Resprosyn (2022). https://github.com/alan-turing-institute/reprosyn
17. Jordon, J., Yoon, J., Van Der Schaar, M.: PATE-GAN: generating synthetic data with differential privacy guarantees. In: International Conference on Learning Representations (2019)
18. Meeus, M., Guepin, F., Cretu, A.M., de Montjoye, Y.A.: Achilles' heels: vulnerable record identification in synthetic data publishing. arXiv preprint arXiv:2306.10308 (2023)
19. de Montjoye, Y.A., Hidalgo, C.A., Verleysen, M., Blondel, V.D.: Unique in the crowd: the privacy bounds of human mobility. Sci. Rep. **3**(1), 1–5 (2013)
20. Nowok, B., Raab, G.M., Dibben, C.: synthpop: bespoke creation of synthetic data in R. J. Stat. Softw. **74**, 1–26 (2016)
21. Office for National Statistics: Census microdata teaching files (2011). https://www.ons.gov.uk/census/2011census/2011censusdata/censusmicrodata/microdatateachingfile
22. Pyrgelis, A., Troncoso, C., De Cristofaro, E.: Knock knock, who's there? Membership inference on aggregate location data. arXiv preprint arXiv:1708.06145 (2017)
23. Ronny, K., Barry, B.: UCI machine learning repository: adult data set (1996). https://archive.ics.uci.edu/ml/datasets/Adult
24. Salem, A., Zhang, Y., Humbert, M., Berrang, P., Fritz, M., Backes, M.: ML-Leaks: model and data independent membership inference attacks and defenses on machine learning models. arXiv preprint arXiv:1806.01246 (2018)
25. Sankararaman, S., Obozinski, G., Jordan, M.I., Halperin, E.: Genomic privacy and limits of individual detection in a pool. Nat. Genet. **41**(0), 065–067 (2009)
26. Shokri, R., Stronati, M., Song, C., Shmatikov, V.: Membership inference attacks against machine learning models. In: 2017 IEEE Symposium on Security and Privacy (SP), pp. 3–18. IEEE (2017)
27. Stadler, T., Oprisanu, B., Troncoso, C.: Synthetic data-anonymisation groundhog day. In: 31st USENIX Security Symposium (USENIX Security 22), pp. 1451–1468 (2022)
28. Tucker, A., Wang, Z., Rotalinti, Y., Myles, P.: Generating high-fidelity synthetic patient data for assessing machine learning healthcare software. NPJ Digit. Med. **3**(1), 1–13 (2020)
29. Xu, L., Skoularidou, M., Cuesta-Infante, A., Veeramachaneni, K.: Modeling tabular data using conditional GAN. In: Wallach, H., Larochelle, H., Beygelzimer, A., d'Alché-Buc, F., Fox, E., Garnett, R. (eds.) Advances in Neural Information Processing Systems, vol. 32. Curran Associates, Inc. (2019). https://proceedings.neurips.cc/paper_files/paper/2019/file/254ed7d2de3b23ab10936522dd547b78-Paper.pdf
30. Yale, A., Dash, S., Dutta, R., Guyon, I., Pavao, A., Bennett, K.P.: Assessing privacy and quality of synthetic health data. In: Proceedings of the Conference on Artificial Intelligence for Data Discovery and Reuse, pp. 1–4 (2019)
31. Yale, A., Dash, S., Dutta, R., Guyon, I., Pavao, A., Bennett, K.P.: Privacy preserving synthetic health data. In: ESANN 2019-European Symposium on Artificial Neural Networks, Computational Intelligence and Machine Learning (2019)
32. Zhang, J., Cormode, G., Procopiuc, C.M., Srivastava, D., Xiao, X.: PrivBayes: private data release via Bayesian networks. ACM Trans. Database Syst. **42**(4) (2017). https://doi.org/10.1145/3134428

Patient-Centric Health Data Sovereignty: An Approach Using Proxy Re-Encryption

Bruno Rodrigues[1] , Ivone Amorim[2]([✉]) , Ivan Silva[2] ,
and Alexandra Mendes[3]

[1] Faculty of Engineering, University of Porto, Porto, Portugal
up202103390@edu.fe.up.pt
[2] PORTIC – Porto Research, Technology & Innovation Center, Polytechnic of Porto,
4200-374 Porto, Portugal
{ivone.amorim,ivcps}@sc.ipp.pt
[3] Faculty of Engineering, University of Porto, Porto & HASLab/INESC TEC, Porto,
Portugal
alexandra@archimendes.com

Abstract. The exponential growth in the digitisation of services implies the handling and storage of large volumes of data. Businesses and services see data sharing and crossing as an opportunity to improve and produce new business opportunities. The health sector is one area where this proves to be true, enabling better and more innovative treatments. Notwithstanding, this raises concerns regarding personal data being treated and processed. In this paper, we present a patient-centric platform for the secure sharing of health records by shifting the control over the data to the patient, therefore, providing a step further towards data sovereignty. Data sharing is performed only with the consent of the patient, allowing it to revoke access at any given time. Furthermore, we also provide a *break-glass* approach, resorting to Proxy Re-encryption (PRE) and the concept of a centralised trusted entity that possesses instant access to patients' medical records. Lastly, an analysis is made to assess the performance of the platform's key operations, and the impact that a PRE scheme has on those operations.

Keywords: data-sovereignty · cryptography · PRE · access delegation · e-health · PHR

1 Introduction

The ever growing digitisation of services that we use daily, as well as the increasing interest in data crossing and sharing to improve processes, services, and

---

This work was partially supported by the Norte Portugal Regional Operational Programme (NORTE 2020), under the PORTUGAL 2020 Partnership Agreement, through the European Regional Development Fund (ERDF), within project "Cybers SeC IP" (NORTE-01-0145-FEDER-000044).

S. Katsikas et al. (Eds.): ESORICS 2023 Workshops, LNCS 14398, pp. 199–215, 2024.
https://doi.org/10.1007/978-3-031-54204-6_11

achieve new business opportunities, raises concerns regarding how data is handled and processed. In the healthcare sector, data sharing is not only beneficial, but also needed to provide the best care possible to the patients. However, this data is also highly sensitive, which requires special care. Several governmental measures have already been taken to improve and standardise the way in which data is shared, such as the European Data Governance Act [6], GDPR[1] and, more specifically, in personal health information, HIPAA[2] and HITECH[3]. These directives instigate a user-centric paradigm, granting individuals sovereignty over their data.

Several approaches have been proposed for ensuring security and privacy in e-health systems. Conventional encryption techniques based on symmetric and asymmetric encryption like AES and ECC are commonly used [4]. However, these techniques become problematic when data needs to be shared among multiple entities due to redundancy and computational burden [5]. Alternative approaches that incorporate policy constraints, such as Attribute-Based Encryption (ABE), are potential solutions [5], but they come with their own complexities and limitations, such as managing attribute-based keys and overriding policies in emergencies [7]. ABE also lacks the fine-grained access control necessary for a patient-centric sovereign approach.

Proxy Re-Encryption (PRE) is a cryptographic solution for secure data sharing without prior knowledge of the recipient. Unlike ABE, it does not rely on policies or attributes. PRE converts a ciphertext to a recipient's key without revealing the plaintext to the intermediary entity. It is particularly useful in semi-trusted cloud environments [17]. In e-health, PRE has already been used to securely share medical records [19,20,23,26], including in emergency scenarios [19]. However, challenges remain in terms of revocability, computational effort, and safeguarding emergencies [26]. Existing solutions for emergency scenarios are limited and rely on assumptions that may impact efficiency and reliability.

In this context, it is necessary to develop a platform that addresses the aforementioned concerns. This includes enabling more control over the data by the patient while ensuring the safety of that data, even in semi-trusted environments. This contributes to the collaborative aspect of e-health and thus enables better treatments and advancements in the healthcare sector.

In this paper, we present a platform that leverages PRE to enhance health data sharing. Umbral's PRE [16] is used as the foundation for re-encryption processes, through which we achieve unidirectionality and non-interactivity, ensuring secure re-encryption from the patient to the data user (e.g., practitioners or health centres) without requiring the data user's private key. This approach centres on the expressed consent of the patient to data sharing, eliminating the need for prior identification of authorised parties - a drawback identified in previous solutions. Additionally, our platform offers revocability options, such as

[1] https://data.europa.eu/eli/reg/2016/679/oj.
[2] https://www.cdc.gov/phlp/publications/topic/hipaa.html.
[3] https://www.hipaajournal.com/what-is-the-hitech-act/.

time-based access limits and patient-initiated access revocation. Importantly, the revocation of access does not require changes to the encrypted healthcare database, distinguishing our platform from the ones that rely on identity and attribute-based PRE schemes.

Furthermore, in the context of healthcare, it is crucial to ensure data sharing in emergency situations when explicit patient consent may not be possible. Our platform addresses this challenge by incorporating a trusted entity for data access when patient authorisation is infeasible.

In summary, our main contributions are:

- A patient-centric platform, that empowers patients with sovereign control over their health data, enabling granular access control and facilitating the sharing of health records only with explicit consent.
- Robust data protection using Umbral's PRE, ensuring secure and encrypted health data sharing without compromising the data user's private key.
- A robust access revocation mechanism that enables time-based access limits and supports manual revocation by the patient at any time and with immediate effect.
- A break-glass mechanism to ensure seamless emergency data access.

The remainder of this paper is organised as follows. Section 2 introduces basic concepts and definitions, as well as the classification and properties of PRE schemes. Furthermore, an analysis is made concerning the framework on which the access delegation mechanism is based. Section 3 presents the current picture of the PRE and the advancements regarding break-glass scenarios. Section 4 details the proposed solution and its implementation. Section 5 is concerned with the performance test, respective results, and discussion. Lastly, Sect. 6 presents the conclusions and future work.

2   Proxy Re-Encryption

PRE is a cryptographic technique that enables a third-party entity, named proxy, to delegate access to encrypted data, without being able to infer the plaintext content of that data. This is achieved by transforming a ciphertext encrypted under one key into a ciphertext encrypted under a different key.

2.1   Syntax and Basic Definitions

Since PRE can be seen as a way to delegate decryption rights to a party, it is possible to categorise the different entities according to the delegation relation they possess with each other. The *delegator* is the entity that owns the data and delegates decryption rights. The *proxy* is the intermediary entity in the delegation process, which uses a Proxy Re-encryption Key (PRK) to transform the ciphertext encrypted under the delegator's public key into a ciphertext that can be decrypted only by using the delegatee's private key. Finally, the *delegatee* is the entity that accesses the information through delegation of decryption rights by the delegator.

Definition 1 (PRE). *A PRE scheme can be defined based on five different algorithms:*

- **KeyGen** — *On input of a security parameter n, the key generation algorithm KeyGen outputs a public/private key pair (pk_A, sk_A) for a given user A.*
- **ReKey** — *On input of a public/private key pair (pk_A, sk_A) for user A and a public/private key pair (pk_B, sk_B) for user B, a PRK $rk_{A \to B}$ is computed.*
- **Encrypt** — *Given the input of a public key pk_A and a message $m \in M$, the encryption algorithm outputs a ciphertext $c_A \in C_1$.*
- **ReEncrypt** — *On input of a ciphertext $c_A \in C_1$ and a PRK $rk_{A \to B}$, the re-encryption algorithm ReEncrypt transforms a ciphertext $c_A \in C_1$ into a ciphertext $c_B \in C_2$.*
- **Decrypt** — *Given a private key sk_A from user A and a ciphertext $c_A \in C_S$ ($S \in \{1, 2\}$) from user A, the same executes the decryption algorithm and outputs the original message $m \in M$.*

According to Qin et al. [18], a PRE scheme can be classified based on its abilities. For example, regarding its directionality, we say that the scheme is *unidirectional* if it enables the delegator's ciphertext to be re-encrypted into the delegatee's ciphertext but not vice versa. Otherwise, we call it *bidirectional*. The multi-use/single-use classification focuses on the number of times the PRK can be used to re-encrypt data. In *multi-use* schemes, the PRK can be utilised to perform several re-encryptions. In the case of a *single-use* scheme, the PRK can only be used to perform a single transformation. Interactivity dictates whether the re-encryption is computed using just the public key from the delegatee (*non-interactive* scheme) or both the public and private keys (*interactive* scheme). Depending on the scenario of utilisation, some properties may be more desirable than others.

Other authors classify PRE schemes according to their way of functioning [9,10]. For example, an Identity-Based PRE (IB-PRE) scheme derives public keys from identity attributes (e.g. email). The messages are encrypted using an identity string from the delegatee. Attribute-Based PRE (AB-PRE) schemes allow transforming a ciphertext defined by a set of attributes or access policies into another ciphertext with a different set of attributes.

2.2 Umbral's PRE Scheme

The Umbral PRE scheme is, in its essence, a threshold PRE scheme. This scheme features an Elliptic Curve Integrated Encryption Scheme (EICS-KEM) inspired in ANSI X9.63 [1] and proposes several improvements over the original PRE scheme proposed by Blaze et al. [3], namely unidirectionality, non-interactivity, and verifiability. It relies on the concept of semi-trusted proxies, also known as ursulas. Being a threshold PRE scheme, it splits the PRK according to shares. The *threshold* portion of the scheme dictates the minimum number of those shares required to decrypt the information.

Splitting the PRK across multiple proxies brings some benefits namely eliminating a single point of failure, in case of a malfunction or compromise of one of the proxies the PRK is still safeguarded.

The re-encryption processes in our platform are supported by pyUmbral [15], a Python-based implementation of Umbral.

Figure 1 presents an overview of the main processes and data flows involved in the Umbral PRE scheme. This system beholds seven main processes: *Encapsulation, Encryption, Generate PRK fragments, Re-encapsulation, Decapsulation,* and *Decryption*. These processes are supported by three major cryptographic methods: Key Encapsulation Mechanism (KEM), Data Encapsulation Mechanism (DEM), and Shamir Secret Sharing (SSS) [21].

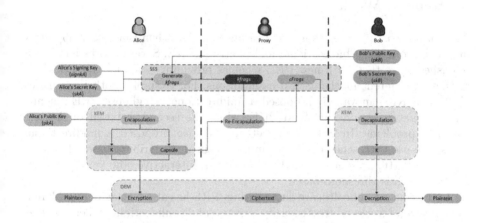

Fig. 1. Procedural overview of pyUmbral PRE scheme

The first step in this process is *Encapsulation*. This is achieved through the use of a Key Encapsulation Mechanism (KEM), in this case, a loosely inspired implementation of ECIES-KEM introduced by Shoup [22]. The KEM is fed with Alice's public key pk_A and outputs a symmetric key K and a *capsule*.

With the capsule and the symmetric key K, the *Encryption* process is performed using a Data Encapsulation Mechanism (DEM) which uses Authenticated Encryption with Additional Data (AEAD). This outputs a ciphertext encrypted with the symmetric key.

When the data is encrypted and stored in the cloud, in order for the access delegation to occur, there is a need to generate a PRK. This is performed by the *Generate PRK fragments* process resorting to the notions present in Shamir Secret Sharing [21], Alice's private key and signing key $signk_A$, and Bob's public key pk_B. This enables the generation of the PRK fragments or *kFrags*. The number of fragments is defined by the number of shares.

The *kFrags* are stored by the proxy for further use in the *Re-encapsulation* process. This process is responsible for generating the *cFrags* which enables Bob to gain access to the file at a later stage. To generate the *cFrags* just the capsule and the *kFrags* are needed. This is due to the fact that this PRE scheme performs the re-encryption over the capsule.

Lastly, once Bob wants to retrieve a file, the *Decapsulation* process needs to happen. This process resorts to SSS in order to reconstruct the symmetric key k. To do so, Alice's public key, Alice's verifying key vk_A for signature verification of the *cFrags*, Bob's private key sk_B, and the *capsule* are needed. Through the use of a Key Derivation Function within the KEM, it is possible to derive the symmetric key K which together with the ciphertext is passed to the DEM. The DEM performs the *Decryption* process and outputs the plaintext content of the file that Bob can now use.

3   Related Work

The notion of PRE made its first appearance in 1998 when Blaze et al. [3] introduced the concept of bidirectional and multi-use PRE. Several works have been published since then with new PRE schemes providing new functionalities and relying on different mathematical assumptions. For example, both Hanaoka et al. [8] and Kirshanova [11] proposed a unidirectional, single-use PRE scheme, but the first relies on threshold PKE, while the second is based on lattice-hardness problems. In 2015, Liang et al. [14] also proposed a unidirectional and single-use PRE scheme, which can be classified as attribute-based. Later, in 2017, Nuñez [16] presented a unidirectional, non-interactive, and verifiable PRE scheme which is threshold-based.

In the context of healthcare data sharing, PRE has also been widely explored. In fact, several works address security, privacy, and confidentiality when it comes to the design and implementation of e-health systems. However, there is still a lack of development concerning safeguarding emergency scenarios in the context of e-health systems [26]. Works that address this kind of scenario in its design, refer to this as break-glass approaches. In 2017, Au et al. [2] proposed a framework for the secure sharing of Personal Health Records (PHRs) that relies on attribute-based PRE and which addresses emergency scenarios. The break-glass capabilities are provided with ABE. In this scheme, the emergency department attribute is always appended to the policy that encrypts the patient PHR, thus providing instant access to the entity from the moment the same is uploaded. The problem with this approach, and in general with ABE approaches, is that they present some caveats, namely key management and resorting to other mechanisms in break-glass approaches. This is due to the fact that emergency normally means an exception to a policy and, thus, overriding that same policy might be a hefty task in some implementations. In 2019, Yang et al. [25] also proposed an approach that is based on an attribute-based PRE, and provided self-adaptive access control, meaning that the system can automatically adapt to normal or emergency situations. However, their break-glass mechanism resorts to a *password-based* paradigm. This approach raises some concerns, namely in the assumption that the individual that stores the password has the necessary means to ensure its secrecy. More recently, in 2022, Li et al. [13] proposed a system for IoT sensors combining PRE and PKE with equality test, permitting searches under different public keys and secure data sharing. However, it does not discuss emergency situations. In the same year, Ren et al. [20], proposed a non-interactive, multi-use, certificateless PRE for sharing health data in a cloud environment. Even though their approach gives full control to the data owner, it has two important drawbacks, namely it is interactive and does not propose a break-glass mechanism. Also in 2022, Xue [24] published a secure data sharing and authorised Searchable framework for e-healthcare systems. This framework lies on a conditional and unidirectional PRE scheme with keyword search. It is also idealised for managing sensible data from medical wearable devices. This platform has some disadvantages namely regarding the PRK generation performance. Also, this work does not address emergency situations. Finally, in 2022, Li et al. [12] propose a framework which is also based on attribute-based PRE that features break-glass capabilities. However, it leaves open the possible solution for revocability. That being said, there is a need to develop a solution that can cope with all the aforementioned concerns and that contributes to a more reliable and robust break-glass approach.

4 Patient-Centric Health Data Sovereignty

In this section, we introduce the envisioned solution for a patient-centric platform that enables health data sovereignty through PRE. The subsequent section presents the architecture of the solution, followed by a description of the processes involved in the key operations for access delegation.

4.1 Proposed Solution

The proposed solution consists of four main nodes: the client, the resource server, the proxy server, and the authorization server, as depicted in Fig. 2.

The client node hosts the client-side application developed with Next.js[4]. This client node communicates with the server nodes via Representation State Transfer (REST) and the Hypertext Transfer Protocol (HTTP). The business logic is divided between the resource and proxy server nodes. The resource server is based on the FastAPI framework[5] running in a Python environment. This server is trusted by the data delegator and it is responsible for assisting the client-side operations, namely feeding the data the client node needs to display the information to the user. The resource server node also performs some core operations such as the initial encryption and final decryption of the Electronic Health Record (EHR) stored in the database server node hosted in a cloud environment (MongoDB[6]) as well as the management of delegation requests (accept or decline). Some other complementary operations are also performed such as the generation of the PRK which is stored afterwards by the proxy

---

[4] https://nextjs.org/.
[5] https://fastapi.tiangolo.com/.
[6] https://www.mongodb.com/.

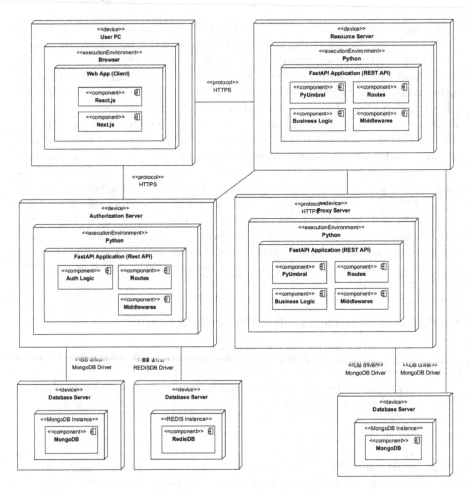

Fig. 2. Deployment diagram of the architecture

server node, and the signature verification of the PRK fragments and capsule fragments.

The proxy server is solely responsible for the process of EHR delegation, being used for the re-encryption of the capsules and the storage of the PRK.

The authorisation server is responsible for performing the authentication of the different users of the platform as well as the issuing and claims verification of the authorisation tokens. These tokens are subsequently used to consume the APIs provided by the resource and proxy server nodes. This node is also associated with two persistence nodes. An in-memory database (REDIS[7] instance) for persisting and performing the lookup of the refresh tokens and a MongoDB

---

[7] https://redis.com/.

instance for storing general purpose user information such as name, email, password, public and verifying keys and roles.

4.2 Authentication/Authorisation

The authorisation is performed by resorting to JSON Web Tokens (JWT) which are signed using HMAC SHA256. This ensures the tokens can not be tampered with or changed, thus enabling secure transmissions between parties.

The authentication flow comprises a traditional email/password authentication, where each user needs to provide a valid email and password. In case of successful authentication, a pair of tokens are issued (access/refresh token) containing some claims needed to support the client-side application. These claims follow the standards and restrictions defined in Request for Comments 7519[8]. Besides the pair of tokens, a Cross-site Request Forgery token is also sent for further protection in requests that require cookies. The refresh token is also sent in a cookie configured with the *secure* and *httpOnly* flags to ensure it is only transmitted through HTTPS and not available to JavaScript in case of a Cross-site Scripting vulnerability in the client-side application.

Since JWT tokens are self-contained, there is no natural way of revoking them. In order to tackle this problem anti-theft mitigation techniques were implemented: *refresh token rotation* and *token reuse detection*.

4.3 Access Delegation Scenario

Access delegation is the core problem tackled in this work. The next sections dissect the access delegation flow from the moment the file is uploaded by the patient to the moment the plaintext content is retrieved by the healthcare provider. For demonstration purposes, the step-by-step process between two entities, Alice (delegator) and Bob (delegatee), is presented.

Upload of an EHR. The access delegation starts with the upload of an EHR by Alice. When Alice uploads a new EHR, which can be a Portable Document Format (PDF) or an image, the resource server encrypts the file using a symmetric key resulting from the encapsulation process and stores it together with the capsule, resulting from the *encapsulation* process, and an associated *userId*.

Another process that is also performed in this step and further detailed in Sect. 4.4 is the safeguarding of emergency situations. Besides the persistence of the file in the database, a PRK is also generated in order to provide access to the predefined trusted entity. This ensures that the trusted party possesses the means to access the file from the moment it is uploaded and that no extra input from the user is needed in this regard. This PRK is sent to the proxy for subsequent use.

Bob Requests Access to an EHR. When Bob wants to access Alice's uploaded EHR, he needs to formalise his intentions by issuing a share request to the resource server containing the EHR's *resourceId*. In this step, the system

---

[8] https://datatracker.ietf.org/doc/html/rfc7519#section-4.

checks if Bob is the owner of the EHR. This prevents a user from performing a share request to itself, something that violates the business rules of the platform since if the file is owned by a given user, it automatically has access to it and no share request is needed.

Once this validation is performed, and provided with the *resourceId*, the resource server generates a share request that includes the *resourceId*, the *delegatorId* and the *delegateeId*, as well as a *status* that is set to pending by default. **Alice Answers the Share Request.** Now that Bob asked Alice for access to the EHR, Alice is now capable of answering the share request. Depending on Alice's answer, the execution flow might have two outcomes:

Accept Scenario. — In case of an acceptance, Alice needs to generate the PRK required to re-encrypt the capsule and further enable Bob to have access to the plaintext content of the EHR. To achieve such a feat, Alice requires her secret key and signing key pair, needed to verify the signature of the *kFrags* and *cFrags* at a later stage, as well as Bob's public key. Notice that just the public key is needed, due to the non-interactivity property of this PRE scheme. Lastly, since the underlying scheme of the access delegation mechanism is a threshold PRE scheme, there is also the need to provide a *threshold* which defines the minimum number of shares needed to decrypt the capsule and the number of *shares* which dictates the number of outputted PRK fragments. This last aforementioned operation outputs the *kFrags*, which are sent to the proxy along with a *shareId* bundling the PRK to a specific share request. Both attributes are persisted by the proxy for further use once Bob retrieves the EHR.

The share request operation ends with the status update of the share request, which is defined as accepted, together with an arbitrary expiration date defined by Alice. This expiration date is optional, being possible to share an EHR indefinitely or temporarily, in which case the share request is automatically revoked through a cron job once that date is transposed. This ensures the time-based access delegation aspect that this work contributes to.

Decline Scenario — In case Alice declines the share request, the status is updated accordingly and no other action is performed.

Bob Retrieves the EHR. Now that Alice explicitly delegated access to the EHR, Bob is now capable of retrieving it. To do so, Bob performs a request to the resource server, which requires Bob's secret key and the *resourceId*, which uniquely identifies the EHR. A file ownership verification is also performed since the decryption steps are different for a delegator and a delegatee, where the former does not have the need to re-encrypt the *capsule*.

As stated previously, ownership trails different paths regarding execution flow. With that said, the following can happen whether the user is or not a data owner.

Data Owner. — In case the user that requests the file is a data owner, a hybrid decryption scenario is performed where the data owner's private key is used to decapsulate the private key used to initially encrypt the file being retrieved, thus no re-encryption takes place.

Not a Data Owner. — If the user is not the data owner, meaning they are a delegatee, a collaborative operation between the resource and proxy servers is required to take place. For this specific scenario, Bob needs to ask the proxy to re-encrypt the capsule using the previously generated PRK. To that purpose, the resource server retrieves the EHR details and sends the capsule to the proxy server. The proxy, equipped with the capsule and the PRK fragments *kFrags*, performs the *re-encapsulation* process outputting the *cFrags*. These *cFrags* are sent back to the resource server, which validates their signature through Alice's verifying key. Once the capsule fragments are validated, Bob decrypts the file by opening the capsule. This last step encompasses Bob's private key, Alice's verifying key, and the verified *cFrags*. With the plaintext content of the EHR, Bob is now capable of accessing the information.

Some important remarks to highlight are that the secret key used in the sharing process is never shared with the intermediary entity or proxy, making it semi-trusted. Additionally, the proxy only stores the PRK, which alone does not grant it the capability to decrypt the file. Furthermore, even if the stored information such as the capsule, PRK, and ciphertext were to be leaked from the database, the safety and integrity of the EHRs would still be preserved, as they are not sufficient for decrypting the EHRs.

4.4 Break-Glass Approach

Safeguarding emergency scenarios is of paramount importance in a health-related platform. Therefore, we adopted an approach that features a central trustworthy entity responsible for managing the authorisation in emergency scenarios. This trustworthy entity is seen as a government entity that is responsible for managing such issues and has full access to the files submitted in the platform.

The implementation is similar to what is described in Sect. 4.3 regarding Alice accepting the share request. However, in this case, there is no explicit acceptance of the share request. When an EHR is uploaded, the trusted entity user is retrieved from the database and a PRK is generated. An accepted share request is automatically created for the trusted entity, which links the PRK to the share request between the patient and the trusted entity.

Regarding the process of retrieving the EHR, it follows a similar procedure as depicted in Sect. 4.3. Just like in a regular file retrieval, since the share request is automatically accepted and the proxy possesses the PRK, the trusted entity requests the proxy to re-encrypt the capsules, enabling the final decryption to take place.

This approach vastly reduces the dependency on external actors, increasing the reliability and availability of the idealised break-glass approach. Having a dedicated entity for this purpose enables instant and swift access to the information if needed.

5   Performance Analysis

In this section, we present the performance tests conducted to evaluate our platform. Given the common concerns of limited hardware infrastructures and sub-optimal conditions in governmental adoption cases, it is important to assess the responsiveness of the key operations offered by the platform. Our main goal is to quantitatively analyze the performance of the most computationally intensive operations and assess the impact of the PRE scheme. As there are no specific regulations, indications, or suggestions regarding performance for this type of platform, our tests are purely quantitative and based on known factors and conditions.

The performance tests were carried out on a deployed version of the platform, hosted in Microsoft Azure using a Free F1 tier running Linux and Python 3.10. While these specifications may be basic, they are sufficient to simulate a sub-optimal environment. In real-world scenarios, it is common for governments to have financial restrictions, making it likely that the platform would be deployed on infrastructure with modest specifications. The tests were conducted using Apache JMeter as the tool of choice.

In the rest of this section, we present the results related to the three most crucial operations of the platform and which involve the use of PRE: file upload, accepting a share request, and file retrieval. Additionally, a brief analysis of the results is also presented.

File Upload. The performance tests depicted in this section aim to evaluate how the different file sizes impact the upload performance of files.

Since the size of EHRs depends on various factors, such as the patient's medical history, the image resolution of the machines used for exams, and the content of the file itself, determining an average file size becomes challenging. Therefore, we conducted our experiments using two different file sizes: 1 MB and 10 MB.

Figure 3 illustrates the results obtained from a series of twenty runs performed for each file size.

It can be observed that a tenfold increase in file size reflected an average increase of 2715 *milliseconds* (ms) when comparing file sizes of 1 MB and 10 MB respectively. The former took an average of 1154 *ms* and the latter an average of 3870 *ms*.

Despite a time of almost four *seconds*, and considering this is not an ideal response time for a REST API, it should be taken into account the complexity of the operations performed. Since this is not a critical operation when it comes to performance, these values are acceptable.

Accepting a Share Request. The acceptance of a share request is a key operation in the platform described in this paper. Although its performance does not possess a high impact on the efficiency of the platform, it does provide valuable information regarding the PRE process. In this operation, the PRK is generated and sent to the proxy for persistence purposes. Notice that, in this case, there was no need to perform the tests for both file sizes since the PRK generation only depends on cryptographic keys.

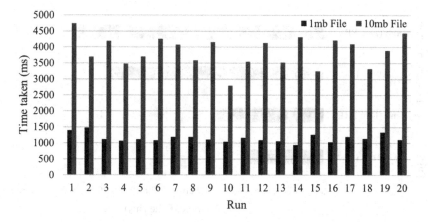

Fig. 3. Performance Tests - File Size Uploads Bar Chart

Regarding the results of these tests, the average time obtained in 20 runs was 869 *ms*. This quick response was expected since the generation of the PRK fragments is a relatively simple operation that depends on the cryptographic key from both ends, the signature, and the number of shares. Additionally, there was not a significant variation among the twenty runs that were performed. This is supported by the low standard deviation of just 188 *ms*.

File Retrieval. This set of tests aims to assess the impact of file sizes and the use of PRE on a file retrieval scenario. The tests were conducted for both regular decryption and PRE decryption. To evaluate the impact of file sizes, the tests were performed for both 1 MB and 10MB file sizes.

Moving on to the obtained results (Fig. 4), a 1 MB file took an average of 903 *ms* to be retrieved while the 10 MB one took an average of 2529 *ms*. Regarding file retrieval with PRE, the 1MB file took an average of 1245 *ms* and 2877 *ms* for the 10MB file.

We have also evaluated the impact of re-encryption on file retrieval operations (Fig. 5) by directly measuring the difference between regular decryption and PRE for each file size. This resulted in an average difference of 342 *ms* for the 1 MB file and 348 *ms* for the other one.

The results of our tests indicate that there is a similar average difference between regular and PRE decryption for both file sizes. This similarity can be attributed to the fact that the re-encryption process only affects the capsule, not the actual file. Since the sizes of the capsule and cryptographic keys are similar in both scenarios, it is expected that the results would be similar as well. The file size does not significantly impact the re-encryption of the capsule, but rather affects the overhead associated with fetching the file from the database and delivering it in the response.

Regarding the obtained results, they were deemed satisfactory since most operations do not possess restrictive requirements when it comes to performance.

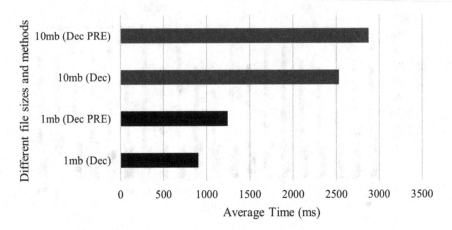

Fig. 4. Performance Tests - Average Time Taken for File Retrieval

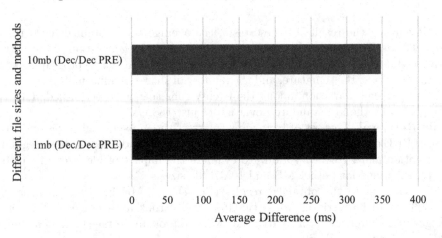

Fig. 5. Performance Tests - Average Impact of PRE in Same Sized Files

Regarding more critical operations such as file retrieval, considering the computational effort and infrastructure complexity required to ensure full correctness with the underlying threshold PRE scheme, the results were deemed satisfactory. It is important to note that these tests were conducted in a shared infrastructure with modest specifications. Thus, it was not possible to control the current workload of the servers during the tests, which may have impacted negatively the aforementioned results.

6   Conclusion

In this paper, we present a PRE-based platform for the secure sharing of e-health, considering a sovereign approach focused on the patient. This approach is achieved by ensuring that the patient's data is only shared with their explicit consent. Furthermore, it also enables robust revocability by the patient, without requiring updates on the encrypted EHR database, further contributing to a user-centric approach. Non-interactivity is also a key characteristic of our platform, which does not require sharing user's private key for the re-encryption process to occur. Another key achievement of our work is the proposed break-glass mechanism. Since some implementations fall short in terms of revocability, and only a few contemplate PRE in emergency scenarios, our solution uses a central trusted entity to which the proxy delegates access from the moment the EHR is uploaded to the platform. This eliminates the need to trust external actors in the system, increasing reliability and allowing swift access to the information in critical situations. There are other key characteristics of our platform worth highlighting. Firstly, it uses symmetric encryption to encrypt the EHR, which is faster than PKE. Secondly, the re-encryption process is performed over the capsule, which tends to have a much smaller size compared to a PHR. The tests that were conducted and our results show that the most demanding task is the upload of the EHR, as expected, because it requires the encapsulation process to occur and the encryption of the EHR. However, the re-encryption process does not show a significant increase when the size of the uploaded files increases. This is because the re-encryption does not involve the EHR. Our platform provides a solution to the sharing of medical data that incorporates key functionalities not covered together in previous literature, such as unidirectionality, non-interactivity, revocability, and a mechanism to deal with emergency situations. This solution contributes to the collaborative aspect of e-health and enables better, and more informed treatments supported by the increased exchange of information between providers.

Regarding future work, it would be beneficial to extend the architecture to accommodate multiple proxies instead of using just one. This could be achieved by utilising a decentralised approach where the proxies work together to re-encrypt the capsules, thus enabling all the benefits that a threshold-based scheme has to offer. Furthermore, additional tests could be performed using different environments and network conditions to cover more use case scenarios.

References

1. American National Standards Institute (ANSI) X9.F1 subcommittee. ANSI X9.63 Public key cryptography for the Financial Services Industry: Elliptic curve key agreement and key transport schemes (5 July 1998), working draft version 2.0
2. Au, M.H., et al.: A general framework for secure sharing of personal health records in cloud system. J. Comput. Syst. Sci. **90**, 46–62 (2017). https://doi.org/10.1016/j.jcss.2017.03.002
3. Blaze, M., Bleumer, G., Strauss, M.: Divertible protocols and atomic proxy cryptography. In: Advances in Cryptology–EUROCRYPT 1998, pp. 127–144 (1998)
4. Edemacu, K., Park, H.K., Jang, B., Kim, J.W.: Privacy provision in collaborative ehealth with attribute-based encryption: survey, challenges and future directions. IEEE Access **7**, 89614–89636 (2019). https://doi.org/10.1109/ACCESS.2019.2925390

5. ENISA: Engineering personal data sharing - emerging use cases and technologies, January 2023. https://www.enisa.europa.eu/publications/engineering-personal-data-sharing

6. European Parliament, C.O.T.E.U.: Regulation (EU) 2022/868 of the European Parliament and of the Council of 30 May 2022 on European data governance and amending Regulation (EU) 2018/1724 (Data Governance Act) (Text with EEA relevance), May 2022. http://data.europa.eu/eli/reg/2022/868/oj/eng, legislative Body: CONSIL, EP

7. Fernández-Alemán, J.L., Señor, I.C., Ángel Oliver Lozoya, P., Toval, A.: Security and privacy in electronic health records: a systematic literature review. J. Biomed. Inf. **46**(3), 541–562 (2013). https://doi.org/10.1016/j.jbi.2012.12.003

8. Hanaoka, G., et al.: Generic construction of chosen ciphertext secure proxy re-encryption. In: Dunkelman, O. (ed.) CT-RSA 2012. LNCS, vol. 7178, pp. 349–364. Springer, Heidelberg (2012). https://doi.org/10.1007/978-3-642-27954-6_22

9. Inbarani, W.S., Shenbagamoorthy, G., Kumar Charlie, C.: Proxy re-encryption schemes for data storage security in cloud- a survey. Int. J. Eng. Res. Technol. (IJERT) **02**(01), 1–5 (2013)

10. Khan, F.: A comparison of proxy re-encryption schemes - a survey. Int. J. Comput. Sci. Inf. Secur. (IJCSIS) **14**, 392–397 (2016)

11. Kirshanova, E.: Proxy re-encryption from lattices. In: Krawczyk, H. (ed.) PKC 2014. LNCS, vol. 8383, pp. 77–94. Springer, Heidelberg (2014). https://doi.org/10.1007/978-3-642-54631-0_5

12. Li, M., Yu, S., Ren, K., Lou, W.: Securing personal health records in cloud computing: patient-centric and fine-grained data access control in multi owner settings. In: Jajodia, S., Zhou, J. (eds.) SecureComm 2010. LNICST, vol. 50, pp. 89–106. Springer, Heidelberg (2010). https://doi.org/10.1007/978-3-642-16161-2_6

13. Li, W., Jin, C., Kumari, S., Xiong, H., Kumar, S.: Proxy re-encryption with equality test for secure data sharing in internet of things-based healthcare systems: Na. Trans. Emerging Telecommun. Technol. **33**, e3986 (2020). https://doi.org/10.1002/ett.3986

14. Liang, K., Fang, L., Wong, D., Susilo, W.: A ciphertext-policy attribute-based proxy re-encryption scheme for data sharing in public clouds: a CP-ABPRE for data sharing in public clouds. Concurrency Comput. Pract. Exp. **27** (2014). https://doi.org/10.1002/cpe.3397

15. NuCypher: pyumbral. https://github.com/nucypher/pyumbral (2018)

16. Nuñez, D.: Umbral: a threshold proxy re-encryption scheme (2017). https://raw.githubusercontent.com/nucypher/umbral-doc/master/umbral-doc.pdf

17. Nuñez, D., Agudo, I., Lopez, J.: Proxy re-encryption: analysis of constructions and its application to secure access delegation. J. Netw. Comput. Appl. **87**, 193–209 (2017). https://doi.org/10.1016/j.jnca.2017.03.005

18. Qin, Z., Xiong, H., Wu, S., Batamuliza, J.: A survey of proxy re-encryption for secure data sharing in cloud computing. IEEE Trans. Serv. Comput. 1 (2016). https://doi.org/10.1109/TSC.2016.2551238

19. Rabieh, K., Akkaya, K., Karabiyik, U., Qamruddin, J.: A secure and cloud-based medical records access scheme for on-road emergencies. In: 2018 15th IEEE Annual Consumer Communications & Networking Conference (CCNC), pp. 1–8 (2018). https://doi.org/10.1109/CCNC.2018.8319175

20. Ren, C., Dong, X., Shen, J., Cao, Z., Zhou, Y.: Clap-pre: certificateless autonomous path proxy re-encryption for data sharing in the cloud. Appl. Sci. **12**(9) (2022). https://doi.org/10.3390/app12094353

21. Shamir, A.: How to share a secret. Commun. ACM **22**(11), 612–613 (1979). https://doi.org/10.1145/359168.359176
22. Shoup, V.: A proposal for an ISO standard for public key encryption. Cryptology ePrint Archive, Paper 2001/112 (2001). https://eprint.iacr.org/2001/112
23. Thilakanathan, D., Chen, S., Nepal, S., Calvo, R., Alem, L.: A platform for secure monitoring and sharing of generic health data in the cloud. Future Gener. Comput. Syst. **35**, 102–113 (2014), special Section: Integration of Cloud Computing and Body Sensor Networks; Guest Editors: Giancarlo Fortino and Mukaddim Pathan
24. Xue, L.: DSAS: a secure data sharing and authorized searchable framework for e-healthcare system. IEEE Access **10**, 30779–30791 (2022). https://doi.org/10.1109/ACCESS.2022.3153120
25. Yang, Y., Zheng, X., Guo, W., Liu, X., Chang, V.: Privacy-preserving smart IoT-based healthcare big data storage and self-adaptive access control system. Inf. Sci. **479**, 567–592 (2019). https://doi.org/10.1016/j.ins.2018.02.005
26. Yüksel, B., Küpçü, A.: Öznur Özkasap: research issues for privacy and security of electronic health services. Futur. Gener. Comput. Syst. **68**, 1–13 (2017). https://doi.org/10.1016/j.future.2016.08.011

PrivacySmart: Automatic and Transparent Management of Privacy Policies

Cristòfol Daudén-Esmel[1,2](✉) (ID), Jordi Castellà-Roca[1,2] (ID),
Alexandre Viejo[1,2] (ID), and Eduard Josep Bel-Ribes[1]

[1] Departament d'Enginyeria Informàtica i Matemàtiques,
Universitat Rovira i Virgili, Tarragona, Spain
{cristofol.dauden,jordi.castella,alexandre.viejo}@urv.cat,
eduardjosep.bel@alumni.urv.cat
[2] UNESCO Chair in Data Privacy, CYBERCAT-Center for Cybersecurity Research
of Catalonia, Av. Països Catalans 26, 43007 Tarragona, Catalonia, Spain

Abstract. Privacy policies and the use of cookies on websites serve important functions but also raise concerns regarding user privacy and tracking. In order to address these concerns and adhere to legal requirements, web service providers utilize pop-ups to obtain user consent based on the notice-and-choice principle. However, a significant issue arises when users accept all policies without thoroughly reading or comprehending them, resulting in difficulties in managing and recalling accepted policies across various websites. To tackle this challenge, we propose PrivacySmart: an innovative system that handles privacy and cookie policy pop-ups for users as they navigate and access online services, all while taking their privacy preferences into account. The system comprises two essential components: a plug-in that necessitates installation on users' browsers and a smartphone application that consolidates all accepted policies from different plug-ins. This system empowers users by granting them control over the policies they have agreed to and the corresponding websites, while avoiding them the policies management overhead. By implementing the tool as a Firefox extension, we have conducted thorough evaluations and obtained promising results from the experiments.

Keywords: Privacy and cookie policies · GDPR · Blockchain and Smart Contracts · Browser plug-in

1 Introduction

Typical income source of web Service Providers (SPs) comes from the ads shown while users access to the provided services and from users' personal data collected while using the service. This personal data, can be sold to third parties which will process it and obtain some benefit, or used to create profiles allowing a personalized advertising [8,12].

Although this information processing enables free online services, it may result in extraction of sensitive data which may jeopardize the individuals' privacy. This fact raised serious concerns about the technical, commercial, political,

S. Katsikas et al. (Eds.): ESORICS 2023 Workshops, LNCS 14398, pp. 216–231, 2024.
https://doi.org/10.1007/978-3-031-54204-6_12

and ethical aspects of personal data collection and analysis by platform owners such as Facebook and other third parties.

In light of the above, the European Union drafted and approved the General Data Protection Regulation (GDPR) [21] to mitigate the abuse of massive collection and processing of the individuals' personal data and, hence, keeping any data-hungry technology company at bay. The main objective of the GDPR is to guarantee specific privacy rights to Data Subjects (natural person to which personal data belongs), ensuring that their personal data "can only be gathered legally, under strict conditions, for a legitimate purpose"; as well as bringing full control back to the data owners.

The scientific community has already paved the way to manage the data processing consent between users and SPs in a GDPR compliance way. In this regard, some authors have already introduced the use of Smart Contracts (SCs) implemented over the blockchain technology (BC) to design and create general-purpose data management and storage schemes which promise to offer features such as transparency, traceability, non-repudiation, integrity, immutability, and decentralization [1,5,6,9,13,16,20,23,28]. However, although these works grant users full control of what is done with their data and solves the *lack of transparency* [2] issue in the current paradigm, they do not offer a practical solution to perform this management in a comfortable way by the user.

In order to fulfill current regulation, online SPs, according to a study carried out on European websites [7], almost two years after the GDPR came into force, 81% of the reviewed sites use pop-up notifications to inform users about their privacy and cookie policies. These privacy and cookie policies pop-ups must generally be managed before accessing the service, thus annoying users and slowing down browsing. Furthermore, a regular Internet user must manage the privacy and cookies preferences of almost every website she visits at least once a year, since according to the ePrivacy Directive[1], persistent cookies should expire after 12 months. Apart from the amount of privacy and cookie policies pop-ups interaction users must perform, they can have some issues when trying to reject most personal data collection and usage policies from SPs. Many websites make the process relatively complicated, making rejecting cookies a matter of performing several clicks, while others directly do not offer the possibility of rejecting them. With all this, users usually end up accepting all cookies usage because it is the easiest and fastest option. In addition, the volume of manually managed privacy and cookie policies is so high that they end up forgetting what have been accepted and on which websites.

1.1   Related Work

As it has been stated, privacy policies and cookies usage management is a tedious and uncomfortable process for users who just want to access to some service in the web [15]. In order to address this, some works have been proposed to facilitate this management. On the one hand, there are proposals that address

---

[1] GDPR Cookies https://gdpr.eu/cookies/.

the consent management between users and Service Providers through the use of smart contracts and the blockchain technologies. On the other hand, some tools have been proposed to facilitate this privacy policies and cookies usage management by simply performing their automatic acceptance or rejection.

There are several proposals in the literature that fall into the first category, systems for the GDPR compliance of the consent management, some relevant examples are [1,5,6,9,13,16,20,23,28]. These schemes follow a similar approach. In particular, they combine a decentralized storage system, the Ethereum blockchain, and smart contracts, in order to provide a dynamic consent management system that targets personal data usage under the GDPR. More specifically, these scheme systems allow individuals to control the collection and usage consent of their personal data throughout the data life-cycle. An example can be found in [5], where authors propose a blockchain-based GDPR-compliant personal data management system that, first, it provides mechanisms for Data Subjects to control and manage their personal data; and, second, it provides publicly accessible and immutable evidences which are useful for a Service Provider to prove the agreements made between a Data Subject and her about the Data Subject's personal data. These evidences might be then used by a Supervisory Authority that performs an auditing procedure on the Service Provider to verify that this entity is doing the data processing exactly as agreed with the affected Data Subjects. However these proposals do not provide a practical solution for users to manage their personal data consent when they access different services on the web, specifically they do not take into account privacy policies and cookies usage pop-ups paradigm which is currently established now.

Focusing on solutions that address automatic management of users' privacy and cookie policies, Vyas et al. propose in [22] a framework for automatically producing privacy policies for users' personal web contents based on a small amount of annotation information. However, this work is limited to the generation of individual policies for each content published into a social network, they do not consider general consent given when accessing different web services that request users' data collection. In a more general ambit, authors in [26,27] present CookiePicker, a system that automatically validates the usefulness of cookies from a Web site and set the cookie usage permission on behalf of users. This system identifies those cookies that cause perceivable changes on a web page as useful, while simply classifying the rest as useless, thus enabling useful cookies and disabling the rest. However, this system does not take into account current paradigm where web service providers do not limit data collection from cookies but from other sources, making the users also to accept their privacy policies. Finally, authors in [14], present a concept for a privacy-friendly cookie setting interface that tries to help users during cookies preferences configuration. Their concept uses an assistant that guides the user to configure their privacy preferences via a series of questions. These preferences will be applied in the cookies configuration to all visited websites. However, the interface just manages the functionalities available in the cookie settings of common browsers, it does not consider available configurations on individual websites, neither the privacy policies that must be accepted on these websites. If a user wants a specific privacy and cookie policies configuration according to her privacy preferences on each website, it must be done manually.

A part from the scientific works trying to address the aforementioned issue with the automatic and transparent management of privacy and cookie policies, modern web browsers also provide users with some solutions. A user can set detailed cookie privacy options for web sites before or during visiting these sites. However, these cookie privacy options use to fail when are used in practice, as they are confusing for regular users [10].

On the other hand, we can find some commercial cookie management software for regular web browsers. While analyzing these tools, we have observed that although they all manage some cookie pop-ups and are convenient to use, they are not so versatile in terms of the number of web pages with which they can interact. For example, Polish Cookie Consent [11] automatically accepts cookie policy/GDPR on websites. On the other hand, Ninja Cookie [4] and Auto Cookie Output [3] have a more restrictive policy by removing cookie banners and rejecting the use of non-essential cookies. Finally, Super Agent [19] automatically fills out website's cookie consent forms on user's behalf based on their preferences. This tool splits optional cookies into three categories (Advertising, Functional and Performance), thus automatically opt out of cookies that are not clearly within any of these categories and let users control the remaining three. Although a combination of these tools could be efficient in terms of cookies acceptance/rejection, they do not offer cookies management, as none offers the possibility of consulting the consent they manage neither take into account privacy policies that also must be managed along with cookies.

After evaluating the available proposals pertaining to privacy policies and the administration of cookie usage, we have come to recognize two main trends. On one hand, there are proposals aimed at addressing consent management between users and service providers, but these often lack practicality. On the other hand, there are tools designed to streamline the management of privacy policies and cookie usage by employing automatic acceptance or rejection mechanisms. However, these tools limit users' ability to maintain comprehensive control over the consents they grant. In light of these findings, there is a clear necessity for a practical solution that enables users to effortlessly and transparently handle privacy policies and cookie usage while retaining full control over all granted consents.

1.2   Contribution and Plan of This Paper

This paper presents the development and deployment of PrivacySmart, a system aimed at effectively handling privacy and cookie policies pop-ups for users engaging with online services. Our system offers an automated and transparent approach to managing these policies, ensuring a seamless user experience during navigation, and registers the provided consent on a Smart Contract deployed on the blockchain. The system comprises two essential components: a plug-in responsible for managing the policies, and a smartphone application that empowers users to exercise control over the acceptance of policies across various websites.

Given a privacy level provided by the user, the designed plug-in must:

- Perform an automatic acceptance of the cookies, according to the privacy level specified by users, thus allowing an easier and faster browsing of the web.
- Register the given consent on each website through a Smart Contract, that will be deployed in the blockchain.
- Be compatible with the main websites privacy and cookie policies pop-ups.

The rest of the paper is organized as follows. First, we introduce and describe our proposed system (Sect. 2). In Sect. 3 we provide the analysis and discussion about the system. Last section (Sect. 4) summarizes the conclusions and future work.

2 Proposal Description

In this section we describe our system for the automatic management of the cookies and personal data usage policies, that compress the agreements between Data Subjects and Service Providers about DSs' personal data, automatically and transparently to the users while they navigate and access to online services.

The plug-in offers several key functionalities. Firstly, it automatically accepts cookies and privacy policies configurations based on user-specified privacy levels, enabling easier and faster web browsing. Secondly, it registers user consent on each website using a Smart Contract, ensuring a secure record of the provided consent. Additionally, the plug-in is compatible with cookie pop-ups from major websites. By effectively identifying cookie and privacy policies configuration pop-ups, the plug-in determines the appropriate selections to align with the user's privacy preferences. This process includes deploying a Smart Contract on the blockchain to record the provided consent, allowing the user to have control and manage accepted privacy and cookie policies for each visited website.

In addition, we provide a smartphone application that consolidates all privacy and cookie policies managed by the plug-in. This application empowers users with complete control over their personal data, giving them a clear overview of the management of their privacy preferences.

2.1 System Architecture Overview

As shown in Fig. 1 we can identify four components on our working environment: our proposed plug-in, the provided smartphone application through which the user has full control of the accepted policies, the blockchain where SCs are deployed, and the web browser where the plug-in is installed and the user uses to access to different websites. The plug-in consists of three main modules: the core module, the pop-up interaction module and the configuration module. First, the core module, consists of a program responsible of identifying the pop-up of the visiting web site, initialize the module responsible of directly interacting with the pop-up and deploy a new SC with the cookies and privacy policies accepted. Then, there is the pop-up interaction module, which consists of a set of scripts, each designed specifically for a concrete pop-up, responsible of accepting/rejecting the cookies and privacy policies on the pop-up and return the configuration set to the main program. Finally, the configuration module allows the user to set-up her privacy preferences, configure the keys used for interacting with the blockchain and manage all consents given by the plug-in trough a UI. On the other hand, the smartphone application plays a crucial role in enhancing user control and convenience. It seamlessly downloads all the consent Smart Contracts (SCs) deployed on the blockchain, effectively summarizing all policies that have been accepted by the plug-ins installed across users' browsers. This consolidated view provides users with a comfortable and user-friendly experience, allowing them to conveniently access and review the collection of accepted policies.

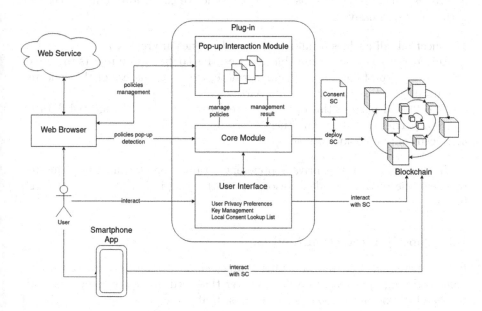

Fig. 1. System Architecture Overview

2.2   User Privacy Preferences

Privacy policies state who will be able to use users' collected data, for which purpose this data can be used and for how long this data can be kept. These policies can be represented at different levels of specification and data granularity like a formal notice or a more structured notice using templates. Formal notice allows Service Providers to set up a more customized privacy policies thus being able to arbitrarily create rules that describe how data will be managed. These policy notices are difficult to interpret, read and perform some automatic matching due to the flexibility on rules description and terms with different names used among different companies. A clear example of this kind of policies are the Terms and Conditions a user must accept when signing up to certain services. On the other hand, on the web environment Service Providers have opted for more structured notice, such as cookies and privacy policies configuration pop-ups. These pop-ups consist of templates provided by some "*cookies providers*" which are easier to interpret and perform an automatic management over them. According to this, in our work, we focus on the management of these web policy pop-ups according to the user's pre-established privacy preferences.

To enhance flexibility and facilitate the policy specification process, we consider using policy templates, as suggested in [18]. These templates represent different privacy levels, defined according to the configuration alternatives that offer the studied pop-ups. These privacy levels can be divided into four main categories, where level one has the most restrictive configuration and level four is the most permissive one:

1. Reject all: all cookies or all non-essential cookies are rejected.
2. Reject profiling cookies and third parties: this configuration rejects the use of cookies for profiling interest. Furthermore, it rejects the use of the collected data by third parties or web site partners.
3. Reject third parties: this option just rejects the use of the collected data by third parties or web site partners.
4. Accept all: all cookies are accepted.

In order to set up this privacy preferences value, the user must be requested to select one of the provided options when the plug-in is installed in the web browser.

2.3   Pop-Up Interaction Module

In the current model, websites offer management of their privacy and cookie policies through pop-ups. In order to cover this need, there are companies, privacy and cookie policies banner providers, that are dedicated to the design of these cookie management pop-ups and provide these tools to other companies which can use them in their websites. In this way, website providers can comply with the GDPR thus presenting the users their privacy policies and a way to grant them.

Each website provider can modify the visual section and the content of the pop-up, by specifying which types of cookies will be used, which data can be collected and which third parties will process the collected data. The main interoperability issue here is that each cookies provider makes its own standard, so the solutions to manage the forms on each website can be very different.

In order to decide which privacy and cookie policies banner providers take into account, we have considered the most used ones according to a study performed by Wrappalyzer [24], where they have analyzed over 1.200.000 websites. The selected ones on this study are Didomi[2], CookieYes[3], CookieNotice[4] and OneTrust[5]. For each of these providers we have implemented a script in the pop-up interaction module responsible of interacting with the banner and manage the consent on users' behalf. The result of the operation is sent back to the Core module, which will record it into an SC. In the case some privacy and cookie policies pop-up does not allow the consent management using a privacy level lower than the one set by the user, the pop-up interaction module, hides the banner without accepting anything, in such a way that the user can access to the web content without being annoyed. This modularity of the system allows the tool to be able to work with more privacy and cookie policies banners of other providers by simply adding specific scripts for them to this module.

2.4   Consent Smart Contract

The Consent SC is responsible for storing the consent managed by the plug-in when it interacts with the web browser pop-up. The SC consists in a single class that holds:

- Web service url: Uniform resource locator of the web page where consent has been managed through the plug-in (*url* argument).
- Privacy level: Integer value that indicates the privacy level established by the user and the one used by the plug-in to perform the acceptance of policy cookies (*privacyLevel* argument).
- Consent validity period: This indicates the dates from which the consent is valid(*beginningDate* and *expirationDate* arguments).

Once the *Consent Smart Contract* instance is created, the following methods can be used to interact with it:

- *whichWeb()* method returns the url value stored in the SC.
- *whichPreference()* method returns the privacy level value stored in the SC.
- *isValid()* method checks that the consent lifetime period has not expired.

2.5   Workflow

The proposed plug-in workflow can be divided into three main phases: the set-up phase, where the plug-in is installed on the web browsers and the user indicates her privacy policy preferences; ii) the navigation phase, when the user accesses to different web pages, and; iii) the control phase, where the user can manage all cookies and privacy policies accepted by the plug-in.

---

[2] Didomi: https://www.didomi.io/es/.
[3] CookieYes: https://www.cookieyes.com/.
[4] Cookie Notice: https://cookiesnotice.com/.
[5] OneTrust: https://www.onetrust.es/.

1. Set-up phase
   User
   (a) Install the plug-in on the web browser.
   (b) Configure the plug-in.
       i. Introduce her privacy policies preferences in the plug-in using the UI.
       ii. Select if she wants to use and existing key pair for the deployment of the SCs or generate a new one. In the first case, the user must input the mnemonic words associated to that key pair and move to step 1d; otherwise, the workflow continues as stated.
   Plug-in
   (c) Execute the BIP-39 protocol [17], such generating 24 mnemonic words and a 512 bits seed, the *BIP-39 seed*.
       NOTE: The user must keep these mnemonic words in a safe place, without them she will not be able to recover the keys or use the same account into another web browser or the smartphone application.
   (d) Execute the BIP-32 protocol [25] using the *BIP-39 seed* as input. This process generates user's Secret Key (SK_u).
   (e) Derives user's Public Key (PK_u) by means of SK_u.
   (f) Create a local consent lookup list. This list is internally used by the plug-in in order to check if privacy and cookie policies have already been managed on a particular website.
2. Navigation phase
   User
   (a) Access to a web page with cookies and privacy policies configuration banner.
   Plug-in - Core module
   (b) If the cookies and privacy policies have already been managed on this web and the consent is valid (*isValid()* method of the Consent SC returns True), no banner will appear so the process ends. Otherwise, if the cookies and privacy policies have already been managed on this web but the consent is not valid (*isValid()* method of the Consent SC returns False), cookies are removed from the browser and the process follows as if the consent has not been manged yet.
   (c) Detect the emerging pop-up and identifies the script in the pop-up interaction module responsible of managing it.
   (d) Initialize the pop-up interaction module script, indicating user's privacy policies preferences.
   Plug-in - Pop-up interaction module
   (e) The script interacts with the pop-up and performs the cookies and privacy policies configuration management, and returns the result to the core module.
   Plug-in - Core module
   (f) The core module deploys a new Consent SC on the blockchain, using the key pair (PK_u, SK_u), indicating the consent granted and the lifetime of the consent. This process returns an identifier of the SC.

(g) The core module adds the web url along with the SC's identifier to the consent lookup list.
3. Management phase
    User
    (a) Requests the consents managed by the plug-in through the UI.
    Plug-in
    (b) The plug-in displays the consent lookup list with all consents managed.
    (c) In the case the user wants to see the details of a given consent, selects it on the display.
    (d) The plug-in gets the consent selected details from the blockchain and displays it to the user.

The provided smartphone application empowers the users with complete control over all privacy and cookie policies managed by various plug-ins installed across their browsers. To ensure a comfortable and user-friendly experience, the application offers these simple functionalities:

1. Add new key pair: This allow users to add a new key pair (PK_i, SK_i) through introducing the mnemonic words provided by the different plug-ins during the set-up phase. By using this mnemonic words, the app will execute BIP-39 and BIP-32 protocols, as in the plug-in Set-up phase, thus recovering the cryptographic keys. After adding a new key pair the app will have full access to all SCs containing the managed policies.
2. Access and Review: Users can conveniently access and review the entire collection of accepted policies through the application. This allows an easy monitoring and management of privacy preferences.

By providing these functionalities, the smartphone application ensures that users have a seamless and user-friendly experience, enabling them to exercise complete control over their privacy and cookie policies across different plug-ins installed on their browsers.

3 Discussion

After implementing the described proposal, we have validated its efficacy through live experiments.

3.1 Implementation

We implemented our plug-in as a Firefox extension coded in JavaScritp[6], HTML[7] and css[8] (source code available in Github[9]). We have chosen Firefox because is

---

[6] JavaScript: https://developer.mozilla.org/en-US/docs/Web/javascript.
[7] HyperText Markup Language: https://developer.mozilla.org/en-US/docs/Web/HTML.
[8] Cascading Style Sheets: https://developer.mozilla.org/en-US/docs/Web/CSS.
[9] Source Code: https://github.com/EduardBel/PrivacySmart.

one of the most used ones, is very extensible and allows programmers to add new or modify existing features. Also scripts in the pop-up interaction module, each responsible of managing the privacy and cookie policies of each banner provider, are coded in JavaScript. Concerning the deployment of the Consent SCs, we have used web3.js library[10], so the plug is able to connect into an existing blockchain. Summarizing, our plug-in is on the browser as an add-on not modifying Firefox's source code. We omit further details on the tool implementation and only describe plug-in's main interfaces (Fig. 2): the plug-in Configuration module main interface and the consent display interface. The configuration module interface, shown in Fig. 2a, allows users to i) manually modify the key pair used to deploy the SCs where the consent is registered; ii) recover an old key pair using the mnemonic words set; iii) change user's privacy preference parameter, and; iv) manage the consents given by the plug-in on the different web sites the user has visited. In order to update the new values for the new key pair or the privacy preference parameter, after adding the new values, the user has to click the "Apply Changes" button. On the same way, if the user wants to see all consents given by the tool, she must click the "Consents Query" button, and the consent display interface will pop-up. Finally, if the user needs to recover an old key pair, she must click the "Recover Wallet" button, and a new interface will appear to introduce the mnemonic words. This UI also shows the user the consent given in the current web site, if any.

The consent display interface shows all privacy and cookie policies managed by the plug-in on the different websites the user has visited. As shown in Fig. 2b, it displays each of the sites, along with the privacy level used on that site and a button in the case the user wants more detailed information of the consent given.

Concerning the smartphone application, it has been coded using Java and web3j library for blockchain interactions. Figure 3, shows the main display interfaces of the application. On the one hand, Fig. 3a shows how the application displays on which websites the policies have been managed by a selected a plug-in (the plug-in has been selected in a previous layout, and these plug-ins are added to the app by specifying the key pair used for deploying the Consent SC). On the other hand, after a user selects a specific website, all information about the consent given is shown as in Fig. 3b.

3.2 Evaluation

We installed our proposed plug-in on a Firefox web browser and used Ganache[11] for the simulation of a public blockchain in order to perform our experiments. On the experiments carried out, although key management system is already implemented, we have used the keys provided by Ganache for the deployment of the ConsentSCs in the blockchain.

---

[10] Web3.js: https://web3js.org/#/.
[11] Ganache: https://trufflesuite.com/ganache/.

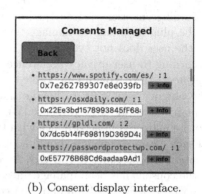

(a) Plug-in configuration module main interface.

(b) Consent display interface.

Fig. 2. PrivacySmart: browser plug-in main interfaces.

(a) Interface for selecting a consent managed from a browser plug-in.

(b) Interface for viewing managed consent information.

Fig. 3. PrivacySmart: smartphone application main interfaces.

In order to determine the correctness of the proposed plug-in, we have evaluated its performance on some websites that use a pop-up offered by the most used privacy and cookie policies banner providers according to [24]. Here we have used different user's privacy parameter values and we have taken into account i) if the plug-in is able to manage the pop-up transparently and on users behalf, so the user does not even notices it, and; ii) if the consent has been performed according to user privacy preferences. In the first parameter (*Transparent Management*, third column in Table 1), our evaluation primarily revolves around the plugin's capability to handle the pop-up discreetly, ensuring that the user remains unaware of its presence. We consider the scenario wherein consent cannot be managed in accordance with the user's specified privacy parameters, and in such cases, the plugin should adeptly conceal the pop-up, preventing any disruption or annoyance to the user. According to the second parameter we evaluate if the consent has been managed according to the user's privacy preference, and the Consent SC has been deployed correctly.

Results obtained, summarized in Table 1, show that our plug-in works perfectly with pop-ups provided by Didomi and OneTrust, allowing users to decide between different privacy preference levels. On the other hand, results obtained in relation to the management of the CookieYes and CookieNotice banners, show that there are pages that do not offer consent management beyond accepting all privacy and coolies policies. If user's privacy preference is set to level 4, it accepts the policy, on any other case the plug-in just hides the pop-up without accepting anything.

4   Conclusions and Future Work

This paper introduces, PrivacySmart, a system designed to seamlessly and transparently manage privacy and cookie policies pop-ups for users during their navigation and access to various online services. The system comprises two components: a plug-in that needs to be installed on each browser used by the user, and a smartphone application that empowers the user to maintain control over the accepted policies across different plug-ins and websites. By using this system, users can navigate the web with ease, as the plug-in automatically handles privacy and cookie policies pop-ups. The smartphone application serves as a centralized tool, enabling users to monitor and manage the acceptance of policies on a per-plug-in and per-website basis. This approach ensures transparency and allows users to maintain control over their privacy preferences throughout their online experiences. We have implemented our design as a Firefox extension and we evaluated its performance on some websites that use a pop-up offered by the privacy and cookie policies banner providers considered in this work. Results show that, although our plug-in has some issue to manage the consent on some websites depending on user's privacy preferences due to the service provider, the tool is able to manage all pop-ups transparently and on users behalf.

Regarding future work, we aim to manage the privacy and cookie policies banners of more service providers and implement the tool for other web browsers to

Table 1. Results of tool performance on websites that use a pop-up offered by the studied privacy and cookie policies banner providers.

Provider	Website	Transparent Management	Privacy level used	Consent Correct
Didomi	marca.com	✓	1	✓
	as.com	✓	1	✓
	elpais.com	✓	2	✓
	giphy.com	✓	2	✓
	reverso.net	✓	3	✓
	elmundo.es	✓	3	✓
	bfmtv.com	✓	4	✓
	societe.com	✓	4	✓
CookieYes	wpmet.com	✓	1	✓
	sliderrevolution.com	✓	2	✓
	tympanus.net	✓	3	✓
	wpdatatables.com	✓	4	✓
	bezkoder.com	✓	3	✓
	wpthemedetector.com	✓	4	✓
			2	X
	styde.net	✓	4	✓
			1	X
CookieNotice	gpldl.com	✓	1	✓
			2	✓
	mailtrap.io	✓	1	X
	osxdaily.com	✓	2	X
	searchengineland.com	✓	3	X
	booster.io	✓	3	X
	wpbuffs.com	✓	3	✓
			4	✓
OneTrust	fiverr.com	✓	1	✓
	gitlab.com	✓	2	✓
	app.slack.com	✓	3	✓
	freepik.com	✓	4	✓
	udemy.com	✓	1	✓
	upwork.com	✓	2	✓
	open.spotify.com	✓	3	✓
	elementor.com	✓	4	✓

increase the number of its users. On the other hand, the proposal that has been presented in this work is a first version of an end user tool for the management of web privacy and cookie policies, we plan to extend the system for the management of general consent under GDPR as stated in [5]. Furthermore we will perform a more in deep discussion taking into account usability of the proposal, a threat analysis of the code and an economic study evaluating over which network the system will be built (Ethereum, Consortium BC, Private BC...) and who will pay for the gas used to deploy the SCs.

Acknowledgments and Disclaimer. This research is supported by the project "HERMES" funded by INCIBE and the European Union NextGenerationEU/PRTR, by project PID2021-125962OB-C32 "SECURING/DATA" funded by MCIN/AEI/10.13039/501100011033/ FEDER, UE, and by the grant 2021SGR 00115 from the Government of Catalonia. The first author is also supported by the Spanish Government under an FPU grant (ref. FPU20/03254).

References

1. Barati, M., Rana, O.: Tracking GDPR compliance in cloud-based service delivery. IEEE Trans. Serv. Comput., 1 (2020). https://doi.org/10.1109/TSC.2020.2999559
2. Bu-Pasha, S., Alen-Savikko, A., Mäkinen, J.S., Guinness, R., Korpisaari, P.: EU law perspectives on location data privacy in smartphones and informed consent for transparency. Eur. Data Prot. Law Rev. **2**(3/2016), 312–323 (2016)
3. CodyMcCodington: Auto cookie optout (2022). https://addons.mozilla.org/en-GB/firefox/addon/auto-cookie-optout/
4. Cookie, N.: Ninja cookie (2020). https://addons.mozilla.org/en-GB/firefox/addon/ninja-cookie/
5. Daudén-Esmel, C., Castellà-Roca, J., Viejo, A., Domingo-Ferrer, J.: Lightweight blockchain-based platform for GDPR-compliant personal data management. In: 5th IEEE International Conference on Cryptography, Security and Privacy, CSP 2021, Zhuhai, China, 8–10 January 2021, pp. 68–73 (2021)
6. Davari, M., Bertino, E.: Access control model extensions to support data privacy protection based on GDPR. In: 2019 IEEE International Conference on Big Data (Big Data), pp. 4017–4024. December 2019. https://doi.org/10.1109/BigData47090.2019.9006455
7. Deloitte: Deloitte: Cookie benchmark study (2020). https://www2.deloitte.com/content/dam/Deloitte/nl/Documents/risk/deloitte-nl-risk-cookie-benchmark-study.pdf
8. Esteve, A.: The business of personal data: Google, Facebook, and privacy issues in the EU and the USA. Int. Data Priv. Law **7**(1), 36–47 (03 2017). https://doi.org/10.1093/idpl/ipw026
9. Faber, B., Michelet, G., Weidmann, N., Mukkamala, R.R., Vatrapu, R.: BPDIMS: a blockchain-based personal data and identity management system. In: Conference: Hawaii International Conference on System Sciences, January 2019. https://doi.org/10.24251/HICSS.2019.821
10. Ha, V., Inkpen, K., Al Shaar, F., Hdeib, L.: An examination of user perception and misconception of internet cookies. In: CHI 2006 Extended Abstracts on Human Factors in Computing Systems, pp. 833–838 (2006)
11. hawkeye116477, krystian3w: Polish cookie consent (2022). https://addons.mozilla.org/en-GB/firefox/addon/polish-cookie-consent/
12. Houser, K., Voss, W.: GDPR: the end of google and Facebook or a new paradigm in data privacy? SSRN Electron. J. (2018). https://doi.org/10.2139/ssrn.3212210
13. Jung, S.S., Lee, S.J., Euom, I.C.: Delegation-based personal data processing request notarization framework for GDPR based on private blockchain. Appl. Sci. **11**(22) (2021). https://doi.org/10.3390/app112210574. https://www.mdpi.com/2076-3417/11/22/10574

14. Kulyk, O., Mayer, P., Volkamer, M., Käfer, O.: A concept and evaluation of usable and fine-grained privacy-friendly cookie settings interface. In: 2018 17th IEEE International Conference on Trust, Security and Privacy in Computing and Communications/12th IEEE International Conference on Big Data Science And Engineering (TrustCom/BigDataSE), pp. 1058–1063. IEEE (2018)
15. McDonald, A.M., Reeder, R.W., Kelley, P.G., Cranor, L.F.: A comparative study of online privacy policies and formats. In: Goldberg, I., Atallah, M.J. (eds.) PETS 2009. LNCS, vol. 5672, pp. 37–55. Springer, Heidelberg (2009). https://doi.org/10.1007/978-3-642-03168-7_3
16. Merlec, M.M., Lee, Y.K., Hong, S.P., In, H.P.: A smart contract-based dynamic consent management system for personal data usage under GDPR. Sensors **21**(23) (2021). https://doi.org/10.3390/s21237994
17. Palatinus, M., Rusnak, P., Voisine, A., Bowe, S.: BIP39: mnemonic code for generating deterministic keys (2013). https://github.com/bitcoin/bips/blob/master/bip-0039.mediawiki
18. Squicciarini, A., Bhargav-Spantzel, A., Czeskis, A., Bertino, E.: Traceable and automatic compliance of privacy policies in federated digital identity management. In: Danezis, G., Golle, P. (eds.) PET 2006. LNCS, vol. 4258, pp. 78–98. Springer, Heidelberg (2006). https://doi.org/10.1007/11957454_5
19. Super Agent, Diogo Minhava: Super agent - automatic cookie consent (2023). https://addons.mozilla.org/en-GB/firefox/addon/super-agent/?utm_source=addons.mozilla.org&utm_medium=referral&utm_content=search
20. Truong, N.B., Sun, K., Lee, G.M., Guo, Y.: GDPR-compliant personal data management: a blockchain-based solution. IEEE Trans. Inf. Forensics Secur. **15**, 1746–1761 (2020)
21. European Union: Regulation (EU) 2016/679 of the European parliament and of the council of 27 April 2016 on the protection of natural persons with regard to the processing of personal data and on the free movement of such data, and repealing directive 95/46/EC (general data protection regulation) (text with EEA relevance). Off. J. Eur. Union L 119 **59**, 1–88 (2016). https://eur-lex.europa.eu/eli/reg/2016/679/oj
22. Vyas, N., Squicciarini, A.C., Chang, C.C., Yao, D.: Towards automatic privacy management in web 2.0 with semantic analysis on annotations. In: 2009 5th International Conference on Collaborative Computing: Networking, Applications and Worksharing, pp. 1–10. IEEE (2009)
23. Wirth, C., Kolain, M.: Privacy by blockchain design: a blockchain-enabled GDPR-compliant approach for handling personal data. In: Reports of the European Society for Socially Embedded Technologies (EUSSET) (2018)
24. Wrappalyzer: Cookie compliance technologies market share (2023). https://www.wappalyzer.com/technologies/cookie-compliance/
25. Wuille, P.: Bip32: Hierarchical deterministic wallets (2012). https://github.com/bitcoin/bips/blob/master/bip-0032.mediawiki
26. Yue, C., Xie, M., Wang, H.: Automatic cookie usage setting with cookiepicker. In: 37th Annual IEEE/IFIP International Conference on Dependable Systems and Networks (DSN 2007), pp. 460–470. IEEE (2007)
27. Yue, C., Xie, M., Wang, H.: An automatic HTTP cookie management system. Comput. Netw. **54**(13), 2182–2198 (2010)
28. Zichichi, M., Ferretti, S., D'Angelo, G., Rodríguez-Doncel, V.: Personal data access control through distributed authorization. In: 2020 IEEE 19th International Symposium on Network Computing and Applications (NCA), pp. 1–4, November 2020. https://doi.org/10.1109/NCA51143.2020.9306721

Try On, Spied On?: Privacy Analysis of Virtual Try-On Websites and Android Apps

Abdelrahman Ragab$^{(\boxtimes)}$ ⓘ, Mohammad Mannan ⓘ, and Amr Youssef ⓘ

Concordia University, Montreal, Canada
{abdelrahman.ragab,m.mannan,amr.youssef}@concordia.ca

Abstract. The use of augmented reality (AR) technology for virtual try-on (VTO) in online shopping is on the rise but its current state of privacy is not well explored. To examine privacy issues in VTO websites and apps, we analyze 138 websites and 28 Android apps that offer VTO. By capturing and analyzing the network traffic, we found that 65% of the websites send user images to a server: 8% to first-party (FP) servers only, and 57% to third-party (TP) servers only or both FP and TP. 18% of apps send user images to a server: 4% to FP servers only, and 14% to TP servers only or both FP and TP. Additionally, 43 websites and 2 apps are confirmed to get the users' images stored, either by the FP website or a TP. 37% of websites are confirmed to use VTO providers which extract facial geometry from received users' images. We also found that 11% of websites featuring VTO violate their own privacy policies, and 25% use a VTO provider that violates its own privacy policy. Privacy policy violations include sharing the user's image to a website's own server, or to a TP server, despite denying so in the privacy policy. Furthermore, 22% of websites use disclaimers that mislead users about what happens to their data when using VTO. We also found 1446 and 931 TP tracking scripts and cookies, respectively, in the analyzed websites. Finally, we identified security vulnerabilities, such as broken authentication, in a VTO provider that can compromise its merchants. These findings underscore the need for greater transparency and clarity from companies using VTO features, and highlight the potential risks to user privacy, even from top brands.

Keywords: virtual try-on · VTO · augmented reality · privacy · security

1   Introduction

According to market research firm `Technavio.com`, the virtual reality (VR), augmented reality (AR), and mixed reality markets are set to grow by US$162.71 billion, between 2021 and 2025 [24]. These technologies enhance the online shopping experience by allowing customers to interact with the product virtually, e.g., to virtually try on clothes [26], visualize products in their own space, and interact with products in a more immersive and realistic way. In June 2020, a survey of U.S. retailers revealed that 20% planned to invest in AR or VR for

S. Katsikas et al. (Eds.): ESORICS 2023 Workshops, LNCS 14398, pp. 232–248, 2024.
https://doi.org/10.1007/978-3-031-54204-6_13

their online stores, up from 8% six months earlier [3]. AR shopping via VTO can also provide benefits for retailers, including increased sales, reduced costs, and improved customer engagement. VTO on websites/apps is very accessible as it does not require expensive headsets; just a web/phone camera. While the popularity of this technology continues to grow, we know little about the current state of privacy and security of such solutions. Feng et al. [6] examined consumers' responses to VTO apps. The results of their study demonstrate that when users have high levels of privacy concerns, they tend to show higher levels of perceived intrusiveness and more negative attitudes towards the app when viewing themselves trying a product using VTO than when viewing professional in-app models wearing the product. This perceived intrusiveness is justified considering that personal data such as user's facial images, body images, or room images become the subject of interest (we refer to any of those types of images as user's image in this study). If these users' images fall into the wrong hands, e.g., by means of leakage, selling, or otherwise, they can be used in nefarious ways such as in fake or depictive videos/images, especially with the advancement of deepfake technologies. Biometric data such as face geometry, which can be obtained from facial images, is particularly used in facial recognition to identify individuals [10]. Additionally, face geometry can be used to extract other information such as age, gender, and health attributes of the individual [14].

Furthermore, it is not well established whether VTO websites and apps are in line with their privacy policies, or if they receive users' images on their servers, process them, or share them with third parties. Previous work such as [23] investigated security and privacy aspects of AR applications and their supporting technologies. They identified some issues, such as the possibility of deception attacks, overload attacks, access control for sensor data, and bystander privacy. Other work [19] investigated authentication mechanisms for AR/VR devices.

In this work, we present a framework (see overview in Fig. 1) for measuring the privacy of websites and Android apps featuring VTO, as well as testing the security of VTO service providers. We analyze 138 websites and 28 Android apps featuring VTO, and we analyze 3 VTO service providers. For the websites featuring VTO, we check if users' images or videos are shared while using the VTO feature, and we check if the observed behavior is in line with the website's privacy policy. In addition to addressing the privacy aspect of the VTO feature, we quantify and classify the third-party cookies and scripts present on each website using an extension that we created and released[1] for the web privacy measurement framework, OpenWPM [5]. We do the same for the apps, but instead of the quantification and classification of cookies and scripts, we check for the presence of tracking libraries. We also test the VTO service providers for security issues such as broken authentication, unauthorized access, and Cross-Site Request Forgery (CSRF). We also check if there are any misconfigurations which can leak users' data.

---

[1] https://github.com/virtualtryon2023/openwpm-cookies-and-scripts-extension.

Contributions and Notable Findings

1. We develop a framework to evaluate the privacy of VTO websites and apps (including top brands), and to test the security of VTO service providers.
2. 90 out of 138 (65%) of the tested websites send the user's image to a server when using the VTO feature, and 79 out of 90 particularly to TP servers including VTO providers, analytics services, and session replay services. For 43 out of 138 (31%) of the websites, the user's image is stored during the VTO. 10 user images are still accessible, with 3 of them still accessible over 2 months after testing. 15 out of 90 (17%) of websites - that send the user's image to a server - violate their own privacy policy and 35 out of 90 (39%) use a VTO service provider that violates its own privacy policy.
3. 6 out of 90 (7%) of websites that send the user's image to a server showed a misleading and false disclaimer that denies the processing, storage or collection of the user's image, or claims that the user's image is not shared and remains on the local device, despite the reality being the opposite. For example, `Prada.com` states "Your Image will not be communicated to PRADA or anyone else and will not be stored by Luxottica. The Image is processed live.", even though it sends the user's image to Adobe Ads.
4. 51 out of 138 (37%) of websites are confirmed to use VTO providers which extract face geometry from received users' images.
5. 1446 out of 2609 (55%) of TP scripts found in 138 websites are trackers. Popular brands such as `Elfcosmetics.com` had the largest number of TP tracking scripts: 29. 931 out of 2487 (37%) of TP cookies found in 138 websites are trackers. E.l.f Cosmetics had the largest number of TP tracking cookies: 40. 55 out of 931 (6%) of cookies are set to the year 9999, and 403 out of 931 (43%) to more than 1 year but less than 5.
6. 5 out of 28 (18%) of tested apps with an overall of 20.5+ million downloads are found to send the user's image to a server, and 4 out of 28 (14%) send it to a TP server. 2 out of 28 (7%) apps get the user's image stored on a server when using the VTO feature. 2 out of 5 of apps that send the user's image to a server violate their own privacy policy.
7. The VTO service provider `Vossle.com` is found to suffer from broken authentication and authorization, where an attacker can get personal information of all merchants using the platform, and can modify the VTO collection of a victim. On sign-up, the user's email and password are leaked to `sentry.io` session replay service.

2   Related Work

Augmented and Virtual Reality. Liebers et al. [12] investigated the use of gaze behavior and head orientation for implicit identification in virtual reality. The personal identifiability of user tracking data during observation of VR videos has also been studied [13,18]. Trimananda et al. [25] focused on Oculus VR (OVR) and provided the first comprehensive analysis of personal data exposed by OVR apps and the platform itself, from a networking and privacy policy perspective. By comparing the data flows collected from the network traffic of 140 apps with statements made in the apps' privacy policies, they found that 68% of OVR data flows were inconsistently disclosed in the privacy policy. Furthermore, they extracted additional context from the privacy policies, and observed that 69% of the consistent data flows have purposes unrelated to the core functionality of apps (i.e., advertising, analytics, marketing, and additional features). Lebeck et al. [11] conducted a qualitative lab study with an immersive AR headset, the Microsoft HoloLens. Through semi-structured interviews, they explored participants' security, privacy, and other concerns.

Virtual Try-On. To the best of our knowledge, this is the first measurement study to look into the privacy and security of websites and apps featuring VTO. Past literature focused on users' perception of VTO technology when shopping online. Feng et al. [6] studied the effect of the users' privacy concerns on their perceived intrusiveness of VTO features, and how it affects their attitude towards VTO apps. Smink et al. [22] studied the perceived informativeness and enjoyment when using VTO in online shopping. Ivanov et al. [9] examined the impact of users' privacy concerns on the intent of adoption of VTO for clothes. They found that a majority of their participants (110 out of 192) "would *ideally* use their own avatar, but choose not to due to privacy concern".

3   Methodology

3.1   Collection of VTO Providers, Websites and Apps

In this section, we outline how we collect our list of VTO service providers' websites, websites featuring VTO, and Android apps featuring VTO. By *VTO service provider's website*, we mean the website of the company providing VTO technology for other websites (clients) to use. A *website/app featuring VTO* is a website/app making use of the VTO feature that is used by end-users. In some cases, some VTO providers have a demo on their website which allows end-users to use the VTO feature. We count such cases under *websites featuring VTO* too and we analyze them as such.

VTO Service Providers. Despite the increasing popularity of VTO, it is still not as ubiquitous, and there are not many VTO service providers. We collect our list of VTO service providers manually using search queries (e.g.,'virtual try on solution') on Google. In total, we find 18 providers. However, we test the security of 3 only because they were the only ones which offer a free trial.

Websites Featuring VTO. In addition to using Google search queries, we see the list of clients on VTO service provider's websites to collect websites featuring VTO. We collect a non-exhaustive list of 138 websites which mostly either offer glasses VTO or makeup VTO. A few websites offered other VTO such as hair and fingernail VTO. We also count websites with features to evaluate skin health - by capturing a user's facial image - as websites featuring VTO.

Android Apps Featuring VTO. To collect Android apps featuring VTO, we query Google's Play Store with relevant keywords (e.g., try on, virtual try on, AR glasses, AR furniture). We also look into the *related apps* section on the app's page, and the list of apps by the same developer. For apps, we look beyond glasses and makeup stores. For example, we also count in apps with clothes try-on, tattoo try-on, furniture AR visualization, hair try-on, shoes try-on, and jewelry try-on. Only apps with at least 1 thousand downloads are considered. We also classify apps to be either *pure VTO* or not.

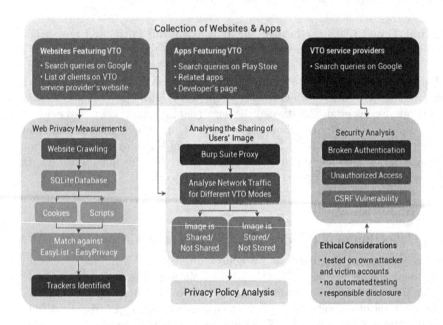

Fig. 1. Overview of analysis framework.

3.2   Analyzing the Sharing of Users' Images on VTO Websites/Apps

We identify 3 different modes through which customers can use the VTO feature. First is live mode, where as long as a user's camera is open, virtual products are placed on their face/body or in the room in real-time. The second mode is image capture, where an image is first captured, then the virtual product is applied. The third mode is image upload, where the user uploads their image from their device before applying the product. We also identify an option to the second and third modes: download/share image, where a user clicks a download/share (to Facebook, WhatsApp, etc.) image button, after applying the VTO effect. We set up a man-in-the-middle-proxy to capture and decrypt HTTP/HTTPS traffic while using the VTO feature in a website/app. For each available mode in a website/app, we capture the network traffic, then analyze the requests and responses. Throughout the experiment for websites, we did not sign-up/in to the website, as it is not required; the VTO feature is available for use without signing in.

To confirm the sending of the users' image, we analyze every request to see if the payload contains the user's image. The payloads containing images are either in JSON format or multi-part file (form-data) format. We look for the strings 'image/jpeg' and 'image/png' in the payload. These strings indicate the beginning of an image encoded in base64 in the case of a JSON payload, and they indicate the field for an image in the form-data payload. To verify it is indeed the user's image, in the case of an image in base64, we convert it to JPEG/PNG format respectively using online tools [15,16]. If the image is in a form-data type of payload, we just save the binary bytes to a JPEG/PNG file. If the image is found to be of the user, then it is confirmed that the user's image is sent to a server. In several cases, the entire request payload is encoded in gzip or zlib format. For gzip, we use Burp Suite's decoder module to decode the payload. In the case of zlib, we use the open source tool *zlib* [1] to decode the payload. A limitation of our method is that although it considers payloads encoded in gzip and zlib, it does not consider other cases such as where the payload is encrypted, in another encoding method, or in other device dependent formats.

We consider that a user's image has been stored in a server in two cases. The first case is when any of the captured outgoing requests (which do not contain the user's image) retrieves the user's image in the response. In the second case, we analyze responses to captured requests after the user's image has been sent to the server for the first time. If any response payload contains a link enabling the viewing or downloading of the user's image or a modified version of it, we infer that the user's image is stored on a server. We do not consider cases where the user's image is obtained from the browser's cache as storing the user's image on a server.

Test Setup. For testing websites, we set up the Burp Suite proxy on a Windows 11 machine, and use Google Chrome to test the websites. For testing Android apps, we use a rooted Samsung Galaxy M02 phone running on Android 13. Communication is established between the Windows 11 machine and the phone via USB connection and ADB (Android Debug Bridge). Burp Suite proxy is used for traffic interception. We use the dynamic instrumentation toolkit Frida [7] to execute scripts to attempt bypassing SSL-pinning where needed.

3.3   Analyzing Privacy Policies w.r.t VTO Feature

Based on our observation while testing the VTO feature of websites/apps, we analyze their privacy policy to see if there is any inconsistency or violation. We classify the standing of a website/app with respect to its privacy policy into *not violated, vague, ambiguous,* or *violated.* We consider that a website has *not violated* its privacy policy if the user's image is not detected to be shared at all, or if no criterion mentioned below is matched. A website with a *vague* standing still does not violate the privacy policy, but there is no direct mention of image collection in the privacy policy. A website will be given an *ambiguous* standing if the privacy policy has contradicting terms, makes no mention of data collection at all, or if the privacy policy is inaccessible. We consider that a website has *violated* its own privacy policy if any of the following defined criteria is matched: (1) *image sharing to server*: the user's image is sent to the website's server despite the privacy policy denying it. (2) *image storing*: the user's image is stored on the website's own server, or an associated cloud storage, despite the privacy policy denying the storing of users' images. (3) *image storage duration*: the duration of storing the user's image exceeds that which is mentioned in the privacy policy. (4) *image sharing to third party*: the user's image is shared with a third-party without consent, despite the privacy policy denying it unless consent is given. (5) *image sharing to analytics services*: the privacy policy mentions the use of tracking and analytics services such as Google Analytics for automatic collection and analysis of the user's behavior and/or system settings, however, the user's image ends up being sent to that service provider. We do not consider the user's image to be normal information nor behavior to be automatically collected and sent to such third-party services.

Based on the above criteria, we also report on websites (clients) which use VTO providers that violate their own privacy policy when being used by the client websites.

3.4   Measurement of Trackers

For websites featuring VTO, we create an extension to the OpenWPM open-source framework [5] and use it to measure third-party (TP) scripts and cookies, and identify trackers. OpenWPM provides raw structured data regarding the crawls and stores it in an SQLite database. Our extension allows us to get the following information about the crawled websites: (1) the number (and details) of distinct first-party and TP cookies per website, (2) the overall number of occurrences of TP cookies across the list of websites, (3) the expiry dates statistics for every TP cookie host domain, (4) the categorization of TP cookies across websites, and (5) the categorization of TP scripts across websites.

To identify TP cookies/scripts, we check their source URL. If the source does not contain the domain name of the first-party website, we consider the cookie/script to be originating from a TP source. We further categorize TP cookies and scripts into one of three categories: *advertisers*, *trackers*, and *unknown*. To categorize advertisers and trackers, we match the source of the detected TP scripts and cookies with the EasyList and EasyPrivacy lists respectively [4], which are lists for known sources of trackers and advertisers. If the source of a cookie/script does not match any entry in the lists, it is categorized as unknown. While it is true that the presented methodology may have misclassified some FP cookies and tracking scripts as TP due to the use of a different domain name by the FP, we mitigate this to some extent by not using exact matching. Rather, we check for the presence of the original FP domain as a substring. So, misclassification may occur only in case the FP uses domain names that do not intersect.

Practically, we found through manual observation that the cookies and trackers that were classified as TP do originate from third parties like analytics, advertising, marketing, and social media companies; there was no misclassification. Also, it should be noted that *Easylist* and *Easy Privacy* lists are not exhaustive and may therefore miss proper classification of some TP scripts and cookies. For Android apps, we check for the presence of tracking libraries (i.e., analytics and session replay services).

Test Setup. We run OpenWPM on an Ubuntu 22 virtual machine (connected to a home network) with 9GB RAM, 32GB HDD, AMD Ryzen 5 4600H 6-core processor (host) for our measurement on June 5, 2023. We run 1 windowed browser (as opposed to a headless browser) and enable the instrumentation for HTTP traffic, cookies, navigation, JavaScript, DNS requests and callstack. We performed stateless crawls (each new page visit uses a fresh browser profile) and enabled bot-mitigation for less bot-like behavior. The crawled data is saved to an SQLite database, which we then process using our extension. For checking tracking libraries in Android apps, we unpack the APK files using the Jadx tool [21] and inspect the libraries used in the source files. The limitation of this approach is that there might be tracking libraries which we were not able to identify due to obfuscation of their names.

3.5   Analysing VTO Service Providers

We consider several security issues for VTO service providers:

Broken Authentication. We remove authentication credentials from sensitive/state changing (e.g., modifying VTO collection) requests and replay them. If the response is the same as when the requests were sent with the credentials, then the website would be considered vulnerable to broken authentication.

Unauthorized Access. We sign in using two accounts: an attacker account and victim account (both belonging to us). We capture a request made by the victim account and replace the credentials with that of the attacker. If the response indicates success, and the victim's account state is changed, then we consider that there is an unauthorized access vulnerability.

CSRF Vulnerability. For a website to be considered vulnerable to CSRF, (1) the server and client should not be communicating via JSON,(2) requests should not require custom headers, and (3) there should be no anti-CSRF token in the request [17]. So, for any PUT and POST request that matches the mentioned criteria, we count the request to be vulnerable to CSRF.

Ethical Considerations and Responsible Disclosure. To not infringe other users' privacy, we create two merchant accounts for the platforms we test: one to represent the attacker and the other to represent the victim. So, whatever test that appears to be intrusive (e.g., modifying the VTO collection of another merchant or retrieving personal information of another merchant) has been done against our own victim account. We also refrain from using active scanning and automated tools when testing for security vulnerabilities. Furthermore, we disclosed the discovered issues with the affected VTO provider, Vossle, in accordance with the CERT Guide to Coordinated Vulnerability Disclosure [8].

4   Results

4.1   Sharing of Users' Images on VTO Featuring Websites

Sending Images to Servers. For all tested websites, upon using the VTO feature, the browser requests the user's permission to use the camera. We found that 90 out of 138 (65%) of the websites send the user's images to a server when using the VTO feature. 79 of them send the user's image to a third-party server. We consider any website or service other than the website being visited to be a third party. For example, VTO service providers, analytics services and session replay services are considered third parties. The majority of the third parties - to which the user's image is sent - are VTO service providers (71 incidents), followed by Google Analytics (9 incidents). Also, there are 2 incidents where the user's image is sent in a Facebook Pixel to `Facebook.com`. We do not know the intention behind sharing users' images with analytics services. Possible reasons include: VTO websites/apps are gathering users' images through an analytics service to e.g., analyze their customer base by inferring users' demographics (e.g., age, gender, ethnicity, etc.), or to feed them into machine learning models for improved user profiling. Besides images, there was one incident where a video of the user is sent to Luxottica server while using its VTO[2] in video capture mode. We found that a user's image can be sent to a server through more than one mode per website. User images are sent to a server in each mode as follows: live mode (40 out of 90, 44%), image upload (41 out of 90, 46%), capture mode (28 out of 90, 31%), and download/share image option (27 out of 138, 30%), respectively.

Image Storing. After analyzing the traffic, we were able to confirm that 43 out of 138 (31%) of the websites either store the user's image themselves or a third-party (associated with the website) stores the image. For 24 of these 43 websites, we detected 25 links (in total) - to access the user's stored image - being sent back from the server. For 10 out of 25 of the links we observed, the user's image is still accessible: 7 over three weeks and 3 over two months since testing. For 6 out of 25 of the links, they expired and accessing them would give an *access denied* error. Access being denied, however, does not necessarily mean

---

[2] https://virtualmirror-xp.luxottica.com/kvbkF86bZsvnGqLmsfUdGj.

that the image is actually deleted. For 9 out of 25 of the links, accessing them after some time gave a *not found* error, which can indicate that the image is deleted.

Session Replay Services. There are 4 incidents on 4 websites where users' images are sent to session replay services: `Transitions.com` sends the user's image to `Contentsquare.com`, `Bvlgari.com` to *Quantum Metric*, `Paireyewear.com` to `Datadoghq.com` and `Lenskart.com` to *Microsoft Clarity*[3] session replay services.

Face Geometry Data. By inspecting the network traffic, we found that 51 websites use VTO providers (including `Fittingbox.com` and `Luna.io`, formerly *Ditto*) which process users' images and extract facial geometry from them. This was confirmed by observing the facial geometry being sent back from the VTO providers' servers to the browser.

4.2 Privacy Policy Analysis w.r.t VTO Feature on Websites

After analysing the privacy policy of the 90 websites which sent the user's image to a server, we found that 15 out of 90 (17%) violate their own privacy policy. 7 out of 15 of them violate their privacy policy on the basis of the criterion *image sharing to analytics services*, as defined in Sect. 3.3, where the websites share the user's images with third-party services such as Google Analytics and Contentsquare session replay service. 6 out of 15 of the violations are on the basis of the criterion *image sharing to third party*. The remaining 2 websites violate their privacy policy on the basis of the criterion *image sharing to server*, and *image storing*, respectively. 36 out of 90 (40%) have a vague standing with regards to their privacy policy. 3 websites have ambiguous standing, and the remaining 36 out of 90 (40%) do not appear to violate their privacy policy.

We found that 35 out of 90 (39%) of the websites - that send the user's image to a server - use a VTO provider which violates its own privacy policy. For example, the VTO provider *Fittingbox* states in its privacy policy "FITTINGBOX will not disclose or store your image; your image is processed live, on your device and only for the duration of the virtual try on experience.". Despite that, we found from the network traffic analysis that it does receive users' images to process them. Many top brands such as `Gunnar.com`, `Fielmann.at`, `Hansanders.nl`, and *Jins*[4] are found to be using *Fittingbox*. Out of the 35 cases where a website uses a VTO provider that violated its own privacy policy, 30 are on the basis of the criterion *image sharing to server* as defined in Sect. 3.3, while the remaining 5 violate the privacy policy on the basis of the criterion *image storage duration*, where the VTO provider (*Perfect Corp*) stores the user's image longer than it claimed. Perfect Corp states in its privacy policy that "If Facebook 'share' function enabled, photo is temporarily stored on Perfect server for 24 h", however,

---

[3] https://clarity.microsoft.com/.
[4] https://us.jins.com.

it was still possible to access the image over 24 h later. After expiring a while beyond the 24 h, it would give an *access denied* error, which may not mean that it has been actually deleted. 46 out of 90 (51%) of the websites - that sent the user's image to a server - do not use VTO providers that violate their own privacy policy. 8 of the websites have a VTO provider which has a vague privacy policy, while just 1 has a VTO provider that has an ambiguous privacy policy.

An alarming observation is that 6 websites (see Table 1) show a pop-up kind of disclaimer upon using the VTO feature which tells the user that their image: will not be uploaded to a server, shared, stored, or that it will be deleted. This disclaimer is made regardless of what is actually stated in the privacy policy. Despite this disclaimer, exactly the opposite occurs; the user's image gets infact sent to a server, stored, or shared with another party. Such disclaimer gives the user false confidence in the website.

We also calculated the overall readability of the privacy policies of the VTO websites which share user's images to a server. We utilized the Flesch-Kincaid Reading Ease metric [2] with readability scores *very easy, easy, fairly easy, standard, fairly difficult, difficult, and very confusing*. Out of the 87 tested privacy policies (3 websites had missing privacy policies), 23, 62 and 2 privacy policies obtained a readability score of very confusing, difficult, and fairly difficult, respectively.

Table 1. Example of tested VTO websites. *PP* in the table header means *privacy policy* and *TP* means *third-party*. A ✓ means *yes*. A blank means *no*. For the privacy policy columns, a ● means *violated*, a ◑ means *ambiguous*, a ◔ means *vague* and a ○ means *not violated*. For the 'violation type' columns, the numbers denote the violations as specified by the criteria defined in Sect. 3.3. The mapping is as follows: (1) *image sharing to server*, (2) *image storing*, (3) *image storage duration*, (4) *image sharing to third party*, (5) *image sharing to analytics services*. A dash '-' means not applicable. The full list of tested websites is available at https://github.com/virtualtryon2023/VTO-Privacy-Analysis.

Website URL	Image sent to TP	Image stored	Own PP	Violation type	VTO provider's PP	Violation type	Misleading disclaimer
www.elfcosmetics.com	✓	✓	○	-	●	3	
virtual-cosme.net	✓		●	4	○	-	
www.aveda.ca	✓	✓	●	5	●	3	
www.madison-reed.com	✓		○	-	●	3	✓
www.punky.com	✓	✓	○	-	●	3	
www.benefitcosmetics.com	✓		●	5	○	-	✓
vto.gunnar.com	✓		○	-	●	1	
www.fittingbox.com			●	1	○	-	
www.transitions.com	✓		●	5	●	1	✓
virtualmirror-xp.luxottica.com		✓	●	2	○	-	
www.bulgari.com	✓		○	-	○	-	✓
www.prada.com	✓		○	-	○	-	✓
drbishop.com	✓		●	4	●	1	
www.peepers.com	✓		●	5	●	1	
edandsarna.com	✓	✓	○	-	○	-	
www.alensa.ie	✓	✓	●	4	●	1	
www.lensmartonline.com	✓	✓	○	-	◑	-	
fyidoctors.com	✓		●	4	●	1	
anrri.com	✓	✓	◑	-	○	-	

4.3   Sharing of Users' Images on VTO Featuring Apps

We had an initial collection of 44 Android apps. 28 out of 44 were deemed to be successfully tested (see the full list of tested apps on our GitHub repository[5]). The others failed due to one of the following reasons: (i) the app does not load even after applying SSL-pinning bypass, (ii) the app not does not load due to unavailability in country or phone compatibility, (iii) the VTO feature is there but does not work, (iv) could not find the button or place within the app to use the VTO feature.

For the successful 28 tests, 5 out of 28 (18%) apps with an overall of 20.5+ million downloads are found to send the user's image to a server, 4 out of 28 (14%) send the image to a third-party server, and 2 out of 28 (7%) are confirmed to store the user's image. 4 out of 5 apps send the user's image to a server in capture mode, and 1 out of 5 send the image in both capture and upload modes. The third parties with which the user's image is shared are: *LogRocket*[6] session replay service, VTO service provider *Luna* (for 2 apps), and some IP address. The image that is sent to a server with an IP address and no domain name is sent over non secure HTTP, which allows any intermediate device between the client and server to intercept and access the image[7]. *Ikea* and *Lenskart* apps are confirmed to store the user's room and personal image, respectively. For *Ikea*, it is confirmed on the basis that an image of the full room view is returned from the backend after processing and remains available afterwards to add AR furniture. Concerning room images, machine learning techniques can now be used for object detection, which can be leveraged to infer information such as the presence of kids (if toys are detected), habits or hobbies (e.g., due to the presence of musical instruments), financial status (if expensive objects or electronics are detected), etc. This data can be used in customer base segmentation. For *Lenskart*, it is confirmed on the basis that an AWS S3 link to access the image is sent back from the backend.

4.4   Privacy Policy Analysis w.r.t VTO Feature on Apps

2 of the 5 apps - that send the user's image to a server - violate their own privacy policy. The app *Yourfit By 3DLook*[8] states in its privacy statement "We will not disclose or share your images with third parties", however, we detected that it did send the user's image to LogRocket session replay service. This violation is on the basis of the criterion *image sharing to third party* as defined in Sect. 3.3. The app *Lenskart: Eyeglasses & More*, which has over 10 million downloads, states "we do not store any personal/sensitive information on our server. This remains safely with you on your phone/other devices.", however, we found that the user's image is sent to a URL with the *lenskart.com* domain, and an accessible AWS S3 link to the image is sent back, proving that the image is in fact stored beyond the user's

---

[5] https://github.com/virtualtryon2023/VTO-Privacy-Analysis.
[6] https://logrocket.com/.
[7] The app has been removed from Google Play as of August 10.
[8] https://3dlook.me/.

device. This violation is on the basis of the criterion *image storing*. 2 out of 5 of the apps - which send the user's image to a server - have a vague and ambiguous privacy policy, respectively. The final app does not violate its privacy policy.

4.5   Measurement of Trackers

Scripts. Overall, we found 2609 third-party (TP) scripts in the 138 websites that we crawled. Using the method described in Sect. 3.4, we categorized 1446 (55%) out of 2609 as trackers, 78 (3%) as advertisers, and the rest are unknown. The top 4 most frequently detected trackers are *googletagmanager.com* (393 out of 1446, 27%), *facebook.net* (180 out of 1446, 12%), *google-analytics.com* (133 out of 1446, 9%), and *hotjar.com* (55 out of 1446, 4%). The *facebook.net* tracker can track user's behavior and share it with third parties [20]. Among the websites with the most TP tracking scripts are websites of popular brands. For example, *E.l.f Cosmetics* has the largest number of TP scripts: 29. See Fig. 3(a) for the top 20 websites with tracking scripts. Furthermore, we found that *E.l.f Cosmetics*'s website has TP tracking scripts from 20 distinct domains, which is the highest number among tested websites. 23 other websites, including *Nars Cosmetics, Jane Iredale, Kits, Madison Reed, Lenscrafter, and Oakley,* have TP tracking scripts from over 10 distinct domains.

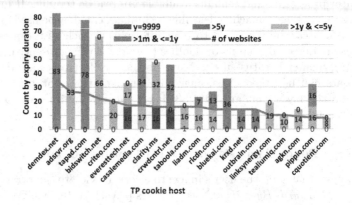

Fig. 2. Expiry of top 20 TP tracker domains sorted by frequency in distinct websites, and the no. of websites in which the top 20 tracker domains are present.

Cookies. We found an overall of 2487 TP cookies in the 138 websites we crawled. 931 (37%) are categorized as trackers, 708 (28%) as advertisers, and the rest are unknown. The most frequently detected tracking domains that have set TP tracking cookies are *demdex.net* (83 out of 931, 8.9%), followed by *clarity.ms* (80 out of 931, 8.6%), then *tapad.com* (78 out of 931, 7.8%). Again, we found popular brands to have a large number of TP cookies in general, and TP tracking cookies in particular. *E.l.f Cosmetics* has the largest number of TP cookies, 121: 40 of which are trackers, and 56 are advertisers (the rest are unknown). Other popular brands such as *Eyeconic*[9] and *Lenscrafters*[10] for eye-wear have 45 and 41 TP tracking cookies, respectively. See Fig. 3(b) for the top 20 websites with tracking cookies. *E.l.f Cosmetics* has its TP tracking cookies from 24 different domains, *Lenscrafters* from 22, and *Eyeconic* from 21. The top three TP tracker domains which occurred in most websites are *demdex.net* (35 out of 138, 25%), *adsrvr.org* (27 out of 138, 20%) and *tapad.com* (26 out of 138, 19%). See Fig. 2 for the number of websites in which the top 20 TP tracker domains are found. We found several TP tracker domains which set cookies with expiry dates to the year 9999. For example, *everesttech.net* and *clarity.ms* have each set such tracking cookies in 16 websites. In the crawled websites, a total of 55 out of 931 (6%) TP tracking cookies are set to the year 9999, 0 to more than 5 years but not 9999, 403 out of 931 (43%) to more than 1 year but less than 5, and 358 out of 931 (38%) to more than one month but less than 1 year. The remaining 115 are less than or equal to 1 month.

Tracking Libraries in Android Apps. We found 19 distinct tracking libraries in the 28 Android apps we tested. Figure 3(c) and 3(d) summarize our findings.

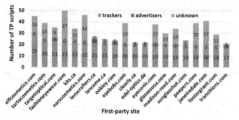

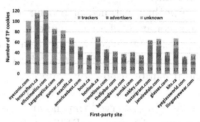

(a) Top 20 count of TP scripts by site and category, sorted by descending order of number of tracking scripts.

(b) Top 20 count of TP cookies by site and category, sorted by descending order of number of tracking cookies.

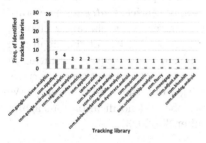

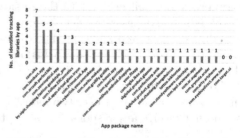

(c) Overall frequency of identified tracking libraries in tested apps.

(d) Number of identified tracking libraries by app.

Fig. 3. Summary of main findings for tracking scripts (a) and cookies (b) in websites, and tracking libraries in apps (c, d).

---

[9] https://www.eyeconic.com/.
[10] https://www.lenscrafters.ca.

4.6 Analysis of VTO Service Providers

Out of the 3 VTO service providers we tested (*Perfect Corp*[11], *Deep AR*[12], *Vossle*), only *Vossle* is found to have major issues. As an end-user who clicks on a generated link for a particular VTO experience of a merchant, the end-user can view (in the response to the GET request) the merchant's personal details such as name, email, mobile number, user id, and the login code associated with the account on sign up, as well as *Shopify*, *Magento* and *WordPress* plugin keys. Assuming a key can be used more than once or a Merchant has not used their key, a non-*Vossle* subscriber could possibly steal a merchant's *Magento* key to use the *Vossle* plugin in their own store. We also found an instance of broken authentication and authorization. Merchants' account IDs are integers starting from 0 onward; meaning, they can be enumerated. This makes it possible to collect personal information of all merchants who use the platform, as there exists an API which retrieves the details of all VTO experiences of a particular merchant using the account ID. The retrieved details include the URL slug of the VTO experience. The URL slug can be used with the previously mentioned API - which requests the VTO experience - to get the personal details of the merchant.

Another instance of broken authentication and authorization is that given the account ID of a victim and removing the authentication parameters from the request, an attacker can create a new VTO experience on behalf of the victim. This can cause confusion to the victim with regards to their VTO collection, and it can be used - for example - to create inappropriate VTO experiences and share it in the name of the victim.

We also observed that no anti-CSRF tokens were used on the *Vossle* website. However, the use of a JWT token instead of session cookies made CSRF attacks possible only in one operation: creating a new VTO experience, where the JWT authentication token is not checked by the website.

A privacy issue we found during sign-up on the platform is that the typed password and email are sent to the session replay service *sentry.io*. The state of the email and password fields gets captured after every character change, including deletion and addition. The different captured states of the email and password fields (as well as other fields) are then sent in one request, resulting in the final state of the email and password being sent to the session replay service.

We informed Vossle about the vulnerabilities but they did not reply. We emailed them again after over two months since the first notification, but again, we did not receive any response (as of September 30, 2023).

5 Conclusion

Based on our analysis, we can conclude that there are concerns regarding the manner in which websites and apps featuring VTO technology manage the privacy of their users, particularly in relation to their images. The majority of tested

---

[11] https://www.perfectcorp.com/business.
[12] https://www.deepar.ai/.

websites send users' images not only to their servers, but also to third-parties as well. The images are stored in many cases, and VTO providers of websites can extract face geometry from users' images. Many VTO featuring websites/apps either violate their own privacy policy or they use a VTO provider that violates its own privacy policy. Furthermore, several websites are found to mislead users by displaying disclaimers - upon using the VTO feature - which are opposite to the reality and do not represent their privacy policies. This is in addition to the lack of clarity in privacy policies as of what really happens to the user's data while using the VTO feature. We also show that there are many third-party tracking scripts and cookies present in VTO websites. Lastly, we found one VTO service provider to be compromising the privacy of its clients by sharing their email and password with a session replay service, and compromising the security of their accounts due to vulnerabilities broken authentication and unauthorized access.

Acknowledgment. This work was supported by the Office of the Privacy Commissioner of Canada (OPC). We also thank the anonymous DPM 2023 reviewers for their insightful feedback and suggestions.

References

1. Cantwell, K.: Zlib: a command-line utility for quickly compressing or decompressing zlib data. https://github.com/kevin-cantwell/zlib
2. Cdimascio: py-readability-metrics. https://github.com/cdimascio/py-readability-metrics/tree/master#flesch-kincaid-grade-level
3. Davis, J.: How 5G will change retail (2021). https://www.insiderintelligence.com/content/how-5g-will-change-retail
4. EasyList: Easylist. https://easylist.to/
5. Englehardt, S., Narayanan, A.: Online tracking: a 1-million-site measurement and analysis. In Proceedings of the 2016 ACM SIGSAC Conference on Computer and Communications Security, CCS 2016. ACM, New York, NY, USA, (2016)
6. Feng, Y., Xie, Q.: Privacy concerns, perceived intrusiveness, and privacy controls: an analysis of virtual try-on apps. J. Interact. Advertising **19**(1), 43–57 (2019)
7. Frida: Frida. https://github.com/frida/frida
8. Householder, A., Wassermann, G., Manion, A., King, C.: CERT® guide to coordinated vulnerability disclosure (2020). https://resources.sei.cmu.edu/asset_files/specialreport/2017_003_001_503340.pdf
9. Ivanov, A., Mou, Y., Tawira, L.: Avatar personalisation vs. privacy in a virtual try-on app for apparel shopping. Int. J. Fashion Des. Technol. Educ. **16**(1), 100–109 (2023)
10. Kaspersky: What is facial recognition - definition and explanation. https://www.kaspersky.com/resource-center/definitions/what-is-facial-recognition
11. Lebeck, K., Ruth, K., Kohno, T., Roesner, F.: Towards security and privacy for multi-user augmented reality: foundations with end users. In: 2018 IEEE Symposium on Security and Privacy. IEEE (2018)
12. Liebers, J., Horn, P., Burschik, C., Gruenefeld, U., Schneegass, S.: Using gaze behavior and head orientation for implicit identification in virtual reality. In: Proceedings of the 27th ACM Symposium on Virtual Reality Software and Technology, New York, NY, USA (2021)

13. Miller, M.R., Herrera, F., Jun, H., Landay, J.A., Bailenson, J.N.: Personal identifiability of user tracking data during observation of 360-degree VR video. Sci. Rep. **10**(1), 17404 (2020)
14. Mirjalili, V., Ross, A.: Soft biometric privacy: retaining biometric utility of face images while perturbing gender. In: 2017 IEEE IJCB, Denver, CO, USA (2017)
15. OnlineJPGTools: Convert base64 to jpeg. https://onlinejpgtools.com/convert-base64-to-jpg
16. OnlinePNGTools: Convert base64 to png. https://onlinepngtools.com/convert-base64-to-png
17. Pagey, R., Mannan, M., Youssef, A.: All your shops are belong to us: security weaknesses in e-commerce platforms. In: Proceedings of the ACM Web Conference 2023, WWW 2023. ACM, New York, NY, USA (2023)
18. Pfeuffer, K., Geiger, M.J., Prange, S., Mecke, L., Buschek, D., Alt, F.: Behavioural biometrics in VR: identifying people from body motion and relations in virtual reality. In: Proceedings of the 2019 CHI Conference on Human Factors in Computing Systems, New York, NY, USA (2019)
19. Roesner, F., Kohno, T., Molnar, D.: Security and privacy for augmented reality systems. Commun. ACM **57**(4), 88–96 (2014)
20. N. Samarasinghe, P. Kapoor, M. Mannan, and A. Youssef. No salvation from trackers: privacy analysis of religious websites and mobile apps. In: Garcia-Alfaro, J., Navarro-Arribas, G., Dragoni, N. (eds.) Data Privacy Management, Cryptocurrencies and Blockchain Technology. DPM CBT 2022 2022. Lecture Notes in Computer Science, vol. 13619. Springer, Cham (2023). https://doi.org/10.1007/978-3-031-25734-6_10
21. Skylot: Jadx. https://github.com/skylot/jadx
22. Smink, A.R., Frowijn, S., van Reijmersdal, E.A., van Noort, G., Neijens, P.C.: Try online before you buy: how does shopping with augmented reality affect brand responses and personal data disclosure. Electron. Commer. Res. Appl. **35**, 100854 (2019)
23. Stephenson, S., Pal, B., Fan, S., Fernandes, E., Zhao, Y., Chatterjee, R.: SoK: authentication in augmented and virtual reality. In: 2022 IEEE Symposium on Security and Privacy. IEEE (2022)
24. Technavio: Augmented reality and virtual reality market by technology, application, and geography - forecast and analysis 2023–2027 (2022). https://www.insiderintelligence.com/content/how-5g-will-change-retail
25. Trimananda, R., Le, H., Cui, H., Ho, J.T., Shuba, A., Markopoul, A.: OVRseen: auditing network traffic and privacy policies in Oculus VR. In: 31st USENIX (2022)
26. Zhang, T., Wang, W.Y.C., Cao, L., Wang, Y.: The role of virtual try-on technology in online purchase decision from consumers' aspect. Internet Res. **29**, 529–551 (2019)

Integrally Private Model Selection
for Support Vector Machine

Saloni Kwatra⬤, Ayush K. Varshney$^{(\boxtimes)}$⬤, and Vicenç Torra⬤

Department of Computing Science, Umeå University, Umeå, Sweden
{salonik,ayushkv,vtorra}@cs.umu.se

Abstract. Today, there are unlimited applications of data mining techniques. According to ongoing privacy regulations, data mining techniques that preserve users' privacy are a primary requirement. Our work contributes to the Privacy-Preserving Data Mining (PPDM) domain. We work with Integral Privacy, which provides users with private machine learning model recommendations and privacy against model comparison attacks. For machine learning, we work with Support Vector Machine (SVM), which is based on the structural risk minimization principle. Our experiments show that we obtain highly recurrent SVM models due to their peculiar properties, requiring only a subset of the training data to learn well. Not only high recurrence, but from our empirical results, we show that integrally private SVM models obtain good results in accuracy, recall, precision, and F1-score compared with the baseline SVM model and the ϵ Differentially Private SVM (DPSVM) model.

Keywords: Integral Privacy · Support Vector Machine ·
Privacy-Preserving Data Mining · Differential Privacy

1 Introduction

Data mining and privacy may initially appear to have two opposing objectives: While privacy aims to protect the confidentiality of personal information, data mining is interested in uncovering knowledge hidden within the data. Finding a way to balance protecting users' sensitive data and extracting valuable knowledge is our goal in this work. Although Privacy-Preserving Data Mining (PPDM) techniques seek to protect users' privacy, doing so may result in decreased data utility. Therefore, while choosing a machine learning model, it is important to consider both the users' goals and the trade-off between data utility and privacy level, which depends on the application of the technique. There has been a lot of research in the direction of PPDM. The concept of k-anonymity [10,11,15,16] is based on group safety. It is a property possessed by anonymized tabular data. When each individual's information in a data release cannot be distinguished from the information of at least k-1 other persons whose information also appears in the release, the data release is said to have the k-anonymity property.

S. Katsikas et al. (Eds.): ESORICS 2023 Workshops, LNCS 14398, pp. 249–259, 2024.
https://doi.org/10.1007/978-3-031-54204-6_14

Differential privacy [2] protects the individual-level information, meaning that the output of a query does not depend much on the addition or deletion of a record in a database. But, in some scenarios, too much addition of noise is needed to suppress the leakage of information about an individual. For example, if the algorithm is computing the mean salaries of the residents of a region. The mean salary would be too high if Mr. Super Rich is present in the database. To protect the salary disclosure of Mr. Super Rich, a lot of noise must be added to the resulting mean, thus making the output mean useless. Next, we have crypto-graphic approaches [9] for providing privacy. These mechanisms apply protocols to facilitate distributed processing like secure multi-party computation [3,6], and sharing of data under privacy guarantees. Nevertheless, they are computationally expensive compared to data obfuscation techniques, and they are not compliant with differential privacy unless we combine the two requirements.

In this work, we have investigated the use of integral privacy as an alternative to differential privacy to achieve a high-utility privacy-preserving approach.

A model that can be learned from different disjoint datasets is integrally private [17]. Integral privacy provides a defense against membership inference attacks by any intruder. Membership inference attack is accessing the records used in the training process [14]. In real life, it is hard to get different datasets that do not share common records. The condition to not share records between datasets is required to avoid membership inference attacks. The first approach for the decision tree was given in [13], where instead of using different datasets, authors have used a sampling approach to build the model space from subsets of varying sizes that do not share records. The approach recommends recurring models as integrally private models.

A similar approach was further applied for linear regression in [12]. This approach needs to find (approximately) model space to recommend integrally private models, which is very time-consuming and can only be done for small datasets due to a limited computational budget. Our main contributions through this paper are as follows.

1. We introduce integrally private model selection with Support Vector Machine (SVM).
2. We propose a method to suggest recurrent SVM models with good utility and privacy guarantees (integrally private).
3. We reduce the computational overhead to recommend the integrally private models which have baseline comparable utility by creating disjoint partitions, where the ratio of the number of instances in each class is the same as the original dataset.
4. We also compared our results with differential privacy to show the superiority of our proposed methodology.

After the introduction, we discuss the background theories. Our proposed methodology will follow this in Sect. 3, results and its analysis with some draw-backs in Sect. 4, and finished with a brief discussion of the future work and conclusion in Sect. 5.

2   Preliminaries

2.1   Support Vector Machine (SVM)

The structural risk reduction principle of statistical learning theory [1] is the foundation for the state-of-the-art binary classification algorithm, Support Vector Machine. Consider a binary classification problem for a dataset $D_{n \times d}$. SVM chooses a hyperplane from a family of hyperplanes that best distinguishes the two classes. The optimal hyperplane of the linear SVM is given as $J(w)$: $w^T x + b = 0$, where $b \in \mathcal{R}$ is the bias term, $w \in \mathcal{R}^n$ is the normal vector of $O(w, b)$. The following optimization problem can be solved to find the optimal hyperplane:

$$J(w) : \min_{w \in \mathbb{R}^n} \frac{1}{2} w^T w + C \sum \max(0, 1 - y_i(w^T x_i + b)) \qquad (1)$$
$$\text{subject to,}$$
$$y_i(w_T x_i + b) \geq 1 - \max(0, 1 - y_i(w^T x_i + b)),$$
$$\text{for } i = 1, 2, ..., d$$

Maximizing the margin corresponds to minimizing the L_2-norm regularization in the first term. The second term corresponds to the total errors for incorrectly classified samples or the errors of incorrectly located samples in the dead zone. Here y_i is the label of ith input with values from $\{+1, -1\}$. C controls the trade-off between maximizing the margin and minimizing the sum of errors. According to the first set of constraints, the data point projections must be at least one unit distant from each other. If this is violated, the error variable must be set to its minimum value to satisfy the constraint, creating a soft-margin hyperplane.

2.2   Model Comparison Attack for SVM and Integral Privacy

With model comparison attack [13], the intruder aims to get access to sensitive information using a membership inference attack. Let D be the original dataset, X be the training set and G be the SVM model generated using the training set X. In a model comparison attack, the intruder has access to the trained model G and the additional number of information S^* about the dataset D ($S^* \in D$). The intruder's aim is to identify maximum records ($\in X$) or completely identify X. In order to do so, the intruder draws a block of samples $S = S_1, S_2, ..., S_a$ where $S_i \subseteq S^*$. Each subsample is a data set that is further used as a training set to generate an SVM model. Intruder compares the generated SVM models with the model G. In the case of SVM, model comparison means the comparison of hyperplane parameters (i.e., weights and bias). After model comparison, if the comparison is successful, the intruder would be able to get the subsample(s) that generate the model G. If only one subsample generates the model G, then the intruder gets complete access to the training set. In case of more than one subsample generating G, a membership inference attack can be done using the intersection analysis, i.e., finding the common records in the subsamples, which leads to model G. This approach was first given for decision trees in [13] where the complete model space (or approximately complete model space) was generated with the information from S^*.

The recently proposed Integral privacy [17] acts as a defense against model comparison attacks. Simply, integrally private models are the models which recur enough (enough can be application dependent), where models are trained on different subsamples which do not share records among them. The condition to not share records among samples is required to avoid any inference using intersection analysis. Let us formally define integral privacy (Fig. 1):

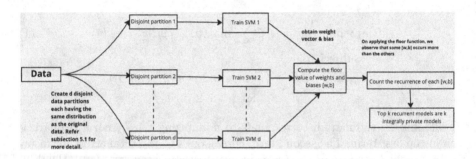

Fig. 1. Flow diagram to obtain Integrally Private selection for SVM

Integral Privacy: Let S^* be the intruder's background knowledge of the data. Let P be the set of samples compatible with the background knowledge. Let $G \in \mathcal{G}$ a model in the model space generated by algorithm A on $S \subseteq P$. Let $Gen^*(G, S^*)$ represent the set of all generators of G which are consistent with the background knowledge S^*. Then, the model G is said to be k-anonymous integrally private if $Gen^*(G, S^*)$ contains at least k elements and

$$\bigcap_{S \in Gen^*(G,S^*)} S = \emptyset \qquad (2)$$

3   Methodology

3.1   Overview

In this paper, we propose IPSVM to build integrally private SVM models. Then, we make a comparison between IPSVM models baseline SVM and DPSVM in terms of accuracy, precision, recall, and F1-score. SVM outputs a vector of weights whose dimension is equal to the number of features and a bias. In order to obtain integrally private models, we apply the floor function over the weights and biases. In this way, we obtain rounded weights and biases, which permits us to obtain recurrence on the models. That is, from different datasets, we obtain the same models. Because of rounding weights and biases, we get good (high) recurrence for the SVM. The following three analyses have been considered.

1. We created smaller disjoint partitions of the dataset. We tested IPSVM on the smaller test set obtained from disjoint sub-partitions without applying the floor function.
2. We also tested the efficacy of IPSVM on the whole test set of the data to compare it with the baseline model without applying the floor function.
3. After applying the floor function, we obtain one set of model parameters (w, b) for each set of recurrent models. We show that even after applying the floor function, the results are reasonably good in comparison with the baseline SVM model and DPSVM.

3.2 Datasets

In our work, we have considered 5 different datasets for binary classification. They are described in Table 1.

Table 1. Description of datasets

Data	Records	Features	Partitions	Ratio $\frac{\text{Positive instances}}{\text{Negative instances}}$
Cod-rna	59535	9	60	0.67
Shuttle	54489	6	100	0.83
Skin segmentation	245057	4	200	0.79
SUSY	200000	9	150	0.45
Sepsis-Survival	129392	4	110	0.91

Originally, SUSY and the shuttle dataset have a dimension of 18 and 10, respectively. We applied Principal Component Analysis (PCA) to reduce the dimensions to 9 and 6, respectively. Also, the shuttle data was a multi-class data with 7 classes. We converted it into binary classification data by combining the samples from two majority classes, which were 45586 and 8903.

3.3 Creation of Partitions

The data-centric approach [8] suggests that data of good quality can generate good results. Our approach is inspired by the data-centric approach in [18], which suggests same-class distribution can lead to baseline comparable results even with 0.2% to 2% of the original dataset. In order to generate integrally private SVM models, we partition the data into same-class distributions. We do as follows: we randomly sample the original binary class dataset to generate a smaller partition that has the same ratio between the number of instances in positive and negative classes. This condition allows us to learn from the instances of the two classes and, as we will see later, increases the number of recurrences of the SVM model. For all the datasets in Table 1, we have generated disjoint samples of varying sizes while keeping the ratio between the classes the same. The sample size for each sample is also given in Table 1. Note that the partitions do not share any record among them, i.e., all the partitions are disjoint, which is a stricter condition than required for integral privacy. This suggests our results will hold (or even improve) if partitions are mutually disjoint. I.e., all partitions do not share any common record. The sample size must be carefully chosen to generate enough samples, and each sample must have enough instances, which can result in a well-learned model. Further work in the direction of a minimum number of instances required to learn a well-learned model may improve the size of each sample.

3.4   Integrally Private SVM (IPSVM)

Recent works based on the concept of Integral Privacy [12,13] recommended recurrent models using different partitioning schemes than ours. The number of sub-partitions created in both works [12] and [13] were immensely large. For example, the cod-rna dataset has 59535 records, and according to [13], the number of sub-partitions needed to create the (approximated) model space would be very large. We use a sub-sampling scheme, which is exceptionally computationally efficient compared to past works. We describe the approach for creating sub-partitions in Subsect. 3.3.

The steps for obtaining the integrally private SVM (IPSVM) models are as follows:

1. Create d disjoint sub-partitions of the data in such a way that the distribution of each sub-partition matches with the original data.
2. Train d SVMs on each sub-partitions and obtain weight vector w and bias b for each sub-partition.
3. Compute the floor value of w and b.
4. Count the recurrence of each pair of $[w, b]$. Extract top k-recurrent models, called integrally private models.

Since the dual solution of SVM is typically sparse, the SVM only requires a portion of the entire number of data points to identify the ideal hyperplane. This characteristic is known as sparsity. As the classifier depends only on a small portion of the dataset, the training set can be made small, which also fastens the training speed of the SVM model [4,5]. **Because of the aforementioned property of SVM, we obtain highly recurrent SVM models with good utility when trained on smaller data partitions.** Refer Sect. 3 for more detail.

4   Results

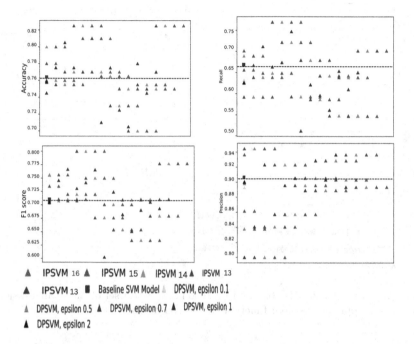

Fig. 2. Accuracy, Recall, F1-score, and Precision on the test set of the smaller disjoint data without applying the floor function on SUSY dataset

Choosing models with high representability guarantees high model utility and privacy as per the definitions of Integral Privacy. Our experimental results show that our approach obtained SVM models with a high recurrence. We show the Top 5 recurrent models in our results.

1. We compare the performance of integrally private models with the baseline SVM model and the DPSVM for $\epsilon = \{0.1, 0.5, 0.7, 1, 2\}$. The dotted line in the graphs, which goes just below the baseline model, provides a clear demarcation between the models performing poorer than the baseline and the models performing better or equivalent to the baseline.

2. We show the accuracy, precision, recall, and F1-score of the integrally private models, the baseline SVM model, and the DPSVM for various values of ϵ on the cod-rna dataset in Fig. 3, SUSY dataset in Fig. 2, and shuttle dataset in Fig. 5. To be noted, IPSVM 6 in the legend of the figures means that Integrally Private SVM models have six recurrences, the same for others.

3. We can deduce from our results on the cod-rna data in Fig. 3, the SUSY data in Fig. 2, the shuttle data in Fig. 5, F1-score on the Sepsis-Survival data and the Skin-Non Skin data in Fig. 4 that we obtain recurrent models in high

256   S. Kwatra et al.

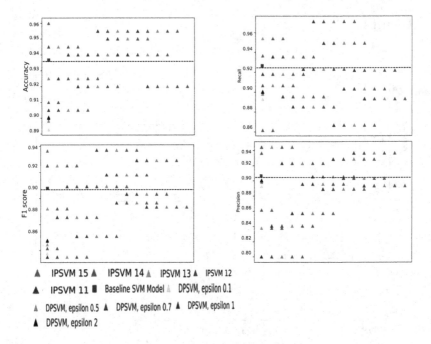

Fig. 3. Accuracy, Recall, F1-score, and Precision on the test set of the smaller disjoint data without applying the floor function on cod-rna dataset

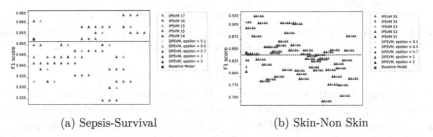

(a) Sepsis-Survival   (b) Skin-Non Skin

Fig. 4. F1-score on the test set of the smaller disjoint data without applying the floor function on Sepsis-survival and Skin-Non Skin dataset

numbers. We explain high numbers with an example of the Sepsis-Survival dataset in Fig. 4. We created 110 disjoint partitions and got recurrences like 17, 16, 15, and 14. Given the number of disjoint partitions, the models were recurrent enough. The performance of recurrent models surpasses DPSVM and is comparable with the baseline SVM model. It is to be noted that we obtain these results when we do not apply the rounding operation on weights and bias of the SVM models. The test set for obtaining the performance metrics was from smaller disjoint partitions (Due to smaller test sets in the figures mentioned above, the performance of the recurrent or integrally private models is sometimes better than the baseline SVM model).

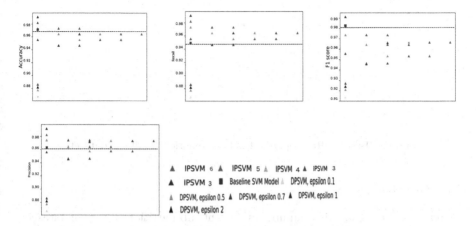

Fig. 5. Accuracy, Recall, F1-score, and Precision on the test set of the smaller disjoint data without applying the floor function on shuttle dataset

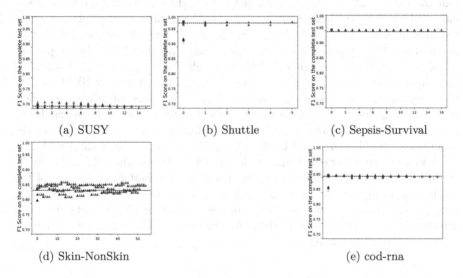

(a) SUSY   (b) Shuttle   (c) Sepsis-Survival

(d) Skin-NonSkin   (e) cod-rna

Fig. 6. F1-score on the test set of the whole data without applying the floor function to all the datasets

4. We show the F1-scores on the test set from the complete data for cod-rna, SUSY, shuttle, Skin-Non Skin, and Sepsis-Survival dataset in Fig. 6. The F1 score for the Sepsis-Survival dataset for DPSVM, epsilon = 0.1, was lesser than 0.2. Hence, it could not fit in the scale of the Y-axis. The F1-scores shown in Fig. 6 prove the efficacy of integrally private models. We also show the F1-scores after applying the rounding operation on weights and biases in Fig. 7. So, we get one F1 score for each set of recurrent models. The results show that applying the floor function does not deteriorate the performance of the SVM model. Hence, recurrent models serve both utility and privacy.

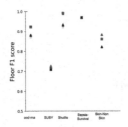

Fig. 7. F1-score after applying the floor function to all the datasets

4.1 Drawbacks

We may not have a sufficient number of disjoint sub-partitions for small datasets, as we create disjoint sub-partitions so that each sub-partition has the same distribution as the original data. For higher-dimensional data, we will get fewer recurrent models for SVM. The solution is to apply dimensionality reduction techniques like Principal Component Analysis (PCA) before creating sub-partitions. We also observed this for SUSY in Fig. 2 and Shuttle dataset in Fig. 5, that the number of recurrent models increases after applying PCA. We apply the rounding operation on weights and biases to obtain the recurrence. Because of the rounding operation, we get recurrence in good amounts for SVM models. Here lies the trade-off between utility and privacy. From the privacy perspective, applying floor function to the weights and biases is good, especially for the privacy of the clients participating in Federated Learning (FL) [7]. In the client-server architecture of FL, the clients do not share their data and only share model parameters by training the model locally on their data. There are various data reconstruction attacks on knowing the model parameters of the machine learning models. Therefore, it is good from the privacy perspective not to share the exact weight and biases in the process of FL. Nevertheless, this privacy comes at the expense of degrading the utility of the datasets, which are more sensitive to the weights.

5 Conclusion and Future Work

In our work, we studied integrally private model selection with SVM. Due to the property of sparsity in SVM, we obtained high recurrence. We would also like to examine the recurrence with other recent variants of SVM and other machine learning techniques. We would also like to extend integral privacy in the domain of Federated Learning (FL) [7], in which different devices learn a machine learning model collaboratively without transferring their data. Only model parameters are shared with the aggregation server. Even though the data is not shared, sharing model parameters leads to substantial leakage. Hence, applying integral privacy to FL is promising future work.

References

1. Cortes, C., Vapnik, V.: Support-vector networks. Machine learning **20**(3), 273–297 (1995)
2. Dwork, C.: Differential privacy: a survey of results. In: Agrawal, M., Du, D., Duan, Z., Li, A. (eds.) TAMC 2008. LNCS, vol. 4978, pp. 1–19. Springer, Heidelberg (2008). https://doi.org/10.1007/978-3-540-79228-4_1
3. Goldreich, O.: Secure multi-party computation. Manuscript. Preliminary Version **78**, 110 (1998)
4. Jung, H.G., Kim, G.: Support vector number reduction: survey and experimental evaluations. IEEE Trans. Intell. Transp. Syst. **15**(2), 463–476 (2013)
5. Kwak, N.: Principal component analysis based on l1-norm maximization. IEEE Trans. Pattern Anal. Mach. Intell. **30**(9), 1672–1680 (2008)
6. Lindell, Y.: Secure multiparty computation for privacy preserving data mining. In: Encyclopedia of Data Warehousing and Mining, pp. 1005–1009. IGI global (2005)
7. McMahan, B., Moore, E., Ramage, D., Hampson, S., y Arcas, B.A.: Communication-efficient learning of deep networks from decentralized data. In: Artificial Intelligence and Statistics, pp. 1273–1282. PMLR (2017)
8. Ng, A.: MLOps: from model-centric to data-centric AI (2021). https://www.deeplearning.ai/wp-content/uploads/2021/06/MLOps-From-Model-centric-to-Data-centricAI
9. Pinkas, B.: Cryptographic techniques for privacy-preserving data mining. ACM SIGKDD Explor. Newsl. **4**(2), 12–19 (2002)
10. Samarati, P.: Protecting respondents identities in microdata release. IEEE Trans. Knowl. Data Eng. **13**(6), 1010–1027 (2001)
11. Samarati, P., Sweeney, L.: Protecting privacy when disclosing information: k-anonymity and its enforcement through generalization and suppression, Tech. rep. (1998)
12. Senavirathne, N., Torra, V.: Approximating robust linear regression with an integral privacy guarantee. In: 2018 16th Annual Conference on Privacy, Security and Trust (PST), pp. 1–10. IEEE (2018)
13. Senavirathne, N., Torra, V.: Integrally private model selection for decision trees. Comput. Secur. **83**, 167–181 (2019)
14. Shokri, R., Stronati, M., Song, C., Shmatikov, V.: Membership inference attacks against machine learning models. In: 2017 IEEE Symposium on Security and Privacy (SP), pp. 3–18. IEEE (2017)
15. Sweeney, L.: Achieving k-anonymity privacy protection using generalization and suppression. Int. J. Uncertainty Fuzziness Knowl. Based Syst. **10**(05), 571–588 (2002)
16. Sweeney, L.: k-anonymity: a model for protecting privacy. Int. J. Uncertainty Fuzziness Knowl. Based Syst. **10**(05), 557–570 (2002)
17. Torra, V., Navarro-Arribas, G., Galván, E.: Explaining recurrent machine learning models: integral privacy revisited. In: Domingo-Ferrer, J., Muralidhar, K. (eds.) PSD 2020. LNCS, vol. 12276, pp. 62–73. Springer, Cham (2020). https://doi.org/10.1007/978-3-030-57521-2_5
18. Varshney, A.K., Torra, V.: Integrally private model selection for deep neural networks. In: Strauss, C., Amagasa, T., Kotsis, G., Tjoa, A.M., Khalil, I. (eds.) Database and Expert Systems Applications. DEXA 2023. Lecture Notes in Computer Science, vol. 14147. Springer, Cham (2023). https://doi.org/10.1007/978-3-031-39821-6_33

Differentially Private Traffic Flow Prediction Using Transformers: A Federated Approach

Sargam Gupta$^{(\boxtimes)}$ and Vicenç Torra

Department of Computing Science, Umeå University, Umeå, Sweden
{sgupta,vtorra}@cs.umu.se

Abstract. Accurate traffic flow prediction plays an important role in intelligent transportation management and reducing traffic congestion for smart cities. Existing traffic flow prediction techniques using deep learning, mostly LSTMs, have achieved enormous success based on the large traffic flow datasets collected by governments and different organizations. Nevertheless, a lot of these datasets contain sensitive attributes that may relate to users' private data. Hence, there is a need to develop an accurate traffic flow prediction mechanism that preserves users' privacy. To address this challenge, we propose a federated learning-based temporal fusion transformer framework for traffic flow prediction which is a distributed machine learning approach where all the model updates are aggregated through an aggregation algorithm rather than sharing and storing the raw data in one centralized location. The proposed framework trains the data locally on client devices using temporal fusion transformers and differential privacy. Experiments show that the proposed framework can guarantee accuracy in predicting traffic flow for both the short and long term.

Keywords: Federated Learning · Traffic Flow Prediction · Differential Privacy · Temporal Fusion Transformer · Time Series Data

1 Introduction

Urban transportation is a vital part of everyday life. Traffic congestion on roads is one of the major concerns in today's transportation system. Most of the people traveling on the road utilize their own observations for selecting an optimum time and path to commute. In the absence of accurate traffic flow predictions, this leads to longer commute times and delays. Hence, everybody requires a timely and accurate traffic flow prediction. Using accurate traffic flow prediction techniques, we can use historic traffic data to predict future road conditions that can be utilised in different location-based services.

This study was partially funded by the Wallenberg AI, Autonomous Systems and Software Program (WASP) funded by the Knut and Alice Wallenberg Foundation.

© The Author(s) 2024
S. Katsikas et al. (Eds.): ESORICS 2023 Workshops, LNCS 14398, pp. 260–271, 2024.
https://doi.org/10.1007/978-3-031-54204-6_15

Even after being such an essential part of Intelligent Transport Management, traffic flow prediction is difficult and quite challenging. First of all, the nature of the traffic data is spatiotemporal. The models predicting the traffic flow must capture both the time-series information and spatial features of the location. Secondly, the traffic flow in a particular region is highly dependent on many different external factors like which day of the week is it or is there any special event happening on a particular day. Hence, these factors need to be considered. Thirdly, most of the existing works can only do a short-term prediction for about the next 30 to 50 min which might not be enough time for the commuters to plan their journey route. Lastly and most importantly, a lot of the historic traffic data may contain some sensitive information about the vehicle which may reveal some private information Hence, it is very essential to build a framework for traffic flow prediction that gives accurate predictions and at the same time preserves sensitive information.

Most of the traffic data is collected by the sensors deployed on the road. This collected data is stored at a central location over which a traffic prediction model is trained. This intrudes on the privacy of the data collected and increases the prediction duration Hence, to address the above-mentioned issues, we propose a novel federated differentially private traffic flow prediction framework based on Temporal Fusion Transformers. The contributions of this paper are summarized as follows:

- We propose a novel privacy-preserving traffic flow prediction framework that integrates Federated Learning (FL), Differential Privacy (DP) and Temporal Fusion Transformers (TFTs). This framework gives accurate and timely predictions without actually sharing the raw data collected from the sensors.
- We incorporate various static information like the day of the week and the calendar holidays within the region which improve the accuracy of the prediction.
- We have included the long-term prediction of traffic flow in a region that was missing in the existing literature.

We use two evaluation metrics (Mean Squared Error and Mean Absolute Error) on a real-world dataset for the simulation of the proposed framework. From the obtained results we can clearly see that our proposed algorithm has a higher performance when compared with the existing works.

The remaining part of this paper is organized as follows. Section 2 reviews some basic concepts needed in understanding the paper. In particular, we discuss FL, DP, and TFTs. Section 3 describes, in brief, some existing literature on traffic flow prediction. Our suggested prediction mechanism is described in Sect. 4. Section 5 describes the dataset and simulation settings for experiments. In Sect. 6, we provide and discuss the results. Section 7 gives the conclusion and future directions.

2   Preliminaries

2.1   Federated Learning

The concept of FL was proposed by Google [5] in 2016 which allows building a collaborative model from distributed data without actually sharing and storing it at a centralized location thereby preserving the privacy and security of the data.

Assuming M clients $\{C_1, C_2, \ldots, C_M\}$, Yang *et al.* [18] define federated learning as a process of constructing collaborative model M_{Fed} with accuracy A_{Fed} such that

$$|A_{Fed} - A_{Cen}| < \delta \tag{1}$$

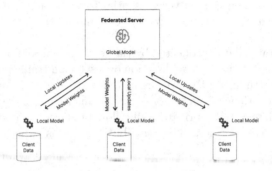

Fig. 1. Federated Learning

where A_{Cen} is the accuracy of centralized machine learning on the centralized dataset $D = D_1 \cup D_2 \cup \cdots \cup D_M$ and δ is a non-negative real number if Eq. (1) holds. The FL algorithm is said to have δ-accuracy loss [18]. There are mainly two categories of FL - one, where data at clients have the same features but different samples, called horizontal FL, and second, called vertical FL, where clients have different feature spaces. In our proposed solution, we work with horizontal FL.

In each communication round, the server transmits the global model parameters to the selected clients. These clients perform the local model training on their own individual dataset and send their updated parameters to the server which then aggregates the differences to the global model. This communication stops when convergence is achieved. The system architecture of FL is represented in Fig. 1.

2.2   Differential Privacy

Differential Privacy [2] is considered as the de facto standard of privacy by most researchers in the field of privacy. DP can provide strong privacy guarantees if the selected values of ε and δ are good. The formal definition of differential privacy is given as follows. An algorithm M is said to be (ε, δ) - differentially private if

$$P(M(D \in S) \leq e^{\varepsilon} P(M(D') \in S) + \delta \tag{2}$$

where D and D' are neighbouring datasets and S is an arbitrary subset of outputs of M. ε is the privacy budget and δ is the relaxation term. A smaller value of ε enforces stronger privacy.

2.3 Temporal Fusion Transformers

Transformers are the state of art deep learning models that were proposed recently in 2017 [16]. They use the self-attention mechanism for different types of tasks. Though they were originally proposed for natural language processing models but several different versions of transformers have become popular over the time. The major advantage of using the transformer models over the traditionally used LSTMs [4] in sequential processing tasks is that they require much less training time due to parallelization. One such type of transformer is the TFT.

TFTs were proposed by Lim et al. [7] in 2020. This model is specifically designed for interpreting and predicting the time-series data. It has several novel architectures that have improved the prediction performance for time series considerably. The TFTs consider different types of inputs like static inputs which could be the never-changing information like the ids of sensors, known inputs which are known even after the input time like a day of the week and holidays, and observed values.

The main modules of the TFT architecture are:

- Gating module: This module helps in filtering out the not-so-necessary complex details in the model formed and hence reducing the complexity of the trained model.
- Variable Selection Network: This module, being true to its name, is used for the feature selection mechanism.
- Static information encoder: This encodes the static information in the problem considered for prediction.
- LSTM encoder-decoder layers: Since our main input is sequential in nature, hence it is worthwhile to consider using LSTM layers to process the temporal information well.
- SeqtoSeq layer and Multi-head attention module: They are used for capturing the short-term and long-term dependencies in the data respectively.

3   Related Work

In this section, we discuss the most relevant research in the field of traffic flow prediction. In the initial studies related to traffic flow prediction, most researchers used traditional machine learning algorithms to solve the time-series problem. Gary et al. [1] proposed a K-Nearest Neighbour approach for short-time traffic flow prediction. Another Bayesian network-based [14] approach was proposed by Sun et al. which took into consideration the adjacent road links to analyze the traffic better. A few more machine learning-based approaches were proposed based on Support Vector Machines (SVMs) [6] and Autoregressive Integrated Moving average (ARIMA) [13] but none of them was accurate enough. This could be because of the complicated relationship between features, volume, and uncertainty of the traffic flow data. Hence, researchers started exploring some deep-learning techniques for time-series prediction [11]. Since, the time-series data is sequential in nature, hence, researchers found that Recurrent Neural Networks (RNNs) could be good at capturing the temporal features in traffic flow prediction. Ma et el. [9] proposed a bidirectional LSTM to capture the time features better while Fu et al. RNNs indeed performed better than traditional machine learning algorithms. Another set of researchers used Convolutional Neural Networks (CNNs) and demonstrated good ability to capture the features in the field of computer vision. Zhang et al. [21] used CNNs for predicting urban traffic flow and captured the correlations of traffic with each road in a city. Some researchers tried combining properties of both CNNs and RNNs like Zhang et al. [20] which used the ST-ResNet, to collectively forecast the inflow and outflow of crowds in a city. Xia et al. [17] proposed a distributed WND-LSTM model in MapReduce that can predict traffic flow for distributed traffic networks. All these models could predict the traffic flow with a decent accuracy but all of them were centralized models and hence did not take data privacy into consideration. Since data privacy is a major concern, hence it is very important to find out an alternative to these models. FL being an emerging field attracted a lot of researchers' eyes. Liu et al. [8] proposed a federated learning-based highway traffic prediction using GRUs. FL, though, is more secure when compared to the centralized approach but it is still not enough. To ensure more privacy in FL approaches Yang et al. [19] proposed privacy-preserving Additive Homomorphic Encryption (AHE) in FL. AHE is a good way of securing the FL environment but it is very computationally intensive and slow and hence cannot be used in timely traffic flow prediction. To overcome these Qi et al. [12] proposed a blockchain-based federated learning approach combined with GRUs and Tang et al. [15] proposed a differential privacy-based federated learning approach with LSTMs for short-term prediction. Though LSTM models are reasonably accurate but training them is difficult as they have a larger number of parameters and cannot parallelize the task. Hence, we propose transformer-based models to predict short-term as well as long-term traffic flows in conjugation with privacy protection.

4   Differentially Private Federated Traffic Flow Prediction Using Temporal Fusion Transformers

In this section, we propose two variants of a new federated traffic flow prediction framework. The two variants differ only in the noise added to them.

Suppose we have m different sensors located in different parts of the city. Each sensor collects the traffic flow data D_i from its region. Each client's data D_i is not shared with anyone and is only used by the client for training their model. Each sensor constructs a TFT model on the dataset D_i. Then, the model updates are sent to the aggregating server where we use the FedAVG [10] algorithm to aggregate these parameters. These aggregated parameters form the global model. This global model is then sent back to the clients. This results in learning from each other's datsets without actually knowing the data.

4.1   Client-Side Training

Figure 2 presents the client-side training steps. Each client collects road traffic data every hour. When feeding this input to the TFT, we segregate the inputs into different types. The first type is the static input values which is the detector id and road number. Then, we input the known inputs. These values are the one that we know even after the prediction time like the hour of the day, day of the week, month, holiday or not etc. Lastly, we input the observed value. This is the value that we want our model to predict after training. In our case, this observed value is the number of vehicles on the road at any particular time. The data format file is created and we set the look back historical window and the prediction length of our model. We then set the hyperparameters which include the number of LSTM layers, dropout rate, minibatch size and number attention heads. Lastly, we train our TFT model and obtain the model parameters.

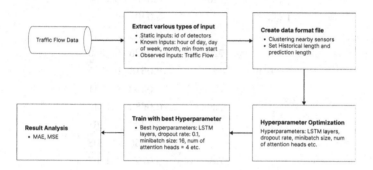

Fig. 2. Client side architecture

4.2   Model Perturbation

When the TFT model is trained on the client, then to ensure the security of the sensitive information we apply ε differential privacy on the client-side trained TFT model. More concretely, we supply the Gaussian mechanism and add noise to the parameters. In our experiments, we add the noise with varying values of epsilon from 0.1 to 0.9 and see how it impacts the global model's prediction accuracy.

4.3   Aggregation Algorithm

Since, aggregation is the key component of this framework, we use the FedAVG algorithm [10] for secure parameter aggregation. It is one of the simplest yet effective and very popular aggregation algorithms. Every iteration of the algorithm starts with initializing a global model to all the clients. The clients train on that model with their own local datasets and obtain a new updated model. The updates in the model parameters of these updated local models are then sent to the global server. The global server aggregates these updates by performing a weighted average of their values. This forms a new global model. Again this updated global model is sent back to the clients for local training. This process continues iteratively until it reaches convergence. Once, the converged model is ready we use this model to predict on the data to evaluate its performance.

Table 1. Prediction results of the proposed model without DP

	Time Step	MSE	MAE
Centralized	24	0.0117	0.0567
	72	0.0134	0.0562
	720	0.0178	0.0713
2 Clients	24	0.0240	0.0931
	72	0.0435	0.1098
	720	0.0466	0.1536
4 Clients	24	0.0495	0.1589
	72	0.0639	0.1795
	720	0.0726	0.1689
6 Clients	24	0.0515	0.1525
	72	0.0552	0.1541
	720	0.0680	0.1640
8 Clients	24	0.0442	0.1461
	72	0.0556	0.1608
	720	0.0721	0.1667

5   Dataset and Experimental Settings

We are using the real-world public dataset collected by Caltrans Performance Measurement System (PeMS) (http://pems.dot.ca.gov) in California. This dataset contains the traffic flow information from the San Francisco Bay area freeways. The data is collected from 862 different sensors located on the highway system. The data is available for two years from 2015 to 2016 with a reading of traffic on roads after every hour. We used three months of data from January 2015 to March 2015 for training the TFT model and predicting the values for the following one day, three days and one month. We have used the Darts TFT [3] python library for implementing the TFT code. For simulating the federated settings we clustered the sensors located in a nearby region in proximity to each other into a single client. The values for the different TFT hyperparameters for the experiments were set as input chunk length as 64, output chunk length as 8, hidden size as 64, LSTM layers as 1, num attention heads as 4, dropout as 0.1, batch size as 16 and epochs=3. The proposed algorithm is simulated for 2, 4, 6 and 8 clients. We also apply DP on the client-side models with different ε values (0.1, 0.5 and 0.9) to show how it impacts the prediction results. For the evaluation of our results, we used Mean Squared Error and Mean Absolute Error.

$$MSE = 1/M \sum_{i}^{M} (actual_i - predicted_i)^2 \tag{3}$$

$$MAE = 1/M \sum_{i}^{M} |actual_i - predicted_i| \tag{4}$$

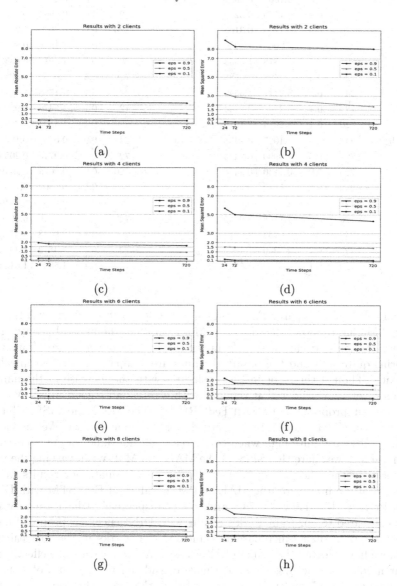

Fig. 3. Comparison of epsilon values for DP

6   Results and Analysis

The results of the experiments described are presented below.

Table 2. Prediction results of the proposed model with DP

Clients	Time Step	Eps	MSE	MAE	Clients	Time Step	Eps	MSE	MAE
2 Clients	24	0.9	0.1808	0.3321	6 Clients	24	0.9	0.0898	0.2245
	72	0.9	0.1746	0.3298		72	0.9	0.0905	0.2242
	720	0.9	0.1706	0.3103		720	0.9	0.0980	0.2249
	24	0.5	3.2065	1.4260		24	0.5	1.1510	0.8403
	72	0.5	2.8518	1.3553		72	0.5	1.0912	0.8333
	720	0.5	1.8467	1.0783		720	0.5	1.0094	0.8054
	24	0.1	8.9417	2.3549		24	0.1	2.1788	1.1221
	72	0.1	8.2561	2.2964		72	0.1	1.6476	0.9995
	720	0.1	8.2084	2.1916		720	0.1	1.4634	0.9617
4 Clients	24	0.9	0.1027	0.2458	8 Clients	24	0.9	0.0768	0.1975
	72	0.9	0.0990	0.2440		72	0.9	0.0715	0.2056
	720	0.9	0.1140	0.2436		720	0.9	0.0679	0.2019
	24	0.5	1.5119	0.9814		24	0.5	0.8602	0.7552
	72	0.5	1.4715	0.9699		72	0.5	0.8055	0.7119
	720	0.5	1.4168	0.9445		720	0.5	0.7056	0.6606
	24	0.1	5.6733	1.9114		24	0.1	2.9688	1.3788
	72	0.1	4.9860	1.7923		72	0.1	2.3772	1.3330
	720	0.1	4.3179	1.6547		720	0.1	1.5631	1.0145

In Table 1, we compared the results of our proposed framework with the centralized Model. It shows the MSE and MAE values of the model by varying the number of clients. It can be seen from the results that our federated framework performs quite well and the obtained values are comparable to the centralized approach. Though the error increases slightly with the increase in the number of clients yet we consider that remains within reasonably good limits. We also compare our proposed work with FedGRU [8]. The MAE and MSE values in their work are 7.96 and 101.49 respectively for the same dataset. We can clearly see that these are quite high when compared with the values of our approach.

In Table 2, we share the values of the MAE and MSE when varying the value of ε for adjusting the privacy budget. In order to evaluate our results we can report from the literature, the MAE and MSE values of FedLSTM with Differential Privacy [15]. They are 7.65 and 100.47 respectively which are very high when compared to our framework's results with DP. Hence, our proposed model performs better than other baselines and existing works in the literature. In Fig. 3, we have plotted the values of MSE and MAE to measure the effectiveness of our model after adding noise. We have considered three values of ε, in our experiments: 0.1,0.5 and 0.9. Please note that the lower the value of ε, more is the noise added. We can see from Table 2 that with the highest ε value, the noise added is less, thus the error values are low and vice versa. We can also observe that with the increase in the number of clients, the values of MAE and MSE show a reducing trend which makes our proposed framework suitable to be used in FL settings with large number of clients. Also, when comparing our error values with existing FedLSTM with DP [15], our values are smaller. Therefore, our approach is better.

7 Conclusion and Future Works

This paper presents a novel federated traffic flow prediction framework based on temporal fusion transformers and differential privacy which can make timely and accurate long-term as well as short-term predictions. The proposed federated framework is privacy-preserving as it does not promote any data sharing, is resistant to membership inference attacks, linkage attacks, and backdoor attacks and also satisfies differential privacy guarantees. This work is compared with some existing works and centralized models on the PEMS Dataset. Our results are comparable to the centralized ML algorithms yet preserve the privacy of the client's data. In the future, we would like to investigate more about the impact of different experiment settings on the proposed framework. We will also consider taking into account the spatial and weather information into account while traffic flow prediction.

References

1. Davis, G.A., Nihan, N.L.: Nonparametric regression and short-term freeway traffic forecasting. J. Transp. Eng. **117**(2), 178–188 (1991). https://doi.org/10.1061/(ASCE)0733-947X(1991)117:2(178)
2. Dwork, C., McSherry, F., Nissim, K., Smith, A.: Calibrating noise to sensitivity in private data analysis. In: Halevi, S., Rabin, T. (eds.) Theory of Cryptography, pp. 265–284. Springer, Berlin Heidelberg, Berlin, Heidelberg (2006). https://doi.org/10.1007/11681878_14
3. Herzen, J., et al.: Darts: User-friendly modern machine learning for time series. J. Mach. Learn. Res. **23**(124), 1–6 (2022). http://jmlr.org/papers/v23/21-1177.html
4. Hochreiter, S., Schmidhuber, J.: Long short-term memory. Neural Comput. **9**(8), 1735–1780 (1997). https://doi.org/10.1162/neco.1997.9.8.1735
5. Konecny, J., McMahan, H.B., Ramage, D., Richtárik, P.: Federated optimization: distributed machine learning for on-device intelligence (2016). https://arxiv.org/abs/1610.02527
6. Li, C., Xu, P.: Application on traffic flow prediction of machine learning in intelligent transportation. Neural Comput. Appl. **33**(2), 613–624 (2020). https://doi.org/10.1007/s00521-020-05002-6
7. Lim, B., Arik, S.O., Loeff, N., Pfister, T.: Temporal fusion transformers for interpretable multi-horizon time series forecasting. Int. J. Forecast. **37**, 1748–1764 (2020)

8. Liu, Y., Zhang, S., Zhang, C., Yu, J.J.: FedGRU: privacy-preserving traffic flow prediction via federated learning. In: 2020 IEEE 23rd International Conference on Intelligent Transportation Systems (ITSC), pp. 1–6 (2020). https://doi.org/10.1109/ITSC45102.2020.9294453

9. Ma, C., Dai, G., Zhou, J.: Short-term traffic flow prediction for urban road sections based on time series analysis and LSTM BILSTM method. IEEE Trans. Intell. Transp. Syst. **23**(6), 5615–5624 (2022). https://doi.org/10.1109/TITS.2021.3055258

10. McMahan, B., Moore, E., Ramage, D., Hampson, S., Arcas, B.A.y.: Communication-Efficient Learning of Deep Networks from Decentralized Data. In: Singh, A., Zhu, J. (eds.) Proceedings of the 20th International Conference on Artificial Intelligence and Statistics. Proceedings of Machine Learning Research, vol. 54, pp. 1273–1282. PMLR (2017)

11. Miglani, A., Kumar, N.: Deep learning models for traffic flow prediction in autonomous vehicles: a review, solutions, and challenges. Veh. Commun. **20**, 100184 (2019). https://doi.org/10.1016/j.vehcom.2019.100184. https://www.sciencedirect.com/science/article/pii/S2214209619302311

12. Qi, Y., Hossain, M.S., Nie, J., Li, X.: Privacy-preserving blockchain-based federated learning for traffic flow prediction. Futur. Gener. Comput. Syst. **117**, 328–337 (2021). https://doi.org/10.1016/j.future.2020.12.003

13. Shekhar, S., Williams, B.: Adaptive seasonal time series models for forecasting short-term traffic flow. Transp. Res. Rec. **2024**, 116–125 (2008). https://doi.org/10.3141/2024-14

14. Sun, S., Zhang, C., Yu, G.: A bayesian network approach to traffic flow forecasting. IEEE Trans. Intell. Transp. Syst. **7**(1), 124–132 (2006). https://doi.org/10.1109/TITS.2006.869623

15. Tang, H., Xue, N., Wang, G.: Differentially private decentralized traffic flow prediction approach based on federated learning. In: Proceedings of the 2022 10th International Conference on Information Technology: IoT and Smart City, pp. 280–285. ICIT 2022, Association for Computing Machinery, New York, NY, USA (2023). https://doi.org/10.1145/3582197.3582244

16. Vaswani, A., et al.: Attention is all you need. In: 31st Conference on Neural Information Processing Systems (NIPS 2017) (2017)

17. Xia, D., et al.: A distributed WND-LSTM model on mapreduce for short-term traffic flow prediction. Neural Comput. Appl. **33**(7), 2393–2410 (2020). https://doi.org/10.1007/s00521-020-05076-2

18. Yang, Q., Fan, L., Yu, H. (eds.): Federated Learning. LNCS (LNAI), vol. 12500. Springer, Cham (2020). https://doi.org/10.1007/978-3-030-63076-8

19. Yang, Q., Liu, Y., Chen, T., Tong, Y.: Federated machine learning: concept and applications. ACM Trans. Intell. Syst. Technol. **10**(2), 1–19 (2019). https://doi.org/10.1145/3298981

20. Zhang, J., Zheng, Y., Qi, D.: Deep spatio-temporal residual networks for citywide crowd flows prediction. In: AAAI 2017: Proceedings of the Thirty-First AAAI Conference on Artificial Intelligence, pp. 1655–1661 (2017). https://doi.org/10.1609/aaai.v31i1.10735. https://ojs.aaai.org/index.php/AAAI/article/view/10735

21. Zhang, J., Zheng, Y., Qi, D., Li, R., Yi, X.: DNN-based prediction model for spatio-temporal data. In: Proceedings of the 24th ACM SIGSPATIAL International Conference on Advances in Geographic Information Systems. SIGSPACIAL 2016, Association for Computing Machinery, New York, NY, USA (2016). https://doi.org/10.1145/2996913.2997016, https://doi.org/10.1145/2996913.2997016

Analyzing Continuous K_s-Anonymization for Smart Meter Data

Carolin Brunn[1]([✉]), Saskia Nuñez von Voigt[1], and Florian Tschorsch[2]

[1] Distributed Security Infrastructures, Technische Universität Berlin,
Berlin, Germany
{c.brunn,saskia.nunezvonvoigt}@tu-berlin.de
[2] Privacy and Security, Technische Universität Dresden, Dresden, Germany
florian.tschorsch@tu-dresden.de

Abstract. Data anonymization is crucial to allow the widespread adoption of some technologies, such as smart meters. However, anonymization techniques should be evaluated in the context of a dataset to make meaningful statements about their eligibility for a particular use case. In this paper, we therefore analyze the suitability of continuous k_s-anonymization with CASTLE for data streams generated by smart meters. We compare CASTLE's continuous, piecewise k_s-anonymization with a global process in which all data is known at once, based on metrics like information loss and properties of the sensitive attribute. Our results suggest that continuous k_s-anonymization of smart meter data is reasonable and ensures privacy while having comparably low utility loss.

1 Introduction

The suitability of data anonymization techniques, such as k-anonymity [20], must be evaluated in the context of a dataset to make meaningful statements. In particular, the data types, the granularity, and distribution have an impact on the efficiency of data anonymization and affect the fundamental trade-off between data privacy and data utility.

For smart meter data, the efficiency of data anonymization remains unclear as the application scenario and the data pose a challenge. While smart meters (SMs) become increasingly important to enable dynamic resource management of various energy sources, the type of data differs from other relational data sources. SMs generate a data stream derived from continuous sensor data, measuring consumption of electric energy, gas, and water. SM data, therefore, comprises sensitive, personal data that require privacy protection. In addition, the application scenario dictates a distributed architecture with distributed data sources.

Supported by the Federal Ministry of Education and Research of Germany (Project 16KISA034).

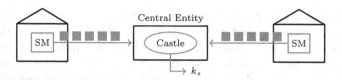

Fig. 1. Centralized architecture with smart meters forwarding measurements to a central entity for anonymization.

In this paper, we investigate the continuous anonymization of SM data and assess the efficiency of k_s-anonymity for the anonymization in this scenario. The concept of k_s-anonymity is an extension of k-anonymity for data streams [3]. In particular, we use the widely recognized algorithm for stream anonymization, CASTLE [3], and study its characteristics and suitability. For our study, we consider a typical SM architecture in which distributed SMs send their data to a central entity (CE). We evaluate the suitability of k_s-anonymity for SM data based on metrics such as information loss and range of the sensitive attribute, and compare the performance of continuous piecewise anonymization with an idealized anonymization as baseline.

Our results suggest that k_s-anonymity is a reasonable choice for anonymizing smart meter data. Based on our metrics, the performance of continuous data anonymization appears to be comparable to our baseline. Further analysis of the diversity of consumption measurements shows that in most clusters, the values of the sensitive attribute are distributed over a wide range and are not clustered around a single consumption value. Additionally, we note that the prioritization of attributes during the anonymization process differs. This should be taken into account in any case, but can also be exploited to shape the process to a certain degree.

The paper is organized as follows. After introducing our problem statement as well as k_s-anonymity and CASTLE in Sect. 2 and 3, we present our evaluation in Sect. 4. In Sect. 5 we conclude the paper.

2   Problem Statement and Related Work

Problem Statement. Our goal is to analyze whether continuous k_s-anonymization is suitable for SM data. Since the data type differs from other relational data sources in some crucial characteristics, this is everything but obvious. The SMs generate continuous data streams consisting of measurements of user consumption, e.g., electricity consumption. Different strategies can be applied to discretize the data stream, such as measuring the current consumption value in fixed intervals or aggregating the entire consumption between two measurement time points. Thus, SM data has different characteristics, such as the temporal granularity of the measurements.

For our evaluation, we use a realistic architecture in which distinct SMs measure the consumption and forward the data directly to a CE, e.g., the energy provider. Figure 1 visualizes this architecture. The CE requires accurate data for billing purposes. In order to facilitate further processing by third parties, e.g., for district management, the data is collected and anonymized centrally before it is forwarded. For this scenario, we assume a trustworthy CE that handles the data confidentially and publishes anonymized data correctly.

Related Work. There are several approaches to avoid profiling and disclosure of information based on smart meter measurements. For instance, load balancing and shaping prevent characteristic traces in consumption data, while other approaches focus on achieving privacy by design with specific architectures [2,4]. Another focus is on protecting privacy by anonymizing consumption data, e.g., with k-anonymity [20] or differential privacy [6,9].

Differential privacy relies on adding statistical noise to recorded data points or to the entire combined dataset, thus offering consumers the ability to include their data in a dataset without fear of negative repercussions. For an accurate data analysis, it is important that the added noise does not influence the data quality and distribution. To ensure this, many data points are needed [7,9]. However, for certain use-cases and applications, these requirements are out of proportion to the benefits that can be derived from the data [5,9].

k-anonymity, on the other hand, works even on relatively small datasets, and furthermore, the original measurements are preserved instead of being statistically altered, which could have had negative impact on energy grid operators, for example [7,9,14]. For these reasons, we choose to focus in this paper on k-anonymity instead of differential privacy.

Another recent approach to load prediction while maintaining data privacy is Federated Learning [8,13]. Here, a global model is trained locally on devices without sharing raw data. This can be particularly useful when a local model is needed, such as for real-time actions. However, the approach requires certain computational resources, more communication between the devices, and a coordinating central entity. Therefore, k-anonymity appears to be a viable alternative when resources are limited.

One algorithm to achieve k-anonymity for streaming data is the one analyzed in this paper—CASTLE. Several other algorithms exist, some of which also address challenges of CASTLE, such as [10,16–18,21]. However, to the best of our knowledge, there are no studies that evaluate the suitability of k_s-anonymity specifically for smart meter data.

3 k_s-Anonymity and CASTLE

We focus on k_s-anonymity [3], which is an extension of k-anonymity [20] for streaming data. The main idea is to modify and group data items in such a way that groups comprise at least k entries that are indistinguishable from each other—an Equivalence Class (EQ). k_s-anonymity [3] extends this idea and requires that a published anonymized stream comprises EQs with at least k distinct individuals, not just k entries.

CASTLE [3] is an established algorithm to achieve k_s-anonymity by assigning incoming data points, called tuples, to clusters that represent their generalization. The tuples are specified in a metric space defined by the so-called Quasi-identifiers (QIs) [20]. The clusters are EQs, where all data points share the same generalized values for each QI attribute. Each cluster must contain at least k distinct individuals. CASTLE either creates a new cluster or assigns the tuple to an existing cluster by minimizing the information loss. As information loss metric, CASTLE uses the Generalized Loss Metric [11]. For cluster generalization, QI attributes either form intervals, in the case of continuous attributes, or they are generalized to their lowest common ancestor with respect to their corresponding domain generalization hierarchy (DGH) for categorical attributes. A DGH is a directed tree structure that defines hierarchical values for such categorical attributes. CASTLE also uses a delay constraint δ that specifies the maximum time that can pass before a tuple needs to be generalized and published. The clusters that were anonymized with CASTLE can then be published and used for further processing, e.g., by third-party data processors.

We can already observe that during the anonymization process, the QIs are used for the generalization. At the same time, please note that the sensitive attribute is not considered in the process. This could enable attacks if users in a cluster have different consumption ranges that differ significantly from each other.

4 Evaluation

Methodology. For our evaluation, we use a dataset of electricity consumption measurements that is publicly available at the UCI Machine Learning Repository.[1] The dataset consists of consumption data from 370 clients, measured every 15 min between 2011 and 2015. Based on the consumption profiles in the dataset, we infer that the set comprises data of individual households, and larger consumers such as schools, hospitals, or small industry.[2] The original dataset contains only measurement data and timestamps and no additional information about

---

[1] https://doi.org/10.24432/C58C86.

[2] The magnitude of consumption values suggests that the values are given in Watt instead of kW as noted in the description of the dataset.

Table 1. SM measurements with exemplary k_s-anonymization

(a) Original data tuples

UID	Address	Time	Value
1	...2105845	09:15	20.5
2	...3101575	09:15	36.5
3	...2104112	09:15	16.8
4	...8108000	09:15	87.5
5	...9103000	09:15	20.5
6	...1108030	09:30	87.5
7	...2102059	09:30	20.5

(b) Exemplary 5-anonymization of Table 1a

Address	Time	Value
[...1108030, ...3101575]	[09:15, 09:30]	20.5
[...1108030, ...3101575]	[09:15, 09:30]	36.5
[...1108030, ...3101575]	[09:15, 09:30]	16.8
[...1108030, ...3101575]	[09:15, 09:30]	87.5
[...1108030, ...3101575]	[09:15, 09:30]	20.5

clients. We therefore added synthetic addresses, modeling a district in Berlin, where zip code, street, and house number are encoded in an integer value. Thus, each data tuple is of the form (*consumption, unique identifier (UID), address, timestamp*). Due to its size, we sampled the dataset (weeks 46 & 47 of November 2014) resulting in 164 102 tuples.

In our simulations, we apply k_s-anonymity to this dataset. During the anonymization process, the UID is removed. The consumption value, which is the sensitive attribute, is retained and never changed. The remaining attributes, indicating the time and location, are the QIs that are generalized. To this end, when published, the anonymized tuples per QI each have only the range between the minimum and maximum value that existed within their corresponding cluster. Table 1 shows exemplary SM data and a potential anonymization with $k = 5$. For better readability, we do not include all QI attributes in this example.

We use the publicly available CASTLEGUARD implementation [19]. When disabling the differential privacy feature (which we did), it resembles the CASTLE algorithm. Since we identified potential bugs, we made some minor adaptations to the code,[3] e.g., in the function `merge_clusters`. We provide our code including the respective changes as well as the dataset on GitHub.[4]

We simulated a distributed k_s-anonymization with CASTLEGUARD for different $\delta \in \{100, 400\}$ and $k \in \{10, 25, 50, 100\}$. Since we sampled the data set, $\delta = 100$ includes data of approximately 15 min and $\delta = 400$ data of one hour. We compare this to a global k_s-anonymization process in which all data tuples are known in advance and then clustered all at once. The latter is simulated using the ARX anonymization tool [1].

---

[3] We have reached out to the developers to discuss the bugs/changes.

[4] https://github.com/carolin-brunn/dpm-castle-analysis.

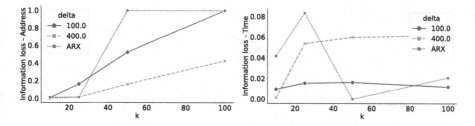

Fig. 2. Average information loss for quasi-identifying attributes.

Information Loss. For our evaluation, we use information loss as utility metric. Specifically, we use the Generalized Loss Metric (GLM) [11], which is also used for estimating the information loss in CASTLE. Here, the cluster range of a generalized attribute is compared to the overall range of this attribute. For each entry, the information loss of an attribute is defined as $\frac{u_i-l_i}{U-L} \in [0,1]$, where u_i or l_i is the upper or lower limit of entry i's attribute generalization, and U or L is the overall upper or lower limit of this attribute, respectively. For our evaluation, we calculate the average information loss across all clusters per attribute.

Figure 2 shows the average information loss of all clusters for varying k and δ of the *address* (left plot) and *time* (right plot) attribute, respectively. We observe that the information loss is highest for the *address* attribute in most settings. The clusters must always contain k distinct individuals that all have different addresses. Thus, whenever a cluster is created, the *address* attribute needs to be generalized. This condition leads to a different behavior than that of the remaining attributes. The information loss increases for the *address* with an increasing k. This is expected since an increasing k requires more distinct individuals with different addresses. We also observe that for CASTLE, the information loss increases as the ratio between k and δ increases. Presumably, CASTLE is forced to join very different clients, if many clients have to be extracted from a relatively small sliding window. Overall, it is noticeable that the *address* information loss is comparable for ARX and CASTLE. For lower k, ARX has a lower information loss than CASTLE's sequential generalization with $\delta = 100$. However, for larger k and δ the advantage of ARX fades. For $\delta = 400$, CASTLE consistently finds better clusters that result in a lower information loss when compared to ARX.

For the *time* attribute, the information loss of ARX and CASTLE is comparable. Note, however, that in the beginning ARX has a higher information loss than CASTLE. ARX's poor performance seems counterintuitive, but can presumably be explained by its anonymization strategy. ARX chooses the same generalization level for all values of the same attribute. Consequently, one cluster that requires a higher level of generalization may cause all other clusters that could be formed with a lower generalization to be published with the unnecessary generalization.

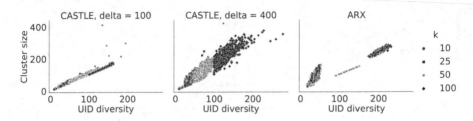

Fig. 3. Cluster size [tuples] in relation to the UID diversity.

In general, the results suggest that CASTLE is a reasonable alternative to a global generalization with ARX, especially for larger δ. Nevertheless, attribute ranges seem crucial for the prioritization when generalizing attributes. Consequently, analyzing the exact behavior of CASTLE with attributes of different magnitudes and diverse parameter settings is necessary to find optimal settings for the anonymization of smart meter data, which we will investigate in the remainder.

UID Diversity. Next, we compare the size of the published clusters and the diversity of unique identifier (UID) values in these clusters. The k value is also the minimum number of distinct UIDs required per cluster. Therefore, a larger UID diversity means a larger number of distinct individuals that protect each other from information disclosure. In contrast, very large clusters with a low UID diversity indicate that many data tuples correspond to the same individuals. This could compromise privacy as a person may have similar consumption values, resulting in low diversity of consumption values and potentially disclosing information.

Figure 3 shows the cluster size in tuples against the UID diversity. The two plots on the left show the results of two simulations with CASTLE, while the plot on the right shows the results of the global anonymization with ARX. The different colors and markers represent the different values of k. For ARX, we observe that the UID diversity of most clusters is between $2 \cdot k$ and $2.5 \cdot k$. Moreover, the clusters generated with ARX are about the size of their UID diversity.

For CASTLE, we observe that δ significantly influences the cluster sizes. For better visibility, we excluded a few clusters that were larger than 500, which were most likely caused by an unfavorable combination of tuples due to an expiring δ. In Fig. 3, the cluster size increases with larger δ, while the range of UID diversity remains about the same. We suspect that this is caused by the nature of the dataset. The extracted sample includes about one-third of the available data points, i.e., measurements of about 120 clients per time point, and each client appears on average 1–2 times per hour. One hour corresponds to approx. 490 data points. Thus, for $\delta = 100$, each client that appears has about 1 data point in the sliding window when the clusters are created. Consequently, the cluster size and UID diversity are about the same. For $\delta = 400$, the sliding window can

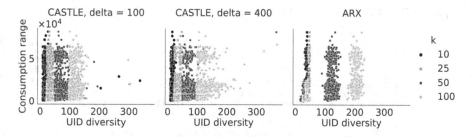

Fig. 4. Consumption range against UID diversity per cluster.

contain several tuples per client. In this case, multiple time points belonging to the same client, are mostly included in the same cluster, resulting in larger clusters with the same UID diversity. This is also reflected by our information loss analysis of the *time* above.

Consumption Range. Next, we analyze the diversity and distribution of the sensitive attribute, i.e., electricity consumption. Our initial analysis showed that almost all settings resulted in a diversity of the sensitive attribute that at least approximately matches the UID diversity, suggesting a high level of privacy protection. Please note that we deliberately refrain from using *l*-diversity [15] as metric in this paper, since *l*-diversity was designed for categorical but not numerical attributes. It particularly does not take the range or similarity of numerical values into account as was previously described in [12]. Consequently, the *l*-diversity results could lead to a distorted notion of privacy protection.

Instead, we consider the range e of the sensitive attribute in the clusters inspired by (k, e)-anonymity [22]. Figure 4 shows the consumption range (sensitive attribute) against the UID diversity. Again, the two plots on the left show the results obtained with CASTLE, while the plot on the right shows ARX' results. The different colors and markers represent the different values of k, which is also the minimum required UID diversity of the clusters.

For CASTLE, we see that k and the UID diversity only slightly influence the consumption range. Indeed, a certain UID diversity exhibits all different ranges of the sensitive attribute.

The same applies for ARX. Independent of k, the clusters exhibit all different ranges. The consumption of individual households is expected to be in smaller ranges typical for the number of members in a household. Compared to that, larger clients such as schools or industry have larger consumption with more variance. The results in Fig. 4 suggest that different types of clients are included in many clusters for both processing strategies.

Consumption Proximity. Information about the range does not capture the distribution of the sensitive attribute. We therefore analyze the difference between neighboring consumption values in a cluster by analyzing their relative

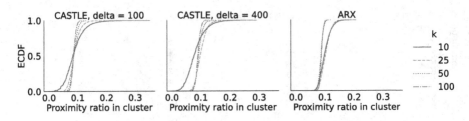

Fig. 5. Average proximity ratio of tuples in clusters.

ϵ-neighborhood with $\epsilon = 0.2$, as described in [12]. We calculate the *proximity ratio* as the average percentage of tuples in a cluster that have other tuples in this cluster within 0.2-neighborhood. This could facilitate a proximity breach, which means that an attacker can infer that the sensitive attribute lies within a small interval [12]. We assume that clusters provide privacy protection if distinct household types are included, thus, eliminating the risk of revealing information about the household due to too many similar values. For this reason, we choose to evaluate the 0.2-neighborhood based on the average daily consumption of different types of households.[5] With 0.2-neighborhood, we include a broad range of consumption values that are likely to occur for the same household type, and thus bear the risk of revealing information if only these were clustered together, while preventing different household types from being labeled as proximate.

Figure 5 shows the distribution of these values as empirical cumulative distribution plots. The larger the k, the fewer tuples are in 0.2-neighborhood of each other, indicating better privacy protection since the values of the sensitive attribute are less similar within a cluster. We observe no substantial difference between the results obtained with CASTLE and ARX, for $k = 10$, the clusters generated by CASTLE show even less proximity than those of ARX. This means that the privacy obtained with the sequential k_s-anonymization is comparable to the global anonymization realized with ARX.

5   Conclusion

In this paper, we analyzed the suitability of k_s-anonymity for smart meter data in a centralized architecture. Our results suggest that the continuous k_s-anonymization with CASTLE is comparable to a global anonymization with ARX. Both strategies achieve low information loss and diverse clusters that are needed to provide privacy protection. We therefore consider k_s-anonymity as a reasonable approach for smart meter data anonymization. Especially when the exact values and course of measurements are needed, k_s-anonymity might prove to be more practical than differential privacy or federated learning. The exact influence of

---

[5] https://www.destatis.de/EN/Themes/Society-Environment/Environment/
Material-Energy-Flows/Tables/electricity-consumption-households.html,   Last
accessed 11 August 2023.

certain parameters, such as window size, require further research in order to find optimal settings for specific use cases. Additionally, the constraints of numerical data such as electricity consumption must be considered and suitable metrics for the evaluation of the privacy of anonymized data have to be chosen. For instance, we suggest analyzing range and proximity instead of l-diversity only.

References

1. ARX homepage. https://arx.deidentifier.org/. Accessed 14 Jun 2023
2. Alshohoumi, F., Sarrab, M., Al-Hamdani, A., Al-Abri, D.: Systematic review of existing IoT architectures security and privacy issues and concerns. Int. J. Adv. Comput. Sci. Appl. **10**(7), 232–251 (2019). https://doi.org/10.14569/IJACSA.2019.0100733
3. Cao, J., Carminati, B., Ferrari, E., Tan, K.: CASTLE: continuously anonymizing data streams. IEEE Trans. Dependable Secur. Comput. **8**(3), 337–352 (2011). https://doi.org/10.1109/TDSC.2009.47
4. Chanal, P.M., Kakkasageri, M.S.: Security and privacy in IoT: a survey. Wirel. Pers. Commun. **115**(2), 1667–1693 (2020). https://doi.org/10.1007/s11277-020-07649-9
5. Dwork, C.: Differential privacy: a survey of results. In: Agrawal, M., Du, D., Duan, Z., Li, A. (eds.) TAMC 2008. LNCS, vol. 4978, pp. 1–19. Springer, Heidelberg (2008). https://doi.org/10.1007/978-3-540-79228-4_1
6. Dwork, C.: Differential privacy in new settings. In: Proceedings of the 21st Annual ACM-SIAM Symposium on Discrete Algorithms, SODA 2010, Austin, Texas, pp. 174–183. SIAM (2010). https://doi.org/10.1137/1.9781611973075.16
7. Eibl, G., Engel, D.: Differential privacy for real smart metering data. Comput. Sci. Res. Dev. **32**(1–2), 173–182 (2017). https://doi.org/10.1007/s00450-016-0310-y
8. Fekri, M.N., Grolinger, K., Mir, S.: Distributed load forecasting using smart meter data: federated learning with recurrent neural networks. Int. J. Electr. Power Energy Syst. **137**, 107669 (2022). https://doi.org/10.1016/j.ijepes.2021.107669
9. Gough, M., Santos, S.F., AlSkaif, T., Javadi, M.S., Castro, R., Catalão, J.P.S.: Preserving privacy of smart meter data in a smart grid environment. IEEE Trans. Ind. Inform. **18**(1), 707–718 (2022). https://doi.org/10.1109/TII.2021.3074915
10. Guo, K., Zhang, Q.: Fast clustering-based anonymization approaches with time constraints for data streams. Knowl. Based Syst. **46**, 95–108 (2013). https://doi.org/10.1016/j.knosys.2013.03.007
11. Iyengar, V.S.: Transforming data to satisfy privacy constraints. In: Proceedings of the 8th ACM SIGKDD International Conference on Knowledge Discovery and Data Mining, Edmonton, Alberta, Canada, pp. 279–288. ACM (2002). https://doi.org/10.1145/775047.775089
12. Li, J., Tao, Y., Xiao, X.: Preservation of proximity privacy in publishing numerical sensitive data. In: Proceedings of the 2008 ACM SIGMOD International Conference on Management of Data, Vancouver, Canada, pp. 473–486. ACM (2008). https://doi.org/10.1145/1376616.1376666
13. Lin, J., Ma, J., Zhu, J.: Privacy-preserving household characteristic identification with federated learning method. IEEE Trans. Smart Grid **13**(2), 1088–1099 (2022). https://doi.org/10.1109/TSG.2021.3125677
14. Lou, X., Yau, D.K.Y., Tan, R., Cheng, P.: Cost and pricing of differential privacy in demand reporting for smart grids. IEEE Trans. Netw. Sci. Eng. **7**(3), 2037–2051 (2020). https://doi.org/10.1109/TNSE.2020.2971723

15. Machanavajjhala, A., Kifer, D., Gehrke, J., Venkitasubramaniam, M.: L-diversity: privacy beyond k-anonymity. ACM Trans. Knowl. Discov. Data **1**(1), 3-es (2007). https://doi.org/10.1145/1217299.1217302

16. Mohamed, M.A., Ghanem, S.M., Nagi, M.H.: Privacy-preserving for distributed data streams: towards L-diversity. Int. Arab J. Inf. Technol. **17**(1), 52–64 (2020). https://doi.org/10.34028/iajit/17/1/7

17. Mohamed, M.A., Nagi, M.H., Ghanem, S.M.: A clustering approach for anonymizing distributed data streams. In: 2016 11th International Conference on Computer Engineering & Systems (ICCES), Cairo, Egypt, pp. 9–16. IEEE (2016). https://doi.org/10.1109/ICCES.2016.7821968

18. Pallas, F., Legler, J., Amslgruber, N., Grünewald, E.: RedCASTLE: practically applicable k_s-anonymity for iot streaming data at the edge in node-red. In: Proceedings of the 8th International Workshop on Middleware and Applications for the Internet of Things, M4IoT@Middleware 2021, Virtual Event, Canada, pp. 8–13. ACM (2021). https://doi.org/10.1145/3493369.3493601

19. Robinson, A., Brown, F., Hall, N., Jackson, A., Kemp, G., Leeke, M.: CASTLEGUARD: anonymised data streams with guaranteed differential privacy. In: 2020 DASC/PiCom/CBDCom/CyberSciTech, Calgary, AB, Canada, pp. 577–584. IEEE (2020). https://doi.org/10.1109/DASC-PICom-CBDCom-CyberSciTech49142.2020.00102

20. Sweeney, L.: k-anonymity: a model for protecting privacy. Int. J. Uncertain. Fuzziness Knowl. Based Syst. **10**(5), 557–570 (2002). https://doi.org/10.1142/S0218488502001648

21. Yang, L., Chen, X., Luo, Y., Lan, X., Wang, W.: IDEA: a utility-enhanced approach to incomplete data stream anonymization. Tsinghua Sci. Technol. **27**(1), 127–140 (2022). https://doi.org/10.26599/TST.2020.9010031

22. Zhang, Q., Koudas, N., Srivastava, D., Yu, T.: Aggregate query answering on anonymized tables. In: 2007 IEEE 23rd International Conference on Data Engineering, Istanbul, Turkey, pp. 116–125 (2007). https://doi.org/10.1109/ICDE.2007.367857

Towards Real-World Private Computations with Homomorphic Encryption: Current Solutions and Open Challenges

Michela Iezzi[1]([✉]), Carsten Maple[2], and Andrea Leonetti[1]

[1] Banca d'Italia, Rome, Italy
michela.iezzi@bancaditalia.it
[2] The Alan Turing Institute, London, UK
cmaple@turing.ac.uk

Abstract. There is an increasing need to share sensitive information within and beyond organisations. Protecting this information is vital for commercial and regulatory reasons. Homomorphic Encryption (HE) has come to the fore as a mechanism to enable the sharing of confidential data in a secure and private manner. Multiple open-source libraries are now publicly available, providing organisations with the tools to utilise the advantages of HE. While research devoted much effort to the academic and cryptographic aspects of HE schemes, research explicitly focusing on real-world financial applications is comparably rare. There is a need to provide a comparative analysis and related benchmarking of the most suitable HE libraries, having fixed the functional and non-functional requirements of the enterprise application of interest. We consider the motivation and background for HE and discuss the most promising open-source HE libraries. Having introduced real-world use cases in a financial context, we then illustrate outstanding challenges and how we plan to circumvent open points, introducing HELT (Homomorphic Encryption Libraries Toolkit).

Keywords: Homomorphic Encryption · Private computation · Real-world applications

1 Introduction

Financial institutions create, process, and control significant amounts of data. This data can have significant value, especially when combined with other sources or types of data. Such sources include other financial institutions and service organisations, government and regulatory bodies, and other units within their own organisation. However, sharing such data is not always possible for legal,

The views and opinions expressed in this paper are those of the authors and do not necessarily reflect the official policy or position of Banca d'Italia.

regulatory or commercial reasons. As such, methods are required that allow the use and analysis of this data in a confidential manner. Homomorphic Encryption (HE) is a promising approach to the problem of computation of confidential data. Since the introduction of Fully Homomorphic Encryption (FHE) in 2009 [13], much effort has been devoted to optimising the drawbacks brought by the enhancements introduced by the work of Gentry. In this direction, the academic community has developed many libraries to test and allow HE use. The first versions of these libraries were not ready for enterprise and real-world applications. HE realises not only the protection of data *in-transit* or *at-rest* but also *in use*. It represents paramount progress in data analysis due to the increasing usage of personal data and its applications in everyday life. Moving to a more specific context, we can observe how financial institutions and services have access to structured and unstructured personal data due to their varied duties. Furthermore, fintech companies and public institutions could also use public cloud services. It appears more evident that legal instruments, e.g., Non-Disclosure Agreements (NDA) [18], are not protective enough for data owners and financial counterparties. There is a demand for more stable and sound technology solutions to the problem of confidentiality of personal data, such as PETs (Privacy Enhancing Technologies). Of course, HE is only one of the available PETs on the market. We focus on this cryptographic technique taking into account two different motivations: (i) many PETs fail with the so-called *privacy-utility trade-off*: an amount of leakage about confidential data should be accepted to obtain valuable results from the computation [27]; (ii) the recent and consistent investments in the HE field in the last years [20].

Despite attempts to make HE libraries more user-friendly, building enterprise-ready applications that act on homomorphically encrypted data still requires a range of technical experts: (i) the *data analyst*, which could either be a data scientist or an artificial intelligence expert, or a (typically untrusted) researcher that may be external to the organisation; (ii) the *software developer*, which helps in the integration of the new application in the already existing legacy environment, provided all the functional and non-functional constraints; (iii) the *cryptographer*, which is pivotal to choose the suitable library and to choose the right HE context, that as we will see in the remainder of the paper, is not an easy task for a non-cryptographer. Moreover, new and existing enterprise applications should be translated into a HE-friendly format to support the computation. It is not easy to make these three actors work together. Furthermore, an expert skilled in all these aspects is yet to be available in the market. Enterprises need a solution to fix this gap, at least partially.

This paper conveys the idea that it is necessary to build open-source benchmarking tools that allow understanding of some crucial issues:

- if the existing HE libraries are usable for the data analyst;
- which library fits a given application;
- what means integrating them with the existing enterprise environment.

We propose a two-step approach for adopting HE in an enterprise context to reach this objective. The first step is providing the data analyst with encrypted confidential data and an HE environment with selected open-source libraries. The cryptographer will guide the analyst in building the proper analysis in a HE-friendly format. A phase of control of the results by the Data Owner may be envisaged to avoid re-identification due to analyses aimed at extracting confidential data. The second step will provide an HE toolbox where some standard functions, e.g., the primitive blocks of statistical computations or some simple machine learning or Natural Language Processing tools, are implemented, given a chosen library, and then exposed to the data analyst, apart from a set of parameters. This step should be carefully implemented, considering the functional and non-functional requirements of the involved actors. The choice of parameters is challenging because the HE context highly depends on the target application and the employed data. The goal is to provide a set of rules and predefined parameters. This paper is a starting point for analysing some available HE libraries. It represents a short work-in-progress report for developing a playground where the data analysts, helped by the cryptographers in the initial phase, can experiment with which library is more suitable for the selected application.

Outline. The remainder of the paper is organised as follows. Section 2 describes the industrial context we are touching. Section 3 introduces a proper background for HE. In Sect. 4, we describe the main libraries, giving a valuable overview of implemented schemes and their parameters. Section 5 discusses the requirements for a possible HE benchmarking tool. In Sect. 6, we review the main results available in the literature. Finally, Sect. 7 concludes the paper and gives directions for future work.

2   Industrial Context

Although HE has been successfully employed in medicine [33], we focus on the financial institutions' context. Indeed, governments and institutions have access to confidential data for their purposes. Among institutions, we will consider the case of a central bank, which owns different confidential assets, like datasets about companies, balance sheets of banks and intermediaries, payment systems data, suspicious transactions data, and many others. These datasets are instrumental in ensuring that a central bank acts, e.g., as the supervisory authority or is proficient in economic research, collaborating with academia and other statistics institutions. Each dataset has a different data owner who is the only one in charge of manipulating and analysing the data. The possibility of collaboration between external actors, such as data scientists or academic researchers, and the sharing of confidential assets with other institutions and academia are challenging. It may undergo ad-hoc remote processing systems [4] or anonymisation processes [7]. Furthermore, the confidential nature of the data assets cannot fully unravel the potential of public cloud computing. In Fig. 1, the depicted use cases are locked due to the confidential nature of the data.   We can deduce that, in

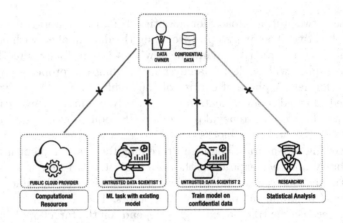

Fig. 1. Locked enterprise use cases due to privacy concerns.

the financial context, two are the main scenarios that ask for a solution based on HE [17,32], as in Fig. 2:

- *private outsourcing computation*, where an institution may decide to use public cloud resources to execute computational intensive tasks on confidential data;
- *privacy preserving data science*, where an external actor (that may be a machine learning expert, a researcher from another institution, or a data scientist from the same institution that is not the data owner) has to perform tasks like, e.g., Private Prediction as a Service (PPaaS), Private Training as a Service (PTaaS), or statistical analysis on confidential data.

Moreover, the use of HE in this second scenario protects confidential data from untrusted third parties and the intellectual property of the algorithm developed by the external actor [5]. Public cloud resources could enable this scenario, especially in the case of PTaaS. We may deal with these different situations in these three scenarios: (i) encrypted data, plain model, (ii) encrypted data, encrypted model, and (iii) multiple encrypted data from different data owners. Multikey Homomorphic Encryption could enable the last one [21]. With their different use cases, these scenarios can represent practically relevant HE applications in our industrial context. Sharing a statistical dataset ensuring confidentiality requires fixing functional and non-functional requirements that enable a wise choice of the HE library to support private computation. In the case of private computation with HE, confidential data will undergo a new data-processing pipeline: as we will see in Sect. 3, working with homomorphically encrypted data requires a phase of Encoding before Encryption; the classical Extract-Transform-Load (ETL) process should be complemented with these two phases before sharing data between counterparties. The design of these phases is closely tied to the nature of data (e.g., textual or numeric, structured or unstructured) and the application we need to deploy: having a benchmarking environment will help

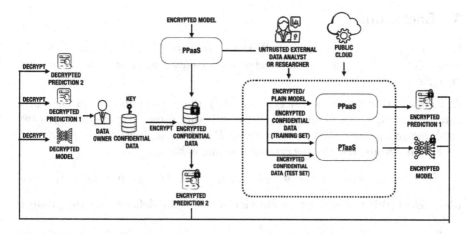

Fig. 2. Private Prediction as a Service (PPaaS) and Private Training as a Service (PTaaS)

choose the most appropriate HE library for each application. In Table 1, we gathered the requirements from the point of view of the three actors that are involved in our design process, as seen in 1: (i) the data analyst, (ii) the data owner, and (iii) the software developer. From this requirements gathering, we will exclude the cryptographer that will set up the HE test environment and assist these actors in the application deployment.

Table 1. Requirements for private computation with Homomorphic Encryption.

Actor	Requirement
Data Analyst	Usability
	Documentation and toy examples
	Parameters setting
	Programming language
	Ease of data preparation phase
	Confidentiality of models
Data Owner	Data confidentiality
	Correctness of results
	Performance
	Cloud/on-premise solution
Software Developer	Integration in the enterprise environment
	Code maintenance and upgrade

3   Background

We introduce the main results of HE theory to pose a common language for the remainder of the paper. The interested reader may find an in-depth discussion in [1,22].

A Primer. Homomorphic Encryption (HE) allows computation on encrypted data by employing an *homomorphism*, a structure-preserving map between two algebraic groups, i.e., the plaintext group P and the ciphertext group C.

For an asymmetric HE encryption scheme, it holds:

$$Encr(pk_{encr}, p_1 \diamond p_2) = Encr(pk_{encr}, p_1) \circ Encr(pk_{encr}, p_2) = c_1 \circ c_2 \quad (1)$$

where $Encr(\cdot)$ is the encryption function, $\diamond$ and $\circ$ are defined over the group P and C.

Equation 1 means that computing $\diamond$ over plaintexts p_1 and p_2 is equivalent to computing $\circ$ on related ciphertexts c_1 and c_2.

HE schemes are required to work with complex functions, not just single operations. Beyond key generation, encryption, and decryption functions, the HE scheme defines an *evaluation function* as follows, $Eval(pk_{eval} f, [c_1, c_2])$, where the function f should belong to the set of the admissible functions for that particular scheme to be correct:

$$p_1 \diamond p_2 = Decr(sk, c_1 \circ c_2) \quad (2)$$

To this end, the function f should be polynomial, i.e., expressible as a combination of multiplications and additions; in other words, the function f has to be *homomorphic-ready*. For practical applications of our interest, such as machine learning tasks or statistical analysis, this is not to be taken for granted: many approximation techniques for complex f have been explored, such as (i) Taylor expansion series approximation, (ii) Chebychev polynomials, (iii) look-up table, (iv) least squares.

Lattice and Ring-Based Cryptography. The security of HE schemes relies on the hardness of known problems on lattices that act as the basis for their construction. Learning With Errors (LWE) and Ring Learning With Errors (RLWE) are the most relevant.

Roughly, the encryption operation can be seen as adding random noise to the plaintext, and the decryption operation is recovering the plaintext after filtering the noise using the secret key. The random noise grows as the number of operations increases. When the number of multiplications exceeds a fixed depth, the noise becomes a burden for correct decryption that cannot be ensured anymore. Noise growth is typically associated with a noise budget that depends on the type of scheme. Furthermore, an unwanted expansion in the ciphertext and the key size happens during computation. Moreover, the hardness of these problems contributes to the computational complexity of the HE scheme.

Bootstrapping and Optimizations. When the depth of the function to be homomorphically evaluated is not known a priori, e.g., if we are dealing with a neural network, LHE is not enough, and *bootstrapping*, introduced by Gentry in 2009 [13], is the instrument to efficiently transform an LHE scheme with certain properties to an FHE scheme.

The *bootstrapping* operation reduces noise and allows correct decryption for any function. A second level of homomorphic encryption with a noise budget greater than the first level is applied to the ciphertext. Then, it is possible to decrypt the ciphertext with respect to the first encryption key, removing accumulated noise and restoring a new noise budget. The sufficient condition to apply bootstrapping to an LHE scheme is that the decryption circuit of the latter is included in the set of admissible functions to be evaluated. Various optimisations have been proposed to overcome the described inherent limits; we will find them optional in many libraries:

- *modulus-switching*, that prevents the ciphertext from growing without control.
- *key-switching*, that enables the revert of the new secret key to the original secret key, decreasing the size of the ciphertext.
- *relinearization*, that reduces the size of the ciphertext modulus.

These optimisation techniques mostly manage noise in LHE schemes and are employed when the depth of the circuit to be evaluated is known in advance. At the same time, bootstrapping cannot be avoided in all other use cases.

HE Schemes. HE schemes are classically classified into four main classes, depending on the type and the number of elementary operations. For real-world applications, we are mainly interested in (i) *Leveled Homomorphic Encryption (LHE)* schemes, where additions, multiplications, and their combination are allowed but only up to a fixed number, and (ii) *Fully Homomorphic Encryption (FHE)* schemes, where both addition and multiplication are allowed, without limits on the number of operations.

Various HE schemes have been implemented in HE libraries, mainly based on LWE or RLWE problems. One of the first is the BGV scheme that works over the integers, based on the LWE problem, and it is characterised by noise and ciphertext growth. Other popular schemes are, e.g., (i) CKKS which allows working with real numbers, and (ii) TFHE, which is based on the hardness of LWE assumption over the torus and provides fast bootstrapping.

Usually, LHE schemes are more practical and ensure a good trade-off between computational complexity, performance time, and privacy preservation. This is true in all the use cases characterised by the fixed depth of the computation.

Encoding Raw Input Data. Input data to be encrypted could have many different formats, highly dependent on the chosen HE scheme. Batching allows the packing of many plaintexts into a single ciphertext, enabling parallel homomorphic computation and slot-wise operations in a SIMD fashion. Each value is independently encoded in a slot inside an array. Binary representation of plaintexts is often available. More sophisticated encoding methods can be found for schemes based on the TFHE scheme, where binary or real values for each slot are taken on the torus.

4 Available Libraries

This section presents an overview of the HE libraries we will compare. We choose the following seven libraries considering various features, as stated in Table 1. We excluded from our analysis wrappers or compilers; we aim to explore HE libraries already employed in the research community [17]. All the libraries are open-source since they are still at a research level. These libraries are addressed to a developer with advanced cryptographic skills: defining a cryptographic context where HE parameters for the selected scheme are chosen is necessary. Table 2 and 3 summarise supported operations and main features for each library, except for OpenFHE, that we plan to include in our future work.

4.1 HElib

HElib is an open-source C++ library developed by IBM and the Algorand Foundation. Two schemes are available: leveled and fully BGV for integers and leveled CKKS for real and complex numbers. Packing enables the construction of an LHE scheme and an FHE with bootstrapping where available. Another type of representation is the binary one, which is used only for the BGV scheme and could be employed for FHE and LHE.

The encryption context creation requires setting many parameters, which are inherently tight to the inner logic of the library; even if in HElib scripts and utilities are available to help the developer, this choice is challenging for a non-cryptographer. This is true especially for the BGV scheme, while CKKS default parameters are present. It is worth remarking that in HElib, noise and time of execution are two parameters that need to be optimised, and typically the size and the depth of the SIMD circuits are descriptive of these constraints. We first fix the bound on the noise, i.e., the depth of the circuits, and then optimise the running time. Noise is also tightly related to the security level, which is recommended to be fixed at 128 bits.

4.2 SEAL

SEAL [28] is an open-source C++ library developed at Microsoft. The available schemes are BFV for integers and CKKS for real values. SEAL provides only the leveled mode, so the type of computation should be known in advance to balance the encoding and encryption parameters correctly. The encoding happens in two ways, depending on the selected HE scheme. A batch encoder is employed for the BFV scheme, while for the CKKS scheme, a CKKS encoder is implemented. The encryption context creation usually needs three parameters, which also influence the encoding phase. Two parameters are common to both BFV and CKKS schemes and alter both noise budget and performance, and the third parameter is peculiar to the chosen scheme. Contextually to the encryption context, the SEAL library creates a modulus switching chain, a set of encryption parameters derived from the original ones, which improves performance and communication cost in the BFV scheme. In the CKKS scheme, the modulus switching prevents

Table 2. Admitted operations for each library. CT stands for ciphertext, PT stands for plaintext.

Library	HE Scheme	CT + PT	CT + CT	CT * PT	CT * CT	Column shift	Row shift	Binary circuit
HElib	BGV bin.	✗	✓	✗	✓	✓	✗	✓
	BGV pack	✓	✓	✓	✓	✓	✗	✗
	CKKS	✓	✓	✓	✓	✓	✗	✗
SEAL	BFV	✓	✓	✓	✓	✓	✓	✗
	CKKS	✓	✓	✓	✓	✓	✗	✗
PALISADE	BGV	✓	✓	✓	✓	Rotate	Rotate	✗
	BFV	✓	✓	✓	✓	✗	✗	✗
	CKKS	✓	✓	✓	✓	Rotate	Rotate	✗
	FHEW	✗	✗	✗	✗	✗	✗	✓
	RGSW	✗	✓	✗	✓	✓	✗	✓
Concrete	LWE	✓	✓	✓	External product	Rotate	Rotate	✓
	GLWE	✓	✓	✓	External product	Rotate	Rotate	✓
LATTIGO	CKKS	✓	✓	✓	✓	Rotate	Rotate	✗
	BGV	✓	✓	✓	✓	Rotate	Rotate	✗
	BFV	✓	✓	✓	✓	Rotate	Rotate	✗

noise growth. A valuable feature of SEAL is the automatic parameter selection, which helps the user fix the parameters based on the state-of-the-art attacks against RLWE.

4.3 PALISADE

PALISADE [19] was born as a Sponsored Project of NumFOCUS, a nonprofit charity in the United States, and has the contributions of various cryptographers and developers coming from, e.g., Duality Technologies or the HE community. It is an open-source C++ library built on lattice-based cryptography. It is designed to be modular and extensible, providing a well-documented codebase and a transparent system to choose parameters, encryption schemes, and data encoding methods. The various features are offered in terms of capabilities that the user has to enable, e.g., Encryption, SWHE, and LHE; for each of these capabilities, the list of available schemes and related operations are given, as summarised in Table 2. Various representations for polynomials are available; the recommended one is DCRTPoly, where the Chinese Remainder Theorem format represents polynomial coefficients. Various encoding types are available in PALISADE, like Integer, Fractional, or Packed encoding. The creation of context depends on the enabled capability and related HE scheme, and it requires the choice of ring dimension, multiplicative depth, and batch size for schemes like BGV, BFV, and CKKS.

Table 3. HE main features.

Library	Lang	Multithread	SIMD	Multi-key	Mod Switch	Key Switch	Bootstr	Relin
HElib	C++	✓	✓	✗	✓	✓	BGV	✓
SEAL	C++	✓	✓	✗	✓	✗	✗	✓
PALISADE	C++	✓	✓	✗	✓	✓	✓	BGV
TFHE	C++	✓	✗	✗	✗	✓	✓	✗
Concrete	Rust	✗	✓	✗	✗	✓	✓	✗
Lattigo	Go	✗	✗	✓	✓	✓	CKKS	✓

4.4   OpenFHE

The PALISADE project is converging into the OpenFHE open-source project [6], which is supported by DARPA and has as contributors many of the leading developers of the major open-source HE libraries. It is a C++ library that supports the most useful HE schemes and is based on the hardness of the RLWE problem.

The available schemes are (i) BGV and BFV for modular arithmetic over finite fields, (ii) CKKS for vectors of real and complex numbers, (iii) DM, and CGGI, for boolean circuits and decision diagrams. SIMD packing is available for both vectors of integers and real numbers. This library foresees bootstrapping for all HE schemes in future versions. Each scheme runs in AUTO and MANUAL modes to overcome inherent difficulties in setting parameters and applying optimisations such as modulus/key switching, rescaling for CKKS, or bootstrapping. Integration with the existing compilers is easy to obtain. Multiple backends, e.g., GPU and FPGA, provide hardware acceleration support. It also enables multi-party versions of such HE schemes.

We plan to include OpenFHE in our future benchmarking tool.

4.5   TFHE

TFHE (Fast Fully Homomorphic Encryption Library over the Torus) [11] is a C/C++ library, which improves the bootstrapping time to 0.1 s, as in [10,12]. It implements a generalisation of LWE and RLWE on the Torus.

TFHE provides both leveled and bootstrapping modes; bootstrapping is executed after every boolean operation. The inputs are integer values, and the user decides the precision of the plaintext representation, i.e., the number of bits. The key management is facilitated since only two keysets are required: (i) the Secret Keyset, which is used to encrypt and decrypt confidential data symmetrically, and (ii) the Cloud Keyset, which is used to perform computation and bootstrapping on the ciphertexts. The user has to rewrite the required computation as a boolean circuit using the available binary gates. The encryption context is automatically created by specifying the security level and using the related default parameters.

4.6 Concrete

Concrete [35] is an open-source Rust library developed at Zama. It implements a discretised TFHE version for machine learning tasks and neural networks. This library allows keeping invariant the topology of the original neural network to be evaluated without the need to change it to make it more homomorphic-friendly, as mentioned in Sect. 2. The key enhancement is Programmable Bootstrapping (PBS), which permits the computation of any function, even the non-linear ones, during the bootstrapping phase, resetting the noise simultaneously. PBS is possible if the function can be decomposed and expressed as a linear combination of univariate functions using methods like Ridge decomposition or Kolmogorov superposition theorem. The encoding feature in Concrete is different from TFHE: each array slot is encoded as real Torus elements modulo 1, i.e., real numbers between 0 and 1. Creating an encryption context in Concrete means choosing parameters like the dimension of the vector of integers (LWE) or polynomials (RLWE) and the standard deviation of the noise distribution added to the body value; these two parameters influence the computation time, the ciphertext overhead, and the number of bits of precision that remains available. Recently, Concrete has been enriched with a module on the top of the Concrete library, Concrete ML, to enable machine learning-based applications.

4.7 LATTIGO

LATTIGO [26] is an entirely Go-based HE library developed at EPFL and based on RLWE schemes. The Go programming language has many valuable features: it works well with concurrent systems and is as efficient as C++, despite being more accessible to code. The encryption context creation is easily obtained using default parameters available for 128-bit of security. The ability to efficiently deal with concurrency makes Lattigo one of the HE libraries that offers multi-party computation (MPC) for both implemented schemes, BFV and CKKS, taking in input both integers and real values, with packed representation. Another unique characteristic is that bootstrapping is available for CKKS.

5 Towards Real-World HE Applications: HELT

There are many challenges in developing real-world HE applications starting from scratch. Apart from well-known HE issues like computational costs and performance concerns, more support tools for developers and ready-to-use frameworks for data analysts are needed. Many efforts are currently devoted to providing user-friendly APIs to develop privacy-preserving data science applications quickly, and the vendors are trying to satisfy this enterprise requirement. Notable examples are the IBM Security HE Services or Zama's roadmap for Concrete [16,34].

Another trend is the development of HE Compilers, which should provide high-level functions that prevent the user from working with HE parameters setting or operations on cyphertexts [31]. However, compilers or DS-ready environments are not general-purpose. Another critical aspect is the selection of HE parameters because it influences the security level, the compactness of the scheme, and the performance. The HE standard, which is in progress, provides tables of recommended parameters to guide the data scientist in the choice [3]. Furthermore, in literature, there are some recent contributions to guide the developers in setting the so-called HE context: [8,25] make a significant step forward in developing a parameter generator that is readily usable in the PALISADE library; the drawback is that it is library dependent and works only for the BGV scheme, which is indeed a state-of-the-art FHE scheme but is not flexible enough to be employed in all business applications. Furthermore, as investigated in [17], many primitives that are part of the business application should be rewritten to be fully HE-ready: this applies to activation functions for machine learning tasks, as well as to simple statistics primitives, such as mean, variance, or linear regression. This is highly tied to integrating or replacing novel privacy-preserving applications with HE in an enterprise or legacy context, which is challenging to achieve.

In Fig. 3, it is depicted the typical protocol for a HE-based application [9, 15,24]: Besides the HE setup, which considers several exchanges between client and server, we would like to highlight that the additional data encoding and encryption is a significant phase of the HE pipeline, as seen in Sect. 2.

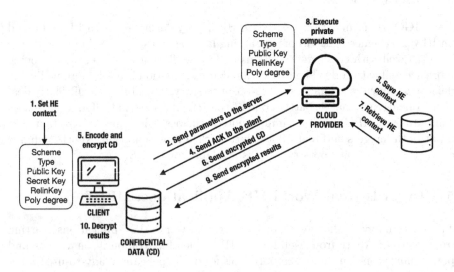

Fig. 3. HE pipeline for a privacy-preserving computation.

Our answer to some of these concerns is the development of the *Homomorphic Encryption Libraries Toolkit* (HELT); this paper represents a work-in-progress report of our experience so far. The purpose of this toolkit will be to compare and benchmark a set of selected HE libraries, which are the ones described in

Sect. 4. HELT is designed as a Docker-based toolkit: each HE library has its directory containing the package with preliminary benchmarks and a Docker file. The user will create a container for each library, solving dependency problems efficiently. Furthermore, a configuration file is provided with suggested HE context parameters that the expert user can modify. In our first version, we plan to compare the libraries by the available HE schemes and their functionalities. The starting point is the computation of simple metrics like the execution time of every single operation, the creation time for the HE context, and the creation time for the keys for every library. At the moment, we ran different tests on the same HE scheme within the same library, changing the parameters. We also measured the dimension in bytes of the generated keys and ciphertext created. The second step is to implement a set of HE-ready building blocks tailored to our business needs and, simultaneously, modular enough to be reused in various enterprise contexts. HELT will also enable us to understand the transition readiness of some critical applications that use confidential data from the standard enterprise environment in the HE domain. Furthermore, we would like to evaluate the selected libraries against the business requirements given in Sect. 2. One of the first conclusions drawn from our analysis is that: (i) HE schemes like BFV and BGV are employable for applications that make use of input that are in the form of strings or integers; (ii) the CKKS scheme is desirable when dealing with machine learning tasks; (iii) the TFHE scheme is robust when there is the need to compare ciphertext, and it is possible to translate the comparison in binary circuits.

Our next steps encompass the following:

– the integration of the OpenFHE library;
– the test of the multikey HE functionality where available, e.g., in Lattigo;
– the investigation of the data integrity problem: we can resort, e.g., to a solution that uses an attached checksum to the ciphertext to detect attacks.

6   Related Work

A few papers about benchmarking HE libraries are available; none encompass comparison frameworks for the financial and statistical applications in scenarios like the ones depicted in Sect. 2. One of the first works about benchmarking is the HEtest framework [30], which tests the main bottlenecks of HE libraries. However, this tool includes only HElib, although the authors remark that it is extensible to other libraries. Melchor et al. [2] compare a modified version of HElib, SEAL, and FV-NFLib to work with large plaintext moduli. The paper is insightful in providing some remarks about the library choice and implementation recommendations. Marrone et al. [23] propose a testbed oriented to evaluate the performance of HE-based applications towards the specific adopted library. Takeshita et al. take a similar approach in HEProfiler [29], focusing on the CKKS scheme. In [14], Gouert et al. answer the problem of the lack of comparison tools for developers proposing Terminator 2 Benchmarking Suite, a compiler that converts benchmarks written in T2, a domain-specific language, into encrypted programs running on HElib, SEAL, LATTIGO, TFHE, and PALISADE. To our knowledge, none of the reviewed works includes Concrete and OpenFHE libraries inside their benchmarking tools.

7   Conclusion

Homomorphic encryption can preserve data privacy while performing complex computations on it. Nonetheless, it has several challenges in its employment in real-world applications, particularly in the financial context. We described some use cases of interest. The industrial community needs a comparative open-source tool of the most useful HE libraries to gradually let the data analyst be independent of a cryptographer while developing an enterprise application. We propose a two-step approach. Firstly, we aim to provide a HE playground for the data analyst, and the cryptographer is still present to guide the analyst in selecting HE parameters. Then, an environment with built-in homomorphic functions and APIs should be available for the data analyst, apart from a set of HE parameters. We give the reader background for HE theory and describe the most promising HE libraries and their main characteristics. Finally, we describe the requirements and challenges for an HE library in an industrial context, introducing our seminal idea for HELT.

References

1. Acar, A., Aksu, H., Uluagac, A.S., Conti, M.: A survey on homomorphic encryption schemes: theory and implementation. ACM Comput. Surv. (Csur) **51**(4), 1–35 (2018)
2. Aguilar Melchor, C., Kilijian, M.-O., Lefebvre, C., Ricosset, T.: A comparison of the homomorphic encryption libraries HElib, SEAL and FV-NFLlib. In: Lanet, J.-L., Toma, C. (eds.) SECITC 2018. LNCS, vol. 11359, pp. 425–442. Springer, Cham (2019). https://doi.org/10.1007/978-3-030-12942-2_32
3. Albrecht, M., et al.: Homomorphic encryption security standard. Tech. rep., HomomorphicEncryption.org, Toronto, Canada (November 2018)
4. Applied Research Team: Blind learning environment. Tech. rep., Bank of Italy, Rome, Italy (June 2022). https://www.bankit.art/assets/downloads/BLE_Unrestricted.pdf (Accessed 21 June 2023)
5. Armknecht, F., et al.: A guide to fully homomorphic encryption. Cryptology ePrint Archive (2015)
6. Badawi, A.A., et al.: Openfhe: Open-source fully homomorphic encryption library. Cryptology ePrint Archive, Paper 2022/915 (2022)
7. Bellomarini, L., Blasi, L., Laurendi, R., Sallinger, E.: Financial data exchange with statistical confidentiality: a reasoning-based approach. In: Proceedings of the 24th International Conference on Extending Database Technology, EDBT 2021, Nicosia, Cyprus, 23–26 March 2021, pp. 558–569 (2021)
8. Biasioli, B., Marcolla, C., Calderini, M., Mono, J.: Improving and automating bfv parameters selection: An average-case approach. Cryptology ePrint Archive, Paper 2023/600 (2023). https://eprint.iacr.org/2023/600

9. Bos, J.W., Lauter, K., Naehrig, M.: Private predictive analysis on encrypted medical data. J. Biomed. Inform. **50**, 234–243 (2014)
10. Chillotti, I., Gama, N., Georgieva, M., Izabachène, M.: Tfhe: fast fully homomorphic encryption over the torus. J. Cryptol. **33**(1), 34–91 (2020)
11. Chillotti, I., Gama, N., Georgieva, M., Izabachène, M.: TFHE: fast fully homomorphic encryption library (August 2016). https://tfhe.github.io/tfhe/
12. Chillotti, I., Gama, N., Georgieva, M., Izabachène, M.: Faster fully homomorphic encryption: Bootstrapping in less than 0.1 seconds. Cryptology ePrint Archive, Paper 2016/870 (2016), https://eprint.iacr.org/2016/870
13. Gentry, C.: Fully homomorphic encryption using ideal lattices. In: Proceedings of the Forty-first annual ACM Symposium on Theory of Computing, pp. 169–178 (2009)
14. Gouert, C., Mouris, D., Tsoutsos, N.G.: Sok: New insights into fully homomorphic encryption libraries via standardized benchmarks. Cryptology ePrint Archive, Paper 2022/425 (2022)
15. Han, K., Hong, S., Cheon, J.H., Park, D.: Logistic regression on homomorphic encrypted data at scale. In: Proceedings of the AAAI Conference on Artificial Intelligence, vol. 33, pp. 9466–9471 (2019)
16. IBM: Ibm security homomorphic encryption services (2023). https://www.ibm.com/security/services/homomorphic-encryption, (Accessed 30 June 2023)
17. Iezzi, M.: Practical privacy-preserving data science with homomorphic encryption: an overview. In: 2020 IEEE International Conference on Big Data (Big Data), pp. 3979–3988. IEEE (2020)
18. Iezzi, M.: The evolving path of "the right to be left alone" - when privacy meets technology. In: 2021 Third IEEE International Conference on Trust, Privacy and Security in Intelligent Systems and Applications (TPS-ISA), pp. 225–234 (2021)
19. Library, PHES: Library (2023). https://palisade-crypto.org/software-library/
20. Lloyd, J.: Homomorphic encryption: the future of secure data sharing in finance? (2022). https://www.turing.ac.uk/blog/homomorphic-encryption-future-secure-data-sharing-finance (Accessed 30 June 2023)
21. López-Alt, A., Tromer, E., Vaikuntanathan, V.: On-the-fly multiparty computation on the cloud via multikey fully homomorphic encryption. In: Proceedings of the Forty-fourth Annual ACM Symposium on Theory of Computing, pp. 1219–1234 (2012)
22. Marcolla, C., Sucasas, V., Manzano, M., Bassoli, R., Fitzek, F.H., Aaraj, N.: Survey on fully homomorphic encryption, theory and applications (2022)
23. Marrone, S., Tortora, A., Bellini, E., Maione, A., Raimondo, M.: Development of a testbed for fully homomorphic encryption solutions. In: 2021 IEEE International Conference on Cyber Security and Resilience (CSR), pp. 206–211 (2021)
24. Masters, O., et al.: Towards a homomorphic machine learning big data pipeline for the financial services sector. Cryptology ePrint Archive (2019)
25. Mono, J., Marcolla, C., Land, G., Güneysu, T., Aaraj, N.: Finding and evaluating parameters for bgv. Cryptology ePrint Archive (2022)
26. Mouchet, C.V., Bossuat, J.P., Troncoso-Pastoriza, J.R., Hubaux, J.P.: Lattigo: A multiparty homomorphic encryption library in go. In: Proceedings of the 8th Workshop on Encrypted Computing and Applied Homomorphic Cryptography, pp. 64–70. No. CONF (2020)
27. Sankar, L., Rajagopalan, S.R., Poor, H.V.: An information-theoretic approach to privacy. In: 2010 48th Annual Allerton Conference on Communication, Control, and Computing (Allerton), pp. 1220–1227. IEEE (2010)

28. Microsoft SEAL (release 4.1). https://github.com/Microsoft/SEAL (Jan 2023), microsoft Research, Redmond, WA
29. Takeshita, J., Koirala, N., McKechney, C., Jung, T.: Heprofiler: an in-depth profiler of approximate homomorphic encryption libraries (2022)
30. Varia, M., Yakoubov, S., Yang, Y.: Hetest: A homomorphic encryption testing framework. In: Financial Cryptography Workshops (2015)
31. Viand, A., Jattke, P., Hithnawi, A.: Sok: fully homomorphic encryption compilers. In: 2021 IEEE Symposium on Security and Privacy (SP), pp. 1092–1108. IEEE (2021)
32. Wood, A., Najarian, K., Kahrobaei, D.: Homomorphic encryption for machine learning in medicine and bioinformatics. ACM Comput. Surv. (CSUR) **53**(4), 1–35 (2020)
33. Wood, A., Shpilrain, V., Najarian, K., Kahrobaei, D.: Private naive bayes classification of personal biomedical data: Application in cancer data analysis. Comput. Biol. Med. **105**, 144–150 (2019)
34. Zama (2022). https://www.zama.ai/post/introducing-the-concrete-framework (Accessed 30 June 2023)
35. Zama: Library (2023). https://github.com/zama-ai

AddShare: A Privacy-Preserving Approach for Federated Learning

Bernard Atiemo Asare[✉], Paula Branco, Iluju Kiringa, and Tet Yeap

Faculty of Computer Science, University of Ottawa, Ottawa, Canada
{basar092,pbranco,iluju.kiringa,tyeap}@uottawa.ca

Abstract. Centralized machine learning methods that depend on data from multiple sources have faced serious privacy issues. Federated learning (FL), which enables decentralized machine learning by training models on local devices while keeping data private and simply sharing model weights with a central server, has therefore come to be recognized as a promising alternative. However, maintaining the privacy of training data does not protect privacy as training data can be inferred from model weights. To overcome this difficulty, we propose AddShare an FL system that protects the privacy of the local model weights while allowing the computation of a global model. Leveraging state-of-the-art techniques, AddShare uses additive secret-sharing, providing a simple yet efficient method to safeguard sensitive information without compromising predictive accuracy. Moreover, additional components are integrated to ensure lower computational costs and increase privacy. We conducted extensive experiments across multiple datasets that yielded very promising results for AddShare. AddShare did not adversely impact model accuracy compared to the widely-used FedAvg algorithm. Simultaneously, the privacy of the models is ensured and the computational cost is reduced through the implementation of groups while using a single aggregating server, a capability not available in other related solutions.

Keywords: federated learning · privacy preservation · secure aggregation · additive secret sharing · encryption

1 Introduction

FL has demonstrated its potential in preserving privacy while enabling collaboration among multiple parties to train machine learning models. FL achieves this by allowing the exchange of model-related data while keeping the raw data of the parties private [18]. FL is important in scenarios where collaboration is required but privacy is paramount, such as cyber security firms teaming up to improve anomaly detection. This approach offers many benefits, such as accommodating privacy and security concerns, reducing the communication and computation costs of training, and enabling decentralized decision-making [20]. Despite the fact that FL aims to preserve privacy by ensuring that clients' data never leaves their premises, several studies (e.g., [8]) have shown that it is still possible to reconstruct private data from machine learning parameters. This undermines the primary objective of FL, which is to keep clients' data confidential.

Among the various privacy-preserving techniques proposed for FL, secure multiparty computation (SMC) is a promising approach that allows multiple parties to jointly compute a function on their private inputs without revealing any information about them. By using SMC in FL, the participants can securely share their model updates while keeping their data confidential. This protects the privacy of the individuals and enhances the trust and fairness of the overall learning process. However, the implementation of SMC in FL can be challenging due to the computational and communication overheads and the need to ensure the correctness and security of the computation. Therefore, it is important to develop practical and efficient methods for using SMC in FL and evaluate their performance and robustness under different scenarios.

In this paper, we present a novel framework called AddShare that addresses the challenge of privacy-preserving in FL by combining conventional FL techniques with additive secret sharing. Specifically, Our framework, called AddShare, is unique in its simplicity, speed, scalability, and efficiency. It enables decentralized model aggregation while maintaining strict privacy guarantees for local client data. We implement our framework and ran comprehensive tests on well-known datasets including CIFAR10, F-MNIST, MNIST, and SVHN to confirm AddShare's efficacy. Our results show that AddShare reaches accuracy levels comparable to models trained only using the FedAvg method. Additionally, rather than integrating all participating clients in the secret-sharing process, we instead execute the process among subgroups, which is a unique idea in our framework. This strategy lowers the cost of communication while improving the speed of the FL process.

This paper is organized as follows. In Sect. 2, we present an overview of existing related approaches. Section 3 introduces our proposed AddShare approach to address privacy concerns within FL. Section 4 describes the empirical evaluation carried out, and Sect. 5 discusses the results obtained. Finally, Sect. 6 concludes the paper.

2   Background and Related Work

2.1   Federated Learning Attacks

We investigate three types of FL attacks: reconstruction, inference, and communication interception attacks. These categories pose significant risks to participant data security and privacy [4]. Our aim is to develop effective countermeasures to protect FL process confidentiality, integrity, and privacy by understanding these threats.

Reconstruction attacks aims to recover initial data used for training an FL model. Attackers seek to reconstruct private data from the model's inputs or outputs. Even if the model is privacy-preserving, this attack might expose private data from the training set. Using the Deep Leaked Gradients algorithm [21],

Table 1. FL Secret Sharing Algorithms

Algorithm	Sharing	Single Server	Multi-Server
SecAgg [3]	Shamir	✓	✗
SecAgg+ [2]	Shamir	✓	✗
SCOTCH [12]	Additive	✗	✓
FedShare [1]	Additive	✗	✓
AddShare	Additive	✓	✗

authors reconstructed almost 100% of initial data through inference. This algorithm rebuilds images and text, inferring data from leaked gradients, even with limited iterations or gradients from an honest client (more details in Sect. 3). Membership inference attacks determine if a data sample was part of an FL model's training set. These attacks use a data record and black-box model access to infer membership [16]. For sensitive data, this attack is highly risky. FL's model exchange between clients and a central server makes it vulnerable to interception [4]. Communication interception attacks involve unauthorized eavesdropping on communication, aiming to access data or model changes.

2.2 Privacy in Federated Learning

Differential privacy [7] provides privacy guarantees by minimizing data impact on output. Sun et al. [17] propose a local differential privacy mechanism for FL, adapting weights updates for deep neural networks. Secure Multi-Party Computation (SMC) preserves FL privacy through cryptographic protocols [3]. Researchers proposed secure function evaluation and secret sharing [3] and some optimized SMC for FL efficiency. Researchers use secret-sharing-based SMC for FL privacy. Approaches like SecAgg, and SecAgg+ apply Shamir's scheme with a single lead server. SCOTCH and FedShare use additive secret sharing with multiple servers. Table 1 compares secret-sharing algorithms for FL, with AddShare being the only additive scheme with a single server.

3 The AddShare Approach

This section presents AddShare, a novel framework where multiple data parties collaborate with a machine learning (ML) service known as the central aggregating server. Our framework is designed to ensure robustness against two distinct threat models: the honest-but-curious server and an external attacker.

3.1 Threat Models

The honest-but-curious server threat model assumes that the server functions as intended but collects extra information beyond its scope [11]. This well-known FL threat model [3] involves scrutinizing model weights for reconstruction attacks. Sharing weights among clients and an aggregator risks interception or tampering of updates in transit. It encompasses external adversaries like hackers, using eavesdropping or man-in-the-middle attacks to access sensitive information. Eavesdroppers can intercept communication to steal intermediate updates or the final model.

3.2   AddShare Algorithm

Our proposed AddShare Algorithm has three main components: (i) additive secret sharing; (ii) encryption; and (iii) generation of groups. The key idea of AddShare is to avoid any client and server to know any client's local weights and to defend against an attacker listening to all communications to recover the client weights. These two goals are achieved through an embedded additive secret-sharing mechanism and the encryption of communications. Finally, the use of groups allows to minimize the communication overhead improving the FL rounds speed. We describe the three main components next.

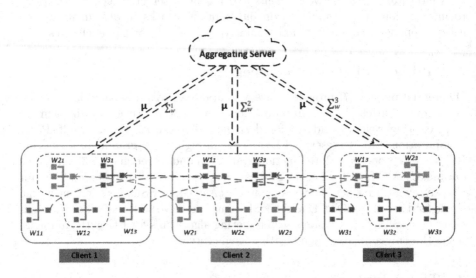

Fig. 1. Overview of the proposed AddShare Algorithm using additive secret sharing for model weights sharing in FL. (Considering a 3-client FL setup, Client 1 builds 3 shares from its local model weights ($W11$, $W12$, and $W13$), keeps one share ($W11$), and sends $W12$ and $W13$ to clients 2 and 3, while also receiving one share from the other clients. The shares are aggregated and sent to the central server.)

Additive Secret Sharing Component. In secret sharing [15], a secret value x is divided into n shares x_1, x_1, ... x_n. The shares are chosen in such a way that, when they are combined, they reveal the original secret value, but any subset of shares less than a threshold k does not reveal any information about

---

Algorithm 1. Generate n shares of a multidimensional array.

Input: n: number of clients entering the sharing process; arr, multidimensional array of shape $(m_1, m_2, \ldots, m_k)$ with the client's local weights.

Output: $shares$: list of size n containing arrays of shape $(m_1, m_2, \ldots, m_k)$ such that $\sum_{k=1}^{n} shares[k] = arr$.

1: $rand\_arr \leftarrow$ array of $n - 1$ randomly generated arrays of shape $(m_1, m_2, \ldots, m_k)$, where each element of $rand\_arr[i]$ is drawn from a uniform distribution between $-|arr[i]|$ and $|arr[i]|$.

2: $nth\_share \leftarrow arr - \sum_{i=1}^{n-1} rand\_arr[i]$

3: $shares \leftarrow (rand\_arr, nth\_share)$

4: Return $shares$

---

the secret. This method can be thought of as a (k, n)-threshold secret sharing scheme, where k is the threshold number of shares necessary for secret retrieval and n is the number of shares. We employ the additive secret sharing [5], a variant of secret sharing whereby all the shares are necessary for secret retrieval. This method can also be thought of as an (n,n)-threshold secret sharing scheme. This method is applied as a privacy preservation protocol in our FL system. After each client has trained a model with the local data, the model weights are shared. Instead of simply sharing the original weights, each client splits the local model weights W into n shares, where n is equal to the number of participating clients in the sharing process. These weight shares are exchanged among the clients. This ensures that each client receives a share of the model weights of other clients, and no client has access to the original model weights of other clients. Each client recomputes the model weights using their local share and the $n - 1$ shares received from the other clients. The reconstructed model weights of client i, which we represent as $\sum_w^i$, are sent to the aggregating server, where they are aggregated using FedAvg [10]. Finally, all clients receive the updated model, μ from the server. Figure 1 displays this process for 3 clients and Algorithm 1 provides the pseudo-code for the steps involved in the additive secret sharing procedure of model weights. We must highlight that the example in Fig. 1 assumes all clients participate in one sharing process, i.e., the total number of clients is the same as the number of clients sharing the weights. In the group component proposed, we discuss a strategy where a total of n clients is considered but the sharing process is carried out in groups where only k clients participate.

Encryption Component. We used the well-known RSA (Rivest-Shamir-Adleman) encryption [14], which uses public keys and the mathematical properties of prime numbers and modular arithmetic to provide secure communication and data encryption. A public key is used for encryption, and a private key is used for decryption. The strength of RSA resides in the computational complexity of factoring huge composite numbers into their prime components, making it a cornerstone of modern encryption.

After generating the shares with the weights of the model, client i encrypts the shares that will be sent to another client j using client j's public key. This allows client j to receive the shares, decrypt them, and aggregate them before sending them to the central server.

The key generation process of RSA encryption involves the following steps:

(a) Prime Number Selection: Select two large prime numbers, p and q.
(b) Modulus Computation: The product of p and q yields the modulus, n.
(c) Euler's Totient Function: Calculate $\phi(n) = (p-1) * (q-1)$.
(d) Public Key: Chose an integer e that is coprime with $\phi(n)$.
(e) Private Key: The private key d is the multiplicative inverse of e modulo $\phi(n)$.

To encrypt the *shares* using RSA encryption, we follow two steps: (i) Public Key Acquisition: the recipient's public key (e, n) is obtained; and (ii) Ciphertext Computation: ciphertext, C is computed using $C = shares^e \bmod n$. To decrypt the ciphertext C and retrieve the original message, two steps must be completed: (i) Private Key Usage: the private key (d, n) is employed; and (ii) Plaintext Computation: Plaintext, *shares* is computed using $shares = C^d \bmod n$.

To mitigate the threat of eavesdroppers, RSA encryption is employed as a safeguard. By encrypting the additive share sent to each client using the client's public key, RSA ensures that only clients possessing the corresponding private key can decrypt and access that model share, preserving the confidentiality and integrity of the FL process. In this paper, client keys are generated offline, and each client securely stores its private keys while sharing the corresponding public keys with other clients.

3.3 Implemented AddShare Variants

Additive Secret Sharing FL. This variant only applies additive secret sharing in the FL process. No encryption is used and no groups of clients are formed. For the n clients, each $i - th$ client splits their model weights into n additive shares using Algorithm 1. Each $i - th$ client keeps one share of their n additive shares and exchanges the $n - 1$ shares left with the other $n - 1$ clients without encrypting the weights. At the end of this exchange process, each $i - th$ client reconstructs the model weights using its local share and the $n-1$ shares received from the other clients. The reconstructed model weights are sent to the central server for aggregation into a global model.

Encrypted Additive Secret Sharing FL. Building upon the previous variant, in this case, we combine the benefits of both encryption and additive secret sharing. The same additive secret sharing process is followed but the clients encrypt the shares before transmitting them to the other clients using each client's public key. This ensures the weight's privacy during the FL process.

Additive Secret Sharing FL with Groups. This variant introduces the concept of subgroup-based additive secret-sharing FL. Instead of performing additive secret sharing among all n clients, participants are divided into smaller subgroups

Table 2. Characteristics of the datasets used in our experiments.

Reference	Dataset	# Classes	Train Size (per client)	Total Train Size
[9]	CIFAR10	10	1000	60000
[6]	MNIST	10	1200	70000
[19]	F-MNIST	10	1200	60000
[13]	SVHN	10	1465	73257

of size k (e.g., subgroups of 3, 5, and 10) executed by the aggregating server. The additive secret sharing is performed only within each subgroup. This decreases the number of communications as instead of building n shares to send to $n-1$ clients, only k shares are needed and $k-1$ shares are sent. The resulting model updates are then sent to the central server for aggregation into a global model.

Encrypted Additive Secret Sharing FL with Groups. Extending the previous variant, this approach combines all components of AddShare including subgroup-based additive secret-sharing FL with encryption. Clients encrypt their additive shares and transmit them securely within their subgroups.

4   Empirical Evaluation

We selected four multiclass datasets to evaluate the effectiveness of the proposed approaches. Each dataset was randomly shuffled and partitioned into 50 equal-sized independently and identically distributed (IID) subsets, one for each client. Detailed information on the used datasets can be seen in Table 2. For all the used datasets, the pixel values were normalized to the $[0, 1]$ interval.

Each client used the LeNet-5 architecture, which consists of 7 layers, including 2 convolutional layers, 2 pooling layers, and 3 fully connected layers. We used Adam's optimizer with a learning rate of 0.001 and a batch size of 10 for each client. The federated process runs for 50 clients and 10 rounds. For each round, we trained each node's model for 2 epochs and recorded accuracy, training time, and the secret sharing time. We assigned a maximum running time of 6 days for each pair of dataset and FL strategy. Experiments that did not complete under this time are marked with *. We implement the learning script in Python using Tensorflow and Keras.

We compared the performance of 6 variants: (i) FedAvg system; (ii) FedAvg with additive secret-sharing; (iii) FedAvg with additive secret-sharing in subgroups; (iv) encrypted FedAvg system; (v) encrypted FedAvg with additive secret-sharing; and (vi) encrypted FedAvg with additive secret-sharing in subgroups (our AddShare proposal with the three components). For the variants that use subgroups we tested them with 3 different subgroup sizes of 3, 5, and 10. Thus, we tested a total of 10 alternative implementations. For the variants using encryption, we used the RSA of the models' weights during the transmission process. We selected accuracy as the overall performance assessment metric,

Table 3. Overall results of the 10 FL alternatives on CIFAR10 Dataset.

Experiments	Server Avg.		Client Avg.		
	Accuracy	FL Time (s)	Accuracy	Training Time (s)	SS Time (s)
FedAvg	0.426	139.440	0.381	1.559	No SS applied
FedAvg Encrypted	0.426	1156.671	0.381	1.347	No SS applied
AddShare - All	0.426	142.627	0.380	1.395	0.106
AddShare - G3	0.348	121.448	0.257	1.056	0.007
AddShare - G5	0.375	121.208	0.320	1.168	0.011
AddShare - G10	0.374	123.299	0.317	0.998	0.027
AddShare Encrypted - All	*	*	*	*	*
AddShare Encrypted - G3	0.348	1564.897	0.261	0.925	0.011
AddShare Encrypted - G5	0.374	3232.966	0.316	1.069	0.016
AddShare Encrypted - G10	0.374	7182.971	0.316	0.892	0.034

Table 4. Overall results of the 10 FL alternatives on F-MNIST Dataset.

Experiments	Server Avg.		Client Avg.		
	Accuracy	FL Time (s)	Accuracy	Training Time (s)	SS Time (s)
FedAvg	0.787	129.551	0.762	1.526	No SS applied
FedAvg Encrypted	0.787	855.573	0.761	1.490	No SS applied
AddShare - All	0.787	133.600	0.760	1.817	0.083
AddShare - G3	0.739	109.302	0.708	1.091	0.006
AddShare - G5	0.754	109.635	0.729	1.093	0.015
AddShare - G10	0.753	109.987	0.730	1.096	0.016
AddShare Encrypted - All	*	*	*	*	*
AddShare Encrypted - G3	0.738	1142.256	0.706	1.331	0.016
AddShare Encrypted - G5	0.754	2335.041	0.729	1.400	0.014
AddShare Encrypted - G10	0.754	5432.993	0.729	1.075	0.030

Table 5. Overall results of the 10 FL alternatives on SVHN Dataset.

Experiments	Server Avg.		Client Avg.		
	Accuracy	FL Time (s)	Accuracy	Training Time (s)	SS Time (s)
FedAvg	0.739	228.763	0.700	1.734	No SS applied
FedAvg Encrypted	0.739	1243.891	0.702	1.884	No SS applied
AddShare - All	0.739	231.587	0.701	1.725	0.103
AddShare - G3	0.606	199.185	0.536	1.345	0.013
AddShare - G5	0.633	204.532	0.579	1.229	0.013
AddShare - G10	0.633	203.169	0.580	1.214	0.024
AddShare Encrypted - All	*	*	*	*	*
AddShare Encrypted - G3	0.606	1616.384	0.425	1.012	0.013
AddShare Encrypted - G5	0.631	3584.688	0.578	1.121	0.027
AddShare Encrypted - G10	0.631	6714.204	0.576	0.771	0.114

which we assess on the central server and the clients. We also observe the computational time in seconds for each FL round, as well as the training time and the secret sharing time in the clients.

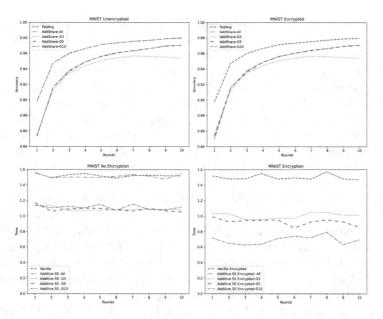

Fig. 2. Accuracy (top) and running time in seconds (bottom), per FL round for MNIST dataset. Non-encrypted variants are on the left and encrypted variants are on the right.

5   Results and Discussion

All our code and results are freely available at https://github.com/baasare/ADDSHARE-DPM23. Tables 3, 4, and 5 present the overall performance and time results of all alternatives tested for each of the four datasets considered. Figures 2 display the running time recorded per FL round and the accuracy per round for the MNIST dataset (similar results were obtained on the other three datasets).

The accuracy trends depicted in Fig. 2 showcase the progressive improvement in accuracy for each experiment. The other three datasets not shown here present a similar trend. Interestingly, across all datasets, the difference in accuracy between the baseline FedAvg and AddShare when using all clients is minimal and remains relatively stable as the experiments unfold. This suggests that incorporating the AddShare approach within the FL process does not significantly impact the performance of the models. Still, we observe a tendency to exhibit lower performance scores when smaller groups are considered for the AddShare approach. In fact, when using groups of 3 clients, the performance tends to be lower for all datasets, irrespective of the usage of encryption. When comparing the impact of using subgroups in AddShare, we observe a clear advantage of using this component. For all datasets, using AddShare with groups reduces significantly the running time when compared to using FedAvg and AddShare with all clients. This last option with encryption did not finish running in 6 days while the same variants with subgroups completed in less than 1 day (with and without encryption). This decrease in running time can be ascribed to a reduction in the communication rounds during the exchange of weight shares among clients when performing additive secret-sharing. However, the results are different when encryption is used. In this case, we observe that FedAvg with encryption takes on average less time per FL round than any of the AddShare alternatives. This shows that when adding encryption to AddShare there is a trade-off that needs to be considered regarding the time efficiency.

Analyzing in more detail how RSA encryption affects the FL process makes it clear that, despite adding an extra degree of security against eavesdroppers, the time required for the encryption process is indeed costly. An important factor to take into account in the context of FL is the time cost associated with RSA encryption. A balance must be achieved between privacy protection and computing efficiency while security remains of the greatest significance. It can be important to balance the advantages of improved security against the potential increase in running time induced by RSA encryption, depending on the particular use case and the available computational resources. Still, we must highlight that when comparing the AddShare variants, we observe that the usage of groups makes the AddShare variant with encryption significantly less time-consuming when compared to the alternative of not using groups.

Overall, our experiments show that AddShare with groups and encryption is the solution that provides the best trade-off between data privacy and time efficiency. Our results show that this AddShare variant maintains good performance accuracy while keeping the running time manageable and relatively close to the standard approaches.

6   Conclusion

We presented AddShare, a practical and secure aggregation protocol designed to ensure privacy in FL. AddShare addresses the challenge of aggregating model weights in an FL system without compromising the privacy of individual clients' models, while also preserving the performance of the training process. Moreover, no client is able to recover any of the other clients' weights. This ensures that sensitive information remains protected throughout the FL process, mitigating the risk of privacy breaches. Our solution incorporating additive secret sharing with encryption and groups of clients provides guarantees against specific threat models including the honest-but-curious server and eavesdropper attackers. Our results demonstrate that the incorporation of AddShare does not adversely affect the performance of the FL system, ensuring privacy without sacrificing accuracy. The introduced concept of executing AddShare among subgroups has an outstanding impact in terms of reducing communication costs. This optimization enhances the scalability and efficiency of the FL system by distributing the computational burden across smaller, more manageable groups.

References

1. Khojir, H.F., et al.: FedShare: secure aggregation based on additive secret sharing in federated learning. In: International Database Engineered Applications Symposium Conference, Heraklion, Crete Greece, 2023, pp. 25–33. ACM (2023). https://dl.acm.org/doi/10.1145/3589462.3589504

2. Bell, J.H., et al.: Secure single-server aggregation with (poly)logarithmic overhead. In: Proceedings of the 2020 ACM SIGSAC Conference on Computer and Communications Security, pp. 1253–1269 (2020)
3. Bonawitz, K., et al.: Practical secure aggregation for privacy-preserving machine learning. In: Proceedings of the 2017 ACM SIGSAC Conference on Computer and Communications Security, pp. 1175–1191 (2017)
4. Bouacida, N., Mohapatra, P.: Vulnerabilities in federated learning. IEEE Access 9, 63229–63249 (2021). https://doi.org/10.1109/ACCESS.2021.3075203
5. Choudhury, A., Patra, A.: Secret sharing. In: Secure Multi-Party Computation Against Passive Adversaries. Synthesis Lectures on Distributed Computing Theory, pp. 17–31. Springer, Cham (2022). https://doi.org/10.1007/978-3-031-12164-7_3
6. Deng, L.: The MNIST database of handwritten digit images for machine learning research. IEEE Sig. Process. Mag. 29(6), 141–142 (2012)
7. Dwork, C.: Differential privacy. In: Bugliesi, M., Preneel, B., Sassone, V., Wegener, I. (eds.) ICALP 2006. LNCS, vol. 4052, pp. 1–12. Springer, Heidelberg (2006). https://doi.org/10.1007/11787006_1
8. Gongye, C., Fei, Y., Wahl, T.: Reverse-engineering deep neural networks using floating-point timing side-channels. In: 2020 57th ACM/IEEE Design Automation Conference (DAC) (2020). https://doi.org/10.1109/dac18072.2020.9218707
9. Krizhevsky, A.: Learning multiple layers of features from tiny images. University of Toronto (2009)
10. McMahan, H.B., et al.: Communication-efficient learning of deep networks from decentralized data. In: Proceedings of the 20th International Conference on Artificial Intelligence and Statistics, April 2017, pp. 1273–1282. PMLR (2017). ISSN 2640-3498. https://proceedings.mlr.press/v54/mcmahan17a.html
11. Moore, E., et al.: A survey on secure and private federated learning using blockchain: theory and application in resource-constrained computing. arXiv arXiv:2303.13727 [cs], March 2023
12. More, Y., et al.: SCOTCH: an efficient secure computation framework for secure aggregation. arXiv arXiv:2201.07730 [cs], February 2022
13. Netzer, Y., Wang, T., Coates, A., Bissacco, A., Wu, B., Ng, A.: Reading digits in natural images with unsupervised feature learning. In: NIPS Workshop on Deep Learning and Unsupervised Feature Learning 2011 (2011)
14. Rivest, R.L., Shamir, A., Adleman, L.: A method for obtaining digital signatures and public-key cryptosystems. Commun. ACM 21(2), 120–126 (1978)
15. Shamir, A.: How to share a secret. Commun. ACM 22(11), 612–613 (1979). https://doi.org/10.1145/359168.359176
16. Shokri, R., et al.: Membership inference attacks against machine learning models. arXiv arXiv:1610.05820 [cs, stat], March 2017
17. Sun, L., Qian, J., Chen, X.: LDP-FL: practical private aggregation in federated learning with local differential privacy. arXiv arXiv:2007.15789 [cs], May 2021
18. Thursday: Federated learning: collaborative machine learning without centralized training data. https://ai.googleblog.com/2017/04/federated-learning-collaborative.html
19. Xiao, H., et al.: Fashion-MNIST: a novel image dataset for benchmarking machine learning algorithms. arXiv arXiv:1708.07747 [cs, stat], September 2017
20. Yang, Q., et al.: Federated machine learning: concept and applications. ACM Trans. Intell. Syst. Technol. 10(2), 1–19 (2019)
21. Zhao, B., et al.: iDLG: improved deep leakage from gradients. arXiv arXiv:2001.02610 [cs, stat], January 2020

Secure Multiparty Sampling of a Biased Coin for Differential Privacy

Amir Zarei$^{(\boxtimes)}$ (ID) and Staal A. Vinterbo (ID)

Norwegian University of Science and Technology, Trondheim, Norway
{amir.zarei,staal.vinterbo}@ntnu.no

Abstract. Sampling a biased coin is a key primitive in designing secure multiparty computation (MPC) for differentially private mechanisms. We explore privately sampling a biased coin from l unbiased coins and offer an unconditionally secure MPC protocol for this task that can be implemented using either $7.5l - 4$ (when l is even) or $7.5l - 1.5$ (when l is odd) multiplications in 7 rounds. This protocol assumes control over the choice of the underlying field size and is compatible with any linear secret sharing scheme with a multiplication protocol. The protocol is also secure against active adversaries when the underlying secret sharing scheme is secure. Eriguchi and colleagues proposed a protocol to generate noise for differential privacy, incorporating a sub-protocol for biased coins. Replacing their sub-protocol with ours significantly reduces communication needs as the number of multiplications needed per biased coin becomes roughly 3/8 of the original.

Keywords: Secure Multiparty Computation · Differential Privacy

1 Introduction

Differential privacy [1] is a standard framework for privacy-protective analysis of data from individuals. Intuitively, differential privacy requires an analysis algorithm to introduce random noise to mask individual contributions. This noise can be applied individually or in aggregate, called local and centralized models. The local model enables individuals to achieve privacy independently, while the centralized model, although requiring a trusted party, introduces less overall noise [2]. A goal is to combine the local model's privacy with the centralized model's utility. To this end, Dwork et al. [3] investigate secure MPC for differentially private algorithms, showing that a shared biased coin is an essential primitive for generating noise according to discrete probability distributions.

Secure MPC based on secret sharing fits many real-world trust scenarios and can readily be reasoned about. However, it can be resource-intensive, requiring significant inter-party communication. This challenge has inspired various solutions in the realm of differential privacy [3–5]. We contribute to this line of work by reducing the communication and round complexities in computing a shared biased coin, thereby improving the efficiency of generating shared noise from discrete probability distributions, a standard practice in current differential privacy applications [5,6].

S. Katsikas et al. (Eds.): ESORICS 2023 Workshops, LNCS 14398, pp. 310–320, 2024.
https://doi.org/10.1007/978-3-031-54204-6_19

1.1 Other Background and Related Works

A coin with bias α is a random bit that takes value 1 with probability α. The traditional method for openly sampling such a coin first samples a uniformly random number $r \in [0,1]$, then outputs 1 if $r \leq \alpha$ and 0 otherwise. A secure MPC implementation of this method that achieves statistical error at most 2^{-l} is to discretely sample l unbiased coins, consider these coins as the binary form of r, then compare the binary form of r and α. Dwork et al. [3] mention this implementation can be realized using $O(l)$ multiplications. Seeking improvement, Champion et al. [5] propose an MPC method for generating many biased coins. However, their method relies on oblivious RAM data structures and cannot be directly applied to secure MPC protocols based on secret sharing [4].

Eriguchi et al. [4] provide a secure MPC realization of the differentially private geometric mechanism based on secret sharing over $\mathbb{Z}_p$. As a core building block of this protocol, they present a technique for sampling a biased coin that depends on generating l unbiased coins. For this, they rely on two existing protocols for sampling unbiased coins, providing two examples of protocols for sampling a biased coin, one using $O(l)$ multiplications discussed possible by Dwork et al. Their primary choice for sampling unbiased coins is a protocol introduced by Schoenmakers et al. [7], which does not fail and costs $5nl$ multiplications for n parties. The second, offered by Damgård et al. [8], costs $2l$ multiplications but fails with a probability of order p^{-1}. Depending on which of these is used to generate unbiased coins, their biased coin protocol requires $(5n + 19)l$ multiplications [4] in 11 rounds [16] or $20l$ multiplications in 10 rounds to generate one biased coin. As the geometric distribution measures the probability of taking N biased coins to obtain success, their protocol for generating a geometric sample requires $(5n + 19)lN + 17N + 5n + 3$ or $(20)lN + 17N + 5n + 3$ multiplications, depending on the choice of how the unbiased coins are generated. This example emphasizes the importance of simplifying biased coin generation to reduce the complexity of creating a geometric sample.

1.2 Contribution

This paper improves the efficiency of secure MPC of sampling a biased coin by reducing the comparison of $r \leq \alpha$ to extract the least significant bit of a secret shared value, inspired by solutions of Reistad et al. [13,14]. This provides an unconditional secure MPC protocol compatible with any linear secret sharing scheme over $\mathbb{Z}_p$, where $l = \lceil \log_2 p \rceil$. The protocol can be realized using either $7.5l - 4$ (when l is even) or $7.5l - 1.5$ (when l is odd) multiplications in 7 rounds, assuming control over the field size p, i.e., p must be selected as a Mersenne prime or other primes close to powers of 2. The protocol's security is upheld against active adversaries, matching the level of security provided by the underlying secret sharing scheme. Our solution significantly reduces the number of multiplications and rounds needed to generate a biased coin compared to the solutions of Eriguchi et al. [4]. We also exemplify how our protocol can reduce the communication complexity of secure MPC differentially private mechanisms. These claims are detailed in Sect. 4.

2 Preliminaries

This section will establish the framework, notations, and complexity metrics used in our study, and outlines the sub-protocols underlying our proposed protocol.

2.1 Setting, Basic Notation and Complexity

We assume an unconditionally secure, linear secret sharing scheme allowing values of the finite field $\mathbb{Z}_p$ for some prime $p > 2$ to be shared among $n > 2$ parties. We also assume this scheme incorporates a secure, constant-round multiplication protocol for shared values. Such a scheme can be implemented by Shamir's secret sharing [9], and the protocols of Ben-Or et al. [10]. The security property of the scheme is inherited, i.e., if this is unconditionally secure against active adversaries, then so is the proposed protocol. This scheme functions as a trusted third party, immune to tampering or corruption, and enables parties to share data, conduct arithmetic operations, and reveal data. This third party can be instantiated as an ideal functionality, adopting the characteristics of an Arithmetic Black Box (ABB), similar to the one proposed by Damgård et al. [11]. Using an ABB allows protocol constructions to focus on primary tasks without worrying about the security of underlying primitives. The protocol described here can then be applied to any scheme equivalent to this ideal functionality, implying that security is shown by ensuring no leaks when values are revealed and that the underlying primitives are secure by assumption.

The notation $[\![a]\!]$ indicates that $a \in \mathbb{Z}_p$ is shared among the parties, and l stands for the number of bits required for p, with $l = \lceil \log_2 p \rceil$. For shared values $[\![a]\!]$ and $[\![b]\!]$, and a public constant c, $[\![a]\!] + [\![b]\!]$, $[\![a]\!] + c$, and $c[\![a]\!]$ are performed by each party locally, while the product $[\![a]\!][\![b]\!]$ needs one multiplication (protocol) invocation. Additionally, shared values can be revealed to a chosen set of parties. The XOR of shared bits $[\![a]\!]$ and $[\![b]\!]$ is computed as $[\![a]\!] \oplus [\![b]\!] = [\![a]\!] + [\![b]\!] - 2[\![a]\!][\![b]\!]$ using one multiplication invocation. $[\![a]\!]_B$ refers to a uniformly random bitwise shared element, i.e., $([\![a_{l-1}]\!], \dots, [\![a_0]\!])$. For $[\![a]\!]_B$, the sum $\sum_{i=0}^{l-1} 2^i [\![a_i]\!]$ follows a uniform distribution over $\mathbb{Z}_p$. $[\![a]\!]_b$ denotes l uniformly random shared bits, i.e., $([\![a_{l-1}]\!], \dots, [\![a_0]\!])$. For $[\![a]\!]_b$, $\sum_{i=0}^{l-1} 2^i [\![a_i]\!]$ may not follow a uniform distribution over $\mathbb{Z}_p$, i.e., $\sum_{i=0}^{l-1} 2^i [\![a_i]\!] \geq p$ may occur; thus, a reduction modulo p is required. Publicly known value α can be split into bits as α_B. Given $[\![a]\!]_b$ and α_B, the XOR of bits in their j-th bit-position is denoted by $\alpha_j \oplus [\![a_j]\!] = \alpha_j + [\![a_j]\!] - 2\alpha_j [\![a_j]\!]$ (with the subscripts B and b being dropped off for readability).

The complexity analysis will focus on round and communication complexities. The former is represented by the number of sequential invocations of the multiplication protocol. The latter includes the overall number of times the multiplication protocol is invoked, an often-used proxy for the amount of data sent by the parties. Multiplication invocations that can be executed in parallel count as a single round. Multiplication by constants and addition require no communication and is regarded without cost. The complexity of revealing is considered negligible compared with the multiplication protocol and is disregarded. Rounds for revealing values are ignored as in other works.

2.2   Known Primitives

The following primitives require generating random values that may fail. However, the failure probability, typically of order p^{-1}, is negligible and ignored as p is sufficiently large (see Damgård et al. [8] for further discussion).

Random Element Generation. The parties can create a uniformly random shared value $[\![r]\!]$ via the RAN_p protocol of Damgård et al. [8]. In RAN_p, each party distributes a random value r_i, and $[\![\sum_{i=1}^{n} r_i \bmod p]\!]$ becomes a random shared value unknown to all the parties. The complexity of this protocol is bounded by one multiplication invocation in one round. Damgård et al. [8] also introduce an element inversion technique wherein $[\![r]\!]$ and $[\![r^{-1}]\!]$ can be created by generating two random shared elements $[\![r]\!]$ and $[\![s]\!]$, then computing and revealing their product. The protocol fails if $rs = 0$; otherwise, $[\![r]\!]$ is a non-zero shared element. Also, $[\![r^{-1}]\!]$ can be computed without cost as $[\![r^{-1}]\!] = (rs)^{-1}[\![s]\!]$. Seeing rs does not leak information about $[\![r]\!]$ as $[\![s]\!]$ is a uniformly random value. Three multiplications and two rounds bound the complexity of this technique.

Prefix Product Computation. Given k non-zero shared values $[\![a_1]\!], ..., [\![a_k]\!]$, the parties can compute prefix products as $[\![b_j]\!] = \prod_{i=1}^{j} [\![a_i]\!]$ for $j \in \{1, ..., k\}$ using the method of Damgård et al. [8] with the improvement by Reistad et al. [12,13]. The method sets $r_0 = 1$ and generates k random non-zero shared elements $[\![r_i]\!]$, their inverses $[\![r_i^{-1}]\!]$, and the masks $[\![s_i]\!]$ by the inversion technique. Then, it computes $[\![r_{i-1}]\!][\![s_i]\!]$ for $i \in \{1, ..., k\}$ in parallel with previous computation. Later, it masks each $[\![a_i]\!]$ and reveal the result as $m_i = [\![a_i]\!][\![r_{i-1}r_i^{-1}]\!]$ for $i \in \{1, ..., k\}$. $[\![r_{i-1}r_i^{-1}]\!]$ can be done without cost as $[\![r_{i-1}r_i^{-1}]\!] = [\![r_{i-1}s_i]\!] \cdot (r_i s_i)^{-1}$. Finally, it locally computes the prefixes as $[\![b_j]\!] = [\![r_j]\!] \cdot \prod_{i=1}^{j} m_i$ for $j \in \{1, ..., k\}$. Privacy of $[\![a_i]\!]$'s is ensured as they are masked by $[\![r_i^{-1}]\!]$'s. The complexity is $5k$ multiplications in 3 rounds. Specifically, preparing for the prefix product, including computing $[\![r_i]\!]$'s, $[\![r_i^{-1}]\!]$'s, $[\![s_i]\!]$'s and $([\![r_{i-1}]\!][\![s_i]\!])$'s needs $4k$ multiplications in the first two rounds. Then, masking a_i's needs k multiplications in the third round.

Random Bit(s) Generation. The parties can create a uniformly random shared bit $[\![b]\!]$ using the RAN_2 protocol of Damgård et al. [8]. The parties first generate a uniformly random shared value $[\![r]\!]$ and reveal its square. The protocol fails if $r^2 = 0$; otherwise the parties can compute $[\![b]\!]$ as $[\![b]\!] = 2^{-1}((\sqrt{r^2})^{-1}[\![r]\!] + 1)$, where $0 \leq \sqrt{r^2} \leq \frac{p-1}{2}$. The complexity is bounded by two multiplications and two rounds. Additionally, the parties can generate l uniformly random shared bits $[\![r]\!]_b = ([\![r_{l-1}]\!], ..., [\![r_0]\!])$ by l invocations of RAN_2 in parallel, costing $2l$ multiplications in 2 rounds [8].

Random Bitwise Element Generation. The parties can generate a uniformly random bitwise shared element $[\![r]\!]_B \in \mathbb{Z}_p$ by generating l bits using l

parallel invocations of RAN_2, then verifying that these bits represent a value less than p [8]. This verification may fail, so multiple attempts may be needed. The studies of [8,12,15] assumed four attempts to ensure that overall failure probability is negligible in the number of generated elements, imposing $52l + 24\sqrt{l}$ multiplications in 7 rounds [15]. However, if p can be chosen sensibly, e.g., as a Mersenne prime or other primes close to powers of two, the failure probability can be reduced to negligible in l, eliminating the need for verification, and reducing the complexity to $2l$ multiplications in 2 rounds [8].

Least Significant Bit Extraction. The parties can obtain the least significant bit of a secret shared input $[\![X]\!]$, where $[\![X]\!] < \sqrt{4p}$ using the LSB protocol of Reistad [13]. This protocol involves creating a random bitwise shared mask $[\![s]\!]_B$, then computing and revealing m as $[\![m]\!] = [\![s]\!]_B + [\![X]\!]$. Decomposing $[\![s]\!]_B$ as $[\![s]\!]_B = 2^{l-1}[\![s_{l-1}]\!] + 2^{l-2}[\![s_{l-2}]\!] + [\![\hat{s}]\!]_B$ ensures that $[\![\hat{m}]\!] = [\![\hat{s}]\!]_B + [\![X]\!] < 2^{l-2} + \sqrt{4p} < p$ never needs a modulo p reduction, thus $[\![X_0]\!] = [\![\hat{s}_0]\!]_B \oplus [\![\hat{m}_0]\!]$. Four possible values for $[\![\hat{m}]\!]$ exist based on m, $[\![s_{l-1}]\!]$, and $[\![s_{l-2}]\!]$. Thus, $[\![\hat{m}_0]\!]$ can be computed as,

$$[\![\hat{m}_0]\!] = (1 - [\![s_{l-1}]\!] - [\![s_{l-2}]\!] + [\![\hat{s}]\!])m_0 + ([\![s_{l-2}]\!] - [\![\hat{s}]\!])(m_0 \oplus (m < 2^{l-2}))$$

$$+([\![s_{l-1}]\!] - [\![\hat{s}]\!])(m_0 \oplus (m < 2^{l-1})) + [\![\hat{s}]\!](m_0 \oplus (m < 2^{l-1} + 2^{l-2})),$$

where $[\![\hat{s}]\!] = [\![s_{l-1}]\!][\![s_{l-2}]\!]$. Revealing $[\![\hat{m}_0]\!]$ may disclose information about $[\![X]\!]$. Also, $[\![s]\!]_B$ is a uniformly random secret shared value, so $[\![m]\!]$ is also a uniformly random value and does not leak any information. As for complexity, $[\![s]\!]_B$ requires $2l$ multiplications and 2 rounds, given control over the selection of p. Computing $[\![\hat{m}_0]\!]$ and going from $[\![\hat{m}_0]\!]$ to $[\![X_0]\!]$ requires two multiplications in two sequential rounds. Overall, the protocol requires $2l + 2$ multiplications in 4 rounds.

3   The Sampling Technique

This section will present a sampling technique to generate a shared biased coin and a protocol for its implementation.

We assume the field size p is a Mersenne prime or a prime close to powers of two and $l = \lceil \log_2 p \rceil$, b denotes a coin with bias $\alpha \in (0,1)$ and α_B indicates the binary form of α, a public input to the protocol. The sampling technique consists of 3 steps. First, it generates l uniformly random shared bits $[\![r]\!]_b = ([\![r_{l-1}]\!], ..., [\![r_0]\!])$ using RAN_2. Second, it transforms the comparison $[\![r]\!]_b > \alpha_B$ into computing $[\![X]\!]$ such that $[\![X]\!] < 2^{\frac{l+1}{2}}$ and the least significant bit $[\![X_0]\!]$ of $[\![X]\!]$ is equivalent to the result of $[\![r]\!]_b > \alpha_B$ (further details in the next subsection). Lastly, it extracts $[\![X_0]\!]$ by the LSB protocol. Once this is done, $[\![\hat{b}]\!] = 1 - [\![X_0]\!]$ is the realization of coin b within the statistical difference at most 2^{-l} when $([\![r_{l-1}]\!], ..., [\![r_0]\!])$ are sampled uniformly from $\{0, 1\}$. Correctness of the sampling technique stems from the above discussion and Sect. 3.1. Privacy is assured by the underlying secret sharing scheme, with the fact that the only values revealed occur in the primitives, which have been considered in Sect. 2.2.

3.1   Computing $[\![X]\!]$

Let $[\![r]\!]_b$ and α_B be two l-bit values. The main idea for computing $[\![r]\!]_b > \alpha_B$ is to first compute a value $[\![x_i]\!]$ for each bit-position i as follows:

$$[\![x_i]\!] = [\![r_i]\!](1 - \alpha_i)2^{\sum_{j=i+1}^{l-1} \alpha_j \oplus [\![r_j]\!]}, \tag{1}$$

then extracting the least significant bit $[\![X_0]\!]$ from

$$[\![X]\!] = \sum_{i=0}^{l-1} [\![x_i]\!]. \tag{2}$$

The correctness of the above is given in the following theorem, which is heavily based on Theorem 1 in Reistad et al. [13].

Theorem 1. *Given l uniformly random shared bits $[\![r]\!]_b$ and a publicly known value α_B, $[\![\hat{b}]\!] = 1 - [\![X_0]\!]$ is a shared coin with bias α.*

Proof (sketch). $[\![x_i]\!]$ is either 0 or a distinct power of 2. $[\![x_i]\!] = 1$ occurs if and only if $[\![r_i]\!]$ is set and α_i is not set, and $\sum_{j=i-1}^{l-1} \alpha_j \oplus [\![r_j]\!] = 0$ (indicating that the bit-position i is the most significant differing bit position). Later, in computing $[\![X]\!]$, at most one $[\![x_i]\!]$ is odd when $[\![x_i]\!] = 1$, and it exists if $[\![r]\!]_b > \alpha_B$. Finally, $[\![\hat{b}]\!] = 1 - [\![X_0]\!]$ yields a shared coin with bias α. ☐

To compute $[\![x_i]\!]$'s, $2^{\sum_{j=i+1}^{l-1} \alpha_j \oplus [\![r_j]\!]}$ is performed for each bit-position i. This can be done by rewriting the exponentiation of Eq. (1) as,

$$\prod_{j=i+1}^{l-1} (1 + (\alpha_j \oplus [\![r_j]\!])), \tag{3}$$

which can be computed by the prefix product primitive of Sect. 2.2. The transformation from the exponentiation to the prefix product is possible as all terms $(1 + (\alpha_j \oplus [\![r_j]\!]))$ are invertible (they are either 1 or 2).

There is still an outstanding issue to address: as a result of Eq. (2) $[\![X]\!] < 2^{l-1}$, while to apply the LSB protocol, we assume $[\![X]\!] < 2^{\frac{l+1}{2}} < \sqrt{4p}$. To deal with this problem, Reistad et al. [13,14] outline an advanced version of the previously described method. While rooted in the original method, this extended technique differentiates itself by evaluating pairs of bit-positions rather than individual ones. Consequently, $[\![r_i]\!](1 - \alpha_i)$ will be altered such that $r_i > \alpha_i$ for 2 bits at a time, and $\alpha_j \oplus [\![r_j]\!]$ will only output 0 if both corresponding pairs of bits are equal. The advantage of this extended technique is twofold: it cuts the occurrences of $[\![x_i]\!]$ by half and ensures that $[\![X]\!] < 2^{\frac{l+1}{2}}$. This, in effect, substantially trims the number of multiplications in computing $[\![X]\!]$. We now elaborate on a variation of this extended technique, including an alternation relevant to our specific requirements.

Equation (4) is the two-bit version of Eq. (1). This is computed only for *odd* bit-positions $i < l$, with the assumption that l is *even*,

$$[\![x_i]\!] = [\![u_i]\!] 2^{\sum_{j=((i-1)/2)+1}^{(l/2)-1} (\alpha_{2j} \oplus [\![r_{2j}]\!]) \vee (\alpha_{2j+1} \oplus [\![r_{2j+1}]\!])}, \tag{4}$$

where

$$[\![u_i]\!] = [\![r_i]\!] \wedge (\neg \alpha_i) \vee (\neg(\alpha_i \oplus [\![r_i]\!])) \wedge [\![r_{i-1}]\!] \wedge (\neg \alpha_{i-1}). \tag{5}$$

Equation (5) is simply a comparison circuit for 2-bit numbers. This expression can be written in terms of arithmetic as follows,

$$[\![u_i]\!] = [\![r_i]\!](1 - \alpha_i) + (1 + 2\alpha_i [\![r_i]\!] - [\![r_i]\!] - \alpha_i)[\![r_{i-1}]\!](1 - \alpha_{i-1}). \tag{6}$$

Furthermore, the exponentiation of Eq. (4) can be written as,

$$[\![v_i]\!] = \prod_{j=((i-1)/2)+1}^{(l/2)-1} (1 + ([\![w_{2j}]\!] + [\![w_{2j+1}]\!] - [\![w_{2j}]\!][\![w_{2j+1}]\!])), \tag{7}$$

where $[\![w_{2j}]\!] = \alpha_{2j} \oplus [\![r_{2j}]\!]$, $[\![w_{2j+1}]\!] = \alpha_{2j+1} \oplus [\![r_{2j+1}]\!]$ and for the odd bit-position $i = l - 1$, we set $v_{l-1} = 1$. Finally, we can obtain the least significant bit $[\![X_0]\!]$ of

$$[\![X]\!] = \sum_{i=0}^{(l/2)-1} [\![x_{2i+1}]\!] = \sum_{i=0}^{(l/2)-2} [\![v_{2i+1}]\!][\![u_{2i+1}]\!] + v_{l-1}[\![u_{l-1}]\!]. \tag{8}$$

The complexity of computing $[\![X]\!]$ is $1.5l - 2$ multiplications in three rounds, plus $4(0.5l - 1)$ multiplications and two rounds for preparing the prefix product in Eq. (7) as it takes on $0.5l - 1$ inputs. Specifically, $0.5l$ multiplications are needed to compute the multiplications of Eq. (6) that can be parallelized in one round. These multiplications can be reused to calculate the terms of the prefix product in Eq. (7). Next, $0.5l - 1$ multiplications are required to mask the inputs of the prefix product in Eq. (7) (as explained in Sect. 2.2, the prefixes are locally computed by the parties without cost). Finally, $0.5l - 1$ multiplications are used to compute the multiplications of Eq. (8) that can be parallelized (in Eq. (8), v_{l-1} is publicly known, so $v_{l-1}[\![u_{l-1}]\!]$ can be considered costless). Privacy of computing $[\![X]\!]$ is trivial: information leaks when a value is revealed. This occurs only in the sub-protocols that have been accounted for.

To complete our discussion of the two-bit version of Eq. (1), we also consider the case where l is *odd*. For this, Eq.(9) is the two-bit version of Eq.(1), which is computed only for *even* bit-positions $i < l$,

$$[\![x_i]\!] = [\![u_i]\!] 2^{\sum_{j=(i/2)+1}^{(l-1)/2} (\alpha_{2j} \oplus [\![r_{2j}]\!]) \vee (\alpha_{2j-1} \oplus [\![r_{2j-1}]\!])}. \tag{9}$$

Then, Eqs.(6), (7) and (8) are replaced with Eqs. (10), (11) and (12), respectively, where

$$[\![u_i]\!] = \begin{cases} [\![r_i]\!](1 - \alpha_i) & i = 0, \\ [\![r_i]\!](1 - \alpha_i) + (1 + 2\alpha_i [\![r_i]\!] - [\![r_i]\!] - \alpha_i)[\![r_{i-1}]\!](1 - \alpha_{i-1}) & i = 2k, \end{cases} \tag{10}$$

Protocol 1. Sampling a coin with bias α

Inputs: α_B and $l = \lceil \log_2 p \rceil$.
Output: A shared coin $[\![\hat{b}]\!]$ with bias α.

1. The parties run RAN_2 to generate $[\![r_i]\!]$ for $i \in \{0, 1, ..., l-1\}$.
When l is *even*:
   2. The parties compute $[\![u_i]\!] = [\![r_i]\!](1-\alpha_i)+(1+2\alpha_i[\![r_i]\!]-[\![r_i]\!]-\alpha_i)[\![r_{i-1}]\!](1-\alpha_{i-1})$
     for $i = 2k+1, k \in \{0, 1, ... (l/2)-1\}$.
   3. The parties compute $[\![v_i]\!] = \prod_{j=((i-1)/2)+1}^{(l/2)-1}(1 + ((\alpha_{2j} \oplus [\![r_{2j}]\!]) + (\alpha_{2j+1} \oplus$
     $[\![r_{2j+1}]\!]) - (\alpha_{2j} \oplus [\![r_{2j}]\!])(\alpha_{2j+1} \oplus [\![r_{2j+1}]\!])))$ for $i = 2k+1, k \in \{0, 1, ..., (l/2)-2\}$,
     where $v_{l-1} = 1$.
   4. The parties compute $[\![x_i]\!] = [\![u_{2i+1}]\!][\![v_{2i+1}]\!]$ for $i \in \{0, 1, ..., (l/2)-2\}$, where
     $[\![x_{(l/2)-1}]\!] = v_{l-1}[\![u_{l-1}]\!]$.
   5. The parties locally compute $[\![X]\!] = \sum_{i=0}^{(l/2)-1}[\![x_i]\!]$.
When l is *odd*:
   2. The parties compute $[\![u_i]\!] = [\![r_i]\!](1-\alpha_i)+(1+2\alpha_i[\![r_i]\!]-[\![r_i]\!]-\alpha_i)[\![r_{i-1}]\!](1-\alpha_{i-1})$
     for $i = 2k, k \in \{1, ... ((l-1)/2)\}$, where $[\![u_0]\!] = [\![r_0]\!](1-\alpha_0)$.
   3. The parties compute $[\![v_i]\!] = \prod_{j=(i/2)+1}^{(l-1)/2}(1+((\alpha_{2j} \oplus [\![r_{2j}]\!]) + (\alpha_{2j-1} \oplus [\![r_{2j-1}]\!])-$
     $(\alpha_{2j} \oplus [\![r_{2j}]\!])(\alpha_{2j-1} \oplus [\![r_{2j-1}]\!])))$ for $i = 2k, k \in \{0, 1, ..., ((l-1)/2)-1\}$, where
     $v_{l-1} = 1$.
   4. The parties compute $[\![x_i]\!] = [\![u_{2i}]\!][\![v_{2i}]\!]$ for $i \in \{0, 1, ..., ((l-1)/2)-1\}$, where
     $[\![x_{(l-1)/2}]\!] = v_{l-1}[\![u_{l-1}]\!]$.
   5. The parties locally compute $[\![X]\!] = \sum_{i=0}^{(l-1)/2}[\![x_i]\!]$.
6. The parties run LSB with input $[\![X]\!]$ and obtain $[\![X_0]\!]$.
7. The parties locally compute $[\![\hat{b}]\!] = 1 - [\![X_0]\!]$ and output $[\![\hat{b}]\!]$.

$k \in \{1, 2, ... (l-1)/2\}$, and

$$[\![v_i]\!] = \prod_{j=(i/2)+1}^{(l-1)/2} (1 + ([\![w_{2j}]\!] + [\![w_{2j-1}]\!] - [\![w_{2j}]\!][\![w_{2j-1}]\!])), \qquad (11)$$

where $[\![w_{2j}]\!] = \alpha_{2j} \oplus [\![r_{2j}]\!]$, $[\![w_{2j-1}]\!] = \alpha_{2j-1} \oplus [\![r_{2j-1}]\!]$ and for the even bit-position $i = l - 1$, we set $v_{l-1} = 1$. Finally,

$$[\![X]\!] = \sum_{i=0}^{(l-1)/2}[\![x_{2i}]\!] = \sum_{i=0}^{((l-1)/2)-1}[\![v_{2i}]\!][\![u_{2i}]\!] + v_{l-1}[\![u_{l-1}]\!]. \qquad (12)$$

The complexity of computing $[\![X]\!]$ involves $1.5(l-1)$ multiplications in three rounds, plus $4(0.5(l-1))$ multiplications and two rounds for preparing the prefix product in Eq. (11) as it takes on $(0.5(l-1))$ inputs. Specifically, $0.5(l-1)$ multiplications are used to compute the multiplications of Eq. (10) that can be parallelized in one round. Later, $0.5(l-1)$ multiplications are required to mask the inputs of the prefix product in Eq. (11) in one round. Finally, $0.5(l-1)$ multiplications are needed to compute the multiplications of Eq. (12) that can be parallelized in one round.

3.2   The Protocol and Overall Complexity Analysis

Protocol 1 serves to implement the sampling technique. It uses sub-protocols to generate random bits (RAN_2), to compute prefix product, and to extract the least significant bit (LSB) from Sect. 2.2.

As for complexity, we can generate $[\![s]\!]_B$ (needed for the LSB protocol) using $2l$ multiplications in parallel with generating $[\![r]\!]_b$ using $2l$ multiplications in the first two rounds. Preparing for the prefix product costs $2l - 4$ (when l is even) or $2l - 2$ (when l is odd) multiplications which can also be parallel with previous computations. Next, we can compute $[\![X]\!]$ using $1.5l - 2$ (when l is even) or $1.5(l - 1)$ (when l is odd) multiplications in 3 rounds. Finally, $[\![X_0]\!]$ can be computed using 2 multiplications applying the LSB protocol in 2 rounds. Overall, $7.5l - 4$ (when l is even) or $7.5l - 1.5$ (when l is odd) multiplications in 7 rounds are required to generate one shared coin with bias α using the sampling technique, assuming control over the choice of p.

4   Comparison

This section will compare the biased coin protocol presented by Eriguchi et al. [4] with our proposed protocol. Eriguchi et al.'s protocol generates l uniformly random shared bits by combining the parties' local random bits using $5nl$ multiplications. We refer to this method as RandBits 1. Another technique for this, RandBits 2 (discussed in Sect. 2.2), generates l uniformly random shared bits by performing l simultaneous invocations of RAN_2, resulting in a total cost of $2l$ multiplications. Recall that this technique may fail with a p^{-l} probability. Using RandBits 1, Eriguchi et al.'s protocol can be implemented with $(5n + 19)l$ multiplications [4] and 11 rounds [16], whereas RandBits 2 enables the implementation using $20l$ multiplications and 10 rounds.

Table 1 compares the complexity of our solution to that of Eriguchi et al. [4], assuming that both protocols use RandBits 2.

Table 1. Complexity of biased coin protocols using RandBits 2

Presented in	Rounds	Multiplications		Statistical diff.	Security
[4]	10	$20l$		2^{-l}	Unconditional
This paper	7	l is even $7.5l - 4$	l is odd $7.5l - 1.5$	2^{-l}	Unconditional

"This paper" refers to the presented protocol in this paper. This protocol requires fewer multiplications and rounds than the previous solution [4]. To generate one biased coin, this protocol needs approximately 3/8 and 7/10 of the multiplications and rounds used in [4]. For our protocol, the field size must be chosen as a Mersenne prime or other primes close to powers of two. Although Mersenne primes become sparse for larger values, using them works for smaller values of l (i.e., $l \in [60, 520]$), commonly used in practice [5]. Moreover, other primes close to powers of two also yield satisfactory results [8]. Both protocols provide the same security guarantee against passive adversaries and can similarly be extended to handle stronger adversary models. Furthermore, both protocols have a failure probability on the order of p^{-1}, attributed to using RandBits 2 and the inversion technique. However, this failure probability can be deemed negligible by selecting a sufficiently large p.

Unbiased coins $[\![r]\!]_b = ([\![r_{l-1}]\!], ..., [\![r_0]\!])$ can be generated using RandBits 1, eliminating the RandBits 2 failure probability. Even with this modification, our protocol requires fewer multiplications and rounds than Eriguchi et al.'s protocol, as shown in Table 2, assuming both protocols use RandBits 1 for n parties. To use RandBits 1, each party must distribute shares for her l inputs. In the complexity analysis of our protocol in Table 2, following Eriguchi et al., we equate the complexity of this step to l parallel multiplications in one round.

Table 2. Complexity of biased coin protocols using RandBits 1

Presented in	Rounds	Multiplications		Statistical diff.	Security
[4]	11	$(5n + 19)l$		2^{-l}	Unconditional
This paper	8	l is even $(5n + 6.5)l - 4$	l is odd $(5n - 6.5)l - 1.5$	2^{-l}	Unconditional

Incorporating our biased coin protocol into Eriguchi et al.'s protocol for generating symmetric geometric noise significantly reduces communication complexity. With $p = 2^{61} - 1$ and $N = 75$, using our protocol requires about half as many multiplications as the original. To fairly compare, we assumed both protocols used RandBits 2 and $n = 3$ for this example. Even using RandBits 1, using our protocol results in roughly 1.6 times fewer multiplications.

5   Summary

This paper has presented an efficient, unconditionally secure MPC protocol for sampling a biased coin in shares. The main idea of the sampling process is to take a public bias in bits as an input, generate a stream of random bits, and then transform the comparison of these two to the extraction of the least significant bit of a secret shared value as a shared biased coin. The complexity of our protocol is $7.5l - 4$ (when l is even) or $7.5l - 1.5$ (when l is odd) invocations of the multiplication protocol carried out in 7 rounds, assuming control over the selection of the underlying field size. The provided protocol represents progress by requiring fewer multiplication protocol invocations and rounds than the solutions by Eriguchi et al. [4]. This progress is important as the protocol is fundamental in constructing secure MPC for differentially private mechanisms.

References

1. Dwork, C., Roth, A.: The algorithmic foundations of differential privacy. Foundations and Trends® in Theoretical Computer Science, vol. 9, pp. 211–407 (2014). https://doi.org/10.1561/0400000042
2. Duchi, J.C., Jordan, M.I., Wainwright, M.J.: Local privacy and statistical minimax Rates. In: IEEE 54th Annual Symposium on Foundations of Computer Science, pp. 429–438 (2013). https://doi.org/10.1109/FOCS.2013.53
3. Dwork, C., Kenthapadi, K., McSherry, F., Mironov, I., Naor, M.: Our data, ourselves: privacy via distributed noise generation. In: Vaudenay, S. (ed.) EUROCRYPT 2006. LNCS, vol. 4004, pp. 486–503. Springer, Heidelberg (2006). https://doi.org/10.1007/11761679_29
4. Eriguchi, R., Ichikawa, A., Kunihiro, N., Nuida, K.: Efficient noise generation to achieve differential privacy with applications to secure multiparty computation. In: Borisov, N., Diaz, C. (eds.) FC 2021. LNCS, vol. 12674, pp. 271–290. Springer, Heidelberg (2021). https://doi.org/10.1007/978-3-662-64322-8_13
5. Clement, C., Kamath, G., Steinke, T.: The discrete gaussian for differential privacy. J. Priv. Confidentiality 12 (2022). https://doi.org/10.29012/jpc.784
6. Differential Privacy Team Google: Secure Noise Generation (2020). https://github.com/google/differential-privacy/blob/main/common_docs/Secure_Noise_Generation.pdf
7. Schoenmakers, B., Tuyls, P.: Efficient binary conversion for paillier encrypted values. In: Vaudenay, S. (ed.) EUROCRYPT 2006. LNCS, vol. 4004, pp. 522–537. Springer, Heidelberg (2006). https://doi.org/10.1007/11761670_31
8. Damgård, I., Fitzi, M., Kiltz, E., Nielsen, J.B., Toft, T.: Unconditionally secure constant-rounds multi-party computation for equality, comparison, bits and exponentiation. In: Halevi, S., Rabin, T. (eds.) TCC 2006. LNCS, vol. 3876, pp. 285–304. Springer, Heidelberg (2006). https://doi.org/10.1007/11681878_15
9. Shamir, A.: How to share a secret. Commun. ACM 22, 612–613 (1979)
10. Ben-Or M., Goldwasser S., Wigderson, A.: Completeness theorems for noncryptographic fault-tolerant distributed computations. In: Proceedings of the Twentieth Annual ACM Symposium on Theory of Computing, pp. 1–10. ACM Press, New York (1988). https://doi.org/10.1145/62212.62213
11. Damgård, I., Nielsen, J.B.: Universally composable efficient multiparty computation from threshold homomorphic encryption. In: Boneh, D. (ed.) CRYPTO 2003. LNCS, vol. 2729, pp. 247–264. Springer, Berlin, Heidelberg (2003). https://doi.org/10.1007/978-3-540-45146-4_15
12. Reistad, T.I., Toft, T.: Secret sharing comparison by transformation and rotation. In: Desmedt, Y. (ed.) ICITS 2007. LNCS, vol. 4883, pp. 169–180. Springer, Heidelberg (2009). https://doi.org/10.1007/978-3-642-10230-1_14
13. Reistad, T.I.: Multiparty comparison-an improved multiparty protocol for comparison of secret-shared values. In: SCITEPRESS 2009, vol. 1, pp. 325–330 (2009)
14. Reistad, T.I., Toft, T.: Linear, constant-rounds bit-decomposition. In: Lee, D., Hong, S. (eds.) ICISC 2009. LNCS, vol. 5984, pp. 245–257. Springer, Heidelberg (2010). https://doi.org/10.1007/978-3-642-14423-3_17
15. Toft, T.: Constant-rounds, almost-linear bit-decomposition of secret shared values. In: Fischlin, M. (ed.) CT-RSA 2009. LNCS, vol. 5473, pp. 357–371. Springer, Heidelberg (2009). https://doi.org/10.1007/978-3-642-00862-7_24
16. Eriguchi, R., Ichikawa, A., Kunihiro, N., Nuida, K.: Efficient noise generation protocols for differentially private multiparty computation. IEEE Trans. Dependable Secure Comput. 01, 1–16 (2022). https://doi.org/10.1109/TDSC.2022.3227568

CBT 2023

Foreword from the CBT 2023 Program Chairs

This volume contains the proceedings of the 7th International Workshop on Cryptocurrencies and Blockchain Technology (CBT 2023), which was organized within the satellite activities of the 28th European Symposium on Research in Computer Security (ESORICS 2023), which took place in The Hague, The Netherlands, from the 25th to the 29th of September, 2023.

The CBT workshop started in 2017 with the aim of providing a forum for researchers with a specific focus on the use of cryptocurrencies and blockchain technologies in areas such as the identification and tracking of distributed autonomous organizations. Papers published in previous venues carefully analyzed current issues in such domains and proposed scientific updates to consolidate security and privacy in the blockchain research area.

In response to the call for papers, CBT 2023 received 18 submissions. All the submissions were carefully reviewed by the 32 members of the program committee and with the help of some additional reviewers. All submissions were evaluated based on their significance, novelty, and technical quality. Based on the reviews and the online discussion phase, six papers were accepted for presentation at the workshop.

As in the previous years, the CBT workshop was held in conjunction with the Data Privacy Management (DPM) workshop. The program was complemented with an invited keynote by Michal Choras from the Bydgoszcz University of Science and Technology, complementing as well the program of the 18th DPM Workshop on Data Privacy Management (DPM 2023), the 9th CyberICPS Workshop on the Security of Industrial Control Systems & of Cyber-Physical Systems (CyberICPS 2023), and the 7th Workshop on SECurity and Privacy Requirements Engineering (SECPRE 2023). The keynote of Prof. Choras contributed to establish synergies and a great atmosphere between the workshops' attendees. This was also materialized with an important novelty with respect to past editions of the CBT post-proceedings, which are now in a joint volume with other ESORICS workshops. Having a joint proceedings volume with all the workshops has been seen as a beneficial way to gain more relevance and presence in our community, which shall also contribute to more stable and consistent publication of future ESORICS workshops.

The organization of CBT 2023 was made possible through the support received from Institut Polytechnique de Paris (Télécom SudParis and the SAMOVAR laboratory), the BART initiative (supported by Inria, SystemX, and Institut Mines-Télécom), volunteers from TU Delft and the University of Murcia. Special thanks go to the Spanish Ministry of Universities linked to the European Union through the NextGenerationEU program under the Margarita Salas postdoctoral fellowship program (172/MSJD/22). We would like to thank all the authors who submitted papers to the workshop, as well as all the workshop attendees and all the people involved in the organization of CBT 2023. Then, we are grateful to the Program Committee members and the external reviewers for their help in providing detailed and timely reviews of the submissions. Our gratitude goes as well to Kaitai Liang and Georgios Smaragdakis, General chairs of ESORICS 2023, Jérémie Decouchant and Stjepan Picek, Workshop chairs of ESORICS 2023, and all the ESORICS 2023 local organization volunteers, for all their help and support. Last but by no means least, we also thank Springer and Ronan Nugent for their presence at the event and all their support throughout the entire publication process.

October 2023

Pantaleone Nespoli
Joaquin Garcia-Alfaro

7th International Workshop on Cryptocurrencies and Blockchain Technology – CBT 2023

PC Chairs

Joaquin Garcia-Alfaro   Institut Polytechnique de Paris, France
Pantaleone Nespoli   Universidad de Murcia, Spain

Program Committee

Lennart Ante	Blockchain Research Lab, Germany
Daniel Augot	Inria Saclay, France
Artem Barger	IBM Research, Israel
Alex Biryukov	University of Luxembourg, Luxembourg
Rainer Böhme	Universität Innsbruck, Austria
James Chiang	Technical University of Denmark, Denmark
Jeremy Clark	Concordia University, Canada
Mauro Conti	University of Padua, Italy
Vanesa Daza	Universitat Pompeu Fabra, Spain
Nour El-Madhoun	EPITA Engineering School, France
Kaoutar Elkhiyaoui	EURECOM, France
Joshua Ellul	University of Malta, Malta
Paula Fraga	University of A Coruna, Spain
Victor Garcia	Universitat Oberta de Catalunya, Spain
Hannes Hartenstein	Karlsruher Institut für Technologie, Germany
Jordi Herrera-Joancomarti	Universitat Autonoma de Barcelona, Spain
Jiasun Li	George Mason University, USA
Daniel-Xiapu Luo	Hong Kong Polytechnic University, China
Shin'ichiro Matsuo	Georgetown University, USA
Darya Melnyk	Aalto University, Finland
Jose Luis Muñoz-Tapia	Universitat Politècnica de Catalunya, Spain
Guillermo Navarro-Arribas	Universitat Autònoma de Barcelona, Spain
Dongming Peng	University of Nebraska-Lincoln, USA
Cristina Pérez-Solà	Universitat Oberta de Catalunya, Spain
Motoyoshi Sekiya	Fujitsu Limited, USA
Matteo Signorini	Nokia Bell Labs, France
Weidong Shi	University of Houston, USA
Hitesh Tewari	Trinity College Dublin, Ireland

Florian Tschorsch	Technische Universität Berlin, Germany
Eirini Tsiropoulou	University of New Mexico, USA
Dimitrios Vasilopoulos	IMDEA Software Institute, Spain
Edgar Weippl	SBA Research, Austria

Steering Committee

Rainer Böhm	Universität Innsbruck, Austria
Joaquin Garcia-Alfaro	Intitut Polytechnique de Paris, France
Hannes Hartenstein	Karlsruher Institut für Technologie, Germany
Jordi Herrera-Joancomartí	Universitat Autònoma de Barcelona, Spain

Additional Reviewers

Marc Guzmán-Albiol	Universitat Politècnica de Catalunya, Spain
Oliver Stengele	Karlsruher Institut für Technologie, Germany
Rafael Genés-Durán	Universitat Politècnica de Catalunya, Spain
Vinod P. Nair	University of Padua, Italy
Matthias Grundmann	Karlsruher Institut für Technologie, Germany
Ankit Gangwal	University of Padua, Italy

Transaction Fee Mechanism for Order-Sensitive Blockchain-Based Applications

Mohammad Sadegh Nourbakhsh$^{(\boxtimes)}$ ⓘ, Feng Hao ⓘ, and Arshad Jhumka ⓘ

University of Warwick, Coventry, UK
{Mohammad-Sadegh.Nourbakhsh,feng.hao,H.A.Jhumka}@warwick.ac.uk

Abstract. Demand for blockchains such as Bitcoin and Ethereum far exceeds supply, thereby requiring a selection mechanism that, from a transaction pool, chooses a subset of transactions to be included "on-chain". Historically, every transaction submitted to the pool is associated with a bid (in the blockchain's native currency). A miner then decides which set of transactions from the pool should be included in a block. When the block is published, the bid of each included transaction is transferred from its creator to the miner. However, in newer applications such as *decentralised finance (DeFi)*, transaction inclusion in a block is no longer sufficient. In fact, the order in which the transaction is executed is of paramount importance. While research exists on mitigating transaction ordering manipulations, there is a lack of work on transaction fee mechanisms (TFMs) that are order-robust. This paper investigates order-robust TFMs from a mechanism design perspective and shows several impossibility results. For instance, we demonstrate that the recent EIP-1559 TFM is not incentive-compatible for order-sensitive transactions. On the other hand, we present and prove a necessary condition for an order-robust TFM.

Keywords: Blockchain · Transaction fee mechanism · Ordering · Incentive compatibility · Utility maximization

1 Introduction

Blockchain and distributed ledger technologies (DLT) have gained immense popularity since the development of Bitcoin in 2009 [10]. These technologies offer an open, distributed, trustless, and tamper-resistant ledger that serves as the foundation for a new generation of financial services. Beyond facilitating transactions, blockchain enables the design and deployment of complex financial services and tools through smart contracts, particularly on platforms like Ethereum. The market capacity of blockchain technology reached a record-breaking 3 trillion dollars in November 2021 [1].

Ordering is a crucial aspect of traditional financial markets, and its significance extends to blockchain-based financial services. In these services, the order of transactions holds equal importance and can significantly impact users' profitability. To illustrate the transaction ordering problem, we present the following use case:

Example 1 (Eggs in sandwich shop).   In a small town with limited egg availability, a sandwich shop operates by buying eggs from suppliers at the same price they sell them. The price of sandwiches containing eggs fluctuates based on the quantity of remaining eggs. Customers place orders on-site, and there is a maximum queue size at the shop, with the owner deciding which subset of customers can enter when the queue exceeds its capacity. In this scenario, Alice desires an omelette, Rachel wants a hotdog, Kevin orders a tuna sandwich, and Bob requests an egg mayo sandwich. Charlie is the supplier of eggs to the shop. Assuming all customers can stand in line, the order in which they join the queue becomes significant because the price of their sandwiches is influenced by the number of remaining eggs. For instance, if Charlie sells his eggs before Alice and Bob, he will receive a lower payment compared to selling them after the customers who specifically desire eggs. Likewise, if Alice stands behind Bob in the queue, she will pay a higher price for her sandwich compared to if she stands before Kevin. The positions of Kevin and Rachel in the queue are inconsequential as the prices of their sandwiches are unaffected by the number of remaining eggs.

Ordering's impact on users' outcomes can lead them to strategically execute transactions before or after a specific set of transactions in order to maximize their profits or utility. In traditional finance, front-running involves leveraging early access to market information for personal gain [6]. Similarly, in the blockchain system, front-running refers to submitting a transaction that is executed ahead of certain pending transactions, while back-running involves submitting a transaction to be executed after a particular set of transactions. These actions can introduce instability in order-sensitive blockchain applications.

Unlike traditional finance, where front-running typically requires exclusive and sometimes illicit access to stock data, the transparent nature of blockchain allows anyone to observe recently mined transactions and monitor the mempool, which serves as a shared buffer for transactions awaiting inclusion in blocks. This transparency creates opportunities for front-running, and the potential profitability of such opportunities attracts various users to the blockchain ecosystem.

Users exploit reordering opportunities to increase profits, resulting in competitive priority gas auctions (PGA) and higher transaction fees [5]. The mempool becomes a vulnerable space where reordering attacks can occur, known as the "dark forest" [12]. However, PGAs can negatively impact blockchain throughput and transaction fees for other transactions in blocks.

Our research primarily centres on Nakamoto-style consensus blockchain systems, wherein a randomly chosen miner is tasked with selecting and ordering transactions within each block. Consequently, we examine the incentives of agents, including both users and miners, at the block-level timescale. While it is conceivable for a group of agents to collude and employ sophisticated order manipulation strategies, the likelihood of such collusion is relatively low, mainly due to the random selection of miners for each block.

Miners in blockchain systems are incentivized through block rewards and transaction fees to maintain the blockchain's security. Various mechanisms have been proposed for transaction allocation and payment methods to miners since the emergence of Bitcoin. These mechanisms fall under the Transaction Fee Mechanism (TFM), which determines user fees for block inclusion and miners' rewards for transaction allocation. However, existing TFMs are mainly tailored for cryptocurrency systems like Bitcoin that overlook the significance of transaction order in blockchain applications such as *decentralized finance* (DeFi). As a result, there are currently no TFMs specifically designed to address the needs of order-sensitive blockchain applications used in financial services.

This paper introduces a generalized model for TFM analysis that incorporates the impact of transaction ordering on agents' utilities. Currently, there is no existing TFM model that accounts for the state of transactions within a block. Our novel model is general enough to allow formalization and analysis of existing TFMs, helping to establish correctness conditions based on incentive compatibility. By applying this framework, we prove that the current TFM in Ethereum, namely *EIP-1559*, is not user incentive-compatible (UIC) for order-sensitive blockchain-based applications. Additionally, we prove that there is no deterministic TFM that satisfies both off-chain agreement proof and UIC. On the positive side, we identify a necessary condition for a TFM to be UIC.

2 Related Works

The TFM holds a pivotal role in blockchain systems, defining transaction costs and network security. Initially, the prevalent TFM in Bitcoin and Ethereum was the first price auction (FPA) [10]. However, Ethereum shifted to a posted-price TFM [15].

Prior TFM research mainly concentrated on the Bitcoin blockchain. Lavi et al. proposal [7] introduced a monopolistic auction for the Bitcoin TFM, where users in a block pay the minimum bid. However, it was shown by Andrew et al. [19] that in this auction, strategic bidding leads to zero revenue as users increase. Another TFM by Lavi et al. [7] is the Random Sampling Optimal Price (RSOP), addressing the user incentive compatibility (UIC) issue, but not myopic miner incentive compatible (MMIC).

To transcend TFM limitations, Basu et al. proposed a generalized second price auction-based TFM [3] aiming for UIC. This TFM is not MMIC, but as users increase, deviation revenue converges to zero. Moreover, Basu et al. [2] proposed Stablefees, an alternative TFM grounded in the second price auction. In a different vein, Chung et al.'s burning second price auction [4] confirms a random set of transactions in a block.

EIP-1559 marks a significant departure from the FPA and serves as the pioneering TFM implemented in a large-scale blockchain system. Comparative analyses have extensively examined the features of EIP-1559 in relation to FPA and other potential TFMs for Ethereum [14]. Furthermore, research has focused on assessing the stability of EIP-1559 and the influence of its base fee [8,13]. Empirical studies have been conducted to investigate transaction fees, consensus security, and the impact of EIP-1559 on the Ethereum blockchain ecosystem [9]. Although EIP-1559 has introduced positive attributes such as predictable fees and enhanced user experience, it has overlooked the impact of transaction ordering on agents' utilities. Notably, empirical evidence reveals that the extraction of miner extractable value (MEV) remains unaffected following the implementation of EIP-1559 [9].

Despite the efforts to improve TFMs, none of the proposed mechanisms has considered the effect of transaction orders on users' revenue by assuming a constant value for a transaction.

Several research papers in the field of blockchain systems have tackled the issue of order manipulation, considering it a problem in the context of changing transaction orders. For instance, [6] introduced the concept of front-running in blockchain systems and provided insights into the front-running behaviour exhibited by miners within the Ethereum blockchain.

The emergence of users actively seeking front-running opportunities has led to the rise of a competitive phenomenon known as the priority gas auction (PGA) within blockchain systems [5]. Additionally, the concept of miner-extractable value (MEV) is introduced by Daian et al. [5], which quantifies the potential profit that miners can obtain by manipulating the order of transactions in the blockchain. To assess the extent of extracted value within the Ethereum blockchain, empirical studies have been conducted [12,17].

Exclusive mining services have emerged as a response to the challenges posed by order manipulation and MEV extraction in blockchain systems [16]. These services involve collusion between users and a specific miner, where users transmit their transactions directly to the service through a private channel instead of broadcasting them across the network. However, recent research has revealed that exclusive mining services not only facilitate the extraction of MEV but also provide significant benefits to the participating miners, amplifying their advantage in order manipulation and MEV extraction [11].

3   System Model

In this paper, we consider the blockchain system as responsible for maintaining the current state and executing a precisely ordered sequence of transactions that both read from and modify this state. There are four main components in the process, namely (i) users, (ii) miners, (iii) mempool and (iv) blockchain.

Users: Users are represented as agents responsible for generating transactions to be executed within the blockchain system. Each user is identified by a unique label c_i, ranging from 1 to N. Transactions generated by user c_i are denoted as tx_i and can encompass various actions such as buying stocks or selling shares.

Mempool: The mempool in the blockchain serves as a buffer where verified transactions are stored. When a transaction is generated by a user, it undergoes verification and is then added to the mempool. We assume that each user has at most one transaction in the mempool at any given time. Hence, a transaction tx_i generated by user c_i is represented as a 3-tuple: $\langle b_i, g_i, v_i \rangle$, where:

- b_i denotes the bid per unit size, indicating the amount the user c_i is willing to pay for executing the transaction.
- g_i represents the visible size of the transaction.
- v_i corresponds to the valuation of the transaction, indicating the maximum value that user c_i is willing to pay for the execution of tx_i. It is also referred to as the private value of the transaction.

We will revisit this transaction model when considering transaction ordering.

Miners: Miners select a subset of verified transactions from the mempool to form a block, which has a maximum size denoted by G. The transactions within the block are executed in the specified order, leading to updates in the blockchain's state.

When a block is added to the blockchain, the miner receives a payment determined by the bids associated with each transaction in the block. Therefore, we assume that miners are rational and will select transactions in a manner that maximizes their payment.

Blockchain: A blockchain is a sequence of blocks denoted as $B_1, B_2, \ldots, B_{k-1}$, with the initial block called the *genesis* block (B_1). The current block being added to the blockchain is B_k, and the entire block history is denoted as H.

4   Background

In this section, we provide a brief overview of the TFMs from an unordered set of transactions in a block. TFM models proposed by [4,15] focused on the allocation of transactions to the block. Historically, a TFM is formalized as a 3-tuple of rules: (i) Allocation rule, (ii) payment and (iii) miner revenue rule.

Definition 1 (Allocation rule). *The allocation rule is a function x from the on-chain history H and mempool M to a binary value $x_i(H, M)$ for each pending transaction $tx_i \in M$. $x_i(H, M) = 1$ means that transaction tx_i is allocated to the current block B_k.*

A trivial allocation will be to allocate all transactions to a block. However, this may exceed the maximum permissible size of a block (G). Thus, we have the notion of a feasible allocation.

Definition 2 (Feasible allocation rule). *An allocation rule is feasible if, for every possible history H and mempool M:*

$$\sum_{tx_i \in M} g_i \cdot x_i(H, M) \leq G \tag{1}$$

where G is the maximum permissible size of a block.

A feasible allocation rule is responsible for assigning transactions to a block while respecting the maximum block size. The payment rule determines how transaction fees are transferred when a transaction is added to the blockchain.

Definition 3 (Payment rule). *A payment rule is a function p from the on-chain history H and allocated transactions in B_k to a non-negative number $p_i(H, B_k)$ for each transaction tx_i in B_k.*

$p_i(H, B_k)$ indicates the cost (per unit size) of allocating tx_i in block B_k that user c_i should pay.

Definition 4 (Miner revenue rule). *A miner revenue rule is a function Mr from the on-chain history H and allocated transactions in B_k to a non-negative number $Mr_i(H, B_k)$ for each transaction tx_i in B_k.*

$Mr_i(H, B_k)$ indicates the price (per unit size) of allocating tx_i in block B_k for the miner.

Definition 5 (Transaction fee mechanism (TFM)). *A transaction fee mechanism (TFM) is a triple (x, p, Mr) in which x is a feasible allocation rule, p is a payment rule, and Mr is a miner revenue rule.*

The definitions provided earlier assume a constant value for transactions in a block, regardless of their order. However, in decentralized financial systems such as decentralized exchanges, the order of transactions within a block can greatly affect the utility and profit of users. To address this, a new model is needed that takes into account the impact of transaction ordering on agent utilities.

5   Theory

In this section, we now revisit some previous definitions in the context of transactions (re)ordering in a block.

5.1   Order Oriented Private Value

Previous studies on TFMs have often assumed that a user's valuation of a transaction remains constant once it is included in a block. However, this assumption may not hold true for order-sensitive applications like DeFi. To address this, we introduce the concepts of order-robustness and order-sensitivity, which classify transactions based on whether their valuation depends on the presence and order of other transactions in the block.

Definition 6 (T-order robust transaction). *Transaction tx_i is order-robust in sequence T if, changing tx_i's position in the sequence T without changing $T \backslash \{tx_i\}$, the private value of tx_i remains constant, i.e., $T = T_p \cdot tx_i \cdot T_s$ and $T' = T_{p'} \cdot tx_i \cdot T_{s'}$, where $(T = T' \wedge T_p \neq T_{p'} \wedge T_s \neq T_{s'})$, the valuation of tx_i in T is the same as in T'.*

Remark 1. If tx_i is T-order robust, tx_i is T'-order robust, for every $T' \sqsubseteq T$, where $\sqsubseteq$ denotes subsequence.

We denote the set of all possible sequences of a set X by $\bar{X}$.

Definition 7 (Order-robust transaction). *Given a set of transactions in block B_k, a transaction $tx_i \in B_k$ is said to be order-robust in B_k if it is T-order robust for every possible sequence T of the transactions in B_k, i.e., $\forall\, T \in \bar{B}_k$, tx_i is T-order robust.*

Definition 8 (Order-sensitive transaction). *A transaction $tx_i \in B_k$ is said to be order-sensitive in a transactions block B_k if tx_i is not order-robust in B_k.*

Definition 9 (Biggest order-sensitive subsequence (BOS)). *The biggest order-sensitive subsequence of a transaction tx_i (BOS_i) is the biggest subsequence $T \sqsubseteq \bar{B}_k$ such that removing each $tx_j \in T$ changes tx_i's private value.*

Example 2. In the sandwich shop Example 1, assume the maximum queue size is 3 and Alice's transaction tx_A (omelette):

- Given $B_k = \{Alice, Rachel, Kevin\}$, tx_A is T-order-robust in the sequence $T = \langle Rachel, Alice, Kevin \rangle$ as the private value of tx_A is constant in every place in $T \backslash \{Alice\} = \{Rachel, Kevin\}$.

- Given $B_k = \{Alice, Rachel, Bob\}$, tx_A is order-sensitive as there exists $T' = \langle Rachel, Bob, Alice \rangle$, tx_A is not T'-order-robust & $BOS_A = \{Bob\}$ in T'.

- Kevin's transaction tx_K is order-robust in $(B_K \subseteq \{Alice, Bob, Charlie, Kevin, Rachel\} \wedge |B_k| = 3 \wedge tx_K \in B_k)$, as it is T-order robust for every possible $T \sqsubseteq \bar{B}_k$.

Definition 10 (Sensitive mempool). *We say that a mempool $\mathcal{M}$ is a sensitive mempool if there is at least one order-sensitive transaction in the mempool $\mathcal{M}$, i.e., $\exists B_k \subseteq \mathcal{M}, \exists tx_i \in B_k$ such that tx_i is order-sensitive in B_k.*

5.2   Generalized TFM Modelling

A TFM is a crucial component of the blockchain protocol that determines which transactions are included in a block and their order within the block. It also specifies the transaction fees users need to pay for inclusion and the revenue received by the miner. To capture the impact of transaction ordering, we modify the TFM by introducing a *placement* rule, which considers the order of transactions. The placement rule serves as an allocation rule that incorporates transaction order. Placement rule captures the effect of the order of transactions in a block. For the same subset of transactions, different placement sequences may have different outcomes for both users (with order-sensitive transactions) and the miner. Additionally, we generalize the payment rule and miner revenue rule to account for transaction orders. The modified rules are as follows:

Definition 11 (Placement rule). *The placement rule is a function X from the on-chain history H and mempool M to a binary vector $X_i(H, M)$ for each pending transaction $tx_i \in M$.*

- $X_i(H, M)[s]$ *indicates the value of the placement vector $X_i(H, M)$ for the order s. $X_i(H, M)[s] = 1$ if tx_i is found in order s in B_k, 0 otherwise.*
- *We denote by s_i, the rank of transaction tx_i in the block B_k, i.e., $X_i(H, M)[s_i] = 1$. If tx_i is not in the block, then $s_i = 0$ and $X_i(H, M)[s_i] = 0$.*
- *$X(H, M)$ is the placement matrix such that each row is a placement vector of a transaction in the mempool.*

$$X(H, M) = \begin{bmatrix} \cdots \\ \cdots \\ \cdots \\ X_i(H, M) \\ \cdots \\ \cdots \end{bmatrix}$$

- *Block B_k is then given as:*

$$B_k = X^T \cdot M \tag{2}$$

However, the placement rule may attempt to place a transaction in more than one place. Thus, we need to constrain the placement rule, to give rise to a feasible placement rule.

Definition 12 (Feasible placement rule). *A placement rule is feasible if, for every possible history H and mempool M:*

1. The placement rule should place each transaction tx_i in at most one place.

$$\forall tx_i \in M : \sum_{\forall s} X_i(H, M)[s] \leq 1 \tag{3}$$

2. The placement rule should assign each place in the block sequence to one transaction. Denoting the number of transactions in B_k by S, none of the places before S should remain empty, i.e., all ranks are allocated.

$$\forall j, 1 \leq j \leq S, \exists tx_k \in M \cdot X_k[H, M][j] = 1 \tag{4}$$

3. Two transactions cannot have the same rank in the block.

$$\forall tx_i, tx_j \in B_k, i \neq j \cdot s_i \neq s_j. \tag{5}$$

4. The placement rule should place transactions in a block with a cumulative size smaller or equal to the size of the block.

$$\sum_{tx_i \in M} g_i \cdot x_i(H, M)[s_i] \leq G \tag{6}$$

While a placement rule is proposed by a TFM, miners still have complete control over the placement of transactions in the block.

Definition 13 (Payment rule). *A payment rule is a function P from the on-chain history H and ordered transactions in B_k through the placement matrix X, to a non-negative number $P_i(H, B_k, X)$ for each transaction tx_i in order s_i of B_k.*

$P_i(H, B_k, X)$ *indicates the cost (per unit size) of an included transaction tx_i through placement matrix X in block B_k that user i should pay.*

Definition 14 (Miner revenue rule). *A miner revenue rule is a function Mr from the on-chain history H and placed transactions, through a feasible placement rule, in B_k to a non-negative number $mr_i(H, B_k, X)$ for each transaction tx_i with placement vector x_i in B_k. $mr_i(H, B_k, x_i)$ indicates the prize (per unit) of placing tx_i in order s_i of block B_k for the miner.*

Example 3 (Payment and (miner) revenue in sandwich shop). In the sandwich shop Example 1, Alice will pay $P_A(H, B_k, X)$ which is a function of the number of eggs in the shop (H), and placed people (X) in the current queue (B_k).

Alice's payment $P_A(H, B_k, X)$ where X is placing transactions in $B_k = \{Alice, Rachel, Bob\}$ is different from $P_A(H, B_k, X')$ where X' is placing transactions in $B_k' = \{Charlie, Alice, Bob\}$.

The sandwich shop's revenue from serving an omelette for Alice is Mr_A (H, B_k, X). Same as above, the revenue is a function of placing people in the queue.

Definition 15 (Generalized Transaction Fee Mechanism (GTFM)). *A generalized transaction fee mechanism (GTFM) is a triple (X, P, Mr) in which X is a feasible placement rule, P is a payment rule, and Mr is a miner revenue rule.*

Based on the proposed Generalized TFM modelling, we aim to model several previously known and proposed TFMs using the rules proposed in the previous section. Our objective is to demonstrate that our proposed model can accurately represent these existing TFMs.

Example 4 (First price auction (FPA) [10]). The (intended) placement rule for FPA is to include a feasible subset of transactions that maximizes the sum of the size-weighted bids. The payment rule is equal to the miner revenue rule and both are independent of blockchain history and other transactions in the block.

$$- P_i(B_k) = Mr_i(B_k) = b_i$$

$$
\begin{aligned}
\underset{X_i}{\arg\max} \quad & \sum_{tx_i \in M} X_i(H, M)[s_i].b_i.g_i \\
\text{s.t.} \quad & \sum_{tx_i \in M} X_i(H, M)[s_i].g_i \leq G
\end{aligned}
\tag{7}
$$

FPA's lack of UIC is evident [15], even without accounting for the impact of transaction ordering on users' utilities.

Example 5 (EIP-1559 [18]).   EIP-1559 TFM is the current TFM of the Ethereum blockchain. The (intended) placement rule for EIP-1559 is to include a feasible subset of transactions that maximizes the sum of the size-weighted bids condition on which they bid at least the base fee. The base fee is "burning" (similar to giving away a small fee) and the miner receives the difference between users' payments and the base fee.

- $r = f(H)$ is the base fee which is a function of the blockchain history.
- $P_i(H, B_k, X) = min\{C_i, r+t_i\}$ which C_i is the fee cap and t_i is the maximum tip the user tends to pay the miner.
- $Mr_i(H, B_k, X) = P_i(H, B_k, X) - r = min\{C_i - r, t_i\}$
-

$$\max_{x_i} \quad \sum_{tx_i \in M} \sum_{\forall s_i} x_i(H, M).min\{C_i - r, t_i\}.g_i$$

$$\text{s.t.} \quad \sum_{tx_i \in M} \sum_{\forall s_i} x_i(H, M).g_i \leq G \tag{8}$$

In EIP-1559, the mechanism designer assumes that the base fee is usually not excessively low. It means that the cumulative size of transactions in the mempool whose private value is more than the base fee is not bigger than the maximum block size.

$$\sum_{tx_i \in M : v_i \geq r} g_i \leq G \tag{9}$$

5.3   Agents' Utilities and Incentive Compatibility

Based on our proposed generalized TFM modelling, considering the order-based private value of the transactions, we present formal definitions of the utilities of miners and users, who act as rational agents in the blockchain system and aim to optimize their utilities by adhering to the rules of the TFM. Our focus is on agents' incentives at the level of a single block. We assume that the addition of a transaction to the block has a common marginal cost μ, known to all users. Given these assumptions, rational users aim to optimize their utility by bidding for the intended placement of their transactions.

Miners. In this paper, we consider a simplified model of miners' behaviour in which they have the ability to add fake transactions to the mempool without incurring any cost. We assume that miners are myopic and their utility is intended for the current block. This simplified model allows us to analyze the incentives for miners in the short term and examine how they can optimize their utility through TFM rules. The utility function of a miner (Eq. 10) shows that the utility of a miner depends on two arguments that the miner can control to maximize its utility. The first argument is the selection of transactions and their ranks in a block. The second part is adding fake transactions and their ranks to the block. A miner maximizes its utility by controlling both mentioned arguments based on the miner revenue rule of a TFM. Though a TFM is specified by the protocol designer based on a given placement rule, miners may choose to deviate from that rule. Thus, to ensure that miners are truthful, we require the TFM to be incentive-compatible.

Definition 16 (Myopic miner utility). *For a $TFM(X, P, Mr)$, on-chain history H, mempool M, and fake transactions F, utility of a myopic miner is:*

$$
U_{miner}(B_k, F) := \underbrace{\sum_{tx_i \in B_k \cap M} Mr_i(H, B_k, X_i) \cdot g_i}_{miner's\ revenue}
$$

$$
- \underbrace{\sum_{tx_i \in B_k \cap F} P_i(H, B_k, X_i) \cdot g_i}_{fee\ for\ miner's\ fake\ transactions} \tag{10}
$$

$$
- \underbrace{\mu \sum_{tx_i \in B_k} g_i}_{marginal\ costs} .
$$

The first term shows all ordered real transactions revenues. The second term indicates the cost to the miner of adding its fake transactions to the block. The last sum indicates the marginal cost of adding transactions.

Definition 17 (Incentive compatibility for myopic miner (MMIC)). *A $TFM(X, P, Mr)$ is incentive-compatible for a myopic miner (MMIC) if for every on-chain history H and mempool M, a myopic miner maximizes its utility (10) following the placement rule without creating any fake transactions, i.e., $F = \emptyset$. Then, $B_k = X^T \cdot M$*

Users. Assuming rationality, users bid in order to maximize their utility. In light of the order-robust and order-sensitive classifications, we can formally define users' utility as a function of their private value and the payments made through the TFM's payment rule. Specifically, as noted earlier, the private value of a given transaction may depend on the presence and order of other transactions in the block. In fact, the transaction's private value is a function of its BOS in the block. By incorporating the placement matrix into the utility function, we can account for the impact of transaction order on users' valuations and thereby more accurately model their behaviour within the TFM framework.

Definition 18 (User utility function). *For a $TFM(X, P, Mr)$, on-chain history H and mempool M, the utility of user i, the owner of transaction tx_i, with private value v_i and bid b_i is:*

$$
u_i(b_i) := \begin{cases} (v_i - b_i).g_i, & s_i \neq 0 \\ 0 & otherwise \end{cases} \tag{11}
$$

In this paper, we do not assume that the private value is a constant. Rather, the private value v_i of a transaction tx_i depends on the expected private value V_i of tx_i, based on the last block, and on the (preceding) transactions that affects its value in the current block B_k, i.e., $v_i(V_i, BOS_i)$

Users are rational agents who aim to maximize their utilities by adhering to TFM rules. It is important to consider that miners also prioritize their own utilities when placing transactions within a block. Therefore, we must examine whether utility maximization is feasible through TFM rules. For TFM rules to be effective, they must be incentive-compatible for users. In order to define this incentive compatibility, we first define the symmetric Ex Post Nash Equilibrium.

Definition 19 (Symmetric Ex Post Nash Equilibrium (Symmetric EPNE)). *Fix a $TFM(X, P, Mr)$ and block history H. A bidding strategy $b^*(\cdot)$ is a symmetric ex-post Nash equilibrium (symmetric EPNE), if for every mempool M, bidding $b^*(v_i)$ maximizes the utility (11) of user c_i conditioned on all $c_j \neq c_i$ following strategy $b^*(v_j)$.*

The existence of a symmetric EPNE in a TFM means that, if all users c_j follow b^*, c_i will not have any incentive to deviate. We can define incentive compatibility for users based on the existence of symmetric EPNE bidding strategy.

Definition 20 (Incentive compatibility for users (UIC)). *A TFM (X, P, Mr) is user incentive compatible (UIC) if, for every on-chain history H, and mempool M, there is a symmetric EPNE bidding strategy.*

5.4 Off-Chain Agreements

In a blockchain environment, it is plausible for a miner and a group of users to form an off-chain coalition, with the goal of increasing the collective utility of the coalition. Thus, a TFM should be devised taking this possibility into account.

Definition 21 (Off-chain agreement). *For set C of transactions and miner m, an off-chain agreement (OCA) between C's creators and m specifies:*

1. *A bid matrix b^C, with b_i^C vector to be submitted with the transaction $tx_i \in C$.*
2. *A placing matrix X^C, indicating the transactions that the miner m will place in its block.*
3. *An agreement price B^C, with β_i from transaction tx_i's owner to miner m.*

In an OCA, each transaction tx_i's owner agrees to submit tx_i with an on-chain bid of b_i^C while transferring $\beta_i.g_i$ to the miner m off-chain; the miner, in turn, agrees to mine a block with the agreed-upon sequence of transactions C.

Definition 22 (Joint utility). *for an on-chain history H, the joint utility of a miner and some users with a set of transactions C with placement vector X^C in block B_k is:*

$$u_{joint}(m, C, X^C) = \sum_{tx_i \in C} (v_i - P_i(H, B_k, X) + Mr_i(H, B_k, X)).x_i^T.g_i \quad (12)$$

Definition 23 (OCA-Proof). *A $TFM(X, P, Mr)$ is OCA-proof if, for every on-chain history H, no off-chain agreement between a miner m and any number of users with the transaction set C can increase their joint utility by deviation from TFM rules.*

6 Results

The author of [15] has shown that the EIP-1559 TFM is UIC when the base fee is not excessively low (9) and $min\{v_i, r + \mu\}$ is the users' symmetric EPNE. However, the incentive compatibility is satisfied assuming constant private values for transactions. However, for an order-sensitive mempool, the TFM cannot satisfy incentive compatibility for users.

Theorem 1 (EIP-1559 is not UIC for order-sensitive mempool). *Fix an on-chain History H, a base fee $r = f(H)$, and a marginal cost μ. There is no symmetric EPNE bidding strategy in an order-sensitive mempool.*

Proof. We assume that the base fee is not excessively low, which means that the block size is sufficient to accommodate all transactions present in the mempool where the optimal fee for each transaction exceeds the base fee, i.e., $b^*(.) > r$. The author of [15] has shown that for excessively low base fee, EIP1559 is not UIC. We assume that there is a symmetric EPNE for all users: $b^* = min\{C_i^*, r + t_i^*\}$.

The myopic miner places transactions in the block in order to maximize its revenue (Eq. 8). The not excessively low assumption satisfies the feasible placement condition. Therefore, the miner places all transactions with $b^*(.) > r$ in the block.

As the places of transactions in the block do not affect the miner's revenue (Eq. 8), without loss of generality, we assume that the miner places the transactions in B_k based on their bid b^* in descending order.

As in order-sensitive mempool, there is a subset of order-sensitive transactions, We assume there is an order-sensitive transaction tx_i which is order-sensitive in a sequence $T \subseteq B_k$. The transaction owner can change his bid $b_i > b^*$ to get a higher rank (smaller BOS_i) in T to enhance his utility by increasing its private value $v_i(V_i, BOS_i)$. Therefore, b^* is not an EPNE for an order-sensitive transaction tx_i. Subsequently, there is no symmetric EPNE for users in EIP-1559 and it is not UIC.   □

In light of the fact that EIP-1559 does not satisfy incentive compatibility for users in an order-sensitive mempool, our focus is on identifying a TFM that satisfies incentive compatibility for users. The rationale for prioritizing user incentive compatibility over miner incentive compatibility stems from the fact that miners, as rational agents, have access to the mempool and can maximize their utility by selecting the most profitable set of transactions to include in a block.

Theorem 2. (Impossibility theorem). *For an order-sensitive mempool, there is no deterministic TFM that satisfies both UIC and OCA-proof.*

Proof. In a deterministic TFM, a miner decides about the placement of transactions in the block. If we assume that the order of the transactions is forced by an external protocol, such as an order-fairness protocol. Therefore, the miner is at least responsible for the inclusion of transactions in a block. In both cases, we show that a TFM cannot satisfy UIC and OCA-proof

Assuming two order-sensitive transactions (tx_i, tx_j) exist in the mempool. The miner can make a block B_k in one of the following ways:

1. $S_1 = \langle tx_i, tx_j \rangle \sqsubseteq \bar{B}_k$
2. $S_2 = \langle tx_j, tx_i \rangle \sqsubseteq \bar{B}_k$
3. $S_3 = S_1 \backslash tx_i = \langle tx_j \rangle \sqsubseteq \bar{B}_k$

As we have assumed that the TFM is UIC, there is a symmetric EPNE for both users i and j. Without loss of generality, we can assume that based on the users' bids, the miner makes a block such as (i) following the placement rule. Now the following may happen:

1. The user j increase its transaction's bid convincing the miner to change the block such as (ii). Therefore, as the user can increase its revenue by deviation from the EPNE, the assumption of the existence of a symmetric EPNE and subsequently UIC is incorrect.
2. The user j makes an off-chain agreement with the miner to make the block such as (ii) or (iii). The difference in revenue increase can divide between the miner and the user. Therefore, as there is a possibility of OCA, the assumption of OCA-proof is not correct. Hence, a contradiction.   □

Theorem 3. (Necessary condition for UIC TFM). *A TFM is said to be incentive compatible for users if, for every placed transaction tx_i in block B_k, BOS_i is empty.*

Proof. We consider two cases: (i) if a transaction tx_i is order-robust and (ii) when transaction tx_i is order-sensitive.

- Order-robust: if a transaction tx_i is order-robust, then, by definition, the private value of user u_i is independent of other transactions in the block.
- Order-sensitive: Assume that tx_i is placed at rank $r > s_i$. Since tx_i is order-sensitive, it means that its BOS_i at r is non-empty. This means that the private value of tx_i is lower than the maximum expected private value. To increase the utility of c_i, tx_i is moved higher up. However, when BOS_i is empty when tx_i is ranked at s_i, tx_i is order-robust for that given sequence. Hence, the private value of user c_i is constant, equal to the expected private value, when BOS_i is empty.   □

Corollary 1. (UIC TFM). *If a TFM is UIC for order-robust transactions and if for every order-sensitive transaction tx_i in a block and BOS_i is empty, then TFM is UIC.*

7   Discussion

One of the primary motivations behind the replacement of the first price auction (FPA) with EIP-1559 in the Ethereum blockchain was to achieve incentive compatibility for both users and miners [15]. However, our analysis using the generalized TFM framework reveals that EIP-1559 is not UIC when considering an order-sensitive mempool. This finding is supported by the growing adoption of exclusive mining services such as Flashbots, which indicates a lack of UIC for order-sensitive transactions [9]. Moreover, by disregarding the impact of transaction ordering, existing TFMs fail to satisfy the conditions of MMIC, UIC, and OCA-proof. Moreover, we have extended our results to demonstrate the impossibility of a deterministic TFM that can simultaneously satisfy both user incentive compatibility and OCA-proof conditions.

We have established that the necessary condition for a TFM to be UIC is the absence of any order-sensitive sub-sequence (BOS) within a block. This condition ensures that all transactions in the block are order-robust, providing users with confidence in the value they will receive. Alternatively, a UIC TFM can be achieved by having an order-robust mempool, meaning that services or functionalities within the blockchain system do not rely on transaction orders. This condition was implicitly present in previously considered UIC TFMs.

In this study, we have primarily operated under the assumption that all involved agents, encompassing users and miners, exhibit rational behaviour, driven by their desire to maximize their revenue within the context of a TFM. We acknowledge that this perspective excludes the influence of non-rational agents, including altruistic or malicious actors whose behaviour might deviate from incentive-based rationale. Nonetheless, it is our conjecture that over time, users' behaviour will tend towards rationality. Additionally, we have presumed that miners adhere to myopic decision-making. However, it is pertinent to note that in cases where a substantial coalition of miners collaborates, they might prioritize long-term utility optimization over immediate block-specific gains. Another dimension of limitation in our model pertains to our assumption of each user having a maximum of one transaction within a mempool per block. This assumption disregards scenarios where users may possess multiple transactions, each with potentially varying effects on their revenue contingent upon distinct placements within the block.

8   Conclusion and Future Works

This paper has made significant contributions towards understanding the effect of transactions (re)ordering on blockchain transactions from agents' utility perspectives. By defining the private value of transactions as a function of other transactions in the block, we have captured the impact of order sensitivity. Additionally, we have proposed a generalized TFM modelling approach that considers the placement of transactions in the block. Through our analysis, we have shown that no deterministic TFM can satisfy both UIC and OCA-proof. Furthermore, we have identified and proved a necessary condition for a TFM to satisfy UIC. These findings can help improve the design of TFMs in blockchain systems to prevent order manipulation attacks.

As there exists no deterministic TFM that is UIC for order-sensitive mempool, we will investigate weaker notions of UIC and also a stochastic version of TFMs that are UIC, i.e., the pricing mechanism is varying rather than deterministic.

Our future research will delve into the exploration of alternative forms of UIC within the context of order-sensitive mempools. This involves investigating weaker variations of UIC and exploring stochastic versions of TFMs, where pricing mechanisms become variable rather than deterministic. We plan to address the limitations outlined in Sect. 7, including the incorporation of non-rational agent dynamics. Additionally, we plan to refine our model to account for scenarios where users may have multiple transactions within a mempool for a single block. This refinement will provide a more comprehensive understanding of how transaction order impacts revenue outcomes.

Acknowledgements. The second author is supported by EPSRC (EP/T014784/1).

References

1. Crypto total market cap 2010–2022. https://www.statista.com/statistics/730876/cryptocurrency-maket-value/. Accessed 1 Feb 2022
2. Basu, S., Easley, D., O'Hara, M., Sirer, E.G.: StableFees: a predictable fee market for cryptocurrencies. Manage. Sci. **69**, 6417–7150 (2023)
3. Basu, S., Easley, D.A., O'Hara, M., Sirer, E.G.: Towards a functional fee market for cryptocurrencies. CoRR **abs/1901.06830** (2019). http://arxiv.org/abs/1901.06830
4. Chung, H., Shi, E.: Foundations of transaction fee mechanism design, pp. 3856–3899 (2023). https://doi.org/10.1137/1.9781611977554.ch150, https://epubs.siam.org/doi/abs/10.1137/1.9781611977554.ch150
5. Daian, P., et al.: Flash Boys 2.0: frontrunning in decentralized exchanges, miner extractable value, and consensus instability. In: 2020 IEEE Symposium on Security and Privacy (SP), pp. 910–927 (2020). https://doi.org/10.1109/SP40000.2020.00040
6. Eskandari, S., Moosavi, S., Clark, J.: SoK: transparent dishonesty: front-running attacks on blockchain. In: Bracciali, A., Clark, J., Pintore, F., Rønne, P.B., Sala, M. (eds.) FC 2019. LNCS, vol. 11599, pp. 170–189. Springer, Cham (2020). https://doi.org/10.1007/978-3-030-43725-1_13
7. Lavi, R., Sattath, O., Zohar, A.: Redesigning bitcoin's fee market. ACM Trans. Econ. Comput. **10**(1), 1–31 (2022). https://doi.org/10.1145/3530799
8. Leonardos, S., Monnot, B., Reijsbergen, D., Skoulakis, E., Piliouras, G.: Dynamical analysis of the eip-1559 ethereum fee market. In: Proceedings of the 3rd ACM Conference on Advances in Financial Technologies. p. 114–126. AFT '21, Association for Computing Machinery, New York, NY, USA (2021). https://doi.org/10.1145/3479722.3480993, https://0-doi-org.pugwash.lib.warwick.ac.uk/10.1145/3479722.3480993

9. Liu, Y., Lu, Y., Nayak, K., Zhang, F., Zhang, L., Zhao, Y.: Empirical analysis of EIP-1559: transaction fees, waiting times, and consensus security. In: Proceedings of the 2022 ACM SIGSAC Conference on Computer and Communications Security, CCS 2022, pp. 2099–2113. Association for Computing Machinery, New York, NY, USA (2022). https://doi.org/10.1145/3548606.3559341
10. Nakamoto, S., et al.: Bitcoin. A peer-to-peer electronic cash system (2008)
11. Piet, J., Fairoze, J., Weaver, N.: Extracting Godl [sic] from the salt mines: ethereum miners extracting value. arXiv preprint arXiv:2203.15930 (2022)
12. Qin, K., Zhou, L., Gervais, A.: Quantifying blockchain extractable value: how dark is the forest? In: 2022 IEEE Symposium on Security and Privacy (SP), pp. 198–214 (2022). https://doi.org/10.1109/SP46214.2022.9833734
13. Reijsbergen, D., Sridhar, S., Monnot, B., Leonardos, S., Skoulakis, S., Piliouras, G.: Transaction fees on a honeymoon: Ethereum EIP-1559 one month later. In: 2021 IEEE International Conference on Blockchain (Blockchain), pp. 196–204. IEEE Computer Society, Los Alamitos, CA, USA, December 2021. https://doi.org/10.1109/Blockchain53845.2021.00034, https://doi.ieeecomputersociety.org/10.1109/Blockchain53845.2021.00034
14. Roughgarden, T.: Transaction fee mechanism design for the ethereum blockchain: an economic analysis of EIP-1559. arXiv preprint arXiv:2012.00854 (2020)
15. Roughgarden, T.: Transaction fee mechanism design. ACM SIGecom Exchanges 19(1), 52–55 (2021)
16. Strehle, E., Ante, L.: Exclusive mining of blockchain transactions (2020)
17. Torres, C.F., Camino, R., State, R.: Frontrunner jones and the raiders of the dark forest: an empirical study of frontrunning on the ethereum blockchain. In: USENIX Security 2021, pp. 1343–1359. USENIX Association, August 2021
18. Vitalik Buterin (@vbuterin), E.C.E.: EIP-1559: Fee market change for eth 1.0 chain, April 2019. https://eips.ethereum.org/EIPS/eip-1559
19. Yao, A.C.: An incentive analysis of some bitcoin fee designs. CoRR abs/1811.02351 (2018). http://arxiv.org/abs/1811.02351

Comparison of Ethereum Smart Contract Analysis and Verification Methods

Vincent Happersberger[1]([✉]) [iD], Frank-Walter Jäkel[1] [iD], Thomas Knothe[1], Yvonne-Anne Pignolet[2] [iD], and Stefan Schmid[3] [iD]

[1] Fraunhofer Institute for Production Systems and Design Technology IPK, Berlin, Germany
`vincent.happersberger@ipk.fraunhofer.de`
[2] DFINITY Foundation, Zurich, Switzerland
[3] Technical University of Berlin, Berlin, Germany

Abstract. Ethereum allows to publish and use applications known as smart contracts on its public network.

Smart contracts can be costly for users if erroneous. Various security vulnerabilities have occurred in the past and have been exploited causing the loss of billions of dollars. Therefore, it is in the developer's interest to publish smart contracts that serve their intended purpose only.

In this work, we study different approaches to verify if Ethereum smart contracts behave as intended and how to detect possible vulnerabilities. To this end, we compare and evaluate, different formal verification tools and tools to automatically detect vulnerabilities. Our empirical comparison of 140 smart contracts with known vulnerabilities shows that different tools vary in their success to identify issues with smart contracts. In general, we find that automated analysis tools often miss vulnerabilities, while formal verifiers based on model checking with Hoare-style source code annotations require high effort and knowledge to discover possible weaknesses. Specifically, some vulnerabilities (e.g., related to bad randomness) are not detected by any of the tools. Formal verifiers perform better than automated analysis tools as they detect more vulnerabilities and are more reliable. One of the automated analysis tools was able to find only three out of 16 Access Control vulnerabilities. On the contrary, formal verifiers have a hundred percent detection rate for selected tests.

As a case study with a smart contract without previously known vulnerabilities and for a more in-depth evaluation, we examine a smart contract using a two-phase commit protocol mechanism which is key in many smart contract applications. We use the presented tools to analyze and verify the contract. Thereby we come across different important patterns to detect vulnerabilities e.g. with respect to re-entrancy, and how to annotate a contract to prove that intended the restriction and requirements hold at any time.

Keywords: Ethereum · Smart Contract · Verification methods · Formal Verification · Automated Test Tools · Blockchain

S. Katsikas et al. (Eds.): ESORICS 2023 Workshops, LNCS 14398, pp. 344–358, 2024.
https://doi.org/10.1007/978-3-031-54204-6_21

1   Introduction

The term smart contract initially referred to the automation of general legal contracts. Smart contracts recently gained much interest due to the rise of blockchain technology, especially with the success of Ethereum [58]. Today smart contracts are more known for their use as low-level code scripts running on blockchains, enabling code execution without trusting third parties [37]. The most popular blockchain for smart contracts, Ethereum, provides Solidity, a programming language designed for the development of smart contracts. With this innovation, Ethereum differs from previous blockchain technologies like Bitcoin, enabling more generic decentralized applications instead of only asset transfers. Solidity smart contracts have been used to create governance systems with voting rights, escrow services, decentralized lending, and other financial services. Thousands of smart contracts get deployed on the Ethereum network every day [5].

1.1   Related Work

The verification and analysis of smart contracts have recently received much attention in the literature [7]. Indeed, many vulnerabilities have been observed and reported in the last few years. The vulnerabilities we consider in this paper are collected from [9,39,52], and were studied also in other works [28].

Existing literature revolves around automated analysis tools, formal verification of the source code, approaches using source-code annotations, to byte-code consideration, among other methods.

Security issues in Ethereum smart contracts in general and automated analysis tools to identify those vulnerabilities are studied in [17], using the automated analysis tools Oyente, Securify, Remix, and SmartCheck. The automated analysis tools Osiris, Oyente, and Slither (also studied in this paper) have been analyzed against vulnerable Solidity smart contracts [54], also observing false negatives, see also [10] and [17] for similar studies. Permenev et al. overview current state-of-the-art practices collectively with properties to consider when performing smart contract audits [44], however, their tool is not open source and needs an additional specification file as input together with a smart contract. Further automated analysis tools have been studied in [18,22,42,43] as well. The authors in [18] use SmartBugs to execute automated test tools to compare multiple tools, however, focusing on performance and considering fewer smart contracts, and not discussing formal verifiers. The SmartCheck studied in [22] is deprecated since 2020 and might not work correctly for Solidity version greater than 0.6.0, which applies to our own example in Sect. 4.

The translation from Solidity to Boogie (both considered in this paper) enables verification of Hoare-style annotations [8,55]. This allows for precise reasoning but depends on the inventiveness and know-how of the developer [8]: The more annotations cover the specification, the more precise they are in validation.

Nenad Petrovic et al. present solc-verify as an existing smart contract verification solution as it reasons about source code using the Solidity compiler,

Boogie, and SMT solvers to detect common vulnerabilities [45]; the authors also present a tool that provides annotations but needs input verification rules.

The specification and annotation for smart contracts are often considered the most difficult aspects of verification, and it has also been observed that the same invariants appear in many different contracts and therefore can be reused [11]. In this work, we use formal verifiers which use Hoare logic [47].

Li et al. [53] discuss program-level specification with Hoare-style properties, also covering vulnerabilities and semantic correctness of smart contract functions [53].

The authors of [32] argue that static analysis tools which function on the source code level often do not allow reason about the gas consumption when executing smart contracts, hence making it impossible to analyze vulnerabilities e.g., related to front running or denial of service.

In [56], a tool is presented that works on the source-code level to verify the reliability and security of Ethereum smart contracts, using symbolic execution. With that, it can additionally reason about properties such as gas consumption which allows reasoning about vulnerabilities e.g. denial of service. But similar to other implementations which use Hoare-style annotations these properties still must be manually defined for this approach for the Formal Symbolic Process Virtual Machine-Ethereum (FSPVM-E).

Nehai and Bobot [41] use the language WhyML to compile Why3 contracts translated from Solidity contracts; these contracts contain low-level information such as the gas consumption of a contract's functions. On the generated smart contracts they can annotate allocations to check that functions only use a limited gas amount.

Another option to verify the correctness of smart contracts is formal verification at the byte code level instead of the source code level which we study. This approach finds bugs in the smart contract which result from the compiler itself which translates source code to byte code and afterwards runs the byte code [48]. We also note that smart contracts on Ethereum can be translated or programmed in Java and verified with a dynamic logic called JavaDL [53].

Also, functional correctness properties were studied in the literature, using model checking [33,40], and exploring possible execution paths which can possibly be exploited.

Further formal verification approaches and automated analysis tools are presented in [16,27].

1.2   Contribution

In summary, our paper makes the following contributions. Firstly, we conduct an examination of 140 vulnerable smart contracts using automated analysis tools and analyze the outcomes of this investigation. This data set of smart contracts was grouped into categories, which renders searching for certain vulnerabilities more efficient. With that approach, we were able to investigate the intended behavior of the automated analysis tools which we have recorded in Table 2.

Furthermore, we employ Hoare-style source code annotations on smart contracts within each category in cases where the automated analysis tools failed to detect the vulnerabilities. This allows us to perform formal verification with model checking and compare the results with those obtained from the automated analysis tools.

Furthermore, we analyze the smart contract development process with respect to verifying the contract. As a case study, we consider a smart contract implementing a two-phase commit protocol based on a well-known distributed algorithm to carry out a transaction if all involved parties commit to it. We utilize the proposed methods to apply the previously mentioned automated analysis tools to our featured two-phase commit smart contract and conduct formal verification, enabling us to analyze potential vulnerabilities in this specific context. We focus on the vulnerabilities we studied before and use Hoare-style source code annotations for the application of formal verification annotation.

1.3   Organization

The remainder of this paper is organized as follows. In Sect. 2 we discuss tools from different verification methods. Furthermore, in Sect. 3 we study the findings of each tool on a curated data set containing 140 smart contracts. In Sect. 4 we describe a general verification approach. Afterwards, we simulate the process of a smart contract developer by presenting a contract implementing a two-phase commit scheme and verifying each function with the acquainted methodology. In Sect. 5 we discuss the pros and cons of test tools, their limitations, and their findings. Finally, we conclude this work and discuss future work in Sect. 6.

2   Categorization of Methods

There are several methods to verify that a smart contract works as intended and to find potential vulnerabilities in smart contracts.

An audit typically includes monitoring for common smart contract vulnerabilities like transaction order dependency, integer overflow, unprocessed exceptions/unchecked call-function return, re-entrancy, typographical errors, requirement violation, incorrect inheritance order, and unrestricted action. Furthermore, a comprehensive audit analyses gas consumption, deployment consistency, data and repository consistency, access control, and authorization, operations trail and event generation, token supply manipulation, and data consistency [2,14]. Some audits check for inconsistencies from the white paper and other advanced logic errors that existing automated tools cannot detect [42].

In addition to manual code reviews, tools are used to detect vulnerabilities and problems. In this section, we present the different tools we compare with each other in subsequent sections.

2.1 Automated Analysis Tools

The following automated analysis tools will be used to analyze smart contracts because all of them are open-source and they only need a Solidity smart contract without further annotation or test cases as input, and they detect vulnerabilities and bad practices in smart contracts regardless of the Solidity version.

Oyente. Oyente [35] was developed by Melonport AG in 2016 as one of the first smart contract analysis tools. It uses symbolic execution to detect vulnerabilities. Unlike a specific implementation, where a program operates on a given input and finds only one control flow path, symbolic execution can simultaneously explore multiple paths at the same time when a program normally needs different inputs. The execution is then performed by the symbolic execution engine. Oyente operates directly on the low-level byte code which is executed by the Ethereum Virtual Machine (EVM) and therefore has no direct contact with the high-level Solidity code. Oyente is also the basis for other automated tools like Maian [30] and Osiris [54]. Maian additionally deploys the analyzed smart contracts on a private blockchain to confirm vulnerabilities by sending corresponding transactions to the contracts. With that, it also considers attacks requiring multiple transactions [16,30]. Osiris combines Oyente's symbolic execution with taint analysis. Taint analysis tracks the reproduction of data across the control flow of a program. This technique reduces the number of false positives for tools searching for integer errors to reliably find vulnerabilities caused by integer bugs in Ethereum smart contracts.

Slither. Slither is one of the first open-source static analysis tools for smart contracts built with Solidity and was developed by TrailOfBits [21]. It converts Ethereum smart contracts through their abstract syntax tree that is gained by the Solidity compiler into SlithIR. This is an intermediate representation of the contract where it keeps the semantic information that would be lost by transforming it into byte code. The framework runs multiple vulnerability detectors and therefore can find over 80 different vulnerabilities, errors, and bad practices which can occur in smart contracts.

Mythril. Mythril [12] was published in 2018 as a security analysis tool for Ethereum smart contracts. It detects a wide range of security vulnerabilities in smart contracts for every EVM-compatible blockchain e.g. Hedera, Tron, and Vechain using symbolic execution on EVM bytecode, Satisfiability modulo theories(SMT) solving, and taint analysis. Additionally, it is also used as part of the MythX security analysis platform.

2.2 Model Checking with Hoare-Style Annotation

This formal verification method can be used for systems that can be represented by finite-state models. The user must provide a precise finite-state model of the system and a formally defined property the model should meet. The method checks for every state and system scenario the model can access if the specified property is met. If at any point the assumption is violated a counterexample is provided to show the circumstances under which the system fails. However, if all tests are successful the system model is formally tested for a given property [38].

In this section, two formal verification tools will be presented where both use model-checking methods. The two are publicly available, only need a smart contract as input, and perform automated formal verification using code annotations. Other tools need additional specification files.

Solc-Verify. Solc-verify is a source-level verification tool for Ethereum smart contracts using modular program analysis and SMT solvers. It is an extension to the Solidity compiler (solc) and operates on the source code, not on the Ethereum bytecode which is more common. By this solc-verify can make statements about properties that can only be found in high-level language contracts. The verifier enables automated formal verification by allowing contract invariants, loop invariants, and pre and postcondition annotations [24]. Furthermore, it translates the contract source code to the Boogie Intermediate Verification Language (IVL) and relies on the Boogie verifier to later provide verification conditions to SMT solvers [25].

VeriSol. VeriSol is a Microsoft Research project which automatically checks the correctness of assertions in a Solidity smart contract by also encoding the semantics of contracts into a low-level intermediate verification language Boogie. Afterwards, the tool leverages and extends the verification toolchain for Boogie programs [51,55]. In general, VeriSol uses several model-checking techniques including SAT [29].

3   Empirical Tool Comparison

For the comparison and evaluation between different automated analysis tools and formal verifiers a data set [6] containing a total of 140 different smart contracts subdivided into categories is used. The table below describes these categories. This made it possible to search for certain vulnerabilities and it helps to know where each vulnerability should be expected.

The vulnerabilities are subdivided into two groups with the second group starting after the Denial Of Service vulnerability. Note that the vulnerabilities from the second group cannot be detected by formal verifiers. They need additional information to be trackable which is missing in the source code e.g. the gas consumption of a smart contract. The column name Level describes where the vulnerability occurs. E.g., Front-running vulnerabilities are typically due to the ability of the miners to select which transactions to add to a block and should therefore be handled at the blockchain level (Table 1).

SmartBugs [18,22] was used to run and evaluate all the 140 Solidity files with Oyente, Slither, and Mythril. The results are presented in Table 2.

Table 1. Dataset of 140 vulnerable Solidity smart contracts [6]

Vulnerability Category	Number	Level
Re-entrancy	31	Solidity
Access Control	18	Solidity
Arithmetic	15	Solidity
Unchecked Low-Level Calls	52	Solidity
Denial Of Service	6	Solidity
Bad Randomness	8	Blockchain
Front-running	4	Blockchain
Time Manipulation	5	Blockchain
Short Addresses	1	Ethereum Virtual Machine

Solc-verify and VeriSol are limited to certain pragma versions of smart contracts as well as the compiler version. Moreover, the annotation of smart contracts takes a lot of time, even when the vulnerability to be identified is known. Therefore, we selected for each of the five solidity-level vulnerabilities categories one smart contract where the automated analysis tools did not find any vulnerabilities. For these contracts, we then added the necessary annotations for the formal verifiers manually. This required carefully studying the smart contracts to identify the properties and invariants and state them in the formalism the tools understand.

The run time varies from seconds to minutes per contract. It takes Mythril 49:04 min to run 52 contracts and Oyente 4:15 min. The formal verifiers run within seconds but can only read one smart contract at a time.

Table 2. Comparison between automated tools and formal verifiers. Percentages represent #(successful detection) / #(tested contracts)

Vulnerabilities & Tools	Oyente	Slither	Mythril	solc-verify	VeriSol
Re-entrancy	96%	96%	80%	100%	100%
Access Control	0%	16%	0%	100%	100%
Arithmetic	100%	0%	93%	100%	100%
Unchecked L-L Calls	0%	0%	96%	100%	100%
Denial Of Service	0%	0%	0%	100%	100%
Bad Randomness	0%	0%	0%	0%	0%
Front-running	0%	0%	25%	0%	0%
Time Manipulation	0%	0%	0%	0%	0%
Short Addresses	0%	0%	0%	0%	0%

The specification of annotations for formal verifiers needs knowledge of what the contract should do and what edge cases might occur. The time and effort to annotate a smart contract can vary greatly and is in the order of several hours for a relatively simple contract like the two-phase commit contract presented in the case study below. On the positive side, the understanding of contracts grows.

Verifiers can only detect violations of properties that are annotated. Hence, developers might falsely assume that a contract is secure if the specifications do not cover the expected behaviors. The results show that the effort is worth it and the formal verifiers find vulnerabilities that can not be found by automated analysis tools [1].

The comparison and analysis of the automated analysis tools and formal verifiers clarify that none of the tools are able to detect all of the vulnerabilities. The formal verifiers were able to find the vulnerabilities in the contracts with annotations.

4   Case Study: 2-Phase Commit Smart Contract

In this section, we consider a smart contract that behaves as a coordinator for a two-phase commit (2PC) procedure. Such a mechanism is crucial in many smart contract applications to ensure that an action is only executed if other smart contracts are in agreement with the execution.

2PC is executed in two phases. First, the coordinator asks participants to prepare. The second phase is entered once all participants replied with commit or abort. If all participants replied with ready, the coordinator asks the participants to commit, otherwise, the coordinator instructs them to abort. The participants reply with an acknowledgment when they executed accordingly. Thus a transaction will only take place if all participants vote to commit [36].

In summary, a smart contract with 2PC ensures that a transaction is either executed or aborted based on the votes of the participants within a timeout interval. If one of the participants does not reply in time or votes to abort the transaction will abort.

An existing contract [49] was extended to offer the following functionality. The contract owner can start a voting phase by declaring a time until other participants can call the commitRequest() function to vote for commit or abort by calling the function with a parameter. Public variables commitCounter and abortCounter store the number of votes. After the voting phase has ended the commit() function can be called by the owner with two input parameters, an address to receive funds and the amount to send. The _receiver can be any valid address from the network except the null address, and the amount to be sent to the _receiver e.g. 0.01 gETH equals 10^{16} in uint256. If no participant voted or if at least one participant voted to abort the smart contract will return the funds to the contract owner. If the transaction succeeds there is no error message and the contract owner can start a new voting round.

The contract can be used where a community can decide through voting if a donation e.g. to an institution announced on a website or to a participant should happen and how much should be donated. The contract could be extended e.g.

with some off-chain randomization to choose the receiver or the amount of the donation. Also, the participant role could be restricted how many commit votes are needed to finally commit, and how often the transfer should happen after the voting phase. Additionally, a check that the _receiver cannot be the contract owner (self-transfer) is thinkable.

For the case study, we will use the same automated analysis tools and formal verifiers with Hoare-style source code annotations as above. The contract is deployed on the Goerli test network [26] via remix.ethereum.io [20]. After deployment, the smart contract needs funds to later be able to transfer Ether. To interact with the contract as a participant Metamask [34] was used to transfer and receive funds which are possible to monitor via Goerli Etherscan [19].

4.1 General Approach

In addition to running automated analysis tools on the contract, a manual code review is common during audits. This means each line of code is considered to find vulnerabilities and decide whether the contract is exploitable. Depending on the smart contract complexity this can take multiple days. Additionally, for each line of code that is considered exploitable or vulnerable, a matching Hoare-style source code annotation that picks up the vulnerability is necessary to verify that a possible remedy holds. To choose the right Hoare annotation the specification annotations provided in [3,50] help by listing all possible options and examples of how and where to use them. A downside of this procedure is the time and knowledge needed to seek out, troubleshoot, and check whether vulnerabilities have been fixed with annotations that examine them in detail. But if applied comprehensively this procedure helps to verify the correct execution of smart contracts.

Another approach to verify smart contracts regarding safety is verification of the byte code read by the Ethereum Virtual Machine (EVM) after compiling the high-level source code mostly written in Solidity to machine-readable byte code. The verification of byte code is possible with the help of proof assistants such as Coq and Isabelle/HOL [57]. Both provide formal languages to express mathematical formulas and environments to prove them [13,46]. For this approach, the manual creation of specifications the contract must fulfill is still required.

4.2 Application

For this contract, we follow the above-described procedure to detect vulnerabilities and exploits that can occur in each function.

As a first step, we run the automated analysis tools. They did not find any vulnerabilities besides possible integer overflows[1], but had problems with the current Solidity syntax, and sometimes could not find the pragma version which was implemented. Next, we check for each line of code whether it is exploitable and add applicable Hoare annotations listed in [3,50]. As an example, we use Re-entrancy exploits. They can be prevented with a simple pattern to execute

---

[1] Since Solidity version 0.8.0 uint cannot overflow/underflow anymore [4].

certain instructions before calling other contracts (e.g., decrease cached funds before sending them) or make re-entering a function impossible by violating conditions. Therefore, we consider which functions should be accessible by whom and check if these requirements can be violated or exploited with invariants that must hold at any time. We annotate the contract with an invariant (line 1) to verify that the userBalances that the contract stores never gets in an inconsistent state. The invariant, so the userBalances must always be less or equal to the balance of the contract. With the fixed code where the userBalances variable (line 10) is deducted before the external call (line 8) the invariant holds. Another annotation is useful for the vulnerable function. A precondition (line 4) to prevent self-transfers. This can be necessary since every function is checked independently [23]. Solc-verify correctly outputs without the fix that the conditions might not hold at the end of the function.

```
1 /// @notice invariant __verifier_sum_uint(userBalances) <= address(this).balance
2 contract Reentrancy_insecure {
3        mapping (address => uint) private userBalances;

4        /// @notice precondition msg.sender != address(this)
5        function withdrawBalance() public {
6               uint amountToWithdraw = userBalances[msg.sender];

7               // Here, the caller can call withdrawBalance() again
8               (bool success, ) = msg.sender.callvalue: amountToWithdraw("");
9               require(success);
10              userBalances[msg.sender] = 0;
11       }
12 }
```

If integer variables get modified, we check with pre and postconditions if the modification takes place properly or if the integers can overflow (dependent on the Solidity version). We insert an invariant in line 1 to prove that the function can only be called within a voting phase to prevent access violations. This condition must hold at every time for this function therefore we use an invariant. We check that the commitCounter tracks the number of commits of participants in a voting session and therefore increments itself. Thus we add postconditions and do the same for abort votes. With postconditions we check that the counters increase from their initial value (0) after the function call.

```
1 /// @notice invariant block.timestamp < endOfCommitRequest
2 // count the votings of the participants
3 function commitRequest(bool _agreement) public onlyBeforeEndOfCommitRequest {
4        /// @notice postcondition commitCounter > 0
5        if(_agreement) commitCounter++;
6        /// @notice postcondition abortCounter > 0
7        else abortCounter++;
8 }
```

With the formal verification tools we prove with invariants that restrictions hold at any time e.g. only the owner can call certain functions (access control), only voting within voting phases is possible, the contract has enough funds for transfer and the transfer is successful (unchecked low-level call). Additionally, we check for possible integer overflows, re-entrancy, and correct manipulation of the variables which hold the vote count.

5 Discussion

It stands out that formal verifiers perform better than automated analysis tools. This was expected but some automated analysis tools did not detect what they were intended to. The verifiers can only read one contract at a time and each contract needs specific source code annotations based on the intended behavior. This process is elaborate and we need to be sure we cover the specification. All automated analysis tools have the same problem with detecting the pragma version of a smart contract which cannot be foreseen as it occurs irregularly. Many of today's common security risks come from developers who do not follow recommended development practices [15] and security measures or do not have sufficient knowledge of the Ethereum system [31].

As the comparison and the underlying tests bring forward the automated analysis tools are handy to use but do not cover all of the vulnerabilities we tested. Mythril is one of the three automated analysis tools we used in this work whose run time exceeds the time it took Oyente and Slither to test the data sets by far.

The formal verification tools perform best, especially solc-verify. Both verifiers are able to detect all of the identifiable vulnerabilities we tested for. It is more costly to annotate contracts instead of just running an automated analysis tool on them but it comes with more security, knowledge and brings more code understanding. With the formal verifiers, we could prove the tested smart contracts are vulnerable where the automated analysis tools found no vulnerabilities or marked them insufficiently.

The automated analysis tools sometimes need multiple approaches to run a test and Oyente e.g. gives no output messages for errors. Regular crashes can cause a false interpretation of the results as it might give the impression the contract cannot be tested which might not be the case that we witnessed after several runs.

It seems that the automated analysis tools and the formal verifier VeriSol are not up to date and have problems reading current syntax which made it elaborate to perform tests.

6 Conclusion

We applied the collected knowledge from the vulnerabilities in smart contracts. With the acquainted vulnerabilities, we could limit the spectrum of errors for the two-phase commit smart contract. Additionally, we applied Hoare-style annotations for the case study of the two-phase commit smart contract. With that, we came to the result that with concrete specification annotations formal verification exactly proves the intended behavior of what the contract is designed to do. However the process of defining an extensive and sufficient specification in the form of annotations is elaborate and time-consuming. With our application of the mentioned procedures in our case study of a two-phase commit protocol we came to the conclusion that a mix that combines automated analysis, and formal verification including manual review is the most efficient way to verify the safety of smart contracts.

We recommend using automated analysis tools for initial testing purposes as they are easy and fast to use and already cover many common vulnerabilities. Furthermore, to apply formal verification at the end of the test phase to detect deep-rooted vulnerabilities and verify intended behavior where automated analysis tools are limited. To our consideration, the automated analysis tools performed not as well as presented by the developers and were limited in their findings. Due to different Solidity versions many changes in the source code, e.g. functions needed to be replaced by deprecated functions. This somehow led to the falsification or misinterpretation of the outcomes. We also came to the conclusion that reasoning about possible gas consumption of contracts with their functions and possible compilation bugs is not covered by any tool that we have considered. If there is not enough knowledge for manual verification it is recommended to consider a smart contract audit which might be affordable nowadays considering the costs starting from 500 USD. It is to be seen how Solidity develops and formal verification for smart contracts finds more application. But Solidity improved a lot and has a big community for continuous development and bug fixes nowadays.

In terms of future work, we aim for more research in the field of security of Ethereum smart contracts especially with formal verification methods. This includes tools for automated Hoare-style source code annotations to fully cover possible vulnerabilities. With that, a more independent verification methodology is thinkable. Developers would be able to let a tool mathematically prove the correctness of their smart contract and check if it executes the intended behavior. Furthermore, improvements for the automated analysis tools are highly needed which is also an important topic to which we want to contribute.

References

1. Awosika, E., Richards, S., et al.: Formal verification of smart contracts (2022). https://github.com/ethereum/ethereum-org-website/blob/dev/src/content/devel opers/docs/smart-contracts/formal-verification/index.md
2. InterFi Network: Smart-Contract-Audits (2023). https://github.com/interfinet work/smart-contract-audits
3. Hajdu, A., et al.: Solc-verify-readme.md (2021). https://github.com/SRI-CSL/ solidity/blob/boogie/SOLC-VERIFY-README.md

4. chriseth et al.: Version 0.8.0 (2020). https://github.com/ethereum/solidity/releases/tag/v0.8.0
5. agaperste et al.: Smart Contracts Created (Granular) (2023). https://dune.com/queries/688911
6. J.F.F., et al.: Smartbugs-Curated (2022). https://github.com/smartbugs/smartbugs-curated/tree/main/dataset
7. Almakhour, M., Sliman, L., Samhat, A.E., Mellouk, A.: Verification of smart contracts: a survey. Pervas. Mob. Comput. **67**, 101227 (2020)
8. Antonino, P., Roscoe, A.: Formalising and verifying smart contracts with solidifier: a bounded model checker for solidity. arXiv preprint arXiv:2002.02710 (2020)
9. Antonopoulos, A.M., Wood, G.: Mastering Ethereum: Building Smart Contracts and Dapps. O'reilly Media (2018)
10. Behan, S.: Solidity Smart Contract Testing with Static Analysis Tools. Master's thesis, Dublin, National College of Ireland (2022). https://norma.ncirl.ie/5932/. Submitted
11. Bernardi, T., et al.: Wip: finding bugs automatically in smart contracts with parameterized invariants (2020)
12. Bernhard Mueller, F.I.E.A.: Mythril (2017). https://github.com/ConsenSys/mythril
13. Bertot, Y., Castéran, P.: Interactive theorem proving and program development. In: Coq'Art: The Calculus of Inductive Constructions. Springer (2013)
14. CertiK: Certik - Securing the web3 World (2022). https://www.certik.com/
15. Chriseth, Liu, D., et al · Solidity (2016). https://github.com/ethereum/solidity/blob/develop/docs/security-considerations.rst
16. Di Angelo, M., Salzer, G.: A survey of tools for analyzing ethereum smart contracts. In: 2019 IEEE International Conference on Decentralized Applications and Infrastructures (DAPPCON), pp. 69–78. IEEE (2019)
17. Dika, A., Nowostawski, M.: Security vulnerabilities in ethereum smart contracts. In: 2018 IEEE International Conference on Internet of Things (iThings) and IEEE Green Computing and Communications (GreenCom) and IEEE Cyber, Physical and Social Computing (CPSCom) and IEEE Smart Data (SmartData), pp. 955–962. IEEE (2018)
18. Durieux, T., Ferreira, J.F., Abreu, R., Cruz, P.: Empirical review of automated analysis tools on 47,587 ethereum smart contracts. In: Proceedings of the ACM/IEEE 42nd International Conference on Software Engineering, pp. 530–541 (2020)
19. Ethereum. Goerli Testnet Explorer (2015). https://goerli.etherscan.io/
20. Ethereum. The Native IDE for Web3 Development (2018). https://remix.ethereum.org/
21. Feist, J., Grieco, G., Groce, A.: Slither: a static analysis framework for smart contracts. In: 2019 IEEE/ACM 2nd International Workshop on Emerging Trends in Software Engineering for Blockchain (WETSEB), pp. 8–15 (2019). https://doi.org/10.1109/WETSEB.2019.00008
22. Ferreira, J.F., Cruz, P., Durieux, T., Abreu, R.: Smartbugs: a framework to analyze solidity smart contracts. In: Proceedings of the 35th IEEE/ACM International Conference on Automated Software Engineering, pp. 1349–1352 (2020)
23. Hajdu, A.: Solidity Summit Demo (2022). https://github.com/hajduakos/solidity-summit-demo

24. Hajdu, Á., Jovanović, D.: solc-verify: a modular verifier for Solidity smart contracts. In: Chakraborty, S., Navas, J.A. (eds.) Verified Software. Theories, Tools, and Experiments. LNCS, vol. 12301, pp. 161–179. Springer, Cham (2020). https://doi.org/10.1007/978-3-030-41600-3_11

25. Hajdu, Á., Jovanović, D., Ciocarlie, G.: Formal specification and verification of solidity contracts with events. arXiv preprint arXiv:2005.10382 (2020)

26. Happersberger, V.: Contract of the two-phase commit smart contract (2023). https://goerli.etherscan.io/address/0x6e972a23da401321820ff121c2e41e43140b3dd1/#code

27. Harz, D., Knottenbelt, W.: Towards safer smart contracts: a survey of languages and verification methods. arXiv preprint arXiv:1809.09805 (2018)

28. He, D., Deng, Z., Zhang, Y., Chan, S., Cheng, Y., Guizani, N.: Smart contract vulnerability analysis and security audit. IEEE Network 34(5), 276–282 (2020). https://doi.org/10.1109/MNET.001.1900656

29. Ivančić, F., Yang, Z., Ganai, M.K., Gupta, A., Ashar, P.: Efficient sat-based bounded model checking for software verification. Theoret. Comput. Sci. 404(3), 256–274 (2008)

30. Nikolic, I.: Maian (2018). https://github.com/ivicanikolicsg/MAIAN

31. Kaleem, M., Mavridou, A., Laszka, A.: Vyper: a security comparison with solidity based on common vulnerabilities. In: 2020 2nd Conference on Blockchain Research and Applications for Innovative Networks and Services (BRAINS), pp. 107–111 (2020). https://doi.org/10.1109/BRAINS49436.2020.9223278

32. Kalra, S., Goel, S., Dhawan, M., Sharma, S.: Zeus: analyzing safety of smart contracts. In: NDSS, pp. 1–12 (2018)

33. Kongmanee, J., Kijsanayothin, P., Hewett, R.: Securing smart contracts in blockchain. In: 2019 34th IEEE/ACM International Conference on Automated Software Engineering Workshop (ASEW), pp. 69–76 (2019). https://doi.org/10.1109/ASEW.2019.00032

34. Lee, W.M.: Using the metamask chrome extension. In: Beginning Ethereum Smart Contracts Programming, pp. 93–126. Springer (2019)

35. Luu, L., Chu, D.H., Olickel, H., Saxena, P., Hobor, A.: Making smart contracts smarter. In: Proceedings of the 2016 ACM SIGSAC Conference on Computer and Communications Security, pp. 254–269 (2016)

36. Marks, B., Yang, H., Na, Y.: Two-phase commit using blockchain (2022). https://www.scs.stanford.edu/22spcs244b/projects/TwoPhase%20Commit%20Using%20Blockchain.pdf

37. Mohanta, B.K., Panda, S.S., Jena, D.: An overview of smart contract and use cases in blockchain technology. In: 2018 9th International Conference on Computing, Communication and Networking Technologies (ICCCNT), pp. 1–4 (2018). https://doi.org/10.1109/ICCCNT.2018.8494045

38. Murray, Y., Anisi, D.A.: Survey of formal verification methods for smart contracts on blockchain. In: 2019 10th IFIP International Conference on New Technologies, Mobility and Security (NTMS), pp. 1–6. IEEE (2019)

39. NCC Group + Contributors: Dasp - Top 10. https://dasp.co/

40. Nehaï, Z., Piriou, P.Y., Daumas, F.: Model-checking of smart contracts. In: 2018 IEEE International Conference on Internet of Things (iThings) and IEEE Green Computing and Communications (GreenCom) and IEEE Cyber, Physical and Social Computing (CPSCom) and IEEE Smart Data (SmartData), pp. 980–987 (2018). https://doi.org/10.1109/Cybermatics_2018.2018.00185

41. Nehaï, Z., Bobot, F.: Deductive proof of industrial smart contracts using why3. In: Sekerinski, E., et al. (eds.) Formal Methods. FM 2019 International Workshops: Porto, Portugal, 7–11 October 2019, Revised Selected Papers, Part I, pp. 299–311. Springer, Cham (2020). https://doi.org/10.1007/978-3-030-54994-7_22

42. Perez, D., Livshits, B.: Smart contract vulnerabilities: does anyone care? arXiv preprint arXiv:1902.06710, pp. 1–15 (2019)

43. Perez, D., Livshits, B.: Smart contract vulnerabilities: vulnerable does not imply exploited. In: USENIX Security Symposium, pp. 1325–1341 (2021)

44. Permenev, A., Dimitrov, D., Tsankov, P., Drachsler-Cohen, D., Vechev, M.: Verx: safety verification of smart contracts. In: 2020 IEEE Symposium on Security and Privacy (SP), pp. 1661–1677 (2020). https://doi.org/10.1109/SP40000.2020.00024

45. Petrović, N., Tošić, M.: Semantic approach to smart contract verification. Facta Univ. Ser. Automat. Control Robot. 19(1), 021–037 (2020)

46. Ribeiro, M., Adão, P., Mateus, P.: Formal verification of ethereum smart contracts using Isabelle/HOL. In: Nigam, V., et al. (eds.) Logic, Language, and Security: Essays Dedicated to Andre Scedrov on the Occasion of His 65th Birthday, pp. 71–97. Springer, Cham (2020). https://doi.org/10.1007/978-3-030-62077-6_7

47. Roşu, G., Ştefănescu, A.: From hoare logic to matching logic reachability. In: Proceedings of the Formal Methods: 18th International Symposium (FM 2012), Paris, 27–31 August 2012, pp. 387–402. Springer, Cham (2012)

48. Runtime Verification. Smart Contract Analysis and Verification (2023). https://runtimeverification.com/smartcontract

49. Serca, I.A.: Implementing 2 phase commit (2pc) with solidity (2018). https://ethereum.stackexchange.com/questions/54950/implementing-2-phase-commit-2pc-with-solidity

50. Lahiri, S.: Verisolcontracts.sol (2019). https://github.com/microsoft/verisol/blob/master/Test/regressions/Libraries/VeriSolContracts.sol

51. Lahiri, S., ellab123, et al.: verisol. https://github.com/microsoft/verisol

52. SmartContractSecurity + Contributers. SWC registry smart contract weakness classification and test cases (2020). https://swcregistry.io/

53. Tolmach, P., Li, Y., Lin, S.-W., Liu, Y., Li, Z.: A survey of smart contract formal specification and verification. ACM Comput. Surv. 54(7), 1–38 (2022). https://doi.org/10.1145/3464421

54. Torres, C.F., Schütte, J., State, R.: Osiris: hunting for integer bugs in ethereum smart contracts. In: Proceedings of the 34th Annual Computer Security Applications Conference, pp. 664–676 (2018)

55. Wang, Y., et al.: Formal verification of workflow policies for smart contracts in azure blockchain. In: Chakraborty, S., Navas, J.A. (eds.) Verified Software. Theories, Tools, and Experiments: 11th International Conference, VSTTE 2019, New York City, NY, USA, July 13–14, 2019, Revised Selected Papers, pp. 87–106. Springer, Cham (2020). https://doi.org/10.1007/978-3-030-41600-3_7

56. Yang, Z., Lei, H., Qian, W.: A hybrid formal verification system in coq for ensuring the reliability and security of ethereum-based service smart contracts. IEEE Access 8, 21411–21436 (2020). https://doi.org/10.1109/ACCESS.2020.2969437

57. Hirai, Y.: Ethereum-Formal-Verification-Overview (2018). https://github.com/pirapira/ethereum-formal-verification-overview

58. Zou, W., et al.: Smart contract development: challenges and opportunities. IEEE Trans. Softw. Eng. 47(10), 2084–2106 (2021). https://doi.org/10.1109/TSE.2019.2942301

CHAUSSETTE: A Symbolic Verification of Bitcoin Scripts

Vincent Jacquot[(✉)] and Benoit Donnet

University of Liège, Montefiore Institute, Liège, Belgium
{vjacquot,benoit.donnet}@uliege.be

Abstract. The Bitcoin protocol relies on scripts written in SCRIPT, a simple Turing-incomplete stack-based language, for locking the money carried over the Bitcoin network. This paper explores the usage of symbolic execution for finding transactions that permit to redeem the money without being the legitimate owner. In particular, we show in detail how using insecure scripts could have led to security breaches, resulting in bitcoins theft. Our contributions include (*i*) a quantification of the vulnerable script instances over the full Bitcoin history up to Feburary, 4th 2023; (*ii*) the development and open source publication of a symbolic execution tool, called CHAUSSETTE; (*iii*) the description of how to use CHAUSSETTE to perform the attack; and, (*iv*) a discussion around a way to secure vulnerable money.

1 Introduction

Bitcoin, the first decentralized cryptocurrency has been deployed in 2008 [42]. While numerous cryptocurrencies followed thereafter [12,26], Bitcoin is the largest by market cap: half a trillion USD as of April 2023 [28]. Since then, the development of cryptocurrencies has generated a popular enthusiasm. In particular, for Bitcoin, multiple and various use cases have been implemented both by the academic and developers community [7] [5, Chapter 7]. Among others, we can cite lotteries [9,39], multiparty computations [3,11], or contingent payments [8,38].

In parallel to this enthusiasm, cryptocurrencies have been the subject, throughout the years, of several hijacking [33,35]. According to TRM Labs analysis, 2022 was a record-setting year for crypto hacks, with about $3.7 billion in stolen funds, including 10 hacks involving $100 million or more [47].

One key aspect of Bitcoin is that all applications share the common property of being handled by scripts written in the SCRIPT programming language. Indeed, Bitcoin relies fully on scripts to check the ownership and the validity of money expenses. These scripts are subject to bugs or vulnerabilities [13], introducing the risk of getting hacked and losing money.

In this paper, we provide a security analysis performed on the whole Bitcoin *blockchain* using CHAUSSETTE, a symbolic execution tool we developed. CHAUSSETTE explores all the paths a script's execution might take and searches for a

B. Donnet—This work is supported by the CyberExcellence project funded by the Walloon Region, under number 2110186.

set of input values that allow a money transfer. In addition, we publicly release the CHAUSSETTE code.[1]

Our analysis shows that numerous scripts, more than three hundred thousand, do not properly secure the money they are in charge of. In particular, these insecure scripts allow people other than the true owner to spend the money. In total, tens of bitcoins could have been stolen.

The remainder of this paper is organized as follows: Sect. 2 provides a comprehensive guide on the main building blocks of the Bitcoin protocol and SCRIPT; Sect. 3 introduces CHAUSSETTE, with the results of the analysis on the whole blockchain. The attacks we found are carefully described and quantified; Sect. 5 discusses a potential solution to secure vulnerable funds; Sect. 6 positions this paper with respect to the state of the art; finally, Sect. 7 concludes this paper by summarizing its main achievements.

2   Background

In this section, we provide the required background for the remainder of the paper. In Sect. 2.1, we discuss the main concepts on which the Bitcoin protocol [42] (hereafter abbreviated as BTC), is built. In Sect. 2.2, we provide a comprehensive guide on the mechanisms used to verify the ownership of the currency defined by the protocol. the bitcoin (hereafter abbreviated as ฿).

2.1   The Bitcoin Protocol

The Bitcoin protocol (BTC) defines a decentralized digital currency that enables payments to anyone, anywhere in the world. The *satoshi* is the smallest possible division and equals one hundred millionth of a bitcoin (฿).

BTC runs over a decentralized network of nodes running a consensus algorithm for updating a public ledger of financial transactions. Those transactions are grouped into blocks which are chained together and form the *blockchain*.

Transactions are verified and blocks are created by special nodes called *miners*. In every new block, a given number of new ฿ is created and attributed to the miner as a reward. Initially, the reward was set to 50 ฿ and this value is halved every 210,000 blocks [5, Chapter 10]. Additionally, every transaction specifies a transaction fee paid to the miner which includes the transaction in the block.

BTC is designed to produce a block every ten minutes on average [5, Chapter 10]. The transactions that are broadcasted on the network wait in the *mempool* for a block to be mined.

A transaction is composed of a set of $n > 0$ inputs: $i_0, \ldots, i_{n-1}$ and $m > 0$ outputs: $o_0, \ldots, o_{m-1}$. The rightmost transaction represented in Fig. 1 is composed of two inputs and two outputs. Every output is defined by a script that locks the money and its value in satoshis. Here, the two outputs respectively lock 10^7 and $9,096,749$ satoshis. Every input refers to an output from a previous transaction and contains a proof of ownership. From that point, the referred

---

[1] See https://gitlab.uliege.be/bitcoin/symbolic_execution.

Fig. 1. The satoshis unlocked by the two inputs in the right-most transaction are split between two outputs. The transaction fee is attributed to the miner who includes the transaction into the block.

outputs' values are considered spent. Thus, the miners will reject any further transaction containing an input spending one of them. The two inputs claim respectively $5,882,892$ and $13,218,618$ satoshis from previous outputs. The sum of the values unlocked by the n inputs of a transaction has to be greater or equal to the sum of the values of the m outputs. The difference of the two sums (in the example: $4,761$ satoshis) is the transaction fee that is rewarded to the miner including the transaction into the block.

2.2 The Bitcoin Script Language

BTC defines a stack-based language, SCRIPT, to determine whether an input is allowed to spend or not an output. This language instructions are encoded over one byte and support a wide range of general functionalities such as cryptographic, arithmetic, or branching operations [19]. Some other operations allow pushing byte vectors onto the stack. When used as numbers, byte vectors are interpreted as little-endian variable-length integers with the most significant bit determining the integer sign [19].

Every input and output contains a script, which are both concatenated and executed by the miners. If no error occurs and the script returns `True`, the input is allowed to spend the money. Any non-zero value is interpreted as *True*, but its default representation is the byte vector $0x01$ [20]. On the other hand, `False` is represented by any representation of 0, such as an empty byte vector (its default representation [20]), $0x00$, or $0x80$ (negative zero). BTC specifies a set of standard scripts [14] that are well known and secure methods to lock an output. While the use of standard scripts is recommended, users can implement their own, i.e., non-standard, scripts to support their specific needs.

Figure 2 illustrates the process of validation for an output locked with a standard PUBKEY script. By extension, the output and the corresponding input are said to be of type PUBKEY.

Firstly, the miner extracts the input and output scripts, that are provided in hexadecimal format in Fig. 2. Then, the scripts are parsed and concatenated. The parsing is straightforward: the first opcode 48 (72 in decimal) in the input script indicates the following 72 bytes stand for a constant. This completes the parsing of the input script. The output script starts with the opcode 41 that indicates a

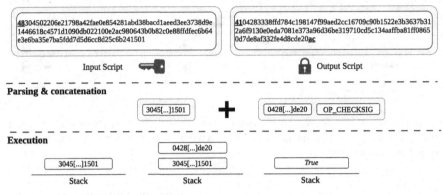

1. CONSTANTS: The constants are pushed onto the stack.
2. OP_CHECKSIG: The operator pops a public key and a signature from the stack.
                 If the signature is valid for the public key and the transaction, *True* is pushed onto the stack. Otherwise, *False* is pushed.

Fig. 2. Claim of a PUBKEY output.

constant of 65 bytes is following. Finally, the last opcode is *ac* standing for the operator OP_CHECKSIG [19].

The miner's last step is to execute the concatenation of the input and output script. The constants are pushed on the stack in LIFO order. OP_CHECKSIG pops two elements from the stack. The first one is assumed to be a public key and the second one a signature. A hash digest is obtained from the transaction. The exact parts of the transaction that are considered to produce the hash [16] are not discussed in this paper. The signature used by OP_CHECKSIG must be a valid signature for this hash and public key. If it is, *True* is pushed onto the stack. Otherwise, *False* is pushed onto the stack.

We also need to cover two other standard scripts defined by BTC: SCRIPT-HASH [2] and WITNESS_V0_SCRIPTHASH [37] which require an extra verification rule.

Every SCRIPTHASH and WITNESS_V0_SCRIPTHASH input contains a second script called the *redeem script*. In SCRIPTHASH (resp. WITNESS_V0_SCRIPT-HASH) inputs, the redeem script is included as the last constant inside the input script (resp. in the witness data, i.e. an optional data array in the input). For example, in Fig. 3, the constant $5121022afc[...]52ae$ is the redeem script. For the sake of simplicity, we do not present the raw hex script, but rather its parsed version. Note that this example stands for one particular instance. Redeem scripts are not restricted to the use of a standard MULTISIG script. In fact, redeem scripts might also be non-standard.

As usually, the miners will execute the input and output script together as illustrated at step 1 in Fig. 3. The redeem script is just interpreted as a constant. Then, a few extra steps are required for the transaction to be valid. The redeem script is parsed again. In the current example, the first byte is 51 that represents the instruction OP_1 and the second byte indicates the presence of a 33-byte constant: $022afc[...]$. To finish, 52 and *ae* stand for the instructions OP_2 and

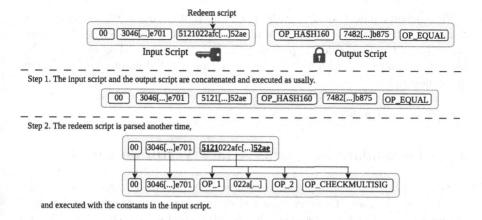

Fig. 3. Claim of a SCRIPTHASH output whose redeem script is a standard MULTISIG script.

OP_CHECKMULTISIG. Finally, the parsed redeem script is executed with the remaining input data. This second execution must also run without errors and return *True* for the input to be valid.

3   Data Collection Methodology

Measurements were run on a computer equipped with an AMD 3600X processor running Ubuntu 20.04.5 at 4.4 GHz using 16 GB. We ran a BTC node on the machine to obtain the full blockchain. The client used was the C++ reference implementation [18] version v22.0.0. This client offers a convenient command line interface to fetch the transactions in JSON format. The blockchain was analyzed from block 0 to 775,000 (included). This latter was published on February 4th, 2023 at 13:14:22 UTC.

Unfortunately, the command line interface does not include much information about the transactions' inputs in the results as they just point to an output [17]. In fact, the type and value of the corresponding output are not included. To circumvent the issue, instead of relying on existing pieces of code, such as Blocksci [32] (no longer supporterd by its authors as of November 2020 [31]) we developed our own tool to parse the blockchain and annotate the inputs (our code is freely available[2]). The annotation is composed of two phases.

During the first phase, the blockchain is parsed exactly once. Unspent outputs are collected and cached in a UTXO (Unspent Transaction Outputs) set in RAM. Because of the RAM constraints, this set can only contain a maximum number of outputs. When the set is full, the oldest unspent outputs are evicted from the cache. The inputs are annotated with their corresponding output, if this latter is in the set.

---

[2] https://gitlab.uliege.be/bitcoin/symbolic_execution.

The second phase consists in labeling the inputs that were not annotated during the first phase. The RAM is filled with as many of these inputs as possible. Then, the blockchain is parsed to find their corresponding outputs. This procedure is repeated with another batch of unannotated inputs until all inputs are annotated.

Our code performed the two phases in roughly 48 h. Our code will be released upon paper acceptance.

4   Non-standard Scripts as Attack Vector on Bitcoin

In this section, we expose how non-standard scripts can be used as an attack vector to steal funds. Those custom scripts (see Sect. 2.2) are implemented by the users or services to protect their funds. They can be involved either in inputs as a redeem script or in outputs. As with every piece of code, they are subject to bugs and vulnerabilities.

Figure 4a exposes a few metrics to give an order of magnitude of the different scripts' usage. 433,458 outputs are locked with a non-standard script, which represents 0.019% of all the outputs. 24,394,307 WITNESS_V0_SCRIPTHASH [37] and 634,004,474 SCRIPTHASH [2] outputs have been used. From these 658.3 million outputs (29% of all outputs), 16.4M are unspent. Amongst the 641.9 million inputs spending the outputs, 3,435,086 redeem scripts (0.15% of all outputs) are non-standard. This gives a total of 3,868,544 non-standard scripts found in the blockchain.

Finally, the probability distribution function (PDF) per output type is provided in Fig. 4b. Most of the variations in usage come from the fact that all the standard scripts have been defined at different points in time. For example, SCRIPTHASH was defined in January 2012 [2] (roughly after block 160,000) and took a long time to be widely adopted.

While still popular, the usage of outputs requiring a redeem script decreases over time for the benefit of simpler locking methods such as PUBKEYHASH and WITNESS_V0_KEYHASH scripts.

While the usage of non-standard scripts stays low in proportion, this still concerns numerous outputs. More importantly, the majority of ₿ is held by a small number of Virtual Asset Service Providers (VASP), because many BTC users rely on them to manage their cryptocurrency [27]. A malicious VASP could start using on purpose a vulnerable non-standard script to protect the funds of their customers. Then, this could be used as a back door to steal the money and the VASP could claim to be under attack.

In the following subsections, two attacks on non-standard scripts are described. The tool implemented to perform these attacks is described priorly at Sect. 4.1. The first attack targets the non-standard output scripts (Sect. 4.2) and the second one targets the non-standard redeem scripts (Sect. 4.3).

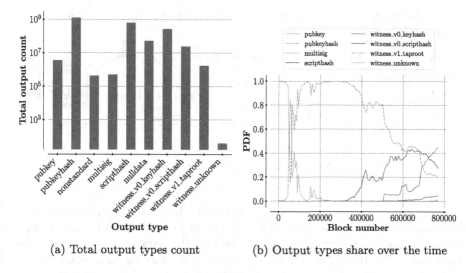

(a) Total output types count   (b) Output types share over the time

Fig. 4. Distribution of the BTC outputs up to block 775,000.

Table 1. Path and opcodes count of the non-standard scripts.

	Mean	Std Dev	95% CI
Path Count	5.622	2.87	±0.003
Opcodes Count	15.35	10.47	±0.01

4.1 CHAUSSETTE: A SCRIPT Symbolic Execution Tool

Symbolic execution is a way of analyzing a program to determine what inputs cause each part of a program to execute. Symbolic execution employs satisfiability-modulo theory (SMT) [40] constraint solvers to determine the feasibility of a path condition and generate concrete solutions for it.

Contrarily to miners who execute scripts on concrete values to check the validity, our symbolic execution tool, called CHAUSSETTE, executes scripts on symbols and returns scripts' output as a function in terms of these symbolic inputs. Then, CHAUSSETTE uses Z3 [41], an SMT solver, to find a set of concrete values for which the script output is True. For example, while a miner would execute the concatenation of an input script and an output script, CHAUSSETTE only considers the output script and searches for values for which the output script returns *True*.

This technique is particularly suitable for the Bitcoin script language as many of the usual limitations do not apply. Indeed, the scripts are usually quite simple (see Table 1), so the number of feasible paths stays computationally manageable. Additionally, the Bitcoin language does not implement arrays [19] that are usually trickier to represent symbolically [43]. Finally, no operator interacts with their environment as a regular program on a machine would, e.g., by making system calls or receiving signals [19].

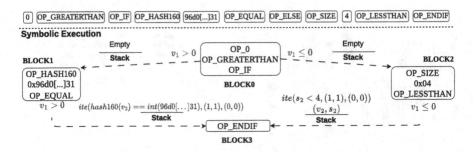

Fig. 5. Example of CHAUSSETTE execution.

Due to space constraints, we do not describe how CHAUSSETTE deals with every operator. Instead, we present how CHAUSSETTE deals with the script illustrated in Fig. 5. CHAUSSETTE's goal is to find the data that will redeem the money locked by this script. We use the acronym *ite* standing for If-Then-Else, such that the expression $ite(a, b, c)$ is evaluated to b if a is *True*, c otherwise. Finally, byte vectors used by SCRIPT are represented as tuples (v, s), where v is the integer interpretation of the vector and s its size in bytes. The default representation of *False* is the empty byte vector $(val = 0, size = 0)$, while the default representation of *True* is $(1, 1)$ (see Sect. 2.2).

As a first step, CHAUSSETTE builds the control flow graph for the script. The opcodes are grouped into blocks of consecutive instructions, these blocks are chained together to represent all the possible paths. The full list of opcodes that might alter the execution flow is [OP-IF, OP-NOTIF, OP-RETURN, OP-VERIFY] [19]. These two latter are special in the sense that they may invalidate the execution. To represent this feature in our model, we create a special final block ERROR-BLOCK that pushes 0 (*False*) onto the stack and does not point to any block. Thus, whenever this block is visited, the top stack is necessarily *False* and invalidates the execution accordingly. The informed reader will notice that some branching operators are missing from the above list, such as OP_CHECKSIGVERIFY, OP_EQUALVERIFY, etc. The reason is that these operators ending with "verify" can be replaced by two operators. For example, the operator OP_CHECKSIGVERIFY can be replaced with the operators OP_CHECKSIG OP_VERIFY without any logic change [19].

The script is decomposed into four blocks: BLOCK0 containing the operators [OP-0 OP-GREATERTHAN OP-IF] that points to BLOCK1 and to BLOCK2 respectively composed of [OP-HASH160 96d0[...]31 OP-EQUAL] and [OP-ELSE OP-SIZE 4 OP-LESSTHAN]. These two blocks point to the final block of the script: BLOCK4 composed of [OP-ENDIF].

The second step is the symbolic execution. We cover in detail in the next paragraphs the execution for blocks 0, 1, 2, and 3. Figure 5 illustrates for each block the set of constraints and the state of the stack after execution which are passed to the child blocks.

BLOCK0. The first block to be executed is the entry point of the script. Firstly, OP-0 pushes the empty vector $(0,0)$ onto the stack. Then, OP-GREATERTHAN tries to pop two elements from the top of the stack. As only one element is on the stack, CHAUSSETTE will generate on the fly a symbolic BTC byte vector. This symbolic vector is represented with a tuple (v_1, s_1), where v_1 stands for its integer value interpretation and s_1 is the number of bytes. Finally, OP-GREATERTHAN pushes another symbolic vector onto the stack represented with the tuple: $ite(v_1 > 0, (1,1), (0,0))$. Finally, OP-IF pops this symbolic vector. Contrarily to a regular execution, both child blocks, BLOCK1 and BLOCK2, will be executed with a different set of constraints: respectively $v_1 > 0$ and $v_1 \leq 0$. Additionally, the state of the stack, that is currently empty, is passed to the children.

BLOCK1. As OP-HASH160 tries to pop an element from an empty stack, a symbolic vector (v_2, s_2) is generated. OP-HASH160 pushes the 20-byte vector [19] $(hash160(v_2), 20)$ onto the stack, where $hash160$ is an uninterpreted function taking one integer as an argument and returning one integer. As a remainder, an uninterpreted function is a function that has no other property than its name and a n-ary form. It allows any interpretation that is consistent with the constraints over the function. Then, the constant $96d0[...]31$ is pushed onto the stack. OP-EQUAL pushes the vector $ite(hash160(v_2) == int(96d0[...]31), (1,1), (0,0))$. Finally, the set of constraints and the state of the memory are passed to BLOCK3.

BLOCK2. A symbolic vector (v_2, s_2) is generated as OP-SIZE needs an element and the stack is empty. OP-SIZE pushes onto the stack the element itself (v_2, s_2), then the size of this element $(s_2, min\_bytes\_encoding(s_2))$ where $min\_bytes\_enco - ding$ is a function returning the size needed to encode s_2. Then, the concrete byte vector $(4,1)$ is pushed onto the stack. Finally, OP-LESSTHAN pops two elements from the stack and pushes $ite(s_2 < 4, (1,1), (0,0))$ on it. No additional constraint is added to the path. As done for BLOCK1, the state of the memory and the set of constraints are passed to BLOCK3.

BLOCK3. As this block has several parents, we need to reconcile both paths' constraints and memories. The parents' constraints are merged using a logical OR. This gives us the expression $v_1 > 0$ OR $v_1 \leq 0$, which simplifies into *True*, which is expected as any execution of the script goes through that block. The memories are reconciled using *ite* expressions. For example, *top*, the top stack element, becomes:

$$top = ite(v_1 > 0, \, ite(hash160(v_2) == int(96d0[...]31), (1,1), (0,0))$$
$$ite(s_2 < 4, (1,1), (0,0)))$$

The last step consists in using Z3 to find values such as $top \neq 0$. Because of the nature of uninterpreted functions, $hash160$ is not constrained and Z3 can evaluate $hash160(v_2) == int(96d0[...]31)$ to *True*. This is equivalent to assuming

Table 2. Patterns for which the votes were not unanimous. The 3rd column designates the number of scripts for which CHAUSSETTE found a solution to unlock them.

Pattern	Script count	Vulnerable script count
OP-CONSTANT OP-CHECKLOCKTIMEVERIFYOP-DROP	15	7
OP-CONSTANT OP-CONSTANT	2	1
CONSTANT CONSTANT CONSTANT OP-CHECKMULTISIG	18	3

we have the ability to perform a preimage attack, which is infeasible [36] for RIPEMD-160 and SHA256, the two hash functions being used by SCRIPT [19]. The trick is to add a final constraint $hash160(v_2) \neq int(96d0[...]31)$. Thus, Z3 will return a solution made of concrete values such as $v_1 < 0$ *and* $s_2 == 4$. In order to redeem the money locked by this script, two constants in the input script are required: the first one being a constant of 4 bytes, the second one being a negative value of any size.

We conclude this subsection with the results of CHAUSSETTE on the 3,868,544 non-standard scripts found. Despite the quantity, most scripts are very similar and can be grouped into 780 patterns. Two scripts containing the same opcodes, but differing only in the constants are said to be generated from the same pattern. In order to speed up the computation, up to 100 scripts (some patterns have fewer than 100 script instances) from every pattern have been randomly selected to be analyzed by CHAUSSETTE with a 30-second timeout. The final security tag attributed to the pattern is voted by majority and propagated to all the script instances generated from this pattern. A pattern can either be considered unsafe if a solution allowing the script to be unlocked is found, safe otherwise.

Apart from three patterns (see Table 2), the votes per pattern were unanimous. These three instances correspond to cases where the constant plays a predominant role in the semantic. For example, in the third pattern, the first constant designates the number of valid signatures the owner must present [19]. In three cases, this constant is 0, making the script vulnerable.

In total, CHAUSSETTE ran 16,138 script over 14,549.65 s ($\sim$4 h). Aggregating the run time per pattern, we obtain a 95% confidence interval for the run time per pattern of $1.33_{\pm 0.2448}$ s.

Moreover, due to the small number of patterns, we have inspected every one of them manually to assert the security tag correctness. We define as a positive a pattern tagged unsafe and a safe pattern as negative. Table 3 contains all the analysis results. Nine patterns over the 780 exceed the 30-second timeout, with five being manually analyzed as unsafe and four as safe. Two patterns use the only opcode that CHAUSSETTE does not support: OP-ROLL, one being safe and the other one unsafe. In total, eleven patterns and the 2,114 related scripts cannot be analyzed by CHAUSSETTE. Therefore, CHAUSSETTE is able to analyze 98.59% of the patterns discovered and 99.94% of the scripts that relate to these patterns.

Table 3. Results of the CHAUSSETTE analysis over the 780 patterns.

		Manual security tag		Total
		Positive	Negative	
CHAUSSETTE security tag	Positive	176	3	**179**
	Negative	2	588	**590**
	Timeout	5	4	**9**
	Not supported	1	1	**2**
Total		**184**	**596**	**780**

Over the 771 patterns CHAUSSETTE manages to analyze within 30 s, we detected three false positives (FP) and two false negatives (FN) for 176 true positives (TP) and 588 true negatives(TN). Considering only the patterns that CHAUSSETTE is able to analyze within 30 s, the recall of CHAUSSETTE is 0.9888 and its precision is 0.9832.

The origin of false positives and false negatives can be traced back to our model that does not always perfectly align with reality. In general, a false positive arises when the model lacks certain constraints, leading it to be overly permissive in its formulation of a solution.

To ease reproducibility and future improvement of the current state of the art, CHAUSSETTE is publicly released upon paper acceptance.[3] Additionally, access to the analyzed scripts will be granted on demand to researchers.

4.2   Non-standard Output Scripts

To perform this attack, the attacker needs to keep up-to-date a real-time UTXO (Unspent Transaction Outputs) set. In April 2023, it is composed of roughly 88M outputs [25] which is manageable for any decent computer. For every unspent output, CHAUSSETTE will return whether this script can be unlocked and the values of the constants to include in the input script.

Note that CHAUSSETTE does not generate the input script by itself, but this could be very easily implemented to fully automate the attack.

This attack can even be upgraded to a replay attack. Let us suppose an output o requires finding a value y such that its $sha256$ hash is x and does not involve any signature verification. As stated in the previous section, CHAUSSETTE is designed to assume that preimage attacks are impossible. However, in the very specific context of BTC, the legit owner must publish the input containing this value y in a transaction t. This transaction t is broadcasted and is waiting in the mempool to be included into the blockchain. One could sniff the mempool very easily, as every full node maintains one. Moreover, most clients propose a very convenient way to fetch this data [15]. Then, one would publish another transaction t' claiming the same output o', but proposing a higher transaction fee to incentive miners to include t' rather than t into the blockchain.

---

[3] See https://gitlab.uliege.be/bitcoin/symbolic_execution.

Table 4. Non-standard output scripts: security analysis results.

	Script count	Pattern count	Total value locked
Vulnerable to symbolic execution	220,554	18	1.94675 ฿
Vulnerable to replay attacks	62	11	2.349736 ฿
Safe	203,485	39	3962.236896 ฿
Unspendable	9,357	16	0.639538 ฿

Table 5. Non-standard input scripts: security analysis results.

	Script count	Pattern count	Total value locked
Vulnerable	153, 310	194	51.07 ฿
Safe	3,281,776	514	2.192923×10^6 ฿

The results in Table 4 summarize the attack's severity. The 433,458 scripts can be grouped into 84 distinct patterns. From the Sect. 4.1, it has been shown that eighteen of them are unsafe, and the 1.947 ฿ protected by the 220,554 scripts derived from them can be unlocked by anyone. On the other hand, the upgraded version of the attack could have been used to steal 2.35 ฿ from 62 scripts. In total, from the 10.63 vulnerable, 9.62 ฿ have been spent, leaving 1.01 ฿ vulnerable. Finally, 9,357 outputs have been proven to be impossible to spend and result from either a malformed script or a script designed to be unspendable [1]. This category also encompasses scripts whose execution was invalidated because of reserved opcodes [19].

4.3   Non-standard Redeem Scripts

This second attack involves sniffing the mempool as for the previous replay attack in order to find inputs spending SCRIPTHASH and WITNESS_V0_SCRIPT-HASH outputs. As a reminder from Sect. 2.2, these outputs include a value x and the miners check that the hash of the redeem script equals to this x.

The attacker only needs to parse the mempool to find a transaction t spending one SCRIPTHASH or WITNESS_V0_SCRIPTHASH output. If the redeem script does not involve any signature operators, the attacker can just publish a transaction t' with the same input, a larger transaction fee, and a different output to steal the money. Because miners tend to include transactions that maximize their profit, t' is more likely to be included than t [5, Chapter 2].

Table 5 contains the results of the analysis on the 3,435,086 non-standard redeem scripts we found. 51.07 ฿ have been spent with an input that could have been attacked, i.e., the redeem script does not involve any signature. While, this only represents an insignificant percentage (0.0023289%) of the total money that has flown through these outputs, it still represents a decent incentive for hackers.

There are exactly 16.4M unspent SCRIPTHASH and WITNESS_V0_SCRIPT-HASH outputs, and they lock a total value of 5.46M ฿. This value is provided by TRM Labs[4], as it was faster to ask them rather than set up a UTXO set. This represents the only third-party data we used in this paper. Thus, it represents 26% of the 21M ฿ that will ever be mined [5, Chapter 1]. Unless they are including an x value already encountered in the blockchain, the corresponding redeem script is unknown. Thus, it is unfortunately impossible to know for every one of them if they are safe or not.

But, the presence of 153,310 vulnerable scripts over the 641.9M spent SCRIPTHASH and WITNESS_V0_SCRIPTHASH outputs, gives a vulnerability ratio of 0.000238838. Assuming the same ratio holds for the 16.4M unspent outputs, we are able to provide an estimation of 1,304 ฿ that might be stolen.

5   Attempts to Secure BTC

This section starts with recommendations to secure the future published scripts against the attacks we have just described (Sect. 5.1). Then, a discussion on how to secure scripts that are already published is proposed (Sect. 5.2).

5.1   Recommendations

At first, companies and individuals should consider if they really need to use non-standard scripts because innovation introduces new risks as demonstrated in Sect. 4. In case the need is real, the use of tools such as CHAUSSETTE is necessary to assert the security.

As a rule of thumb, script developers should ensure that every possible path involves at least one signature operation. Moreover, they should keep in mind that relying only on pre-image hashes is not sufficient to guarantee security. Indeed, a transaction containing a secret is going to be made public before being included in the blockchain.

5.2   Securing Published Scripts

Unfortunately, there is no perfect solution for the published scripts that are currently vulnerable. However, this section explores a potential solution.

Let us consider the following context. Bob owns some ฿ in a SCRIPTHASH output. To spend it, Bob needs to publish the redeem script in an input in a transaction t and suppose this script is vulnerable as described in Sect. 4. From that moment, this transaction t is broadcasted, but not yet included in the blockchain as it is waiting for a miner to include it in a block. As far as we know, there is no mechanism implemented to prevent an attacker (Alice) performing a replay attack as described in Sect. 4.

---

[4] https://www.trmlabs.com/.

Such a situation has already been discussed in 2013 by the BTC community as they faced the same issue [45]. A few outputs (see 37k7toV1Nv4DfmQbm Z8KuZDQCYK9x5KpzP) were designed to be awarded to the first person finding a collision for *sha*1. The redeem script did not involve any signatures, thus making an attack possible.

By applying the same solution suggested in the thread, Bob would not broadcast t, but instead he would mine a block by itself and include t in it. The redeem script would become public at the same time as the output will be spent. Attacking this vulnerable output would require rewriting BTC history which is computationally impossible unless Alice owns 51% of the computation power [5, Chapter 10].

Unfortunately, this solution is impractical nowadays as the amount of computing resources to mine a block is greatly higher than in 2013 [24]. As an alternative, Bob could reach out to a known ₿ mining company [6] and provide them with proof of ownership. The mining company would not broadcast t and would include the transaction moving Bob's fund to a secured address directly in a block. The downside of this solution is that it relies on the ability to trust the mining company. From the moment this company is in possession of t, they could simply modify it to steal the money.

6   Related Work

Blockchain security has attracted the attention of the research community those last years. Numerous tools, such as Mythril [29], Securify [48], Manticore [46], and Oyente [30] have been developed to analyze and report security issues in Ethereum smart contracts. These tools also employ some symbolic analysis of the code.

To the best of our knowledge, no tool designed for BTC exists. A prototype tool [34] has been developed, but it only covers a portion of SCRIPT language and was tested on two real BTC scripts.

Bartoletti and Zunino [10] define a theory of liquidity and a verification technique for contracts expressed in BitML, a high level DSL (Domain Specific Language) for smart contracts that compile into BTC transactions.

Finally, Andrychowicz et al. [4] discuss a framework for modeling the BTC contracts using timed automata. They provide two BTC contracts that are modeled manually as an example. Unfortunately, no automation process has been provided yet.

7   Conclusion

While BTC is considered safe by most people, this paper highlighted vulnerabilities in non-standard scripts written in SCRIPT that could have led to the theft of 55.36 ₿, 1.57M US dollars worth on April, 26th 2023 [23]. A comprehensive guide on SCRIPT and its role in securing ฿ and the detailed attacks was provided. Moreover, a proposal to secure the ฿ that might still be vulnerable has been given.

The BTC blockchain was parsed up to block 775,000 and 3,868,544 non-standard scripts have been found. These scripts can be grouped into 780 patterns.

CHAUSSETTE, our symbolic execution tool, is capable of analyzing 99.94% of the BTC scripts within 30 s with a precision and a recall of respectively 0.9832 and 0.9888. Moreover, CHAUSSETTE highlights the presence of numerous insecure patterns used to secure ฿.

Potential future works include, but are not limited to, the application of CHAUSSETTE to assert other UTXO blockchains' security which are also using SCRIPT [21,22] or the application of symbolic execution techniques to account-based blockchains.

Ethical Considerations.. The researches discussed in this paper have been conducted in accordance to ethical considerations in blockchain network measurements [44]. Further, to avoid any security issue, the vulnerable scripts are not released publicly. Finally, CHAUSSETTE must be seen as a tool for also assessing vulnerability risks in using non-standard scripts.

References

1. Andresen, G.: Bitcoin core release notes 0.9.0. https://github.com/bitcoin/bitcoin/blob/master/doc/release-notes/release-notes-0.9.0.md. Accessed 20 Apr 2023
2. Andresen, G.: Pay to script hash. BIP 16, Bitcoin (January 2012)
3. Andrychowicz, M., Dziembowski, S., Malinowski, D., Mazurek, L.: Fair two-party computations via bitcoin deposits. In: Proceedings of the Financial Cryptography and Data Security (FC) (March 2014)
4. Andrychowicz, M., Dziembowski, S., Malinowski, D., Mazurek, L.: Modeling bitcoin contracts by timed automata. In: Proceedings of the Formal Modeling and Analysis of Timed Systems (FORMATS) (September 2014)
5. Antonopoulos, A.: Mastering Bitcoin. O'Reilly Media, Inc. (2014)
6. Arrieche, A., Henn, P.: Who are the biggest bitcoin mining companies? https://capital.com/biggest-global-crypto-bitcoin-mining-companies-ranking-btc#:~:text=What%20are%20the%20famous%20bitcoin,according%20to%20data%20from%20CompaniesMarketCap. Accessed 08 May 2023
7. Atzei, N., Bartoletti, M., Cimoli, T., Lande, S., Zunino, R.: Sok: unraveling bitcoin smart contracts. In: Proceedings of the Principles of Security and Trust (POST) (April 2018)
8. Banasik, W., Dziembowski, S., Malinowski, D.: Efficient zero-knowledge contingent payments in cryptocurrencies without scripts. In: Proceedings of the European Symposium on Research in Computer Security (ESORICS) (September 2016)
9. Bartoletti, M., Zunino, R.: Constant-deposit multiparty lotteries on bitcoin. In: Proceedings of the Financial Cryptography and Data Security (FC) (April 2017)
10. Bartoletti, M., Zunino, R.: Verifying liquidity of bitcoin contracts. In: Proceedings of the Principles of Security and Trust (POSRT) (April 2019)
11. Bentov, I., Kumaresan, R.: How to use bitcoin to design fair protocols. In: Proceedings of the Advances in Cryptology (CRYPTO) (August 2014)

12. Binance. Binance Coin Whitepaper. https://www.exodus.com/assets/docs/binance-coin-whitepaper.pdf. Accessed 02 May 2023
13. Bistarelli, S., Mercanti, I., Santini, F.: An analysis of non-standard bitcoin transactions. In: Proceedings of the Crypto Valley Conference on Blockchain Technology (CVCBT) (June 2018)
14. Bitcoin Community. Bitcoin improvement proposals. https://github.com/bitcoin/bips. Accessed 30 Mar 2023
15. Bitcoin Community. getrawmempool - bitcoin. https://developer.bitcoin.org/reference/rpc/getrawmempool.html. Accessed 01 June 2023
16. Bitcoin Community. Op checksig. https://en.bitcoin.it/wiki/OP_CHECKSIG. Accessed 07 Aug 2023
17. Bitcoin Community. RPC API Reference. https://developer.bitcoin.org/reference/rpc/. Accessed 11 Apr 2023
18. Bitcoin Community. Running a Full Node. https://bitcoin.org/en/full-node. Accessed 30 Mar 2023
19. Bitcoin Community. Script. https://en.bitcoin.it/wiki/Script. Accessed 30 Mar 2023
20. Bitcoin Core Developers. Bitcoin Core - interpreter.cpp. https://github.com/bitcoin/bitcoin/blob/80f4979322b574be29c684b2e106804432420ebf/src/script/interpreter.cpp#L412. Accessed 28 Apr 2023
21. Bitcoin Core Developers. Dogecoin - script.cpp. https://github.com/dogecoin/dogecoin/blob/master/src/script/script.cpp. Accessed 02 May 2023
22. Bitcoin Core Developers. Litecoin - script.cpp. https://github.com/litecoin-project/litecoin/blob/master/src/script/script.cpp. Accessed 02 May 2023
23. blockchain.com: Bitcoin Price. https://www.blockchain.com/explorer/assets/btc. Accessed 26 Apr 2023
24. blockchain.com. Total hash rate (TH/s). https://www.blockchain.com/fr/explorer/charts/hash-rate. Accessed 26 Apr 2023
25. blockchain.com. Unspent transaction outputs. https://www.blockchain.com/fr/explorer/charts/utxo-count. Accessed 18 Apr 2023
26. Buterin, V.: Ethereum Whitepaper. https://ethereum.org/en/whitepaper/. Accessed 02 May 2023
27. Chainalysis: 60% of bitcoin is held long term as digital gold. What about the rest?, https://blog.chainalysis.com/reports/bitcoin-market-data-exchanges-trading/. Accessed 13 Apr 2023
28. CoinMarketCap. Coinmarketcap. https://coinmarketcap.com/fr/. Accessed 26 Apr 2023
29. ConsenSys. Mythril. https://github.com/ConsenSys/mythril. Accessed 12 Apr 2023
30. Enzyme Finance. Oyente. https://github.com/enzymefinance/oyente. Accessed 12 Apr 2023
31. Kalodner, H., et al.: Blocksci. https://github.com/citp/BlockSci. Accessed 07 Aug 2023
32. Kalodner, H., et al.: BlockSci: dsign and applications of a blockchain analysis platform. In: Proceedings of the USENIX Security Symposium (August 2020)
33. Kessler, S.: Axie infinity's Ronin blockchain overhauls tech, expands to new game studios a year after $625m hack. https://www.coindesk.com/tech/2023/03/30/axie-infinitys-ronin-blockchain-overhauls-tech-expands-to-new-ip-on-anniversary-of-600m-hack/. Accessed 02 May 2023

34. Klomp, R., Bracciali, A.: On symbolic verification of bitcoin's script language. In: Proceedings of the Data Privacy Management, Cryptocurrencies and Blockchain Technology (DPM) (September 2018)

35. Korn, J.: Another crypto bridge attack: nomad loses $190 million in chaotic hack. https://edition.cnn.com/2022/08/03/tech/crypto-bridge-hack-nomad/index. html. Accessed 02 May 2023

36. Li, Y., Liu, F., Wang, G.: New records in collision attacks on RIPEMD-160 and SHA-256. In: Proceedings of the International Conference on the Theory and Applications of Cryptographic Techniques (EUROCRYPT) (April 2023)

37. Lombrozo, E., Lau, J., Wuille, P.: Segregated witness (consensus layer). BIP 141, Bitcoin (December 2015)

38. Maxwell, G.: The first successful zero-knowledge contingent payment. https://bitcoincore.org/en/2016/02/26/zero-knowledge-contingent-payments-announcement/. Accessed 12 Apr 2023

39. Miller, A.K., Bentov, I.: Zero-collateral lotteries in bitcoin and ethereum. In: Proceedings of the IEEE European Symposium on Security and Privacy Workshops (EuroS&PW) (April 2016)

40. Monniaux, D.: A survey of satisfiability modulo theory. In: Proceedings of the Computer Algebra in Scientific Computing (SASC) (September 2016)

41. de Moura, L., Bjørner, N.: Z3: an efficient SMT solver. In: Proceedings of the International Conference on Tools and Algorithms for the Construction and Analysis of Systems (TACAS) (March–April 2008)

42. Nakamoto, S.: Bitcoin: a peer-to-peer electronic cash system (2008). http://www.bitcoin.org/bitcoin.pdf

43. Perry, D., Mattavelli, A., Zhang, X., Cadar, C.: Accelerating array constraints in symbolic execution. In: Proceedings of the ACM SIGSOFT International Symposium on Software Testing and Analysis (ISSTA) (July 2017)

44. Tang, Y., Li, K., Wang, Y., Chen, J.: Ethical challenges in blockchain network measurement research. In: Proceedings of the Workshop on Ethics in Computer Security (EthiCS) (February 2023)

45. Todd, P.: Topic: REWARD offered for hash collisions for SHA1, SHA256, RIPEMD160 and other. https://bitcointalk.org/index.php?topic=293382.0. Accessed 26 Apr 2023

46. Trail of Bits: Manticore. https://github.com/trailofbits/manticore. Accessed 12 Apr 2023

47. TRM Labs. Looking back at 2022 and towards 2023 to see what the future holds for digital assets policy (December 2022). https://www.trmlabs.com/post/looking-back-at-2022-and-towards-2023-to-see-what-the-future-holds-for-digital-assets-policy. Accessed 26 Apr 2023

48. Tsankov, P., Dan, A., Drachsler-Cohen, D., Gervais, A., Bünzli, F., Vechev, M.: Securify: practical security analysis of smart contracts. In: Proceedings of the ACM SIGSAC Conference on Computer and Communications Security (CCS) (October 2018)

A Simple Single Slot Finality Protocol
for Ethereum

Francesco D'Amato⬡ and Luca Zanolini(✉)⬡

Ethereum Foundation, Zug, Switzerland
{francesco.damato,luca.zanolini}@ethereum.org

Abstract. Currently, Gasper, the implemented consensus protocol of
Ethereum, takes between 64 and 95 slots to finalize blocks. Because of
that, a significant portion of the chain is susceptible to reorgs. The possibility to capture MEV (Maximum Extractable Value) through such
reorgs can then disincentivize honestly following the protocol, breaking
the desired correspondence of honest and rational behavior. Moreover,
the relatively long time to finality forces users to choose between economic security and faster transaction confirmation. This motivates the
study of the so-called single slot finality protocols: consensus protocols
that finalize a block in each slot and, more importantly, that finalize the
block proposed at a given slot within such slot.

In this work we propose a *simple, non-blackbox* protocol that combines a synchronous dynamically available protocol with a partially synchronous finality gadget, resulting in a consensus protocol that can finalize one block per slot, paving the way to *single slot finality* within
Ethereum. Importantly, the protocol we present can finalize the block
proposed in a slot, within such slot.

Keywords: Ethereum · single slot finality · ebb-and-flow · consensus

1 Introduction and Related Work

Traditional Byzantine consensus protocols, such as PBFT [5], are devised in a
partial synchronous network model [8], in the sense that they always guarantee
safety, but they guarantee liveness only after GST. In this setting, however,
participants in the protocol are fixed, known in advance, and without possibility
to go *offline*.

Dynamic participation (among systems' participants) has lately become an
essential prerequisite for developing permissionless consensus protocols. This
concept, initially formalized by Pass and Shi via their *sleepy model*, [15] encap-
sulates the ability of a system to handle participants joining or leaving during a
protocol execution. In particular, a consensus protocol that preserves safety and
liveness while allowing dynamic participation is called *dynamically available*.

One problem of such protocols, as a result of the CAP theorem [9,11], is
that they do not tolerate network partitions; no consensus protocols can both

S. Katsikas et al. (Eds.): ESORICS 2023 Workshops, LNCS 14398, pp. 376–393, 2024.
https://doi.org/10.1007/978-3-031-54204-6_23

satisfy liveness (under dynamic participation) and safety (under temporary network partitions). Simply put, a consensus protocol (for state-machine replication) cannot produce a single chain that concurrently offers dynamic availability and guarantees transaction finality in case of asynchronous periods or network partitions. Because of that, dynamically available protocols studied so far are focused on a synchronous model [6,12,13].

To overcome this impossibility result, Neu at al. [14] introduce a family of protocols, referred to as *ebb-and-flow* protocols, which operate under two confirmation rules, and outputting two chains, one a prefix of the other. The first confirmation rule defines what is known as the *available chain*, which provides liveness under dynamic participation (and synchrony). The second confirmation rule defines the *finalized chain*, and provides safety even under network partitions. Interestingly, such family of protocols also captures the nature of the Ethereum consensus protocol, Gasper [4], in which the available chain is output by (the confirmation rule of) LMD-GHOST [17], and the finalized chain by the (confirmation rule of the) *finality gadget* Casper FFG [3]. However, the (original version of) LMD-GHOST is actually not secure [14] even in a context of full-participation.

Motivated by finding a (more secure) alternative to LMD-GHOST, and following the ebb-and-flow approach, D'Amato *et al.* [6] devise a synchronous dynamically available consensus protocol, Goldfish, that, combined with a generic (partially synchronous) finality gadget, implements an ebb-and-flow protocol. Moreover, Goldfish is reorg resilient: blocks proposed by honest validators are guaranteed inclusion in the chain. However, Goldfish is brittle to temporary asynchrony [7], in the sense that even a single violation of the bound of network delay can lead to a catastrophic failure, jeopardizing the safety of *any* previously confirmed block, resulting in a protocol that is not practically viable to replace LMD-GHOST in Ethereum. In other words, Goldfish is not *asynchrony resilient*.

To cope with the problem of Goldfish, D'Amato and Zanolini [7] propose RLMD-GHOST, a provably secure synchronous protocol that does not lose safety during *bounded* periods of asynchrony and which tolerates a weaker form of dynamic participation, offering a trade-off between dynamic availability and asynchrony resilience. Their protocol results appealing for practical systems, where strict synchrony assumptions might not always hold, contrary to what is generally assumed with standard synchronous protocols.

In this work we build upon the work of D'Amato and Zanolini [7], and we devise a protocol that combines RLMD-GHOST with a partially synchronous finality gadget. In particular, we give the following contributions. We devise a secure and reorg-resilient ebb-and-flow protocol [14] as a potential substitute for the current Ethereum consensus protocol, Gasper [4], which can finalize (at most) one block per slot. In particular, our protocol can finalize the block proposed in the current slot, within such slot, paving the way to *single slot finality* [2] protocols for practical use within Ethereum. Finally, we expand upon the *generalized sleepy model* [7] introduced by D'Amato and Zanolini [7], adjusting it to accommodate a partially synchronous setting. We refer to the resulting model as the *generalized partially synchronous sleepy model*. This enhanced model not only extends the original sleepy model, first presented by Pass and Shi [15], but it also introduces stronger and more generalized constraints related to the corruption and sleepiness power of the adversary. Furthermore, our model integrates the concept of partial synchrony, setting it apart from the model proposed by D'Amato and Zanolini [7]. Our security results will be proven within this extended model.

The remainder of this work is structured as it follows. In Sect. 2 we present our system model. Prerequisites for this work are presented in Sect. 3; we recall RLMD-GHOST as originally presented by D'Amato and Zanolini [7], state its properties, and show a class of protocols, called *propose-vote-merge* protocols, that groups together (a variant of) LMD-GHOST, (a variant of) Goldfish, and RLMD-GHOST under an unique framework. Protocol specifications are described in Sect. 4. In particular, we show how to slightly modify RLMD-GHOST to interact with a finality gadget, and then present the full protocol. In Sect. 5 we formally prove the properties that our protocol satisfy. Finally, in Sect. 6 we enable our protocol to finalize the block proposed in the current slot through *acknowledgments*, messages sent by participants in the consensus protocol, but only relevant to external observers. Conclusions are drawn in Sect. 7. Missing proofs can be found in the full version of this work.

2   Model and Preliminary Notions

2.1   System Model

We consider a set of n *validators* $v_1, \ldots, v_n$ that communicate with each other through exchanging messages. Every validator is identified by a unique cryptographic identity and the public keys are common knowledge. Validators are assigned a protocol to follow, consisting of a collection of programs with instructions for all validators. A validator that follows its protocol during an execution is called *honest*. Each validator has a *stake*, which we assume to be the same for every validator. If a validator v_i fails to serve the role assigned to it or tries to deliberately deviate from the protocol, i.e., v_i is *Byzantine*, and a proof of this misbehavior is given, it loses a part of its stake proportional to the severity of the fault (v_i gets *slashed*). We assume the existence of a probabilistic poly-time adversary $\mathcal{A}$ that can choose up to f validators to corrupt over an entire protocol execution. Corrupted validators stay corrupted for the remaining duration of the protocol execution, and are thereafter called *adversarial*. The adversary $\mathcal{A}$ knows the the internal state of adversarial validators. The adversary is *adaptive*: it chooses the corruption schedule dynamically, during the protocol execution.

We assume that a best-effort gossip primitive that will reach all validators is available. In a protocol, this primitive is accessed through the events "sending a message through gossip" and "receiving a gossiped message." Moreover, we assume that messages from honest validator to honest validator are eventually received and cannot be forged. This includes messages sent by Byzantine validators, once they have been received by some honest validator v_i and gossiped around by v_i.

Time is divided into discrete *rounds*. We consider a partially synchronous model in which validators have synchronized clocks but there is no a priori bound on message delays. However, there is a time (not known by the validators), called *global stabilization time* (GST), after which message delays are bounded by Δ rounds. Moreover, we define the notion of *slot* as a collection of 4Δ rounds. The adversary $\mathcal{A}$ can decide for each round which honest validator is *awake* or *asleep* at that round [15]. Asleep validators do not execute the protocol and messages for that round are queued and delivered in the first round in which the validator is awake again. Honest validators that become awake at round r, before starting to participate in the protocol, must first execute (and terminate) a *joining protocol* (Sect. 3), after which they become *active*. All adversarial validators are always awake, and are not prescribed to follow any protocol. Therefore, we always use active, awake, and asleep to refer to honest validators. As for corruptions, the adversary is adaptive also for sleepiness, *i.e.*, the sleepiness schedule is also chosen dynamically by the adversary. Moreover, there is a time (not known by the validators), called *global awake time* (GAT), after which all validators are always awake.

We assume that every message has an *expiration period* η [6,7]. More specifically, for a given slot t and a constant $\eta \in \mathbb{N}$ greater than or equal to 0, the *expiration period* for slot t is the interval $[t - \eta, t - 1]$. Only messages sent within this time frame influence the behavior of the protocol at slot t. Furthermore, during each protocol execution slot, only the most recent messages sent by validators are considered.

We require that, for some fixed parameter $1 \leq \tau \leq \infty$, the following condition, referred by D'Amato and Zanolini [7] as τ-*sleepiness at slot t*, holds for any slot t *after* GST:

$$|H_{t-1}| > |A_t \cup (H_{t-\tau,t-2} \setminus H_{t-1})| \tag{1}$$

with H_t, A_t, and $H_{s,t}$ are the set of active validators at round $4\Delta t + \Delta$, the set of adversarial validators at round $4\Delta t + \Delta$, and the set of validators that are active *at some point* in slots $[s,t]$, *i.e.*, $H_{s,t} = \bigcup_{i=s}^{t} H_i$ (if $i < 0$ then $H_i := \emptyset$), respectively. Note that $f = \lim_{t \to \infty} |A_t|$. In other words, we require the number of active validators at round $4\Delta(t - 1) + \Delta$ to be greater than the number of adversarial validators at round $4\Delta t + \Delta$, together with the number of validators that were active at some point between rounds $4\Delta(t - \tau) + \Delta$ and $4\Delta(t-2) + \Delta$, but not at round $4\Delta(t - 1) + \Delta$.

Intuitively, this condition is designed to work with a protocol that applies expiration to its messages, with the period set as $\eta = \tau$. The messages taken into consideration at slot t originate from slots $[t - \tau, t - 1]$. Among these, the only messages sent by honest validators that can be relied upon come from H_{t-1}. However, unexpired messages from honest validators, who were inactive in slot $t - 1$, could potentially aid the adversary.

Note that our approach diverges from the *generalized sleepy model* proposed by D'Amato and Zanolini [7]. Specifically, we require that Eq. 1 only holds after GST and we refer to this model as the *generalized partially synchronous τ-sleepy model* (or wlog, when the context is clear, as the τ-*sleepy model* for short). Finally, we say that an execution in the generalized partially synchronous sleepy model is τ-*compliant* if it satisfies τ-sleepiness (Eq. 1).

2.2 Validator Internals

View. A *view* (at a given round r), denoted by $\mathcal{V}$, is a subset of all the messages that a validator has received until r. The notion of view is *local* for the validators. For this reason, when we want to focus the attention on a specific view of a validator v_i, we denote with $\mathcal{V}_i$ the view of v_i (at a round r).

Blocks and chains. Let's consider two chains, ch_1 and ch_2. We denote $\mathsf{ch}_1 \prec \mathsf{ch}_2$ if ch_1 acts as a prefix to ch_2. When block B is at the end of chain ch, we refer to it as the *head of* ch, and we equate the entire chain with B. Therefore, if $\mathsf{ch}' \prec \mathsf{ch}$ and A is the head of ch', we also express this as $\mathsf{ch}' \prec B$ and $A \prec B$.

Fork-choice functions. A *fork-choice function* is a deterministic function, denoted as FC. This function, when given a view $\mathcal{V}$ and a slot t as inputs, produces a block B. If B is a block extending $\mathsf{FC}(\mathcal{V}, t)$, then $\mathsf{FC}(\mathcal{V} \cup B, t)$ equals B. The result of FC is referred to as the *head of the canonical chain* in $\mathcal{V}$, and the chain with B as its head is referred to as the *canonical chain* in $\mathcal{V}$. Every validator keeps track of its canonical chain and updates it using FC, according to its local view. The canonical chain for validator v_i at round r is represented as ch_i^r. In this work we will focus our attention on a specific class of fork-choice functions based on GHOST [16]. D'Amato and Zanolini [7] characterize a GHOST-based fork-choice function by a view filter FIL, which takes as input a view $\mathcal{V}$ and a slot t, and outputs $(\mathcal{V}', t)$, where $\mathcal{V}'$ is another view such that $\mathcal{V}' \subseteq \mathcal{V}$. Then, $\mathsf{FC}(\mathcal{V}, t) := \mathrm{GHOST}(\mathsf{FIL}(\mathcal{V}, t))$, i.e., $\mathsf{FC} := \mathrm{GHOST} \circ \mathsf{FIL}$.

2.3 Security

Security Parameters. In this work we treat λ and κ as the security parameters related to the cryptographic components utilized by the protocol and the protocol's own security parameter, respectively. We also account for a finite time horizon, represented as T_{hor}, which is polynomial in relation to κ. An event is said to occur with *overwhelming probability* if it happens except with probability which is $\mathrm{negl}(\kappa) + \mathrm{negl}(\lambda)$. The properties of cryptographic primitives hold true with a probability of $\mathrm{negl}(\lambda)$, signifying an overwhelming probability, although we will not explicitly mention this in the subsequent sections of this work.

Confirmed Chain. The protocols we consider always specify a *confirmation rule*, with whom validators can identify a *confirmed prefix* of the canonical chain. Alongside the canonical chain, validators then also keep track of a *confirmed chain*. We refer to the confirmed chain of validator v_i at round r as Ch_i^r (cf. ch_i^r for the canonical chain).

Definition 1 (Secure protocol [6]). *We say that a protocol outputting a confirmed chain Ch is secure after time T_{sec}, and has confirmation time T_{conf}[1], if Ch satisfies:*

Safety *For any two rounds $r, r' \geq T_{\text{sec}}$, and any two honest validators v_i and v_j (possibly $i = j$) at rounds r and r' respectively, either $\mathsf{Ch}_i^r \prec \mathsf{Ch}_j^{r'}$ or $\mathsf{Ch}_j^{r'} \prec \mathsf{Ch}_i^r$.*

Liveness *For any rounds $r \geq T_{\text{sec}}$ and $r' \geq r + T_{\text{conf}}$, and any honest validator v_i active at round r', $\mathsf{Ch}_i^{r'}$ contains a block proposed by an honest validator at a round $> r$.*

A protocol satisfies τ-safety and τ-liveness if it satisfies safety and liveness, respectively, in the τ-sleepy model, i.e., in τ-compliant executions. A protocol satisfies τ-security if it satisfies τ-safety and τ-liveness.

We now recall the definitions of *dynamic availability* and *reorg resilience* from [7]. We consider them only under network synchrony, *i.e.*, for $\mathsf{GST} = 0$, as this is the only setting in which we utilize them. Note that it is customary to only analyze dynamic availability with $\mathsf{GST} = 0$, when analyzing the behavior of ebb-and-flow protocols.

Definition 2 (Dynamic availability). *We say that a protocol is τ-dynamically-available if and only if it satisfies τ-security with confirmation time $T_{\text{conf}} = O(\kappa)$ when $\mathsf{GST} = 0$. Moreover, we say that a protocol is dynamically available if it is 1-dynamically-available, as this corresponds to the usual notion of dynamic availability.*

Definition 3 (Reorg resilience). *An execution with $\mathsf{GST} = 0$ satisfies reorg resilience if any honest proposal B from a slot t is always in the canonical chain of all active validators at rounds $\geq 4\Delta t + \Delta$. A protocol is τ-reorg-resilient if all τ-compliant executions with $\mathsf{GST} = 0$ satisfy reorg resilience.*

Definition 4 (Accountable safety). *We say that a protocol has accountable safety with resilience $f > 0$ if, upon a safety violation, it is possible to identify at least f responsible participants. In particular, it is possible to collect evidence from sufficiently many honest participants and generate a cryptographic proof that identifies f adversarial participants as protocol violators. Such proof*

---

[1] If the protocol satisfies liveness, then at least one honest proposal is added to the confirmed chain of all active validators every T_{conf} slots. Since honest validators include all transactions they see, this ensures that transactions are confirmed within time $T_{\text{conf}} + \Delta$ (assuming infinite block sizes or manageable transaction volume).

cannot falsely accuse any honest participant that followed the protocol correctly. Finally, we also say that a chain is f-accountable if the protocol outputting it has accountable safety with resilience f. If a protocol Π outputs multiple chains $\mathsf{Ch}_1, \ldots, \mathsf{Ch}_k$, *we say that* Ch_i *is f-accountable if* Π_i *is, where* Π_i *is the protocol which runs* Π *and outputs only* Ch_i.

Ebb-and-flow Protocols. Neu *et al.* [14] propose a protocol with two confirmation rules that outputs two chains, one that provides liveness under dynamic participation (and synchrony), and one that provides accountable safety even under network partitions. This protocol is called *ebb-and-flow* protocol. We present a generalization of it, in the τ-sleepy model.

Definition 5 (τ-secure ebb-and-flow protocol)
A τ-secure ebb-and-flow protocol *outputs an available chain* chAva *that is τ-dynamically-available if* $\mathsf{GST} = 0$, *and a finalized (and accountable) chain* chFin *that, if $f < \frac{n}{3}$, is always safe and is live after* $\max\{\mathsf{GST}, \mathsf{GAT}\}$. *Moreover, for each honest validator v_i and for every round r,* chFin_i^r *is a prefix of* chAva_i^r.

3   Propose-vote-merge Protocols

The aim of this work is to present a secure ebb-and-flow [14] protocol that can finalize (at most) one block per slot and, in particular, that can finalize within slot t the block proposed in t. This is achieved by revisiting the *propose-vote-merge* protocol RLMD-GHOST introduced by D'Amato and Zanolini [7] as the basis for our protocol implementation. Propose-vote-merge protocols proceed in *slots* consisting of k rounds[2], each having a proposer v_p, chosen through a proposer selection mechanism among the set of validators. In particular, at the beginning of each slot t, the proposer v_p proposes a block B. Then, all active validators (also referred as *voters*) vote after Δ rounds. Every validator v_i has a buffer $\mathcal{B}_i$, a collection of messages received from other validators, and a view $\mathcal{V}_i$, used to make consensus decisions, which admits messages from the buffer only at specific points in time.

Propose-vote-merge protocols are defined through a deterministic fork-choice function FC, which is used by honest proposers and voters to decide how to propose and vote, respectively, based on their view at the round in which they are performing those actions. It is moreover used as the basis of a *confirmation rule* (Sect. 4.2), which defines the output of the protocol, and thus with respect to which the security of the protocol is defined. In the case of RLMD-GHOST, its fork-choice function RLMD-GHOST considers the last (non equivocating) messages sent by validators that are not older than $t - \eta$ slots (for an expiration

---

[2] D'Amato and Zanolini [7] implement RLMD-GHOST with fast confirmation with $k = 3\Delta$ (Appendix B [7]). However, we will consider $k = 4\Delta$, following the approach taken by D'Amato *et al.* [6] when presenting Goldfish with *fast confirmation*. We will show how RLMD-GHOST with fast confirmation can be changed into its variant with $k = 4\Delta$ in Sect. 4 while presenting our protocol.

period η), in order to make protocol's decisions. In particular, the filter function $\mathsf{FIL}_{\mathrm{rlmd}}(\mathcal{V}, t)$ removes *all but the latest messages within the expiry period* $[t - \eta, t)$ *for slot* t, *from non-equivocating validators*, i.e., $\mathsf{FIL}_{\mathrm{rlmd}} = \mathsf{FIL}_{\mathrm{lmd}} \circ \mathsf{FIL}_{\eta\text{-exp}} \circ \mathsf{FIL}_{eq}$. Here, $\mathsf{FIL}_{\mathrm{lmd}}(\mathcal{V}, t)$ removes all but the latest votes of every validator (possibly more than one) from $\mathcal{V}$ and outputs the resulting view, i.e., it implements the *latest message* (LMD) rule, $\mathsf{FIL}_{\eta\text{-exp}}(\mathcal{V}, t)$ removes all votes from slots $< t - \eta$ from $\mathcal{V}$ and outputs the resulting view, and $\mathsf{FIL}_{eq}(\mathcal{V}, t)$ removes all votes by *equivocating validators in* $\mathcal{V}$ [1], i.e., validators for which $\mathcal{V}$ contains multiple, equivocating, votes for some slot t.

A propose-vote-merge protocol proceeds in three phases:

PROPOSE: In this phase, which starts at the beginning of a slot, the proposer v_p merges its view $\mathcal{V}_p$ with its buffer $\mathcal{B}_p$, i.e., $\mathcal{V}_p \leftarrow \mathcal{V}_p \cup \mathcal{B}_p$, and sets $\mathcal{B}_p \leftarrow \emptyset$. Then, v_p runs the fork-choice function FC with inputs its view $\mathcal{V}_p$ and slot t, obtaining the head of the chain $B' = \mathsf{FC}(\mathcal{V}_p, t)$. Proposer v_p extends B' with a new block B, and updates its canonical chain accordingly, setting $\mathrm{ch}_p \leftarrow B$. Finally, it broadcasts the message $[\text{PROPOSE}, B, \mathcal{V}_p \cup \{B\}, t, v_p]$.

VOTE: Here, every validator v_i that receives a proposal message $[\text{PROPOSE}, B, \mathcal{V}, t, v_p]$ from v_p merges its view with the proposed view $\mathcal{V}$, by setting $\mathcal{V}_i \leftarrow \mathcal{V}_i \cup \mathcal{V}$. Then, it broadcasts votes for some blocks based on its view. We omit, for the moment, for which blocks a validator v_i votes: it will become clear once we present the full protocol.

MERGE: In this phase, every validator v_i merges its view with its buffer, i.e., $\mathcal{V}_i \leftarrow \mathcal{V}_i \cup \mathcal{B}_i$, and sets $\mathcal{B}_i \leftarrow \emptyset$.

The MERGE phase, along with all other operations involving views and buffers discussed in the previous section, are implemented using the *view-merge* technique [6,7,10]. The idea behind the view-merge technique involves synchronizing the views of all honest validators with the view $\mathcal{V}_p$ of the proposer for a specific slot *before* the validators broadcast their votes in that slot.

D'Amato *et al.* [6] introduce the notion of *active* validators[3]: awake validators that have terminated a *joining protocol* at a round r, described as it follows. Assuming a propose-vote-merge protocol proceeding in slots of $k = 4\Delta$ rounds, when an honest validator v_i wakes up at some round $r \in (4\Delta(t-1) + 3\Delta, 4\Delta t + 3\Delta]$, it immediately receives all the messages that were sent while it was asleep, and it adds them into its buffer $\mathcal{B}_i$, without actively participating in the protocol yet. All new messages which are received are also added to the buffer $\mathcal{B}_i$. Validator v_i then waits for the *next view-merge opportunity*, at round $4\Delta t + 3\Delta$, in order to merge its buffer $\mathcal{B}_i$ into its view $\mathcal{V}_i$. At this point, v_i starts executing the protocol. From this point on, validator v_i becomes *active*, until either corrupted or put to sleep by the adversary. We consider such a joining protocol when describing our propose-vote-merge protocol.

---

[3] Observe that D'Amato *et al.* [6] actually refer to *awake* validators to indicate what we call active, and to *dreamy* validators to indicate what we call awake (but not active).

4   Protocol Specification

4.1   Data Structures

We consider five message types: PROPOSE, BLOCK, CHECKPOINT, HEAD-VOTE, and FFG-VOTE. We make no distinctions between network-level representation of blocks and votes, and their representation in a validator's view, *i.e.*, there is no difference between BLOCK and *-VOTE messages and blocks and votes, and we usually just refer to the latter. We describe the objects as tuples (DATA-TYPE, ...) with their data type as a tag, but in practice mostly refer to them without the tag. We use dot notation to refer to the fields. For the tag, we do so simply with .tag, for the other fields we use the generic names specified in the object descriptions below, to access the different fields, *e.g.*, $B.t$ is the slot of block B. In the following, t is a slot and v_i a validator.

Blocks and Checkpoints. A block is a tuple $B = (\text{BLOCK}, b, t, v_i)$, where b is a *block body*, *i.e.*, the protocol-specific content of the block[4]. A checkpoint is a tuple $\mathcal{C} = (\text{CHECKPOINT}, B, t)$, where B is a block and $\mathcal{C}.t \geq B.t$.

Votes. A head vote is a tuple $[\text{HEAD-VOTE}, B, t, v_i]$, where B is a block. An FFG vote is a tuple $[\text{FFG-VOTE}, \mathcal{C}_1, \mathcal{C}_2, v_i]$, where $\mathcal{C}_1, v_2$ are checkpoints, $\mathcal{C}_1.t < \mathcal{C}_2.t$, and $\mathcal{C}_1.B \prec \mathcal{C}_2.B$. We refer to the two checkpoints as *source* and *target*, respectively, and to FFG votes as *links* between source and target. When v_i is clear from context, we also write $\mathcal{C}_1 \to \mathcal{C}_2$ for the whole vote, *e.g.*, we say that v_i casts a $\mathcal{C}_1 \to \mathcal{C}_2$ vote.

Proposals. A proposal is a tuple $[\text{PROPOSE}, B, \mathcal{V}, t, v_i]$ where B is a block and $\mathcal{V}$ a view. We refer to $\mathcal{V}$ as a *proposed view*.

Gossip Behavior. Votes and blocks are gossiped at any time, regardless of whether they are received directly or as part of another message. For example, a validator receiving a vote also gossips the block that it contains, and a validator receiving a proposal also gossips the blocks and votes contained in the proposed view. Finally, a proposal from slot t is gossiped only during the first Δ rounds of slot t.

4.2   Confirmation Rule

A confirmation rule allows validators to identify a *confirmed prefix* of the canonical chain, for which safety properties hold, and which is therefore used to define the output of the protocol. Since the protocol we are going to present outputs two chains, the available chain chAva and the finalized chain chFin, we have two confirmation rules. One is *finality*, which we introduce in Sect. 4.3, and defines chFin. The other confirmation rule, defining chAva, is the one adopted by

---

[4] For simplicity, we omit a reference to the parent block.

RLMD-GHOST, in its variant supporting fast confirmation[5]. It is itself essentially split in two rules, a *slow* κ-deep confirmation rule, which is live also under dynamic participation, and a *fast optimistic rule*, requiring $\frac{2}{3}n$ honest validators to be awake, *i.e.*, a stronger assumption than just τ−compliance. Both rules are employed at round $4\Delta t + 2\Delta$, and chAva is updated to the highest block confirmed by either one, so that liveness of chAva only necessitates liveness of one of the two rules. In particular, τ-compliance is sufficient for liveness. On the other end, safety of chAva requires both rules to be safe.

4.3   FFG Component

As mentioned above, a propose-vote-merge protocol is characterized by a fork-choice function that identifies for every slot the current head of the canonical chain for a given validator. Moreover, we described two kind of votes that a validator v_i executes in the VOTE phase: a HEAD-VOTE, used to vote for the head of the canonical chain, i.e., the output of the fork-choice function evaluated at the current slot, and an FFG-VOTE, used by the *FFG-component* of our protocol[6].

The FFG component of our protocol aims at finalizing one block per slot by counting FFG-VOTES cast at a given slot.

Justification. We say that a set of $\frac{2}{3}n$ distinct FFG votes $\mathcal{C}_1 \rightarrow \mathcal{C}_2$ is a *supermajority link* between $\mathcal{C}_1$ and $\mathcal{C}_2$. We say that a checkpoint C is *justified* if there is a chain of $k \geq 0$ supermajority links $(B_{\text{genesis}}, 0) \rightarrow \mathcal{C}_1 \cdots \rightarrow \mathcal{C}_{k-1} \rightarrow C$. In particular, $(B_{\text{genesis}}, 0)$ is justified. Finally, we say that a block B *is justified* if there exists a justified checkpoint $\mathcal{C}$ with $\mathcal{C}.B = B$.

Slashing. The slashing rules are the same as in Casper FFG. Validator v_i is slashable (see Sect. 2) for two *distinct* FFG votes $(\mathcal{C}_1, \mathcal{C}_2, v_i)$ and $(\mathcal{C}_3, \mathcal{C}_4, v_i)$ if either: $\mathbf{E_1}$ (Equivocation) $\mathcal{C}_2.t = \mathcal{C}_4.t$ or $\mathbf{E_2}$ (Surround voting) $\mathcal{C}_3.t < \mathcal{C}_1.t < \mathcal{C}_2.t < \mathcal{C}_4.t$.

Latest Justified Checkpoint and Block. A checkpoint is justified in a view $\mathcal{V}$ if $\mathcal{V}$ contains the chain of supermajority links justifying it. We refer to the justified checkpoint C of highest slot $C.t$ in $\mathcal{V}$ as the *latest justified checkpoint* in $\mathcal{V}$, or $\mathcal{LJ}(\mathcal{V})$, and to $\mathcal{LJ}(\mathcal{V}).B$ as the *latest justified block* in $\mathcal{V}$, or $LJ(\mathcal{V})$. Ties are broken arbitrarily (the occurrence of a tie implies that $\frac{n}{3}$ validators are slashable for equivocation). For brevity, we also use $\mathcal{LJ}_i$ to refer to $\mathcal{LJ}(\mathcal{V}_i)$, the latest justified checkpoint in the view $\mathcal{V}_i$ of validator v_i.

---

[5] With some minor changes, as RLMD-GHOST still has 3Δ rounds per slots, by requiring an optimistic assumption on network latency in order for fast confirmations to be live.

[6] The component of our protocol that outputs chFin is almost identical to Casper [3], the *friendly* finality gadget (FFG) adopted by the Ethereum consensus protocol Gasper [4]. This is the reason why we decided to use the *FFG* terminology already accepted within the Ethereum ecosystem.

Finality. A checkpoint $\mathcal{C}$ is *finalized* if it is justified and there exists a supermajority link $\mathcal{C} \rightarrow \mathcal{C}'$ with $\mathcal{C}'.t = \mathcal{C}.t + 1$. A block B is finalized if there exists a finalized checkpoint $\mathcal{C}$ with $B = \mathcal{C}.B$.

4.4   Voting

Fork-choice. Similarly to Gasper [4], we adopt an hybrid *justification-respecting* fork-choice, namely HFC, building upon RLMD-GHOST [7] fork-choice function. $HFC(\mathcal{V}, t)$ starts from $LJ(\mathcal{V})$, the *latest justified block* in $\mathcal{V}$, instead of B_{genesis}, and then proceeds as RLMD-GHOST, *i.e.*, it runs GHOST using the view filtered by FIL_{rlmd}. Formally, we can define it by using another view filter, FIL_{FFG}, *i.e.*, HFC = RLMD-GHOST ∘ FIL_{FFG}. $FIL_{\text{FFG}}(\mathcal{V}, t)$ outputs $(\mathcal{V}', t)$, where $\mathcal{V}'$ filters out blocks in $\mathcal{V}$ that conflict with $LJ(\mathcal{V})$. In other words, it filters out *branches which do not contain* $LJ(\mathcal{V})$, so $LJ(\mathcal{V})$ is guaranteed to be canonical.

Algorithm 1. HFC, the justification-respecting fork-choice function

1: **function** HFC($\mathcal{V}, t$)
2:      **return** RLMD-GHOST($FIL_{\text{FFG}}(\mathcal{V}, t)$)
3: **function** FII$_{\text{FFG}}(\mathcal{V}, t)$
4:      $\mathcal{V}' \leftarrow \mathcal{V} \setminus \{B \in \mathcal{V}, B.\text{tag} = \text{BLOCK} : LJ(\mathcal{V}) \not\prec B \wedge B \not\prec LJ(\mathcal{V})\}$
5:      **return** $(\mathcal{V}', t)$

Voting Rules. Consider a validator v_i voting at slot t. Head votes work exactly as in RLMD-GHOST, or any propose-vote-merge protocol, *i.e.*, validators vote for the output of their fork-choice: when it is time to vote, validator v_i casts vote [HEAD-VOTE, $HFC(\mathcal{V}_i, t), t, v_i$]. FFG votes always use the *latest justified checkpoint as source*. The target block is the *highest confirmed descendant of the latest justified block, or the latest justified block itself if there is none.* The target checkpoint is then $\mathcal{C}_{\text{target}} = (\arg\max_{B \in \{LJ_i, \text{chAva}\}} |B|, t)$, with $|B|$ being the height of block B, and the FFG vote of v_i is [FFG-VOTE, $\mathcal{LJ}_i, \mathcal{C}_{\text{target}}, v_i$], voting for the link $\mathcal{LJ}_i \rightarrow \mathcal{C}_{\text{target}}$.

4.5   Protocol Execution

Our protocol is implemented in Algorithm 2 and it works as it follows. Note that the PROPOSE and HEAD-VOTE phases are *exactly* as in a generic propose-vote-merge protocol (see Sect. 3). Moreover, a slot t in our protocol begins at round $4\Delta t$. At any time, the finalized chain chFin$_i$ of validator v_i just consists of the finalized blocks according to its view $\mathcal{V}_i$, so we omit explicit updates to chFin in the following.

Algorithm 2. Single slot finality protocol – code for validator v_i

---

1: **State**
2:      $\mathcal{V}_i \leftarrow \{\mathcal{B}_{\text{genesis}}\}$: view of validator v_i
3:      $\mathcal{B}_i \leftarrow \emptyset$: buffer of validator v_i
4:      $\text{ch}_i \leftarrow \mathcal{B}_{\text{genesis}}$: canonical chain of validator v_i
5:      $t \leftarrow 0$: the current slot
6:      $r \leftarrow 0$: the current round
      PROPOSE
7: **at** $r = 4\Delta t$ **do**
8:      **if** $v_i = v_p^t$ **then**
9:          $\mathcal{V}_i \leftarrow \mathcal{V}_i \cup \mathcal{B}_i$, $\mathcal{B}_i \leftarrow \emptyset$, $B' \leftarrow \text{HFC}(\mathcal{V}_i, t)$
10:          $B \leftarrow \text{NewBlock}(B')$, $\text{ch}_i \leftarrow B$
11:          send message [PROPOSE, B, $\mathcal{V}_i \cup \{B\}$, t, v_i] through gossip
      HEAD-VOTE
12: **at** $r = 4\Delta t + \Delta$ **do**
13:      $\text{ch}_i \leftarrow \text{HFC}(\mathcal{V}_i, t)$
14:      send message [HEAD-VOTE, $\text{HFC}(\mathcal{V}_i, t)$, t, v_i] through gossip
      CONFIRM AND FFG-VOTE
15: **at** $r = 4\Delta t + 2\Delta$ **do**
16:      $B_{\text{fast}} \leftarrow B_{\text{genesis}}$
17:      $S_{\text{fast}} \leftarrow \{B \prec \text{ch}_i : |\{v_j : \exists B' \succ B : [\text{HEAD-VOTE}, B', t, v_j] \in \mathcal{B}_i\}| \geq \frac{2}{3}n\}$
18:      **if** $S_{\text{fast}} \neq \emptyset$ **then:**
19:          $B_{\text{fast}} \leftarrow \underset{S_{\text{fast}}}{\arg\max} |B|$
20:          **if** $\neg(B_{\text{fast}} \prec \text{chAva}_i \wedge \text{ch}_i^{\lceil \kappa} \prec \text{chAva}_i)$ **then:**
21:              $\text{chAva}_i \leftarrow \underset{\text{ch} \in \{\text{ch}_i^{\lceil \kappa}, B_{\text{fast}}\}}{\arg\max} |\text{ch}|$
22:      $C_{\text{target}} \leftarrow (\underset{B \in \{LJ_i, \text{chAva}_i\}}{\arg\max} |B|, t)$
23:      send message [FFG-VOTE, $\mathcal{LJ}_i$, C_{target}, v_i] through gossip
      MERGE
24: **at** $r = 4\Delta t + 3\Delta$ **do**
25:      $\mathcal{V}_i \leftarrow \mathcal{V}_i \cup \mathcal{B}_i$
26:      $\mathcal{B}_i \leftarrow \emptyset$
27: **upon** receiving a gossiped message [PROPOSE, B, $\mathcal{V}$, t, v_p^t] **do**
28:      $\mathcal{B}_i \leftarrow \mathcal{B}_i \cup \{B\}$
29:      **if** $r \in [4\Delta t, 4\Delta t + \Delta]$ **then**
30:          $\mathcal{V}_i \leftarrow \mathcal{V}_i \cup \mathcal{V}$
31: **upon** receiving a gossiped BLOCK B **or** a gossiped *-VOTE V from v_j **do**
32:      $\mathcal{B}_i \leftarrow \mathcal{B}_i \cup \{B\}$ **or** $\mathcal{B}_i \leftarrow \mathcal{B}_i \cup \{V\}$

PROPOSE: At round $4\Delta t$, proposer v_p merges its view $\mathcal{V}_p$ with its buffer $\mathcal{B}_p$, i.e., $\mathcal{V}_p \leftarrow \mathcal{V}_p \cup \mathcal{B}_p$, and sets $\mathcal{B}_p \leftarrow \emptyset$. Then, v_p runs the fork-choice function HFC with inputs its view $\mathcal{V}_p$ and slot t, obtaining the head of the chain $B' = \text{HFC}(\mathcal{V}_p, t)$. Proposer v_p extends B' with a new block B, and updates its canonical chain accordingly, by setting $\text{ch}_p \leftarrow B$. Finally, it broadcasts the proposal [PROPOSE, B, $\mathcal{V}_p \cup \{B\}$, t, v_p].

HEAD-VOTE: In rounds $[4\Delta t, 4\Delta t + \Delta]$, a validator v_i, upon receiving a proposal message (PROPOSE, B, $\mathcal{V}$, t, v_p) from v_p, merges its view with the proposed view $\mathcal{V}$ by setting $\mathcal{V}_i \leftarrow \mathcal{V}_i \cup \mathcal{V}$. At round $4\Delta t + \Delta$, even if no proposal is received, validator v_i updates its canonical chain by setting $\mathsf{ch}_i \leftarrow \mathrm{HFC}(\mathcal{V}_i, t)$, and casts the head vote (HEAD-VOTE, $\mathrm{HFC}(\mathcal{V}_i, t)$, t, v_i).

CONFIRM: At round $4\Delta t + 2\Delta$, a validator v_i selects for fast confirmation the highest *canonical* block $B_{\mathsf{fast}} \prec \mathsf{ch}_i$ such that B_i contains $\geq \frac{2}{3}n$ votes from slot t for descendants of B_{fast}, from distinct validators. It then updates its confirmed chain chAva_i to the highest between B_{fast} and $\mathsf{ch}_i^{\lceil \kappa}$, the κ-deep prefix of its canonical chain, *as long as this does not result in updating chAva_i to some prefix of it* (we do not needlessly revert confirmations).

FFG-VOTE: At round $4\Delta t + 2\Delta$, after updating chAva_i, a validator v_i casts the FFG vote (FFG-VOTE, $\mathcal{LJ}_i$, $\mathcal{C}_{\mathsf{target}}$, v_i), where $\mathcal{C}_{\mathsf{target}} = (\underset{B \in \{\mathcal{LJ}_i, \mathsf{chAva}_i\}}{\arg\max} |B|, t)$

MERGE: At round $4\Delta t + 3\Delta$, every validator v_i merges its view with its buffer, *i.e.*, $\mathcal{V}_i \leftarrow \mathcal{V}_i \cup \mathcal{B}_i$, and sets $\mathcal{B}_i \leftarrow \emptyset$.

5 Analysis

Algorithm 2 works in the generalized partially synchronous sleepy model, and is in particular a τ-secure ebb-and-flow protocol, *if we strengthen τ-compliance to require that less than $\frac{n}{3}$ validators are ever slashable for equivocation*, for reasons that will be explained shortly. For $\mathsf{GST} = 0$, we show in Sect. 5.1 that, if the execution is τ-compliant in this stronger sense, then all the properties of RLMD-GHOST [7] keep holding. In Sect. 5.2 we show that the finalized chain chFin is $\frac{n}{3}$-accountable, and thus always safe if $f < \frac{n}{3}$. Moreover, if $f < \frac{n}{3}$, chFin is live after $\max\{\mathsf{GST}, \mathsf{GAT}\}$.

Before proceeding with the analysis under synchrony and partial synchrony, we state without proof the *view-merge property*, which follows from the usage of the view-merge technique, since it enables proposers to synchronize the view of honest voters with theirs. It corresponds to Lemma 2 as presented by D'Amato and Zanolini [7], with an addition regarding synchronization of the latest justified checkpoint.

Lemma 1. *Suppose that t is a slot with an (honest) active proposer and that network synchrony holds in rounds $[4\Delta t - \Delta, 4\Delta t + \Delta]$. Say the proposed block is B, and the latest justified checkpoint in the view of the proposer is $\mathcal{LJ}_p$. Then, at round $4\Delta t + \Delta$, all active validators broadcast a HEAD-VOTE for the honest proposal B of slot t. Moreover, $\mathcal{LJ}_i = \mathcal{LJ}_p$ for any such active validator v_i.*

5.1 Synchrony

Throughout this part of the analysis, we assume that $\mathsf{GST} = 0$, and that $< \frac{n}{3}$ validators are ever slashable for equivocation, by which here we mean signing multiple HEAD-VOTEs for a single slot, rather than violating $\mathbf{E_1}$. In other words, we are not concerned about equivocation with FFG-VOTEs, but rather with HEAD-VOTEs, which can similarly be declared a slashable offense. Observe that, in RLMD-GHOST with fast confirmations (Appendix B [7]), this assumption is strictly needed for safety (and only for clients which use fast confirmations), but for example not for reorg resilience or liveness, because fast confirmations do not affect the canonical chain. On the other hand, the protocol we present here utilizes confirmations as a prerequisite for justification, and justification does affect the canonical chain, since HFC filters out branches conflicting with the latest justified block. Therefore, we require that $< \frac{n}{3}$ validators are ever slashable for equivocation for all of the properties which we are going to prove. As already mentioned, to avoid stating it repeatedly, we further restrict η-compliant executions to those executions in which the assumption holds.

Our single slot finality protocol implemented in Algorithm 2 uses the HFC fork-choice function, dealing with checkpoints and justifications. However, one could implement it using also different fork-choice functions. In particular, we show that by substituting HFC with RLMD-GHOST (with equal expiration period η), $i.e.$, if we ignore justifications and consider the $vanilla$ fork-choice function introduced by D'Amato and Zanolini [7], then the resulting protocol is equivalent to the RLMD-GHOST protocol with fast confirmation (Appendix B [7]). This because FFG votes have no effect at all, and as such it is η-reorg-resilient, and η-dynamically-available. Moreover, the following two results about fast confirmations (Appendix B [7]) also apply.

Theorem 1 (Reorg resilience of fast confirmations). *Let us consider an η-compliant execution with* GST $= 0$. *A block fast confirmed by an honest validator at a slot t is always in the canonical chain of all active validators at rounds $\geq 4\Delta(t+1) + \Delta$.*

Theorem 2 (Liveness of fast confirmations). *An honest proposal B from a slot t in which $|H_t| \geq \frac{2}{3}n$ is fast confirmed by all active validators at round $4\Delta t + \Delta$.*

We show that, under synchrony, $i.e.$, with GST $= 0$, these properties are preserved by our justification-respecting protocol, which uses HFC instead. To do so, we show that for every η-compliant execution, Algorithm 2 using FC $=$ RLMD-GHOST and Algorithm 2 using FC $=$ HFC are $equivalent$, i.e., the sequence of outputs of Algorithm 2 is the same regardless of which fork-choice function is used. All properties of Algorithm 2 with FC $=$ RLMD-GHOST in such η-compliant executions then also apply to Algorithm 2 with FC $=$ HFC. In particular, it is also η-reorg-resilient and η-dynamically-available, and it also satisfies reorg resilience and liveness of fast confirmations, $i.e.$, Theorems 1 and Theorem 2 hold.

Theorem 3 (Execution equivalence). *Let us consider an η-compliant execution with* GST $= 0$ *and with Algorithm 2 using* FC $=$ HFC. *Furthermore, let* us consider the same execution, with the same adversarial strategy and random-ness, with Algorithm 2 using FC = RLMD-GHOST. The sequence of outputs of the two algorithms correspond exactly.

5.2   Partial Synchrony

Throughout this section we assume that $f < \frac{n}{3}$. First, we prove that the final-ized chain is accountably safe, exactly as done in Casper [3]. Then, we show that honest proposals made after $\max(\mathsf{GST}, \mathsf{GAT}) + \Delta$ are justified within their proposal slot, which implies liveness of the finalized chain.

Theorem 4 (Accountable safety). *The finalized chain* chFin *is accountably safe, i.e., two conflicting finalized blocks imply that at least $\frac{n}{3}$ adversarial valida-tors can be detected to have violated either* $\mathbf{E_1}$ *or* $\mathbf{E_2}$.

Lemma 2. *If an honest proposer v_p proposes a block B at a slot t after* $\max(\mathsf{GST}, \mathsf{GAT}) + \Delta$, *and the latest justified checkpoint in the view of the pro-poser is $\mathcal{LJ}_p$, then the checkpoint (B, t) is justified in all honest views at round $4\Delta t + 3\Delta$, by supermajority link $\mathcal{LJ}_p \rightarrow (B, t)$.*

Theorem 5 (Liveness). *Consider two consecutive slots t and $t+1$ with honest proposers after* $\max(\mathsf{GST}, \mathsf{GAT}) + 4\Delta$. *The block B proposed at slot t is finalized at the end of slot $t + 1$.*

6   Single Slot Finality

The protocol implemented in Algorithm 2 is a an η-secure ebb-and-flow protocol which (at best) finalizes a block in every slot, but it does not achieve *single slot finality*, i.e., it cannot finalize a proposal *within its proposal slot*. At best, it lags behind by one slot, finalizing a proposal from slot t at the end of slot $t + 1$. A straightforward extension of our protocol which achieves single slot finality is one with 5Δ rounds per slot, allowing for an additional FFG voting phase. This would be very costly in Ethereum, for two reasons. First, it would in practice significantly increase the slot time, because each voting round requires aggregat-ing hundreds of thousands (if not millions) of BLS signatures, likely requiring a lengthier multi-step aggregation process. Moreover, it would be expensive in terms of bandwidth consumption and computation, because such votes would have to all be gossiped and verified by each validator, costly even if already aggregated. For these reasons, we describe here an alternative way to enhance to protocol for the purpose of achieving single slot finality, without suffering from the drawbacks just described. We introduce a new type of message, *acknowl-edgment*, and a new slashing condition alongside it. Acknowledgments do not influence the protocol in any way, except in case of slashing, and are mainly intended to be consumed by external observers which want to have the earli-est possible finality guarantees. Therefore, they do not need to be gossiped to and verified by all validators. They can then simply be gossiped in smaller sub-networks (similar to the *attestation subnets* which Ethereum employs today), requiring limited bandwidth and verification resources. If an observer wants to have faster finality guarantees than they could have by simply following the chain or listening to the global gossip, they can opt to participate in all such sub-networks, and collect all acknowledgments. As doing so is permissionless, it can also be expected that aggregate acknowledgments, or equivalent proofs, might become available through some other channels.

Acknowledgment. An *acknowledgment* is a tuple $[\text{ACK}, \mathcal{C}, t, v]$, where $\mathcal{C}$ is a checkpoint with $\mathcal{C}.t = t$. We also refer to this as an acknowledgment *of* $\mathcal{C}$. A *supermajority acknowledgment of* $\mathcal{C}$ is a set of $\geq \frac{2}{3}n$ distinct acknowledgments of $\mathcal{C}$. At round $4\Delta t + 3\Delta$, after merging the buffer $\mathcal{B}_i$, validator v_i broadcasts the acknowledgment $[\text{ACK}, \mathcal{LJ}_i, t, v_i]$ if $\mathcal{LJ}_i.t = t$, i.e., if $\mathcal{LJ}_i$ has been justified in the current slot. An observer which receives a supermajority acknowledgment of a *justified* checkpoint $\mathcal{C}$ *may* consider $\mathcal{C}$ to be finalized.

Slashing rule for finality voting. When validator v_i broadcasts an acknowledgment of $(\mathcal{C}, t)$, it *acknowledges* that, at the end of slot t, it knows about $\mathcal{C}$ being justified. Since the FFG voting rules prescribe that the source of an FFG vote should be the latest known justified checkpoint, subsequent FFG votes with a source whose slot is $< t$ constitute a provable violation, which is analogous to surround voting. Accordingly, we formulate a third slashing rule, which ensures that finality via a supermajority acknowledgment is accountably safe. In particular, validator v_i is slashable for an FFG vote $(\mathcal{C}_1, \mathcal{C}_2)$ and an acknowledgment $(\mathcal{C}, t)$, if they satisfy $\mathbf{E_3}$, i.e., $\mathcal{C}_1.t < \mathcal{C}.t < \mathcal{C}_2.t$. In other words, the link $\mathcal{C}_1 \to \mathcal{C}_2$ *surrounds* the acknowledged checkpoint.

Theorem 6 (Accountable safety with acknowledgments). *The finalized chain is accountably safe even when it is updated via acknowledgments as well, i.e., two conflicting finalized checkpoints imply that more than $\frac{n}{3}$ adversarial validators can be detected to have violated $\mathbf{E_1}$, $\mathbf{E_2}$, or $\mathbf{E_3}$.*

Theorem 7 (Single Slot Finality). *An honest proposal from a slot t after $\max(\text{GST}, \text{GAT}) + 4\Delta$ is finalized in round $4\Delta(t+1)$ by a supermajority acknowledgment.*

7   Conclusions

In this work, we have made significant strides towards realizing a secure and reorg-resilient ebb-and-flow protocol that has the potential to replace Ethereum's current consensus protocol, Gasper. We have provided a comprehensive analysis and modifications to D'Amato and Zanolini's RLMD-GHOST protocol, integrating it with a partially synchronous finality gadget. In particular, our protocol introduces a novel approach for achieving single slot finality.

Another significant contribution of our work lies in the expansion of the generalized sleepy model introduced by D'Amato and Zanolini. Our generalized partially synchronous sleepy model introduces stronger constraints related to the adversary's corruption and sleepiness power and incorporates the concept of partial synchrony. This extension not only enhances the original model but also provides a generalized framework suitable for a wider array of practical scenarios.

However, despite the security guarantees of our protocol, we acknowledge that it is not (yet) practical for real-world implementation. This challenge is due to the current structure of Ethereum, which employs a large pool of validators. Requiring every validator to vote at each slot would necessitate extensive message exchanges – a process that is far from optimal given the scale of Ethereum's network. Therefore, while our current findings represent a crucial stride towards an improved consensus protocol, they also highlight the need for additional research. Specifically, we need to focus on how we can refine the voting mechanism to better manage and aggregate the messages involved in this process.

References

1. Asgaonkar, A.: Remove equivocating validators from fork choice consideration. https://github.com/ethereum/consensus-specs/pull/2845
2. Buterin, V.: Paths toward single-slot finality (2023). https://notes.ethereum.org/@vbuterin/single_slot_finality
3. Buterin, V., Griffith, V.: Casper the friendly finality gadget. CoRR abs/1710.09437 (2017). http://arxiv.org/abs/1710.09437
4. Buterin, V., et al.: Combining GHOST and Casper (2020)
5. Castro, M., Liskov, B.: Practical byzantine fault tolerance. In: Seltzer, M.I., Leach, P.J. (eds.) Proceedings of the Third USENIX Symposium on Operating Systems Design and Implementation (OSDI), New Orleans, Louisiana, USA, February 22–25, 1999, pp. 173–186. USENIX Association (1999)
6. D'Amato, F., Neu, J., Tas, E.N., Tse, D.: No more attacks on proof-of-stake ethereum? CoRR abs/2209.03255 (2022). https://doi.org/10.48550/arXiv.2209.03255
7. D'Amato, F., Zanolini, L.: Recent latest message driven ghost: Balancing dynamic availability with asynchrony resilience (2023). https://arxiv.org/abs/2302.11326
8. Dwork, C., Lynch, N.A., Stockmeyer, L.J.: Consensus in the presence of partial synchrony. J. ACM **35**(2), 288–323 (1988)
9. Gilbert, S., Lynch, N.A.: Brewer's conjecture and the feasibility of consistent, available, partition-tolerant web services. SIGACT News **33**(2), 51–59 (2002)
10. Kane, D., Fackler, A., Gagol, A., Straszak, D.: Highway: efficient consensus with flexible finality. CoRR abs/2101.02159 (2021). https://arxiv.org/abs/2101.02159
11. Lewis-Pye, A., Roughgarden, T.: Resource pools and the CAP theorem. CoRR abs/2006.10698 (2020). https://arxiv.org/abs/2006.10698
12. Malkhi, D., Momose, A., Ren, L.: Byzantine consensus under fully fluctuating participation. IACR Cryptol. ePrint Arch, p. 1448 (2022)

13. Momose, A., Ren, L.: Constant latency in sleepy consensus. In: Yin, H., Stavrou, A., Cremers, C., Shi, E. (eds.) Proceedings of the 2022 ACM SIGSAC Conference on Computer and Communications Security, CCS 2022, Los Angeles, CA, USA, November 7–11, 2022, pp. 2295–2308. ACM (2022)

14. Neu, J., Tas, E.N., Tse, D.: Ebb-and-flow protocols: a resolution of the availability-finality dilemma. In: 42nd IEEE Symposium on Security and Privacy, SP 2021, San Francisco, CA, USA, 24–27 May 2021, pp. 446–465. IEEE (2021)

15. Pass, R., Shi, E.: The sleepy model of consensus. In: Takagi, T., Peyrin, T. (eds.) Advances in Cryptology – ASIACRYPT 2017: 23rd International Conference on the Theory and Applications of Cryptology and Information Security, Hong Kong, China, December 3-7, 2017, Proceedings, Part II, pp. 380–409. Springer International Publishing, Cham (2017). https://doi.org/10.1007/978-3-319-70697-9_14

16. Sompolinsky, Y., Zohar, A.: Secure high-rate transaction processing in bitcoin. In: Böhme, R., Okamoto, T. (eds.) Financial Cryptography and Data Security: 19th International Conference, FC 2015, San Juan, Puerto Rico, January 26-30, 2015, Revised Selected Papers, pp. 507–527. Springer Berlin Heidelberg, Berlin, Heidelberg (2015). https://doi.org/10.1007/978-3-662-47854-7_32

17. Zamfir, V.: Casper the friendly ghost. a correct-by-construction blockchain consensus protocol. https://github.com/ethereum/research/blob/master/papers/cbc-consensus/AbstractCBC.pdf

Timely Identification of Victim Addresses in DeFi Attacks

Bahareh Parhizkari[1]([✉])[ID], Antonio Ken Iannillo[1][ID],
Christof Ferreira Torres[2][ID], Sebastian Banescu[3][ID], Joseph Xu[3][ID],
and Radu State[1][ID]

[1] SnT, University of Luxembourg, Esch-sur-Alzette, Luxembourg
bahareh.parhizkari@uni.lu
[2] ETH Zurich, Zürich, Switzerland
[3] Quantstamp, Inc., San Franciso, USA

Abstract. Over the past years, Decentralized Finance (DeFi) protocols have suffered from several attacks. As a result, multiple solutions have been proposed to prevent such attacks. Most solutions rely on identifying malicious transactions before they are included in blocks. However, with the emergence of private pools, attackers can now conceal their exploit transactions from attack detection. This poses a significant challenge for existing security tools, which primarily rely on monitoring transactions in public mempools. To effectively address this challenge, it is crucial to develop proactive methods that predict malicious behavior before the actual attack transactions occur. In this work, we introduce a novel methodology to infer potential victims by analyzing the deployment bytecode of malicious smart contracts. Our idea leverages the fact that attackers typically split their attacks into two stages, a deployment stage, and an attack stage. This provides a small window to analyze the attacker's deployment code and identify victims in a timely manner before the actual attack occurs. By analyzing a set of past DeFi attacks, this work demonstrates that the victim of an attack transaction can be identified with an accuracy of almost 70%.

Keywords: Ethereum · Smart Contracts · DeFi · Victims · Attacks

1 Introduction

Blockchain and smart contract-based financial systems and applications, commonly called Decentralized Finance (DeFi) protocols, have made remarkable progress in capturing usage and attracting investments, resulting in exponential growth in the amount of capital staked within them. A persistent problem in these financial systems is the loss of funds through the unintended use of smart contracts. These are often referred to as hacks and exploits.

Companies providing DeFi services employ various strategies to protect their products against hacks. These encompass a range of approaches, such as developing secure development practices, conducting security audits, and bug bounties. However, it is crucial to note that despite utilizing these methods, achieving

S. Katsikas et al. (Eds.): ESORICS 2023 Workshops, LNCS 14398, pp. 394–410, 2024.
https://doi.org/10.1007/978-3-031-54204-6_24

100% security cannot be guaranteed. They must acquire information about ongoing security incidents as soon as possible to ensure they can take appropriate actions, such as pausing the protocols to limit the damage before significant financial damage occurs.

Numerous studies focus on designing tools to detect attacks on smart contracts by monitoring transactions on the public mempool and avoiding suspicious transactions from being recorded on the ledger [12,14,18,29,30,35]. However, these defensive methods become useless when attacker execute their transactions via private pools. It could impede companies from reacting against attacks promptly, particularly during the execution phase.

An essential aspect of DeFi security is detecting exploits while they are happening or before they happen (i.e., prevention). Typical exploits generally involve the following steps: deployment of malicious contracts, attack execution, and funds extraction. In a recent attack on Euler Finance [1], hackers utilized private pools to drain $197 million. However, they deployed the malicious smart contract a few blocks prior to initiating the attack transaction, providing a crucial window for intervention and prevention. Another instance is the attack on the Rubic exchange [7], resulting in a $1.4 million loss. During this incident, attackers deployed a malicious contract and promptly executed the attack transaction after deploying it via private pools. However, prevention could be achieved since the attack transaction occurred one block after the contract creation transaction. In such situations, the most viable option is detecting attack characteristics during the rescue time window between creating a malicious smart contract and the execution of the first exploit transaction. This can be achieved by analyzing the features of newly created smart contracts to distinguish malicious smart contracts from benign ones. For example, Forta recently introduced an ML bot [17] that utilizes machine learning prediction models to analyze the deployment bytecode (i.e., binary code sent to the network for the creation of a smart contract) of newly created smart contracts. Nevertheless, an important aspect is still lacking: when an ongoing attack is detected, what actions can we take to prevent the attacker from further exploiting the victim? This involves a combination of the following steps: 1) stopping the execution of malicious transactions, 2) detecting and informing the victim of the attack, and promptly notifying them about the ongoing attack. This enables the victim to take remedial actions, including identifying and fixing the exploited vulnerabilities. While Forta's ML bot [17] provides alerts on potential attacks, it does not offer an approach to identify the victims of the attacks.

In this work, we aim to address this limitation by proposing a solution that automates the identification of targeted addresses by analyzing malicious smart contracts deployed by attackers. We aim to quantify the percentage of victims that could be identified and alerted before an attack occurs, allowing for proactive intervention to minimize the hack's impact. In both previously explained attacks on Euler Finance and Robic Exchange, the victim's address was hardcoded inside the deployment bytecode of the malicious contract. Therefore, the victim could be identified prior to the attack transaction. Through exploring 117 attacks across four chains, we discovered that in almost 80% of cases, the victim's address emerged before the first attack transaction. Nevertheless, numerous attack contracts contain a large number of potential victims to consider. In this research, our goal is to overcome the limitations of existing attack detection methodologies on DeFi by solving the victim identification problem. The contributions of this paper are the following:

1. We investigate the usage of private pools for malicious purposes in the DeFi ecosystem.
2. We propose a novel methodology to identify victims before being exploited by malicious contracts.
3. We evaluate and compare two methods used to extract the victims' addresses from the set of potential victims of a malicious contract.

The paper is organized as follows. Section 2 provides information on smart contracts, including their bytecode and an explanation of private and public transaction pools. Section 3 discusses our motivations for performing this research and examines the current trend of utilizing private pools for malicious purposes. Section 4 outlines our methodology and algorithms. Section 5 presents the evaluation of our results. In Sect. 6, we compare our findings with relevant existing works. Finally, Sect. 7 concludes the paper.

2 Background

2.1 DeFi and Smart Contracts

Smart contracts are lines of code that are stored within a blockchain and can be executed through transactions. Ethereum [33] was the first blockchain to introduce Turing-complete smart contracts, and its implementation has been crucial in the development of decentralized finance (DeFi) [32]. Smart contracts are executed within decentralized blockchains. Without the requirement for a trusted third-party involvement, they lead to a less costly and more efficient execution. [37] Ethereum leverages the Ethereum Virtual Machine (EVM) for the execution of smart contracts, which are compiled to EVM bytecode. DeFi encompasses various financial services enabled through smart contracts, such as lending, borrowing, and trading.

Smart contracts hold a balance of cryptocurrency or tokens, and this capability is particularly relevant in DeFi. For example, users might deposit funds into a smart contract to participate in a lending pool. The smart contract holds these funds and manages their distribution according to its programmed logic. DeFi allows for functionalities such as liquidity pools, where multiple users deposit funds, and the smart contract automatically handles the pooling and distribution of assets.

A smart contract can also store data, known as the contract's state. For example, in a lending protocol, a smart contract could store information regarding the total amount of funds lent out and the interest rates. These state variables can be read or modified through functions within the smart contract. When a user interacts with the contract, for instance, by lending assets, the contract updates the relevant state variables by changing, for instance, the total amount of funds lent.

Smart contracts can also call functions and send transactions to other smart contracts. This ability to interact, often referred to as composability, is crucial for building complex decentralized applications where multiple smart contracts work together. For instance, a decentralized exchange might use one smart contract to manage user balances, another to handle order matching, and another to execute trades. These contracts need to communicate with each other to function cohesively.

Following Ethereum, several other blockchains have also adopted smart contracts with EVM compatibility, enabling developers to deploy Ethereum smart contracts with minimal modifications. As the pioneer of smart contracts, Ethereum is the most adopted blockchain for DeFi applications. However, it often suffers from high transaction fees and network congestion due to its popularity. In this paper, we consider three other EVM-compatible blockchains: Binance Chain [3], Polygon [6], Arbitrum [2]. At the time of writing, Ethereum has a Total Value Locked (TVL) of about 24B USD, BSC has a TVL of about 3B USD, Polygon has a TVL of about 884M USD, and Arbitrum has a TVL of about 2B USD [4]. TVL refers to the amount of cryptocurrency or assets held within a smart contract, a set of smart contracts, or a whole blockchain and it's usually expressed in USD.

2.2   Attacker Model

When examining DeFi attacks on EVM-compatible blockchains, the attack process can typically be divided into three main stages: deployment of malicious contract, attack execution, and funds extraction.

In the deployment stage, the attacker deploys a malicious smart contract onto the blockchain. The smart contract contains the logic and instructions required to exploit vulnerabilities contained within the victim's smart contract.

After deployment, the attacker executes the attack by triggering the logic contained in the malicious smart contract. This can be performed either at deployment time via the constructor or via a separate transaction. The constructor embeds code that is executed only once, namely during deployment. Attackers might embed the attack logic within the constructor itself to execute the attack during deployment. Alternatively, the attacker embeds the attack logic into a normal function and invokes it via a separate transaction after the malicious contract has been deployed. This method gives the attacker more control over the timing of the attack. It may be used to exploit more complex vulnerabilities or to coordinate with other events on the blockchain. During the attack execution, the malicious contract may interact with the victim contracts in various ways, such as by manipulating oracle data, performing reentrancy attacks, or exploiting flaws in the business logic of the contract to bypass access control checks, all aiming to create an illicit advantage for the attacker.

After the successful exploitation, the attacker seeks ways to extract the illegally obtained funds or assets. This might involve: extracting funds directly to the attacker's wallet address, using additional smart contracts to obscure the source of the transactions to make tracing more difficult, or converting the stolen assets through decentralized exchanges and mixing services to obfuscate the traces further.

2.3 Private Pools

Maximal Extractable Value (MEV) is a concept that refers to the profit a user can make through their ability to include, exclude, or reorder transactions within certain blocks [22]. For instance, users can engage in practices like front-running, where they observe a profitable transaction in the mempool and create another transaction with a higher gas price to benefit from the knowledge of the pending transaction [31]. MEV has implications for blockchain security, fairness, and transaction finality.

Flashbots [15] is a research and development organization aiming to mitigate the negative externalities of MEV. It provides a communication channel called Flashbots Relay, through which users can send their transactions directly to block producers without broadcasting them via the public mempool. This mechanism allows for a more efficient way to capture MEV. In 2022, more than 80% of MEV extraction was happening via Flashbots and 13.2% was coming from other private pools [31].

Attackers can also leverage private pools and transaction relay systems to conduct their malicious activities with more privacy and precision [21]. Indeed, private pools allow transactions to be executed privately before being broadcast to the public blockchain. Thus, attackers can hide their activities until the attack has been completed, obscuring the malicious contract's interactions from any tools that monitor the public mempool. Some private transaction pool providers, such as Flashbots and Eden Networks are already operating on Ethereum, and we expect this trend to grow in other chains, either.

3 Motivation

Despite the emergence of numerous attack analysis and detection tools over the past years, the DeFi ecosystem continues to experience a growing trend in both the rate of attacks and loss of funds. According to Immunefi's 2022 crypto loss report [20], hackers exploited vulnerabilities in 134 different contracts of several chains, including Ethereum and BSC, resulting in $3,773,906,837 in losses throughout the year. It highlights that even though we can detect attacks, we still lack in preventing attackers from fulfilling their malicious intentions and protecting funds against such exploitation. While various existing tools identify suspicious behavior by monitoring chain activities, they still fall short in automatically detecting the actual victims and notifying them on time.

We investigated a dataset of 69 attacks on Ethereum occurred between 2020 and 2023 on the Ethereum blockchain to determine if they utilized private pools for execution (Fig. 1). To do this, we focused on Flashbots [15] and Eden networks [16] as two major private pool providers on Ethereum. We extracted the attack transactions and checked whether they were relayed through Flashbots or Eden network's private pools. We found that none of these attacks originated from Eden networks. However, we observed a rising trend in attacks executed on Flashbots' private pools. Out of all 26 attacks we analyzed in 2022, 13 or 50% of them were executed through Flashbots, while only 2 out of 21 attacks in 2021 were executed through Flashbots. Considering the available data, we expect a potential increase in the future usage of Flashbots' private pool.

Our analysis revealed that attackers increasingly utilize private pools to execute malicious transactions, allowing them to conceal their malicious activities from monitoring tools. This highlights the importance of proactively analyzing malicious contracts and preventing such attacks. Research by Zhou et al. [38] analyzed 192 attacks and discovered that 56% of the hackers are not executing attacks automatically, providing defenders with a rescue time frame. Rescue time is the time frame between deploying a malicious smart contract and the first malicious transaction. This rescue time window provides an opportunity to prevent malicious activities. For instance, for the recent attack on Euler Finance [1], the attackers managed to drain $197,000,000 through a flash loan attack. Even though the hackers used private pools to execute attack transactions, they deployed the attack contract a few blocks before executing the actual attack transactions, providing a short rescue time window.

The increasing use of private pools by attackers and a rescue time window highlight the importance of identifying victims' addresses in malicious contracts. Identifying the addresses of potential victims makes it possible to notify them and take proactive measures to protect their funds before the attack is executed.

4 Methodology

To achieve the goal of identifying victims' addresses prior to hack transactions and through the analysis of malicious smart contracts, we have developed a novel methodology consisting of the following three consecutive steps: (1) extracting potential victims' addresses; (2) extracting deployers' addresses; (3) determining the actual victims.

4.1 Extracting Potential Victims' Addresses

To execute a malicious transaction targeting specific victims, the victims' addresses should be provided to the malicious contract beforehand. There are four different approaches for a hacker to communicate victims' addresses to malicious contracts:

1. Including victim addresses in the deployment bytecode during contract creation. In this way, the victim addresses are hardcoded into the bytecode of the malicious contract itself.

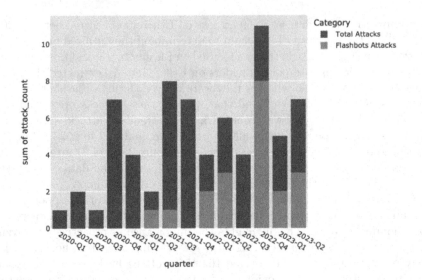

Fig. 1. The progression of attacks performed through private pools and on Ethereum over time, compared to the total number of attacks. Each bar represents the number of attacks that occurred within one quarter of the year.

2. Importing them during the deployment of the malicious contract. Victim addresses can be passed as parameters to the constructor of the malicious contract during its creation.
3. Sending them by some other initialization transactions before malicious transaction.
4. Sending victim addresses as parameters during the execution of the malicious transaction.

We manually analyzed all malicious contracts in our dataset over four different chains and we realized that in the majority of attacks (79.49%), the hackers specify the victim's address either in the malicious smart contracts or its constructor's parameters. Only 20.51% of attacks rely on the attack transaction to specify the victim as well. None of these attackers transmitted the victim's address for the first time through any transaction other than the first attack transaction or the contract creation transaction.

Thus, the first step of our methodology is to extract all hardcoded addresses from the deployment bytecode and the parameters of the malicious contract's constructor. To achieve this goal, we extract the deployment bytecode of malicious smart contracts, convert them to readable opcodes, and extract all hex strings with a length of 20 that was loaded with the operand of Push20. Additionally, we extracted all 20-byte values found within the inputs of the contract creation transaction. Then, we examined each extracted address to determine if an active contract was associated with it. For our analysis, we define an active contract as a contract with at least one transaction.

From the creation transactions of the malicious contract, we extracted a set of active contracts, which we refer to as potential victims. Note that external-owned accounts (EOAs), non-active contracts, and non-addresses were excluded as potential victims, as they cannot be targeted in an attack.

4.2   Extracting Deployers' Addresses

The average number of potential victims for a malicious smart contract is 9.63, making extracting the actual victim challenging. To visually represent this distribution, we present the Fig. 2, illustrating the frequency of the potential victims associated with each malicious contract. In the worst-case scenario, a malicious contract included more than 40 potential victims.

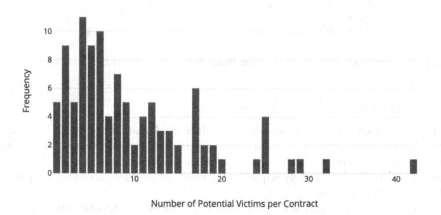

Fig. 2. Frequency of Number of Potential Victims in Different Attacks.

Note that the number of actual victim addresses in a single attack often exceeds one. However, we have observed that all victim addresses are usually associated with the same project. For example, let us consider the recent attack on Euler Finance [1], an Ethereum-based borrowing and lending platform. It suffered from a Flash loan attack on 13th March 2023, resulting in a substantial loss of $196,000,000. Through the analysis of the deployment bytecode of the corresponding malicious smart contract, we extracted 25 potential victims. Out of all these potential victims, we discovered that only five unique deployers deployed 15. Figure 3 represents all the potential victims of the attack on Euler Finance. Seven are deployed by the same deployer address, all belonging to the victim project.

Therefore, the methodology's second step extracts each potential victim's deployer address, indicating affiliation to a specific DeFi project.

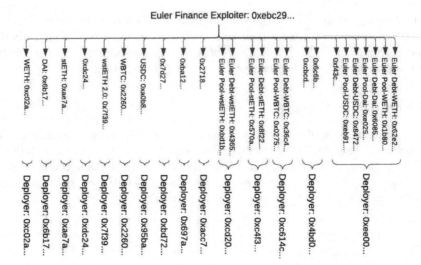

Fig. 3. Potential victims of Attack on Euler Finance clustered by their deployers.

4.3 Determining Actual Victims

The third stage of our methodology involves analyzing the potential victims identified in the preceding steps in order to detect the actual victims. This stage is based on the hypothesis that a significant association exists between the number of contracts deployed by a particular deployer and the probability of that deployer being the victim.

This subsection presents the Dominant Deployer Identification (DDI) method, which can be enhanced with the ERC20 exclusion criterion.

The DDI method focuses on the number of contracts deployed by each deployer. By examining the deployment bytecode of malicious smart contracts, this method aims to identify the deployer associated with the highest number of deployed contracts within each malicious smart contract and designate all of their contracts as victims. One key advantage of this method is its simplicity. It relies on a straightforward metric, the number of contracts deployed, to determine the deployer with the highest deployment activity. The method provides a direct approach to identifying victim addresses by singling out this deployer. In cases where there is a tie between two or more different deployers for the highest number of deployed contracts, the method does not label any deployer as a victim. This limitation may result in the omission of potential victim addresses, potentially reducing the effectiveness of the identification process. We introduced the following method to fix the limitations of tied deployers for the highest number of deployed contracts. This method aim to filter out potential victims that are less likely to be the actual victim.

The DDI method with the ERC20 exclusion criterion considers that ERC20 tokens are often implemented using smart contract libraries that have undergone extensive code audits and are considered more robust and secure. This method leverages this characteristic by filtering out ERC20 token contracts from the pool of potential victims associated with deployers. By excluding ERC20 tokens, the method aims to narrow down the set of potential victim addresses to those less likely to have vulnerabilities or be targets of attacks. This filtering process assumes that reusing well-audited smart contract libraries reduces the risk of exploitation. After the filtering phase, the method counts the number of contracts deployed by each deployer and follows the same procedure as the DDI method without the ERC20 exclusion criterion. The advantage of adding this filtering is that it introduces an additional layer of consideration by prioritizing contracts that are more likely to be secure. By excluding ERC20 tokens, the method focuses on contracts with a higher likelihood of being victims. However, it is essential to acknowledge that this method assumes ERC20 token contracts are more secure due to extensive code audits. While this assumption is generally valid, it does not guarantee absolute certainty.

In the next section, we will evaluate the application of this methodology and compare the effectiveness of the two proposed methods.

5   Evaluation

5.1   Dataset

To perform our analysis, we manually collected and labeled a dataset consisting of 117 smart contract attacks. All these attacks occurred between 2020 and 2023, and we gathered them from four different blockchains: 69 attacks occurred on Ethereum, 28 of them were on BSC, 13 on Polygon, and finally 7 occurred on Arbitrum. We analyzed the attacks documented in the Rekt database [8] and extracted various data points such as deployment bytecode, runtime bytecode, constructor parameters, and victim addresses of each attack. Table 1 provides a detailed overview of our dataset and depicts the distribution of extracted attacks across each chain.

According to our findings, out of all 117 attacks analyzed in our dataset, we discovered that in 86 cases, the victim addresses were communicated through deployment bytecode, and in 7 cases it was communicated through the constructor's parameters. during contract creation; while initial hack transactions revealed victim addresses in the remaining 24 attacks. We found that in all 117 attacks, the victim address could be found in the malicious contract's deployment bytecode, the constructor's inputs, or the initial attack transaction. Our results clearly indicate that by analyzing contract creation transactions, we have the potential to detect victim addresses for almost 80% of the attacks. However, in the remaining attacks, the victim's address remains unknown until the occurrence of the initial attack transaction.

Table 1. Number of smart contract attacks in our dataset, categorized by chain name.

Chain	Victim address's communication method			Total
	Deployment Bytecode	Constructor Parameters	Attack Tx	
Ethereum	53	3	13	69
Binance	17	3	8	28
Polygon	10	1	2	13
Arbitrum	6	0	1	7
Total	86	7	24	117
	73.50%	5.98%	20.51%	100%

5.2   Results

We implemented a script to execute our methodology on smart contracts' deployment bytecode. The script extracts all potential victims, cluster them based on deployer addresses, and utilizes the Dominant Deployer Identification (DDI) technique on these potential victims. If there is a single dominant set of addresses, the script labels them as the victim. This means we identified a single deployer who deployed the highest number of deployed contracts within the malicious smart contract. Otherwise, if multiple sets of addresses are dominant, we will analyze them using the two specified victim determination methods we explained in Sect. 4.3.

We evaluated the script on all 117 malicious contracts and calculated the confusion matrix for each of the two methods. Table 2, demonstrates the corresponding measures. As can be observed, we successfully identified the victims of 62 attacks out of all 117 attacks, using the DDI approach and without the ERC20 exclusion criterion. The DDI approach combined with the ERC20 exclusion criterion was able to identify the victims of 65 attacks. Furthermore, the DDI approach without the ERC20 exclusion criterion correctly identified 21 attacks where the victim's address wasn't present in the deployment bytecode. However, when using the DDI approach with the ERC20 exclusion criterion, we identified 19 attacks where the victim's address was not present in the deployment bytecode.

We can assess the effectiveness of the two methods by comparing their precision and recall. As predicted, incorporating the filtering analysis method resulted in an increase in the number of false positives but a decrease in the number of false negatives, resulting in a higher recall, but lower precision. Note that the importance of recall's absolute value is greater than that of precision. This is because false negatives can lead to significant financial loss. False positives, on the other hand, are relatively less costly. Until a specific threshold, such as a weekly occurrence, is crossed, project owners might tolerate false positive reports; however, a false negative report could directly result in a huge financial loss and warrants closer attention.

Table 2. Results on the comparison of DDI Performance, with and without ERC20 exclusion criterion on the Dataset of hacks, across four different chains.

Chain	Measure	Methods	
		DDI	DDI + ERC20 exclusion criterion
Ethereum	Number of Attacks	69	69
	True Positive	33	36
	False Positive	7	9
	False Negative	16	13
	True Negative	13	11
	Accuracy	66.67%	68.12%
Binance	Number of Attacks	28	28
	True Positive	17	17
	False Positive	3	3
	False Negative	3	3
	True Negative	5	5
	Accuracy	78.57%	78.57%
Polygon	Number of Attacks	13	13
	True Positive	6	6
	False Positive	0	0
	False Negative	5	5
	True Negative	2	2
	Accuracy	61.54%	61.54%
Arbitrum	Number of Attacks	7	7
	True Positive	6	6
	False Positive	0	0
	False Negative	0	0
	True Negative	1	1
	Accuracy	100%	100%
Total	Number of Attacks	117	117
	Attacks with Hardcoded Victims	93	93
	True Positive	62	65
	False Positive	10	12
	False Negative	24	21
	True Negative	21	19
	Precision	86.11%	84.42%
	Recall	72.09%	75.58%
	Accuracy	70.94%	71.79%
	F1 score	78.48%	79.75%

Nonetheless, when evaluating the F1 score, which represents the harmonic mean of precision and recall, we observe that the F1 score of DDI with the ERC20 exclusion criterion is 79.75%, hence surpassing the F1 score of DDI without the ERC20 exclusion criterion which is 78.48%.

We have identified some limitations that challenge our ability to identify the victims of all attacks. The first limitation refers to attacks where the actual victim's address is transmitted solely through the first attack transaction. It makes it impossible to identify the victims in the contract creation phase. Second, attackers might combine the contract creation and execution in a single transaction, leaving no rescue time to identify the attack before the execution of the attack. Within our dataset, we found only one instance of such an attack where contract creation and the malicious transaction occurred in the same transaction. It was the Reentrancy attack on Rari Fuse on Arbitrum [5], which took place on 30th April 2022. Another limitation is the dataset size. As shown in the table, the ERC20 exclusion criterion yielded noticeable improvements in the True Positive rate for Ethereum but did not affect Polygon. It is due to the volume of data available on Ethereum compared to Polygon and BSC. However, it is worth noting that our DDI method successfully extracted all victim addresses of attacks in Arbitrum, despite the smaller dataset for that chain.

6   Related Work

Smart Contract Attacks. A plethora of tools have been proposed to detect and analyze attacks on smart contracts. ECFCHECKER [19] was the first tool to enable the runtime detection of reentrancy attacks via a modified version of the EVM. SEREUM [28] also proposed a modified version of the EVM, but which could protect already deployed smart contracts by blocking reentrancy attacks. ÆGIS [12,13] generalize SEREUM's idea by leveraging a smart contract to maintain and distribute a list of rules that are written using a domain-specific language to detect and block smart contract attacks at runtime. Perez et al. [23] use Datalog to study and analyze the bytecode of vulnerable smart contracts of past attacks. Similar to ECFCHECKER and SEREUM, SODA [11] uses a modified Ethereum client to inject custom modules for the online detection of malicious transactions. ETHSCOPE [34] adds dynamic taint analysis to an Ethereum client and replays historical transaction data which then stores traces into an Elasticsearch database which can be queried for past attacks. Zhou et al. [39] analyzed real-world attacks and defenses adopted in the wild based on the transaction logs produced by an uninstrumented EVM and decoupling decoupling adversarial actions from adversarial consequences. TxSPECTOR [35] adopts the Datalog facts proposed by Brent et al. [9] to detect and analyze malicious transactions post-mortem. Similarly, HORUS [14] also leverages Datalog to detect attacks against smart contracts but leverages dynamic taint analysis to capture attacks that span across multiple transactions. [36] Zheng et al. present XBlock-ETH – a framework that generates Ethereum datasets in the form of CSV files consisting of transactions, smart contracts, and token transfers, which can then be further leveraged to detect attacks. Wang et al. [29] propose BLOCKEYE a real-time attack detection system for DeFi projects, which performs symbolic reasoning on the data flow of smart contract states, e.g., asset price, and flags a transaction as a potential attack if a violation is detected on a critical invariant. Zhou et al. [38] analyzed close to 200 real-world incidents and concluded that the average rescue time frame for most smart contract attacks is 1±4.1 h, with the longest rescue time frame being 26.5 h. Forta [17] tries to leverage the same fact as we do, namely that there is a rescue window that allows them to detect malicious deployment bytecode before an attacker can perform the actual attack. They use a detection bot that uses a machine learning model to detect malicious smart contract creations based on a contract's disassembled EVM opcodes. Wang et al. [30] propose a deep-learning-based attack detection system called DeFiScanner that leverages information emitted via events during transaction execution to cluster if a transaction is an attack or not. Gai et al. [18] present a tool called BLOCKGPT, which leverages a large language model to detect abnormal transactions from traces that are captured during the execution of a transaction. Qin et al. [25] describe a methodology for whitehat hackers to monitor the public mempool and to copy and frontrun attacker transactions before they can have an impact on the victim contracts. Moreover, Qin et al. [26] introduce execution property graphs for EVM transactions and leverage graph traversal techniques to detect if a transaction is malicious or not. Most of the solutions that been proposed so far either take too long to analyze transaction which makes them impractical to be used as real-time attack detection systems, or they depend on the monitoring of pending transactions in the mempool which attackers can avoid by leveraging private pools. Moreover, most of the aforementioned tools focus on detecting attacks but not identifying victim addresses. However, identifying victim addresses is crucial as this allows for them to be rescued.

Private Transactions. Lyu et al. [21] collected private transactions at a large scale and performed analysis on their characteristics, such as transaction costs, miner profits, as well as security impacts. Lyu et al. [21] find that although private transactions were proposed to protect end users from attacks, they find that only 18.1% of private transactions have been used for that purpose. Qin et al. [27] provide a theoretical analysis of network congestion in the presence of private pools, and conclude that as opposed to Flashbots' claims, private pools do not reduce network congestion. Weintraub et al. [31] show however that Flashbots does at least reduce gas prices in some instances. Moreover, they also show that a large number of MEVs are being extracted via private pools such as Flashbots. Piet et al. [24] and Capponi et al. [10] analyze the profit distribution within Flashbots and conclude, similarly to Weintraub et al. [31], that miners are making most of the profit. Weintraub et al. [31] measures MEV ex- traction before and after the inception of Flashbots and concludes that searchers were making more profit prior to Flashbot sand that the number of searchers using Flashbots is decreasing.

7 Conclusion

We investigated whether we can identify victims of attacks by analyzing the deployment bytecode of malicious smart contracts. We introduced a comprehensive methodology that involved extracting potential victims from deployment bytecode and identifying the actual victims. By analyzing 117 attacks on DeFi across four different blockchain networks, we discovered that in over 80% cases, the victim address is present within the malicious smart contracts even before the first attack transaction occurs. To refine our approach, we introduced a technique that involved identifying the dominant deployer among all potential victims and filtering out ERC20 tokens, considered proven secure tokens, to improve the accuracy of our findings. In future work, we aim to improve accuracy by formalizing heuristics, refining analysis methods, and expanding our dataset.

References

1. $197 million stolen: Euler finance flash loan attack explained. https://blog.chainalysis.com/reports/euler-finance-flash-loan-attack, Accessed 26 Jun 2023
2. Arbitrum: Scaling Ethereum. https://arbitrum.io Accessed 29 Jun 2023
3. BNB Smart Chain: A Parallel BNB Chain to Enable Smart Contracts. https://www.bnbchain.org/en/smartChain Accessed 29 Jun 2023
4. DefiLlama. https://defillama.com Accessed 29 Jun 2023
5. Fuse Exploit Post Mortem. https://medium.com/@JackLongarzo/fuse-exploit-post-mortem-76ce18d8974 Accessed 30 Jun 2023
6. Polygon: Blockchains for mass adoption. https://polygon.technology Accessed 29 Jun 2023
7. Rubic dex aggregator hack leads to $1.4m of user funds stole. https://www.binance.com/en/feed/post/134920 Accessed 16 Aug 2023
8. Top crypto hacks-rekt database. https://defiyield.app/rekt-database Accessed 29 Jun 2023
9. Brent, L., et al.: Vandal: A scalable security analysis framework for smart contracts. arXiv preprint arXiv:1809.03981 (2018)
10. Capponi, A., Jia, R., Wang, Y.: The evolution of blockchain: from lit to dark. arXiv preprint arXiv:2202.05779 (2022)
11. Chen, T., et al.: Soda: A generic online detection framework for smart contracts. In: Proceedings of the Network and Distributed System Security Symposium (NDSS'20) (2020)
12. Ferreira Torres, C., Baden, M., Norvill, R., Fiz Pontiveros, B.B., Jonker, H., Mauw, S.: Ægis: Shielding vulnerable smart contracts against attacks. In: Proceedings of the 15th ACM Asia Conference on Computer and Communications Security, pp. 584–597 (2020)
13. Ferreira Torres, C., Baden, M., Norvill, R., Jonker, H.: ÆGIS: Smart Shielding of Smart Contracts. In: Proceedings of the 2019 ACM SIGSAC Conference on Computer and Communications Security, pp. 2589–2591 (2019)
14. Ferreira Torres, C., Iannillo, A.K., Gervais, A., State, R.: The eye of horus: Spotting and analyzing attacks on ethereum smart contracts. In: Financial Cryptography and Data Security: 25th International Conference, FC 2021, Virtual Event, March 1–5, 2021, Revised Selected Papers, Part I 25. pp. 33–52. Springer (2021)

15. Flashbots: Flashbots docs. https://docs.flashbots.net/flashbots-auction/overview Accessed 29 Jun 2023
16. Flashbots: Flashbots docs. https://docs.edennetwork.io Accessed 26 Jun 2023
17. Forta-Network: How forta's predictive ml models detect attacks before exploitation. https://forta.org/blog/how-fortas-predictive-ml-models-detect-attacks-before-exploitation Accessed 13 Jun 2023
18. Gai, Y., Zhou, L., Qin, K., Song, D., Gervais, A.: Blockchain large language models. arXiv preprint arXiv:2304.12749 (2023)
19. Grossman, S., et al.: Online detection of effectively callback free objects with applications to smart contracts. In: Proceedings of the ACM on Programming Languages 2(POPL), 48 (2017)
20. Immunefi: Immunefi crypto losses report. https://immunefi.com/reports Accessed 26 Jun 2023
21. Lyu, X., Zhang, M., Zhang, X., Niu, J., Zhang, Y., Lin, Z.: An empirical study on ethereum private transactions and the security implications. arXiv preprint arXiv:2208.02858 (2022)
22. Mazorra, B., Reynolds, M., Daza, V.: Price of mev: towards a game theoretical approach to mev. In: Proceedings of the 2022 ACM CCS Workshop on Decentralized Finance and Security, pp. 15–22 (2022)
23. Perez, D., Livshits, B.: Smart contract vulnerabilities: Vulnerable does not imply exploited. In: 30th USENIX Security Symposium (USENIX Security 21). USENIX Association, Vancouver, B.C. (Aug 2021)
24. Piet, J., Fairoze, J., Weaver, N.: Extracting godl [sic] from the salt mines: Ethereum miners extracting value. CoRR abs/2203.15930 (2022)
25. Qin, K., Chaliasos, S., Zhou, L., Livshits, B., Song, D., Gervais, A.: The blockchain imitation game. arXiv preprint arXiv:2303.17877 (2023)
26. Qin, K., et al.: Towards automated security analysis of smart contracts based on execution property graph. CoRR abs/2305.14046 (2023)
27. Qin, K., Zhou, L., Gervais, A.: Quantifying blockchain extractable value: How dark is the forest? In: 43rd IEEE Symposium on Security and Privacy, SP 2022, San Francisco, CA, USA, May 22–26, 2022, pp. 198–214. IEEE (2022)
28. Rodler, M., Li, W., Karame, G., Davi, L.: Sereum: Protecting existing smart contracts against re-entrancy attacks. In: Proceedings of the Network and Distributed System Security Symposium (NDSS'19) (2019)
29. Wang, B., et al.: Blockeye: Hunting for defi attacks on blockchain. In: 2021 IEEE/ACM 43rd International Conference on Software Engineering: Companion Proceedings (ICSE-Companion), pp. 17–20. IEEE (2021)
30. Wang, B., Yuan, X., Duan, L., Ma, H., Su, C., Wang, W.: Defiscanner: spotting defi attacks exploiting logic vulnerabilities on blockchain. IEEE Transactions on Computational Social Systems (2022)
31. Weintraub, B., Torres, C.F., Nita-Rotaru, C., State, R.: A flash(bot) in the pan: measuring maximal extractable value in private pools. In: Barakat, C., Pelsser, C., Benson, T.A., Choffnes, D.R. (eds.) Proceedings of the 22nd ACM Internet Measurement Conference, IMC 2022, Nice, France, October 25–27, 2022, pp. 458–471. ACM (2022)
32. Werner, S., Perez, D., Gudgeon, L., Klages-Mundt, A., Harz, D., Knottenbelt, W.: Sok: decentralized finance (defi). In: Proceedings of the 4th ACM Conference on Advances in Financial Technologies, pp. 30–46 (2022)
33. Wood, G., et al.: Ethereum: a secure decentralised generalised transaction ledger. Ethereum project yellow paper 151(2014), 1–32 (2014)

34. Wu, L., et al.: Ethscope: A transaction-centric security analytics framework to detect malicious smart contracts on ethereum. arXiv preprint arXiv:2005.08278 (2020)
35. Zhang, M., Zhang, X., Zhang, Y., Lin, Z.: Txspector: Uncovering attacks in ethereum from transactions. In: USENIX Security Symposium (2020)
36. Zheng, P., Zheng, Z., Wu, J., Dai, H.: Xblock-eth: Extracting and exploring blockchain data from ethereum. IEEE Open J. Comput. Soc. 1, 95–106 (2020)
37. Zheng, Z., et al.: An overview on smart contracts: challenges, advances and platforms. Futur. Gener. Comput. Syst. 105, 475–491 (2020)
38. Zhou, L., et al.: Sok: Decentralized finance (defi) attacks. Cryptology ePrint Archive (2022)
39. Zhou, S., Yang, Z., Xiang, J., Cao, Y., Yang, Z., Zhang, Y.: An ever-evolving game: Evaluation of real-world attacks and defenses in ethereum ecosystem. In: 29th USENIX Security Symposium (USENIX Security 20), pp. 2793–2810. USENIX Association (Aug 2020)

On the (Not So) Surprising Impact of Multi-Path Payments on Performance And Privacy in the Lightning Network

Charmaine Ndolo[1][(✉)] and Florian Tschorsch[1,2]

[1] Humboldt -Universität Zu Berlin, Berlin, Germany
c.n.ndolo@hu-berlin.de, florian.tschorsch@tu-dresden.de
[2] Technische Universität Dresden, Dresden, Germany

Abstract. The Lightning network (LN) addresses Bitcoin's scalability issues by providing fast and private payment processing. In order to mitigate failures caused by insufficient channel capacities, LN introduced multi-path payments. To the best of our knowledge, the effect of multi-path payments remains unclear. In this paper, we therefore study the impact of multi-path payments on performance and privacy. We identify metrics quantifying the aforementioned properties and utilise them to evaluate the impact of multi-path payments. To this end, we develop a simulator implementing pathfinding in LN using single and multi-path payments as well as various pathfinding algorithms. We find that, while the success rate of multi-path payments is up to 20% higher, the impact of multi-path payments on performance otherwise remains within limits. On the other hand, the impact on privacy appears to be greater, e.g., multi-path payments are more likely to encounter an on-path adversary and the relationship anonymity is more likely to be compromised by colluding intermediate hops. However, multi-path payments are less likely to be deanonymised based on the path lengths.

1 Introduction

Layer 2 solutions such as the Lightning network (LN) [21] offer a solution to Bitcoin's scalability problem by means of a payment channel network (PCN). A PCN is a network of off-chain payment channels, each between two parties, in which funds can move in either direction as long as both parties agree. LN facilitates fast payment processing by limiting the need for global consensus to a subset of states [21]. In addition to speed, privacy is a focal objective in LN leading to various privacy-enhancing measures. For instance, while channel capacities are announced to the public network, the individual endpoints' balances are kept private. LN also supports multi-hop payments allowing the routing of payments over multiple intermediate nodes.

Finding such paths is an essential part of LN and is delegated to the sender of a payment. i.e., multi-hop payments are source-routed. The pathfinding algorithm in LN is typically accomplished using Dijkstra's shortest path algorithm [5]

© The Author(s), under exclusive license to Springer Nature Switzerland AG 2024
S. Katsikas et al. (Eds.): ESORICS 2023 Workshops, LNCS 14398, pp. 411–427, 2024.
https://doi.org/10.1007/978-3-031-54204-6_25

and a fee-based cost function.[1] Given the uncertainty over balances, a path chosen by a sender, may fail due to insufficient balances along the way. To ameliorate this challenge, a lot of effort has been devoted to the question of efficient routing, e.g., [2,22,26] and notably [20] whose authors proposed the selection of paths based on the probability of a payment succeeding.

It has been shown that LN generally performs well with lower payment volumes, but suffers from degradation with increasing payment volumes due to a lack of channels with sufficiently high capacity [3,31]. As a response, the network introduced *multi-path payments (MPP)* and *atomic multi-path payments (AMP)* as an alternative payment scheme [6,8,18]. Such payments allow splitting a payment amount into multiple payment parts of lesser value and thereby maximise on the entire available flow between sender and receiver. A crucial difference between MPPs and AMPs is that the former use the same payment hash for all parts and AMPs are atomic.

To the best of our knowledge, the relationship between performance and privacy in conjunction with multi-path payments remains open. Privacy in LN has been shown to be susceptible to various attacks such as balance-revealing [4,9] and deanonymisation attacks [11,15,23]. It is probable that multi-path payments may heighten privacy concerns due to payment data traversing the network on multiple occasions, e.g., with respect to correlation attacks.

In this work, we study the impact of multi-path payments on performance and privacy in LN empirically using network simulations. We include fee and probability-based pathfinding in our analysis as the pathfinding algorithm plays a role in the outcome of key routing parameters. Among others, we find that high-volume payments are more likely to succeed as multi-path payments which are also less likely to be deanonymised based on the path lengths. Where applicable, we contextualise our results with earlier research. The main contributions of this work can be summarised as follows:

1. we identify various metrics to quantify performance and privacy in the LN;
2. we compare the single and multi-path payments w.r.t the identified metrics in combination with fee and probability-based pathfinding algorithms; and
3. we implement an LN simulator providing us with empirical, simulation-based results on the impact of multi-path on performance and privacy in LN.

The remainder of this paper is structured as follows. Section 2 provides an overview of LN as well as our methodology including the identified metrics for performance and privacy. We present and discuss our results in Sect. 3 and Sect. 4. We summarise related literature in Sect. 5 and conclude in Sect. 6.

2   Network Model

Once a (bidirectional) channel in LN has been established between two parties, an arbitrary number of payments can be made between them. By opening a

---

[1] https://github.com/lightning/bolts/blob/master/07-routing-gossip.md#requirements-9.

channel, a fixed number of funds is committed – known as the *capacity* – which can be disposed of freely within the channel. Transactions between the two channel endpoints alter the parties' *balances*, i.e., each node's share of the channel's capacity. Motivated by privacy concerns, node balances are kept private.

For reasons mainly related to practicability, LN is not a complete network in which every pair of nodes has a channel. Instead, channels form a PCN that enables routing payments between parties via multiple intermediate hops. Multi-hop routing requires that there must be a set of channels linking the sender and the recipient and essentially boils down to a shortest path problem. The PCN is therefore commonly modelled and reasoned about as a (directed) graph [3,28].

Definition 1 (The Lightning network graph). *The LN graph is a directed multigraph* $G = (V, E)$ *where* V *is the set of Lightning nodes and* E *the multiset of payment channels in the network.*

Note that while channels are bidirectional, attributes such as each node's fee structure make it necessary to distinguish the direction of an edge in G when reasoning about pathfinding. Hence, it is necessary to define G as a directed graph. G is a multigraph as, in practice, a pair of nodes may have more than one channel between them.

Payments in Lightning are source-routed, i.e., the sender is responsible for finding a path to the recipient, and is typically accomplished using some form of Dijkstra's shortest path algorithm [5]. The LN specification, Basis of Lightning Technology (BOLT) [1], defines the edge weights using a fee-minimising cost function based on channel capacities, fees and locking duration. At the time of writing, routing nodes in LN charge two types of fees – a *base fee* that is due regardless of the amount in question as well as a *proportional fee* that is scaled by the amount to be forwarded. Given the cost function, a shortest path search algorithm is expected to return the cheapest path between two nodes. Due to the uncertainty over balances, this cost function often leads to failed payments as a result of insufficient liquidity [20].

Based on the observation that channels with higher capacity provide a higher chance of success, Pickhardt et al. propose to select paths based on the *success probability* [20], which is the product of the involved channels' individual success probabilities. The lower the ratio of payment amount and channel capacity, the higher the success probability. In this case, a shortest path search algorithm returns the channel with the highest probability of success.

Further design details of payment channels in general and PCNs in particular, e.g., on the atomicity of multi-hop payments, can be found in [1,13,21,29].

2.1   Performance Metrics

In the following, we describe metrics quantifying the performance of LN and PCNs in general. While some of the described metrics can already be found in existing literature, we identify additional metrics that encapsulate the *utility* and *usability* of the network from a user's perspective.

We begin with the *success rate* as a rudimentary measure of performance which we define as the ratio of successful payments and the total number of payments [16]. Furthermore, we study the amount of *transaction fees* due for successful multi-hop payments. In the case of multi-part payments, we consider each part individually. The *path length* is a well-known measure of network topologies and quantifies the number of edges (channels) a payment traverses before arriving at its recipient. Similar to the transaction fees, we consider the partial payment paths independently. The path length is only relevant to successful payments as failed payments do not have a complete path between sender and receiver. As a final performance metric, we use the *number of payment attempts* as an indicator of routing efficiency. We define the number of payment attempts as the number of Hashed Timelock Contracts (HTLCs) triggered by a single payment before it eventually succeeds or fails. We define the number of attempts for a multi-path payment as the sum of all parts' attempts.

2.2 Privacy Metrics

Although LN (and layer 2 solutions in general) strives for improved privacy, compared to on-chain solutions, recent works have identified shortcomings in the privacy provided by LN [13,23,29,30]. We compile measures quantifying privacy in LN in what follows.

Unless stated otherwise, we assume an *honest but curious (HBC)* adversary. Such an adversary is a legitimate participant in LN who will not deviate from the protocol but will try to infer as much as possible from observed messages [17]. Given that an HBC adversary has limited capabilities, we consider these properties to be a lower bound on privacy in the network.

Observation rate: We quantify how often an *on-path* adversary observes payments using what we call the *observation rate*. The observation rate is the proportion of the number of payments that encountered an adversary in any of their attempted paths and the total number of payments. This metric has previously been studied in [29]. In the case of multi-path payments, we define the observation rate as the proportion of payments that include such a node in at least one of their parts' attempted paths.

A high observation rate is a result of either a high number of watchers or, more plausibly based on the properties of LN channel graph [12,23,27], routing hubs that forward a great number of payments.

Sender and Receiver Inference: After analysing the length of payment paths in LN, Kappos et al. set up a formula defining the probability that a node's predecessor and successor in a payment's path are the respective payment endpoints [10]. The formula is based on the path length probability distribution and estimates the probabilities Pr_s^{succ} and Pr_s^{fail} of correctly identifying the sender of successful and failed payments [10]. The probabilities Pr_r^{succ} and Pr_r^{fail} for the payment's destination are calculated analogously.

Shorter, unsuccessful paths lead to the highest probabilities whereas longer, successful paths exhibit the lowest probabilities. We propose to extend this measure to multi-path payments by handling payment parts as individual payments.

Relationship Anonymity: Tikhomirov et al. examine the probability of a successful path being vulnerable to a confirmation attack [29], i.e., a path $s, i_1, ..., i_n, d$ in which the hops i_1 and i_n are under adversarial control. We extend this measure to payments by characterising a payment as vulnerable if at least one of its paths is vulnerable in that both the first and last hops are controlled by an adversary. The measure is identical to the one in [29] for single payments as they have exactly one path if successful. Assuming an on-path adversary is able to correlate payments, e.g., using common identifiers such as the condition to fulfil an HTLC, successfully deanonymising one payment path is sufficient to determine the sender-recipient pairs for the remaining parts.

Path Diversity: We introduce *path diversity* as a further measure of privacy in the LN, i.e., we want to identify how (dis)similar the paths of a multi-path payment are with respect to the routing nodes and edges. It does not make much sense to examine single payments in this context as there is only one path for each such payment. Path diversity is desirable from a privacy standpoint in order to reduce the number of payments being observed by the same node so as to, e.g., hamper correlation attacks. A lack of path diversity is also suggestive of an (over)reliance on some nodes and edges which is unhealthy for a network in respect to resilience. However, path diversity also means more nodes are involved in delivering a given payment likely leading to an increase of the observation rate.

We propose to quantify the path diversity for a set of payment paths using the *effective path diversity (EPD)* measure defined by Rohrer et al. [25]. The EPD is the degree to which a set of paths between the same source s and destination d share common intermediate nodes and edges. It is an aggregation of path diversities for a set of paths between a given node pair (s, d) and defined as

$$EPD = 1 - e^{-\lambda k_{sd}} \in [0, 1), \quad k_{sd} = \sum_{i=1}^{k} D_{min}(P_i), \qquad (1)$$

where k is the number of paths and $D_{min}(P_i)$ is the minimum diversity of path i when measured against all previously selected paths. The constant λ scales the impact of k_{sd} based on the utility of added diversity. Lower marginal utility is indicated by a high value of λ (> 1) whereas a low value of λ represents a higher marginal utility. We argue that lower values of λ are more representative of the significance of diverse paths in LN.

2.3 Network Simulations

In order to analyse the effects of the different payment types combined with different pathfinding approaches, we developed a tool to simulate pathfinding and payment delivery in LN using algorithms similar to those used in practice. The simulator is publicly available in our accompanying Git repository.[2] The simulator reads LN snapshots to reconstruct the PCN according to the network model in Def. 1. It supports probability-weighted [20] and fee-weighted

---

[2] https://github.com/cndolo/lightning-simulator.

pathfinding[3] as well as single and multi-path payments. The simulator implements a *trial-and-error* loop and attempts to deliver a failed payment by looking for an alternative path until the set of possible paths is exhausted. In case of ambiguity in the Lightning specification, e.g., on the maximum number of parts a payment may be split into, we followed LND's implementation as it is the most commonly used client [32]. To this end, the simulator only attempts to split payments greater than 10k sat and into at most 16 parts.

We utilised a channel graph dated 15th May 2023, which contains $18,820$ nodes and $134,838$ edges and was collected from our own well-synchronised LN node. We discarded nodes and edges without essential data for the simulation such as fee structure and reduced the graph to its largest strongly connected component leading to a graph with $14,453$ nodes and $134,782$ edges.

Given the private nature of node balances, the simulator splits the channel capacity into two balance values following a uniform distribution at the beginning of a simulation (see [20] for discussions on the distribution of capacities) and updates the node balances after every successful payment delivery. We simulate various payment volumes following the categorisation of payments in [7] as actual volumes are unknown, i.e., *micro* payments, *medium* payments and *macro* payments. We chose not to make assumptions about patterns between transacting parties and simulated $5,000$ transactions between random sender-receiver pairs for each selected amount ranging between 100 sat and 10 million (m) sat. We repeated each simulation scenario multiple times with different seeds for the random number generator, i.e., for each set of $5,000$ sender-receiver pairs, the channel graph was initialised before simulating payment delivery of each amount with all four combinations of pathfinding algorithm and payment type.

While the results in this work are based on an implementation of MPP in that the same payment identifier is used for all parts, the results can be generalised to AMP, e.g., by assuming an attacker is able to identify related parts. Furthermore, the simulator ensures that all multi-path payments are atomic, i.e., either all parts succeed or no funds are moved at all.

3   Impact on Performance

We present and discuss our results pertaining to the performance of LN based on the metrics presented in Sect. 2.1. All in all, our simulations confirmed either what previous works have already established or what we can expect given what we know about the network. We omit some charts due to space constraints but provide interactive versions of all charts in our accompanying repository.[4]

3.1   Success Rate

We observe that the choice of pathfinding method is not significant for the success of the simulated payments. Instead, the payment amount – limited by channel

---

[3] https://github.com/lightning/bolts/blob/master/07-routing-gossip.md#htlc-fees.
[4] https://cndolo.github.io/lightning-simulator.

capacities – is the decisive factor. The type of payment plays a secondary role for the success rate in that larger payments are more successful when routed as multi-path payments. Most failures in LN are due to an insufficient maximum flow between sender and receiver, i.e., there is no path between sender and receiver where all of the path's edges have enough capacity to forward the requested amount [3]. Clearly, multi-path payments are at an advantage over single payments when it comes to utilising the maximum flow because a payment can be delivered via multiple paths.

As the payment amount increases, probability-weighted payments begin to show a very slight advantage of up to 2% over their respective fee-weighted counterparts. Multi-path payments start to separate themselves at payment volumes $\geq$10k sat when payments may actually be split and succeed approximately 20% more often than their single counterparts. However, less than 2% of the payments worth 5m sat and greater succeeded regardless of payment type.

3.2 Transaction Fees

In general, we noticed that the amount of absolute fees increases with the payment amount. Furthermore, paths selected based on the success probability are more expensive than fee-weighted paths. This is not surprising and indeed expected given that fee-weighted pathfinding selects paths by minimising the total amount of fees whereas probability-weighted pathfinding disregards the fees.

While multi-path payments mostly incur slightly higher fees than comparable single payments, the additional cost of splitting a payment seems to be negligible. The difference is partly due to the *base* fees charged by some nodes in LN. In the absence of base fees, we expect close to no difference between single and multi-path payments provided that all parts take paths with similar fee policies. Tochner et al. found that fee policies in LN mostly follow the same structure [30].

The necessity of the base fee in LN has been questioned [19], however, it is yet to be eliminated completely. At the time of writing, 50% of the channels in LN have adopted this proposal and do not charge a base fee.[5] The impact of base fees becomes clearer when looking at the charged fees relative to the payment volume. Lower payment volumes such as 100 sat were the most expensive regardless of the pathfinding method or payment type.

3.3 Path Length

The distribution of the successful paths' lengths is depicted in Fig. 1. At lower payment volumes, some fee-weighted paths are significantly longer than probability-weighted paths with some even at the maximum permitted hop count of 20.

For payment volumes of up to 100k sat, all combinations yield a constant median path length of 5. The median path length drops to 4 at payment volumes $\geq$500k sat for single and $\geq$5m sat for multi-path payments. In anticipation

---

[5] According to https://lnrouter.app/graph/zero-base-fee.

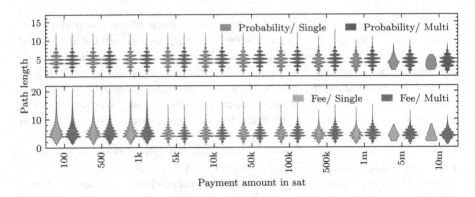

Fig. 1. The distribution of successful payments' path lengths.

of discussions on privacy in Sect. 4.2, shorter paths have a negative impact on privacy in LN. The results presented here align with findings presented in [10].

3.4 Payment Attempts

The total number of payment attempts recorded during simulation of the different combinations for various amounts is shown in Fig. 2. The total number of attempts remains almost constant for all simulated amounts. As the payment volume increases, we notice that the number of attempts made by single payments gradually decreases for payments greater than 50k sat. In cases where no capable routes are found, payments fail without recording any attempts thus leading to the decline in the number of attempts for single payments. This claim is supported by the results in Sect. 3.1 where we recorded an almost zero success rate for the highest payment amounts. When looking at the percentage of successful attempts, we find that, while the total number of attempts remains almost constant, most of the HTLCs initiated by multi-path payments are not fulfilled in contrast to single payments.

Furthermore, probability-weighted pathfinding requires marginally fewer attempts, which becomes evident as the payment amount increases. This is because of the fundamental premise that probability-weighted pathfinding prefers channels with endpoints that are more likely to have sufficient routing balance leading to fewer iterations of the trial-and-error loop.

3.5 Insights

- The payment volume plays the most significant role in the success of a payment. We observe a previously confirmed inverse relationship between the payment volume and success rate [3,31]. The type of payment plays a secondary role with multi-path payments able to deliver up to 20% more high-volume payments than single payments.

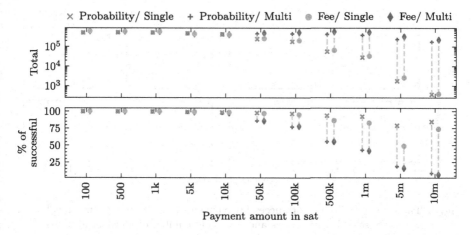

Fig. 2. The total number of HTLC attempts and the percentage of successful attempts.

- The impact of multi-path payments on fees proved to be marginal. In light of the gradual elimination of base fees, we expect the additional fees accrued by multi-path payments to diminish. Furthermore, our simulations show that the pathfinding algorithm plays a vital role in the accumulated fees as routes computed based on the success probability are significantly more expensive than fee-weighted payments. While the main result is not unexpected, we have been able to quantify that probability-weighted paths charge between 3% and 10% more than fee-weighted paths in relative fees.
- Our results on path lengths indicate that it is not quite determined by the payment type but more by the pathfinding approach. The payment amount in question plays a minor role although the difference between the median path lengths for different amounts is not significant.
- We find that the number of additional payments triggered by multi-path payments is reasonable, however, a quick glance at the relative values shows that more and more of these attempts are futile as the payment volume increases. The heightened success rate comes at the price of more network activity. Furthermore, we establish that probability-weighted pathfinding is more efficient than fee-weighted pathfinding with regard to the number of payment attempts.

4   Impact on Privacy

As the outcome of some of the discussed privacy measures is heavily dependent on an adversary's standing in the network, we executed our simulations with two different adversary selection strategies on the same set of payments. Similar to [11] and [14], we characterised up to 20 nodes as adversaries based on betweenness centrality and random selection. Note that the betweenness centrality was computed without weights.

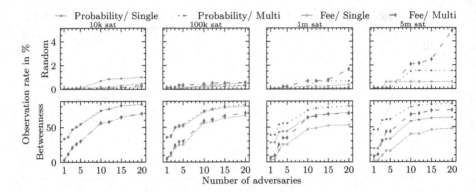

Fig. 3. The observation rate for successful payments for selected payment volumes, various adversary selection strategies and a varying number of adversarial nodes.

4.1 Observation Rate

Figure 3 shows the observation rate for successful payments using two different adversary selection strategies. Unsurprisingly, the random selection of adversaries results in a very low observation rate whereas central nodes observe a high number of payments. These results are to be expected given the underlying scale-free topology [3,23] of the channel graph and hint at the presence of routing hubs.

The observation rate is higher for multi-path payments and is highest with probability-weighted pathfinding. With only 15 adversarial nodes, over 70% of the payments were observed by a central adversary. These findings are indicative of a relation between centrality and capacity because probability-weighted pathfinding deliberately looks for high capacity channels (in proportion to the payment's value).

An explanation for the higher observation rate when using multi-path payments is the triggered payment attempts (cf. Fig. 2). Accordingly, multi-path payments have a higher observation rate than single payments and are otherwise identical with regard to the different pathfinding methods.

From a privacy standpoint, the presence of hubs is indeed problematic as these central watchers observe a fair share of the payments allowing them to gather an abundant amount of information. For instance, such a node could profile users in the case of regular payments of a certain amount taking the same (sub-)path. The importance of path diversity in the network becomes evident.

4.2 Sender and Receiver Inference

Having studied the odds of encountering an adversary on a payment's path, we examine what information can be gained by such an observation. The probabilities of correctly deanonymising the sender are depicted in Fig. 4. Recall that payment parts are handled individually and that the probabilities for receiver deanonymisation Pr_r are equal to the corresponding Pr_s.

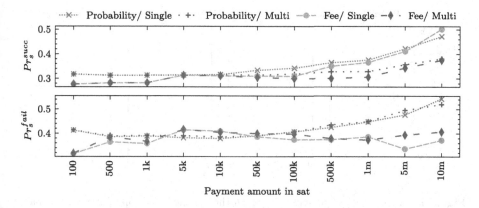

Fig. 4. The probability Pr_s that a node's predecessor is the payment's sender.

Successful, single payments are more likely to be deanonymised with the probabilities increasing for higher payment amounts. It may seem counter-intuitive that the sender of multiple payment parts is harder to deanonymise but it is resultant of the individual parts' path lengths and how often they occur. There are fewer successful single payments at higher volumes and given that the density of single payments' path lengths around the median increases (see Fig. 1), the probability of a path being of that length rises. Besides, this measure does not try to correlate observed payments.

We also observe that the probabilities Pr_s^{succ} generally increase as the payment volume increases. Given that we know from Sect. 3.3 that the path lengths not only tend to get shorter as the payment volume increases but also same-length paths become more common, Pr_s^{succ} is expected to increase. As every additional edge increases the risk of payment failure, the availability of short, liquid paths is a desirable property for a PCN like Lightning. However, precisely this property has a negative impact on the anonymity.

The odds shift slightly when looking at the probabilities Pr_s^{fail} for failed paths in that fee-weighted paths are easier to deanonymise than probability-weighted paths for payments >1k sat and <100k sat. Outside of this range, probability-weighted paths continue to be more likely to be deanonymised. We also find that Pr_s^{fail} for the two payment types do not differ greatly when using the same pathfinding approach and establish that the pathfinding method is decisive for the sender/receiver inference of failed payments.

4.3 Relationship Anonymity

The percentage of payments vulnerable to deanonymisation based on colluding intermediate hops is shown in Fig. 5. Similar to [29], we find that a random selection of adversaries does not compromise the relationship anonymity. On the other hand, the impact of central adversaries is already evident at just a handful

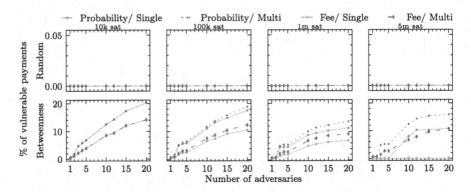

Fig. 5. The percentage of payments in which the first and last hop of at least one part are adversarial.

of adversaries. 20 adversaries, corresponding to ≪ 1% of the node population, are sufficient to compromise up to 20% of the payments.

As the payment amount increases, the overall share of vulnerable payments decreases, however, the anonymity of multi-path payments is more likely to be compromised. As shown in Fig. 6, the number of payment parts increases thereby increasing the attack surface (in comparison to single payments). With respect to the different pathfinding algorithms, probability-weighted paths are more vulnerable to such a confirmation attack. We hypothesise that this is because its search optimises for shorter paths with relatively high capacity which places well-connected nodes with high-capacity channels at an advantage. This claim is supported by the slight decrease in vulnerable payments as the payment amount increases driving the shortest path search algorithm to deviate to less-preferred paths.

We conclude that the pathfinding approach plays a significant role for relationship anonymity as probability-weighted paths are clearly more susceptible to attacks. Multi-path payments are also more vulnerable to deanonymisation attacks than single payments in case of compromised intermediaries.

4.4 Path Diversity

We applied the EPD measure to every set of paths taken by multi-path payments using different values of λ reflecting the utility of diverse paths and depict the results in Fig. 7. The number of paths k is the number of parts a payment was split into. In general, and regardless of the pathfinding approach, the utilised paths exhibit diversity ranging between 0 and 0.6 for the smallest and greatest tested λ respectively. For payments below 500k sat and 1m sat, the EPD values for fee and probability pathfinding are all 0, which can be attributed to the fewer number of parts needed to complete payments. These scores imply that paths contain very few disjoint hops, e.g., detours around a bottleneck channel, and are otherwise identical.

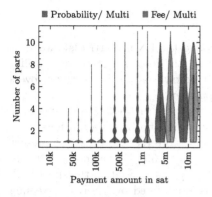

Fig. 6. The number of parts successful multi-path payments were delivered in.

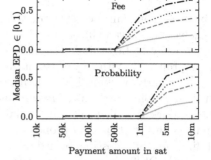

Fig. 7. The median EPD for multi-path payments using various λ.

The EPD values increase as the payment amount increases and show a clear correlation between the number of parts and the diversity. As visible in Fig. 6, the number of parts increases as the payment amount increases. Although higher values of λ result in higher EPD values, the overall progression of the EPDs remains the same. We argue that lower values of λ best signify the utility of diverse paths with respect to the privacy of the Lightning channel graph.

4.5 Insights

- High-centrality nodes observe a fair share of the payments especially when using probability-weighted pathfinding. Furthermore, the observation rate for multi-path payments is higher than that of single payments. The higher observation rate is due to the number of triggered HTLCs and payment parts. A tug-of-war between performance and privacy appears to be evident.
- Our results point to the influence of the payment type on the sender and receiver inference of successful payments based on path length probabilities. We established that successful single payments are more likely to be compromised by a predecessor/successor attack while the pathfinding method plays a bigger role for failed payments.
- In contrast, we find that relationship anonymity is more likely to be compromised by colluding intermediate nodes when using multi-path payments.
- We find that a higher number of payment parts has a positive impact on the path diversity which can lead to better privacy, e.g., by bypassing correlation attacks. Simultaneously, the presence of more diverse paths means a payment has a higher chance of traversing different observation points leading to a higher share of vulnerable paths.

5 Related Work

Given the abundance of literature on PCNs and the LN in particular, we limit ourselves to relevant literature that deals with the interaction between utility and privacy in Lightning. To the best of our knowledge, no prior work covers these properties with regard to multi-path payments.

In an early work on LN, Martinazzi studies the structural properties of the channel graph shortly after its mainnet launch and finds, among others, that the network is resilient to random failures [14]. More recent works also present findings on the structural properties of LN [3,23,27,30]. For example, Béres et al. find that it is possible to deduce transacting parties based on the short path lengths PCN [3]. Kappos et al. study the privacy offered by LN [10], revealing privacy attacks and formalising the findings presented in [3].

Tang et al. study the interplay between privacy and utility in PCNs and show fundamental limits of the established trade-off [28]. They argue that PCNs must choose either low privacy or low utility and cannot offer profound privacy and utility simultaneously. Additionally, Malavolta et al. prove the trade-off between privacy and concurrency in PCNs [13] and show that PCNs can only achieve non-blocking progress at the expense of privacy.

The authors of [18] investigate the utility of multi-path payments for the successful delivery of payments in LN and show that splitting payments leads to a higher success rate. The authors of [20] investigate payment splitting and discuss when and how to split a payment. They conclude that payment splitting is only beneficial for large payments.

Similar to our work, multiple previous works follow an empirical approach and are based on network simulators [3,10,11,24]. However, they either make simplifying assumptions about the routing algorithm, payment distribution or updates to the channel graph during simulation. In addition, the simulator developed in this work contributes to the state of the art by implementing support for multiple payment schemes as well as different pathfinding algorithms.

6 Conclusion

We identified performance and privacy metrics for PCNs and studied the impact of multi-path payments on performance and privacy in LN empirically. In part, we confirm earlier results such as the relationship between the success rate and payment volume. Having recorded notable differences in the fees, number of payment attempts, and path lengths, we find that the choice of pathfinding algorithm has a greater impact on performance than on privacy. Our results indicate that the impact of multi-path payments on performance generally remains within limits, although multi-path payments have a higher success rate. Our results point to a greater impact of multi-path payments on privacy, e.g., the higher chance of encountering an on-path adversary. Remarkably, while such payments are more susceptible to confirmation attacks, they are also less likely to be deanonymised by a simple predecessor/successor attack than single payments. In summary, multi-path payments are especially useful for the delivery of high-volume payments which, however, comes with concerns on privacy. Both payment types showed weaknesses with regard to privacy due to the structure of the channel graph making it difficult to mark one superior to the other.

References

1. Bolt: Basis of lightning technology (lightning network specifications). https://github.com/lightning/bolts
2. Bagaria, V., Neu, J., Tse, D.: Boomerang: redundancy improves latency and throughput in payment-channel networks. In: Bonneau, J., Heninger, N. (eds.) Financial Cryptography and Data Security: 24th International Conference, FC 2020 , Kota Kinabalu, Malaysia, February 10–14, 2020 Revised Selected Papers, pp. 304–324. Springer International Publishing, Cham (2020). https://doi.org/10.1007/978-3-030-51280-4_17
3. Béres, F., Seres, I.A., Benczúr, A.A.: A cryptoeconomic traffic analysis of bitcoins lightning network (2019). http://arxiv.org/abs/1911.09432
4. Biryukov, A., Naumenko, G., Tikhomirov, S.: Analysis and probing of parallel channels in the lightning network. In: Eyal, I., Garay, J. (eds.) Financial Cryptography and Data Security: 26th International Conference, FC 2022, Grenada, May 2–6, 2022, Revised Selected Papers, pp. 337–357. Springer International Publishing, Cham (2022). https://doi.org/10.1007/978-3-031-18283-9_16
5. Dijkstra, E.W.: A note on two problems in connexion with graphs. Numer. Math. **1**, 269–271 (1959)
6. Eckey, L., Faust, S., Hostáková, K., Roos, S.: Splitting payments locally while routing interdimensionally. IACR Cryptol. ePrint Arch. p. 555 (2020). https://eprint.iacr.org/2020/555
7. Ersoy, O., Roos, S., Erkin, Z.: How to profit from payments channels. In: Bonneau, J., Heninger, N. (eds.) Financial Cryptography and Data Security: 24th International Conference, FC 2020 , Kota Kinabalu, Malaysia, February 10–14, 2020 Revised Selected Papers, pp. 284–303. Springer International Publishing, Cham (2020). https://doi.org/10.1007/978-3-030-51280-4_16
8. Fromknecht, C., Osuntokun, O.: Bolt 21: Atomic multi-path payments. https://github.com/cfromknecht/lightning-rfc/blob/bolt-amp/21-atomic-multi-path-payments.md
9. Herrera-Joancomartí, J., Navarro-Arribas, G., Ranchal-Pedrosa, A., Pérez-Solà, C., García-Alfaro, J.: On the difficulty of hiding the balance of lightning network channels. In: Proceedings of the 2019 ACM Asia Conference on Computer and Communications Security, AsiaCCS 2019, Auckland, New Zealand, July 09–12, 2019.,pp. 602–612. ACM (2019)
10. Kappos, G., Yousaf, H., Piotrowska, A., Kanjalkar, S., Delgado-Segura, S., Miller, A., Meiklejohn, S.: An empirical analysis of privacy in the lightning network. In: Borisov, N., Diaz, C. (eds.) Financial Cryptography and Data Security: 25th International Conference, FC 2021, Virtual Event, March 1–5, 2021, Revised Selected Papers, Part I, pp. 167–186. Springer Berlin Heidelberg, Berlin, Heidelberg (2021). https://doi.org/10.1007/978-3-662-64322-8_8
11. Kumble, S.P., Epema, D.H.J., Roos, S.: How lightning's routing diminishes its anonymity. In: ARES 2021: The 16th International Conference on Availability, Reliability and Security, Vienna, Austria, August 17–20, 2021. pp. 13:1–13:10. ACM (2021)

12. Lin, J., Primicerio, K., Squartini, T., Decker, C., Tessone, C.J.: Lightning network: a second path towards centralisation of the bitcoin economy (2020). https://arxiv.org/abs/2002.02819
13. Malavolta, G., Moreno-Sanchez, P., Kate, A., Maffei, M., Ravi, S.: Concurrency and privacy with payment-channel networks. In: Proceedings of the 2017 ACM SIGSAC Conference on Computer and Communications Security, CCS 2017, Dallas, TX, USA, October 30 - November 03, 2017, pp. 455–471. ACM (2017)
14. Martinazzi, S.: The evolution of lightning network's topology during its first year and the influence over its core values (2019). https://arxiv.org/abs/1902.07307
15. Nisslmueller, U., Foerster, K., Schmid, S., Decker, C.: Toward active and passive confidentiality attacks on cryptocurrency off-chain networks. In: Proceedings of the 6th International Conference on Information Systems Security and Privacy, ICISSP 2020, Valletta, Malta, February 25–27, 2020, pp. 7–14. SCITEPRESS (2020)
16. Papadis, N., Tassiulas, L.: Blockchain-based payment channel networks: Challenges and recent advances. IEEE Access **8**, 227596–227609 (2020)
17. Paverd, A.J., Martin, A.C.: Modelling and automatically analysing privacy properties for honest-but-curious adversaries (2014)
18. Piatkivskyi, D., Nowostawski, M.: Split payments in payment networks. In: Garcia-Alfaro, J., Herrera-Joancomartí, J., Livraga, G., Rios, R. (eds.) Data Privacy Management, Cryptocurrencies and Blockchain Technology: ESORICS 2018 International Workshops, DPM 2018 and CBT 2018, Barcelona, Spain, September 6-7, 2018, Proceedings, pp. 67–75. Springer International Publishing, Cham (2018). https://doi.org/10.1007/978-3-030-00305-0_5
19. Pickhardt, R., Richter, S.: Optimally reliable & cheap payment flows on the lightning network (2021). https://arxiv.org/abs/2107.05322
20. Pickhardt, R., Tikhomirov, S., Biryukov, A., Nowostawski, M.: Security and privacy of lightning network payments with uncertain channel balances (2021). https://arxiv.org/abs/2103.08576
21. Poon, J., Dryja, T.: The bitcoin lightning network: Scalable off-chain instant payments (Jan 2016), https://lightning.network/lightning-network-paper.pdf
22. Rohrer, E., Laß, J.-F., Tschorsch, F.: Towards a concurrent and distributed route selection for payment channel networks. In: Garcia-Alfaro, J., Navarro-Arribas, G., Hartenstein, H., Herrera-Joancomartí, J. (eds.) Data Privacy Management, Cryptocurrencies and Blockchain Technology: ESORICS 2017 International Workshops, DPM 2017 and CBT 2017, Oslo, Norway, September 14-15, 2017, Proceedings, pp. 411–419. Springer International Publishing, Cham (2017). https://doi.org/10.1007/978-3-319-67816-0_23
23. Rohrer, E., Malliaris, J., Tschorsch, F.: Discharged payment channels: quantifying the lightning network's resilience to topology-based attacks. In: 2019 IEEE European Symposium on Security and Privacy Workshops, EuroS&P Workshops 2019, Stockholm, Sweden, June 17–19, 2019,. pp. 347–356. IEEE (2019)
24. Rohrer, E., Tschorsch, F.: Counting down thunder: timing attacks on privacy in payment channel networks. In: AFT '20: 2nd ACM Conference on Advances in Financial Technologies, New York, NY, USA, October 21–23, 2020, pp. 214–227. ACM (2020)
25. Rohrer, J.P., Jabbar, A., Sterbenz, J.P.G.: Path diversification: a multipath resilience mechanism. In: 7th International Workshop on Design of Reliable Communication Networks, DRCN 2009, Washington, DC, USA, October 25–28, 2009, pp. 343–351. IEEE (2009)

26. Roos, S., Moreno-Sanchez, P., Kate, A., Goldberg, I.: Settling payments fast and private: Efficient decentralized routing for path-based transactions. In: 25th Annual Network and Distributed System Security Symposium, NDSS 2018, San Diego, California, USA, February 18–21, 2018. The Internet Society (2018)

27. Seres, I.A., Gulyás, L., Nagy, D.A., Burcsi, P.: Topological analysis of bitcoin's lightning network. In: Mathematical Research for Blockchain Economy, 1st International Conference, MARBLE 2019, Santorini, Greece, May 6–9, 2019, pp. 1–12. Springer (2019)

28. Tang, W., Wang, W., Fanti, G., Oh, S.: Privacy-utility tradeoffs in routing cryptocurrency over payment channel networks. Proc. ACM Meas. Anal. Comput. Syst. 4(2), 29:1–29:39 (2020)

29. Tikhomirov, S., Moreno-Sanchez, P., Maffei, M.: A quantitative analysis of security, anonymity and scalability for the lightning network. In: IEEE European Symposium on Security and Privacy Workshops, EuroS&P Workshops 2020, Genoa, Italy, September 7–11, 2020, pp. 387–396. IEEE (2020)

30. Tochner, S., Schmid, S., Zohar, A.: Hijacking routes in payment channel networks: A predictability tradeoff (2019). https://arxiv.org/abs/1909.06890

31. Waugh, F., Holz, R.: An empirical study of availability and reliability properties of the bitcoin lightning network (2020). https://arxiv.org/abs/2006.14358

32. Zabka, P., Foerster, K., Schmid, S., Decker, C.: Empirical evaluation of nodes and channels of the lightning network. Pervasive Mob. Comput. 83, 101584 (2022)

SECPRE 2023

SECPRE 2023 Preface

This volume contains revised versions of the papers presented at the seventh International Workshop on SECurity and Privacy Requirements Engineering (SECPRE 2023), which was co-located with the 28th European Symposium on Research in Computer Security (ESORICS 2023), held in The Hague, the Netherlands on September 28th, 2023.

Data protection regulations, the complexity of modern environments (such as IoT, IoE, Cloud Computing, Big Data, Cyber-Physical Systems, etc.) and the increased level of user awareness in IT have forced software engineers to identify security and privacy as fundamental design aspects, leading to the implementation of more trusted software systems and services. Researchers have addressed the necessity and importance of implementing design methods for security and privacy requirements elicitation, modeling, and implementation in recent decades in various innovative research domains. Today, Security by Design (SbD) and Privacy by Design (PbD) are established research areas that focus on these directions. The new GDPR Regulation sets even stricter requirements for organizations regarding its applicability. SbD and PbD play a very critical and important role in assisting stakeholders in understanding their needs, complying with the new legal, organizational, and technical requirements, and finally selecting the appropriate measures to fulfill these requirements. SECPRE aimed to provide researchers and professionals with the opportunity to present novel and cutting-edge research on these topics.

SECPRE 2023 attracted 7 high-quality submissions, each of which was assigned to 3 referees for single-blind review; the review process resulted in 4 papers being selected for presentation and inclusion in these proceedings. The topics covered included organizational and technical aspects of privacy in cloud computing, IoT, and Mobile technologies.

We would like to express our thanks to all those who assisted us in organizing the event and putting together the program. We are very grateful to the members of the Program Committee for their timely and rigorous reviews. Thanks are also due to the Organizing Committee of the event. Last, but by no means least, we would like to thank all the authors who submitted their work to the workshop and contributed to an interesting set of proceedings.

September 2023

John Mylopoulos
Christos Kalloniatis
Annie Antón
Stefanos Gritzalis

Organization

General Chairs

Annie Antón   Georgia Institute of Technology, USA
Stefanos Gritzalis   University of Piraeus, Greece

Program Committee Chairs

John Mylopoulos   University of Ottawa, Canada
Christos Kalloniatis   University of the Aegean, Greece

Program Committee

Travis Breaux   Carnegie Mellon University, USA
Sabrina De Capitani di Vimercati   Università degli Studi di Milano, Italy
Vasiliki Diamantopoulou   University of the Aegean, Greece
Carmen Fernandez-Cago   University of Malaga, Spain
Eduardo Fernandez-Medina   University of Castilla-La Mancha, Spain
Maritta Heisel   University of Duisburg-Essen, Germany
Jan Jürjens   University of Koblenz-Landau, Germany
Maria Karyda   University of the Aegean, Greece
Costas Lambrinoudakis   University of Piraeus, Greece
Tong Li   Beijing University of Technology, China
Haralambos Mouratidis   University of Brighton, UK
Liliana Pasquale   University College Dublin, Ireland
Michalis Pavlidis   University of Brighton, UK
David Garcia Rosado   University of Castilla-La Manca, Spain
Pierangela Samarati   Università degli Studi di Milano, Italy
Nicola Zannone   Eindhoven University of Technology,
                                         The Netherlands

Creating Privacy Policies from Data-Flow Diagrams

Jens Leicht$^{(\boxtimes)}$, Marvin Wagner, and Maritta Heisel

paluno - The Ruhr Institute for Software Technology, University of Duisburg-Essen,
Duisburg, Germany
{jens.leicht,marvin.wagner,maritta.heisel}@uni-due.de

Abstract. Privacy policies are often used to fulfill the requirement of
transparency of data protection legislation like the General Data Protection Regulation of the European Union. The privacy policies are used
to describe how the data subject's data are handled by the data controller. Domain and legal experts mostly create these policies manually.
We propose a tool-supported method to improve the creation of accurate
privacy policies based on information from the development phase of a
system. During privacy and security threat analyses information about
system behavior is collected in form of data-flow diagrams. These diagrams describe which data flows from where to where within the system
and to which external actors.

Based on this data-flow information we can create the basic structure
of a privacy policy, already containing the data-flows. The extracted
information is one of the most important parts of a privacy policy, providing transparency when data is transferred to external parties.

Keywords: Privacy Policy · Data-Flow Diagram · LINDDUN ·
Privacy Impact Analysis · Model-Based

1 Introduction

Privacy policies are an important tool for service providers to comply with data
protection legislation, like the General Data Protection Regulation of the European Union (GDPR) [5]. The creation of privacy policies is a time consuming
and complex process, which we support by reusing information from the software
development process.

Data-flow diagrams (DFDs) contain important information about the transfer of data in the context of a piece of software or a complete system. Information regarding internal data processing is also present in DFDs. This information
covers some of the details that data controllers need to provide to data subjects
via privacy policies. We present an automated method, including tool-support,
which enables data controllers to retrieve relevant privacy policy information
from their DFDs.

DFDs are often created in the context of privacy requirements engineering
or privacy impact analyses, as required by the GDPR. They are also relevant in

S. Katsikas et al. (Eds.): ESORICS 2023 Workshops, LNCS 14398, pp. 433–453, 2024.
https://doi.org/10.1007/978-3-031-54204-6_26

security threat modeling approaches, meaning that they are an important model for privacy- or security critical software. For example, the LINDDUN method [4] makes use of DFDs to identify privacy threats. Since DFDs are created during the analysis we can use them with a minimal overhead to extract privacy relevant information from them, supporting policy authors in the creation of privacy policies. Updating the privacy policies based on updated DFDs can also improve the accuracy of the privacy policy when the system design changes.

Our method to derive parts of privacy policies from DFDs uses the Prolog-Layered Privacy Language (P-LPL) for the created privacy policies. In previous work we used P-LPL to perform automated GDPR-compliance checks on policies, providing feedback to the policy authors [12]. These compliance-checks are part of the Privacy Policy Compliance Guidance (PriPoCoG) framework. This framework also includes an access control methodology called P2BAC [11] which supports the enforcement of P-LPL privacy policies. By using P-LPL, we ensure compatibility with the PriPoCoG-framework.

The paper is structured as follows. We start with relevant background information in Sect. 2. Our concept is presented in Sect. 3, followed by a look at our DFD tool in Sect. 4. Next, we discuss related work in Sect. 5. Finally, we close this paper with a conclusion and a look at future work in Sect. 6.

2   Background

In this section we provide short introductions to the terminology used by the General Data Protection Regulation of the European Union (GDPR), the LINDDUN privacy threat modeling approach, data-flow diagrams, privacy policies, and the Eclipse Modeling Framework.

2.1   GDPR Terminology

The General Data Protection Regulation (GDPR) [5] introduces some terminology in the context of data handling and privacy policies, which we use throughout the paper to distinguish different roles and actors.

Data Subject is the person whose data are processed by the service provider (data controller). This is the person that we need to inform about any data handling, which is mostly done using privacy policies.

Data Controller is the person or legal entity in charge of controlling the data handling. This can be the service provider itself or a person/entity operating in the name of the service provider. The data controller specifies the privacy policy to inform its data subjects.

Data Processor (Data Recipient) is an external entity that processes some data on behalf of the data controller. Since the data processors receive the data from the controller, we also call these data recipients in the context of privacy policies.

Purpose is an explanation describing the reason for which data are processed. Privacy policies contain purposes explaining to the data subjects why their data are being handled.

2.2   LINDDUN

LINDDUN is a privacy threat modeling approach. The name is derived from the different types of privacy threats considered in the threat analysis: Linkability, Identifiability, Non-repudiation, Detectability, Disclosure of information, Unawareness (and Unintervenability), Non-compliance. The LINDDUN approach provides three methods for performing privacy analyses. In this paper we reference the LINDDUN Pro method, which uses data-flow diagrams to systematically analyze a system regarding privacy.

The LINDDUN Pro method begins with the definition of DFDs based on a high-level system description. It provides privacy threat trees and catalogues, which are used to identify threats in the DFDs. After identifying possible misuse scenarios and assessing and prioritizing identified risks, the method elicits privacy requirements and selects appropriate privacy enhancing technologies (see [4] for further details on the LINDDUN approach).

2.3   Data-Flow Diagrams

Data-flow diagrams (DFDs) are diagrams using five components that describe which process or external actor has access to which data by modeling data-flows within and out of the system. DFDs were introduced by DeMarco [3]. The following elements can be used in DFDs:

Process represents a system-internal process that handles some data. It is visualized by a circle (cf. *Data Bundling* in Fig. 1).

Actor represents an entity that may send or receive data. Actors are visualized by rectangles (cf. *Data Processor* and *Internal Data Miner* in Fig. 1).

Storage is used to represent internal data bases, file systems, or files that store some data they receive from processes or actors. They are visualized differently depending on the implementation of the DFD editor. We use the notation introduced by DeMarco [3], two horizontal lines surrounding the label of the storage (cf. *Database* in Fig. 1).

Data-Flow is a directed line between two diagram elements (process, actor, or storage), which is either annotated with a label or a list of data that flow along this connection (cf. *DF1* to *DF5* in Fig. 1). We use labels and provide tables with mappings from labels to their corresponding lists of data (cf. right-hand side of Fig. 2). The origin of a data-flow is called source, and the destination of a data-flow is called sink.

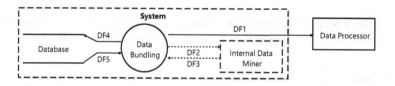

Fig. 1. Exemplary data-flow diagram.

Trust Boundary is a segment of a data-flow diagram surrounded with a dashed line (cf. *System* in Fig. 1). This segment can have different meanings, which should be defined when creating the DFD. We primarily use trust boundaries to differentiate internal processes, which are directly controlled by the data controller, from external actors.

All the above-described elements, except for the trust boundary, can optionally be marked as out-of-scope. This means that the elements are not considered in the analysis but might still be helpful in understanding the data-flows. Out-of-scope elements use a dashed outline/line (cf. *Internal Data Miner*, *DF2*, and *DF3* in Fig. 1). We also do not consider these elements when translating a DFD into a privacy policy.

2.4   Privacy Policies

To comply with the transparency requirements of the GDPR many data controllers make use of privacy policies.

Textual Policies. A commonly used form of privacy policies is the textual form. Data controllers verbally describe how they process the data subject's data and explain the reasons behind the processing (purposes). Excerpts from the Amazon.de privacy policy can be found in Listings 1, 2, and 3 in Sect. 3.2. We use a more formal and computer processable form of privacy policies as described below.

P-LPL Policies. The Prolog-Layered Privacy Language (P-LPL) [12] is a derivative of the Layered Privacy Language (LPL) [6] and provides a computer processable form for expressing GDPR-compliant privacy policies. P-LPL is part of the Privacy Policy Compliance Guidance (PriPoCoG)-framework [12], which provides GDPR-compliance checks for P-LPL policies, as well as access control based on these policies using P2BAC [11].

P-LPL policies use a hierarchical structure to arrange processing purposes, which we make use of as described in Sect. 3.5. All elements of a P-LPL policy have titles and descriptions that are used for the policy representation towards the data subjects.

3   Methodology

In this section we present the general concept and provide a detailed explanation of the generation of privacy policy information from data-flow diagrams.

3.1   Concept

Creating privacy policies from DFDs is achieved by performing the following steps:

1. **Creation of DFDs of the system behavior using our tool (cf. Sect. 4).** This can be done as part of privacy or security threat analyses, e.g., using LINDDUN [4] or STRIDE [9], or independently of any threat modeling technique. During privacy impact analyses (PIAs), DFDs also play an important role. The DFDs created in this step also help document the system behavior. If the DFDs have shared components, for example, recurring actors, these shared components need to be imported from the main model (cf. Sect. 4) to prevent duplicate elements representing the same entity. During this step it is important to not introduce ambiguities in the DFDs, e.g., the term *address* can have many different interpretations of what data are included in an address. Travis Breaux's and Mitra Bokaei-Hosseini's Ontology of Personal Information[1] (OPI) shows that these ambiguities can occur for many terms used in data flows and privacy policies. The solution is to name each data element as precisely as possible. Alternatively, a mapping table could be introduced revealing what data is contained in a specific term. Ambiguities in the DFDs result in the same ambiguities in the privacy policy.

2. **Importing combined model into privacy policy editor.** All DFDs created within a project using our tool share a single model. Hence, they can be visualized in a single Privacy Data-Flow Diagram representing all data-flows of the system. That diagram can be imported into our privacy policy editor (cf. Sect. 3.6).

3. **Creation of intermediate privacy policy.** The editor extracts all available information from the diagram, as explained in Sect. 3.5 below. Since the extracted information is not sufficient to create a complete privacy policy, we call it an intermediate privacy policy.

4. **Manually completing the privacy policy.** The policy author can now manually edit the intermediate policy, entering further details. The final output is a P-LPL policy that can be checked for GDPR-compliance using PriPoCoG [12].

Deriving the main components of a privacy policy from DFDs modeling the system behavior has the following benefits: *1.* The complexity of the task of creating a privacy policy is reduced. *2.* The resulting policy can be checked for GDPR-compliance using the PriPoCoG-framework. *3.* The resulting policy accurately describes the actual system behavior. The chance of discrepancies between policy and system behavior is reduced. *4.* If the system is adapted and the DFDs are updated according to the new system behavior, the policy can be updated, too. Thus, further improving the accuracy of the policy.

In the security engineering context (e.g., STRIDE [9]) DFDs become more complex compared to DFDs from the privacy engineering context (e.g., LINDDUN). This increased complexity leads to more detailed, and therefore more complex, privacy policies. However, the use of a purpose hierarchy, as described in Sect. 3.5 (Step 4) below, increases the comprehensibility of such detailed privacy policies. The top-level purposes give a general overview over the data

---

[1] https://opi.cs.cmu.edu/show/address.

processed by a data controller, whereas the sub-purposes can provide more details to the interested reader.

In the future, layered DFDs could be used to create a more abstract top-level DFD that is more suitable for the privacy policy creation. The details needed in the security context could then be placed in lower-level DFDs, refining the processes presented in the top-level DFD.

In the following we introduce a running example which we use as a guide through the process of extracting privacy policy-relevant information from DFDs.

3.2   Running Example

As a running example we use two sections of the *Amazon.de* [1] privacy policy and create a DFD from the described behavior. In general, the DFDs for our approach will not be created based on existing privacy policies, but instead from actual system behavior. We just make use of an existing privacy policy, as we have no insights into the actual system behavior of the *Amazon.de* systems. In our running example we focus on the delivery of products, as well as the processing of payments. All other mentioned processing purposes will not be considered in this paper. Listing 1 shows how *Amazon.de* describes the purposes for which they process personal data. In Listing 2 we can see in which cases the personal data of the data subject are transferred to third-party service providers. Amazon also receives updated personal data from some third-party service providers, e.g., a corrected delivery address from delivery partners (cf. Listing 3).

> "Purchase and delivery of products and services. We use your personal information to take and handle orders, deliver products and services, process payments, and communicate with you about orders, products and services, and promotional offers ."

Listing 1. Excerpt from the *Amazon.de* privacy policy (purposes) [1].

> "Third party service providers: We employ other companies and individuals to perform functions on our behalf. Examples include fulfilling orders for products or services, delivering packages, [...], processing payments [...]."

Listing 2. Excerpt from the *Amazon.de* privacy policy (data processors) [1].

> "updated delivery and address information from our carriers or other third parties, which we use to correct our records and deliver your next purchase or communication more easily"

Listing 3. Excerpt from the *Amazon.de* privacy policy (data from other sources) [1].

Since the *Amazon.de* privacy policy is not very detailed in stating which data are transferred to which third-party service provider, we assume that the following data are transferred for the purposes *product delivery* and *payment processing*:

- **product delivery**
  - Name
  - Address
  - Phone Number
  - E-Mail Address

- **payment processing**
  - Amount due
  - Name
  - Address
  - Bank Account Number

A data-flow diagram for this scenario is shown in Fig. 2. This diagram differs from a normal DFD because it was created using our DFD-tool and already contains annotations, which we explain in further detail in Sects. 3.4 and 4.3 below. Without annotations the actor *Data Subject* and its related data-flows would not be greyed-out. The storages *Orders* and *Transactions* are greyed-out because the diagram shown is a *PrivacyDataFlowDiagram* (cf. Sect. 4.3).

The data subject places an order by providing all necessary information: Order(the items ordered), Name, Address, Phone Number, Mail Address, and Bank Account Number (*DF1*). Order details are processed by *Order Processing* and stored in *Orders* (*DF2 + DF3*).

The *Payment Processing* process receives Order, Name, Address, and Bank Account Number from *Order Processing* (*DF7*) and forwards the Amount due (extracted from Order), Name, Address, and Bank Account Number to the *Bank* (*DF8*). Transaction details of the bank transfer are returned to the *Payment Processing* process and used to decide whether the product delivery should be triggered (*DF9*). All transaction-related information (Order, Name, Address, Bank Account Number, and Transaction Details are stored in *Transactions* (*DF10 + DF11*). Transaction Details, Name, and Address will be forwarded to the *Tax Authorities* if required (*DF13*).

The Transaction Confirmation (based on the success of a transaction) is internally (i.e., inside the Amazon.de trust boundary) forwarded to the process *Order Processing* (*DF12*) and from there stored in *Orders* (*DF2 + DF3*). *Order Processing* forwards Name, Address, Phone Number, and E-Mail Address to the *Parcel Service* for product delivery (*DF4*). The *Parcel Service* returns

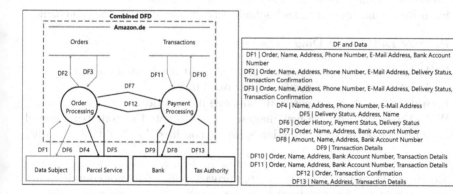

Fig. 2. left: Combined data-flow diagram for our running example, data subject and storages are greyed-out based on annotations (cf. Sect. 3.4); right: Data-flows and their corresponding data.

the current delivery status, as well as a potentially updated address and name (cf. Listing 3) to the *Order Processing* process (*DF5*), which is then stored in *Orders* (*DF2* + *DF3*). The *Data Subject*, receives an Order History (based on the past orders stored in *Orders*), a Payment Status (based on the *Transaction Confirmation*), and the Delivery Status (*DF6*).

3.3   Validation Conditions

To reduce the number of errors that can happen during the process of defining DFDs as well as extracting privacy policy information from such diagrams, we define validation conditions. These conditions can be checked manually, especially when drawing DFDs by hand. However, we also implement these validation conditions in our DFD-tool, as described in Sect. 4.4, so that they can be checked by the tool when creating the DFDs.

We identified the following 14 validation conditions. Some of these conditions are relevant for data-flow diagrams in general, and some are introduced to be able to transform data-flow diagrams into privacy policies. Conditions 1 to 10 apply to data-flow diagrams in general. Conditions 11 to 14 are specific to Privacy Data-Flow Diagrams.

General Data-Flow Diagrams:

1. Each data-flow needs a source and a sink.
2. Each data-flow needs at least one assigned data-element.
3. Processes need to be located inside a trust boundary.
4. Storages need to be located inside a trust boundary.
5. Source and sink of a data-flow must not both be of type storage.
6. Source and sink of a data-flow must not both be of type actor.
7. Source and sink of a data-flow need to be different.
8. An actor must be source or sink of at least one data-flow.
9. An element cannot be inside more than one trust boundary.
10. Elements cannot be inside and outside a trust boundary at the same time.

Privacy Data-Flow Diagrams:

11. Each data-element needs to be referenced by at least one data-flow.
12. Each data-flow diagram needs at least one process.
13. Each data-flow diagram needs at most one data subject.
14. When the combined data-flow diagram contains more than one trust boundary, only one of the trust boundaries can be considered as the data controller.

Condition 11 ensures that the created privacy policy does not contain unnecessary information about data that is not actually flowing anywhere. Adding such unnecessary information would clutter the resulting privacy policy, reducing transparency towards the data subject. Condition 12 ensures that information from the data-flow diagram can be combined into a purpose inside the privacy policy (cf. Sect. 3.5). A process is also required for a data-flow analysis to be sensible, as data-flows without a process (directly between actors) will not be of interest for the party conducting the analysis. Such a data-flow would only be relevant for a data-flow analysis conducted by the actors themselves. Condition 13 assures that the data subject used in the diagrams represents a single data subject, which is congruent with a privacy policy that represents all necessary information about the data of the single data subject reading the policy. Finally, condition 14 assures that trust boundaries, used for example for groups of external actors, are not considered to be part of the system. This means that the combined Privacy DFD has at most one trust boundary representing the data controller's system. Any additional trust boundary will be considered external.

3.4   Annotated Data-Flow Diagram

In addition to creating the data-flow diagrams using our tool, privacy policy authors will need to annotate the data-flow diagrams. The overhead, however, is very small as they only need to mark the one actor representing the data subject, as well as the trust boundary that represents the data controller. It is also possible that the DFDs contain no actor representing the data subject. In this case only the trust boundary of the data controller needs to be annotated in the DFDs.

Optionally, authors can add descriptions for each element in the diagram. These descriptions are used to create user-friendly representations of the elements inside the privacy policy. For the basic privacy policy elements: purpose, data, and data recipient the descriptions are used directly to describe these elements. Data-flows do not have a direct representation in the privacy policy. Hence, we combine all data-flow descriptions in the description of the purpose, which is part of the policy.

Further information that may be required for a GDPR-compliant privacy policy needs to be entered manually using our work-in-progress privacy policy editor, which we describe in more detail in Sect. 3.6 below. Missing information includes, for example, the rights of the data subject or information about data controllers or data protection officers. An alternative way of entering some of the additional information could be to further annotate the diagrams. However, we expect a better usability when entering the data using the policy editor, instead of further annotating the diagrams.

3.5   Intermediate Policy

The combined data-flow diagram (cf. Step 2 in Sect. 3.1 and Sect. 4.3) is exported from our DFD-tool as an XML-file. This file is then imported into our privacy policy editor (cf. Sect. 3.6) which extracts all available information from the XML-file and creates the corresponding privacy policy elements as described below.

Table 1. Summary of the elements of the DFD shown in Fig. 2.

Process	Data-Flows	Data	Actors
Order Processing	DF1-DF7, DF12	Order, Name, Address, Phone Number, E-Mail Address, Bank Account Number, Delivery Status, Order History, Payment Status, Transaction Confirmation	Parcel Service
Payment Processing	DF7-DF13	Order, Name, Address, Bank Account Number, Amount, Transaction Details, Transaction Confirmation	Bank, Tax Authority

Table 1 provides an overview of the processes shown in Fig. 2, their related data-flows, and the data included, as well as the actors involved in these data-flows. The intermediate policy (listed in Table 2) is created based on the information shown in Table 1 using the following procedure:

1. For each data-element used in the combined DFD, a corresponding element is created in the policy editor. If source or sink of all data-flows containing a data-element are marked as out-of-scope, the data-element will not be translated into the privacy policy. The same applies if all relevant data-flows themselves are marked out-of-scope. The name of the data-element as well as the optional description annotation are used to pre-fill the editor with additional information about the element.
2. For each actor that is either sink or source of a data-flow from or to a process inside the data controller (annotated trust boundary, cf. Section 3.4), a data recipient element is created in the policy editor. Actors that are marked as out-of-scope and the data subject are not translated into the policy.
3. A purpose element is created for each pair of *process* and *actor* that are connected via a data-flow. Again, data-flows marked out-of-scope and to or from the data subject are not considered here. *Processes*, that do not have any external actor as data recipient, are still translated to corresponding purposes in the policy. These purposes describe data processing by the data controller and are therefore also relevant for a privacy policy. The data-elements of all incoming and outgoing data-flows of such processes are added to the resulting purpose.
4. If a *process* is connected to multiple *actors*, an additional purpose is created, that combines all purposes created for this *process* in the previous step. The purposes created during this step of the translation are arranged in a purpose hierarchy, which, for our running example, is shown as a screenshot from our privacy policy editor in Fig. 3. For the process *Payment Processing* two purposes are created (*Bank* and *Tax Authority*) and combined in the main *Payment Processing* purpose.
5. The descriptions of the purposes, if supplied in the annotated DFDs (cf. 3.4), are created based on the description of the *process*, as well as the descriptions of the data-flows from and to the *process*. Listings 4 and 5 show the exem-

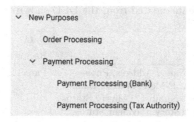

Fig. 3. Purpose hierarchy of the intermediate policy.

plary descriptions of *DF8* and *DF9*. Combined with the description of the *Payment Processing* process, the resulting description of the corresponding child purpose *Payment Processing (Bank)* is shown in Listing 6.

6. For hierarchical purposes, the descriptions are a concatenation of the descriptions of the child purposes. Listing 7 shows the description of the parent purpose *Payment Processing* combining Listing 6 with the description of the second child purpose *Payment Processing (Tax Authority)*.

7. Finally, data and data recipients are assigned to the corresponding purposes. This assignment is based on all data-flows between a process and an actor. The hierarchical purposes that combine multiple purposes are assigned with the union of data-elements and data recipients of their child purposes.

This translation procedure is supported by our DFD-tool as well as our privacy policy editor. However, it can also be applied to any DFD and any form of privacy policy, e.g., when manually translating DFDs into a policy.

" Data are transferred to our bank to process the payment for your order."

Listing 4. Exemplary description of DF8.

" The bank gives us access to transaction details after a payment has been processed ."

Listing 5. Exemplary description of DF9.

" We process your data in order to carry out financial transactions for the payment of your orders. Data are transferred to our bank to process the payment for your order. The bank gives us access to transaction details after a payment has been processed."

Listing 6. Exemplary description of the child purpose *Payment Processing (Bank)*.

" We process your data in order to carry out financial transactions for the payment of your orders. Data are transferred to our bank to process the payment for your order. The bank gives us access to transaction details after a payment has been processed. We forward your data to the tax authority as required by law ."

Listing 7. Exemplary description of the parent purpose *Payment Processing*.

Table 2. Policy elements created from the DFD shown in Fig. 2 (cf. Table 1).

Purpose	Data	Data Recipients	Sub-purposes
Order Processing	Order, Name, Address, Phone Number, E-Mail Address, Bank Account Number, Delivery Status, Order History, Payment Status, Transaction Confirmation	Parcel Service	-
Payment Processing	Order, Name, Address, Bank Account Number, Amount, Transaction Details, Transaction Confirmation	Bank, Tax Authority	Payment Processing (Bank), Payment Processing (Tax Authority)
Payment Processing (Bank)	Amount, Name, Address, Bank Account Number, Transaction Details	Bank	-
Payment Processing (Tax Authority)	Name, Address Transaction Details	Tax Authority	-

Table 2 shows for each purpose created what data are used for this purpose and who the data recipients are. Additionally, for the purpose *Payment Processing* its sub-purposes *Payment Processing (Bank)* and *Payment Processing (Tax Authority)* are shown. The parent purpose contains all data-elements, as well as all data recipients of its children. We explain how this information is used in the privacy policy editor in Sect. 3.6 below.

3.6   Privacy Policy Editor

The intermediate policy discussed in the previous section can be used in our privacy policy editor to create a GDPR-compliant privacy policy. The policy author can load the intermediate policy to fill parts of the privacy policy with the information gathered from the DFDs. An excerpt from the main page of our currently work-in-progress policy editor is shown in Fig. 4. The editor highlights the data, data recipients, and purpose tiles in red, because these contain some of the information from the intermediate policy, but there is still information missing for a complete privacy policy.

The overall policy additionally requires the following information:

- essential policy information (e.g., the language used or a reference to a textual privacy policy),
- information about the data controllers,
- information about data protection officers,
- a list of rights that the controller grants the data subjects,
- and information regarding the competent supervisory authority.

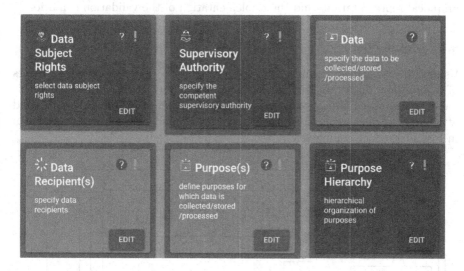

Fig. 4. Excerpt from the main page of the PriPoCoG privacy policy editor pre-filled with information from the DFD shown in Fig. 2.

The data-elements imported from the DFDs are missing the following information: data type, sensitivity level (e.g., explicit, sensitive, or non-sensitive). The data recipients are missing information regarding their classification as either a person, legal entity, or public authority. Regarding the purposes, authors need to decide whether the data subject must accept the purpose, or whether this is optional. Purposes additionally lack information regarding data retention and the legal bases on which a purpose is based.

Although the above-mentioned information needs to be added manually, most of the policy is filled with the information from the DFDs. The purposes and their corresponding data and data recipients are the largest part of the privacy policy. The proportion between the pre-filled elements and the data to be added manually depends on the size of the system under consideration.

Once the policy author enters the missing information manually the tiles will turn green to show that these parts of the privacy policy are complete. The grey tiles indicate that no information has yet been entered in these categories. When sufficient information is entered, the policy can be checked for GDPR-compliance. We explain how we perform compliance-checks on the privacy policy in [12].

4   Tool Support

To help users of our approach create DFDs, we provide a graphical editor. It is based on the *Eclipse Modeling Framework (EMF)*[2] and *Sirius*[3]. Sirius builds on EMF and the *Acceleo Query Language (AQL)*. AQL is a specification language similar to the *Object Constraint Language (OCL)*[4]. The elements of an EMF metamodel can be filtered, created, deleted, and manipulated with AQL. In the following we describe the main elements of the metamodel, as well as the different graphical representations and the implementation of the validation conditions.

4.1   Metamodel

Using EMF we defined the metamodel shown in Fig. 5, which defines all elements of a data-flow diagram. To reduce the complexity of the metamodel for this paper, we removed two abstract classes that are used to introduce some shared attributes. Each element of the model has a name and a description (not shown in Fig. 5 to reduce complexity).

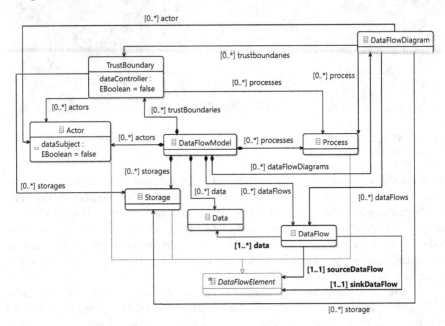

Fig. 5. EMF-metamodel describing all elements of a data-flow diagram and their relations.

---

[2] https://www.eclipse.org/modeling/emf/.
[3] https://www.eclipse.org/sirius/.
[4] https://www.omg.org/spec/OCL/.

Our main element is *DataFlowModel*. It contains all other elements. Furthermore, we have the elements *TrustBoundary*, *Actor*, *Storage*, *Data*, *DataFlow*, *Process*, and *DataFlowDiagram*, which are contained in the element *DataFlowModel*. The elements: *Actor*, *Process*, *Storage*, and *DataFlow* have a boolean attribute *OutOfScope*(not shown in Fig. 5 to reduce complexity), because some elements may not be relevant or out-of-scope for a data-flow analysis.

In addition to all standard elements of a DFD, we added a boolean attribute to the *Actor* element: *dataSubject*. This attribute is used to exclude actors that represent the data subject from further processing of the diagram. The data subject is not a data recipient in the context of a privacy policy; hence, we exclude it from our translation process. Additionally, we added a boolean attribute *dataController* to the *TrustBoundary*. We use this attribute to highlight the trust boundary of the data controller. For multiple DFDs, we decide that *Actor*, *Storage*, *DataFlow*, and *Process* can be assigned to the element *DataFlowDiagram*. Thus, we can obtain a better overview by showing smaller DFDs that together form the whole model (cf. Fig. 7 vs. Fig. 2).

Similarly, we assign elements to the *TrustBoundary*, because in this way we can define which elements are inside the trust boundary. A *DataFlow* can take place between two *DataFlowElements* which can be *Storage*, *Process*, or *Actor* and mandatorily needs a *sourceDataFlow* and a *sinkDataFlow*. Additionally, *DataFlow* must be assigned at least one or more elements of *Data*. These restrictions, requiring at least one element are highlighted in **bold** in Fig. 5.

The metamodel is part of the editor's back-end and is not visible to the user of the tool.

4.2   Model Instance

An instance of the metamodel is a data-flow model. It contains instantiated metamodel elements from a concrete data-flow model. The model instance can be created and modified via graphical representations, described below. Additionally, the editor allows storing the results of the modeling process persistently.

The tree view of the model instance from our running example is shown in Fig. 6. It contains all elements of the model. The tree view of the model instance is not comprehensible for the user. Therefore, we provide a graphical editor.

A data-flow model can contain multiple DFDs, which can have shared elements. These shared elements occur only once in the data-flow model, but are referenced by each DFD they appear in. An example of such shared elements are the processes and the data-flows *DF7* and *DF12* in Fig. 7, which only appear once in the combined DFD (cf. Fig. 2) and the tree view instance in Fig. 6.

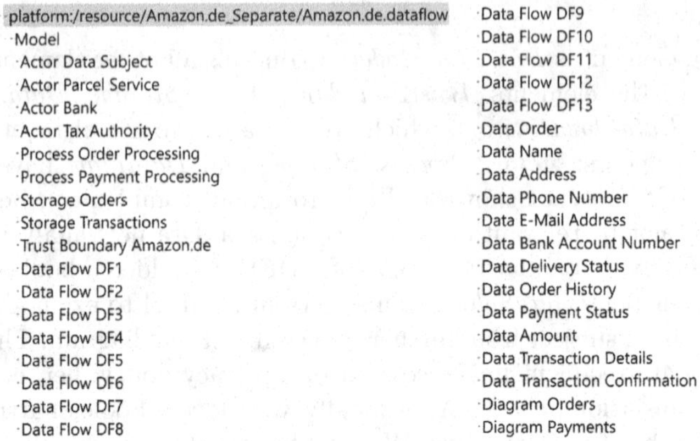

platform:/resource/Amazon.de_Separate/Amazon.de.dataflow
· Model
· Actor Data Subject
· Actor Parcel Service
· Actor Bank
· Actor Tax Authority
· Process Order Processing
· Process Payment Processing
· Storage Orders
· Storage Transactions
· Trust Boundary Amazon.de
· Data Flow DF1
· Data Flow DF2
· Data Flow DF3
· Data Flow DF4
· Data Flow DF5
· Data Flow DF6
· Data Flow DF7
· Data Flow DF8

· Data Flow DF9
· Data Flow DF10
· Data Flow DF11
· Data Flow DF12
· Data Flow DF13
· Data Order
· Data Name
· Data Address
· Data Phone Number
· Data E-Mail Address
· Data Bank Account Number
· Data Delivery Status
· Data Order History
· Data Payment Status
· Data Amount
· Data Transaction Details
· Data Transaction Confirmation
· Diagram Orders
· Diagram Payments

Fig. 6. Tree view of the model instance from our running example (cf. Fig. 2).

The model instances are part of the backend, too. The user of the tool only interacts with the graphical representations, described in the following.

4.3 Graphical Representations

We have three different graphical representations of the model instance. All three representations share the fact that trust boundaries, which are marked as data controllers, are highlighted in red. Trust boundaries that do not represent the data controller are drawn in black.

We have two graphical representations for DFDs called *DataFlowDiagram* and *PrivacyDataFlowDiagram.*

Both diagrams are almost equal. The *DataFlowDiagram* represents a selected part of the entire model. Only the elements which are assigned to the *DataFlowDiagram* are shown. This gives the user a clear overview. This representation is used for general purpose data-flow diagrams. The DFDs in Fig. 7 are created using the *DataFlowDiagram* representation.

The *PrivacyDataFlowDiagram* has two special properties compared to the DFD representation. We grey-out all storages, the data subject, and all dataflows which have storages or the data subject as source or sink. They are greyed-out because they are not relevant for the translation into a privacy policy.

Additionally, we have a main diagram called *DataFlowMainDiagram* where all elements are represented at once in a combined DFD. The represented elements are the union of all elements from the separate DFDs. This main diagram gives a complete overview of the entire model. However, the large number of elements can be overwhelming for the user. Hence, we recommend defining separate DFDs first. The *DataFlowMainDiagram* representation uses a *PrivacyDataFlow-Diagram* representation for the combined model. The DFD shown in Fig. 2 is the *DataFlowMainDiagram* combining the two separate DFDs for *Order Processing* and *Payment Processing* shown in Fig. 7. The combined diagram is used for exporting the DFDs to the privacy policy editor (cf. Sect. 3.6).

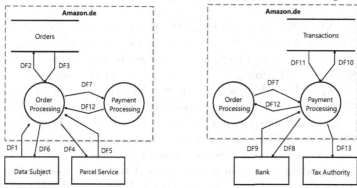

Fig. 7. left: Data-flow diagram for *Order Processing*; right: Data-flow diagram for *Payment Processing*.

4.4 Implemented Validation Conditions (VCs)

The validation conditions of Sect. 3.3 are implemented in the editor using AQL. They are checked automatically after a trigger of the user.

Listing 8 shows the AQL implementation of VC 14 as an example: *"When the combined data-flow diagram contains more than one trust boundary, only one of the trust boundaries can be considered as the data controller."*

```
aql:  self.trustBoundaries->size()>1 implies self.
      trustBoundaries->one(t | t.dataController=true)
```

Listing 8. AQL implementation of VC 14.

The context of the VC is the element *DataFlowModel* (see Fig. 5). Therefore, *self* is of type *DataFlowModel*. The first part *self.trustBoundaries− >size()>1* is evaluated to true or false. If we have more than one trust boundary in our model, it is evaluated to true. If the first part is true, the second part after the ***implies*** *self.trustBoundaries − > one(t|t.dataController=true)* needs to be true. This is the case if the set of all trust boundaries contains exactly one trust boundary where the attribute *dataController* is set to *true*.

The other VCs are implemented similarly or covered by the constraints specified in the metamodel.

5 Related Work

Robles-González et al. propose a framework extending LINDDUN, specifically targeting identification and authentication processes [13]. We do not extend the privacy threat analysis, but instead make use of the documentation created during this process. Even extended/derived frameworks like the one of Robles-González et al. are compatible with our proposed method, as long as they continue to use data-flow diagrams for their privacy analyses.

Before LINDDUN was proposed in the privacy context, Microsoft created STRIDE in the context of security threat modeling [9]. This security threat model also uses data-flow diagrams and hence is also compatible with our method. Since STRIDE focusses on security instead of privacy, the resulting privacy policy may be lacking some data transfers, that may be identified using LINDDUN. However, using DFDs from STRIDE will still support privacy policy authors when defining a policy, as many data-flows will be covered by the STRIDE DFDs, preparing large parts of the privacy policy.

Since we support privacy policy authors in the process of creating privacy policies, by providing a tool-supported method to extract policy information from DFDs, we also want to mention the work of Hjerppe et al. [7]. They provide a method for automatically creating LPL-policies from annotated source code. Depending on the size of a project it might be more viable to use the annotated source code to generate the privacy policy. However, in projects where a privacy impact analysis or privacy threat modeling using LINDDUN is applied, our method transforms knowledge created during these analyses into useful content for a privacy policy.

Kunz et al. also use a model-based approach in the privacy context [10]. They propose *Privacy Property Graphs* for privacy threat analyses. These privacy property graphs are created from static code analysis and are enriched data-flow diagrams. This provides the potential for an adapted version of our work presented in this paper. This adaptation could take the automatically generated privacy property graphs as input to prepare the privacy policies with less manual overhead.

Wang et al. analyzed 120 android apps concerning discrepancies between privacy policies and app behavior [14]. They identified 21 strong and 18 weak violations of the provided privacy policies. This means that 39 apps did not behave as described in their accompanying privacy policies. Using our approach and DFDs modeling the app behavior these inaccuracies in the policies could be prevented.

With the same goal Andow et al. proposed a different approach for the analysis of such discrepancies [2]. They also take the data recipient into account when verifying the behavior of the application. With this detail considered they analyzed 13796 applications and came to the conclusion that 42.4% of these applications had discrepancies between app behavior and privacy policy.

GDPR-compliance in systems and privacy policies is also considered an important topic by the European Union. It, for example, funded a recent research project for the assessment of GDPR-compliance. Completed in 2021, the DEFeND[5] project supports data controllers in the planning, design, and operational phases.

---

[5] https://www.defendproject.eu/.

6   Conclusion and Future Work

Conclusion. We presented our tool-supported method for the extraction of privacy policy information from data-flow diagrams. This allows policy authors to reuse information from privacy and security threat analyses when creating privacy policies for their services.

Our method and tool improve the creation of privacy policies by automatically extracting information regarding data-flows from these diagrams and providing this information as purposes and data recipients in our privacy policy editor. DFDs from the security engineering context can be more complex compared to the ones from the LINDDUN approach. Using a purpose hierarchy, we can combine the detailed information contained in these DFDs into more general purposes, which better fit a privacy policy.

Although the policy author still needs to enter some information manually, a large part of the privacy policy can be pre-filled using our approach. The definition of purposes and their data and data recipients takes up a large part of the policy definition process. This time-consuming task is made easier by importing the information from the DFDs.

Additionally, extracting this information from models representing the system behavior can improve the accuracy of the privacy policies. When the policies are not created independently of the system they more closely represent the actual system behavior.

Future Work. The approach we presented in this paper can be extended to support layered DFDs. This could further improve the purpose hierarchy created from the DFDs.

The integration of further privacy-related methods into the privacy policy creation process is a promising task for the future. The aim is to extract as much policy information as possible from work that has already been done during the development of a system. Thus, we reduce the overhead occurring in the privacy policy creation process.

Another goal for the future is the combination of different automated privacy policy creation approaches, like the one by Hjerppe et al. [7] with our DFD-approach. Combining different approaches could further reduce the overhead needed for the creation of privacy policies.

Besides the approach by Hjerppe et al., privacy property graphs (PPGs) by Kunz et al. [10] could also be used to extract privacy policy information. This could be achieved by adapting the methodology presented in this paper to take PPGs as input. This approach could potentially increase the amount of information extracted from the diagrams, as PPGs are enriched data-flow diagrams that contain additional information, which may be relevant for privacy policies.

Since DFDs are not part of UML[6] an extension of UML, standardizing DFDs, would be beneficial for future developments around DFDs. The UMLsec extension by Jürjens [8] is a good example for the benefits of a standardized notation.

Acknowledgement. We thank Julien Lukasewycz for his useful input during the development of our approach, as well as writing this paper. We further thank the reviewers of this paper for their valuable input regarding the paper itself as well as the approach we presented.

References

1. Amazon Europe Core: Amazon.de privacy policy (2022). https://www.amazon.de/gp/help/customer/display.html?nodeId=201909010&language=en_GB. Accessed 02 July 2023
2. Andow, B., et al.: Actions speak louder than words:Entity-Sensitive privacy policy and data flow analysis with PoliCheck. In: 29th USENIX Security Symposium (USENIX Security 20), pp. 985–1002 (2020)
3. DeMarco, T.: Structure analysis and system specification. In: Broy, M., Denert, E. (eds.) Pioneers and Their Contributions to Software Engineering, pp. 255–288. Springer Berlin Heidelberg, Berlin, Heidelberg (2001). https://doi.org/10.1007/978-3-642-48354-7_9
4. Deng, M., Wuyts, K., Scandariato, R., Preneel, B., Joosen, W.: A privacy threat analysis framework: supporting the elicitation and fulfillment of privacy requirements. Requirements Eng. **16**(1), 3–32 (2011). https://doi.org/10.1007/s00766-010-0115-7
5. European Parliament, Council of the European Union: Regulation 2016/679 of the European Parliament and of the Council of 27 April 2016 on the protection of natural persons with regard to the processing of personal data and on the free movement of such data, and repealing Directive 95/46/EC (General Data Protection Regulation). Official Journal of the European Union L119, 1–88 (2016). https://eur-lex.europa.eu/legal-content/EN/TXT/?uri=OJ:L:2016:119:TOC
6. Gerl, A.: Modelling of a privacy language and efficient policy-based de-identification. Thesis, Universität Passau (2020). https://nbn-resolving.org/urn:nbn:de:bvb:739-opus4-7674
7. Hjerppe, K., Ruohonen, J., Leppänen, V.: Extracting LPL privacy policy purposes from annotated web service source code. Softw. Syst. Model. **22**(1), 331–349 (2023)
8. Jürjens, J.: UMLsec: Extending UML for secure systems development. In: UML 2002 - The Unified Modeling Language: Model Engineering, Concepts, and Tools 5th International Conference Dresden, Germany, September 30-October 4, 2002 Proceedings, pp. 412–425. Springer (2002)
9. Kohnfelder, L., Grag, P.: The threats to our products. Tech. rep., Microsoft Corporation (2009). https://nbn-resolving.org/urn:nbn:de:hbz:464--20210712-090625-4
10. Kunz, I., Weiss, K., Schneider, A., Banse, C.: Privacy property graph: towards automated privacy threat modeling via static graph-based analysis. Proc. Privacy Enhanc. Technol. **2**, 171–187 (2023)

---

[6] The Unified Modeling Language: https://www.omg.org/spec/UML/.

11. Leicht, J., Heisel, M.: P2BAC: Privacy policy based access control using P-LPL. In: Mori, P., Lenzini, G., Furnell, S. (eds.) 9th International Conference on Information Systems Security and Privacy, pp. 686–697. SciTePress (2023). https://doi.org/10.5220/0011788500003405

12. Leicht, J., Heisel, M., Gerl, A.: PriPoCoG: guiding policy authors to define GDPR-compliant privacy policies. In: Trust, Privacy and Security in Digital Business: 19th International Conference, TrustBus 2022, Vienna, Austria, August 24, 2022, Proceedings. pp. 1–16. Springer (2022)

13. Robles-González, A., Parra-Arnau, J., Forné, J.: A LINDDUN-based framework for privacy threat analysis on identification and authentication processes. Comput. Security **94**, 101755 (2020)

14. Wang, X., Qin, X., Hosseini, M.B., Slavin, R., Breaux, T.D., Niu, J.: Guileak: Tracing privacy policy claims on user input data for android applications. In: Proceedings of the 40th International Conference on Software Engineering, pp. 37–47 (2018)

Up-to-Date Threat Modelling for Soft Privacy on Smart Cars

Mario Raciti[1,2]([✉])[ID] and Giampaolo Bella[2][ID]

[1] IMT School for Advanced Studies Lucca, Lucca 55100, Italy
mario.raciti@imtlucca.it
[2] Università degli Studi di Catania, Catania 95125, Italy
giamp@dmi.unict.it

Abstract. Physical persons playing the role of car drivers consume data that is sourced from the Internet and, at the same time, themselves act as sources of relevant data. It follows that citizens' privacy is potentially at risk while they drive, hence the need to model privacy threats in this application domain.

This paper addresses the privacy threats by updating a recent threat-modelling methodology and by tailoring it specifically to the *soft privacy* target property, which ensures citizens' full control on their personal data. The methodology now features the sources of documentation as an explicit variable that is to be considered. It is demonstrated by including a new version of the de-facto standard LINDDUN methodology as well as an additional source by ENISA which is found to be relevant to soft privacy. The main findings are a set of 23 domain-independent threats, 43 domain-specific assets and 525 domain-dependent threats for the target property in the automotive domain. While these exceed their previous versions, their main value is to offer self-evident support to at least two arguments. One is that LINDDUN has evolved much the way our original methodology already advocated because a few of our previously suggested extensions are no longer outstanding. The other one is that ENISA's treatment of privacy aboard smart cars should be extended considerably because our 525 threats fall in the same scope.

Keywords: risk assessment · automotive · LINDDUN · ENISA

1 Introduction

Modern smart cars are full-fledged, interconnected nodes of a computerised ecosystem, often referred to as the Internet of Everything. The data that people generate while driving qualifies as personal data because it can be referred to drivers, and sometimes to their digital identity specifically. Therefore, it falls under the requirements of the General Data Protection Regulation in Europe, and of similar juridical prescriptions worldwide. The integration of various sensors, cameras, and communication systems in modern vehicles creates new opportunities for privacy breaches, raising concerns about data protection measures and corresponding risks.

© The Author(s), under exclusive license to Springer Nature Switzerland AG 2024
S. Katsikas et al. (Eds.): ESORICS 2023 Workshops, LNCS 14398, pp. 454–473, 2024.
https://doi.org/10.1007/978-3-031-54204-6_27

It follows that people's privacy may be put at stake when they become car drivers. While *hard privacy* concerns the various techniques to protect a subject's personal data from everyone else, such as anonymisation and minimisation, *soft privacy* pertains to the range of practices to be followed for the subject to share their personal data with someone else while keeping full control, such as consent mechanisms and impact assessments. Our research rests on the observation that privacy issues in the automotive domain are not fully understood at present, although they are certain to demand GDPR compliance. Compliance may be addressed in terms of privacy risk assessment, which in turn demands privacy threat modelling, hence the general motivation for this paper, which is spelled out more in detail in the sequel of this Section.

1.1 Context and Motivation

Privacy is a complex and multifaceted concept that may be interpreted in different ways in different contexts, yet we take it as a fundamental human right in the first place. In a GDPR fashion, we may summarise privacy as the right of an individual, that is, the data subject, to control or influence what information related to them may be collected, processed and stored, and by whom and to whom that information may be disclosed. Privacy and security are distinct concepts that should not be used interchangeably. While threat modelling has traditionally been approached from a security perspective, a challenge for all privacy threat modelling approaches comes from the following question: "how to consider the impact on data subjects involved in the privacy threat?" This aspect is stressed in law and regulation compliance, i.e., in the Data Protection Impact Assessment (DPIA), required under the GDPR, to help identify, assess, and mitigate privacy risks associated with data processing activities. Arguably, a DPIA would benefit from a privacy threat model.

Threat modelling is challenging as the analyst faces various problems, such as completeness and threat explosion. On the one hand, completeness may be impactful because failing to account for specific threats would cause pitfalls to the subsequent risk assessment. On the other hand, the pursuit of completeness can result in a phenomenon known as threat explosion, characterised by an overwhelming number of threats that may be irrelevant, infeasible, or redundant with each other. Completeness and redundancy are considered by our previous work that features *threat embracing* [16]. Briefly, if two or more threats are described by labels that are deemed to be redundant in terms of their semantic similarity by the analyst's scrutiny, then these threats can be semantically merged into one.

Furthermore, as we shall see below, there is a lack of privacy threat taxonomies for smart cars in the state of the art, hence a clear motivation to push towards the advancement of a privacy threat modelling framework tailored for the automotive domain. Therefore, we modelled soft privacy threats for the automotive domain through a novel methodology that features a combinatoric approach [17]. In short, we produced a final list of threats by taking a domain-dependent approach and by leveraging the threats from various sources, including in particular the LINDDUN state-of-the-art privacy threat modelling framework [23] and ENISA's "Good practices for security of smart cars" [7]. In particular, although the ENISA report is among the most relevant sources about car cybersecurity in Europe, its treatment of privacy is very limited, hence the need for a deeper close-up.

However, LINDDUN has recently been significantly updated, hence the results from our previous work demand an accurate revision. More precisely, LINDDUN has increased the number of soft privacy threats and, in consequence, an up-to-date list of soft privacy threats for the automotive domain must be modelled. It could be pursued by leveraging the new version of the LINDDUN methodology, an approach that would bring the useful byproduct of checking how LINDDUN has evolved over time, particularly whether in the same direction we advocated [16].

1.2 Research Question and Contributions

Following the context and motivation given above, this paper focuses on soft privacy in the automotive domain from the threat modelling perspective. With the aim of advancing previous research, this paper addresses the core research question:

RQ *What are the soft privacy threats for the automotive domain?*

The following treatment answers the research questions by advancing an improvement of our innovative privacy threat modelling methodology [17] and applying it to the current landscape of the automotive domain. A key advantage of our methodology lies in its combinatoric approach, which offers two key benefits: the elicitation of domain-independent threats by analysing relevant sources from the state of the art; the elicitation of domain-dependent threats by combining a generic threat knowledge base with domain-specific assets. Furthermore, by incorporating five variables into the analysis, our privacy threat modelling methodology ensures that the direction pursued by the analyst remains focused and aligned with the desired outcome. The variables act as guiding principles, allowing the analyst to make informed decisions based on relevant and reliable information. The updated methodology adopts the mentioned ENISA report on smart cars as a source of specific and comprehensive knowledge on the automotive domain, and OWASP's "Calculation of the complete Privacy Risks list v2.0" [13]. In addition, these sources are augmented with the new version of LINDDUN and with an additional representative of the state of the art, namely the ENISA "Threat Taxonomy v2016" [6]. Therefore, the new methodology rests on a significantly extended, domain-independent threat knowledge base.

This paper contributes an updated version of our privacy threat modelling methodology and provides an updated list of 23 soft privacy threats that are domain-independent, thereby extending the 17 that we made available when we adopted the original LINDDUN [16]. Because LINDDUN's soft privacy threats have increased from 9 to 17 over its two versions, our proposed extensions of it have decreased from 8 to 6. As we shall detail below, this can be taken as an indication that LINDDUN has evolved in the direction we advocated.

Moreover, our novel 23 threats are also combined with 43, rather than 41 as before, specific assets of the automotive domain, so as to produce, by appropriate combinations, a total of 525 domain-dependent soft privacy threats for the automotive domain — each combination instantiates a given threat to each of the assets that are deemed affected by the threat. These represent a substantial extension to the existing threat taxonomy introduced by the ENISA report on smart cars, which is rather scant in terms of privacy featuring only a couple of privacy threats. It could be argued that a better understanding of privacy within the automotive domain is achieved.

1.3 Article Summary

The organisation of the manuscript follows a simple waterfall style. Section 2 outlines the related work, and Sect. 3 gives an overview of LINDDUN and its latest changes. Section 4 describes our novel privacy threat modelling methodology. Section 5 demonstrates the methodology by applying it to the automotive domain along with a case study, and Sect. 6 concludes.

2 Related Work

The challenges implicated by threat modelling led Wuyts et al. [27] to highlight the problems of current knowledge bases, such as limited semantics and lack of instantiating logic. Also, the authors discussed the requirements for a privacy threat knowledge base that streamlines threat elicitation efforts.

Furthermore, it is also noteworthy to recall that the process of threat modelling inherently implies assumptions and arbitrary decisions. Landuyt et al. [23] highlighted the influence of assumptions to the outcomes of the analysis during the risk assessment process, more precisely in the threat modelling phase in the context of a LINDDUN privacy threat elicitation.

In addition, several attempts were made for the purposes of threat modelling in the automotive domain. Vasenev et al. [24] were among the first to apply an extended version of STRIDE [12] and LINDDUN [5] to conduct a threat analysis on security and privacy threats in the automotive domain. In particular, the case study is specific to long term support scenarios for over-the-air updates. Moreover, this work suggests that the privacy topic in the automotive domain has not reached the same level of maturity as cybersecurity.

In general, threat modelling is part of a wider process, that is risk assessment. Wang et al. [25] proposed a threat-oriented risk assessment framework tailored for the automotive domain, with the aim, among the others, of overcoming assumptions and subjectivity. This framework can be considered a precursor to ISO/IEC:21434 [10], which was defined a year later. Also, the authors applied STRIDE and the attack tree method for the threat modelling.

Moreover, Chah et al. [2] applied the LINDDUN methodology to elicit and analyse privacy requirements of CAV system, while respecting the privacy properties set by the GDPR. Such attempt represents a solid baseline for the broader process of privacy risk assessment tailored for the automotive domain. Finally, Bella et al. [1] advanced a dedicated risk assessment framework for privacy risks in modern cars. They proposed a double assessment, combining an asset-oriented ISO approach with a threat-oriented STRIDE approach.

The above works addressed crucial topics such as threat elicitation, threat knowledge base, privacy threat analysis and privacy risk assessment, both in general and specifically tailored to the automotive domain. However, to the best of our knowledge, there are no works advancing privacy threat modelling upon the basis of the de-facto standard LINDDUN, in its new version, with the aim of eliciting both domain-independent and domain-dependent soft privacy threats. These are the distinctive features of the present contribution.

3   A Primer on (The New) LINDDUN

It is convenient to provide an introduction to LINDDUN before proceeding with the description of our methodology. LINDDUN is a privacy threat modelling methodology, inspired by STRIDE, that supports analysts in the systematical elicitation and mitigation of privacy threats in software architectures. LINDDUN privacy knowledge base represents one of its main strengths, and it is structured according to the 7 privacy threat categories encapsulated within LINDDUN's acronym [5]. Recently, LINDDUN has been updated, and it is now available under three flavours from a lean to an in-depth approach: LINDDUN GO, LINDDUN PRO and LINDDUN MAESTRO. In particular, LINDDUN GO comes in the form of a card deck representing the most common privacy threats; LINDDUN PRO takes on a systematic and exhaustive approach, supported by the knowledge base; LINDDUN MAESTRO targets an enriched system description to enable more precise threat elicitation, yet it is still under development.

The first notable difference with the old version lies on the acronym, which puts more emphasis on the privacy threat types rather than on the privacy properties affected by threats. In fact, for the sake of comparison, the acronym that was previously expanded as *Linkability, Identifiability, Non-repudiation, Detectability, Disclosure of information, Unawareness*, and *Non-compliance*, has now been revised as follows:

- *Linking:* associating data items or user actions to learn more about an individual or group.
- *Identifying:* learning the identity of an individual.
- *Non-repudiation:* being able to attribute a claim to an individual.
- *Detecting:* deducing the involvement of an individual through observation.
- *Data Disclosure:* excessively collecting, storing, processing or sharing personal data.
- *Unawareness & Unintervenability:* insufficiently informing, involving or empowering individuals in the processing of personal data.

– *Non-compliance:* deviating from security and data management best practices, standards and legislation.

The framework considers the state-of-the-art privacy threat types according to the privacy threat properties introduced by Pfitzmann [14]. These are categorised as hard privacy and soft privacy properties. In particular, unlinkability, anonymity and pseudonymity, plausible deniability, undetectability and unobservability, and confidentiality (hiding data content, including access control) are under the umbrella of hard privacy; user content awareness (including feedback for user privacy awareness, data update and expire) together with policy and consent compliance are, on the other hand, soft privacy properties.

LINDDUN provides a set of threats specific to privacy, named as "threat catalogue", in the form of threat trees. These privacy threat trees are inspired by the Secure Development Lifecycle (SDL) [9] and reflect common attack patterns [26] on the basis of state-of-the-art privacy developments, structured according to LINDDUN or STRIDE threat category and, in the previous version of LINDDUN, also to Data Flow Diagram (DFD) element type. In fact, the consideration of the DFD interactions has become more implicit in the new version of the framework, as the threat trees have become independent of the DFD element type, thus resulting in a significant diminution of the number of nodes as a side effect. The new guidance on how to link the Data Flow Diagram interactions rests now solely on the LINDDUN mapping table.

Threat trees provide a formal way to describe the security of systems based on a variety of attacks. Basically, the root node represents the ultimate goal, e.g., the threatening to a property, the children nodes embody different ways of achieving that goal, namely refinements, hence leaves represent basic-level attacks that can not be further refined. In addition, non-leaf nodes can be conjunctive (logic AND) or disjunctive (logic OR) [20].

In the new version of LINDDUN, threat trees provide support to reason about applicability (criteria), factors that determine threat impact (impact), and examples of each characteristic pertaining to the threat (examples). The framework provides a different view of the threat trees in terms of detail, as it is possible to consult each tree at three different levels: Basic, Examples, All details.

An example tree is presented in Fig. 1 for the Linking threat, which can be achieved through $L.1$ "Linked data", e.g., IP address, and $L.2$ "Linkable data", e.g., browser fingerprint. Both of these provide various attack paths which are not necessarily limited to the LINDDUN property analysed, namely Linking could lead to Identifying threats if we consider $L.1.1$ "Unique identifier".

We believe that the new version of LINDDUN represents a step forward from a GDPR perspective, as we can identify two LINDDUN privacy threat types, i.e., Unawareness & Unintervenability (threats against data subject rights) and Non-compliance (violations against data protection principles), which tightly align with the European regulation by including as many as 17 threats. In the previous version of LINDDUN, these two types were already bound to soft privacy, but only included 9 threats. Moreover, these soft privacy threats were lacking relevant

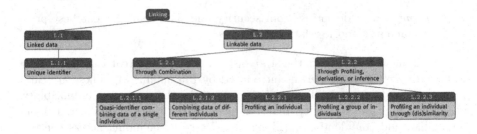

Fig. 1. Example of a LINDDUN threat tree: Linking.

aspects, such as those related to data subject controls, consent, and violation of regulations, which are now caught by the new threat knowledge base. On the other hand, the remaining types target more technical privacy threats, gathered under the umbrella of hard privacy, and as such contribute more directly to the selection of "appropriate technical and organisational protection measures".

Despite LINDDUN threat trees may lack some formal semantics and have minimal selection criteria to express potential threats [27], they still aim at providing a valuable overview of potential threat types that seeks to be general, hence suitable for a privacy threat analysis of any application domain. Moreover, the application of LINDDUN may lead to a high number of threats that may not be relevant, feasible, or important, thereby being labor-intensive and time-consuming, especially for complex or large systems. Hence, the advantage of having a catalogue of privacy threats, which are broad and applicable to various domains, may result in the problem of threat explosion.

4   A Privacy Threat Modelling Methodology

This Section advances an improvement of our privacy threat modelling methodology [17]. Our methodology incorporates both domain-independent and domain-specific knowledge and considers the potential consequences on the privacy of individuals as its cornerstone. The pivotal approach that our methodology relies upon is a combinatoric one with the aim of eliciting both domain-independent threats and domain-dependent threats. In particular, the former embody a generic threat knowledge base that consists of what is already known at present, whilst the domain-specific threats are derived from the first. Furthermore, in its previous version, our methodology identified four variables that contribute to model privacy threats, i.e., the specific privacy property, the threat agents, the application domain and the level of detail.

The new version is enriched by considering an additional variable, that is, the document source. The inclusion of five essential variables in our methodology orient the analysis, thus providing practical guidance to the analyst. Figure 2 depicts the updated methodology, while a description of the new introduced variable is provided below along with an outline of the combinatoric approach and a summary the other variables.

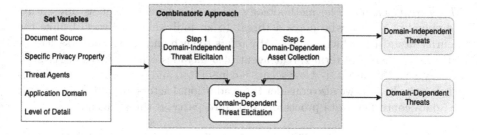

Fig. 2. Diagram of our updated privacy threat modelling methodology.

The Document Source. In privacy threat modelling, the knowledge base is crucial for both threats and assets to be elicited. Threats and assets may be derived from different sources, e.g., state-of-the-art reports, scientific contributions, guidelines, et cetera. Therefore, the document source of the threats/assets that the methodology seeks to gather can be either *internal* or *external* to the analyst's institution. In the case of internal document source, threats/assets may arise from the analyst's expertise, knowledge of the particular institutional context, or insights into the specific system or domain being assessed. On the other hand, the external document source involves gathering threats/assets from external references, such as established best practices or recognised industry standards. This allows the analyst to leverage existing knowledge and insights from a broader community of experts.

A combination of both internal and external document sources may also be possible, for instance, when the analyst enucleates a new threat/asset being inspired from one or more external sources. In such a case, we refer to the document source of that threat/asset as *hybrid*. Furthermore, the document source variable provides the means to keep track of the version of the threats, for example, the *year* in which the specific threat list is published. Moreover, when considering two or more different document sources, it may likely happen that some threats within such lists are inherently embraceable. Hence, threat embracing remains crucial for a proper merge of different document sources.

The Specific Privacy Property. Privacy relates to the control that individuals have over their personal information, including how it is collected, used, and shared. According to the state of the art [4,5], we can distinguish between two degrees of privacy, i.e., hard privacy and soft privacy. Briefly, while hard privacy focuses on minimising the risks associated with the collection and retention of personal data, soft privacy focuses on the appropriate use and sharing of personal data while respecting individuals' rights to control their data. It is clear that, in addition to hard privacy and soft privacy, *cybersecurity* plays a major, complementary role in terms of protection against the unauthorised access of data.

The Threat Agents. The methodology refers to a threat agent as any entity, individual or group, who poses a threat to an individual's privacy. Unlike the security literature, which traditionally refers to such entities as "adversaries" or "attackers", here the term threat agent also includes other sources of risks for privacy, as a threat agent is less security-connotated and not limited to malicious actors only. In fact, we also consider three additional actors directly from GDPR, i.e., data controller, data processor, and third party as threat agents.

The Application Domain. The application domain in threat modelling identifies two prevailing approaches, i.e., domain-dependent and domain-independent. Domain-dependent threat modelling is specific to a particular application domain, such as healthcare, finance, or automotive, and it takes into account the unique characteristics of the domain itself, thus it may be more accurate and effective. On the other hand, domain-independent threat modelling is not specific to any application domain and can be applied to a wide range of systems. LINDDUN, for example, is a domain-independent methodology. A combination of the two approaches may offer a more effective and efficient analysis, picking the advantages of both.

The Level of Detail. The level of detail of the statement describing a threat becomes relevant in the context of threat modelling and, subsequently, in risk assessment exercises with respect to the likelihood estimation of a threat. However, the most appropriate level of detail, that is, the choice of employing semantic relations, such as hypernyms or hyponyms, should be considered within the main picture, and the analyst will choose it with some inevitable bias.

4.1   The Combinatoric Approach

The five variables introduced by our privacy threat modelling methodology are crucial in the execution of the combinatoric approach, as they contribute to follow the direction desired by the analyst. The approach consists of three steps:

1. Domain-Independent Threat Elicitation
2. Domain-Dependent Asset Collection
3. Domain-Dependent Threat Elicitation

The first step involves the collection of domain-independent threats from relevant document sources. The second step consists of the collection of a list of assets for the target domain from relevant document sources.

The third and last step aims at producing a list of domain-specific threats. In particular, for each domain-independent threat elicited in Step 1, this step associates to it the assets enumerated in Step 2. The sheer association expresses the object of the threat that was domain-independent in the first place, thereby making it domain-dependent. In other words, the domain-independent threat is instantiated over each of the assets it affects, producing a domain-dependent threat.

While relevant examples will be given in the next Section, if $dit_1, \ldots, dit_n$ is the list of domain-independent threats produced by Step 1, then the number of domain-dependent threats that arise can be calculated as follows:

$$affected\_assets(dit_1) + \ldots + affected\_assets(dit_n).$$

5 Demonstration in the Automotive Domain

We apply our updated privacy threat modelling methodology to address the research question. In particular, we propose an exercise to focus on soft privacy with the new version of LINDDUN. While this paper details the key elements and findings, the full treatment is available online [15]. The exercise is detailed below. In particular, we set the variables discussed through Sect. 4 as follows:

S: External
P: Soft Privacy
T: Attacker, Data Controller/Processor, Third Party
D: Domain-Dependent – Automotive
L: Abstract

5.1 Domain-Independent Threat Elicitation

Soft privacy is the target property, therefore we must consider the LINDDUN threats that refer to such property, i.e., U(nawareness & unintervenability) and N(on-compliance), as a first document source. For each node of the U-N property trees, we annotate the pertaining threat in a table. It is convenient to provide a brief and general explanation of these threats, referring to the new descriptions provided by their sources. In particular, U(nawareness & unintervenability) refer to situations where individuals are not adequately informed, involved, or empowered in the processing of their personal data. N(on-compliance) refers to situations where a system deviates from security and data management best practices, standards, and legislation. It primarily focuses on the organisational and operational management context in which a system or service operates.

As one of the aims in eliciting the list of soft privacy threats is completeness, we may also want to extend the list of domain-independent threats by adding other *external* document sources. In particular, our previous work [17] included the 8 threats that were found [16] to be outstanding with respect to the old version of LINDDUN. In detail, they account for the 2 threats from the ENISA report that fall under the "Legal" category, i.e., "Failure to meet contractual requirements" and "Violation of rules and regulations/Breach of legislation/Abuse of personal data", and the 6 threats from the "Calculation of the complete Privacy Risks list v2.0" [13] document, i.e., "Consent-related issues", "Inability of user to access and modify data", "Insufficient data breach response", "Misleading content", "Secondary use", "Sharing, transfer or processing through 3rd party".

These threats relate to soft privacy as per the definition of soft privacy that we covered previously in Sect. 4. Moreover, some of them are embraceable with the new threat catalogue proposed by LINDDUN. In particular, we notice that "Violation of rules and regulations/Breach of legislation/Abuse of personal data" is now *embraceable* with several threats such as "Regulatory non-compliance" and "GDPR"; "Consent-related issues" is now *embraceable* with "Invalid consent"; "Inability of user to access and modify data" with "Lack of data subject control"; "Insufficient data breach response" with "GDPR". Hence, we can discard those threats, since they are already contemplated in the new LINDDUN threat trees, and keep the following ones: "Failure to meet contractual requirements", "Misleading content", "Secondary use", "Sharing, transfer or processing through 3rd party".

Moreover, we also consider here the ENISA "Threat Taxonomy v2016" [6] as another *external* document source, as it is relevant to enrich the domain-independent threat knowledge base. We pick the threats that specifically target soft privacy. These can be found under the "Legal" category, i.e., "Violation of laws or regulations/Breach of legislation", "Failure to meet contractual requirements", "Unauthorized use of IPR protected resources", "Abuse of personal data", and "Judiciary decisions/court orders". Again, three of such threats are already included in the more recent ENISA report on smart cars. In fact, "Failure to meet contractual requirements" is repeated and "Violation of laws or regulations/Breach of legislation" is embraced with "Abuse of personal data" into one single threat. Hence, we can add the following threats to the final list: "Unauthorized use of IPR protected resources", "Judiciary decisions/court orders". It is noteworthy that these additions are still possible without consequences on the domain variable, as such threats are general privacy threats, i.e., they ignore domain specific entities. Hence, such threats can be analysed in relation with (virtually) any application domain.

In summary, we elicited a total of 23 soft privacy threats from the selected document sources, i.e., LINDDUN, ENISA and OWASP. Table 1 shows such threats — the 6 that are highlighted are those that we do not deem embraceable with the current LINDDUN threats, hence represent our updated proposal for an extension to it. Moreover, while the 2 threats in italics are actually new (as they originate from the newly considered ENISA source), the remaining 4 already were among the 8 that we suggested before [16]. It means that we managed to embrace half of the previous suggestions to current LINDDUN threats, something that we interpret as evidence that LINDDUN has been extended coherently with what we advocated.

5.2 Domain-Dependent Asset Collection

For Step 2, we leverage two *external* document sources from the state of the art, i.e., the assets identified in the work proposed by Bella et al. [1] and ENISA's taxonomy of the key assets in the automotive domain. The former presents the following list of assets:

Table 1. Domain-independent soft privacy threats elicited in Step 1.

S	Threat
U	Unawareness of processing
	Unawareness as data subject
	Unawareness as a user sharing personal data
	Lack of data subject control
	Lack of data subject control – Preferences
	Lack of data subject control – Access
	Lack of data subject control – Rectification/erasure
N	Regulatory non-compliance
	GDPR
	Insufficient data subject controls
	Violation of data minimization principle
	Unlawful processing of personal data
	Invalid consent
	Lawfulness problems not related to consent
	Violation of storage limitation principle
	Improper personal data management
	Insufficient cybersecurity risk management
ENISA	Failure to meet contractual requirements
	Unauthorized use of IPR protected resources
	Judiciary decisions/court orders
OWASP	Misleading content
	Secondary use
	Sharing, transfer or processing through 3rd party

- *Personally Identifiable Information:* any data that could potentially be used to identify a particular individual, such as full name, date, and place of birth, driving licence number, phone number, mailing, and email address.
- *Special categories of personal data:* data about the driver, e.g., racial or ethnic origin, political opinions, religious or philosophical beliefs, trade union membership, genetic data, biometric data, data concerning health or data concerning sex life or sexual orientation (GDPR art. 9).
- *Driver's behaviour:* driver's driving style, e.g., the way the driver accelerates, speeds up, turns, brakes.
- *User preferences:* data regarding cabin preferences, e.g., seating, music, windows, heating, ventilation and air conditioning (HVAC).
- *Purchase information:* driver's financial information, such as credit card numbers and bank accounts.

- *Smartphone data:* data that the vehicle and driver's smartphone exchange with each other via the mobile application and short-range wireless connections such as Wi-Fi and Bluetooth (contact book, phone calls, text messages).
- *GPS data:* vehicle geolocation history and route tracking.
- *Vehicle information:* vehicle information such as carmaker, model, vehicle identification number (VIN), licence plate and registration.
- *Vehicle maintenance data:* data about the maintenance and status of vehicle components such as kilometres travelled, tyre pressure, oil life, brake, suspension, and engine status.
- *Vehicle sensor data:* data analysed and calculated by car sensors, such as distance sensors, crash sensors, biometric sensors, temperature sensors and internal and external cameras.

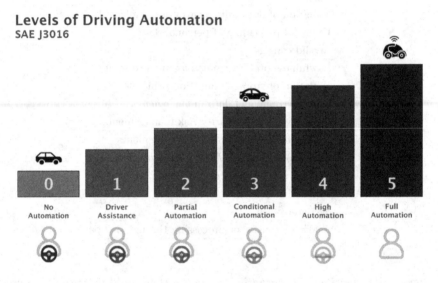

Fig. 3. Vehicles automation levels as defined in SAE J3016.

The report by ENISA focuses on Automated Driving System-Dedicated Vehicle (ADS-DS) [19], i.e., semi-autonomous and autonomous cars, and V2X communications, pertaining to SAE Level 4 and Level 5. Figure 3 depicts the SAE levels of driving automation. The focus of the study is on smart cars that, as connected systems, have the necessary capabilities to autonomously perform all driving functions under certain (or all) conditions, and are able to communicate with their surroundings including other vehicles, pedestrians and Road-Side Units (RSU). Moreover, the key concepts analysed by ENISA do not only concern passenger cars but also commercial vehicles (e.g. buses, coaches, etc.), including self-driving, ride-sharing vehicles that can be shared with other users.

The assets proposed by ENISA are categorised in: "Car sensors and actuators", "Decision Making Algorithms", "Vehicle Functions", "Software management", "Inside vehicle Communication Components", "Communication Networks and Protocols", "Nearby External Components", "Network and Domain Isolation Features", Servers", "Systems and Cloud Computing", "Information", "Humans", "Mobile Devices". For the sake of brevity, we only quote the descriptions of the assets under the "Information" category:

- *Sensors data* refers to data that is gathered by the different smart car sensors and which will be transmitted to the appropriate ECU for processing.
- *Keys and certificates* refers to the different keys and certificates used for security purposes (such as authentication, securing the exchanges, secure boot, etc.). Keys are stored in devices embedded in the vehicle (e.g. ECU) and/or in servers depending on their use.
- *Map data* refers to the information about the car environment. Map data allows us to increase the passenger safety by correlating its information with the sensor data. Contrary to GNSS, which gives only information about the geolocalisation, map data gives information about the surrounding environment.
- *V2X information* refers to the various information exchanged via V2X communications (e.g. emergency vehicle approaching, roadworks/collision warning and traffic information).
- *Device information* refers to the various information related to a device embedded in a smart car (e.g. ECU, TCU) or connected devices (e.g. smartphones, tablet). This includes information such as type, configuration, firmware version, status, etc., of different smart car sensors and which will be transmitted to the appropriate ECU for processing.
- *User information* refers to smart cars user (e.g. driver, passenger, etc.) information such as name, role, privileges and permissions.

Moreover, soft privacy is part of privacy, which is related to security, thereby all the assets proposed by ENISA may be virtually involved in the execution of the combinatoric approach.

During the execution of this step, within the list proposed by Bella et al., we identified some assets that are embraceable with the ENISA taxonomy. In particular, "Personally Identifiable Information" is *embraceable* with "User information"; "Smartphone data" with "Device information"; "GPS data" with "Map data"; "Vehicle sensor data" with "Sensor data". Thereby, we explicitly picked the following assets from the paper contribution: "Special categories of personal data", "Driver's behaviour", "User preferences", "Purchase information", "Vehicle information', "Vehicle maintenance data". The last two were not available before. The remaining assets, according to our scrutiny, are already contemplated in the ENISA taxonomy.

Overall, we elicited a total of 43 assets, a small increase on the 41 that we had before [17].

5.3   Domain-Dependent Threat Elicitation

In the last step, we conjugate the findings from the previous steps. For each domain-independent threat elicited in Step 1, we assign the assets from Step 2 that we deem to be potentially affected by that particular threat. In general, a threat may apply to multiple assets, therefore for some threat-asset pairs we annotate multiple assets or, in case all assets are affected, we add the label "All assets" for the sake of brevity. In particular, most assets that we deem to be potentially affected by the soft privacy threats fall under the ENISA category "Information".

While the full results are available online [15], we present an exemplification of some noteworthy domain-dependent threats, with the additional aim of providing the rationale behind the related threat-asset(s) associations:

dit_{i_1} *Unawareness of processing* refers to the lack of awareness or understanding about how personal data is being processed. It affects various assets, such as sensors data, map data, V2X information, device information, user information, special categories of personal data, user preferences, purchase information, vehicle information, and vehicle maintenance data.

dit_{i_2} *Lack of data subject control – Preferences* specifically refers to the lack of control individuals have over their preferences. It affects assets such as user preferences and purchase information. When individuals cannot control or manage their preferences effectively, their privacy in relation to their preferences can be at risk.

dit_{i_3} *Regulatory non-compliance* encompasses all assets. It refers to the failure to comply with relevant privacy regulations or laws. When organizations do not adhere to the required privacy standards, all assets can be affected, leading to potential privacy breaches.

dit_{i_4} *GDPR* is also associated with all assets. It specifically refers to non-compliance with the General Data Protection Regulation (GDPR), a data protection law in the European Union. Violations of GDPR can lead to severe penalties and legal consequences.

dit_{i_5} *Violation of data minimization principle* refers to the violation of collecting and processing only the necessary data. It affects assets such as sensors data, map data, V2X information, device information, user information, special categories of personal data, user preferences, and purchase information, vehicle information, and vehicle maintenance data.

dit_{i_6} *Unlawful processing of personal data* covers all assets. It occurs when personal data is processed unlawfully or without a legal basis. When personal data is processed in violation of applicable laws or regulations, it poses a significant privacy risk to all assets involved.

dit_{i_7} *Lawfulness problems not related to consent* is associated with all assets. It highlights issues of lawfulness in data processing that are not specifically related to consent. These problems may include processing of personal data without a valid legal basis or exceeding the scope of permitted processing activities, such as automated decision-making on sensitive personal data.

dit_{i_8} *Improper personal data management* is associated with user information and special categories of personal data. It signifies improper management practices regarding personal data, including inadequate safeguards, inappropriate handling, or unauthorised access. Improper data management can lead to privacy breaches, data leaks, or unauthorised use of sensitive information.

dit_{i_9} *Failure to meet contractual requirements* refers to a breach of contractual requirements by Tier 1 and/or Tier 2 car components or software suppliers, thus encompassing all assets. Such threat may lead to financial, safety, privacy and/or operational impacts.

$dit_{i_{10}}$ *Sharing, transfer or processing through 3rd party* refers to the sharing or transferring of various assets to third parties that increases the likelihood of unauthorised access, misuse, or breaches. It is clear that the affected assets belong to the ENISA "Information" category and include special categories of personal data, driver's behaviour, user preferences, purchase information, vehicle information, and vehicle maintenance data.

As an outcome of this exemplification, the resulting number of domain-dependent threats would be:

$$affected\_assets(dit_{i_1}) + \ldots + affected\_assets(dit_{i_{10}}) =$$
$$10 + 2 + 43 + 43 + 10 + 43 + 43 + 2 + 43 + 12 = 251$$

5.4 Case Study

This Section presents a case study that relies on the latest breaking news and articles about privacy incidents in the automotive domain. In particular, we employ classical web searches as a source of relevant information by building queries as "privacy automotive", "automotive breach", "smart car privacy", et similia, in the *News* search filter offered by Google. If we matched some news with a soft privacy threat from the previous exercise, then we would be able to give some statistics about the occurrences of such threat, hence inferring an estimation of its likelihood. For the sake of brevity, we only present some illustrative examples of news that matched with one or more of the proposed soft privacy threats. The following examples extend our previous case study [17] and provide a different reading of the pieces of news in common, in light of the new threat list.

A data breach at Toyota Motor's Indian business [18] might have exposed some customers' personal information. "Toyota Kirloskar Motor (TKM) has been notified by one of its service providers of an incident that might have exposed personal information of some of TKM's customers on the internet". This perfectly embodies a threat that we find in Table 1, i.e., "GDPR", stemming from an inadequate response to a data breach that does not comply with GDPR.

Furthermore, we find another news that represents multiple threats: "GDPR", "Lack of data subject control", "Insufficient data subject controls" and

"Violation of data minimization principle". The Dutch Data Protection Authority (DPA) investigated Tesla's camera-based "Sentry Mode" security system [8], which is designed to protect the vehicle against theft or vandalism while it is parked. It does this by taking footage with four cameras on the outside of the vehicle. This specific threat has now received a mitigation measure from the manufacturer, as the company altered security cameras to be more privacy-friendly and avoid GDPR violations. Originally, when Sentry Mode was enabled, this system was on by default. The cameras continuously filmed everything around a parked Tesla and stored one hour of footage each time.

In addition, we also found a review [22] that perfectly matched with the implications related to several soft privacy threats from the previous exercise. The article discusses a suggestion for a new feature to be added to the Ring Car Cam. The author proposes an Alexa-based voice command that would temporarily turn off the interior camera and microphone. This suggestion is based on the author's wife's volunteer work, which involves discussing private and privileged information about children's legal cases on the phone. The author's wife currently uses the physical privacy shutter to prevent the camera from recording video and audio inside the car. However, she sometimes forgets to flip the shutter up or down. Therefore, the author proposes a hands-free privacy trigger that would allow the user to enable or disable privacy mode with a voice command. This feature would eliminate the need for the user to physically manipulate the shutter, making it easier to maintain privacy while driving.

Moreover, we found a match for the "Improper personal data management" threat, as Toyota Japan [21] disclosed a significant data breach that occurred due to a cloud misconfiguration, resulting in the exposure of millions of customers' vehicle details over a decade. The exposed data included personal information, vehicle details, and videos.

Another discovery [3], related at least to the "Insufficient cybersecurity risk management" threat, revealed that BMW may have potentially exposed sensitive files and client data, including customer information, as a result of an unprotected environment and the exposure of configuration files on the official BMW Italy website. Although the information alone may not compromise the website, it could be used for reconnaissance purposes by hackers. As a typical example of interconnection between privacy and security, the exposed configuration file could have allowed threat actors to find other vulnerabilities and access the site's source code.

The same interconnection between privacy and security is also tangible in the National Highway Traffic Safety Administration (NHTSA) warning [11] to carmakers in Massachusetts not to comply with a state law that requires them to share more vehicular telematics data with third parties. This naturally embodies the "Judiciary decisions/court orders" threat. The NHTSA argues that the state law is pre-empted by federal law and could potentially allow hackers to remotely access and control cars, leading to safety risks. The law, known as the "right to repair" law, has been the subject of a court battle between carmakers and the state. The NHTSA's letter represents the federal government's direct involvement in the case and raises concerns about the potential dangers of open access to vehicle telematics. The litigation is likely to face further delays due to the NHTSA's intervention.

5.5 Evaluation

In this Section, we evaluate the findings from the previous experiment. The application of the combinatoric method to the automotive domain yielded notable results, which are available online [15], as stated above. In particular, we produced a novel, refined list of soft privacy threats that are domain-dependent. In fact, we associate the generic threat knowledge base pertaining to soft privacy, collected at the end of Step 1, with the automotive-specific assets collected at the end of Step 2, thus obtaining domain-specific soft privacy threats for modern cars with a homogeneous level of detail and dependent on the automotive domain, at the end of Step 3. A confirmation of the practicality and relevance of such threats for the automotive domain was proven by means of web searches. This answers the research question.

Furthermore, the newly introduced variable in our privacy threat modelling methodology represents a foundational improvement for both Step 1 and Step 2, as the choice of the source document(s) requires a thorough examination.

In addition, it is important to emphasise that a crucial difference between the new list and the old list of threats found: among the 8 threats added to the list in our previous work, 4 were deemed to be embraceable with the new LINDDUN threat catalogue. Hence, LINDDUN is clearly moving towards the direction that we hoped, and we are confident that their threat knowledge base will continuously improve in such a positive direction. Also, this supports the case that embracing is relevant and useful, especially when the analyst considers different document sources.

Our new list of threats enriches the broader threat knowledge base in the automotive domain over soft privacy. While we cannot claim that no more valid candidates exist, our final list of threats is complete with respect to the state-of-the-art knowledge base on soft privacy threats. Notably, such base features the new LINDDUN threat catalogue and the relevant taxonomies by ENISA. Our output is now available for the international community's evaluation.

6 Conclusions

This paper faced the challenge of privacy threat modelling by focusing specifically on soft privacy and on the automotive domain. Its research question found an answer through the development of an updated version of a previous threat modelling methodology, which now revolves around five rather than four variables. These variables help the analyst make well-informed decisions upon the basis of a solid foundation of relevant and reliable data.

The methodology was demonstrated on a case study from the automotive domain, taking into account a new version of LINDDUN, which yields a de-facto privacy threat model, and an additional, relevant source by ENISA. As a result, as many as 23 domain-independent threats, 43 domain-specific assets and 525 domain-dependent threats for soft privacy in the automotive domain were produced [15].

These results support the arguments that LINDDUN has evolved coherently with what we advocated before and that ENISA's privacy threats can be extended dramatically. Such arguments, in turn, represent a major leap forward in the modelling of soft privacy threats on smart cars.

Aknowledgements. Giampaolo Bella acknowledges financial support from: PNRR MUR project PE0000013-FAIR.

References

1. Bella, G., Biondi, P., Tudisco, G.: A double assessment of privacy risks aboard top-selling cars. Automotive Innovation, pp. 1–18 (Jan 2023). https://doi.org/10.1007/s42154-022-00203-2
2. Chah, B., Lombard, A., Bkakria, A., Yaich, R., Abbas-Turki, A., Galland, S.: Privacy threat analysis for connected and autonomous vehicles. Procedia Comput. Sci. **210**, 36–44 (2022). https://doi.org/10.1016/j.procs.2022.10.117, https://www.sciencedirect.com/science/article/pii/S1877050922015733, the 13th International Conference on Emerging Ubiquitous Systems and Pervasive Networks (EUSPN) / The 12th International Conference on Current and Future Trends of Information and Communication Technologies in Healthcare (ICTH-2022) / Affiliated Workshops
3. Cybernews: Bmw exposes clients in italy (2023). https://cybernews.com/security/bmw-exposes-italy-clients/
4. Danezis, G.: Introduction to Privacy Technology (2008). http://www0.cs.ucl.ac.uk/staff/G.Danezis/talks/Privacy_Technology_cosic.pdf
5. Deng, M., Wuyts, K., Scandariato, R., Preneel, B., Joosen, W.: A privacy threat analysis framework: supporting the elicitation and fulfillment of privacy requirements. Requirements Eng. **16**(1), 3–32 (Mar 2011). https://doi.org/10.1007/s00766-010-0115-7
6. ENISA: Threat Taxonomy (2016). https://www.enisa.europa.eu/topics/cyber-threats/threats-and-trends/enisa-threat-landscape/threat-taxonomy/view
7. ENISA: Good Practices for Security of Smart Cars (2019). https://www.enisa.europa.eu/publications/smart-cars
8. Europe, A.N.: Tesla escapes fine from dutch watchdog after automaker alters security cameras (2023). https://europe.autonews.com/automakers/tesla-alters-cameras-avoid-dutch-fine-over-privacy-violations
9. Howard, M., Lipner, S.: The Security Development Lifecycle, vol. 34. Microsoft Press (June 2006). https://doi.org/10.1007/s11623-010-0021-7
10. ISO: ISO/IEC 21434 - road vehicles - cybersecurity engineering (2021)
11. Law, B.: New us agency joins fray over massachusetts repair law, car data (2023). https://news.bloomberglaw.com/privacy-and-data-security/new-us-agency-joins-fray-over-massachusetts-repair-law-car-data
12. Microsoft: The STRIDE threat model (2009). https://learn.microsoft.com/en-us/previous-versions/commerce-server/ee823878%28v=cs.20
13. OWASP: Top 10 Privacy Risks (2021). https://owasp.org/www-project-top-10-privacy-risks/

14. Pfitzmann, A., Hansen, M.: A terminology for talking about privacy by data minimization: Anonymity, unlinkability, undetectability, unobservability, pseudonymity, and identity management (Aug 2010). http://dud.inf.tu-dresden.de/literatur/Anon_Terminology_v0.34.pdf
15. Raciti, M., Bella, G.: Github repository with complete outcomes (2023). https://github.com/tsumarios/Privacy-Threat-Modelling-Research/tree/main/SECPRE23
16. Raciti., M., Bella., G.: How to model privacy threats in the automotive domain. In: Proceedings of the 9th International Conference on Vehicle Technology and Intelligent Transport Systems - VEHITS, pp. 394–401. INSTICC, SciTePress (2023). https://doi.org/10.5220/0011998800003479
17. Raciti., M., Bella., G.: A threat model for soft privacy on smart cars. In: Proceedings of the 2nd Workshop on Automotive Cyber Security - ACSW (In press). https://doi.org/10.48550/arXiv.2306.04222
18. Reuters: Toyota's indian unit warns of a possible customer data breach (2023). https://www.reuters.com/technology/toyotas-indian-unit-warns-possible-customer-data-breach-2023-01-01/
19. SAE: Taxonomy and Definitions for Terms Related to Driving Automation Systems for On-Road Motor Vehicles (J3016_202104) (2021). https://www.sae.org/standards/content/j3016_201806/
20. Schneier, B.: Attack trees. Dr. Dobb's J. 24(12), 21–29 (1999)
21. TechCrunch: Toyota Japan exposed millions of vehicles' location data for a decade (2023). https://techcrunch.com/2023/05/12/toyota-japan-exposed-millions-locations-videos/
22. underscored, C.: The ring car cam takes ring's great security smarts on the road (2023). https://edition.cnn.com/cnn-underscored/reviews/ring-car-cam
23. Van Landuyt, D., Joosen, W.: A descriptive study of assumptions made in linddun privacy threat elicitation. In: Proceedings of the 35th Annual ACM Symposium on Applied Computing, pp. 1280–1287. SAC '20, Association for Computing Machinery, New York, NY, USA (2020). https://doi.org/10.1145/3341105.3375762
24. Vasenev, A., Stahl, F., Hamazaryan, H., Ma, Z., Shan, L., Kemmerich, J., Loiseaux., C.: Practical security and privacy threat analysis in the automotive domain: Long term support scenario for over-the-air updates. In: Proceedings of the 5th International Conference on Vehicle Technology and Intelligent Transport Systems - VEHITS, pp. 550–555. INSTICC, SciTePress (2019). https://doi.org/10.5220/0007764205500555
25. Wang, Y., Wang, Y., Qin, H., Ji, H., Zhang, Y., Wang, J.: A systematic risk assessment framework of automotive cybersecurity. Automotive Innovation 4(3), 253–261 (Aug 2021). https://doi.org/10.1007/s42154-021-00140-6
26. Wuyts, K., Joosen, W.: Linddun privacy threat modeling: a tutorial (Jul 2015), technical Report (CW Reports)
27. Wuyts, K., Sion, L., Van Landuyt, D., Joosen, W.: Knowledge is power: systematic reuse of privacy knowledge for threat elicitation. In: 2019 IEEE Security and Privacy Workshops (SPW), pp. 80–83 (2019). https://doi.org/10.1109/SPW.2019.00025

Security and Privacy for Mobile Crowdsensing: Improving User Relevance and Privacy

Cihan Eryonucu$^{(\boxtimes)}$ and Panos Papadimitratos

Networked Systems Security Group, KTH Royal Institute of Technology,
Stockholm, Sweden
{eryonucu,papadim}@kth.se
https://www.eecs.kth.se/nss

Abstract. Mobile crowdsensing (MCS) leverages smart devices for diverse data collection tasks, ranging from noise measurements to traffic congestion levels. However, with security and privacy a prerequisite for deployment, creating a diverse ecosystem, considering user specifics, providing adequate privacy to task initiators, and enhancing user control are key factors for MCS systems to achieve their full potential. We introduce our secure and privacy-preserving architecture for MCS, designed to address these challenges, improving user control, relevance, and privacy. Our work utilizes a variant of identity-based encryption to capture user characteristics and attributes, enabling secure task enrollment and eligibility enforcement while reinforcing task initiator privacy. This study emphasizes modularity as a design goal, enabling system entities to function without relying upon others while supporting all security and privacy requirements of MCS stakeholders. We finally evaluate feasibility and efficiency to show that the proposed system is practical.

Keywords: Mobile Crowdsensing · Security · Privacy

1 Introduction

Mobile crowdsensing (MCS) is revolutionizing the way data is gathered, by harnessing the ubiquity and connectivity of smart devices equipped with user-friendly interfaces and diverse sensing capabilities. MCS applications range from noise measurement [12] and environmental radiation monitoring [3] to traffic congestion levels [14] and popular times of businesses and places [11].

While the use of MCS offers a multitude of benefits, it also raises concerns. Privacy, as user-contributed data often expose sensitive information, e.g., frequently visited places [20], and security, as collected data can be manipulated, e.g., through Sybil-based attacks, leading to false information provided to users of popular apps [6]. Data verification is crucial to sift maliciously or erroneously submitted data [10,21], complemented by accountability mechanisms for offending users while protecting users' privacy, is another issue. Incentives should

S. Katsikas et al. (Eds.): ESORICS 2023 Workshops, LNCS 14398, pp. 474–493, 2024.
https://doi.org/10.1007/978-3-031-54204-6_28

encourage user participation without connecting them to the submitted data. The primary challenge is crafting a comprehensive solution for MCS that coordinates the aforementioned concerns while maximizing the advantages of MCS. To this end, secure and privacy-preserving (S&P) MCS architectures offer decentralized solutions with system entities separated by operational roles. Despite the efforts of the research community [5,16,18,23], several challenges remain for S&P MCS architectures to address.

In spite of a good understanding of requirements [7] and significant efforts in the literature, the complexity of addressing all requirements simultaneously is challenging. Some [4,27–29] consider specific requirements in isolation without considering their integration with the rest, others [8,18,25] striving for comprehensive solutions, but there are still important aspects, like TI privacy, that necessitate further exploration.

Typically, the MCS service providers are regarded as single, unified entities [5,18] or a firmly interconnected network with multiple entities [8,25] with various collaborating entities responsible for specific services e.g., credentials, remunerations, etc. While these entities depend on each other for proper functionality, there is no mechanism to utilize them individually, leading to poor usability of the MCS system. Furthermore, users have weak influence over the MCS policies, specifically regarding selecting the security, privacy, or utility policies best suited to them, which in turn hinders user relevance, trust, and participation in the system.

To tackle the identified challenges while retaining the advantages of the S&P MCS architectures, we propose a fresh design look and leverage attribute-based cryptography (ABC). We capture the properties of the participants in a verifiable manner, enabling secure task release, hiding task information from incompetent users, and task eligibility enforcement, barring incapable users from tasks to which they cannot reliably contribute. We also highlight the importance of modularity as a design goal, an aspect that received little attention from the literature. Modularity entails allowing a multiplicity of actors to instantiate different parts of the architecture without compromising the system's integrity or functionality. Our contributions are summarized as follows:

- We improve the user relevance in MCS by incorporating user characteristics in a privacy-preserving and verifiable way into the broad system design. By harnessing ABC, we imprint user properties (computational power, sensory capabilities, and reputation) into the credentials to enable task eligibility enforcement and ensure the quality of contributions.
- We enhance task initiators' privacy by designing a secure task release mechanism to make the tasks accessible and visible *only* to users with adequate capabilities.
- Lastly, we evaluate our system's feasibility and efficiency, future-proofing the system's practicality and compatibility with extensions.

2   System and Adversary Model

System Model: We start by introducing general MCS system entities (actors).

- **Task Initiators (TIs)** are organizations, such as government agencies, non-profit organizations, private companies, and academic institutions. TIs launch their campaigns, seeking to collect data from contributors to form knowledge about phenomena and activities. Tasks specify various parameters for data collectors, such as the required sensors, data format, the area(s) of interest, task duration, remuneration budget, and a minimum number of users. Task areas can be defined using geographical coordinates or regions, i.e., historical quarters, municipalities, cities, etc.
- **Contributors**, participants, or users are individuals with mobile sensing devices providing the raw measurements needed to gain insights regarding tasks. Each contributor is unique, with characteristics based on location, demographics, motivation, expertise on the task, and the mobile computing and sensing platform (e.g., smartphone).
- **Security and Privacy Infrastructure** provides necessary technical platforms, software, and other resources to support user registration, task enrollment, data collection, and remuneration management. The infrastructure is the facilitator between TIs and contributors. Third-party stakeholders may participate in the infrastructure as identity providers (IdPs) and certificate authorities (CAs), providing authentication to their users, government agencies regulating sensitive data collection tasks, or data aggregators collecting and processing the collected data. We dissect and define the S&P infrastructure entities' roles in Sect. 5.

Adversary Model

We consider external and internal adversaries aiming to abuse the MCS system. We assume MCS infrastructure entities are *honest-but-curious*, i.e., they follow the defined protocol behavior, but they are curious to learn information about clients; such as sensory capabilities, device/network-specific information, remuneration details, and task enrollment history. Further, they actively try to link users syntactically by observing changes in credentials in use and semantically by inspecting the information, like their whereabouts over time. Malicious infrastructure entities collude to de-anonymize participants. Section 7 discusses the ramifications of such collusions.

External adversaries are non-registered users without access to the system services. They can still mount clogging Denial of Services (DoS) attacks[1], eavesdrop on communication, send unauthorized/forged and replay legitimate contributions, and try to collect other users' rewards.

Internal adversaries are the users and TIs, all with valid credentials, or attackers who gain unauthorized access by other means, e.g., hacking devices, making them relatively stronger compared to external attackers. Such adversaries are interested in learning information about other contributors, such as identifying the task participation history, user sensor profiling, submitting inaccurate data to pollute the data collection process, and tracking user-submitted data. The adversaries may try to obtain task information they cannot participate in. They

---

[1] Such attacks are beyond the scope of this work.

also try to obtain unfair payments, i.e., intentionally submitting faulty data, double submissions, and remuneration for someone else's submission.

3 Security and Privacy Requirements

To realize a secure and privacy-preserving MCS architecture, we consolidate the following requirements based on the literature [5,7,8].

R1 Privacy-preserving participation: Privacy preservation covers separate core requirements that make up the general design goal. In prior works, these core requirements are often addressed in isolation or in combination but seldom in their entirety. Core privacy requirements include **(a)** identity privacy, covering both digital and real user identities; **(b)** location privacy, concealing users' whereabouts throughout the process; **(c)** device privacy, hiding device-specific identifiers; **(d)** data privacy, ensuring the unlinkability of the submitted data; **(e)** network anonymity, keeping sender's networking identifiers (e.g., IP addresses) confidential, which can be integrated with device privacy; lastly, **(f)** TI privacy, protecting the task description and the TI identity from unsuited users; **(g)** task enrollment secrecy, hiding the tasks participants are involved in. Collectively, these facets of privacy form full privacy protection.

R2 Fair and private incentives: User contributions should be compensated. Incentives could take multiple forms, ranging from monetary rewards to reputation to access to resources i.e., querying task results. Incentives should not be linked to user contributions (privacy) and should be resilient against potential exploitation from malicious or self-serving users (fairness).

R3 Communication integrity, confidentiality, and authenticity: Communication among system entities and users should be across secure channels that guarantee data integrity, confidentiality, and authenticity.

R4 Access control: The system should define the roles of the actors and these roles should be adhered to. Users should be able to access data (aggregates) from different tasks, choose, and contribute to tasks they are authorized for based on the prerequisites outlined for each task by the TI. We additionally require user properties to be verifiable as a basis for user access.

R5 Data verification: The contributed data quality must be verified to ensure the formed knowledge truthfulness. Data quality is assessed based on the submitted data itself combined with auxiliary information on time and context (location, system, and environment conditions).

R6 Accountability: Users and infrastructure entities are responsible for their actions within the system. Misbehaving users should be evicted and their credentials revoked accordingly. Likewise, malicious system entities should be identified. Accountability acts as a bedrock for building trust among participants, TIs, and third-party stakeholders (e.g., IdPs, CAs), which strengthens the integrity of the system.

4 Related Work

Often, the literature claims a particular requirement is addressed when, in fact, separate, albeit related, issues are addressed. This is most evident in privacy-preserving participation (R1), with some studies defining privacy as user identity [5,23], while others define it as data privacy [4,29]. These two requirements deserve separate consideration. To illustrate the overview of the literature, Table 1 shows the comparison between the most complete S&P MCS architectures, to the best of our knowledge.

AnonySense [23], one of the early architectures in the literature, aims to uphold privacy by severing the link between users and their submitted measurements. However, AnonySense does not provide a robust revocation and data verification mechanism, allowing adversaries to pollute the data collection persistently. Moreover, it does not consider the device and TI privacy. PEPSI [5] employs identity-based encryption to safeguard user privacy as well as TI privacy, but it does not address user location privacy and accountability. Furthermore, PEPSI is vulnerable to collusion attacks from users and TIs [13].

RPPTD [4], a privacy-preserving truth discovery framework without a trusted third party and non-colluding entities, has the users add noise to the sensed measurement before signing them. While the system assumes the existence of ground truth, it does not deal with incentives, user and TI privacy, and accountability. PRICE [29] offers another privacy-preserving truth discovery scheme emphasizing secure and privacy-aware incentivization, but it does not address accountability and anonymity.

Table 1. Features in secure and privacy-preserving MCS architectures. ●: Feature present. ◐: Not fully addressed/considered. ○: Feature missing

Name	Sybil Resilience	Accountability	Data Verification	Enrollment Secrecy	User Privacy	Location Privacy	Device Privacy	Data Privacy	TI Privacy
This Work	●	●	●	●	●	●	●	●	●
SPPEAR [8]	●	●	●	●	●	●	●	●	○
SPOON [18]	○	○	●	○	●	●	◐	●	●
PRICE [29]	○	○	●	○	○	●	○	●	●
ZebraLancer [16]	◐	◐	○	●	●	○	○	●	●
EPTSense [25]	●	●	●	●	●	○	○	●	○
RPPTD [4]	◐	○	◐	○	○	○	○	●	○
PEPSI [5]	○	○	○	○	●	○	●	○	●
AnonySense [23]	○	○	○	●	●	○	◐	○	○

A number of studies use blockchains as service providers for MCS [26,30]. ZebraLancer [16] allows users to participate anonymously in tasks while ensuring data confidentiality and fair incentives. Although it facilitates revocation, it limits users to submit only a single measurement, creating constraints for real-world applications and hardening compatibility with other systems.

SPOON [18] focuses on precise task allocation paired with reputation management while preserving user privacy. Tasks are allocated to users based on their credits (reputation) and location without revealing any. However, the service provider links users to the tasks, and accountability is not considered. Furthermore, users are assumed not to be able to spoof their device locations.

SPPEAR [8,9], in conjunction with SHIELD [10], is a comprehensive S&P MCS architecture in the literature. SPPEAR enables anonymous contribution to the tasks, supports revocation, and fair remuneration. However, it does not consider TI privacy and user control.

The aforementioned works do not consider modularity and user control as design goals for their system. Although regularly addressed in isolated works, TI privacy and enrollment secrecy are usually of secondary importance in works and seldom addressed together with other requirements [5,8,18,23,25].

5   Architecture Overview

In this section, we give an overview of the system entities in Fig. 1 comprising our architecture. Infrastructure entities are modular; they do one thing and satisfy one requirement, autonomous; operate independently, and handle individual requests without any collaboration from other entities, and flexible; they support multiple policies for actors to pick based on their needs, can change over time, and are involved in different ways (e.g., supplying keys to vehicular communication systems). Consequently, the architecture endorses the separation of duties principle [22].

Task Initator (TI) and Task Announcement Channel (TAC): TIs create tasks, and users select the ones that interest them. TAC facilitates the announcement and browsing of various tasks. The publishing process for tasks can take multiple forms: Tasks are either evaluated by the system or another trusted entity before they are published, or they can be published without restrictions, placing the responsibility of evaluation solely on individual users. For enhanced privacy and security, a *task release* procedure is utilized, configuring tasks to be visible only to users satisfying specific preconditions, e.g., users with a specific type of sensor.

Mobile Client: Users interact with the MCS system and contribute to the tasks with a mobile app on their mobile devices. The app enables users to register, select tasks, collect rewards, and participate in tasks. The platform of the mobile client is not only smartphones, as such apps can be utilized by a broad range of devices, e.g., vehicular systems, UAVs, etc.

Registration Manager (RM): RM serves as the initial point of contact between the mobile client and the infrastructure. With two primary responsibilities, the RM registers new users and validates the presence of devices and users entering the system.

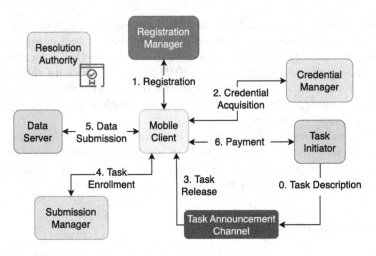

Fig. 1. System model

Credential Manager (CM): Issues and manages long-term credentials (LTCs) for registered participants. CM issues two types of credentials: Anonymous authentication based schemes and public key cryptography (PKC) based primitives. CM also handles credential exchange between external PKIs and identity providers (i.e., Google).

Submission Manager (SM): Tasked with providing users with essential tools and privacy-enhancing technologies (PETs) to submit data in a privacy-preserving manner, most frequently, pseudonyms, digital certificates with anonymized identities. SM can also procure tools required in PETs, i.e., primitives for differential privacy, secure multi-party computation (MPC), etc. SM handles task enrollment requests and, consequently, issues pseudonyms/tools for users.

Data Server (DS): It collects, stores, and aggregates user-collected data. DS also has data verification functionality, sifting the user-submitted data based on the perceived quality and accuracy. Deemed maliciously and wrongly submitted data are excluded and are not included in the task aggregates. DS issues receipts to users upon their data submission.

Resolution Authority (RA): Eviction of users and revocation of their credentials are mediated by the RA. The revocation procedure starts when a user misbehaves and detected by the system entities. The system then revokes the detected users' credentials. The accountability of the potentially compromised or deviant entities is also overseen by the RA.

6   Protocols

The architecture utilizes PKC and attribute-based cryptography (ABC) as protocol building blocks. Each entity has its own key pair and certificate signed by the CM, as well as the public parameters of ABC constructions, to be able to verify attribute-based signatures. Only mobile clients have the attribute-based keys (ABKs) to decrypt task descriptions and authenticate themselves to enroll for tasks. The network connection between entities and clients is secured via server-authenticated transport layer security (TLS). We describe cryptographic preliminaries for protocols before we describe them. Table 2 provides notations and abbreviations.

Table 2. Table of notations

Notation	Description
RM	Registration manager
CM	Credential manager
SM	Submission manager
DS	Data server
TI	Task initiator
RA	Resolution authority
$ABK_{pattern}$	Attribute-based key with *pattern*
t, t_s, t_e	Current, start, and end timestamp
λ	Attribute universe size
l	$User_{id}$ length
n	Number of active tasks
k	Number of IDs in the CRL
$[m]_{pattern}$	Message m encrypted with *pattern*
$\{\cdot\}_{\sigma_{pattern}}, \{\cdot\}_{pattern}$	Signature σ generated with *pattern*
$h(\cdot)$	Hash function
$E_{pattern}(\cdot)$	Encryption function utilizing a *pattern*
$D_k(\cdot)$	Decryption function with key k

6.1   Preliminaries

We utilize ABC as a main form of LTC. We use the JEDI scheme [15] as a building block based on identity-based encryption WKD-IBE [1]. First, we define *patterns*, a λ-sized list of integers and *wildcard* symbols with the following format:

$$pattern = \{P(i); P(i) \in \mathbb{Z}_p^* \cup \{*\}, i \in \{1..\lambda\}\}$$

ABKs, signatures, and ciphertexts have patterns. Patterns play a crucial role in authentication and decryption, facilitated by a 'match' function. We say

$match(pattern_x, pattern_y)$ returns *True* iff $\forall i \in \{1..\lambda\} : (P_x(i) = P_y(i)) \vee$ $(P_x(i) = *)$. The asterisk $(*)$ denotes an optional value in patterns, indicating that the field is capable of matching any value. The optional values can be delegated to be transformed into fixed values, generating a brand-new pattern. Once an optional value is delegated and assigned a specific value, the field becomes final and loses its optional status.

Delegation of patterns gives control to users as it enables them to modify their attributes. Users may use this feature not to disclose some of their existing attributes. In our scheme, we allocate 25 fields specifically for the most common types of sensors typically employed in crowdsensing, i.e., $i = 1$ for Bluetooth, $i = 2$ for GPS, etc. We assign 6 fields to represent the date, time, and week number to specify the ABK validity and facilitate passive revocation. Finally, we designate 64 fields for the $User_{id}$ to aid credential revocation. Owned attributes, such as a microphone, can be proven by generating a signature using those attributes. The patterns reinforce user control, ensure secure task enrollment by matching them with clients' sensory capabilities, establish credential expiration by denoting valid time periods as attributes, and aid in revocation procedures by incorporating $User_{id}$ into the keys.

The utilized functions of the ABC scheme are as follows:

- **setup**(λ): Takes pattern universe size (λ) as input, then initializes and returns the master secret key (msk) and public parameters ($params$).
- **keygen**($msk, params, pattern$): Generates a key $ABK_{pattern}$ with given *pattern* using public parameters and master secret. If the input is another key instead of a msk, a new key, $ABK_{pattern}$, is generated (if the key pattern *matches* the input *pattern*); this is also called key delegation.
- **encrypt**($params, pattern, m$): Encrypts the given message (m) with the *pattern*. Returns the ciphertext as $[m]_{pattern}$. Note that one does not need a key to encrypt a message.
- **decrypt**($ABK_{pattern_u}, [ciphertext]_{pattern}$): Decrypts the ciphertext using the given ABK. $pattern_u$ must *match* the ciphertext pattern for successful decryption.
- **sign**($params, ABK_{pattern_u}, pattern, m$): Generates a signature ($\sigma_{pattern}$) for a message (m) with a specific *pattern*. ABK $pattern_u$ must *match* the signature *pattern*.
- **verify**($params, pattern, \sigma_{pattern}$): Returns true if the signature ($\sigma_{pattern}$) is generated using *pattern*, otherwise false. One does not need an ABK to verify signatures.

6.2   High-Level Overview

We discuss first, in brief, the overall system operations corresponding to Fig. 1, then present in more detail each protocol. Initially, the mobile client registers with the RM, and it undergoes what we term as *Sybil probing* test for verification. Once successfully verified, the RM issues a short-term token to certify the client's sensors and capabilities (Step 1). Using this token, the client acquires an ABK with defined capabilities and a task enrollment ticket from the CM (Step 2). The client then fetches available tasks, decrypts only the ones it can participate in, and picks the desired task (Step 3). The client proves it is capable of carrying out the task by authenticating itself using the ABK and presenting the ticket to enroll in a task. After successful enrollment, the client receives pseudonyms from SM (Step 4). Finally, the client collects measurements and submits data, signing it with a private key corresponding to a pseudonym and receiving a receipt as proof of submission (Step 5). This receipt is then used to request payments from the TI (Step 6).

6.3   Device Registration

The registration manager is the first point of contact between mobile clients and the S&P MCS architecture every time they want to use the system. Its responsibilities encompass user management and coordinating the *Sybil-probing* process.

The purpose of *Sybil-probing* is two-fold: Determining the mobile client's sensory capabilities and safeguarding the system against Sybil devices. The mobile application gathers information about the device's capabilities while simultaneously validating its functioning. The app does not collect unique identifiers associated with the device but rather performs sanity checks [2], detecting the potential sensors that will be utilized by the client. The sensor condition can be established through various steps, including collecting sample data, validating calibration information, and analyzing diagnostic data. It is important to note that only the sensor condition, which involves the presence and capabilities of the sensor, is shared with the RM. No private data pertaining to the device is disclosed. Subsequently, $User_{id}$, condition of the sensors, validity period, token's scope, and a random number, r, are then bundled together and signed by RM to create a short-term token. We define the token format as follows

$$token = \{User_{id}, t_s, t_e, scope, sensors, r\}_{\sigma_{RM}}$$

The scope can be *ABK* for acquiring ABK, *ticket* for using the token as a *task-joining ticket*, and *authenticate* for utilizing the token as a system-wide credential. Specifically, an *ABK* token is used for authenticating the client to the CM, with a short validity period. Once verified, the CM issues an ABK for sensors defined in the token field *sensors*. Only one *ABK* token can be active at any given time per client. The *authenticate* token provides access and authentication for system operations, e.g., obtain pseudonyms, make contributions, etc., allowing clients to engage with different parts of the system without specialized cryptography, which may be crucial for some types of clients (i.e., low-power devices).

The issued tokens are in OAuth2 format [19], the industry-standard framework enabling parties to authenticate to third parties without using user credentials. OAuth2 enables compatibility with existing services and makes adoption easier with external parties easier. Sybil-probing occurs every time a user starts the mobile client and also periodically to verify the client is an actual device.

484   C. Eryonucu and P. Papadimitratos

6.4 Credential Acquisition

The CM is tasked to issue Long-term credentials (LTCs) and task-joining tickets. LTCs are typically issued as ABKs but can be issued as ordinary digital certificates as well. We utilize tickets to enable revocation and regulate access to the tasks. Depending on the use case, both may have extended validity periods, e.g., lasting several days to weeks, compared to tokens issued by the RM.

With an ABK token from the RM, a mobile client can request an ABK. The token, encoded with a sensor list and $User_{id}$, becomes the blueprint for creating the key's pattern. Each sensor field value represents the version number of the corresponding sensor. For instance, if a client possesses Bluetooth 5.1, this would be represented as $P(1) = 51$. If the client does not have a particular sensor, the value for that field is assigned as 0.

The CM has the authority to define the key's validity period, allowing users to utilize the key over an extended timeframe. This flexibility can be demonstrated by, e.g., leaving the key's pattern's day field as optional, ensuring the key remains valid for an entire month. Alternatively, the week number field can be employed to extend the key's validity to span a full week. Finally, the $User_{id}$ fields are set in binary format.

We utilize task-joining tickets as the building block of the revocation process. This is facilitated through the use of authenticated tickets, which securely link clients to their pseudonyms while maintaining their anonymity. The ticket structure is defined as follows:

$$ticket = \{h(User_{id}, t_s, t_e, r), (t_s, t_e)\}_{\sigma_{CM}}$$

The user ID remains confidential as it is hashed together with a random number and the ticket's start and end times. This obfuscates the user's identity while still allowing the CM to disclose it when necessary. The CM dispenses tickets to clients, provided they haven't exceeded the permitted number of tasks. Tickets can be provisioned ahead of time for later usage to enhance user control. One can also utilize tokens with a *ticket* scope instead of tickets.

6.5 Task Release and Enrollment

The system stores task definitions in the task channel. Depending on the TI policies, tasks can be encrypted using their specific policies (patterns) or can be in plaintext. Clients without the capabilities for a particular task cannot decrypt or authenticate with the patterns defined in their ABK, so they can neither access the definitions nor participate in those tasks. We outline the *task release* protocol as follows:

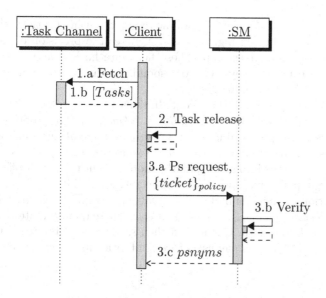

Step 1. The client retrieves encrypted tasks and their associated patterns from the task announcement channel. The client refrains from querying tasks with its preferences as it would reveal its attributes. The TAC returns encrypted tasks bundled with their policies, $[Tasks] = \{[task_i]_{policy_i}; i \in \{1..n\}\}$.

Step 2. The client decrypts all suitable tasks with its ABK whilst disregarding tasks with incompatible patterns. More formally, the client operation can be denoted as $Client : D_{ABK_u}([task_i])$ if $match(ABK_u, policy_i)$ for all $i \in \{1..n\}$. Upon selecting a task to join, the client generates key pairs for the subsequent certificate signing requests (CSRs), with the number and lifetime set as per the task specifics.

Step 3. Upon selecting a task to join, the client generates key pairs for the subsequent certificate signing requests (CSRs), with the number and lifetime set as per the task specifics. The client sends a request for pseudonyms, coupled with the signed task-joining ticket and CSRs. The ticket is signed with the task's policy, validating the client's capability to join the task, while the ticket anonymously binds the client to pseudonyms. CM verifies whether the signature pattern matches the task policy and whether the ticket is authenticated and valid. After the verification, the CM issues and returns pseudonyms to the client.

In step 3.a, the mobile client can also utilize a token with a *ticket* scope to authenticate itself. If the task has a sensory requirement, the token should also encapsulate the sensors. Tokens provide an alternative authentication means for clients, enhancing user control and at the cost of their privacy.

6.6   Data Submission and Remuneration

The mobile client contributes to the tasks by leveraging pseudonyms or tokens. We define each sample authenticated by pseudonym as $s =$

$\{data, loc, radius, t\}_{\sigma_{ps_i}}$, where $data$ represents the required sensing for the task, loc signifies the location of the sensing, $radius$ designates the precision of the position, and t stands for the timestamp. These fields are hashed and subsequently signed using the private key that corresponds to the pseudonym ps_i. Using pseudonyms provides maximum privacy.

Clients can alternatively submit their contributions using a token with a "submit" scope is denoted as $s = \{data, loc, radius, t, token_{\sigma_{RM}}\}$. This approach circumvents the necessity of performing any cryptographic operations, such as generating signatures, on the mobile client, as the tokens are authenticated by the RM. Although using tokens impinges upon the mobile client privacy, it offers better performance, compatibility, and, more importantly, flexibility.

After the verification of the submission, DS creates a receipt for the mobile client formalized as $receipt = \{ID_{receipt}, quality, t\}_{\sigma_{DS}}$ where quality states the assessment of the contributed data. Clients can then send the receipts to TI to redeem them. Alternatively, TI can pay users through forwarding payments over the infrastructure.

6.7   User Revocation

Our architecture revokes the credentials of misbehaving any client (i.e., contributing incorrect measurements to corrupt the collected data), irrespective of the type of credentials they use. Misbehavior detection schemes [10,17], designed specifically for the PS, can be employed to identify such attacks[2]. The inclusion of ABC contributes to the integration of data verification and truth discovery schemes.

Revocation can be tailored to the system needs and can take several forms, ranging from barring clients from a single task to expulsion from MCS. Our architecture allows the revocation of all issued credentials, with the exact revocation strategies being left to the discretion of the system operators.

Upon detection of misbehavior, the RA is alerted to initiate the process. The revocation request includes the malicious client credentials, a pseudonym set, or a token. This is then forwarded to the issuing entity to pinpoint the misbehaving user. The identification process is straightforward if the data submission involves a token, as the $User_{id}$ is tied to the token. For submissions with pseudonyms, the RA consults the SM to obtain the ticket used during the task enrollment. This request also prompts the SM to revoke any remaining pseudonyms linked to the user. This ticket is sent to CM to resolve the $User_{id}$. Finally, CM adds the $User_{id}$ to the credential revocation list (CRL) and informs RM to halt any further credential issuance.

Revoked credentials can no longer be used. This is apparent in the case of revoked tokens, which include the bearer's ID, allowing the verifier to compare the ID with the CRL directly. However, with ABK signatures being anonymous,

---

[2] The construction of these misbehavior detection methods is beyond the scope of this work and therefore is not discussed here.

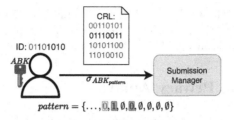

Fig. 2. A client proving it is not revoked. Each colored bit in the signature pattern affirms the user is not on the CRL

a mechanism is required to enable entities to verify whether the signer credentials were revoked.

To demonstrate their credentials are still valid, clients disclose a number of bits of their $User_{id}$, an *unrevoked subset*, to the authentication pattern before signature generation. Given that every $User_{id}$ is unique, if a user is not listed on the CRL, then at least one bit differs from any ID on the list. Revoked clients cannot find such a bit or subset and thus cannot authenticate.

We provide an illustration of the authentication process depicted in Fig. 2. For simplicity, we assume $User_{id}$ is 8-bits long, and four IDs are listed on the CRL. The client examines the CRL to assemble its *unrevoked subset*. The first bit, shaded in red, eliminates the last two entries, also colored red, from the list. The bit colored in green eliminates the top entry, and the blue bit effectively cancels out the remaining entry. Note that the revealed patterns ultimately leak information about the $User_{id}$. The extent of the leakage depends on the ID length, number of revoked IDs in the CRL, and *unrevoked subset* construction. We further explore these relationships in Sect. 8.

We design two primary strategies to devise *unrevoked subsets*: random and greedy bit selection methods. The random method randomly selects $User_{id}$ indices in each iteration, adding them to the subset if they eliminate any $User_{id}$. Then, it updates the list, eliminating the IDs in CRL based on the last added bit, and proceeds to the next iteration until no IDs are left in CRL. However, there is a chance that the method might choose an index that does not eliminate any IDs, exemplified by the 3rd bit of the $User_{id}$ in Fig. 2, and it may not always yield the optimal subset.

We can employ a greedy method to find the least revealing subset. In this method, the client selects the bit that results in the highest ID elimination from the CRL until all IDs are eliminated. The selection process involves identifying the index i that $\min_{i \in \{1..l\}} f_i(ID(i))$ where $f_i(bit)$ finds the frequency (occurrence) of the bit in index i of the CRL and $ID(i)$ returns the $User_{id}$ for the index i. However, there is a drawback with performance as the entire CRL, involving l columns and k rows, is scanned to find the index, remove it, and repeat for the reduced CRL. On average, every selected bit halves the IDs in the CRL. Only the residual list is examined for subsequent iterations, making a logarithmic growth rate and expected subset size of random method $O(log k)$

with k representing the CRL size. The greedy method examines all indices (l columns) in every iteration, resulting in a $O(l * logk)$ complexity. For small-sized lists, revealing a single bit could be sufficient for the subset.

7 Security and Privacy Analysis

We informally analyze how the proposed protocols and architecture achieve the defined requirements. Note that the collusions between entities do not break the requirements; e.g., if some parties need to collude to break an actor's privacy, we still consider the requirement as addressed.

User identities are shared only with the RM during the initial registration, and then the user is assigned to its system ID, i.e. $User_{id}$. The RM only knows about this binding. The $User_{id}$ is revealed only to CM when obtaining tickets and ABKs. Apart from this, the CM does not know anything about the client and its actions.

Clients authenticate anonymously via attribute-based signatures, preventing the SM from linking pseudonym requests revealing a small subset of their IDs during authentication. Further, the presented ticket has its $User_{id}$ masked. All in all, the SM does not know which client requested the pseudonyms for a specific task, nor can it link any two requests to a client. Lastly, the CM issues the tickets without any task information, so task privacy is protected.

Table 3. Colluding entities and their combined intelligence

Entities	Information Exposure	Possible Ramifications (if any)
RM	$User_{id}$	The RM knows the user is registered with id
CM	$sensors$, $User_{id}$	The CM infer that $User_{id}$ has the $sensors$
SM	$psnyms$, $Task_{id}$, $ticket$	The SM infer that an anonymous user has pseudonyms for the $Task_{id}$
DS	s, $receipt$ $psnyms$, $Task_{id}$	The DS know that submissions come from some user for a specific task
RM, CM	$sensors$, $User_{id}$	No new information gained by this collusion
RM, SM	$User_{id}$, $psnyms$ $Task_{id}$, $ticket$	The RM and the SM cannot link any credential with $User_{id}$
RM, DS	$User_{id}$, s, $receipt$ $psnyms$, $Task_{id}$	$User_{id}$ do not have any connection to the pseudonyms, submissions, and receipts
CM, SM	$psnyms$, $Task_{id}$, $ticket$ $sensors$, $User_{id}$	The entities can learn $User_{id}$ with $sensors$ obtained pseudonyms for a task
CM, DS	$User_{id}$, s, $receipt$ $psnyms$, $Task_{id}$	There are no ways to link $User_{id}$ with the $psnyms$
SM, DS	$psnyms$, $Task_{id}$, $ticket$ s, $receipt$	They can infer and track the submissions made by an anonymous user
CM, SM, DS	all	Entities can identify a $User_{id}$'s task participation history and submissions

Mobile clients use pseudonyms for data submission, ideally fresh for each submission. Using the same pseudonym for multiple data submissions allows a curious DS to trivially link the submissions. Issued credentials (tickets, tokens, ABKs, pseudonyms) have non-overlapping validity times to prevent Sybil-based attacks. This limits data submission to one per client at any given time. Unless clients abandon their anonymity by using tokens, making it trivially detectable if they misbehave.

Device identifiers are validated locally on the client devices and are never collected by any entity. Network identifiers can be hidden by the utilization of the TOR network. Tasks can be encrypted to block unwanted parties from seeing the task details. TI identity is only known to the RM at the time of registration. Task creation is done through the TAC using tokens with one-time user IDs **(R1)**.

Receipts are signed by the DS, making it impossible for malicious users to forge them. Furthermore, no receipts can be used twice - they are consumed when used **(R2)**. Communication among any entity is over server-authenticated TLS, except while using pseudonyms during the data submission, thus achieving communication authenticity, integrity, and confidentiality **(R3)**.

Scopes defined on the issued tokens denote the access rights of the clients. Only the CM can generate ABKs with patterns. The task selection will always be limited to the defined sensors on ABK because clients cannot see or join tasks that require sensors they don't have. Tickets provide authorization for participation in tasks **(R4)**.

Data verification schemes deserve their own independent inquiries, so we do not design a new data verification scheme for this work. However, we make our system to be compatible and integrable with such schemes like [10] and utilize them **(R5)**.

The RA resolves any suspected misbehaviors and, if found guilty, initiates the revocation process. Evicted users are prevented from doing any operation within the system since their credentials are revoked, and they cannot get new credentials **(R6)**.

Table 3 provides insight into what MCS colluding entities infer about the users and the implications. No pair of colluding entities can completely deanonymize users. Moreover, the majority of the two-entity collusions do not result in new information leaks compared to their non-colluding states. The only time the system learns everything about the users is when CM, SM, and DS collude. Any other combination of three entities cannot achieve complete de-anonymization. Some of the entities can be run by the same organizations, given there are no privacy/security conflicts. For example, a TI can also employ its own DS with adjustments to the remuneration process, as users should be remunerated. The collaboration of CM, SM, and DS is needed for complete revocation. By adhering to the principle of separation of duties, a system of checks and balances needs to be in place to detect and handle any misbehavior.

8   Implementation and Evaluation

We implemented system entities in JavaScript and Python and developed a
mobile client app for Android devices. We use OpenSSL for cryptographic operations, i.e., to generate ECDSA key pairs for entity digital certificates and
pseudonyms. We implemented a wrapper library for ABC to utilize the core
JEDI pairing library [15] in the mobile environment. We conduct experiments
on smartphones in Xiaomi Redmi 9, released in 2020, an entry-level device with
modest resources, and we host our server entities in an HP Z440 workstation with
96 GB of RAM. All the plotted values are averaged over 200 measurements and
fall within a 95% confidence interval, but we do not show the intervals because
the intervals are too tight (i.e., interval sizes are in the orders of microseconds).

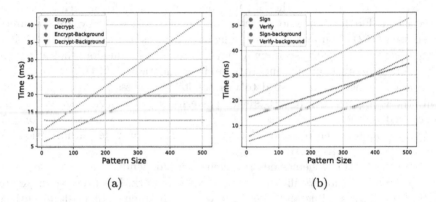

Fig. 3. Impact of pattern size over cryptographic operation latency.

We experiment with protocols using ABC, i.e., task encryption, release, and
enrollment. We wish to understand how the ABC affects the protocols and how it
scales with larger pattern sizes. We additionally investigate how these operations
perform in the background, i.e., when the phone is locked. Figure 3a shows the
execution times for encryption and decryption, averaged over 200 measurements
with an increasing number of patterns. Realistically, tasks are encrypted with
patterns less than size 15, as they only need the required sensors and validity
time. We see that a larger pattern size increases the encryption time; still, the
operation is highly efficient in a mobile environment, even in the background.
Encryption is a rare operation, only used when TAC requires task details from
TIs. Comparatively, decryption is a frequent operation; all suitable tasks are
decrypted by mobile clients when they want to access the tasks. The number
of active tasks at a given time, thus the number of decryptions, varies, but the
decryption time (latency) is low, allowing for many descriptions in a short time,
e.g., 50 task descriptions per second on the background power. This is further
reinforced by the fact that decryption times are unaffected by the pattern size
on the ciphertext, as seen in Fig. 3a.

Figure 3b illustrates the signature generation and verification performance, with varying numbers of patterns. Execution time grows linearly with larger patterns. We can see that the *sign* operation is cheaper than *verify*. This is advantageous for mobile clients, which are usually resource-constrained compared to the server. When in the background, both operations take 1.5 times longer but still grow linearly. Nevertheless, they perform comparably to widely employed PKC schemes [24] and create no major performance issues in the mobile environment.

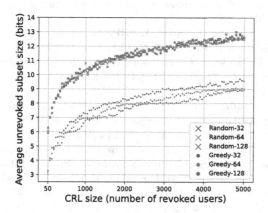

Fig. 4. Impact of CRL size on the number of revealed bits during authentication.

We assess the privacy exposure of the *unrevoked subset* during the task enrollment process. An increase in the number of clients in the CRL requires more bits to validate the IDs's absence in the CRL. We investigate the effect on the number of disclosed bits, considering varying $User_{id}$ bit lengths, for both bit selection methods in Fig. 4. Both method's effect on privacy exposure exhibits a logarithmic trend with respect to the CRL size. The greedy bit selection method discloses 30% fewer bits than the random method. It is noteworthy that the $User_{id}$ length, l, does not influence the random selection method as the unrevoked subset is considerably smaller than l. However, for the greedy method, the larger l means more indices to look for the optimal index, which can yield better results.

9   Conclusion

We presented an S&P MCS architecture focusing on relatively overlooked design goals of TI privacy, user control, and relevance. We brought attention to modularity and interoperability for the MCS architecture entities focusing on their autonomy, flexibility, and usability as a fresh design goal. We evaluated how we addressed the discussed requirements and made experiments to demonstrate the efficiency and practicality of the proposed protocols. Future research directions can include experimentation on tokens, formal analysis, rigid sybil-probing, alternative data submission policies, and security/privacy exposure labels.

References

1. Abdalla, M., Kiltz, E., Neven, G.: Generalized key delegation for hierarchical identity-based encryption. Cryptology ePrint Archive, Paper 2007/221 (2007)
2. Borsub, J., Papadimitratos, P.: Hardened registration process for participatory sensing. In: Proceedings of the 11th ACM Conference on Security & Privacy in Wireless and Mobile Networks. Association for Computing Machinery (2018)
3. Brown, A., Franken, P., Bonner, S., Dolezal, N., Moross, J.: Safecast: successful citizen-science for radiation measurement and communication after Fukushima. J. Radiol. Prot. **36**(2), S82–S101 (2016)
4. Chen, J., Liu, Y., Xiang, Y., Sood, K.: RPPTD: robust privacy-preserving truth discovery scheme. IEEE Syst. J. **16**(3), 4525–4531 (2022)
5. De Cristofaro, E., Soriente, C.: Extended capabilities for a privacy-enhanced participatory sensing infrastructure (PEPSI). IEEE Trans. Inf. Forensics Secur. **8**(12), 2021–2033 (2013)
6. Eryonucu, C., Papadimitratos, P.: Sybil-based attacks on google maps or how to forge the image of city life. In: Proceedings of the 15th ACM Conference on Security and Privacy in Wireless and Mobile Networks (2022)
7. Giannetsos, T., Gisdakis, S., Papadimitratos, P.: Trustworthy people-centric sensing: privacy, security and user incentives road-map. In: 2014 13th Annual Mediterranean Ad Hoc Networking Workshop (MED-HOC-NET) (2014)
8. Gisdakis, S., Giannetsos, T., Papadimitratos, P.: Security, privacy, and incentive provision for mobile crowd sensing systems. IEEE Internet Things J. **3**(5), 839–853 (2016)
9. Gisdakis, S., Giannetsos, T., Papadimitratos, P.: SPPEAR: security and privacy-preserving architecture for participatory-sensing applications. In: ACM Conference on Security and Privacy in Wireless and Mobile Networks (ACM WiSec) (2014)
10. Gisdakis, S., Giannetsos, T., Papadimitratos, P.: SHIELD: a data verification framework for participatory sensing systems. In: ACM Conference on Security & Privacy in Wireless and Mobile Networks (ACM WiSec) (2015)
11. Google: Popular times, wait times, and visit duration. https://support.google.com/business/answer/6263531. Accessed 19 June 2013
12. Grubeša, S., Petošić, A., Suhanek, M., Durek, I.: Mobile crowdsensing accuracy for noise mapping in smart cities. Automatika (2018)
13. Günther, F., Manulis, M., Peter, A.: Privacy-enhanced participatory sensing with collusion resistance and data aggregation. In: Gritzalis, D., Kiayias, A., Askoxylakis, I. (eds.) CANS 2014. LNCS, vol. 8813, pp. 321–336. Springer, Cham (2014). https://doi.org/10.1007/978-3-319-12280-9_21
14. Help, W.: How does waze work? https://support.google.com/waze/answer/6078702. Accessed 17 June 2023
15. Kumar, S., Hu, Y., Andersen, M.P., Popa, R.A., Culler, D.E.: JEDI: many-to-many end-to-end encryption and key delegation for IoT. In: 28th USENIX Security Symposium (USENIX Security 2019). USENIX Association (2019)
16. Lu, Y., Tang, Q., Wang, G.: ZebraLancer: private and anonymous crowdsourcing system atop open blockchain. In: 2018 IEEE 38th International Conference on Distributed Computing Systems (ICDCS) (2018)
17. Luo, T., Huang, J., Kanhere, S.S., Zhang, J., Das, S.K.: Improving IoT data quality in mobile crowd sensing: a cross validation approach. IEEE Internet Things J. **6**(3), 5651–5664 (2019)

18. Ni, J., Zhang, K., Xia, Q., Lin, X., Shen, X.S.: Enabling strong privacy preservation and accurate task allocation for mobile crowdsensing. IEEE Trans. Mob. Comput. 19(6), 1317–1331 (2020)
19. OAuth2: Oauth2 access tokens. https://oauth.net/2/
20. Pournajaf, L., Garcia-Ulloa, D.A., Xiong, L., Sunderam, V.: Participant privacy in mobile crowd sensing task management: a survey of methods and challenges. ACM SIGMOD Rec. 44, 23–34 (2016)
21. Restuccia, F., Ferraro, P., Sanders, T.S., Silvestri, S., Das, S.K., Re, G.L.: FIRST: a framework for optimizing information quality in mobile crowdsensing systems. ACM Trans. Sens. Netw. (TOSN) 15(1), 1–35 (2018)
22. Saltzer, J.H., Schroeder, M.D.: The protection of information in computer systems. Proc. IEEE 63(9), 1278–1308 (1975)
23. Shin, M., Cornelius, C., Peebles, D., Kapadia, A., Kotz, D., Triandopoulos, N.: AnonySense: a system for anonymous opportunistic sensing. Pervasive Mob. Comput. 7, 16–30 (2011)
24. Tschofenig, H., Pegourie-Gonnard, M.: Performance of state-of-the-art cryptography on arm-based microprocessors. In: NIST Lightweight Cryptography Workshop, vol. 2015 (2015)
25. Wu, H., Wang, L., Xue, G., Tang, J., Yang, D.: Enabling data trustworthiness and user privacy in mobile crowdsensing. IEEE/ACM Trans. Networking 27(6), 2294–2307 (2019)
26. Wu, H.T., Zheng, Y., Zhao, B., Hu, J.: An anonymous reputation management system for mobile crowdsensing based on dual blockchain. IEEE Internet Things J. 9(9), 6956–6968 (2022)
27. Yan, X., Zeng, B., Zhang, X.: Privacy-preserving and customization-supported data aggregation in mobile crowdsensing. IEEE Internet Things J. 9(20), 19868–19880 (2022)
28. Zhang, X., Lu, R., Ray, S., Shao, J., Ghorbani, A.A.: Spatio-temporal similarity based privacy-preserving worker selection in mobile crowdsensing. In: 2021 IEEE Global Communications Conference (GLOBECOM) (2021)
29. Zhao, B., Liu, X., Chen, W.N., Liang, W., Zhang, X., Deng, R.H.: PRICE: privacy and reliability-aware real-time incentive system for crowdsensing. IEEE Internet Things J. 8(24), 17584–17595 (2021)
30. Zou, S., Xi, J., Xu, G., Zhang, M., Lu, Y.: CrowdHB: a decentralized location privacy-preserving crowdsensing system based on a hybrid blockchain network. IEEE Internet Things J. 9(16), 14803–14817 (2022)

Review on Privacy and Trust Methodologies in Cloud Computing

Stavros Simou$^{(\boxtimes)}$ ⓘ, Aikaterini-Georgia Mavroeidi ⓘ, and Christos Kalloniatis ⓘ

Privacy Engineering and Social Informatics Laboratory, Department of Cultural Technology and Communication, University of the Aegean, University Hill, 81100 Mytilene, GR, Greece
{ssimou,kmav,chkallon}@aegean.gr

Abstract. The vast adoption of cloud computing has led to a new content in relation to privacy and security. Personal information is no longer as safe as we think and can be altered. In addition, Cloud Service Providers (CSPs) are still looking for new ways to raise the level of trust in order to gain popularity and increase their number of users. In this paper, a systematic literature review was carried out to identify the different methodologies, models and frameworks regarding privacy engineering and trust in cloud computing. A detailed review is produced on the specific area to bring forward all the work that has been carried out the recent years using a methodology with a number of different steps and criteria. Based on the findings from the literature review, we present the state-of-the-art on privacy and trust methodologies in cloud computing and we discuss the existing conventional tools that can assist software designers and developers.

Keywords: Privacy · Trust · Methodologies · Privacy Requirements Engineering Methods · Cloud Computing

1 Introduction

After a hesitant and uncertain start, cloud computing has prevailed over the completion in Information Technology (IT) and became dominant in the field. Although there are certain issues concerning users' privacy and security, due to its transformational nature, cloud computing continues to expand and has been accelerated especially in the pandemic according to Flexera report [1]. The same report highlights the role of cloud computing in the competition and its importance on the ways an organization approaches its cloud strategy.

Cloud computing dominant utilization poses new challenges for both providers and consumers, especially as far as privacy protection is concerned [2]. Users' privacy is of vital importance and the cloud vendor should provide all the necessary actions to warrant that no personal information will alter or leak. Despite the success of cloud technology, vendors still cannot provide transparency to users so that the users be able to know where their data resides, how it is managed and who has access to it, at all times. Razaque et al. [3], agrees that in order to build trust between users and cloud computing, Cloud Service Providers (CSPs) should find ways to preserve data privacy at all times. Several scandals

© The Author(s), under exclusive license to Springer Nature Switzerland AG 2024
S. Katsikas et al. (Eds.): ESORICS 2023 Workshops, LNCS 14398, pp. 494–505, 2024.
https://doi.org/10.1007/978-3-031-54204-6_29

concerning stolen or misused data have been revealed, resulting in the users losing their trust in who they allow to handle their data [4].

The past years a number of researchers focused on finding solutions regarding on one hand the privacy in the cloud and on the other hand, to establish trust between users and companies/providers, among others. Several reviews have already been published regarding privacy requirements methods and trust methods [5–7]. Trust and privacy are two interdependent concepts, as by protecting users' privacy, trust is increased. So, a review which connects both methodologies is needed. Within this paper, a literature review is taking place regarding privacy engineering methodologies and users' trust in cloud computing. A detailed review is produced, based on the review of the area in order to bring forward all the work that has been carried out both in privacy engineering methodologies and users' trust. In addition, this research introduces the privacy engineering methods used for the analysis and elicitation of privacy requirements. Various privacy engineering methodologies have been proposed aiming to support software developers at the early stages of system design.

The remainder of the paper is as follows: Sect. 2 describes the literature review methodology (e.g., search method, keywords, exclusion, and inclusion criteria). In Sects. 3 and 4, a presentation of the existing privacy engineering and trust methodologies in cloud environments is performed while in Sect. 5 a discussion on the findings of the study is presented. Finally, the conclusion of the study is expressed in Sect. 6.

2 Methodology

In order to produce this literature review, a number of different steps were followed. Since there are two areas (privacy and trust methodologies) with different content, the keywords used in the search were divided into two different categories. In this case, two literature reviews were conducted, the first one concerns privacy methods and the second one trust methods. Studies which are written in English were searched in Google Scholar, Scopus, IEEExplore, ACM Digital library and Google.

Two main research questions were addressed. The aim of the first research question is to find which privacy engineering methodologies have been published and which steps have been recorded. The aim of the second research question is to record all trust methodologies and their phases. The search was applied to the titles, abstracts, and keywords of studies to be sure that each study will be appropriate for this research. The document type for both reviews was selected to be "conference papers", "journals", "workshop papers" and "chapters" while the publication stage was "final". The search strategy is presented in Table 1. Due to the large number of results, it was needed to define inclusion and exclusion criteria, as presented in Table 2.

The first keywords were used to search for results in the databases for the privacy methodologies, while the second keywords for the trust methodologies in relation to privacy. Regarding privacy engineering methods, the search string used to collect studies, was constructed using the Boolean OR and the Boolean AND, namely the search terms "privacy requirements engineering" OR "privacy requirements methods" OR "privacy frameworks" OR "privacy approaches" AND "cloud computing", were used. The search was limited to the last twenty years. The search results returned 220 papers, and after

Table 1. Search strategy

Academic databases searched	IEEExplore Scopus ACM Digital library
Other data sources	Google (including google scholar)
Target items	Journals papers Workshop papers Conference papers Chapters
Search applied to	Titles Abstracts Keywords
Language	English
Publication period	From 2000 until today (privacy methods) From 2011 until today (trust methods)

Table 2. Inclusion and exclusion criteria

Eligibility criteria	
Inclusion criteria	Academic journal, conference, workshop, chapter papers which include privacy engineering methodologies and trust methodologies Studies which include steps regarding methods Papers written in English Publication date: since 2011
Exclusion criteria	Duplicates Studies without steps Studies whose full text is not accessible Papers available only in the form of abstracts Short papers Posters

excluding duplicates, studies whose full texts were not accessible, short papers, posters, and papers in the form of abstracts 79 were screened. After reading all these, we came up to 11 papers.

Regarding trust methods, the search string used to collect studies, was also constructed using the Boolean OR and the Boolean AND, namely the search terms "trust methods" OR "trust frameworks" OR "trust approaches" AND "cloud computing" AND "privacy" were used. The searching process was limited to the last years (since 2011) and the language to English. Regarding the second research questions, the search results returned 712 papers. The next stage was to exclude all duplications, not accessible, short papers and posters. From this process, 46 articles were included. The last stage was to exclude all the irrelevant articles by reading them. The remaining papers that meet the criteria in relation to trust methodologies and privacy were 12. According to the results, most of the methodologies have been published during the last ten years. It is important to note that methods regarding trust, were started to be published in 2012. In Fig. 1, the publication date of all methods is presented.

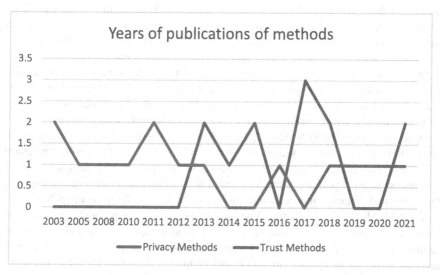

Fig. 1. Privacy and trust methods-publication per year

3 Privacy Requirements Engineering Methods

The consideration of privacy as part of a system's development process is an important aspect towards the development of privacy-aware systems. A number of privacy engineering methods have been developed in order to support privacy requirements elicitation for various software systems.

In [8], LINDDUN, a privacy threat analysis framework, has been described for the elicitation and fulfillment of privacy requirements. LINDDUN first step concerns the design of a data flow diagram and the identification of threats. As authors mention, there are seven types of threats, Linkability, Identifiability, Non-repudiation, Detectability, Information Disclosure, Content Unawareness, Policy, and consent Noncompliance. For the collection of threat scenarios of the system, threat trees and misuse cases are implemented. Developers are supported for the selection of the appropriate techniques for the satisfaction of privacy requirements through privacy-enhancing technologies (PET's).

The method SQUARE for privacy [9] is an extension of the SQUARE methodology [10]. The first approach concerns security requirements, while in SQUARE for privacy also the elicitation and prioritization of privacy requirements is presented. The same steps are used in conjunction with the Privacy Requirements Elicitation Technique (PRET tool) [11], which uses a database of privacy requirements based on privacy laws and regulations. According to Kalloniatis et al. [12], PriS method is a goal-oriented app-roach. PriS considers privacy requirements as organizational goals. This method uses privacy-process patterns to describe the affected organisational processes by the privacy goals. Additionally, the aim is to model organisational processes regarding privacy and to support the selection of the most appropriate techniques and architectures for the sat-isfaction of these processes. In this method, for the identification of privacy goals eight privacy concepts have to be considered, i.e., authentication, authorization, identification, data protection, anonymity, pseudonymity, unlinkability and unobservability. A formal case tool has been developed for the implementation of this method [13].

In [14], a model-based approach which considers privacy and security require-ments has been presented. Specifically, two engineering methods were integrated and Secure Tropos with PriS was developed. Secure Tropos aim is the identification of secu-rity requirements. While privacy concepts are also important, Secure Tropos has been extended by introducing PriS method. Thus, security and privacy requirements are con-sidered in parallel at the early stages of system development [15]. The RBAC framework [16] is an agent-oriented framework. The aim is linking privacy requirements and low-level access control policies. Authors present how to model privacy requirements as constraints and contexts of permissions and users' roles in order to define policies.

The STRAP [17] model is based on a structure analysis of privacy vulnerabilities. It is a goal-oriented approach, and the aim is to support developers to identify privacy requirements during development processes. This method includes four steps, namely, Analysis, Refinement, Evaluation, and Iteration. In [18], i* method is presented which focuses on analyzing, modeling and designing the organisation's processes at the early stages of system design. The target of this method is to design a model which captures all the involved actors and their dependencies. A case tool has been developed for this method, called Organisation Modelling Environment (OME) [19].

An interesting approach was published in 2019, where the aim is to support users to identify the privacy requirements in a software system [20]. The recommender-based privacy requirements elicitation approach EPICUREAN includes modelling and data mining techniques to recommend privacy settings to users and describes three phases, Preparation, Training, Application. The Privacy Criteria Method and the PCM tool [21] support agile software developers to elicit privacy requirements. This method can be used with any requirements specification technique. The PCM tool includes eight steps, i.e., Basic Information Specification, Actors Specification, Trust Relation of Actors Spec-ification, Personal Information Specification, Purpose of Task Context Specification, Privacy Constraint Specification, Risk Scenario Specification, Privacy Mechanism(s) Specification.

In [22], P-RAMS framework is presented for smart-grid-specific privacy require-ments, which extends previous privacy requirements engineering approaches. Authors present a threat tree analysis, which delivers a classification of privacy specific threats. In [23], a Core Ontology for Privacy requirements engineering (COPri) was presented. The aim is to support software developers by providing privacy concepts during the elic-itation of privacy requirements. It includes five main phases, namely, scope & objective identification, Knowledge acquisition, Conceptualization, Implementation, Validation. In 2021, COPri v.2 [24] was proposed which has been extended based on the feedback received from privacy and security experts. Specifically, authors extended the analysis support and the implementation and validation steps.

4 Trust Methodologies

Since the beginning of the cloud computing introduction, users are seeking solutions to keep their data safe and built a level of trust with the ones who host and handle their data. This is a difficult task since it involves different aspects and entities. Nevertheless, many researchers proposed their works and developed trust mechanisms in the cloud. In this section, the trust methodologies, and models, identified in the literature review, are discussed. In order to find recent methodologies and up-to-dated, the years included were dated back to 2011.

In 2013, Wu proposed [25] a trust evaluation model based on the theory of belief functions, also referred Dempster–Shafer evidence theory (D-S) and sliding windows for cloud computing. According to their theory, there is a dynamic form of the interaction evidence, and the trust evaluation involves and depends on interaction between the Cloud Service Provider (CSP) and the Cloud User (CU). The model is simple in execution while the extensibility of the system is improved by allowing only valid interactions to affect the trust degree of entities. The experimental evaluation shows that the success interaction rate of the system is increased due to the identification of the malicious entities and the service provision refusal [25]. The same year Huang categorizes the trust mechanisms for cloud computing in five different categories: reputation based, SLA verification based, transparency mechanisms, trust as a service, and formal accreditation, audit and standards [26]. They developed an informal and abstract framework for analyzing and modeling trust in cloud. A policy-based trust mechanism is used to trust the provider or the service, whenever it conforms to a trusted policy and a presentation of a general structure of evidence-based trust is produced as evidence for trust judgment to support the mechanism.

The following year, the privacy monitoring framework for enhancing transparency in cloud computing [27] is presented by Shabalala. The framework facilitates compliance with privacy laws, regulations and standards, it provides the mechanism that catches the events and alerts the user, and it prevents unauthorized users from accessing confidential data by encrypting data in transit and at rest. It uses an information events and access logs analyzer component to enable user to build a detailed timeline of past events, in relation to its data (where it is stored, who has access, how to protect). The component monitors the operation carried out on the outsourced data. The experimental results show that the framework is easy to use, it provides transparency on how the data is always handled and user awareness [27]. Although the framework could be included in the previous section (Sect. 3), we decided to integrate it in this section since the transparency is a basic ingredient of the trust.

Salih and Lilien, in 2015, proposed a mechanism named Active Privacy Bundles using a Trusted Third Party (APB-TTP) for protecting users' data and privacy in the healthcare field [28]. They use TTPs for maintaining data on the trust levels of visited hosts (VHs) and providing them to APBs upon their request. The issue with this approach is that the authors did not validate the specific mechanism to get a better picture on a real case scenario. Another mechanism to handle users' data in a proper and secure way is presented by Polash and Shiva that focuses on users' transparency in the cloud [29]. It presents the cloud service certification process and moves a step forward by providing a comparative analysis of the existing cloud service certification organization. The authors point out the importance of the confirmation of the standards and best practices the providers follow (cloud service certification process) and present the aspects that can help to increase users' cloud confidence. By doing so, they assist customers to judge the acceptability of a cloud service certification scheme.

Based on the third-party auditor (TPA), Razaque and Rizvi presented a triangular data privacy-preserving (TDPP) model that supports public auditing in cloud environment and provides the line of trust among all the key stakeholders [3]. The model authenticates all the stakeholders, ensures the integrity of the TPA, enforces the Service Level Agreements (SLAs) between users and cloud providers, ensures the message authentication at the provider side and determines the conspiracy role of TPA. The authors provide detailed tests in a variety of different scenarios in order to evaluate the model. The results show that the model effectively develops a TPA-centric trust between users and providers by minimizing the insider threats and increasing fairness in the cloud environment [3].

In 2017, Drucker and Gueron used a Private Trusted Proxy (PTP) to extend the idea of Trusted Proxy (TP) in order to guarantee the data privacy [30]. It uses a secret key that is not shared to an adversary and provides user's confidentiality. Besides the usefulness of the specific scheme, the evaluation tests of the PTP solution seems to be more effective and gives better performances (the time for executing the modeled workload for the entire data as a function of the latency) in relation to the PT solution [30]. The privacy and trust issues between the user and the cloud service provider are also identified by another research [31]. In order to address the issues, a Security Assertion Markup Language (SAML) with Single Sign-On and hash-based encryption algorithm is used. The algorithm provides secure communication between the user and the provider, in that way, the trust issue between them can be overcome. The proposed system also provides a high level of security for user identity management.

Mbanaso and Chukwudebe proposed a configurable policy-based architecture to provide trust, confidentiality and privacy at the same time [32]. The policy mechanism specifies the data to be shared, who is shared with, and the privacy and confidentiality settings of the data. The policy framework also uses Requirements (used to express a party's obligations) and Capabilities (used to express the competences of the relaying party) form elements to guarantee confidentiality, trust and privacy dynamically and concurrently between two or more cooperating entities. Authors are making a number of assumptions in order to provide the required trust and end-to-end privacy and confidentiality.

The use of cloud computing in the healthcare domain is a special case since privacy is of vital importance. Marwan et al. proposed a framework for fueling the integration of cloud applications in the healthcare sector [33]. The framework is based on segmentation and genetic algorithms in order to afford optimal privacy protection. They use a trusted third party to provide secure data exchanges between users and CSPs and Secure Sockets Layer (SSL) technique to establish a secure connection for transmitting medical records. The data is also encrypted before the transfer. Their results show that the framework provides an adequate image analysis using public clouds and improves both security and performance, while ensuring privacy protection [33].

The same year, Tahir and Rajarajan proposed another framework in relation to encryption in the cloud and the trusted servers [34]. The authors use the cryptographic approach of Searchable Encryption (SE) that is based on probabilistic trapdoors and facilitates search over encrypted data stored on the Hyperledger-Fabric, a blockchain technology. The data is encrypted and stored on the blockchain while the search is realized with the use of a privacy-preserving SE. The use of Hyperledger-fabric provides permissioned membership, scalability, higher level of trust and modular architecture. The security analysis that applied on the framework shows that it provides higher level of security and privacy guarantees [34].

Finally, in 2021, Qin et al. suggested that due to the lack of trust among edge computing participants and users' continuous concern over privacy, new solutions need to be presented in the marine field [35]. In order to preserve data privacy, they proposed to use blockchain technology with the federated learning technology to preserve privacy and security under an edge computing framework. The proposed framework on one hand addresses the security issues at node level by using the block chain and on the other a proof of parameters quality (PoQ) consensus mechanism is designed [36].

5 Discussion

Even though a great number of researchers dealt with the issue of trust in cloud computing and proposed various solutions in regards methodologies, frameworks, models and mechanisms, only few of them took under consideration the trust in relation to privacy. Some researchers, in order to develop a policy approach or a framework for the trust in cloud environments, they focused on trust mechanism analysis. They identified different trust attributes and mechanisms and categorized them to address specific aspects of trust. A user can use the framework/policies to compare different services (CSPs) to make trust judgment on the service or the CSP. Comparing different trust mechanisms in the cloud the user can evaluate the level of trust between cloud service providers and choose accordingly. They use techniques to find the level of interaction and assessment between CSPs and consumers to establish the trust degree of the entities. In that way, they identify malicious entities and provide security to all stakeholders. They produce reports to evaluate cloud services' processes and procedures to aware users about the services' standards. The reports provide the cloud service with a certification process resulting in the increase of trust among cloud consumers. They use auditing methodologies to assess CSPs and their services. Cloud users are able to compare the reports, understand the differences and choose the provider that suits him/her.

Other researchers focused on the users control aspect to build trust between user and CSP, using different components for monitoring data while other use Trusted Third Party (TTP) or Third Party Auditors (TPA) for auditing consumers' data on a regular basis. These techniques provide a line of trust among all the key stakeholders and assure privacy in cloud at the required level of trust. The privacy monitoring method can provide the required transparency and enables users to comprehend how their data is handled.

Another approach is the use of cryptography to encrypt stored data. To safely process digital data in an untrusted cloud environment, encryption techniques can be used to ensure confidentiality and privacy protection. This approach guarantees a higher level of security and privacy of the consumers' data, increases the cloud providers' trust and assures the quality and effectiveness of the services. Consumers feel confident using cloud services since their personal and sensitive information cannot be used in case of a breakage. New technologies such as blockchain and federated learning are used to establish trust among participants. These technologies can be used to solve security and privacy issues and establish trust among participants. The encryption technology guarantees the security of data on the chain while the federated learning improves computational efficiency.

The specific solutions cover different areas in relation to applicability. Most of them are used as a generic solution to establish trust between the parties involved. There are also approaches specialized in the demanding sector of healthcare with its sensitive personal data. The people responsible for processing medical digital records should ensure the privacy and confidentiality of the users and maintain trust at all times using appropriate tools and methods. The Marines is another field of applying new technologies to provide privacy protection and increase the level of trust.

The software industry is growing rapidly, and many methodologies and tools have been published in order privacy protection to be ensured while using systems. In the previous Section, a number of them are presented based on the results of the review. They include several processes regarding the elicitation and analysis of privacy requirements which may differ in parts but in general their common aim is to ensure that privacy requirements will be considered from the early stages of the software lifecycle until the late design stages prior to implementation.

Another part which is interesting to mention is the differences regarding the privacy concepts that each method includes. For instance, in PriS eight privacy concepts are reported, namely authentication, authorisation, identification, data protection, anonymity, pseudonymity, unlinkability, and unobservability, while in LINDUUN authors focus on Linkability, Identifiability, Non-repudiation, Detectability, Information Disclosure, Content Unawareness, Policy, and consent Noncompliance. Additionally, there are some methods which do not focus only on privacy. In i* method security requirements are also considered along with privacy requirements. Similarly, Secure Tropos with PriS supports the parallel identification of security and privacy requirements of a system. Several differences can be recognized regarding the content of all methods. STRAP succeeds privacy requirements analysis through a structured analysis of privacy vulnerabilities and it included four steps, while EPICUREAN includes modelling and data mining techniques to recommend privacy settings to users and describes three phases.

6 Conclusion

Cloud computing is an important technology and most of the companies and organizations now days are cloud dependent. The aim of this paper is to introduce a systematic literature review on the existing privacy engineering and trust methodologies in cloud environments. We identify both the privacy engineering methods that have been developed in order to support privacy requirements elicitation for various software systems and the trust methodologies and models that will raise the level of trust between the parties.

A series of privacy methodologies have been introduced in order to support the development of privacy-aware systems. It has been noticed that several steps and requirements are provided but the common part of all privacy requirements engineering methods is to ensure that privacy will be protected in cloud computing systems. Specifically, some of these methods have proposed specific tools to support their aim which can be used by software developers. On the side of trust methods, the purpose is to ensure that trust level will be increased, and many relevant methods are published to achieve it.

The discussion of the findings presented in this paper contributed to a better understanding of cloud environments and specifically on how to preserve privacy and maintain the trust. Even though a number of steps is in the right direction, there is plenty of work to be done in relation to privacy and trust in cloud. The different techniques have been highlighted and they provide appropriate knowledge aiming to support software designers and developers at the early stages of system design.

Acknowledgements. The research project was supported by the Hellenic Foundation for Research and Innovation (H.F.R.I.) under the '2nd Call for H.F.R.I. Research Projects to support Faculty Members & Re-searchers' (Project Number: 2550).

References

1. Flexera, State of the Cloud Report (2021). https://www.flexera.com/blog/cloud/cloud-computing-trends-2022-state-of-the-cloud-report/
2. Cook, A., Robinson, M., Ferrag, M.A.: Internet of cloud: security and privacy issues. In: Mishra, B.S.P., Das, H., Dehuri, S., Jagadev, A.K. (ed.) Cloud Computing for Optimization: Foundations, Applications, and Challenges. SBD, vol. 39, pp. 271–301. Springer, Cham (2018). https://doi.org/10.1007/978-3-319-73676-1_11
3. Razaque, A., Rizvi, S.S.: Triangular data privacy-preserving model for authenticating all key stakeholders in a cloud environment. Comput. Secur. **62**, 328–347 (2016)
4. Kaiser, C., et al.: A vehicle telematics service for driving style detection: implementation and privacy challenges. In: VEHITS, pp. 29–36 (2020)
5. Canedo, E.D., Bandeira, I., Calazans, A., Costa, P., Cançado, E., Bonifacio, R.: Privacy requirements elicitation: a systematic literature review and perception analysis of IT practitioners. Requirements Eng. **27** (2022). https://doi.org/10.1007/s00766-022-00382-8
6. Pattakou, A., Kalloniatis, C., Gritzalis, S.: Security and Privacy under a unified framework: a review. Inter. J. Adv. Sec. **11**(1–2), 39–51 (2018)
7. Ibrahim, F.A., Hemayed, E.E.: Trusted cloud computing architectures for infrastructure as a service: Survey and systematic literature review. Comput. Secur. **82**, 196–226 (2019)
8. Deng, M., Wuyts, K., Scandariato, R., Preneel, B., Joosen, W.: A privacy threat analysis framework: supporting the elicitation and fulfillment of privacy re-quirements. Requirements Eng. **16**(1), 3–32 (2011)
9. Bijwe, A., Mead, N.R.: Adapting the SQUARE Process for Privacy Requirements Engineering, pp. 1–32 (2010)
10. Mead, N.R., Hough, E.D. Ii, T.R.S.: Security Quality Requirements Engineering (SQUARE) Methodology. Carnegie Mellon Software Engineering Institute, Pittsburgh PA (2005)

11. Meis, R., Heisel, M.: Computer-aided identification and validation of intervenability requirements. Information **8**(1), 30 (2017)

12. Kalloniatis, C., Kavakli, E., Gritzalis, S.: Addressing privacy requirements in system design: the PriS method. Requirements Eng. **13**(3), 241–255 (2008)

13. Kalloniatis, C., Kavakli, E., Kontellis, E.: Pris tool: a case tool for privacy-oriented requirements engineering. In: 4th Mediterranean Conference on Information Systems, MCIS, p. 71 (2009)

14. Islam, S., Mouratidis, H., Kalloniatis, C., Hudic, A., Zechner, L.: Model based process to support security and privacy requirements engineering. Inter. J. Sec. Softw. Eng. (IJSSE) **3**(3), 1–22 (2012)

15. Mouratidis, H., Kalloniatis, C., Islam, S., Huget, M.P., Gritzalis, S.: Aligning security and privacy to support the development of secure information systems. J. Univ. Comput. Sci. **18**(12), 1608–1627 (2012)

16. He, Q., Antón, A.I.: A framework for modeling privacy requirements in role engineering. In: 9th International Workshop on Requirements Engineering: Foundation for Software Quality (REFSQ 2003) on Proceedings, pp. 137–146 (2003)

17. Jensen, C., Tullio, J., Potts, C., Mynatt, E.D.: STRAP: a structured analysis framework for privacy. Georgia Institute of Technology (2005)

18. Liu, L., Yu, E., Mylopoulos, J.: Security and privacy requirements analysis within a social setting. In: 11th IEEE International Requirements Engineering Conference 2003 on Proceedings, pp. 151–161. IEEE (2003)

19. Horkoff, J., Yu, Y, Eric, S.K.: OpenOME: an open-source goal and agent-oriented model drawing and analysis tool. iStar **766**, 154–156 (2011)

20. Stach, C., Steimle, F.: Recommender-based privacy requirements elicitation-EPICUREAN: an approach to simplify privacy settings in IoT applications with respect to the GDPR. In: 34th ACM/SIGAPP Symposium on Applied Computing on Proceedings, pp. 1500–1507. Limassol Cyprus (2019)

21. Peixoto, M.M.: Privacy Requirements engineering in agile software development: a specification method. In: REFSQ-2020 Workshops on Proceedings, Pisa Italy (2020)

22. Neureiter, C., Eibl, G., Veichtlbauer, A., Engel, D.: Towards a framework for engineering smart-grid-specific privacy requirements. In: IECON 2013–39th Annual Conference of the IEEE Industrial Electronics Society on Proceedings, pp. 4803–4808. IEEE, Vienna Austria (2013)

23. Gharib, M., Mylopoulos, J.: A core ontology for privacy requirements engineering. arXiv preprint arXiv:1811.12621. (2018)

24. Gharib, M., Giorgini, P., Mylopoulos, J.: COPri v. 2 – A core ontology for privacy requirements. Data Knowl. Eng. **133**, 101888 (2021)

25. Wu, X., Zhang, R., Zeng, B., Zhou, S.: A trust evaluation model for cloud computing. Proc. Comput. Sci. **17**, 1170–1177 (2013)

26. Huang, J., Nicol, D.M.: Trust mechanisms for cloud computing. J. Cloud Comput. Adv. Syst. Appli. **2**(1), 1–14 (2013)

27. Shabalala, M.V., Tarwireyi, P., Adigun, M.O.: Privacy monitoring framework for enhancing transparency in cloud computing. In: 6th International Conference on Adaptive Science & Technology (ICAST), pp. 1–7. IEEE (2014)

28. Salih, R.M., Lilien, L. T.: Protecting users' privacy in healthcare cloud computing with APB-TTP. In: International Conference on Pervasive Computing and Communication Workshops (PerCom Workshops), pp. 236–238. IEEE (2015)

29. Polash, F., Shiva, S.: Building trust in cloud: service certification challenges and approaches. In: Ninth International Conference on Complex, Intelligent, and Software Intensive Systems, pp. 187–191. IEEE (2015)

30. Drucker, N., Gueron, S., Pinkas, B.: Faster secure cloud computations with a trusted proxy. IEEE Secur. Priv. **15**(6), 61–67 (2017)
31. George, J.A., Veni, S., Soomroo, S.: Improving privacy and trust in federated identity using SAML with hash based encryption algorithm. In: 4th IEEE International Conference on Engineering Technologies and Applied Sciences (ICETAS), pp. 1–5. IEEE (2017)
32. Mbanaso, U.M., Chukwudebe, G.A.: Requirement analysis of IoT security in distributed systems. In: 3rd International Conference on Electro-Technology for National Development (NIGERCON), pp. 777–781. IEEE (2017)
33. Marwan, M., Kartit, A., Ouahmane, H.: A cloud-based framework to secure medical image processing. J. Mobile Multimedia, 319–344 (2018)
34. Tahir, S., Rajarajan, M.: Privacy-preserving searchable encryption framework for permissioned blockchain networks. In: IEEE International Conference on Internet of Things (iThings) and IEEE Green Computing and Communications (GreenCom) and IEEE Cyber, Physical and Social Computing (CPSCom) and IEEE Smart Data (SmartData), pp. 1628–1633. IEEE (2018)
35. Qin, Z., Ye, J., Meng, J., Lu, B., Wang, L.: Privacy-Preserving Blockchain-Based Federated Learning for Marine Internet of Things. IEEE Trans. Comput. Soc. Syst. **9**(1), 159–173 (2021)
36. Basha, S.M., Ahmed, S.T., Iyengar, N.C.S.N., Caytiles, R.D.: Inter-locking dependency evaluation schema based on block-chain enabled federated transfer learning for autonomous vehicular systems. In: Second International Conference on Innovative Technology Convergence (CITC), pp. 46–51. IEEE (2021)

Author Index

S. Katsikas et al. (Eds.): ESORICS 2023 Workshops, LNCS 14398, pp. 507–510, 2024.
https://doi.org/10.1007/978-3-031-54204-6

Printed in the United States
by Baker & Taylor Publisher Services